The leading Singaporean series adapted for the National Curriculum

DISCOVERING MATHEMATICS

1C

Teacher Guide

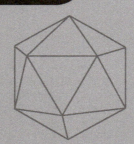

Victor Chow

UK Consultant: Robert Wilne

Singapore Consultant: Berinderjeet Kaur

OXFORD

UNIVERSITY PRESS

OXFORD
UNIVERSITY PRESS

Great Clarendon Street, Oxford, OX2 6DP, United Kingdom

Oxford University Press is a department of the University of Oxford. It furthers the University's objective of excellence in research, scholarship, and education by publishing worldwide. Oxford is a registered trade mark of Oxford University Press in the UK and in certain other countries.

© Oxford University Press and Star Publishing Pte Ltd 2018

The moral rights of the authors have been asserted.

First published in 2018

British Library Cataloguing in Publication Data
Data available

978-0-19-842182-5

1 3 5 7 9 10 8 6 4 2

Paper used in the production of this book is a natural, recyclable product made from wood grown in sustainable forests. The manufacturing process conforms to the environmental regulations of the country of origin.

Printed and Bound by CPI Group (UK) Ltd, Croydon, CR0 4YY

Acknowledgements

The author and publishers would like to thank Jill Borcherds, Lana Laidler and Ann Lui for their contributions to this Teacher Guide. Thanks also to consultants Naomi Norman, Berinderjeet Kaur and Robert Wilne who have advised on the content. All of their contributions and advice have been invaluable.

Editorial team: Dom Holdsworth, Julie Thornton and Sarah Dutton. With thanks also to Katherine Bird and Rosie Day for editorial contributions.

The publishers would like to thank the following for permission to use copyright material:

p137: Tatuasha/Shutterstock; p141: Polygraphus/Shutterstock, p141: MarcelClemens/Shutterstock; p206: ConstantinosZ/Shutterstock; p263: Gemenacom/Shutterstock; p280(T): Paul Tessier/Shutterstock; p280(TC): Freedomnaruk/Shutterstock; p280(C): Judy Ben Joud/Shutterstock; p280(BC): Beboy/Shutterstock; p280(B): Suwin/Shutterstock; p289(T): ORLIO/Shutterstock; p289(C): SW_Stock/Shutterstock; p289(B): Andy Lidstone/Shutterstock; p296: OUP ANZ/Lindsay Edwards; p308: Andrey_Kuzmin/Shutterstock; p316(T): OUP ANZ/Lindsay Edwards; p316(C): Nadezda/Shutterstock; p316(B): Leonello Calvetti/Shutterstock; p321: Altagracia Art/Shutterstock; p326: Ian Dyball/Shutterstock; p328(T): Popartic/Shutterstock; p328(B): David Stuart Productions/Shutterstock; p331: Valzan/Shutterstock; p343: Alexey Grigorev/Shutterstock; p358: IR Stone/Shutterstock; p359: lucadp/Shutterstock; p359: AlexandCo Studio/Shutterstock, p361: Office for National Statistics: https://www.ons.gov.uk/peoplepopulationandcommunity/populationandmigration/populationestimates/articles/overviewoftheukpopulation/mar2017

Cover: Steve Bloom Images/Alamy Stock Photo

CONTENTS

THE DISCOVERING MATHEMATICS SERIES

Discovering Mathematics provides comprehensive support for **three tiers** – Foundation, Middle and Higher – across **all three year groups** in Key Stage 3. The series is an adaptation of the renowned Singaporean secondary series of the same name. The course has been expanded and revised to fully cover the Key Stage 3 National Curriculum. It has been developed by the original Singaporean author team, in conjunction with a large team of UK and Singaporean reviewers and mastery practitioners.

In Singapore, considerable emphasis is placed on using high-quality resources. All secondary schools adopt a textbook series and over 60% of them have chosen *Discovering Mathematics*. This UK adaptation gives you the full suite of resources, as well as an optional programme of professional development.

Student Resources

Student Books and **Workbooks** are available for all three tiers in Years 7–9.

Discovering Mathematics Kerboodle Books provides online access to all nine Student Books for use in school or at home.

Teacher Resources

Teacher Guides are available to support all nine Student Books. Each one contains a Scheme of Work, Notes on Teaching and Fully-worked Solutions for all questions and activities.

Discovering Mathematics Kerboodle contains all nine digital Student Books and videos for front-of-class use, along with interactive assessment resources for students. Additional resources include: digital edition of the Series Guide for Teachers and fully-worked solutions for the Workbooks and Graded Question Banks.

Graded Question Banks, one for each year, provide a bank for additional assessment practice.

Year 7 is shown but equivalent books are available for Year 8 and Year 9.

Series Guide for Teachers, available in print and as a digital edition on Kerboodle, provides a clear summary of the core principles behind mastery, and how to implement it successfully in your school using this series.

Professional Development courses offer practical, expert support to teachers at all stages of their career on how to implement the mastery approach and how to use *Discovering Mathematics*. For more information, email discoveringmathematicspd@oup.com

Algebra Discs are a manipulative pack providing support for number and algebra activities using the Concrete-Pictorial-Abstract (CPA) approach. Each Class Set contains 20 Student Sets, totalling 1600 discs.

HOW TO USE DISCOVERING MATHEMATICS

Teaching for Mastery in *Discovering Mathematics*

Teaching for mastery in *Discovering Mathematics* is:

- for *all* Key Stage 3 maths students: all stages, all levels of attainment
- for *all* secondary maths teachers: experienced and beginning, STEM graduates and non-STEM graduates.

In this series we use 'mastery' in reference to students' outcomes: the learning they develop that is the consequence of the teaching they receive. Students who show mastery in a particular topic or aspect of mathematics are able to solve problems because they have knowledge **THAT**, **HOW** and **WHY** related to that topic.

They have:

- factual knowledge – knowledge THAT (e.g. that the angles in a triangle add up to 180°)
- procedural fluency – knowledge HOW (e.g. how to work out the angles in an isosceles triangle given one of its angles)
- conceptual understanding – knowledge WHY (e.g. why the sum of the angles in a triangle add up to 180°)

We have adapted *Discovering Mathematics* for the UK towards our vision of teaching for mastery for all.

Teaching for mastery prioritises depth over breadth: an insistence that a student truly grasps the fundamental concepts and connections within the mathematics before they move on to the next topic. A lesson for mastery may be focused on one idea only, and that one idea is explored in depth: with examples and followed by consolidation.

Problem-solving is seen as the end goal of a mastery education: the ultimate test that a student has truly grasped the maths. In this section, we'll show how *Discovering Mathematics* supports the mastery approach.

Lesson Design

When designing a maths mastery lesson, decide first what you want students to **think** in the lesson, and then decide what the students will **do**. Both in the Notes on Teaching in this book and in the Student Book, *Discovering Mathematics* encourages this approach. How it does this is described in more detail on the next pages.

1. **Motivating Students' Learning** (see page 3): students are shown upfront how each topic is related to real-life, as well as being encouraged to reflect on their prior learning to develop their knowledge further.

2. **Guided Discovery** (see pages 4–5): students learn best when they discover new concepts for themselves, with guidance from you, the teacher. *Discovering Mathematics* is structured to support this journey of discovery. Not every lesson will look the same, but there are certain elements that are carefully included:
   - the **class activities** and **discussions** to sharpen the students' reasoning, and to prompt them to make connections within the current topic and between others
   - the design and sequencing of the **intelligent practice** that students undertake: the questions, tasks and activities that embed and deepen their factual knowledge, procedural fluency and conceptual understanding.

3. **Concrete-Pictorial-Abstract** (see page 6): the series supports the use of concrete and pictorial representations of a new concept, so students can understand it in the abstract.

4. **Mathematical Language** (see page 7): precise language and vocabulary is introduced, used and reinforced, so that students can express themselves clearly and accurately.

5. **Assessment** (see page 8): activities are included to assess students' learning in the current lesson, to inform design of the next lesson and to allow for rapid intervention to prevent gaps 'in the moment'. Support is given so that *all* students make progress and develop secure and connected knowledge of, fluency with and understanding about the mathematics in each lesson.

Scheme of Work – Chapter 7 Percentages:

Scheme of Work defines lessons to teach in each week

Chapter lengths are different; each one determined by the time required to master key mathematical ideas

Links directly to the Key Stage 3 Programme of Study to show full coverage of the National Curriculum

Extra practice on MyMaths

Links to all series resources

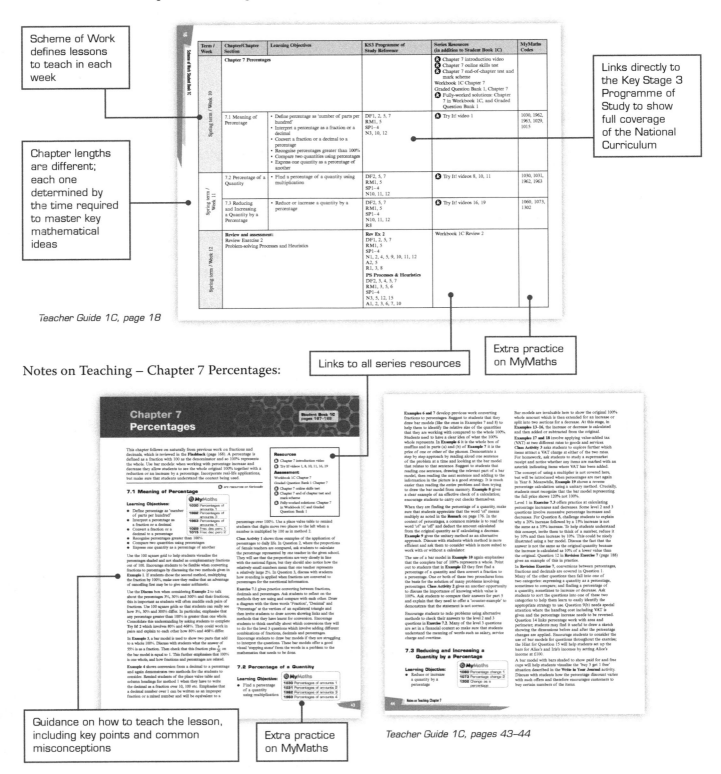

Teacher Guide 1C, page 18

Notes on Teaching – Chapter 7 Percentages:

Guidance on how to teach the lesson, including key points and common misconceptions

Extra practice on MyMaths

Teacher Guide 1C, pages 43–44

Consolidation is provided throughout the **Student Book** as well as in the **Workbook exercises**, **Graded Question Bank exercises** and the **online assessments on Kerboodle**. **Fully-worked solutions** for all exercises, to encourage full understanding, are provided in the Teacher Guide (for the Student Book) and on Kerboodle (for the Workbook and Graded Question Bank).

Motivating Students' Learning

It is vital to show students *why* they learn mathematics, alongside *how*. Although not exclusive to mastery, this is essential to it.

Every Student Book chapter starts with an example of how the maths can be related to real life. This is supported by a **film on the digital book** on Kerboodle

Flashbacks (and **Recall boxes**, see page 4) are a reminder of prior learning. Teaching for mastery requires putting in place strong foundations in students' knowledge. Flashbacks at the start of every chapter are where students and teachers can check those foundations before moving on to the next topic

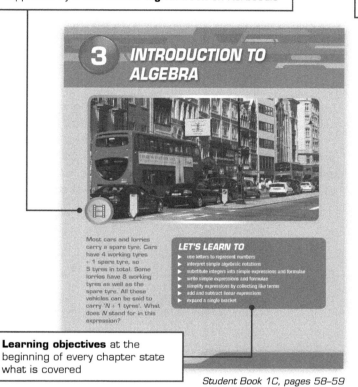

Learning objectives at the beginning of every chapter state what is covered

Student Book 1C, pages 58–59

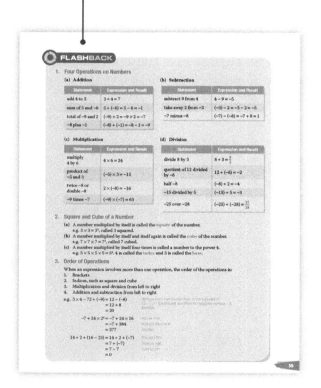

At the end of every chapter, **In a Nutshell** summarises the key learning points that have been covered. This can be used for revision

Maths boxes give interesting facts to enrich learning

Spot Check boxes contain short questions to help clarify any misunderstanding

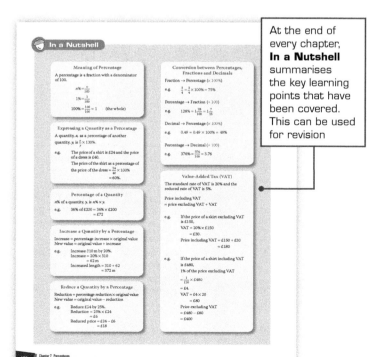

Student Book 1C, page 186

Student Book 1C, pages 225 and 206

Guided Discovery

In Singapore, educators talk about 'Discovery' rather than 'Mastery'. The aim is to **guide** students on a journey of **discovery** to uncover mathematical concepts for themselves. When a student grasps a new concept or operation for themselves, they retain it more reliably than when they are fed it.

In *Discovering Mathematics*, Class Activities in the Student Books allow students to work through the problems with the teacher in class and encourage discussion and group learning. The activities should be mostly done through **pair work** and **small group work**, harnessing peer support. Students start to reason **deliberately before** they have fully understood the technique or procedure they will go on to study.

The **Class Activity** primes and motivates students:

- They want to know **WHY** and so they are eager to know **HOW** – reasoning and explaining is central to mastery.
- The structure ensures that **every** student has to reason and engage with a problem-solving task.
- If the lessons were instead designed 'fluency first, reasoning afterwards', then many students would not reach the reasoning activities before the end of the lesson.

Technology also supports some of the learning experiences in the Class Activities and throughout the series.

Students need **practice** to embed factual knowledge, acquire procedural fluency and develop conceptual understanding that enables them to solve mathematical problems. Practice includes repetition and variation to achieve proficiency and flexibility. It may be in the form of games, simple recall of facts, application of concepts, but above all it should be fun and motivating.

Class Activities usually appear in Teacher Guides in traditional Mathematics textbooks – in *Discovering Mathematics* they occur throughout the Student Books

Objective is clearly defined

Discuss boxes encourage paired and group working

Recall boxes remind students of previous learning

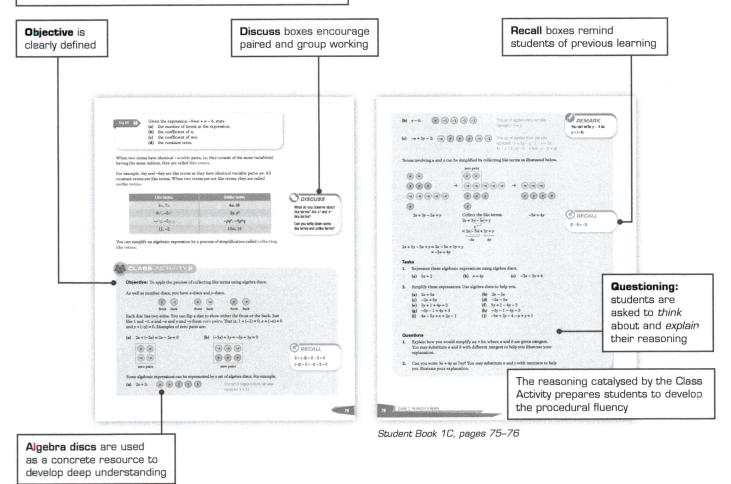

Questioning: students are asked to *think* about and *explain* their reasoning

The reasoning catalysed by the Class Activity prepares students to develop the procedural fluency

Algebra discs are used as a concrete resource to develop deep understanding

Student Book 1C, pages 75–76

In *Discovering Mathematics*, **Examples** with full solutions appear throughout the Student Books. The solutions are always written in full sentences to encourage language development. Additional notes are provided to support understanding and to support the application of the maths in other contexts. The aim is to develop students' confidence and independence.

Examples are always followed by **Try It!** practice questions. They are designed to develop and secure progression in small steps. They allow continuous assessment and rapid intervention.

Fully-worked solutions for all Try It! questions are given in the Teacher Guide. Key Try It! questions also have narrated solution videos on Kerboodle. Both formats show how to present mathematical solutions using precise mathematical language and encourage development of reasoning skills.

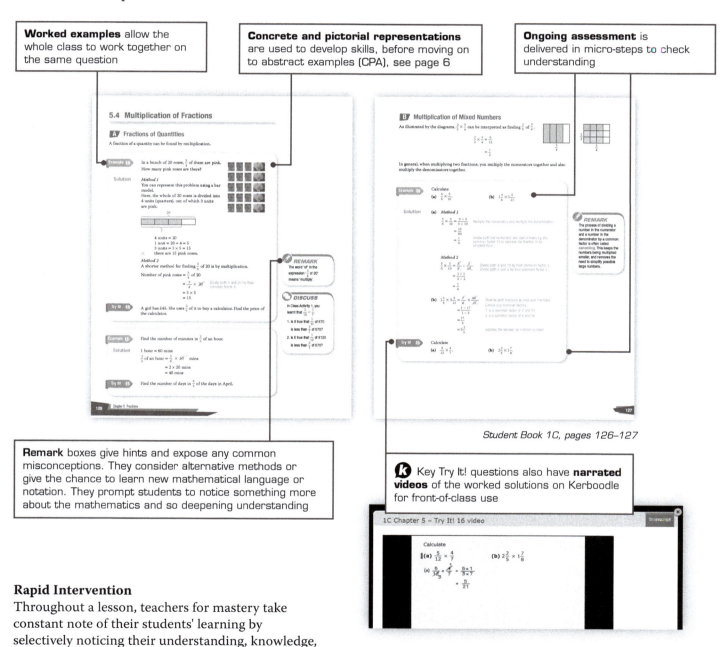

Worked examples allow the whole class to work together on the same question

Concrete and pictorial representations are used to develop skills, before moving on to abstract examples (CPA), see page 6

Ongoing assessment is delivered in micro-steps to check understanding

Remark boxes give hints and expose any common misconceptions. They consider alternative methods or give the chance to learn new mathematical language or notation. They prompt students to notice something more about the mathematics and so deepening understanding

Student Book 1C, pages 126–127

k Key Try It! questions also have **narrated videos** of the worked solutions on Kerboodle for front-of-class use

Rapid Intervention

Throughout a lesson, teachers for mastery take constant note of their students' learning by selectively noticing their understanding, knowledge, misconceptions and progress. Dealing with misconceptions quickly is important – ideally there and then, but certainly that same day. This helps avoid errors becoming embedded.

Concrete-Pictorial-Abstract (CPA) Approach

It matters how students learn. Most students develop secure mathematical knowledge by:

- experiencing **concrete** examples, e.g. by adding five physical objects to another three objects
- moving to **pictorial** representations, e.g. by drawing five objects, and then three more, and grouping them together
- progressing to **abstract** statements using words, e.g. 'five and three makes eight'.

In *Discovering Mathematics*, we believe that *all* students should reason with concrete manipulatives and pictorial representations before doing so with abstract words and symbols. These different representations of mathematical concepts are key to developing deep understanding. Just as teaching for mastery is for all students, so are manipulatives and practical resources.

Word of warning: you and your students will need to invest some time in grasping new pictorial and concrete models for representing mathematics. When teaching for mastery, it's important to introduce new models sparingly, and then to use them consistently.

In *Discovering Mathematics*, we focus on two models: bar models and algebra discs.

Bar Models

Bar models are used throughout the series in problem-solving. It's a big leap for students to take a word-based problem and then formulate an abstract mathematical solution. Bar models are a valuable stepping stone to achieving that. You will need to take time with your students: when they first encounter a bar model, it might even take them longer to solve the problem than without a bar model. But with practice, they'll find the bar model becomes a powerful tool, especially for problems requiring multiplicative reasoning.

Student Book 1C, page 13

Student Book 1C, page 185

Algebra Discs

Algebra discs are presented pictorially in worked examples and class activities throughout the Student Books. A class set of algebra discs is also available as part of this series. The class set contains 20 student sets of double-sided discs, colour-matched precisely with the diagrams in the books. Used together, these pictorial and concrete resources should help guide your students as they explore new algebraic concepts, ultimately helping them to master algebra in its abstract form.

In the example shown here, operations with negative numbers are modelled using algebra discs. Students can manipulate the physical discs to carry out subtractions, and then practise drawing them for calculations such as $5 - (-2)$. Together these support *all* students to develop confident and secure understanding of *why* subtracting any negative quantity is equivalent to adding the corresponding positive quantity.

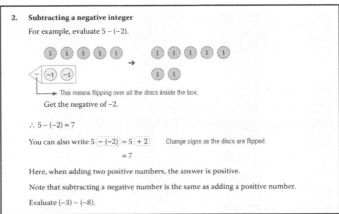

Student Book 1C, page 46

Precise Mathematical Language

Discovering Mathematics places great emphasis on the use of precise mathematical language. Teachers for mastery strive to give all their students the confidence, the vocabulary and the opportunity to explain themselves and justify their mathematical conclusions. This is as relevant in Early Years as it is in Key Stage 3, GCSE and A-level. Maintaining consistent language will support understanding.

> Note that there is no mention of the 'bus stop' method for division – division has no connection with bus stops!

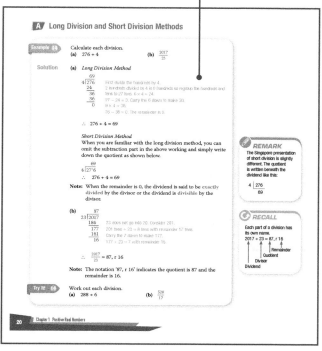

Student Book 1C, page 20

Solutions are given in full sentences in the Student Books, and in the fully-worked solutions in the Teacher Guide and on Kerboodle.

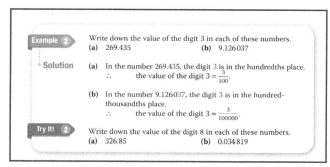

Student Book 1C, page 141

The use of complete sentences encourages students to think clearly, it helps them to grasp the mathematical language, and it allows you, the teacher, to check they have truly understood a given concept.

Mathematical reasoning is encouraged in the approach to questioning.

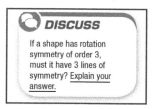

Student Book 1C, page 253

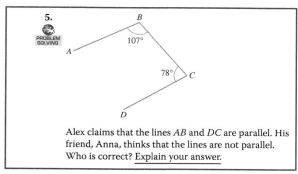

Student Book 1C, page 220

Questions and discussion points ask students to 'Explain' or to 'Justify'. This is an opportunity for students to engage in reasoning and demonstrate their depth of understanding of a concept. This encourages mastery through not just knowing how to do mathematics, but also developing an understanding of *why* it works.

Open questions, which have more than one possible answer, are flagged in the series. These questions encourage depth of understanding and allow students to see that there can be more than one correct answer to a mathematics question.

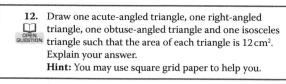

Student Book 1C, page 275

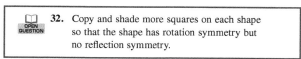

Workbook 1C, page 74

Try encouraging students to create a mathematics glossary in the back of their exercise books. Give them time to add to it when they meet new mathematics vocabulary.

Assessment

Assessment is at the heart of *Discovering Mathematics*. The mastery methodology for assessment is, at its core, straightforward:

1 **Formative assessment**: check students' understanding of a topic and identify weak spots.

2 **Gap-filling**: support students with any weak spots.

3 **Summative assessment**: test students' mastery of the topic.

1 Formative assessment

(a) End-of-chapter section exercises

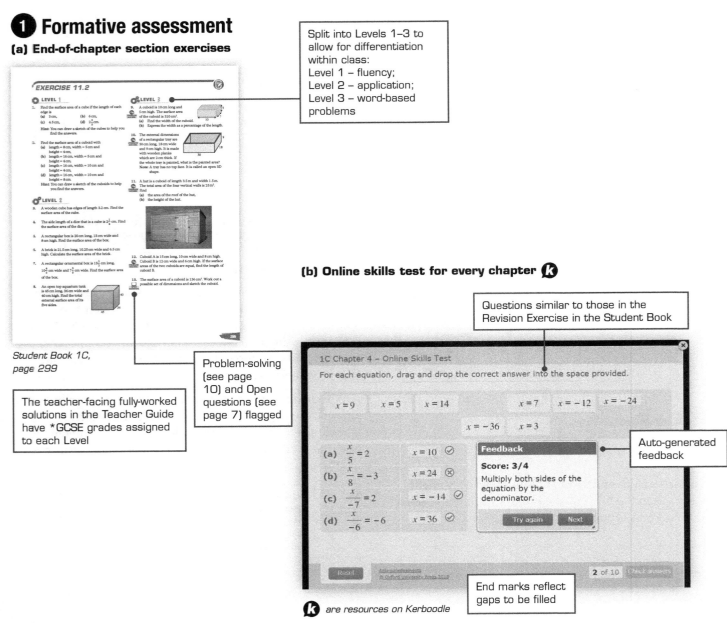

Split into Levels 1–3 to allow for differentiation within class:
Level 1 – fluency;
Level 2 – application;
Level 3 – word-based problems

Student Book 1C, page 299

The teacher-facing fully-worked solutions in the Teacher Guide have *GCSE grades assigned to each Level

Problem-solving (see page 10) and Open questions (see page 7) flagged

(b) Online skills test for every chapter **k**

Questions similar to those in the Revision Exercise in the Student Book

Auto-generated feedback

End marks reflect gaps to be filled

k *are resources on Kerboodle*

2 Gap-filling

Gap-filling can be covered through the Examples and Try It! questions in the Student Books, Try It! videos on Kerboodle and In a Nutshell in the Student Books.

It can be very effective to share students' solutions and explanations with their peers – exemplary ones but also those that reveal a misconception, or those that reach a solution in a novel or sub-optimal way.

❸ Summative assessment

(a) Revision Exercises for every chapter

Covers all content of the chapter

Questions ramp-up in difficulty

The teacher-facing fully-worked solutions in the Teacher Guide have *GCSE grades assigned to each question

Science and Finance contexts flagged to encourage cross-curricular working

Problem-solving questions clearly identified

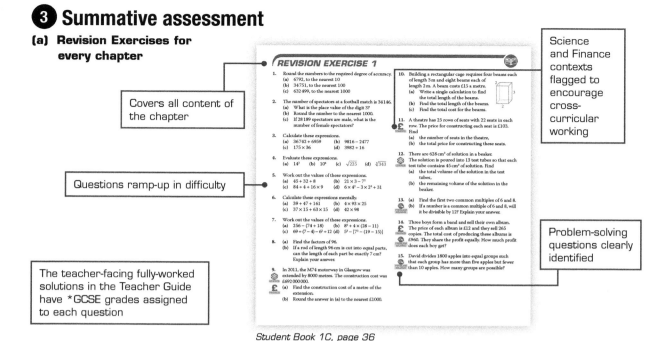

Student Book 1C, page 36

(b) Online end-of-chapter printable test 🄚 (with associated spreadsheet for class monitoring)

Questions taken from the Revision Exercise in the Student Book

Mark scheme provided for teachers with *GCSE grades assigned to each question

Teacher enters class marks into an assessment spreadsheet, which provides GCSE grade analysis

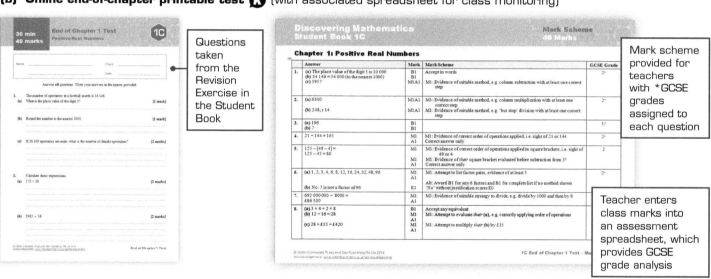

Supplementary Assessment

Additional assessment opportunities can be found throughout the Higher Tier resources in *Discovering Mathematics*.

Student Book:
- Review Exercises appear after every four chapters to support students to answer questions on a range of topics
- Problems in Real-world Contexts question the content of the whole book in real-life situations
- Self-assessment booklet for each Student Book on Kerboodle allows students to reflect on their own strengths and weaknesses 🄚

Workbook:
- Each chapter is matched to the corresponding Student Book chapter
- Questions are split into Levels 1–3 as in the Student Book
- Self-assessment checklist for students to track confidence levels

Graded Question Bank:
- Each chapter directly corresponds to the Student Book chapter for Middle and Higher Tier
- Questions split into Levels 1–3 as in the Student Book
- Also available in editable format on Kerboodle for teachers to make up their own tests 🄚

*GCSE grades are an assessment of actual grade, not a projection to GCSE result.
Three sub-grades are allocated, e.g. 1⁻, 1, 1⁺, 2⁻, 2, 2⁺ etc.

Metacognition

Throughout *Discovering Mathematics*, students are encouraged to reflect on new concepts they've learnt and to test their own understanding. This self-reflection is a proven way of accelerating learning.

A **Write in Your Journal** feature at the end of every chapter asks students to reflect on concepts covered in the chapter and to practise communicating mathematically. We recommend providing a separate exercise book for your students, which they can use exclusively as their mathematics journal.

Discuss boxes appear in each chapter. These provide opportunities for students to work in pairs or groups to think and communicate mathematically.

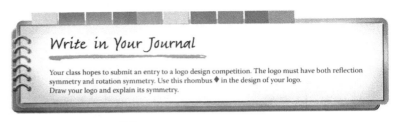

Write in Your Journal

Your class hopes to submit an entry to a logo design competition. The logo must have both reflection symmetry and rotation symmetry. Use this rhombus ◆ in the design of your logo. Draw your logo and explain its symmetry.

Student Book 1C, page 266

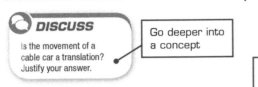

DISCUSS

Is the movement of a cable car a translation? Justify your answer.

Go deeper into a concept

Discuss possible misconceptions

Student Book 1C, page 238

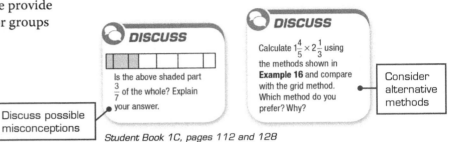

DISCUSS

Is the above shaded part $\frac{3}{7}$ of the whole? Explain your answer.

DISCUSS

Calculate $1\frac{4}{5} \times 2\frac{1}{3}$ using the methods shown in **Example 16** and compare with the grid method. Which method do you prefer? Why?

Consider alternative methods

Student Book 1C, pages 112 and 128

Problem Solving

Skill and confidence at problem-solving is seen as the ultimate goal of a mastery education. It equips students to use mathematics in the real world, through their careers and through their lives.

Every exercise in the series includes problem-solving questions, with an emphasis on real-life contexts. They are all clearly identified in the Student Books, Workbooks and Graded Question Banks.

Every Student Book also has two separate sections dedicated to problem-solving:

1. **Problem-solving Processes and Heuristics** – help students to learn about the steps to take to solve a problem: understand the problem, devise a plan, carry out the plan, and then look back. Examples are given to work through the problem-solving strategies.

7. A rectangular room is 5 m by 4 m and has a height of 3 m.

PROBLEM SOLVING

(a) Find the volume of space in the room.

(b) Jason plans to paint the two longer walls and the ceiling of the room. One tin of paint covers 6 m². How many tins of paint does he need?

Student Book 1C, page 307

2. **Problems in Real-world Contexts** – help students to recognise where mathematics is useful in everyday life, consolidate their learning of problem-solving strategies, and consider what mathematics they have learnt that is relevant to each problem.

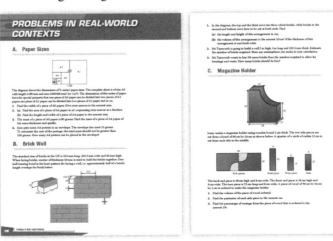

Student Book 1C, pages 338–339

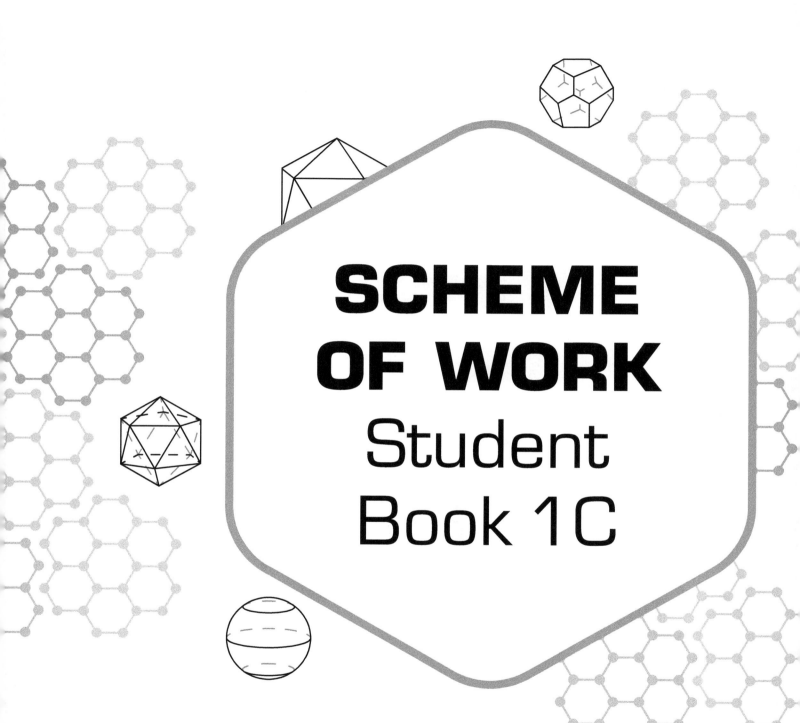

SCHEME OF WORK
Student Book 1C

The *Discovering Mathematics* full series Schemes of Work can be found at www.oxfordsecondary.co.uk/discoveringmathematics

This **Scheme of Work** is for *Discovering Mathematics Student Book 1C*. The detailed Schemes of Work and KS3 POS matching grids for the whole series of *Discovering Mathematics* can be found at www.oxfordsecondary.co.uk/discoveringmathematics

Discovering Mathematics has been adapted from the Singapore series to match fully with the Key Stage 3 Programme of Study (KS3 POS), which is available at www.gov.uk/government/publications/national-curriculum-in-england-mathematics-programmes-of-study

References to the KS3 POS in this Scheme of Work have been abbreviated as follows:
DF – Developing Fluency; **RM** – Reason Mathematically; **SP** – Solve Problems; **N** – Number; **A** – Algebra; **R** – Ratio, Proportion and Rates of Change; **G** – Geometry and Measures; **P** – Probability; **S** – Statistics.

k in the Series Resources column shows content available on *Discovering Mathematics Kerboodle* at www.kerboodle.com.

Term / Week	Chapter/ Chapter Section	Learning Objectives	KS3 Programme of Study Reference	Series Resources (in addition to Student Book 1C)	MyMaths Codes
Autumn term / Week 1	**Chapter 1 Positive Real Numbers**			**k** Chapter 1 introduction video **k** Chapter 1 online skills test **k** Chapter 1 end-of-chapter test and mark scheme Workbook 1C Chapter 1 Graded Question Bank 1, Chapter 1 **k** Fully-worked solutions: Chapter 1 in Workbook 1C, and Graded Question Bank 1	
	1.1 Place Values and Rounding Integers	• Recognise the place values of an integer • Round a number to the nearest 10, 100, 1000	DF1, 2, 5, 7 RM1, 5 SP1–4 N1, 2, 12, 13, 16		1931, 1352, 1840
	1.2 Addition	• Add two positive integers, using: • column method • laws of addition • mental addition	DF2, 5, 7 RM1, 5 SP1–4 N4, 12	**k** Try It! video 43	1020, 1908, 1986
	1.3 Subtraction	• Subtract two positive integers, using: • column method • mental subtraction • Relate addition and subtraction	DF2, 5, 7 RM1, 5 SP1–4 N2, 4, 6, 12		1028, 1908, 1986

Term / Week	Chapter/Chapter Section	Learning Objectives	KS3 Programme of Study Reference	Series Resources (in addition to Student Book 1C)	MyMaths Codes
Autumn term / Week 2	1.4 Multiplication	• Multiply two positive integers, using • grid method and column method • laws of multiplication • mental multiplication	DF2, 5, 7 RM1, 5 SP1–4 N4, 12	ⓚ Try It! video 11	1914, 1916, 1774
Autumn term / Week 3	1.5 Division	• Divide two positive integers, using: • long division and short division methods • mental division • Relate multiplication and division	DF2, 7 RM1, 5 SP1–4 N4, 6, 12	ⓚ Try It! video 18	1905, 1917, 1041, 1775
Autumn term / Week 4	1.6 Index Notation, Square Roots and Cube Roots	• Understand the meaning of square, cube, square root and cube root of a number • Understand index notation	DF1, 2, 7 RM1, 5 SP1–4 N2, 7, 12, 15	ⓚ Try It! videos 21, 23	1053, 1924
	1.7 Order of Operations and Using a Calculator	• Apply the order of operations in calculations • Use calculators to apply operations	DF2, 7 RM1, 5, 6 SP1–4 N4, 5, 12, 15		1167, 1932, 1933
Autumn term / Week 5	1.8 Factors and Multiples	• Identify multiples and factors of numbers • Apply the above concepts to solve daily life problems	DF2, 7 RM1, 5 SP1–4 N3, 12	ⓚ Try It! videos 29, 32	1035, 1032
Autumn term / Week 6	**Chapter 2 Negative Real Numbers**			ⓚ Chapter 2 introduction video ⓚ Chapter 2 online skills test ⓚ Chapter 2 end-of-chapter test and mark scheme Workbook 1C Chapter 2 Graded Question Bank 1, Chapter 2 ⓚ Fully-worked solutions: Chapter 2 in Workbook 1C, and Graded Question Bank 1	
	2.1 Negative Numbers and the Number Line	• Recognise the use of negative numbers in the real world • Represent numbers on a number line	DF2, 5, 7 RM1, 5 SP1–4 N2, 12	ⓚ Try It! video 1	1069, 1776
	2.2 Addition and Subtraction of Integers	• Identify integers and perform addition and subtraction on them	DF2, 5, 7 RM1, 5 SP1–4 N4, 12	ⓚ Try It! videos 5, 7	1068

Term / Week	Chapter/Chapter Section	Learning Objectives	KS3 Programme of Study Reference	Series Resources (in addition to Student Book 1C)	MyMaths Codes
Autumn term / Week 7	2.3 Multiplication, Division and Combined Operations of Integers	• Identify integers and perform multiplication and division on them • Combine operations of integers	DF2, 7 RM1, 5, 6 SP1–4 N4, 5, 12, 15	▶ Try It! video 9	1068
Autumn term / Week 8	**Chapter 3 Introduction to Algebra**			▶ Chapter 3 introduction video ▶ Chapter 3 online skills test ▶ Chapter 3 end-of-chapter test and mark scheme Workbook 1C Chapter 3 Graded Question Bank 1, Chapter 3 ▶ Fully-worked solutions: Chapter 3 in Workbook 1C, and Graded Question Bank 1	
	3.1 Letters to Represent Numbers	• Use letters to represent numbers • Interpret simple algebraic notation	DF2, 3, 4, 5, 7 RM1, 3, 5 SP1–4 N12 A1, 3, 6, 10		1982, 1158, 1179
Autumn term / Week 9	3.2 Substituting Numbers for Letters	• Substitute integers into simple expressions and formulae	DF2, 3, 4, 7 RM1, 3, 5 SP1–4 N12 A1, 2, 3, 5	▶ Try It! videos 9, 13	1187, 1186
	3.3 Writing Algebraic Expressions and Formulae	• Write simple expressions and formulae	DF2, 3, 4, 5, 7 RM1, 3, 5 SP1–4 N12 A1, 2, 3, 5, 6, 10		1158
Autumn term / Week 10	3.4 Like Terms and Unlike Terms	• Simplify expressions by collecting like terms	DF2, 3, 4, 7 RM3, 5 SP1–4 N12 A1, 2, 3, 4		1179
Autumn term / Week 10	3.5 Addition and Subtraction of Linear Expressions	• Add and subtract linear expressions	DF2, 3, 4, 7 RM3, 5 SP1–4 N12 A1, 2, 3, 4	▶ Try It! videos 22, 23, 24	1179

Week	Topic	Objectives		Resources	
Autumn term / Week 10 (continued)	3.6 Expressions with Brackets	• Expand a single bracket	DF2, 3, 4, 7 RM1, 3, 5 SP1–4 N12 A1, 4	⚡ Try It! video 28	1247, 1150
Autumn term / Week 11	**Chapter 4 Simple Equations**			⚡⚡ Chapter 4 introduction video ⚡⚡ Chapter 4 online skills test ⚡ Chapter 4 end-of-chapter test and mark scheme Workbook 1C Chapter 4 Graded Question Bank 1, Chapter 4 ⚡ Fully-worked solutions: Chapter 4 in Workbook 1C, and Graded Question Bank 1	
	4.1 Equations in One Variable	• Understand the concept of equations and balancing • Solve simple equations in one variable	DF2, 4, 5 RM3, 5 SP1–4 N12 A1, 3, 7	⚡ Try It! videos 2, 6	1925, 1154
	4.2 Equations in One Variable with Brackets	• Solve simple equations involving brackets	DF2, 4, 5 RM3, 5 SP1–4 N12 A1, 3, 4, 7	⚡ Try It! video 9	1925, 1928
	4.3 Writing Equations to Solve Problems	• Write simple equations in one variable to solve problems	DF2, 4, 5 RM3, 5 SP1–4 N12 A3, 6, 7	⚡ Try It! videos 11, 14	1158
Autumn term / Week 12	**Review and assessment:** Review Exercise 1		DF1, 2, 3, 4, 7 RM1, 3, 5, 6 SP1–4 N1, 3, 4, 5, 7, 12, 13 A1, 2, 3, 4, 6, 7, 10	Workbook 1C Review 1	

Term / Week	Chapter/Chapter Section	Learning Objectives	KS3 Programme of Study Reference	Series Resources (in addition to Student Book 1C)	MyMaths Codes
	Chapter 5 Fractions			🔾 Chapter 5 introduction video 🔾 Chapter 5 online skills test 🔾 Chapter 5 end-of-chapter test and mark scheme Workbook 1C Chapter 5 Graded Question Bank 1, Chapter 5 🔾 Fully-worked solutions: Chapter 5 in Workbook 1C, and Graded Question Bank 1	
Spring term / Week 1	5.1 Quantities as Fractions	• Use fraction notation and express one quantity as a fraction of another • Convert between improper fractions and mixed numbers	DF1, 2, 5, 7 RM1, 5 SP1–4 N12 R3	🔾 Try It! video 2	1220, 1062, 1019
	5.2 Equivalent Fractions and Comparing Fractions	• Identify equivalent fractions, simplify fractions and compare fractions	DF1, 2, 5, 7 RM1, 5 SP1–4 N2, 3, 12	🔾 Try It! video 8	1042, 1075, 1771
Spring term / Week 2	5.3 Addition and Subtraction of Fractions and Mixed Numbers	• Perform the four operations on fractions and on mixed numbers • Apply fractions in practical situations	DF1, 2, 5, 7 RM1, 5 SP1–4 N4, 12 R3	🔾 Try It! videos 10, 12	1017, 1074
Spring term / Week 3	5.4 Multiplication of Fractions	• Calculate fractions of quantities • Perform the four operations on fractions and on mixed numbers • Apply fractions in practical situations	DF1, 2, 5, 7 RM1, 5 SP1–4 N4, 5, 11, 12 R3	🔾 Try It! video 16	1841, 1046, 1768, 1047, 1769, 1074
	5.5 Division of Fractions and Mixed Numbers	• Find the reciprocal of a number • Perform the four operations on fractions and on mixed numbers • Calculate fractions of quantities • Apply fractions in practical situations	DF1, 2, 5, 7 RM1, 5 SP1–4 N4, 5, 11, 12 R3	🔾 Try It! video 19	1046, 1040, 1074
Spring term / Week 4	5.6 Rational Numbers and Using a Calculator	• Identify fractions as rational numbers	DF1, 2, 7 RM1, 5 SP1–4 N12, 15, 16		1933

Week / term	Chapter 6 Decimals	Learning objectives	References	Resources	
				Chapter 6 introduction video Chapter 6 online skills test Chapter 6 end-of-chapter test and mark scheme Workbook 1C Chapter 6 Graded Question Bank 1, Chapter 6 Fully-worked solutions: Chapter 6 in Workbook 1C and Graded Question Bank 1	
Spring term / Week 5	6.1 Place Values, Ordering and Rounding of Decimal Numbers	• Interpret decimals and write decimals in order of size • Round decimals to the nearest integer	DF1, 2, 5, 7 RM1, 5 SP1–4 N1, 2, 12, 13		1076, 1072, 1004
Spring term / Week 6	6.2 Addition and Subtraction of Decimals	• Use the four operations with decimals	DF1, 2, 7 RM1, 5 SP1–4 N4, 12	Try It! video 7	1380, 1381, 1007
Week 7	6.3 Multiplication of Decimals	• Use the four operations with decimals	DF1, 2, 7 RM1, 5 SP1–4 N4, 12, 15	Try It! video 9	1011, 1382
Spring term / Week 8	6.4 Division of a Decimal by a Whole Number	• Use the four operations with decimals	DF1, 2, 7 RM1, 5 SP1–4 N4, 12		1008
	6.5 Mental Calculation and Conversion between Units	• Convert between units of measure	DF1, 2, 7 RM1, 5 SP1–4 N12 R1	Try It! video 13	1013, 1091
Spring term / Week 9	6.6 Division of a Decimal by a Decimal	• Use the four operations with decimals • Solve real-life problems using decimals	DF1, 2, 7 RM1, 5 SP1–4 N4, 12	Try It! video 21	1923
	6.7 Rational Numbers and Real Numbers	• Convert between decimals and fractions • Identify recurring decimals and real numbers • Solve real-life problems using decimals	DF1, 2, 5, 7 RM1, 5 SP1–4 N9, 12, 15, 16	Try It! video 24	1773, 1016, 1063

Term / Week	Chapter/Chapter Section	Learning Objectives	KS3 Programme of Study Reference	Series Resources (in addition to Student Book 1C)	MyMaths Codes
	Chapter 7 Percentages			📹 Chapter 7 introduction video 📹 Chapter 7 online skills test 📹 Chapter 7 end-of-chapter test and mark scheme Workbook 1C Chapter 7 Graded Question Bank 1, Chapter 7 📹 Fully-worked solutions: Chapter 7 in Workbook 1C, and Graded Question Bank 1	
Spring term / Week 10	7.1 Meaning of Percentage	• Define percentage as 'number of parts per hundred' • Interpret a percentage as a fraction or a decimal • Convert a fraction or a decimal to a percentage • Recognise percentages greater than 100% • Compare two quantities using percentages • Express one quantity as a percentage of another	DF1, 2, 5, 7 RM1, 5 SP1–4 N3, 10, 12	📹 Try It! video 1	1030, 1962, 1963, 1029, 1015
Spring term / Week 11	7.2 Percentage of a Quantity	• Find a percentage of a quantity using multiplication	DF2, 5, 7 RM1, 5 SP1–4 N10, 11, 12	📹 Try It! videos 8, 10, 11	1030, 1031, 1962, 1963
	7.3 Reducing and Increasing a Quantity by a Percentage	• Reduce or increase a quantity by a percentage	DF2, 5, 7 RM1, 5 SP1–4 N10, 11, 12 R8	📹 Try It! videos 16, 19	1060, 1073, 1302
Spring term / Week 12	**Review and assessment:** Review Exercise 2 Problem-solving Processes and Heuristics		**Rev Ex 2** DF1, 2, 5, 7 RM1, 5 SP1–4 N1, 2, 4, 5, 9, 10, 11, 12 A2, 5 R1, 3, 8 **PS Processes & Heuristics** DF2, 3, 4, 5, 7 RM1, 3, 5, 6 SP1–4 N3, 5, 12, 15 A1, 2, 3, 6, 7, 10	Workbook 1C Review 2	

Chapter 8 Angles, Parallel Lines and Triangles

Week	Section	Learning objectives	Codes	Resources	
				Chapter 8 introduction video Chapter 8 online skills test Chapter 8 end-of-chapter test and mark scheme Workbook 1C Chapter 8 Graded Question Bank 1, Chapter 8 Fully-worked solutions: Chapter 8 in Workbook 1C, and Graded Question Bank 1	1081, 1847, 1989, 1990, 1082
Summer term / Week 1	8.1 Points, Lines and Planes	• Describe a point, a line, a line segment, a ray and a plane • Construct lines, line segments and angles using geometry software	DF2 RM5 SP1–4 N12 G3, 5, 13		
	8.2 Angles	• Identify different types of angles • Recognise the properties of vertically opposite angles, angles on a straight line and angles at a point	DF2 RM5 SP1–4 N2, 12 G3, 5, 10, 13, 16		
Summer term / Week 2	8.3 Parallel Lines and Transversals	• Recognise the properties of angles formed by parallel lines and transversals • Find unknown marked angles in a diagram using the above properties	DF2 RM5 SP1–4 N12 G5, 11, 13, 16	Try It! video 7	1109, 1102
Summer term / Week 3	8.4 Triangles	• Classify triangles based on their sides and angles • Understand the general properties of sides and angles of a triangle • Construct triangles where three sides are given	DF2, 7 RM4, 5 SP1–4 N2, 12 G6, 7, 12, 13, 16	Try It! videos 10, 13	1130, 1082, 1090

Term / Week	Chapter/Chapter Section	Learning Objectives	KS3 Programme of Study Reference	Series Resources (in addition to Student Book 1C)	MyMaths Codes
	Chapter 9 Transformations, Symmetry and Congruence			Chapter 9 introduction video Chapter 9 online skills test Chapter 9 end-of-chapter test and mark scheme Workbook 1C Chapter 9 Graded Question Bank 1, Chapter 9 Fully-worked solutions: Chapter 9 in Workbook 1C, and Graded Question Bank 1	
Summer term / Week 4	9.1 Transformations	• Translate, rotate and reflect 2D shapes • Describe translations in vector form • Combine transformations	DF2 RM5 SP1–4 N12 G8	Try It! videos 1, 3, 4	1843, 1127, 1113, 1115, 1839
Summer term / Week 5	9.2 Symmetry	• Recognise and describe reflection symmetry of 2D shapes • Recognise and describe rotation symmetry of 2D shapes	DF2, 7 RM5 SP1–4 N12 G5		1230, 1114, 1116
	9.3 Congruence	• Understand the idea of congruence • Match the sides and angles of two congruent shapes	DF2 RM5 SP1–4 N12 G9	Try It! videos 9, 10	1148
Summer term / Week 6	**Chapter 10 Perimeter and Area of Triangles and Circles**			Chapter 10 introduction video Chapter 10 online skills test Chapter 10 end-of-chapter test and mark scheme Workbook 1C Chapter 10 Graded Question Bank 1, Chapter 10 Fully-worked solutions: Chapter 10 in Workbook 1C, and Graded Question Bank 1	
	10.1 Perimeter and Area of a triangle	• Find the perimeter and area of a triangle	DF2 RM5 SP1–4 N12 G1, 16	Try It! video 3	1110, 1129
	10.2 Circumference of a Circle	• Find the circumference of a circle • Find the perimeter of a semicircle and a quarter of a circle	DF2 RM5 SP1–4 N12, 13, 15 G2, 7, 16	Try It! video 6	1088

Week / term	Section	Objectives	Codes	Resources	Page
Summer term / Week 7	10.3 Area of a Circle	• Find the area of a circle • Find the area of a semicircle and a quarter of a circle	DF2 RM5 SP1–4 N12, 13, 15 G2, 7, 16	⚡ Try It! video 8	1083
	10.4 Perimeter and Area Problems	• Find a length given the perimeter or area of a shape • Solve problems involving perimeters and areas of composite plane figures formed by rectangles, squares, triangles and circles	DF2 RM5 SP1–4 N12, 13, 15 G2, 16	⚡ Try It! videos 10, 14	1129, 1088, 1083
Summer term / Week 8	**Chapter 11 Volume and Surface Area of Cuboids, including Cubes**			⚡ Chapter 11 introduction video ⚡ Chapter 11 online skills test ⚡ Chapter 11 end-of-chapter test and mark scheme Workbook 1C Chapter 11 Graded Question Bank 1, Chapter 11 ⚡ Fully-worked solutions: Chapter 11 in Workbook 1C and Graded Question Bank 1	
	11.1 Nets of Cuboids, including Cubes	• Draw nets of cuboids, including cubes	DF2, 7 RM5 SP1–4 N12 G15		1106, 1107
Summer term / Week 9	11.2 Surface Area of Cuboids, including Cubes	• Calculate the surface area of cuboids, including cubes	DF2, 7 RM5 SP1–4 N12 G15, 16	⚡ Try It! video 3	1107
	11.3 Volume of Cuboids, including Cubes	• Calculate the volume of cuboids, including cubes • Solve problems involving volume and surface area of cuboids, including cubes	DF2, 7 RM5 SP1–4 N12 G1, 16	⚡ Try It! video 9	1137

Term / Week	Chapter/Chapter Section	Learning Objectives	KS3 Programme of Study Reference	Series Resources (in addition to Student Book 1C)	MyMaths Codes
	Chapter 12 Collecting, Organising and Displaying Data			✪ Chapter 12 introduction video ✪ Chapter 12 online skills test ✪ Chapter 12 end-of-chapter test and mark scheme Workbook 1C Chapter 12 Graded Question Bank 1, Chapter 12 ✪ Fully-worked solutions: Chapter 12 in Workbook 1C, and Graded Question Bank 1	
Summer term / Week 10	12.1 Collection of Data	• Recognise different methods of collecting data • Identify and write appropriate survey questions	DF2, 7 RM5 SP1–4 N12		1248, 1249
Summer term / Week 11	12.2 Organisation of Data	• Organise data • Create frequency tables	DF2, 7 SP1–4 N2, 10, 12 S1, 2	✪ Try It! video 4	1385, 1235, 1193
	12.3 Pictograms, Vertical Line Charts and Bar Charts	• Construct, analyse and interpret pictograms, vertical line charts, bar charts and compound bar charts	DF2, 7 SP1–4 N10, 12 S1, 2	✪ Try It! videos 7, 9	1193, 1205
Summer term / Week 12	**Review and assessment:** Review Exercise 3 Problems in Real-world Contexts		**Rev Ex 3** DF2, 7 RM5 SP1–4 N6, 12, 13, 15 A1, 2 G1, 2, 5, 10, 11, 12, 15 S1, 2 **Probs in Real-world Contexts** DF2, 7 RM5, 6 SP1–4 N4, 10, 12, 13, 15 R1, 8 G1, 2, 7, 15 S1	Workbook 1C Review 3	

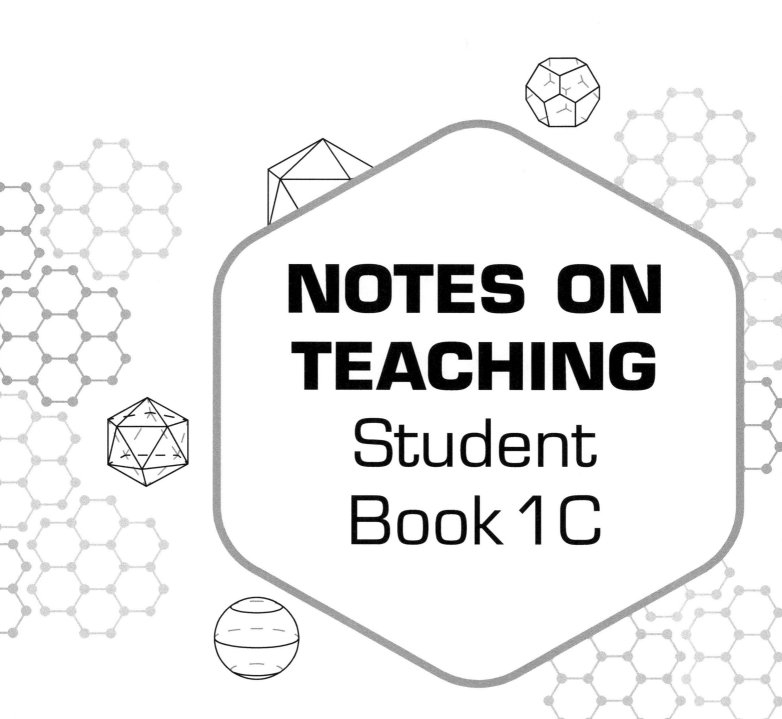

NOTES ON TEACHING
Student
Book 1C

This chapter focusses on number and in particular the underlying properties of the four operations and the relationships between them. The laws covered here will be the foundation for understanding calculations and the progression into algebra later. The bar model is introduced as a visual representation to allow students to see what is happening in the calculations, linking the visual with the abstract. This technique will need developing and practising so that it becomes a tool students are familiar with and happy to apply in different situations.

Students need to be given time to familiarise themselves with the manipulation of numbers in order to improve their agility within calculations. It is important for students to be aware that the equals sign means 'the same on both sides' and not just 'the answer is'.

 are resources on Kerboodle

Resources

k Chapter 1 introduction video

k Try It! videos 3, 11, 15, 21, 23, 29, 32

Assessment

Workbook 1C Chapter 1

Graded Question Bank 1 Chapter 1

k Chapter 1 online skills test

k Chapter 1 end of chapter test and mark scheme

k Fully-worked solutions: Chapter 1 in Workbook 1C and Graded Question Bank 1

1.1 Place Values and Rounding Integers

Learning Objectives:

● Recognise the place values of an integer

● Round a number to the nearest 10, 100 or 1000

MyMaths

1931 Place value beyond 10000
1352 Place value hundreds and thousands
1840 Rounding and accuracy

Students should already be familiar with place value, whole, even, odd and consecutive numbers and the term 'digit' (see parts 1 and 2 of the **Flashback** on page 4). It will be useful to spend some time checking that place value is secure and that students can read large numbers and understand the use of zero as a place holder. Please note that 'ones' is used for the first place value and not 'units'; this is to help with understanding the value of that column and is now being used widely in primary schools.

Class Activity 1 allows students to consider the reasons why a number is rounded in a particular way. Discuss Question 3 with the students and agree how to round a number that is exactly halfway. Drawing number line extracts is a visual way to help students when rounding; use the **Discuss** box (page 7) to check students understand how best to label these. Allow students to make errors, to see if their number line helps them to round and then to adjust if it doesn't. **Exercise 1.1** includes straightforward place value and rounding questions, as well as those set in contexts. Ask students to find their own very large number in real life, and then round it to the nearest 10, 100 and 1000. When tackling Question 14, ask students to discuss and explain why 0 is even.

1.2 Addition

Learning Objective:

● Add two positive integers, using:
   ✳ column method
   ✳ laws of addition
   ✳ mental addition

MyMaths

1020 Adding in columns
1908 More written methods
1986 Mental addition and subtraction

Students should be familiar with the column addition method but may not be familiar with the regrouping of numbers. Regrouping explains how 'carrying' works and will help students understand the mental methods which follow. Try asking students to regroup a number in as many different ways as possible, e.g. $247 = 200 + 40 + 7 = 100 + 130 + 17 = 150 + 80 + 17 = 20 + 200 + 27$ etc. This will help later with mental methods and subtraction.

Work through **Example 3** asking students to check the size of the answers by rounding. Discuss the **Remark** (page 9) and check they are familiar with the approximation sign.

Class Activity 2 explores the properties of addition. Questions 4, 5 and 6 help the students to notice what is happening in the sums and how the addition sums can be manipulated. Reveal that these are the commutative and associative laws and use the bar models to show these laws pictorially. Ask the students to use the names of these laws each time they discuss a manipulation in a question in order to embed the understanding. Work through **Examples 4 and 5** showing how these laws can make a calculation easier to solve. Use the **Discuss** box (page 10) to ask students about the efficiency of the two methods. Encourage students to use these methods to complete

Exercise 1.2, discussing their 'thinking steps' when asked to do a question mentally. Question 12 will be challenging; encourage the use of the bar model to help students visualise the information they have been given and how they can solve the problem.

1.3 Subtraction

Learning Objectives:

- Subtract two positive integers, using:
  - ✲ column method
  - ✲ mental subtraction
- Relate addition and subtraction

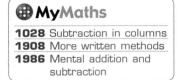

MyMaths
1028 Subtraction in columns
1908 More written methods
1986 Mental addition and subtraction

The column method uses the word 'regroup'; students may be more familiar with decompose, exchange or borrow. Ensure all students understand what you mean by 'regroup' (used mainly in primary schools now).

Class Activity 3 explores the inverse relationship between addition and subtraction. Ask students to draw bar models to show what is happening in each question and to help them see the link between the calculations. Continue to use bar models when discussing **Examples 7 and 8**.

Discuss with students whether subtraction is commutative or associative; make sure they can explain their reasoning for their answer or give a counter-example to prove it is not. The 'It should be noted…' text after Example 8 is very important. Make sure students are aware of the 'not equal to' sign.

Consolidate students' understanding by using **Exercise 1.3**. When completing mental questions, ask students to discuss with each other the strategies they use. Use Question 10 as an opportunity to discuss with students net income and income tax. Question 14 could be completed as a class activity, with a discussion of students' answers.

1.4 Multiplication

Learning Objective:

- Multiply two positive integers, using:
  - ✲ grid method and column method
  - ✲ laws of multiplication
  - ✲ mental multiplication

MyMaths
1914 Short and long multiplication
1916 Long multiplication
1774 Mental multiplication

Both the grid method and column method are shown for multiplication so that students can compare the efficiency of the methods as they move through the examples, first multiplying by a single-digit number and then moving onto multiplying by a two-digit number. Compare what is happening in both methods so that students understand they are equivalent. Students should use their rounding skills to predict the size of an answer before calculating it and then check it is sensible afterwards.

A useful way to promote understanding is to show a bar model and consider the area of rectangles. When using the written method it is useful to write the calculation on each answer line until the students understand the place value of the second line.

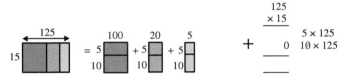

Class Activity 4 considers the properties of multiplication in a similar way to the activity on addition. The key finding to discuss here is Question 7 as this reveals the distributive law. Show this as a bar model (see bottom of page 17) to help students visualise what is happening. It is important to point out that this law works both ways starting with number 1, or with number 2 + number 3. Apply the three laws through **Examples 12 and 13** to consider how to decide which mental strategies to use when solving calculations. Discuss the **Remark** (on page 18) when tackling Example 13, to show how the distributive law can be used when a subtraction is involved.

Students should be encouraged to think of the easiest way to tackle the questions in **Exercise 1.4** so that they apply all the methods discussed. They should discuss their 'thinking steps' when answering the mental calculations.

1.5 Division

Learning Objectives:

- Divide two positive integers, using:
  - ✲ long division and short division methods
  - ✲ mental division
- Relate multiplication and division

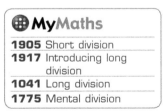

MyMaths
1905 Short division
1917 Introducing long division
1041 Long division
1775 Mental division

Recall the words dividend, divisor, quotient and remainder (see part 6 of the **Flashback** on page 5), and use this terminology frequently when discussing division questions.

Students will have often used short division at primary level rather than long division, so you will need to give some time to work through this long-division method. They may find division difficult because they have two mental models: one of sharing and one of grouping. It may be helpful to use the language of grouping, e.g. for **Example 14**, how many groups of 4 in 27? There are 6 groups of 4 making 24, and you have 3 remaining. (You can show the grouping pictorially on a number line or in an array for those students who are struggling.)

Concentrate first on dividing a double-digit number by a single-digit number so students can become familiar with how to write the method. These should be done both without and with remainders before moving onto three-digit dividends etc.

When students are confident with long division, show them how this can be done using short division. Make a direct comparison between the two methods by answering the same question simultaneously, explaining the reasoning at each step. Work through **Example 15** to put the division into a contextual situation.

Class Activity 5 explores the relationship between multiplication and division. Discuss with students the answers for each question before generalising the inverse relationship between multiplication and division. Work through **Examples 16, 17 and 18** and allow students to complete each Try It! **Class Activity 6** encourages speed and accuracy of mental calculations. This can be repeated with different numbers, after consolidating understanding through **Exercise 1.5**, to see if students can beat their own personal score. Tackling the real-world Questions 8–14 will help students to understand how division can be used to solve problems. Discuss how different students tackle Question 15 and how the answers are related.

1.6 Index Notation, Square Roots and Cube Roots

Learning Objective:

- Understand the meaning of square, cube, square root and cube root of a number
- Understand index notation

MyMaths
1053 Squares and cubes
1924 Higher powers

Use a practical approach with square tiles and cubes to deepen student understanding. Ask students to make a variety of squares with square tiles. What can they tell you about those squares? How many little squares have they used? Is there a quick way of working that out? Then ask them to make a square with 10 tiles. Ask them

to explain why this is not possible. Discuss what square numbers are, then repeat a similar exercise making cubes from smaller cubes. Incorporate **Examples 19 and 20** into this work.

Give students some squares with a known area (use one that is not a perfect square to generate discussion; for example, $20\,cm^2$) and ask if they can work out what the side length would be. Ask students to estimate the side length for those that are not perfect squares. Introduce the square root of a number, linking it to area and side length and using the symbol correctly. Repeat this by giving the volume of cubes, again asking for side length before introducing the cube root symbol.

Make sure that students are aware of the correct use of language and written notation as well as how to use a calculator for these questions.

Using **Examples 22 and 23**, discuss how to find the two integers between which a square root will lie if it is not a whole number. Consolidate this work through **Exercise 1.6**. Questions 10 to 12 may be good questions for collaborative working and discussion of strategies and approaches. In Question 12 discuss the different explanations students give and how the working can be written.

1.7 Order of Operations and Using a Calculator

Learning Objectives:

- Apply the order of operations in calculations
- Use calculators to apply operations

MyMaths
1167 Order of operations
1932 Calculator methods 1
1933 Calculator methods 2

Write a calculation on the board such as $3 + 4 \times 5$ and ask the students to write down the answer on a whiteboard. Ask the class to show their whiteboards and write down the different answers given. Discuss why the answers are different and how the calculations would be written in order to achieve those answers.

Note that students may choose not to perform multiplication and division, and addition and subtraction, from left to right. Sometimes this can make the calculation less difficult. For example, consider the expression $82 \times 51 \div 41$. Finding $82 \div 41$ first (instead of 82×51) makes the calculation easier.

Work through **Examples 24 and 25**. Ask students to practise with their calculators to check they get the same results. Use **Example 26** to discuss with students how to form the calculations from a worded problem. **Exercise 1.7** will give students practice at using the order of operations. Make sure students use a single expression in Questions 12 and 13. As a challenge at the end, ask students to make up worded problems to go with some of the level 2 calculations.

1.8 Factors and Multiples

Learning Objectives:

- Identify multiples and factors of numbers
- Apply the above concepts to solve daily life problems

MyMaths

1035 Multiples

1032 Factors and primes

An opening activity would be to give students 12 square tiles and ask them to make as many different rectangles as possible, recording the dimensions as they build them. Discuss that the product of the dimensions each time gives the total number of squares and therefore each of the dimensions divides exactly into 12. The dimensions can then be named as factors. Discuss how this activity could be done systematically as the starting number of squares increase. When would they know they have found all the factors?

Work through **Examples 27, 28 and 29,** considering how to decide if a number is a factor of a given number and how to find common factors. Use the **Discuss** boxes by Examples 28 and 29 to consider different factors; ask students to work in pairs to discuss what they notice. Encourage students to think carefully about their explanations and reasons, using precise mathematical language.

Introduce the definition of a multiple and work through **Examples 30 and 31**. Check that students understand the word 'product' and that they are able to see the link between factors and multiples.

When looking at common multiples, discuss ways of making the solution more efficient. For example, in **Example 32** students can write down the multiples of both numbers at the same time or they can write down the first few multiples of the larger number first and then write multiples of the smaller number to 'catch it up' until they find a common multiple.

Looking at rules to see if a number is divisible by 3, 5, 6, 9 and 10 will help students when they are finding factors. This can be done as an investigation or a directed piece of work.

Exercise 1.8 will consolidate this work. Questions 13 to 18 will help students understand the usefulness of this area of work. Question 18 extends the thinking and will provide evidence of a student's fluency with this work.

Revision Exercise 1 recaps the work from this chapter and applies it to worded questions in a variety of contexts. Ask students to discuss their answers for Question 13(b) in order to clarify their reasoning. Questions 11 and 13 scaffold a multi-step problem; in each case these problems could be presented without part (a) to increase the challenge.

Questions 32 and 35 in **Workbook 1C Chapter 1** provide the opportunity to discuss how drawing a bar model may help students understand a problem and facilitate an algebraic solution.

The **Write in Your Journal** task helps students to recall and explain their thinking steps in mental calculation questions. Writing annotated examples allows them to revise these strategies at a later date.

The idea of negative numbers is first introduced through some everyday examples, such as winter temperatures, as negative numbers in these situations are likely to be familiar to students. The number line is used as a powerful graphical representation of numbers and helps students to visualise their size in relation to each other. The operations of negative integers are explored using algebra discs as using these manipulatives will consolidate understanding.

k *are resources on Kerboodle*

Resources

k Chapter 2 introduction video

k Try It! videos 1, 5, 7, 9

Algebra discs

Assessment

Workbook 1C Chapter 2

Graded Question Bank 1 Chapter 2

k Chapter 2 online skills test

k Chapter 2 end of chapter test and mark scheme

k Fully-worked solutions: Chapter 2 in Workbook 1C and Graded Question Bank 1

2.1 Negative Numbers and the Number Line

Learning Objectives:

- Recognise the use of negative numbers in the real world
- Represent numbers on a number line

MyMaths

1069 Negative numbers 1
1776 Negative numbers in context

Use the **Flashback** (page 38) as a means of introducing/consolidating the meaning of 'integer'. An intuitive idea of negative numbers arises from situations such as time zones and the temperature scale below zero. **Class Activity 1** could be done by finding pictures on the computer rather than taking photos. Students should be able to classify integers into three groups: positive integers, zero and negative integers. It is important to use 'negative' rather than 'minus' when reading a number (e.g. –8 is read as negative 8), as the sign in front of the 8 does not mean subtract. Careful use of correct language at this stage will help reduce any confusion later when students are calculating.

Students should learn how to draw a number line (see **Remark** page 40). Through **Examples 2 and 3** they should build up the concept of inequality and ordering using the number line. The idea of –3 > –8 can be illustrated by the fact that –8 °C is colder than –3 °C. Spend time here making sure students fully grasp the inequality signs and the meaning of ascending and descending so that these do not get in the way of exploring the concept of negative numbers. Encourage students to close their eyes and visualise the number line with both positive and negative numbers so that they have a mental image for comparing integers later. Discuss with students that not

all number lines go up in steps of 1. Create some number lines with different step lengths and ask students to explain when different ones should be used.

By working through **Exercise 2.1** students will gain an understanding of negative numbers in context and what the negative sign means in each case. Question 20 could be done in pairs with students discussing the problem. Question 21 provides a good discussion for students to understand how the numbers are built. It may be interesting to consider Question 22 as a whole-class discussion.

2.2 Addition and Subtraction of Integers

Learning Objective:

- Identify integers and perform addition and subtraction on them

MyMaths

1068 Negative numbers 2

Algebra discs are introduced in this section to help students add and subtract with negative integers. Spend time with the discs so that students are confident in how to build a positive and a negative number. Vitally important is the understanding of a zero pair which is illustrated on page 43. Ask students to take a mixture of discs and, using zero pairs, work out what overall total they have. Can they use discs to show a positive total, a negative total or a zero total? Discuss the reasoning behind these calculations. Use **Class Activity 2** to manipulate the discs to show how to add two integers with the same sign and with different signs.

Work through **Example 4** making use of the discs if needed for deeper understanding.

Subtraction uses the process of flipping the discs to obtain the negative of a number; when subtracting, a negative number will 'flip' to become positive and a positive number will 'flip' to become negative. This is probably a new idea and therefore one that needs to be discussed in order to understand how it works. This technique is invaluable later when simplifying, adding and subtracting expressions in Chapter 3. Discuss the reasoning used on page 45; look at how the subtraction sign in front flips all the discs in the box. Take time to discuss the concluding sentence before Class Activity 3 to ensure students are happy with the idea that subtraction is equivalent to 'adding the negative'. When mathematicians define arithmetic formally, they specify that: $a - b$ is the same as $a + (-b)$ where $-b$ is the same as $-1 \times b$ and -1 is the additive inverse of 1, so that $1 + (-1) = (-1) + 1 = 0$. So, it is not a coincidence that, for example, $5 - 2$ is the same as $5 + (-2)$: the two calculations are equal by definition. Any calculation 'minuend – subtrahend' is defined to equal 'minuend + negative of subtrahend'. **Class Activity 3** leads students through subtracting a positive integer and subtracting a negative integer by using the algebra discs. Discuss the outcome of these calculations and generalise the results. After discussing this activity, ask students to generate calculations of their own for their partner to solve. Spending time with the discs will consolidate these ideas, using the practical in order to move to the abstract. Work through **Examples 5 to 7** using the discs to support the students' understanding. Through Example 7, draw attention to the need for stating what is denoted by positive and negative numbers. In **Try It! 7** it is important students state which direction is positive before answering the question. Completing levels 1 and 2 of **Exercise 2.2** will help with fluency of calculation, while level 3 will make students think about which calculation is necessary for the context of the question. Encourage use of discs to build confidence. Use Question 11 to discuss students' conclusions.

2.3 Multiplication, Division and Combined Operations of Integers

Learning Objectives:

- Identify integers and perform multiplication and division on them
- Combine operations of integers

⊕ **MyMaths**

1068 Negative numbers 2

Multiplication can be explored by using the grouping and ungrouping of algebra discs. **Class Activity 4** allows students time to practise this and discover how to multiply a positive and a negative integer and also two negative integers. Allow time to discuss any questions students may have about these examples; for example, why $(-2) \times (-3)$ is the same as $-[2 \times (-3)]$. You can see that 'flipping' the discs negates their values. What is

happening arithmetically is that the value on each disc is multiplied by -1 (and this is what happens on the number line: the negative numbers are the reflection, the 'flip', of the positive numbers). Students should be aware of this. Discuss the commutative rule in this context by looking at Question 4 of the activity.

The + or – sign in the brackets defines a number as positive or negative. The brackets separate the number from the operation. Using brackets around negative numbers will help students manipulate the calculations more easily and transfer them onto a calculator more effectively. Show students how to input a negative number into a calculator and distinguish between this and the subtract operation.

Students already know that to find a square root they must find a number which is multiplied by itself to give the number under the square root symbol. Up to this point they have only seen positive numbers in this context, but now they will be able to understand that multiplying a negative by itself will result in a positive answer. Therefore use part (c) of **Example 8** to highlight the negative value of a square root so that students understand a square root will have two solutions. Discuss with students the two solutions to the square root of 9, 25, 100, etc.

Students explore the rules for division of integers by considering division as the inverse of multiplication. Remind students that division by zero is undefined. As students often struggle with division, ask them to write their own division and multiplication facts like those in the middle of page 52.

When performing combined operations on integers, it is crucial that students understand the order of operations in an expression involving brackets and the four operations. Encourage students to write down all the steps as they work through each stage of the calculation until they are confident (as in **Examples 10 and 11**).

Consolidate learning by completing **Exercise 2.3**. The contextual questions in level 3 will enable students to transfer their skills into other subjects and real-world situations. Ask students to think carefully about how they write what they notice for Question 13; encourage full sentences to practise communicating mathematically. They can then share their findings with each other.

Completing **Revision Exercise 2** will increase students' fluency with negative integers. Questions 2 and 3 use addition and multiplication tables to find missing values and involve students working forwards and backwards on calculations. Question 7 provides a good discussion and can be linked to other real-world uses for negative numbers. Discuss Question 10 so that students understand that the bigger total is not always the best one in a given situation.

Completing the table in the **Write in Your Journal** activity and spotting patterns will consolidate students' understanding of the effect of the negative sign when multiplying.

Chapter 3
Introduction to Algebra

Student Book 1C
pages 58–89

It is important to make a smooth transition from arithmetic expressions to algebraic expressions as this can often be a stumbling block for students. The previous two chapters focussed on the structure of the arithmetic work through the use of bar models and algebra discs, and these will prove to be valuable tools when developing understanding of algebraic expressions. Students will generalise simple daily-life scenarios to understand the value of using variables. Constant comparison with the numerical work will build confidence and understanding. The summary table in **Section 3.1** (page 63), comparing the words to the model and the algebraic expression for the four rules, is a very useful review of the key concepts and should be compared to the numerical work in the **Flashback** (page 59) to embed understanding.

---

k are resources on Kerboodle

Resources

k Chapter 3 introduction video
k Try It! videos 9, 13, 22–24, 28
Algebra discs

Assessment

Workbook 1C Chapter 3
Graded Question Bank 1 Chapter 3
k Chapter 3 online skills test
k Chapter 3 end of chapter test and mark scheme
k Fully-worked solutions: Chapter 3 in Workbook 1C and Graded Question Bank 1

3.1 Letters to Represent Numbers

Learning Objectives:

- Use letters to represent numbers
- Interpret simple algebraic notations

⊕ MyMaths

1982 Introduction to algebra
1158 Rules and formulae
1179 Simplifying 1

By exploring some daily-life scenarios in the initial examples, students should find that the use of letters is an easy and efficient way to express a generalised arithmetic expression. Use of age, mass, length and money are all very accessible and relevant to the students.

Ask students if a variable can represent any unknown number. They need to understand that it can and that a variable is used as an unknown quantity. It is important not to confuse students by assigning a letter to an object, for example three apples and four bananas is not $3a + 4b$. Instead a stands for the amount of something, like the amount of apples in a bag, so that $3a$ is the total number of apples in three bags. Ask students if it matters which letter is used for the unknown; for example, does it matter if you use m kg or x kg for the mass of a baby?

Students need to understand the algebraic conventions for expressing addition, subtraction, multiplication and division including the use of positive integer indices. Ask, what is different between $3a$ and a^3? Ensure students understand and can explain why they are different.

Ask students to discuss in pairs or small groups the rules for writing expressions. As a class, create a poster of the rules for the classroom wall.

(For example: write division as $\frac{x}{y}$ rather than $x \div y$; write variables in alphabetical order; variables do not have units; a number next to a letter means multiply.) Make sure that the commutative and associative laws are mentioned here in relation to multiplication so that students are convinced $c \times a \times 4 \times b$ is the same as $4 \times a \times b \times c$ and therefore can be written as $4abc$.

Bar models are a pictorial way of helping students to form expressions, which will help to embed understanding before moving to the abstract, see **Examples 1, 2 and 3**.

Discuss with students the meaning of the brackets in **Example 7** and ensure students can explain for themselves why $(3x)^2$ and $3x^2$ are different.

In problems it is important that students understand that a variable does not have a unit and that only the whole expression does. Therefore, in problems involving units, brackets should be used, for example $(x + 3)$ cm.

Exercise 3.1 develops reasoning from numerical expressions to algebraic expressions. This is done at each level as the questions become more challenging. Completing this whole exercise will be very useful in building understanding. Discuss with students when a numerical answer is possible in a question and when an expression is required.

3.2 Substituting Numbers for Letters

Learning Objective:

- Substitute integers into simple expressions and formulae

⊕ MyMaths

1187 Substitution 1
1186 Substitution 2

This section begins by introducing substitution into expressions before moving on to define formulae. This means students have the opportunity to consolidate their understanding of substitution by substituting into both expressions and formulae. Deepen students' understanding by discussing the meaning of the coefficient for real-life contexts.

Make explicit the definitions of expression (as on page 60) and formula (page 68). Discuss with students 'what is the same' and 'what is different' about an expression and a formula. Make sure they understand and can explain the difference.

Ensure students understand the meaning of the word substitution. Relate it to a sporting substitution to embed the idea of a variable being exchanged for a number. Ask students again what $3x$ means and if necessary suggest they refer to the poster they made in **Section 3.1**. Ask students to explain why if $x = 5$, $3x$ becomes 3×5 and not 35.

Students must consider the order of operations when evaluating. Encourage students to use a bracket to enclose a negative number, so the negative sign is separate from the operation (see **Example 10**). Encourage students to write their solutions vertically lining up equal signs rather than all on one line. Recall the order of operations when discussing **Example 13**.

In **Class Activity 1**, a spreadsheet allows students to compare different expressions. This is an opportunity for students to use spreadsheet notation for formulae. It is also an opportunity to challenge any student's misconceptions regarding expressions. For example, by looking at the spreadsheet they should notice that $(3n)^2$ is not the same as $3n^2$, and they should be able to explain why. **Exercise 3.2** begins with evaluating expressions, before moving on to evaluate formulae. This is another opportunity to discuss the difference between the two. Questions 19 and 20 will challenge students to think about the problem in the given situation. Questions 21 and 22 can be tackled as group activities; challenge students to find the most complicated formulae they can.

3.3 Writing Algebraic Expressions and Formulae

Learning Objective:

● Write simple expressions and formulae

1158 Rules and formulae

Bar models offer visual representations of problems and provide a 'stepping stone' from the words to the abstract algebra. They are used to demonstrate when one quantity is more or less than another, and by how much. They are also used to demonstrate when

one quantity is n times another quantity (where n could be a fraction). Ensure students have plenty of practice using the bar models to support their understanding.

Use **Example 15** to discuss the use of typical mathematical language: 'Express y in terms of x.'

It takes time for students to master the skill of formulating algebraic expressions from word problems so plenty of practice is advisable.

Fully completing **Exercise 3.3** and **Workbook 1C Chapter 3** will develop this skill. Encourage the use of bar models when students find a question challenging, so that they can make sense of the words.

3.4 Like Terms and Unlike Terms

Learning Objective:

● Simplify expressions by collecting like terms

1179 Simplifying 1

Work through **Example 18** and ask students to identify the terms, coefficients and constants in different expressions. Use this language as much as possible when discussing expressions.

Discuss how the terms of an expression can be repositioned to keep the expression equivalent. Students should understand that the sign is attached to the coefficient (which could be an unwritten 1) rather than the variable. The **Discuss** on page 75 is vital; students must recognise that these are unlike terms.

Ask students if (x and x^2) and (a^2b and ab) are two pairs of like or unlike terms. Ask students to write down other terms that would match each of the terms in the brackets. This could be done as a paired activity where one student writes a term and the other has to write a like term that matches it.

Using manipulatives like Cuisenaire™ Rods, where different lengths (colours) represent different variables, and 'algebra through geometry', where x is a square and y a quadrant, help to embed the understanding of like and unlike terms before moving to the abstract.

Class Activity 2 introduces the use of the algebra discs to help with collecting like terms. Students should be familiar with zero pairs from their work on negative integers; this is now extended to include x, $-x$, etc. Using the discs, students can see how expressions can be written in different ways, which is important for manipulation later. Time needs to be spent on this activity so that all students become confident. Again, ask students to make up their own expressions to simplify, to embed this understanding.

Questions at the end of **Class Activity 2** promote student thinking about application of the distributive law. Discuss Question 2 to ensure students understand that $3x + 4y$ cannot be written as $7xy$.

Examples 19 and **20** could be demonstrated through zero pairs using the algebra discs if students need more consolidation.

Question 9 onwards of **Exercise 3.4** can be used to reinforce that the variables in a formula or expression do not include units of measure.

3.5 Addition and Subtraction of Linear Expressions

Learning Objective:

● Add and subtract linear expressions

MyMaths

1179 Simplifying 1

Discuss when a term is linear and when it is not. Students often quickly see that x^2 is not linear but need more convincing about xy.

To build on previous work, each linear expression is initially written in brackets which are then removed and like terms collected.

Recall how flipping discs was used when subtracting negative integers in Chapter 2. The process of flipping algebra discs when dealing with the negative of an expression can help students to understand and remember $-(a + b - c) = -a - b + c$. Remind students at this point that negation is by definition the same as multiplying by -1 (see page 30 in this Teacher Guide). This is explored in **Class Activity 3** before looking at addition and subtraction of expressions. Again, through

the whole activity the discs should be used to consolidate understanding. However, when tackling **Exercise 3.5**, encourage students to use the discs only if they need to.

3.6 Expressions with Brackets

Learning Objectives:

● Expand a single bracket

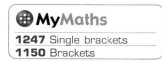

MyMaths

1247 Single brackets
1150 Brackets

Class Activity 4 looks at rewriting expressions with brackets as expressions without brackets. The understanding relies on ungrouping groups, and the algebra discs are used to explain what is happening. It uses previous work on flipping discs when a bracket is being multiplied by a negative. Question 4 brings the students to the understanding that expanding brackets follows the distributive law of multiplication over addition and subtraction.

Revision Exercise 3 allows students to practise the algebraic concepts introduced in this chapter. This is also an opportunity to use the questions to check students' knowledge of language and key algebraic terms they have learnt. The worded questions at the end bring more meaning back to the abstract nature of Questions 1–10, and provide opportunities for students to generate formulae in a variety of contexts and use them to solve problems.

Further practice from **Workbook 1C Chapter 3** will provide challenge and deepen understanding. Question 35 should be tackled by trial and improvement as students will not have solved equations at this point.

The terminology used in algebra needs to be embedded. Ask students to complete the **Write in Your Journal** task to write their own definitions for these words. This will help students distinguish between the words.

A visual approach is used to deepen students' understanding of manipulating equations to find solutions (i.e. roots). For example, bar models (from previous chapters), balancing scales and algebra discs (including zero pairs) are all used. Encourage students to check their answers by substituting solutions back into the equations. Ensure that students understand that 'equals' means 'the same on both sides' as frequently students only interpret the equals sign as meaning 'the answer is'. You can explore this by asking what students think about statements such as 4 = 4 and 4 = 10. Many will say something like 'you mean 4 + 0 = 4' and '4 + 6 = 10' i.e. they will think they have to complete the calculation.

This is a key piece of understanding when manipulating equations. Encourage students to write down the working for each step when solving an equation to help consolidate their learning and show their thinking process.

k *are resources on Kerboodle*

Resources

k Chapter 4 introduction video

k Try It! videos 2, 6, 9, 11, 14
Algebra discs

Assessment

Workbook 1C Chapter 4

Graded Question Bank 1 Chapter 4

k Chapter 4 online skills test

k Chapter 4 end of chapter test and mark scheme

k Fully-worked solutions: Chapter 4 in Workbook 1C and Graded Question Bank 1

4.1 Equations in One Variable

Learning Objectives:

● Understand the concept of equations and balancing

● Solve simple equations in one variable

⊕ My Maths

1925 Equations 1 – one step
1154 Equations 2 – multi-step

Using the **Flashback** (page 91) for guidance, make sure students are confident dealing with negative numbers and substituting into expressions. They also need to remember their work with algebra discs and 'zero pairs' from both Chapter 2 and Chapter 3 so a quick activity involving these could be a helpful reminder.

The bar model helps students visualise the information that is known and the information that is missing. This provides a 'stepping stone' into the algebra. As students move to the formal algebraic representation, the question mark is replaced with the variable x (as on page 92). Discuss with students whether it matters if a different letter is used. Bring in the vocabulary 'solution' and 'root' at the same time, so that students understand they are the same thing. Use the **Remark** box on page 92 to ensure students understand the notation. Checking the solution is correct by working out the LHS and showing it equals the RHS (or vice versa) is an important method, which will be very useful in their later mathematics learning.

Consolidate understanding by asking students to draw a bar model of their own that represents an addition problem. For example, if I bought a drink for 45p and a sandwich for 75p, what would I have spent in total? Repeat this for a subtraction problem; for example, if I had a £5 note and bought a pen for £2, how much change would I get? Move from the bar models into the algebra, writing and solving the equation.

Class Activity 1 demonstrates two methods for solving equations: using a bar model and balancing scales. The balancing scales will require students to use algebra discs and 'zero pairs'. Make sure they check their answer each time by substituting into the original question. Use the **Discuss** box (page 95) to consider further equations containing fractions of x. Avoid suggesting that this may be more of a challenge because it involves a fraction. The visual models and methods are exactly the same as for addition and subtraction. Use both of the methods for all examples and then discuss with students which they prefer and why. You may wish to briefly discuss the limitation of the bar or balance model, that implicitly x is positive. Representing $x + 5 = 2$ as a bar is much harder than $x + 2 = 5$.

Discuss the effect of adding, subtracting, multiplying and dividing both sides of an equation by the same number. The knowledge that the equation remains balanced at every step is the key to solving problems.

Examples 1–4 show the four operations; turning these into a general form using the **Remarks** enriches students' understanding. Discuss the methods used and how the solutions have been set out; use the Try It! for each example to check students' written solutions. **Examples 5 and 6** are both multi-step equations, but whereas Example 5 has only one x term, Example 6 has an x term on both sides, so the first step here is to eliminate x from one side. These multi-step problems are a key development point so discuss further examples with the students.

Exercise 4.1 consolidates the work on single-step equations before moving onto multi-step equations. Encourage students to use a bar model or balancing scales until they are confident to just use the algebraic method. After completing Questions 6 and 7, ask students to write their own questions for a partner to solve in order to give them more practice at two-step problems. Question 11 could be tackled as a class activity using a cloud diagram on the board with $x = -3$ in the cloud. After a few minutes students could start writing their equations on the rays. This can help the less confident to see what equations are being generated and help them to form their own. Change the starting number and try again.

4.2 Equations in One Variable with Brackets

Learning Objectives:

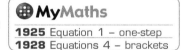

- Solve simple equations involving brackets

1925 Equation 1 – one-step
1928 Equations 4 – brackets

Work through **Examples 7 and 8,** showing both the method given in the solution and also the approach mentioned in the Remark on page 99. Discuss with students (examples) when one way may be better than another. Continue to work through the examples, making sure students check their answer each time by finding the LHS and RHS.

Exercise 4.2 challenges students to tackle quite complex problems involving brackets on both sides of the equation. The level 3 questions bring in worded problems; ask students to discuss their understanding of the questions and to compare their solutions, explaining any differences. Question 9(b) will foster a good discussion about possible values of k. Ask students to compare answers and then decide what rules k must follow in order to provide an integer answer. Further challenge is provided by the later questions in **Workbook 1C Chapter 4.**

4.3 Writing Equations to Solve Problems

Learning Objective:

1158 Rules and formulae

- Write simple equations in one variable to solve problems

Students are asked to solve real-world problems by forming appropriate equations and using algebra to find the solution. **Class Activity 2** allows students to work step by step through two problems. Make sure students recognise the parts of the bar model representing the problem. For example, read the first sentence of the problem, then look at how this is represented on the bar model. Then read the second sentence of the problem and look at how that is represented on the bar model. In this way, students will begin to understand how to read and interpret problems, and how to build their corresponding bar models. Encourage students to check their solutions as well. At the end of this activity ask pairs of students to write down the steps they think would be useful to follow when solving real-world problems. Discuss these as a class and agree the steps required (see page 102).

Work through **Examples 11–14.** For each example draw the bar model then ask students what equation they would write and if there is only one way to write each of the equations. Discuss any alternatives that are given and show the solutions are the same.

Exercise 4.3 consolidates the work by giving the bar model in level 1, before moving onto writing the equations in level 2. The problem-solving questions in level 3 provide a high degree of challenge and require a thorough understanding. Working in pairs and discussing these questions will aid student understanding. If the students find any equations difficult to form, ask them to try drawing a bar model first. This 'tool' will be very useful in future work.

Use **Revision Exercise 4** to assess the skills the students have developed as the questions move from simple equations through to worded problems.

The **Write in Your Journal** activity asks students to write their own problem; this encourages deep thinking skills. For students who find this difficult ask them to write an equation to solve and then to write a worded problem that can go with it.

Review Exercise 1

The purpose of this exercise is to consolidate the learning from the previous four chapters by combining the topics into integrated questions. Encourage the students to show all their working, looking back at previous work to consider the most efficient methods.

The exercise will enable students to become fluent with the skills they have developed. Encourage them to look back at earlier work if they are finding questions challenging and consider which models were helpful in previous chapters. Remind them of the manipulatives and pictures, such as algebra discs, bar models and balancing scales, which helped them to access problems more easily.

Students often make mistakes on a calculator when dealing with negative numbers. Ask students to check their answers to Question 6 with a calculator to allow them to practise this skill. Question 8 could be extended as a whole class activity by asking students, in pairs, to create their own table and questions which can then be given to another pair to work out; this will encourage higher-level thinking. Question 10(c) can be tackled in two ways; ask students to compare the methods and discuss the efficiency of each. Question 15 is likely to be tackled in a variety of ways; ask students to discuss their strategies and explain their thinking, then discuss the merits of each one.

The idea that a fraction represents part of a whole is reinforced throughout this chapter. It is important that the whole is defined; sometimes the whole is a single object, sometimes the whole is a group of objects. Students have the opportunity to revisit negative numbers, by considering negative fractions. They also learn to use a calculator for calculations involving fractions. Make the connection between a fraction and the division it represents to deepen understanding.

k *are resources on Kerboodle*

Resources

k Chapter 5 introduction video

k Try It! videos 2, 8, 10, 12, 16, 19

Assessment

Workbook 1C Chapter 5

Graded Question Bank 1 Chapter 5

k Chapter 5 online skills test

k Chapter 5 end of chapter test and mark scheme

k Fully-worked solutions: Chapter 5 in Workbook 1C and Graded Question Bank 1

5.1 Quantities as Fractions

Learning Objectives:

- Use fraction notation and express one quantity as a fraction of another
- Convert between improper fractions and mixed numbers

MyMaths

1220 Simple fractions
1062 Finding fractions
1019 Improper and mixed fractions

Make sure that the students understand the concept of a whole being a group of objects in the first section on **Proper Fractions** (page 112). Bar models are used to represent the whole, with sections representing the parts. Draw a bar model and ask students to describe it in words and then fractions. The **Discuss** box emphasises the crucial concept that a fraction is a number of *equal* parts of a whole.

When improper fractions are introduced, point out to the students that diagrams show several clearly labelled wholes and a fraction of a whole. Method 2 of **Example 2** makes the clear connection between a fraction and division for converting an improper number to a mixed number.

Take care that students appreciate the concept of proportion when one quantity is being expressed as a fraction of another. Where students are asked to find the number of red marbles as a fraction of the number of green marbles in **Example 3** students need to understand that this is a way of considering one colour as a proportion of the other colours – here there are $\frac{8}{5}$ as many green as red.

Exercise 5.1 enables students to practise interpreting pictorial representations of fractions, writing fractions and converting between mixed numbers and improper fractions. The open Question 12 could be worked on in pairs and the answers compared by the whole class. Return to this question later after covering Section 5.2 and challenge students to make the greatest and least possible fraction with the numbers given. Once students have identified all the possible fractions, ask them to put them in order of size.

5.2 Equivalent Fractions and Comparing Fractions

Learning Objective:

- Identify equivalent fractions, simplify fractions and compare fractions

MyMaths

1042 Equivalent fractions
1075 Comparing fractions
1771 Ordering and simplifying fractions

Students need to be able to find common multiples easily for work finding equivalent fractions; the **Flashback** (page 111) provides a reminder for students. A fraction wall can help students to compare fractions. Link this pictorial representation to work on bar models. Use the **Discuss** boxes (pages 116 and 117) to encourage accurate and clear mathematical communication, giving students the opportunity to explain their thinking and give their reasons, choosing words carefully.

Class Activity 1 demonstrates that fractions can be compared in several different ways. Use the bar models to explore the nature of fractions and the meaning of the number that is the numerator and the number that is the denominator. Students can then use this knowledge to compare fractions which have the same denominator or the same numerator. Using a number line is valuable when negative fractions and mixed numbers are also introduced for comparison.

The level 1 questions in **Exercise 5.2** give practice in simplifying both positive and negative fractions, finding equivalent fractions and comparing fractions. The level 2 questions extend this work to include mixed numbers and improper fractions. Make sure that students notice the negative fractions that appear and remind them that a number line may help them compare these fractions. Consider student responses to Questions 11 and 12 as a whole class to establish that in both cases there is an infinite set of possible answers. Question 15 may generate rich discussion, for example when deciding if the relative size of m and n makes a difference to the answer.

5.3 Addition and Subtraction of Fractions and Mixed Numbers

Learning Objectives:

- Perform the four operations on fractions and on mixed numbers
- Apply fractions in practical situations

MyMaths

1017 Adding subtracting fractions
1074 Mixed numbers

When calculating with fractions, avoid introducing 'quick' alternative methods based on rules. Instead, ensure students further consolidate their understanding of fractions as they work on adding them. Use visual models such as those shown in **Example 9** (page 121) to support students' understanding.

A common misconception is that you simply add/subtract denominators and numerators. Discuss with students why this doesn't work by showing fractions of shapes shaded to demonstrate why, for example, $\frac{1}{5} + \frac{2}{5}$ does not equal $\frac{3}{10}$. Consolidate understanding by saying aloud, 'one-fifth plus two-fifths equals three-fifths'. It might be helpful to make the comparison with £1 plus £2 is £3 or 1 cm plus 2 cm is 3 cm etc. The 'fifths' are the unit in which we are counting.

Discuss mixed number methods with students to help them make a decision whether to convert to improper fractions or deal with whole number parts and fractions separately. Provided that students are secure with negative numbers, the latter method will usually lead to simpler arithmetic.

In completing **Exercise 5.3** students will practise adding and subtracting all types of fractions. They need to deal

with different denominators, mixed numbers and negative answers as they progress through the level 1 and level 2 questions. For the later Questions 9 and 10, remind students to work from left to right when adding or subtracting unless an operation shown in brackets takes priority. (Though of course, always encourage them to look at the question in case there is an obviously better method, for example if solving $\frac{1}{2} + \frac{2}{7} - \frac{1}{2} + \frac{4}{7}$.) If any students are unsure how to start any of the problem-solving Questions 12 to 14, suggest they draw bar models to visualise the problem.

5.4 Multiplication of Fractions

Learning Objectives:

- Calculate fractions of quantities
- Perform the four operations on fractions and on mixed numbers
- Apply fractions in practical situations

MyMaths

1841 Fractions as operators
1046 Multiply divide fractions intro
1768 Starting to multiply fractions
1047 Multiplying fractions
1769 Multiplying fractions by fractions
1074 Mixed numbers

Using a bar model will help students appreciate that finding the unit fraction (e.g. $\frac{1}{4}$) is a first stage to finding any fraction of a quantity. Emphasise the **Remark** on page 126 that 'of' means 'multiply' to help lead students to the more efficient method of multiplication.

Multiplication by integers is dealt with first and then multiplication of two fractions. When teaching multiplication of a fraction by an integer (as in method 2 of **Example 14** on page 126) it may be helpful to write the integer, here 20, with denominator 1 to emphasise that the denominator of the other fraction remains unchanged when multiplied by 1.

Whenever fractions are multiplied, encourage students to cancel before multiplying to make the calculation easier to perform.

Carefully work through **Example 17** (page 128), where the grid method is used for the multiplication of mixed numbers, and point out that there are four calculations to be performed. Drawing a grid ensures that students do not miss parts of the complete calculation and don't fall into the error of multiplying first the whole number, then the fraction parts and finding the total of just these two calculations.

When working through **Exercise 5.4** students have the opportunity to consolidate previous work with negative numbers and apply the correct order of operations. Once completed, students can discuss different approaches to Question 10. They are effectively asked to find $\frac{3}{4}$ of $\frac{1}{5}$ of 40 which could be completed as a single calculation. Contrast this with Question 11 where both fractions to be calculated are of the same whole £1400. For Questions 14 and 15 encouraging students to write $1\frac{3}{5}$ and $3\frac{4}{7}$ as different equivalent improper fractions will open up discussion about the number of possible solutions.

5.5 Division of Fractions and Mixed Numbers

Learning Objectives:

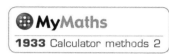

⊕ My Maths

1046 Multiply divide fractions intro
1040 Dividing fractions
1074 Mixed numbers

- Find the reciprocal of a number
- Perform the four operations on fractions and on mixed numbers
- Calculate fractions of quantities
- Apply fractions in practical situations

At the start of work on division, use examples to remind students that to share into a number of groups you can divide by the number of groups or multiply by a fraction. Relating this fraction to the number of groups leads onto the idea of a reciprocal. Explain the meaning of the word reciprocal, emphasising that it is a long word to describe an easy idea.

Use diagrams (as on pages 130 and 131) to demonstrate division by a fraction visually. As with work on multiplication, students must get used to cancelling whenever possible before fractions are multiplied to avoid arithmetic with large numbers.

Dealing with the remainder after division in real-life scenarios, as in **Example 22** and Questions 11, 12 and 13 of **Exercise 5.5**, will need careful explanation so that students do not omit the last step to calculate the remainder fraction of the divisor. Using bar models to represent parts of ribbon in Question 11, parts of drink in Question 12 and cakes or buns in Question 13 may be helpful. In open Question 14, encourage students to consider how the product of the numerators will need

to be a multiple of the product of the denominators to give an integer answer when multiplication takes place. Exercise 5.5 includes not just division but also calculations including more operations so that students can practise applying the correct order of operations. Students should recall that they do not always need to perform multiplication and division, and addition and subtraction, from left to right. Reordering can sometimes make the calculations easier (see page 27 of this Teacher Guide).

5.6 Rational Numbers and Using a Calculator

Learning Objective:

⊕ My Maths

1933 Calculator methods 2

- Identify fractions as rational numbers

Remind students that the division of two integers can always be written as a fraction. The division symbol itself is the same format as a fraction if the two dots are replaced by integers. Encourage students to write a division of their own, and then write it as a fraction.

To practise using a calculator for fraction calculations, students should work through the **Key Sequence** table (page 134) to check that they obtain the same answers. Make sure that students can complete the required key sequence for their particular model of calculator. Careful use of brackets will help ensure accuracy when students complete level 2 questions in **Exercise 5.6**.

Revision Exercise 5 offers further practice with fraction calculations and problem solving. Discuss with students the different methods to compare fractions in Question 1 and encourage them to think about whether to use common numerators or common denominators. For Questions 10 to 15, which are given in various real-life contexts, students will need to decide which operation(s) to use.

The **Write in Your Journal** activity consolidates the use of common numerators to compare fractions. Student explanations will highlight their understanding of how a larger denominator means the whole is split into a greater number of parts and so those parts of the whole will each be smaller.

Student Book 1C
pages 138–166

Throughout the chapter, place value tables and number lines provide visual models for decimals. These help students gain a better understanding of the relative sizes of decimal numbers. Care needs to be taken with language; make sure that students really appreciate the difference between whole number and decimal place values, for example hundreds and hundred*ths*. Laminated empty place value charts and blank number lines may be useful resources for students to write on during some of the class activities.

k *are resources on Kerboodle*

Resources

k Chapter 6 introduction video

k Try It! videos 7, 9, 13, 21, 24

Assessment

Workbook 1C Chapter 6

Graded Question Bank 1 Chapter 6

k Chapter 6 online skills test

k Chapter 6 end of chapter test and mark scheme

k Fully-worked solutions: Chapter 6 in Workbook 1C and Graded Question Bank 1

6.1 Place Values, Ordering and Rounding of Decimal Numbers

Learning Objectives:

● Interpret decimals and write decimals in order of size

● Round decimals to the nearest integer

⊕ MyMaths

1076 Decimal place value
1072 Ordering decimals
1004 Rounding decimals

Column headings given as fractions for decimal place values builds on work covered in the previous fractions chapter. Writing decimals in expanded form helps students see the relative size of the digits in a number. Use the **Remark** and **Discuss** boxes (page 140) to ensure that students appreciate the value of zeros as place holders within a decimal and the redundancy of trailing zeros.

In **Example 2**, highlight that when writing down the value of a digit students should do so in words or with a fraction rather than a decimal e.g. 3 hundredths or $\frac{3}{100}$ rather than 0.03.

Before considering the use of number lines to compare decimals, give the students a number line with only two numbers labelled and ask them to label values marked at equal intervals between them. This will consolidate understanding of number lines and give students confidence to use them for non-integer values.

Using a place value table encourages students to line up digits and decimal points when comparing decimals. Having got into this habit, students may just write the decimal numbers in columns rather than in a table.

Example 4 compares decimals with different numbers of decimal places. Refer to the **Remark** box (page 142) to discuss how trailing zeros can be helpful when comparing decimals.

Using a number line for rounding to the nearest integer will help with later work on bounds. Using the rule to consider the tenths digit as the 'decider' when rounding to the nearest integer will set up the principle for rounding to other degrees of accuracy, e.g. when rounding to the nearest tenth, observe the hundredths digit.

In **Exercise 6.1** as well as comparing positive decimals, students are required to use their knowledge of negative numbers and compare negative decimals too. In Question 10, students need to recognise that in the context of a race, the 'best' time is the least value. Remind students that 0 is an integer for Question 13, where they need to round down to 0. Suggest students draw a number line for Question 15 if they struggle with comparing negative numbers in a real scientific context. Discuss answers to Question 16 as a whole-class activity, insisting that every student offers a different answer in order to demonstrate that there are an infinite number of possibilities.

6.2 Addition and Subtraction of Decimals

Learning Objective:

● Use the four operations with decimals

⊕ MyMaths

1380 Adding decimals mental
1381 Adding decimals in columns intro
1007 Add and subtract decimals

Addition and subtraction of decimals is initially introduced by writing the decimals in expanded form. The example shown gives an improper fraction for the tenths place value; this is then written as a mixed number, which helps students to understand the reason for regrouping in the formal column method. Use **Example 6** to build on students' confidence and understanding of similar calculations using integers instead of fractions. Use part (b) to demonstrate how to find a positive difference first and then adjust when the answer will be negative. Help students to interpret the context of **Example 7** by reading the entire problem aloud. Then read one sentence at a time and ensure students understand it. Look together at the maths associated with each sentence in the problem before moving on to the next.

In **Exercise 6.2**, parts (c) and (d) of both Questions 1 and 2 give students important practice at setting up the column method by lining up the decimal point. Remind students about the usefulness of trailing zeros when the decimals in the calculation have different numbers of digits after the decimal point. For part (d) of both Questions 2 and 3, students will need to deal with finding a negative answer as in **Example 6**.

The Question 6 Hint discourages a column method for 20.00 – 13.75. Discuss the alternative mental method of counting up from £13.75 to the next whole pound and then on to £20. Compare this method with the formal written method, so that students understand why the mental method may be preferable. Another method you may wish to consider is changing £20 – £13.75 to £19.99 – £13.74 which can be easily worked out.

6.3 Multiplication of Decimals

Learning Objective:

- Use the four operations with decimals

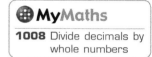

1011 Multiply two decimals
1382 Starting to multiply decimals

Class Activity 1 links decimal calculations to previous work on fractions. For example, by writing 0.6 as $\frac{6}{10}$ and 0.13 as $\frac{13}{100}$, students can see how and why the product of 0.6 and 0.13 is the product of 6 and 13 divided by 1000. Point out to students that the digits are the same as for the product of 6 and 13 but the position of the decimal point is different. Help students to identify that the number of decimal places for the two decimals is the same as the number of decimal places for their product.

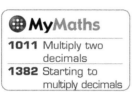

Make sure that students appreciate that extra zeros may need to be added to the right of the decimal point to make up enough decimal places in the product of two decimals. This is described in the third **Remark** beside **Example 8**.

Example 10 provides an opportunity to discuss how work should be set out and the importance of being clear when communicating mathematically. Students need to know that it is not enough to just write down calculations without stating what they tell you, e.g. the total mass of marbles.

The level 1 and 2 questions in **Exercise 6.3** offer practice at multiplying decimals. Remind students to use the correct order for operations in Question 6 and encourage them to check that their answers are reasonable by estimation. Students may need some help interpreting the contexts given in the level 3 questions and they should be encouraged to show their working clearly, as discussed for Example 10. Students could do Question 17 in pairs and then discuss strategies and compare answers as a whole class. Students should be able to place the decimal point easily; if they then struggle, suggest they set out the question as a long multiplication as a starting strategy.

6.4 Division of a Decimal by a Whole Number

Learning Objective:

- Use the four operations with decimals

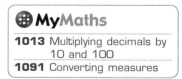

1008 Divide decimals by whole numbers

As with multiplication, **Class Activity 2** consolidates previous work on fractions. Students can see how the structure of dividing the parts of a mixed number separately matches up with the formal division method lining up the decimal points of quotient and dividend, shown in **Example 11**.

Work through **Example 12** and the Try It! Emphasise the use of the trailing zero. This is necessary to complete the division calculation with remainder zero, and will be important for later work with recurring decimals. **Exercise 6.4** gives practice with division including questions set in context for levels 2 and 3. If students struggle with Question 7, suggest first of all drawing a bar model of the problem. Gather together student responses to the open Question 9 and discuss the common features of the answers.

6.5 Mental Calculation and Conversion between Units

Learning Objective:

- Convert between units of measure

1013 Multiplying decimals by 10 and 100
1091 Converting measures

Use **Class Activities 3 and 4** to enable students to see clearly how the digits move in the place value chart when a number is multiplied or divided by powers of 10. It is important that students appreciate that the digits are moving left or right to new place value positions. Encourage this rather than the idea of the decimal point moving.

Example 14 shows students the efficiency of using mental strategies that involve powers of 10; for example using multiplication by 100 and division by 4 to multiply by 25. This is an opportunity to discuss with students other efficient ways of multiplying by involving powers of 10. For example, ask students: what if you were asked to multiply 7.32 by 50? What could you do then? What about 7.32 × 300? What about 7.32 × 250?

Questions 7 and 8 of **Exercise 6.5** offer further practice.

Make sure that students are familiar with the common metric units used in this section. The inclusion of hours, minutes and seconds can be used to make sure that students avoid the common mistake of using 100 minutes for 1 hour during calculations. Discuss with students whether 1 minute and 30 seconds is 1.30 minutes. Encourage students to think about 30 seconds as a fraction in relation to 1 minute so that they can convert 1 minute 30 seconds to 1.5 minutes.

The **Discuss** box on page 157, which matches conversion from a bigger unit to a smaller unit with multiplication and smaller unit to bigger unit with division, encourages students to use a common sense approach to check answers. They need to realise that, for example, the *size* of each m is bigger than the *size* of each cm, so the *number* of m needed is less than the *number* of cm.

The level 2 and level 3 questions in **Exercise 6.5** are problems in real-life contexts that involve conversions of units. For Question 11 discuss how the conversion of litres to millilitres can take place before or after division by 6. Ask students to explain why they chose a particular strategy. A sensible hint for Question 12 is to use a unitary method and find the cost of 1 g of prawns before multiplying by 1000 to get the price for 1 kilogram. For both Questions 14 and 17, students must take care to use either pounds or pence consistently. Collect all student answers for Question 18 and then discuss the highest possible and the lowest possible amounts as an introduction to the concept of upper and lower bounds.

6.6 Division of a Decimal by a Decimal

Learning Objectives:

- Use the four operations with decimals
- Solve real-life problems using decimals

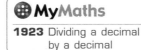
MyMaths
1923 Dividing a decimal
by a decimal

Work here relies on students making the crucial link that a division can be written as a fraction. This can be emphasised by showing that the division symbol itself looks like a fraction with dots replacing the numerator and denominator. Once an equivalent fraction is found with an integer divisor, division of a decimal by a whole number can be carried out as before in Section 6.4. Students can work through **Try It!s 19, 20 and 21** in pairs so they can share and discuss their working. Encourage them to estimate the size of the answer before calculating as a check for their working.

In **Exercise 6.6**, students can refer to **Example 20** to help them explain their method for Question 4. In Question 5 students will need to deal with the remainder and realise that Emma will need an extra jar that will be only partly filled. Discuss the open Question 9 as a whole class; write 0.4 as the fraction $\frac{4}{10}$ and demonstrate that any equivalent fractions will be a division with quotient 0.4.

6.7 Rational Numbers and Real Numbers

Learning Objectives:

- Convert between decimals and fractions
- Identify recurring decimals and real numbers
- Solve real-life problems using decimals

MyMaths
1773 Equivalent fractions 2
1016 Fractions to decimals
1063 Recurring decimals 1

Previous work writing decimal numbers in expanded form gives students clear evidence that all terminating decimals can be converted to a fraction. Discuss with students the two methods for converting fractions to decimals offered in **Example 23**. Encourage them to notice that finding an equivalent fraction with denominator 10, 100, 1000 etc. is most likely to be best if the denominator of the fraction given is itself a factor of 10, 100, 1000 etc.

Emphasise to students the importance of careful notation; the correct placement of the dot above digits for recurring decimals is essential.

Once rational, irrational and real number definitions have been covered you can ask students to draw their own diagram summarising number systems, like that on page 163.

Exercise 6.7 includes work converting between decimals and fractions for both terminating and recurring decimals. For Question 6, ensure that students are able to enter surds and fractions into their calculator. Students could be allowed to use calculators for all questions on recurring decimals if they find the division difficult. Answers for the open Question 11 can be gathered together and discussed, noting that there is an infinite number of rational numbers between 1.4 and 1.5.

Revision Exercise 6 consolidates all the work on decimals. Question 6 gives valuable practice using estimation as a check for calculations. When they carry out division in Question 7, students need to notice that the answers to parts (b) and (d) will be recurring decimals which should be written using the correct notation. Care must be taken with pounds and pence in Question 10. Drawing diagrams labelled with dimensions will help students identify the calculations required in Questions 13 and 14.

The **Write in Your Journal** (page 166) consolidates the work on multiple methods seen throughout this chapter.

Chapter 7
Percentages

This chapter follows on naturally from previous work on fractions and decimals, which is reviewed in the **Flashback** (page 168). A percentage is defined as a fraction with 100 as the denominator and so 100% represents the whole. Use bar models: when working with percentage increase and decrease they allow students to see the whole original 100% together with a reduction or an increase by a percentage. Incorporate real-life applications, but make sure that students understand the context being used.

Resources

k Chapter 7 introduction video

k Try It! videos 1, 8, 10, 11, 15, 19

Assessment

Workbook 1C Chapter 7

Graded Question Bank 1 Chapter 7

k Chapter 7 online skills test

k Chapter 7 end of chapter test and mark scheme

k Fully-worked solutions: Chapter 7 in Workbook 1C and Graded Question Bank 1

7.1 Meaning of Percentage

k are resources on Kerboodle

Learning Objectives:

- Define percentage as 'number of parts per hundred'
- Interpret a percentage as a fraction or a decimal
- Convert a fraction or a decimal to a percentage
- Recognise percentages greater than 100%
- Compare two quantities using percentages
- Express one quantity as a percentage of another

⊕ MyMaths

1030	Percentages of amounts 1
1962	Percentages of amounts 3
1963	Percentages of amounts 4
1029	Frac dec perc 1
1015	Frac dec perc 2

Use the 100 square grid to help students visualise the percentages shaded and not shaded as complementary fractions out of 100. Encourage students to be flexible when converting fractions to percentages by discussing the two methods given in **Example 1**. If students chose the second method, multiplying the fraction by 100%, make sure they realise that an advantage of cancelling first may be to give easier arithmetic.

Use the **Discuss** box when considering **Example 2** to talk about the percentages 3%, 30% and 300% and their fractions; this is important as students will often muddle such pairs of fractions. Use 100 square grids so that students can really see how 3%, 30% and 300% differ. In particular, emphasise that any percentage greater than 100% is greater than one whole. Consolidate this understanding by asking students to complete **Try It! 2** which involves 80% and 468%. They could work in pairs and explain to each other how 80% and 468% differ.

In **Example 3**, a bar model is used to show two parts that add to a whole 100%. Discuss with students what the answer of 55% is as a fraction. Then check that this fraction plus $\frac{9}{20}$ on the bar model is equal to 1. This further emphasises that 100% is one whole, and how fractions and percentages are related.

Example 4 shows conversion from a decimal to a percentage and again demonstrates two methods for the students to consider. Remind students of the place value table and column headings for method 1 when they have to write the decimal as a fraction over 10, 100 etc. Emphasise that a decimal number over 1 can be written as an improper fraction or a mixed number and will be equivalent to a

percentage over 100%. Use a place value table to remind students that digits move two places to the left when a number is multiplied by 100 as in method 2.

Class Activity 1 shows three examples of the application of percentages to daily life. In Question 2, where the proportions of female teachers are compared, ask students to calculate the percentage represented by one teacher in the given school. They will see that the proportions are very closely in line with the national figure, but they should also notice how the relatively small numbers mean that one teacher represents a relatively large 2%. In Question 3, discuss with students how rounding is applied when fractions are converted to percentages for the nutritional information.

Exercise 7.1 gives practice converting between fractions, decimals and percentages. Ask students to reflect on the methods they are using and compare with each other. Draw a diagram with the three words 'Fraction', 'Decimal' and 'Percentage' at the vertices of an equilateral triangle and then invite students to draw arrows showing links and the methods that they have learnt for conversion. Encourage students to think carefully about which conversions they will to do for the level 3 questions which involve adding different combinations of fractions, decimals and percentages. Encourage students to draw bar models if they are struggling to interpret the questions. These bar models offer a good visual 'stepping stone' from the words in a problem to the mathematics that needs to be done.

7.2 Percentage of a Quantity

Learning Objective:

- Find a percentage of a quantity using multiplication

⊕ MyMaths

1030	Percentages of amounts 1
1031	Percentages of amounts 2
1962	Percentages of amounts 3
1963	Percentages of amounts 4

Examples 6 and 7 develop previous work converting fractions to percentages. Suggest to students that they draw bar models (like the ones in Examples 7 and 8) to help them to identify the relative size of the quantities that they are working with compared to the whole 100%. Students need to have a clear idea of what the 100% whole represents. In **Example 6** it is the whole box of muffins and in parts (a) and (b) of **Example 7** it is the price of one or other of the phones. Demonstrate a step by step approach by reading aloud one sentence of the problem at a time and looking at the bar model that relates to that sentence. Suggest to students that reading one sentence, drawing the relevant part of a bar model, then reading the next sentence and adding to the information in the picture is a good strategy. It is much easier than reading the entire problem and then trying to draw the bar model from memory. **Example 8** gives a clear example of an effective check of a calculation; encourage students to carry out checks themselves.

When they are finding the percentage of a quantity, make sure that students appreciate that the word 'of' means multiply as noted in the **Remark** on page 176. In the context of percentages, a common mistake is to read the word 'of' as 'off' and deduct the amount calculated from the original quantity as if calculating a decrease. **Example 9** gives the unitary method as an alternative approach. Discuss with students which method is more efficient and ask them to consider which is more suited to work with or without a calculator.

The use of a bar model in **Example 10** again emphasises that the complete bar of 100% represents a whole. Point out to students that in **Example 12** they first find a percentage of a quantity and then convert a fraction to a percentage. One or both of these two procedures form the basis for the solution of many problems involving percentages. **Class Activity 2** gives an another opportunity to discuss the importance of knowing which value is 100%. Ask students to compare their answers for part 5 and explain that they need to offer a 'counter-example' to demonstrate that the statement is not correct.

Encourage students to redo problems using alternative methods to check their answers to the level 2 and 3 questions in **Exercise 7.2**. Many of the level 3 questions are set in a financial context so make sure that students understand the meaning of words such as salary, service charge and overtime.

7.3 Reducing and Increasing a Quantity by a Percentage

Learning Objective:
- Reduce or increase a quantity by a percentage

MyMaths	
1060	Percentage change 1
1073	Percentage change 2
1302	Change as a percentage

Bar models are invaluable here to show the original 100% whole amount which is then extended for an increase or split into two sections for a decrease. At this stage, in **Examples 13–16**, the increase or decrease is calculated and then added or subtracted from the original.

Examples 17 and 18 involve applying value-added tax (VAT) at two different rates to goods and services. **Class Activity 3** asks students to explore further which items attract a VAT charge at either of the two rates. For homework, ask students to study a supermarket receipt and notice whether any items are marked with an asterisk indicating items where VAT has been added.

The concept of using a multiplier is not covered here, but will be introduced when percentages are met again in Year 8. Meanwhile, **Example 19** shows a reverse percentage calculation using a unitary method. Crucially, students must recognise that the bar model representing the full price shows 120% not 100%.

Level 1 in **Exercise 7.3** offers practice at calculating percentage increases and decreases. Some level 2 and 3 questions involve successive percentage increases and decreases. For Question 8, challenge students to explain why a 20% increase followed by a 15% increase is not the same as a 35% increase. To help students understand this concept, invite them to think of a number, reduce it by 10% and then increase by 10%. This could be nicely illustrated using a bar model. Discuss the fact that the answer is not the same as the original quantity because the increase is calculated as 10% of a lower value than the original. Question 12 in **Revision Exercise 7** (page 188) gives an example of this in practice.

In **Revision Exercise 7**, conversions between percentages, fractions and decimals are covered in Question 1. Many of the other questions then fall into one of two categories: expressing a quantity as a percentage, sometimes to compare; and finding a percentage of a quantity, sometimes to increase or decrease. Ask students to sort the questions into one of these two categories to help them learn to easily identify the appropriate strategy to use. Question 9(b) needs special attention where the handbag cost including VAT is given and the percentage increase needs to be reversed. Question 14 links percentage work with area and perimeter; students may find it useful to draw a sketch showing the dimensions before and after the percentage changes are applied. Encourage students to consider the use of bar models for questions throughout the exercise; the Hint for Question 15 will help students set up the bars for Alice's and Iris's incomes by setting Alice's income at £100.

A bar model with bars shaded to show paid for and free cups will help students visualise the 'buy 3 get 1 free' situation described in the **Write in Your Journal** activity. Discuss with students how the percentage discount varies with such offers and therefore encourages customers to buy certain numbers of the items.

Review Exercise 2

This review exercise combines the work that has been learnt and the methods covered for questions involving fractions, decimals and percentages.

Many of the questions in **Review Exercise 2** require students to convert between fractions, decimals and percentages. Where questions are set in real-life contexts, students may need some support interpreting the contexts and deciding what mathematics to use. The use of a deposit and instalments as a payment method in Question 12 may need some explanation.

Discuss with students the main procedures that they will need to follow: expressing one quantity as a proportion of another, calculating a proportion of a quantity and comparing proportions. In each case, the proportion given or required may be a decimal, fraction or percentage.

Question 4 invites students to compare their method with other students. Ask students to look at their first step to identify whether they found the actual number who drive or cycle first or the percentage who use another means. Discuss how methods are actually equivalent and just involve carrying out the pair of processes required in a different order. Questions 9 and 15 are similar but involve fractions and a mix of fractions and percentages respectively.

Bar models may be helpful throughout the exercise, especially for questions that involve increasing or decreasing a quantity. In Question 14 it is essential that students appreciate that the 100% whole that they are working with is different for the two question parts. For part (b) they are increasing Bowen's salary by 20% but in part (c) Bowen's salary is 85% of the required salary for Carol.

Problem-solving Processes and Heuristics

Student Book 1C
pages 191–199

This section explains how a four-step problem-solving process can be used to help students become good problem solvers.

There are a variety of ways students can tackle problems and the examples here look at how to use different strategies in different situations. Discuss the four-step strategy with the students so they understand what each step involves.

Example 1 uses the 'Look for a Pattern and Make a Table' strategy. Show students the problem and then work through the four steps asking for their contributions at each stage so that you can build up the solution together.

Example 2 uses the 'Draw a Diagram' strategy. Pose this problem to the students and let them have a go unaided before introducing the diagram. Work through the steps using the diagrams and then ask students to comment on how using the diagram has changed the perceived complexity of the problem. **Step 4** 'Looking Back' highlights that this method can also provide easy access to further information not given in the question.

Example 3 uses the 'Draw a Diagram and Write an Equation' strategy. Students are familiar with this from their work on bar models in the algebra chapters so they could try to tackle this in pairs, making sure

they write down each of the four steps. Use the **Discuss** box (page 195) to consider how this problem could be extended.

Example 4 uses the 'Identify Subgoals and Look for a Pattern' strategy. Considering the subgoals and how they relate to each other can help to reduce the amount of work that needs to be done. Ask students what the important difference is between finding numbers ending in 0 and numbers ending in 6 and how this will help them when solving the problem. **Step 4** 'Looking Back' shows how the number of combinations can be found more easily; first by considering tree diagrams and then by using the tree diagrams to show how the number of possibilities can be worked out using multiplication.

Example 5 uses the 'Make a Table and Write an Equation' strategy. (It is vital to the question that students know how many legs a butterfly has.) A table with three columns can easily be set up on a spreadsheet to demonstrate that an answer can be found quickly using this method. Ask students to use formulae to fill cells as efficiently as possible. Now ask students to set the problem up by writing an equation. Compare the two solution methods and ask when each is more useful.

Correct terminology, notation and symbols on geometric diagrams are a very important feature of all work in this chapter. It is therefore very important that the language used during instruction and discussion is precise and unambiguous. Encourage students to use language correctly and ensure that their use of notation is conventional and correct. Students can create a vocabulary list as they work through this chapter.

It is assumed that students know angle properties relating to straight lines from previous work at primary level. Here you extend angle reasoning to properties involving parallel lines and triangles. There is an emphasis on geometric reasoning throughout and students are encouraged to make links between the various properties.

k *are resources on Kerboodle*

Resources

k Chapter 8 introduction video

k Try It! videos 3, 7, 11, 13

Assessment

Workbook 1C Chapter 8

Graded Question Bank 1 Chapter 8

k Chapter 8 online skills test

k Chapter 8 end of chapter test and mark scheme

k Fully-worked solutions: Chapter 8 in Workbook 1C and Graded Question Bank 1

8.1 Points, Lines and Planes

Learning Objectives:

- Describe a point, a line, a line segment, a ray and a plane
- Construct lines, line segments and angles using geometry software

Confirm students understand the definitions of point, line segment and plane given in the first section of the **Flashback** (page 201) by inviting them to give some more examples that they can see around them in the classroom. The diagram of a protractor in the second Flashback section gives an opportunity to discuss the design of a protractor, in particular the inner and outer scales. Students can be asked to write a detailed 'user guide' for a protractor as if they were doing so for someone who had never seen one. Once written, guides can be swapped between students with individuals testing each other's instructions.

Class Activity 1 enables students to use geometry software to really clarify the definitions of point, line, ray and line segment. Tease out precise definitions by asking students what is the same and what is different about a line segment and a line, a line and a ray, and so on. These definitions are summarised clearly in the table after the Class Activity and can be referred to as required.

Example 1 uses sets of points and diagrams to exemplify the definitions. The Note highlights the distinctive feature of rays, which means that rays RP and PR are different, whereas lines RP and PR represent the same line. Use **Try It! 1** to check that students are using the correct conventions to draw lines extending beyond points, line segments joining points and rays extending beyond one

point with an arrowhead. This is also an opportunity to emphasise that straight lines in mathematics should always be drawn with a sharp pencil and a ruler.

Exercise 8.1 consolidates students' drawing skills and their understanding of diagrams. Question 4 enables them to demonstrate understanding of the differences between line segments and rays as discussed in the Example 1 Note. The level 3 Questions 5 and 6 are challenging as students need to present sound geometric reasoning and may need to be reminded to use correct notation for line segments in their assertions. Where students have a problem accessing these questions, suggest that they discuss their reasoning with a partner. For Question 5, offer the prompt: 'Start by writing down what you know about MQ', and for Question 6: 'Look at AC. It is made up of two line segments so start by writing down what you know about AC.' Question 7 ensures that students become familiar with the concept of a line segment of any length being formed of an infinite number of points; part (b) presents a good opportunity for discussion.

8.2 Angles

Learning Objectives:

- Identify different types of angles
- Recognise the properties of vertically opposite angles, angles on a straight line and angles at a point

⊕ MyMaths

1081	Measuring angles
1847	Angles 2
1989	Angles 3
1990	Angles 4
1082	Angle sums

Three-letter angle notation needs to be carefully introduced so that students understand that ∠BAC and ∠CAB are the same. Students should visualise how the direction changes on a route from B to A to C and then trace a route with a finger when interpreting this notation. Emphasise to students that conventionally it is the obtuse/acute angle that is referred to unless the word 'reflex' is added at the front.

Use **Example 2** to make sure that students can use a protractor correctly. Discuss with students how they know which scale to use. Ensure that they understand how to position the vertex of the angle correctly with one of the lines matched up with the line labelled 0 on the protractor scale that they will read from. Encourage students to decide before they measure whether the angle is greater than or less than a 90° right angle.

Encourage students to look carefully at the diagrams showing perpendicular lines, complementary angles and supplementary angles on page 208. The definition of adjacent angles is important and the non-examples given are useful to show students, to consolidate their understanding. It is especially important students understand that when they use the 'angles on a straight line add up to 180°' rule the angles must be adjacent.

Work through **Examples 3–5** emphasising the need to show correct geometric reasoning in working as each property is applied. Discuss with students the fact that there is often more than one approach possible with properties being used in various orders. Examples 3 and 4 both involve setting up and simplifying an equation, linking with work in Chapters 3 and 4.

Exercise 8.2 gives plenty of practice, with Question 6 giving examples where more than one angle property will need to be used. Where students need practice at drawing angles, they can complete Question 3 and should label line segments in accordance with the three-letter angle notation given. The level 2 questions involve setting up and solving equations to find the angles. The clock face in Question 17 requires students to apply proportion and there is plenty of scope for rich extension work considering the angles between the hands at other times. Students must be aware that diagrams are usually not drawn accurately, so missing angles need to be calculated and not measured.

8.3 Parallel Lines and Transversals

Learning Objectives:

- Recognise the properties of angles formed by parallel lines and transversals
- Find unknown marked angles in a diagram using the above properties

MyMaths

1109 Angles in parallel lines

1102 Lines and quadrilaterals

It is important that students know that a transversal intersects any two or more other lines; they do not have to be parallel. The terms corresponding, alternate and co-interior should be introduced in terms of where they are in relation to the transversal before students complete **Class Activity 2** to investigate the special properties of parallel lines. When working through **Examples 6 and 7**, again discuss with students the different approaches that can be used; this is drawn out in the **Remark** associated with Example 6 on page 217. Point out that parallel lines do not have to be horizontal. Indeed, they can be in any orientation, so students may find it helpful to rotate their book to identify pairs of parallel lines and associated transversals with corresponding, alternate and co-interior angles more easily. Discuss with students how drawing extra parallel lines can be helpful, as seen in **Example 8**.

Draw attention to the fact that properties can be used to prove whether a pair of lines are parallel, as shown in **Spot Check** (page 217).

As students work through **Exercise 8.3**, they should identify any extra angles that they use during their working, using three-letter notation. Students could tackle level 3 questions in pairs, so that they have an opportunity to discuss their approach. Ask students to read through each other's work to check that the chain of reasoning is clear to follow. Note that students need geometry software for Question 12.

8.4 Triangles

Learning Objectives:

- Classify triangles based on their sides and angles
- Understand the general properties of sides and angles of a triangle
- Construct triangles where three sides are given

MyMaths

1130 Properties of triangles
1082 Angle sums
1090 Constructing triangles

Students are likely to know the basic properties for special triangles and so the **Discuss** activity on page 221 can be used to consolidate. The 'Types of Triangles' family-tree-style diagram, as shown in the **In a Nutshell** section on page 233, provides a useful summary of classification information. Ask students to make their own copy of this diagram, adding diagrams of examples underneath the labels in the third row.

Prepare students to complete **Class Activity 3** by demonstrating the construction of triangles using a ruler and a pair of compasses following the steps in page 222. Class Activity 3 will then consolidate use of notation for line segments as the students discover the triangle inequality: the sum of two sides is greater than the third side. Students will be able to use this to decide whether any three line segments given can be drawn as a triangle.

When the 'Angles in a Triangle' property is introduced, use the practical activity of tearing angles from a triangle and putting them along a straight edge, as in the **Maths** box on page 225, as a powerful visual image for students. Refer students back to Question 11 in **Exercise 8.3,** which was structured to enable a formal proof to be written using the angle properties previously covered.

Use **Class Activity 4** and **Examples 12 and 13** to demonstrate that the exterior angle property can be a shortcut to solving problems rather than the two-step approach of using the 'Angles in a Triangle' and 'Angles on a Straight Line' properties.

When completing **Exercise 8.4**, encourage students to draw sketches where diagrams are not given. Point out that a sketch does not need to be an accurate size but should still be drawn with a pencil and ruler with any information marked clearly. It is also helpful if students draw sketches bearing in mind the relative sizes of the sides and angles, for example making a 5 cm side clearly longer than a 3 cm side.

Students must look out for notation showing parallel lines and equal sides or angles rather than make assumptions, for example the lines *ED* and *AB* in Question 7(a) are not parallel. Discuss the efficiency of the methods used, for example, in Question 7(b) there are many possible routes to the answer; ask students to come up with the most efficient with the fewest stages. Use Questions 13 and 14 to give students further experience in using geometry software to deduce geometrical properties themselves and then use correct mathematical language to communicate their findings.

Many questions in **Revision Exercise 8** enable students to apply their equation solving skills in a mathematical context. Make sure that they set up equations correctly, using the correct numerical values for angles on a straight line, angles in a triangle and angles at a point. Students might find a bar model helpful here, with the whole bar representing 180° or 360° and the parts representing the smaller angles. Later questions are challenging, so a class discussion of methods used for Questions 1 and 2 will increase student confidence. You could ask students to work in pairs for Question 8 onwards and encourage discussion of geometric reasoning and the possible alternative methods at every opportunity. In some questions, students may find it useful to extend or add lines; for example, extend the pairs of parallel lines in Question 9 and add an extra parallel line through *C* in Question 10.

For the **Write in Your Journal** activity, encourage students to refer to the transversal crossing a pair of parallel lines and the relative positions of pairs of alternate and corresponding angles. Ask students to provide diagrams using correct notation which can be referenced in their written work.

Chapter 9
Transformations, Symmetry and Congruence

Student Book 1C
pages 236–266

This chapter covers the three transformations where the object and image are always congruent. Enlargements are covered later during work on similarity and scale factors. Many students will be familiar with transformations when used to manipulate objects in graphics packages but they must now ensure they use correct mathematical terminology, for example reflect rather than flip and rotate rather than turn. Tracing paper may be useful throughout the chapter for transformations, checking symmetry and testing congruence.

k *are resources on Kerboodle*

Resources
k Chapter 9 introduction video
k Try It! videos 1, 3, 4, 9, 10

Assessment
Workbook 1C Chapter 9
Graded Question Bank 1 Chapter 9
k Chapter 9 online skills test
k Chapter 9 end of chapter test and mark scheme
k Fully-worked solutions: Chapter 9 in Workbook 1C and Graded Question Bank 1

9.1 Transformations

Learning Objectives:
- Translate, rotate and reflect 2D shapes
- Describe translations in vector form
- Combine transformations

MyMaths
1843 Translating
1127 Translating shapes
1113 Reflecting shapes
1115 Rotating shapes
1839 Translating and reflecting

Begin this work by introducing the terminology 'object' and 'image' (and also the use of dash notation on diagrams for the image). Emphasise to students that a translation moves each point on an object to the equivalent point on the image; a common misconception is to describe a translation between the vertices on the object and image that are closest to each other. Give students tracing paper and get them to identify one particular point (usually a vertex) which they move as instructed and then complete the image. Make sure that students understand vector notation and the direction of movement indicated by positive and negative numbers. When writing vectors make sure that students do not include a horizontal line as if they were writing a fraction. In **Example 1**, ensure that students describe the translation in full written sentences using correct terminology to practise communicating mathematically with accuracy.

Throughout this section, **Class Activities 1, 2 and 3** give valuable experience using geometry software and enable students to distinguish between the resulting images for the different transformations.

For reflection, the solution methods given in **Examples 2 and 3** involve counting squares on a grid. Discuss with students how the methods could still work without a grid. Show students how tracing paper is used for reflection by tracing the object and the mirror line then flipping or folding the paper along the mirror line. This will help to emphasise that the object is congruent to the image. When students are dealing with diagonal mirror lines encourage them to turn the book so that the mirror line appears vertical or horizontal.

Check students are familiar with 'clockwise' and 'anticlockwise' to describe direction of rotation.

Section D introduces combinations of transformations. Following on from the Discuss on page 246, ask students to consider when swapping the order of a pair of transformations makes a difference to the image and when it does not.

Questions throughout **Exercise 9.1** allow students to practise carrying out the three transformations on squared paper. Some will find this much easier if larger squared paper is offered. In Questions 7 and 10, make sure that students give a full description of a single named transformation rather than a combination of more than one. Questions 11, 12 and 13 involve combinations of transformations and Question 13 gives ample opportunity for considering how two or more transformations can be combined. Students can use a photo-editing app or other software to experiment easily with multiple and combined transformations.

9.2 Symmetry

Learning Objectives:

- Recognise and describe reflection symmetry of 2D shapes
- Recognise and describe rotation symmetry of 2D shapes

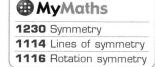

MyMaths

1230 Symmetry
1114 Lines of symmetry
1116 Rotation symmetry

The **Discuss** box on page 250 addresses the common misconception that a diagonal is a line of symmetry for a rectangle. Folding a rectangle of paper will enable students to convince themselves that it is not. Similarly, a cut out parallelogram (ensure it is not a rhombus) can be folded to demonstrate that it has no line of symmetry. Ask students to look around the classroom to find examples of reflection symmetry.

Tracing paper is an invaluable resource for students to use to check rotation symmetry and will be useful throughout **Exercise 9.2**. Ask students to identify some examples of rotation symmetry that they can see in the classroom. When discussing order of rotation symmetry, emphasise that a shape with no rotation symmetry does *not* have rotation symmetry of 0 or 1. It simply has no rotation symmetry. The second **Discuss** box on page 253 ensures that students do not assume that a shape with order of rotation symmetry *n* must have *n* lines of symmetry. Ask students to draw examples where this is the case and also where it is not. The **Exercise 9.2** open Questions 15 and 16 give further opportunity for this discussion.

9.3 Congruence

Learning Objectives:

- Understand the idea of congruence
- Match the sides and angles of two congruent shapes

MyMaths

1148 Congruent triangles

Correct interpretation and use of notation for equal sides and angles on diagrams is essential in this section. Ensure students are confident with the three-letter angle notation, as used in Chapter 8. Discuss **Example 9** with students and ask them to name the corresponding sides and angles to practise this.

The link between congruence and the three transformations, translation, reflection and rotation, is emphasised when students work through **Class Activity 4**. Students may find it difficult to match up corresponding sides and angles whatever the orientation of two congruent shapes, but **Example 10** offers useful practice. Encourage students to notice that the vertices are labelled in alphabetical order and that when describing congruent shapes, the letters denoting corresponding angles and sides match. Tracing paper will be helpful here if students are struggling.

Tessellations are a good way of linking mathematics with art and many students will enjoy the opportunity to be creative in the level 3 questions of **Exercise 9.3**. Question 9 demonstrates a practical use of congruency to determine the width of a river. This process could be replicated in a playground or similar large space.

Revision Exercise 9 consolidates work covered in the chapter, offering more practice at identifying and describing symmetries. You can extend the work on flags in Question 6 by looking at more flags, with the added possibility of a cross-curricular link. Students may need reminding to match up corresponding sides and angles in Questions 11, 12 and 13. Access to square grid paper is essential for Question 7, which is the first time students need to carry out a reflection where the line of reflection passes through the image.

The design of a logo for the **Write in Your Journal** activity gives an opportunity for students to look at existing logos and consider how symmetry often features in effective designs. This activity offers an opportunity for students to use any familiar graphics design software and notice the features which make use of transformations and symmetries.

It is assumed that students will know the mensuration of squares and rectangles from previous work at primary level. Here you extend the concept to find the perimeter and area of triangles, circles and composite shapes. By making connections between the area of a rectangle and triangle, students will derive the formula for area of a triangle. Through investigating the relationship between the diameter and circumference of a circle, students will discover pi and progress to find the formulae for circumference and area of a circle.

In evaluating the perimeters and areas of composite shapes, students should master the technique of dividing the shape into two or more simple shapes. Solving real-world problems will allow students to appreciate the applications of this topic.

(k) are resources on Kerboodle

Resources

(k) Chapter 10 introduction video

(k) Try It! videos 3, 6, 8, 10, 14

Assessment

Workbook 1C Chapter 10

Graded Question Bank 1 Chapter 10

(k) Chapter 10 online skills test

(k) Chapter 10 end of chapter test and mark scheme

(k) Fully-worked solutions: Chapter 10 in Workbook 1C and Graded Question Bank 1

10.1 Perimeter and Area of a Triangle

Learning Objective:

● Find the perimeter and area of a triangle

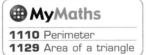

MyMaths

1110 Perimeter
1129 Area of a triangle

The **Flashback** on page 268 will help students to recall the work on squares and rectangles. Substituting into formulae for perimeter and area will also help to recall the work on substitution completed in Section 3.2 (page 66). Make sure students are familiar with the standard notation covered on page 269: using a symbol to stand for 'triangle', labelling sides with lower case letters and the opposite angles with upper case letters.

Discuss with students what is meant by the word perpendicular. Ask them to sort some examples of lines into perpendicular and non-perpendicular, explaining their reasoning. Students sometimes have difficulty recognising perpendicular lines in different orientations so include some that are not vertical/horizontal and also include line segments that would be perpendicular if they were long enough to intersect.

The perimeter of a triangle is consistent with the work students have done on squares and rectangles so is just extending their thinking. One way to remember that perimeter is the outside distance of a shape is to highlight the word rim in pe**rim**eter. Try giving the students a range of triangles, including special triangles, to measure in order to find the perimeter. Ask them to explain how many sides they needed to measure on each one in order to find the perimeter.

Class Activity 1 considers the relationship between the areas of a triangle and a rectangle in order to derive a formula for the area of a triangle. This activity can be introduced practically by giving students a variety of rectangles and asking them to draw a triangle that uses one complete side of the rectangle as the base of the triangle with the remaining vertex on the opposite side of the rectangle. By cutting out the triangle, can they discover the connection between the area of the rectangle and the area of the triangle? Consolidate this with Class Activity 1 and consider the case where the third vertex lies outside the rectangle along the projection of the side opposite the base (as in diagram 3 of the activity). When working through Class Activity 1, point to each vertex as it is read out (e.g. *ABCD*), and encourage students to follow your finger as it points, so that it is absolutely clear which shape is being considered.

Consistently use 'perpendicular height' rather than 'height' whenever discussing the area of a triangle.

Show the students a pair of parallel lines with a fixed base distance for a triangle along one line. Draw a variety of triangles from this base that have the third vertex on the other parallel line, including ones where the triangle has an obtuse angle at the base. Ask students whether all the triangles have the same area and the reason for their answer. Can they draw another triangle that has the same area? How would they draw one with a smaller area or one with a greater area? Make sure they explain their reasoning each time. Use the **Discuss** box at the top of page 272 to consolidate student understanding about the perpendicular height of a triangle. Students might find it helpful to have a cut out triangle that they can hold and rotate to see that 'the base' is not always the base (and the same for the perpendicular height).

Exercise 10.1 (page 273) challenges the students' understanding of base and perpendicular height and makes them think about which measurements are needed to solve the problems. The different orientations of triangles in Questions 2 and 3 will challenge the students' understanding; ask them to explain their reasoning for each question. Question 8 involves constructing with a pair of compasses, this may be an area worth exploring more. If all students attempt Questions 12 and 13 in this exercise, a lovely discussion can be had about the methods and strategies used.

10.2 Circumference of a Circle

Learning Objectives:

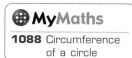

1088 Circumference of a circle

- Find the circumference of a circle
- Find the perimeter of a semicircle and a quarter of a circle

The definition of a circle is important to understand. Ask students one at a time to stand a set distance away from a cone, as more students join ask them what shape they think they are making. This could also be done with counters a set distance from a point. Ask the students to explain why you can draw a circle with a pair of compasses. Make sure that students are confident using the vocabulary associated with circles. Discuss the relationship between the radius and the diameter, agree a definition for each that the students are confident to use.

A common misconception is that a circle has only one side. Discuss with students how many sides they think a circle has. Using geometry software (or pictures of polygons) look at how a regular polygon changes as the number of sides increase, this will lead to the reasoning that a circle is what you get to 'eventually' if you carry on increasing the number of sides.

Class Activity 2 looks at the relationship between the diameter and the circumference of a circle. If students are able to measure circles of various sizes that are more extreme than those they are asked to draw (e.g. circular bin, round cake tin, glue stick, tin of beans, circular table etc.) then the realisation that the circumference divided by the diameter is always about 3 is more powerful.

When you introduce pi as the exact ratio between the circumference and the diameter of a circle, it is interesting to ask students to research mathematicians that have spent time calculating pi and how many decimal places they have found so far. Students could also research why the symbol for pi is used for this number.

Ask students to find pi on their own calculators, discuss the different number of decimal places different

calculators may use for pi. Ask them to use pi in simple calculations so they are confident they know how to use it.

Examples 4–6 use pi as a decimal and a fraction. Explain that answers can also be left in terms of pi and discuss with the students the benefits of using the different values. **Example 6** also looks at using a semicircle or quarter circle within a perimeter question. Highlight that leaving answers in terms of pi until the final stage may result in a more accurate answer because it avoids any rounding errors in intermediate steps.

Exercise 10.2 gives practice at using the formula for the circumference before applying this knowledge to real-world problems. Questions 11–13 are great problem-solving questions which will confirm the fluency of students' skills. Question 14 could be completed as a mini class investigation. Ask students to make a prediction, then give students different radii to test, collate the responses and discuss the result.

10.3 Area of a Circle

Learning Objectives:

1083 Area of a circle

- Find the area of a circle
- Find the area of a semicircle and a quarter of a circle

Develop the area of a circle formula using the circle cut up into parts to form a rectangle (page 279). Getting the students to cut up their own circle, reassemble it into a rectangle and stick it in their books is a worthwhile, if potentially messy, activity. Ask students to explain why the area of the circle and the rectangle are the same. It is useful to use two colours so that students appreciate that the base of the rectangle is half of the circumference, in order to generate the formula.

Example 7 shows how to use the formula for the area of a circle. Ask students which part of the calculation should be completed first.

Before doing **Example 9**, ask students how they would tackle a problem if they were given the diameter instead of the radius. It is important to look at all the examples as they focus on semicircles and quarters of circles as well as circular borders.

As they complete **Exercise 10.3** students will practise using the formula for the area of a circle before moving onto more complex problems. The level 3 questions are more involved; encourage students to read one sentence at a time, and try to make sense of it, before moving onto the next sentence.

Students often struggle with wordier problems because they read the entire problem before looking at a diagram, and there is too much information to keep in short-term memory. So for example, when answering Question 9, suggest that students read the first sentence, which describes the diagram. They should then look at the diagram and ensure they understand the quarters this sentence refers to before they then move onto the second sentence.

10.4 Perimeter and Area Problems

Learning Objectives:

- Find a length given the perimeter or area of a shape
- Solve problems involving perimeters and areas of composite plane figures formed by rectangles, squares, triangles and circles

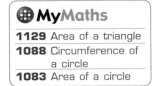

MyMaths

1129 Area of a triangle
1088 Circumference of a circle
1083 Area of a circle

Spend time looking at **Examples 10–12** as they show how to find lengths given perimeters and areas of different shapes. Students will need to practise these, especially with triangles as they often find these the hardest. Ensure students always set up the correct formula with the missing value before trying to solve the problem. Give the students some model answers that have common misconceptions in them and ask them to find the mistakes.

Use real-world examples of the word composite (e.g. doors, glass, concrete) and then relate it to shapes. Show them some composite shapes and ask them to decide how they would split the shape up. Is there more than one way? Is one way easier than another? Ask them

to explain their reasoning. Chose a problem and ask students to split up the shape in as many different ways as possible, find the area each time and prove the answer stays the same.

Work through **Examples 13 and 14** making sure the students do the Try It! questions. Compare their answers to **Try It! 13** to see if any students tackled things differently. Ask them to explain, with reasons, how they built the shape and the efficiency of different methods.

Complete **Exercise 10.4**. It is important to work through all the questions as they offer different challenges for the students. Encourage students to draw diagrams when one is not given so that they can label the information they know in order to help them understand the question. It would be useful to discuss Question 14; ask students to consider 'what is the same and what is different' about triangle *ABC* and triangle *ACD* in order to be able to answer the question.

Revision Exercise 10 will consolidate learning in this chapter. Question 5 is very useful to discuss as students sometimes struggle with the concept of the clock face.

Ask students to copy out the example in **Write in Your Journal** before commenting on the solution. Discussing this solution will further reiterate the importance of the required height being the perpendicular height and remind students to check this when they review their work.

Workbook 1C Chapter 10 combines the work on triangles and circles so that students really have to think about which formulae they need and how to apply them to the solve the given problems. Completing this chapter will demonstrate a strong understanding of this topic.

Ensure students have access to a number of real-world shapes. Give students opportunities to build cuboids and cubes from their nets to provide a better understanding of the idea of surface area. Similarly, use interlocking cubes like Multilink™ to build cuboids and cubes to consider the volume of these 3D solids. Some students find it difficult to visualise a 3D solid from a 2D net, so will benefit from practical work with manipulatives.

Some students may struggle to interpret 2D representations of 3D solids on a page. Give these students lots of opportunities to examine 2D representations and the corresponding 3D solid at the same time using the student book and other sources.

k are resources on Kerboodle

Series Resources

k Chapter 11 introduction video
k Try It! videos 3, 9

Assessment

Workbook 1C Chapter 11
Graded Question Bank 1 Chapter 11
k Chapter 11 online skills test
k Chapter 11 end of chapter test and mark scheme
k Fully-worked solutions: Chapter 11 in Workbook 1C and Graded Question Bank 1

11.1 Nets of Cuboids, including Cubes

Learning Objective:

● Draw nets of cuboids, including cubes

MyMaths
1106 Nets of 3D shapes
1107 Nets, surface area

Pose the question 'Is a square a rectangle?' When students can explain their reasoning, use the **Discuss** box on page 293 to extend their thinking to decide if a cube is a cuboid. Use the **Flashback** (page 292) to check students understand how to find the area of a square and rectangle and can use the formulae. Link the square and square root of a number to the area and side length of a square, similarly the cube and cube root of a number to the volume and side length of a cube.

Provide a collection of real-world 3D objects and ask students to group them into cuboids and non-cuboids, explaining their reasoning as they do so. Introduce the vocabulary from page 293: face, edge, vertex (vertices) shape and solid, and use this language accurately throughout the topic.

Class Activity 1 considers the flat shape created when a cuboid (or cube) is opened out. Using boxes and cutting them up helps students to discover what the net of a shape is. This could also be done using equipment such as Polydron™. Ask students to discuss the answers to the activity Questions 5 and 6 in pairs. Then engage in a whole-class discussion to consolidate understanding.

The **Discuss** box on page 294 is a good challenge for the students. Ask them how many squares will be needed and what rules they will need to follow in order to draw a potential net. Challenge them to see how many they can find. Polydron™ is very useful here for students to test their designs. A useful paired activity is where one student draws a possible net and the other explains if they think it will make a cube and then tests it out. Students then swap roles.

Work through **Examples 1 and 2**, completing the Try It! questions. After Example 2, discuss with students which faces on the cuboid have the same area, how they can describe the position of these faces and how this may help when drawing a net.

Students consolidate their understanding by completing **Exercise 11.1**; it is helpful to provide paper and scissors to use when needed and remind students to always use a ruler and a sharp pencil.

Encourage students to predict which will be nets of cubes in Question 1 *before* they cut out and fold. To help them make their predictions for each net, ask them to choose one face and then imagine the net folding into a cube. Ask which would be the opposite face. Do this for each face on the net. If a student cannot find the opposite face then perhaps it is not a net of a cube. Use a similar approach for Question 2 and cuboids. Question 10 can be used for a class discussion; ask students why they can put the extra square in some places and not others. They can use the same reasoning to help them answer Questions 11 and 12.

11.2 Surface Area of Cuboids, including Cubes

Learning Objective:

1107 Nets, surface area

- Calculate the surface area of cuboids, including cubes

Class Activity 2 helps students to derive the formulae for surface area of a cuboid and a cube. The coloured faces on the net of the cuboid help reinforce which rectangles have the same area.

Work through **Examples 3 and 4**, reminding students about the order of operations when calculating the answers. If students need more practice, then use some real-world cubes and cuboids in the classroom. Ask students to measure them and find their surface area. Emphasise that you are finding an area and so the answers will be in units squared.

Question 2 in **Exercise 11.2** could be extended as a mini investigation. Use this question to discuss the effect on the surface area when the length of one of the sides is doubled. Question 4 of **Workbook 1C Chapter 11** is similar and offers additional scope for discussion. Discuss students' responses to Question 13 of the student book exercise and look at how the different answers may be connected.

Always encourage students to sketch the cuboids and label the sides when tackling word questions. Isometric paper may be used to help students sketch these 2D representations of a cuboid.

11.3 Volume of Cuboids, including Cubes

Learning Objectives:

1137 Volumes of cuboids

- Calculate the volume of cuboids, including cubes
- Solve problems involving volume and surface area of cuboids, including cubes

It is important for students to understand that the volume of a solid is measured in cubic units. Building a variety of 3D solids from Multilink™ (or other practical apparatus) and working out their volumes is an important starting point. **Example 5** considers the volume of two prisms. Discuss with students how they can work out the number of cubes that are used; consider different strategies and discuss their efficiency.

When considering the cuboid on page 301, the coloured layers help students' understanding. Build the cuboid in three different ways: $(5 \times 4) \times 3$ then $(5 \times 3) \times 4$ and then

$(4 \times 3) \times 5$, using coloured layers. Discuss with students the different arrangements and recall that multiplication is associative and commutative.

Use the **Discuss** box on page 301 to ask students to think about the special properties of a cube and how they can use this information to find the formula for the volume of a cube from the formula for a cuboid. Allow them to share their reasoning with a partner before discussing with the class as a whole.

The **Maths** box on page 301 looks at the definition of the gram as the mass of $1\,cm^3$ of water and then calculates the mass of a litre of water. This is needed in **Example 7**.

For **Example 9** and **Try It! 9**, discuss which faces will give the total surface area and draw attention to the difference between the two solids.

Sketches are useful to help visualise a solid when given dimensions. Discuss with students what a sketch is, i.e. that it should be drawn with a ruler and sharp pencil, but does not need to be drawn with accurate lengths.

Level 1 in **Exercise 11.3** gives students practice at finding volumes before increasing the challenge in levels 2 and 3, where questions ask for the surface area and volume of 3D solids.

It may be useful to complete Question 14 as a class. Pose the question 'What is the effect on the volume when one of the sides is doubled in length?' Ask the students to consider what would happen if more than one side was doubled, or one side tripled etc. Question 7 of **Workbook 1C Chapter 11** provides further opportunity to look at the effect on volume when one or more of the side lengths is changed. There is of course scope to discuss and explore other multiples. Using manipulatives such as Multilink™ cubes will help all students grasp this idea.

Engage students in good mathematical discussion and reasoning when tackling the problem-solving Questions 15–18 of Exercise 11.3 and also Questions 7 and 8 in **Revision Exercise 11**; these questions will challenge understanding and fluency. Question 13 of the revision exercise shows a practical application of volume and surface area in a real-world situation. Extend part (c) to discuss the reasons why this may be important.

A lovely investigation can be built from Question 31 in **Workbook 1C Chapter 11**. Ask students to find the volume and surface area of each cube starting with $1 \times 1 \times 1$ and then find the surface area to volume ratio. Use the results of this to explain why elephants have big ears and mice have furry coats.

Using cereal (or other) boxes for the **Write in Your Journal** activity helps students to consider which lengths they are measuring and how these relate to the sides on their net. For a good discussion, try to have a mixture of different boxes, tall and thin, short and fat etc. so that students can compare the volume and surface area for each one. Discuss what they think the cuboid with the smallest surface area for a given volume would look like.

Chapter 12
Collecting, Organising and Displaying Data

Student Book 1C
pages 309–334

This chapter covers methods for collecting, organising and displaying data but stops short of the process of interpretation and comparison of statistics which is covered in Year 9.

There is scope for students to carry out their own surveys and to use real statistical data. Real examples of pictograms, line charts and graphs found in the media can be used to generate discussion. Many links can be made to work students meet in other subjects, particularly science and geography.

Work from Chapter 7 on percentages, expressing one quantity as a percentage of another or a part as a percentage of a whole, is revisited throughout this chapter when interpreting data in frequency tables and charts.

k are resources on Kerboodle

Resources

k Chapter 12 introduction video

k Try It! videos 4, 7, 9

Assessment

Workbook 1C Chapter 12

Graded Question Bank 1 Chapter 12

k Chapter 12 online skills test

k Chapter 12 end of chapter test and mark scheme

k Fully-worked solutions: Chapter 12 in Workbook 1C and Graded Question Bank 1

12.1 Collection of Data

Learning Objective:

● Recognise different methods of collecting data

● Identify and write appropriate survey question

MyMaths
1248 Types of data
1249 Questionnaires

Discuss with students examples of the different methods of data collection. As well as using the examples in the student book, ask students for examples of their own. **Class Activity 1** helps students understand the four different methods of data collection outlined in the first section: taking measurements, observing outcomes, conducting surveys and reading publications. Discuss with students the reliability and accuracy of the different methods and ask them to consider relative costs in terms of both money and time.

Exercise 12.1 (page 314) gives students practice identifying which method of data collection is most suitable in a variety of different contexts. It would be helpful for students to discuss their answers with each other throughout this exercise. When students evaluate questions from questionnaires in Questions 6–9, suggest they refer back to the four points given in the Note in Example 1. Ask students to work with a partner to design the survey form for Question 9. Then ask them to swap with another pair of students, review each other's forms and offer constructive criticism. Discuss **Example 1** on page 312 to ensure that students are aware of the importance of well-designed response boxes which are exhaustive but do not overlap.

12.2 Organisation of Data

Learning Objectives:

● Organise data

● Create frequency tables

MyMaths
1385 Lists and tables 2
1235 Introducing data
1193 Frequency tables and bar charts

Students are likely to be familiar with making tally charts of data from primary school but they must also be clear about how to set up the three columns of a frequency table. **Examples 2 and 3** go through the process for quantitative and qualitative classes. Emphasise to students the importance of checking that the total frequency equals the number of items of data (as highlighted in the **Remark** on page 316). The word frequency should always be used in the final column rather than total or number.

Make sure students appreciate that the purpose of a frequency table is to allow a tally mark to be added for each data value in turn. Instead, some students may be tempted to count the number of each type of data value and then enter the tally and frequency in the table. Discuss with students how accurate this would be, especially when dealing with a lot of data values, and how keeping a tally can avoid errors. Check that students are keeping the 'blocks of 5' separate.

The **Flashback** (page 310) gives a reminder of inequality notation needed for grouped frequency tables. When going through **Example 4**, discuss the class intervals that have been chosen. Students can note that they are uniform and the number of classes is manageable.

Students should be familiar with hours being represented in decimal form like this, but check there is no confusion.

All questions in **Exercise 12.2** (except Question 11) tell students the class intervals to use, but some real-life data collected by the students themselves could give them a chance to make their own decisions about classes. Discuss with students that we often collect data in order to try to answer a question or investigate a claim. What might be the question, or claim, motivating the data collected in the exercises in 12.2? Teachers should note that although grouped continuous data is included in this section, histograms are not covered until later in Key Stage 3.

12.3 Pictograms, Vertical Line Charts and Bar Charts

Learning Objective:

● Construct, analyse and interpret pictograms, vertical line charts, bar charts and compound bar charts

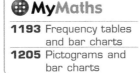

MyMaths

1193 Frequency tables and bar charts
1205 Pictograms and bar charts

Throughout this work, differences and similarities between the three types of chart should be considered and discussed with students. Talk with them about the advantages and disadvantages of using each of pictograms, vertical line charts and bar charts.

Emphasise the importance of having a key for pictograms by discussing how the values represented by a pictogram would change with a different key. When working through the pictograms in **Example 5** and **Try It! 5**, make sure that students appreciate the significance of having a square divided into four sections to represent four magazines and a flower with five petals to represent five plants. Discuss how students would go about choosing a symbol and a 'sensible' key so that data can be shown accurately with parts of symbols. Point out that the use of a symbol for 100 TV sets in **Example 6** means that the pictogram representation is only approximate.

When considering vertical line charts and bar charts, encourage correct labelling by highlighting how the column headings on the tables become the axis labels and how the values in the first column become the line or bar labels. When working through **Examples 7 to 9**, discuss with students the scale used for the frequency axis in each case. It must be linear in all cases, with a scale chosen to make it easy to plot accurately. Emphasise to students that bar charts are used to represent data in distinct categories.

For more able students, you can introduce the terms qualitative data and quantitative data (which includes discrete data and continuous data). Bar charts can be used to represent qualitative data and discrete data. However, for continuous data in class intervals, a bar chart should not be used to represent the data: these should be represented by a histogram.

Make sure that students understand the need for a key for compound bar charts to distinguish between different categories in a class. Discuss the benefits of using a compound bar chart rather than two separate diagrams. Also discuss why the bars are adjacent horizontally not stacked vertically. You could ask when we might choose to arrange them on top of each other. Develop this further when students complete **Class Activity 2**, considering the relative benefits of pictograms and bar charts.

Exercise 12.3 gives students practice at constructing and interpreting all the types of chart covered. Question 12 gives a practical activity for collection of data about different types of shops that could be discussed in class and then set as a homework task.

For questions throughout **Revision Exercise 12**, students need to interpret pictograms, bar charts, vertical line charts and frequency tables. Students must read scales accurately to find frequencies for individual values and carry out calculations using the data obtained. Questions 4, 7 and 8 involve finding percentages; point out that percentages are often used to highlight relative sizes of groups when survey results are presented, particularly in the media. Students need to construct a frequency table for Question 4, but are given the class intervals to use. Discuss the missing axis labels for Question 8, where there is potential for confusion given that both axes have numerical values. Remind students that the vertical axis on a line chart will always be frequency. When students have constructed a pictogram for Question 9, encourage them to discuss the relative merits of the original bar chart and their pictogram.

To complete the first part of the **Write in Your Journal** activity, suggest students write a checklist of important things to consider, which they can tick off as collection and organisation of data is carried out. The second activity, considering advantages and disadvantages of pictograms and bar charts, can be presented as a table with advantages and disadvantages shown in two columns for each type of chart.

In **Review Exercise 3**, the first four questions provide straightforward practice of work involving line segments, angle properties and symmetry. Provide students with tracing paper for symmetry work and suggest that sketching diagrams may be helpful throughout this exercise. Discuss the three-letter notation used in Question 7 to ensure that students identify correct triangles for their area and perimeter calculations. Question 9 includes work to find a radius given the circumference. Make sure that students give evidence to support their decision for which figure has the larger area in part (d).

Encourage students to find the most efficient methods; for example, in Question 10, point out that rather than finding the area of the two quarters and then adding, they could find the area of a semicircle.

Discuss which would be the most appropriate type of bar chart to show both minimum and maximum temperatures for part (c) of Question 11 and remind students of the need for a key. Students may find it useful to cut out a net with the dimensions shown in Question 14, in order to manipulate and fold into a cuboid. Similarly, a paper model of the table top described in Question 15 may be helpful where this type of table is not familiar to students.

Problems in Real-world Contexts

Student Book 1C
pages 338–343

Throughout these problems, there are opportunities to extend the work and incorporate students' own experiences by making links to other curriculum areas such as design and technology, geography and history.

A Paper Sizes

Emphasise to students that, where possible, working with fractions will give more accurate answers. Where solutions to the nearest millimetre are required, care should be taken to avoid premature rounding during working which may affect the accuracy of the final answer.

B Brick Wall

This question gives a rich opportunity for students to consider the crucial need for approximation in building. The 'one-half running bond' technical vocabulary will probably be unfamiliar to most students, although the brick pattern described will not. When students work on Question 1, point out that they should calculate using measurements for bricks in a row where full bricks are used. They could then show by calculation that the brick parts at the ends of the other rows in the diagram will not be exactly half bricks. Question 2 enables plenty of discussion between students about how a reasonable estimate can be reached; encourage them to consider whether mortar should be accounted for and how to deal with the fact that the 2 metre wall will not be an exact number of rows high.

C Magazine Holder

Dealing with the quarter circles for the perimeter of the side pieces is likely to cause the most challenge. Remind students that they need to take the radius of the cut out circle into account when finding the lengths of two of the straight edges. A clearly labelled sketch will be an effective support here.

D The Gherkin

In Question 1(a), make sure students realise that they are to use the information in the question to work out the size of a typical football pitch rather than research

dimensions themselves. Throughout this problem, ask students to check that they round their answers to the various degrees of accuracy required.

E SD Memory Card

Check that students take into account the small half square that is cut out of the corner of the cards when they calculate the volume in Question 2. For Question 3, ask students to sketch the case, which is a cuboid, and label with its dimensions, taking into account the gap allowed around the card.

F Turn Left Sign

Students may find it very helpful to draw a sketch of the arrow shape when finding the area in Question 2. There is opportunity to discuss the variety of ways that the area can be calculated; the arrow shape may be split up or appropriate areas subtracted from the enclosing rectangle. However they choose to do it, students should label a sketch diagram with the dimensions required to find areas for the parts of the shape.

G Window Frame

As students should use $\pi = 3$ in their own calculations, this question becomes more accessible than if greater accuracy was required. Suggest that students draw a sketch of the window frame and label it as they work through to find answers to Question 1. Similarly, a labelled sketch of the square for Question 2 will help ensure that students do not get confused between perimeter and area.

H Population Pyramid for the UK

This diagram is a very rich source of information and may be familiar to students from their geography lessons. Point out that the population scale is measured in thousands so the readings will be estimates. Encourage students to refer to their knowledge of events in history such as the Second World War to offer explanations for features identified in the diagram.

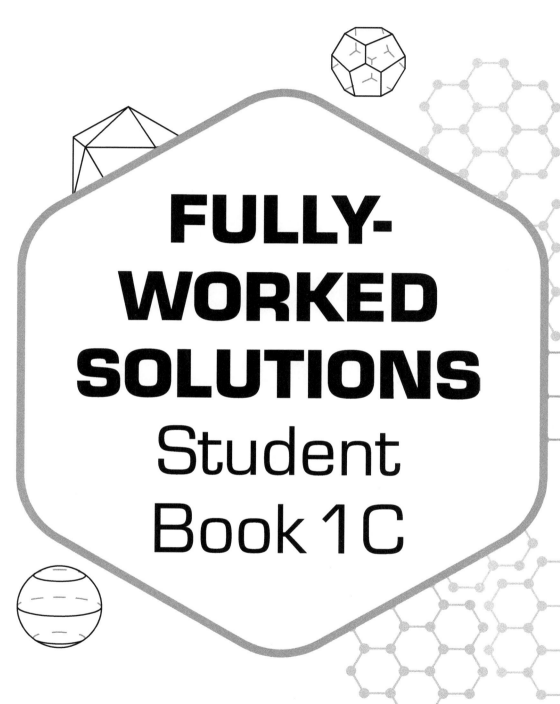

FULLY-
WORKED
SOLUTIONS
Student
Book 1C

Positive Real Numbers

Class Activity 1

Objective: Round numbers to the nearest 10, 100 and 1000.

1.

   380   387   390

   The number line above counts up in tens. 387 is between 380 and 390. Which number, 380 or 390, would you use as an approximation of 387? Explain your answer.

   I would use 390 as an approximation of 387 as 387 is closer to 390 than to 380.

2.

   4700 4720   4800

   The number line above counts up in hundreds. 4720 is between 4700 and 4800. Which number, 4700 or 4800, would you use as an approximation of 4720? Explain your answer.

   I would use 4700 as an approximation of 4720 as 4720 is closer to 4700 than to 4800.

3.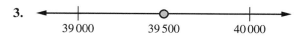

   39 000   39 500   40 000

   The number line above counts up in thousands. 39 500 is between 39 000 and 40 000. Think about which number, 39 000 or 40 000, you would use as an approximation of 39 500.

   39 500 is at the midpoint between 39 000 and 40 000.
   I would use 40 000 as an approximation of 39 500.

Class Activity 2

Objective: To explore some properties of addition.

1. Find the values of these sums.
   (a) (i) $347 + 153$

   $347 + 153 = 500$

   (ii) $153 + 347$

   $153 + 347 = 500$

   (b) (i) $562 + 839$

   $562 + 839 = 1401$

   (ii) $839 + 562$

   $839 + 562 = 1401$

2. Find the sum within the bracket first and then work out the value of each addition.

  (a) (i) $(25 + 39) + 41$

$$(25 + 39) + 41$$
$$= 64 + 41$$
$$= 105$$

        (ii) $25 + (39 + 41)$

$$25 + (39 + 41)$$
$$= 25 + 80$$
$$= 105$$

  (b) (i) $(275 + 429) + 171$

$$(275 + 429) + 171$$
$$= 704 + 171$$
$$= 875$$

        (ii) $275 + (429 + 171)$

$$275 + (429 + 171)$$
$$= 275 + 600$$
$$= 875$$

3. Work out the value of each addition.

  (a) (i) $193 + 68$

$$193 + 68$$
$$= 261$$

$$\begin{array}{r} 193 \\ +\ 68 \\ \hline 261 \\ \hline {\scriptstyle 1\ 1} \end{array}$$

        (ii) $(193 + 7) + 61$

$$(193 + 7) + 61$$
$$= 200 + 61$$
$$= 261$$

  (b) (i) $348 + 175 + 652$

$$348 + 175 + 652$$
$$= 1175$$

$$\begin{array}{r} 348 \\ 175 \\ +\ 652 \\ \hline 1175 \\ \hline {\scriptstyle 1\ 1} \end{array}$$

        (ii) $348 + 652 + 175$

$$348 + 652 + 175$$
$$= 1000 + 175$$
$$= 1175$$

4. What do you observe from the results in Question **1**? Suggest one property of addition from the results.

From the results in Question 1, you see that $347 + 153$ is the same as $153 + 347$, and $562 + 839$ is the same as $839 + 562$.

The order of the two numbers being added together does not affect the sum.

Hence,

number 1 + number 2 = number 2 + number 1.

5. (a) What do you observe from the results in Question **2**? Suggest one property of addition from the results.

From the results in Question 2, you see that (25 + 39) + 41 is the same as 25 + (39 + 41).
Which pairs of numbers are bracketed does not affect the sum.
Hence,
(number 1 + number 2) + number 3 = number 1 + (number 2 + number 3).

(b) Which is easier to calculate: **2(b)(i)** or **2(b)(ii)**? Why?

2(b)(ii) is easier to calculate. Adding 429 and 171 together first gives a multiple of 10 which makes adding the last number easier.

6. (a) What do you observe from the results in Question **3**?

From the results in Question 3, you see that 193 + 68 is the same as (193 + 7) + 61 and 348 + 175 + 652 is the same as 348 + 652 + 175.

(b) Which is easier to calculate: **3(a)(i)** or **3(a)(ii)**? Why?

3(a)(ii) is easier to calculate than 3(a)(i). It is generally easier to find sums which are multiples of 10. By splitting 68 as 7 + 61, you can add 193 and 7 to get 200.

(c) Which is easier to calculate: **3(b)(i)** or **3(b)(ii)**? Why?

3(b)(ii) is easier to calculate than 3(b)(i). By reordering the numbers, you can make the sum of two numbers a multiple of 10 and hence make adding easier.

Class Activity 3

Objective: To recognise the inverse relationship between addition and subtraction.

1. Work out the values of these expressions.
   (a) $25 + 48$

   $25 + 48 = 73$

   (b) $73 - 25$

   $73 - 25 = 48$

   (c) $73 - 48$

   $73 - 48 = 25$

2. Calculate these expressions.
   (a) $367 + 52$

   $367 + 52 = 419$

   (b) $419 - 367$

   $419 - 367 = 52$

   (c) $419 - 52$

   $419 - 52 = 367$

3. Work out the values of these expressions.
   (a) 724 + 156

   724 + 156 = 880
   _____

   (b) 880 − 724

   880 − 724 = 156
   _____

   (c) 880 − 156

   880 − 156 = 724
   _____

4. By observing the above results, if number 1 + number 2 = sum, what is
   (a) sum − number 1,

   sum − number 1 = number 2
   _____

   (b) sum − number 2?

   sum − number 2 = number 1
   _____

5. Find the 3-digit missing number *** in each addition.
   (a)   ***
         $+\ 347$
         $\overline{\ \ 589}$

   589 − 347 = 242
   _____

   (b)   436
         $+\ ***$
         $\overline{\ \ 914}$

   914 − 436 = 478
   _____

Class Activity 4

Objective: To explore some properties of multiplication.

1. Calculate these products.
   (a) (i) 9×13

   $9 \times 13 = 117$
   _____

   (ii) 13×9

   $13 \times 9 = 117$
   _____

   (b) (i) 26×45

   $26 \times 45 = 1170$
   _____

(ii) 45×26

$45 \times 26 = 1170$

---

2. Work out the product within the bracket first and then calculate the value of each expression.

(a) **(i)** $(3 \times 5) \times 7$

$(3 \times 5) \times 7$
$= 15 \times 7$
$= 105$

(ii) $3 \times (5 \times 7)$

$3 \times (5 \times 7)$
$= 3 \times 35$
$= 105$

(b) **(i)** $(2 \times 8) \times 41$

$(2 \times 8) \times 41$
$= 16 \times 41$
$= 656$

(ii) $2 \times (8 \times 41)$

$2 \times (8 \times 41)$
$= 2 \times 328$
$= 656$

---

3. Work out the values of these expressions. For **(i)**, find the sum within the brackets first. For **(ii)**, calculate the multiplication before the addition.

(a) **(i)** $8 \times (3 + 7)$

$8 \times (3 + 7)$
$= 8 \times 10$
$= 80$

(ii) $8 \times 3 + 8 \times 7$

$8 \times 3 + 8 \times 7$
$= 24 + 56$
$= 80$

(b) **(i)** $12 \times (15 + 25)$

$12 \times (15 + 25)$
$= 12 \times 40$
$= 480$

(ii) $12 \times 15 + 12 \times 25$

$12 \times 15 + 12 \times 25$
$= 180 + 300$
$= 480$

---

4. Find the values of these products.
    (a) (i) $5 \times 38 \times 2$

            $5 \times 38 \times 2$
            $= 190 \times 2$
            $= 380$

        (ii) $5 \times 2 \times 38$

            $5 \times 2 \times 38$
            $= 10 \times 38$
            $= 380$

    (b) (i) $4 \times 67 \times 25$

            $4 \times 67 \times 25$
            $= 268 \times 25$
            $= 6700$

        (ii) $4 \times 25 \times 67$

            $4 \times 25 \times 67$
            $= 100 \times 67$
            $= 6700$

5. What do you observe from the results in Question 1? Suggest one property of multiplication from the results.

    From the results in Question 1, you see that $9 \times 13 = 13 \times 9$ and $26 \times 45 = 45 \times 26$.
    Order does not affect the answer in multiplication.
    Hence,
    number 1 $\times$ number 2 = number 2 $\times$ number 1.

6. What do you observe from the results in Question 2? Suggest one property of multiplication from the results.

    From the results in Question 2, you see that $(3 \times 5) \times 7 = 3 \times (5 \times 7)$ and $(2 \times 8) \times 41 = 2 \times (8 \times 41)$.
    The answer is the same when different pairs of numbers are bracketed.
    Hence,
    (number 1 $\times$ number 2) $\times$ number 3 = number 1 $\times$ (number 2 $\times$ number 3).

7. What do you observe from the results in Question 3? Suggest one property involving addition and multiplication from the results.

    From the results in Question 3, you see that $8 \times (3 + 7) = 8 \times 3 + 8 \times 7$ and $12 \times (15 + 25) = 12 \times 15 + 12 \times 25$.
    The answer is the same if each term inside the bracket is multiplied by the number outside the bracket.
    Hence,
    number 1 $\times$ (number 2 + number 3) = number 1 $\times$ number 2 + number 1 $\times$ number 3.

8. (a) What do you observe from the results in Question 4?

        From the results in Question 4, you see that
        $5 \times 38 \times 2 = 5 \times 2 \times 38$ and
        $4 \times 67 \times 25 = 4 \times 25 \times 67$.
        Order does not affect the answer in multiplication.

(b) Which is easier to calculate: **4(a)(i)** or **4(a)(ii)**? Why?

4(a)(ii) is easier to calculate than 4(a)(i). Multiplying by 10 is easier.

(c) Which is easier to calculate: **4(b)(i)** or **4(b)(ii)**? Why?

4(b)(ii) is easier to calculate than 4(b)(i). Multiplying by 100 is easier.

Class Activity 5

Objective: To explore the relationship between multiplication and division.

1. Work out the values of these expressions.
    (a) 8×7

    $8 \times 7 = 56$

    (b) $56 \div 7$

    $56 \div 7 = 8$

    (c) $56 \div 8$

    $56 \div 8 = 7$

2. Work out the values of these expressions.
    (a) 12×6

    $12 \times 6 = 72$

    (b) $72 \div 6$

    $72 \div 6 = 12$

    (c) $72 \div 12$

    $72 \div 12 = 6$

3. Calculate these expressions.
    (a) 13×15

    $13 \times 15 = 195$

    (b) $195 \div 13$

    $195 \div 13 = 15$

    (c) $195 \div 15$

    $195 \div 15 = 13$

4. Consider the above results. If number 1 × number 2 = number 3, what is
   (a) number 3 ÷ number 1,

   number 3 ÷ number 1 = number 2
   _____

   (b) number 3 ÷ number 2?

   number 3 ÷ number 2 = number 1
   _____

Class Activity 6

Objective: To check the speed and accuracy of mental calculation.

You will need a timer. Work out the values of these expressions as quickly and accurately as possible. Add a five-second penalty to your time for each answer you get incorrect.

1. $352 + 143$

   $352 + 143 = 495$
   _____

2. $891 - 247$

   $891 - 247 = 800 - 200 + 91 - 47 = 600 + 44 = 644$
   _____

3. $25 + 36 + 75$

   $25 + 36 + 75 = 25 + 75 + 36 = 100 + 36 = 136$
   _____

4. $734 - 198 - 534$

   $734 - 198 - 534 = 734 - 534 - 198 = 200 - 198 = 2$
   _____

5. $35 + 46 + 75 + 44$

   $35 + 46 + 75 + 44 = 35 + 75 + 46 + 44 = 110 + 90 = 200$
   _____

6. $92 - 47 - 33 + 18$

   $92 - 47 - 33 + 18 = 92 + 18 - (47 + 33) = 110 - 80 = 30$
   _____

7. 57×19

   $57 \times 19 = 57 \times (20 - 1) = 57 \times 20 - 57 = 1140 - 57 = 1083$
   _____

8. 101×48

   $101 \times 48 = (100 + 1) \times 48 = 100 \times 48 + 48 = 4800 + 48 = 4848$
   _____

9. 95×8

   $95 \times 8 = 95 \times 2 \times 2 \times 2 = 190 \times 2 \times 2 = 380 \times 2 = 760$
   _____

10. 86×25

$86 \times 25 = 86 \times 100 \div 4 = 8600 \div 4 = 2150$

---

11. $3 \times 76 + 7 \times 76$

$3 \times 76 + 7 \times 76 = (3 + 7) \times 76 = 10 \times 76 = 760$

---

12. $127 \times 18 - 127 \times 13$

$127 \times 18 - 127 \times 13 = 127 \times (18 - 13) = 127 \times 5 = 127 \times 10 \div 2 = 1270 \div 2 = 635$

---

13. 824×5

$824 \times 5 = 824 \times 10 \div 2 = 8240 \div 2 = 4120$

---

14. 639×25

$639 \times 25 = 639 \times 100 \div 4 = 63\,900 \div 4 = 15\,975$

---

15. $1365 \div 21$

$1365 \div 21 = 1365 \div 3 \div 7 = 455 \div 7 = 65$

---

16. $1024 \div 8$

$1024 \div 8 = 1024 \div 2 \div 2 \div 2 = 512 \div 2 \div 2 = 256 \div 2 = 128$

---

17. $5425 \div 25$

$5425 \div 25 = 5425 \div 5 \div 5 = 1085 \div 5 = 217$

---

18. $9360 \div 20$

$9360 \div 20 = 9360 \div 10 \div 2 = 936 \div 2 = 468$

---

19. $136 \div 7 + 67 \div 7$

$136 \div 7 + 67 \div 7 = (136 + 67) \div 7 = 203 \div 7 = 29$

---

20. $625 \div 8 - 409 \div 8$

$625 \div 8 - 409 \div 8 = (625 - 409) \div 8 = 216 \div 8 = 27$

Try It!

Section 1.1

1. (a) Write the number 320 715 in expanded form.
   (b) Write the number in words.
   (c) What is the value of the digit 2?
   (d) Which digit has the highest value? What is its value?

   Solution
   (a) $320\,715 = 3 \times 100\,000 + 2 \times 10\,000 + 7 \times 100 + 1 \times 10 + 5 \times 1$

   (b) The number is written as: three hundred and twenty thousand, seven hundred and fifteen.

   (c) The place value of the digit 2 is 10 000.
   ∴ the value of the digit 2 is 20 000.

   (d) The digit 3 has the highest value.
   Its value is 300 000.

2. The area of a block of land is $3672\,m^2$. Round the area to the nearest $100\,m^2$.

   Solution
   Area of land
   $= 3672\,m^2$
   $= 3700\,m^2$ (to the nearest $100\,m^2$)

Section 1.2

3. The prices of two cars are £15 398 and £24 156. Find the total price of the cars and check your answer using approximation.

   Solution
   Total price of the cars
   $= £15\,398 + £24\,156$
   $= £39\,554$

   $$\begin{array}{r} 15\,398 \\ +24\,156 \\ \hline 39\,554 \\ \hline \scriptstyle{1\ 1} \end{array}$$

   Check: £15 398 = £15 000 (to the nearest £1000)
   £24 156 = £24 000 (to the nearest £1000)
   £15 398 + £24 156
   ≈ £15 000 + £24 000
   = £39 000
   The answer £39 554 is reasonable.

4. Calculate these sums mentally.
   (a) $677 + 281 + 53 + 49$
   (b) $654 + 387$

   Solution
   (a) $677 + 281 + 53 + 49$
   $= 677 + 23 + 30 + 281 + 19 + 30$
   $= 700 + 300 + 60$
   $= 1060$

   (b) $654 + 387$
   $= 654 + 46 + 300 + 41$
   $= 700 + 300 + 41$
   $= 1000 + 41$
   $= 1041$

5. The volumes of juice in three glasses are $375\,cm^3$, $261\,cm^3$ and $255\,cm^3$. Find the total volume of the juice.

   Solution
   Total volume of juice
   $= 375 + 261 + 255$
   $= 375 + 255 + 261$
   $= 375 + 25 + 30 + 200 + 200 + 61$
   $= 400 + 200 + 200 + 30 + 61$
   $= 800 + 91$
   $= 891\,cm^3$

Section 1.3

6. Work out $8372 - 7245$.

   Solution
   $$\begin{array}{r} \scriptstyle{6\ 1} \\ 8372 \\ -7245 \\ \hline 1127 \end{array}$$
   ∴ $8372 - 7245 = 1127$

7. Find the missing number in each expression.
   (a) $539 + \square = 817$
   (b) $725 - \bigcirc = 246$

   Solution
   (a) $539 + \square = 817$
   $\square = 817 - 539$
   $= 278$

   $$\begin{array}{r} \scriptstyle{7\ 10\ 1} \\ 817 \\ -539 \\ \hline 278 \end{array}$$

   (b) $725 - \bigcirc = 246$
   $\bigcirc = 725 - 246$
   $= 479$

   $$\begin{array}{r} \scriptstyle{6\ 11\ 1} \\ 725 \\ -246 \\ \hline 479 \end{array}$$

8. Evaluate these expressions mentally.
   (a) $456 - 189 - 256$
   (b) $537 - 299$

   Solution
   (a) $456 - 189 - 256$
   $= 456 - 256 - 189$
   $= 200 - 189$
   $= 11$

   (b) $537 - 299$
   $= 537 - 300 + 1$
   $= 237 + 1$
   $= 238$

9. A supermarket has 1328 oranges in stock. After selling 745 oranges, the manager reorders 672 oranges. Find the number of oranges in stock then.

Solution

Number of oranges in stock now
$= 1328 - 745 + 672$
$= 1328 + 672 - 745$
$= 2000 - 745$
$= 2000 - 800 + 55$
$= 1200 + 55$
$= 1255$

Section 1.4

10. Work out the product of 516 and 48.

Solution

Using the column method,

$$
\begin{array}{r}
516 \\
\times 48 \\
\hline
4128 \\
20640 \\
\hline
24768 \\
\end{array}
$$

$516 \times 8 = 4128$
$516 \times 40 = 20640$
$4128 + 20640 = 24768$

$\therefore 516 \times 48 = 24768$

Students could check their solution using estimation:
$516 = 500$ (to the nearest 100)
$48 = 50$ (to the nearest 10)
$516 \times 48 \approx 500 \times 50$
$ = 25000$
The answer 24768 is reasonable.

11. The price of a game console is £329. Find the total price of 46 game consoles.

Solution

Total price of the game consoles
$= 329 \times 46$
$= £15134$

$$
\begin{array}{r}
329 \\
\times 46 \\
\hline
1974 \\
13160 \\
\hline
15134 \\
\end{array}
$$

Students could check their solution using estimation:
$329 = 300$ (to the nearest 100)
$46 = 50$ (to the nearest 10)
$329 \times 46 \approx 300 \times 50$
$ = 15000$
The answer £15134 is reasonable.

12. Calculate these products mentally.
(a) 437×4
(b) $20 \times 69 \times 50$
(c) $8 \times 87 \times 25$

Solution

(a) 437×4
$= 437 \times 2 \times 2$
$= 874 \times 2$
$= 1748$

(b) $20 \times 69 \times 50$
$= 20 \times 50 \times 69$
$= 1000 \times 69$
$= 69000$

(c) $8 \times 87 \times 25$
$= 4 \times 2 \times 87 \times 25$
$= 4 \times 25 \times 2 \times 87$
$= 100 \times 174$
$= 17400$

13. Calculate these expressions mentally.
(a) $38 \times 65 + 62 \times 65$ **(b)** 384×101

Solution

(a) $38 \times 65 + 62 \times 65$
$= (38 + 62) \times 65$
$= 100 \times 65$
$= 6500$

(b) 384×101
$= 384 \times (100 + 1)$
$= 384 \times 100 + 384 \times 1$
$= 38400 + 384$
$= 38784$

Section 1.5

14. Work out each division.
(a) $288 \div 6$
(b) $\dfrac{528}{17}$

Solution

(a)
$$
\begin{array}{r}
48 \\
6\overline{)288} \\
24 \\
\hline
48 \\
48 \\
\hline
0 \\
\end{array}
$$

$\therefore 288 \div 6 = 48$

(b) $\dfrac{528}{17} = 528 \div 17$

$$
\begin{array}{r}
31 \\
17\overline{)528} \\
51 \\
\hline
18 \\
17 \\
\hline
1 \\
\end{array}
$$

$\therefore \dfrac{528}{17} = 31, \text{r } 1$

15. There are 380 ml of an acid in a beaker. The acid is poured into test tubes which can hold 25 ml each. How many test tubes are required to contain all the acid from the beaker?

Solution

$$
\begin{array}{r}
15 \\
25\overline{)380} \\
25 \\
\hline
130 \\
125 \\
\hline
5 \\
\end{array}
$$

$\therefore 380 \div 25 = 15, \text{r } 5$
If 15 test tubes are used, 5 ml of acid will be left in the beaker.
Hence, the number of test tubes required is
$15 + 1 = 16$.

16. Find the missing number in each expression.
    (a) $608 \div \square = 16$
    (b) $\bigcirc \div 13 = 42$

    Solution
    (a) $608 \div \square = 16$
    $\square = 608 \div 16$
    $\square = 38$

$$16\overline{)608} \begin{array}{r} 38 \\ \hline 48 \\ \hline 128 \\ 128 \\ \hline 0 \end{array}$$

    (b) $\bigcirc \div 13 = 42$
    $\bigcirc = 42 \times 13$
    $ = 546$

$$\begin{array}{r} 42 \\ \times\ 13 \\ \hline 126 \\ 420 \\ \hline 546 \end{array}$$

17. Calculate these expressions mentally.
    (a) $716 \div 4$
    (b) $5670 \div 30$
    (c) $910 \div 14$

    Solution
    (a) $716 \div 4$
    $= 716 \div 2 \div 2$
    $= 358 \div 2$
    $= 179$

    (b) $5670 \div 30$
    $= 5670 \div 10 \div 3$
    $= 567 \div 3$
    $= 189$

    (c) $910 \div 14$
    $= 910 \div 2 \div 7$
    $= 455 \div 7$
    $= 65$

18. Work out these products mentally.
    (a) 827×5
    (b) 369×25

    Solution
    (a) 827×5
    $= 827 \times 10 \div 2$
    $= 8270 \div 2$
    $= 4135$

    (b) 369×25
    $= 369 \times 100 \div 4$
    $= 36\,900 \div 2 \div 2$
    $= 18\,450 \div 2$
    $= 9225$

Section 1.6

19. Write down the value of 14^2.

    Solution
    $14^2 = 14 \times 14$
    $ = 196$

20. Write down the value of 10^3.

    Solution
    $10^3 = 10 \times 10 \times 10$
    $ = 1000$

21. Evaluate 3^5.

    Solution
    $3^5 = 3 \times 3 \times 3 \times 3 \times 3 = 243$

22. (a) Find the value of $\sqrt{49}$.
    (b) Find the two consecutive integers that $\sqrt{60}$ lies between.

    Solution
    (a) Since $7 \times 7 = 49$,
    $\sqrt{49} = 7$.

    (b) $7 \times 7 = 49$ and $8 \times 8 = 64$
    $49 < 60 < 64$,
    $\therefore \sqrt{49} < \sqrt{60} < \sqrt{64}$.
    Hence, $7 < \sqrt{60} < 8$.
    $\sqrt{60}$ lies between 7 and 8.

23. (a) Find the value of $\sqrt[3]{27}$.
    (b) Find the two consecutive integers that $\sqrt[3]{200}$ lies between.

    Solution
    (a) Since $3 \times 3 \times 3 = 27$, $\sqrt[3]{27} = 3$.

    (b) $5 \times 5 \times 5 = 125$ and $6 \times 6 \times 6 = 216$
    $125 < 200 < 216$,
    $\therefore \sqrt[3]{125} < \sqrt[3]{200} < \sqrt[3]{216}$.
    Hence, $5 < \sqrt[3]{200} < 6$.
    $\sqrt[3]{200}$ lies between 5 and 6.

Section 1.7

24. Calculate these expressions.
    (a) $8 \times 6 + 14 \div 2$
    (b) $8 \times (6 + 14) \div 2$

    Solution
    (a) $8 \times 6 + 14 \div 2$
    $= 48 + 7$
    $= 55$

    (b) $8 \times (6 + 14) \div 2$
    $= 8 \times 20 \div 2$
    $= 160 \div 2$
    $= 80$

25. Calculate these expressions.
    (a) $97 - 4^3 \div (3 + 1)$
    (b) $28 \times [(9 - 5) + 2]$

    Solution
    (a) $97 - 4^3 \div (3 + 1)$
    $= 97 - 4^3 \div 4$
    $= 97 - 64 \div 4$
    $= 97 - 16$
    $= 81$

    (b) $28 \times [(9 - 5) + 2]$
    $= 28 \times [4 + 2]$
    $= 28 \times 6$
    $= 168$

26. A jar of mass 80 grams is filled with 500 grams of jam. Find the total mass of eight jars of jam.

Solution
Mass of each bottle of jam = $(80 + 500)$ g
Total mass of 8 bottles of jam
= $8 \times (80 + 500)$
= $640 + 4000$
= 4640 grams

Section 1.8

27. Find all the factors of 12.

Solution
Express 12 as a product of two whole numbers.
$12 = 1 \times 12$
$ = 2 \times 6$
$ = 3 \times 4$
$\therefore$ the factors of 12 are 1, 2, 3, 4, 6, 12.

28. Determine whether 5 is a factor of 130.

Solution
Divide 130 by 5 to see if 130 is divisible by 5.

$$\begin{array}{r} 26 \\ 5\overline{)130} \\ \underline{10} \\ 30 \\ \underline{30} \\ 0 \end{array}$$

Since the remainder is 0, 130 is divisible by 5.
$\therefore$ 5 is a factor of 130.

29. Find the common factors of 30 and 45.

Solution
$30 = 1 \times 30 \qquad\qquad 45 = 1 \times 45$
$ = 2 \times 15 \qquad\qquad = 3 \times 15$
$ = 3 \times 10 \qquad\qquad = 5 \times 9$
$ = 5 \times 6$
The factors of 30 are 1, 2, 3, 5, 6, 10, 15, 30.
The factors of 45 are 1, 3, 5, 9, 15, 45.
The common factors of 30 and 45 are 1, 3, 5 and 15.

30. Write down the first six multiples of 7.

Solution
The first 6 multiples of 7 are 7, 14, 21, 28, 35, 42.

31. Determine whether 246 is a multiple of 4.

Solution
Divide 246 by 4 to see if 246 is divisible by 4.

$$\begin{array}{r} 61 \\ 4\overline{)246} \\ \underline{24} \\ 06 \\ \underline{4} \\ 2 \end{array}$$

$246 \div 4 = 61$, r 2

Since the remainder is non-zero, 246 is not a product of 4 and another whole number.
$\therefore$ 246 is not a multiple of 4.

32. Find the first two common multiples of 3 and 5.

Solution
First list some multiples, say the first 10 multiples, of the numbers 3 and 5.
Then find their first two common multiples.
The first 10 multiples of 3 are 3, 6, 9, 12, 15, 18, 21, 24, 27, 30.
The first 10 multiples of 5 are 5, 10, 15, 20, 25, 30, 35, 40, 45, 50.
In the above two lists, 15 and 30 are their common multiples.
(You can get more common multiples like 45, 60, 75, . . . if you list more multiples of each number.)
Hence, the first two common multiples of 3 and 5 are 15 and 30.

Exercise 1.1

Level 1   GCSE Grade **1 / 1⁺**

1. Write each number in expanded form.
(a)   603 180   (b)   6 300 018

Solution
(a) $603\,180 = 6 \times 100\,000 + 3 \times 1000 + 1 \times 100 + 8 \times 10$

(b) $6\,300\,018 = 6 \times 1\,000\,000 + 3 \times 100\,000 + 1 \times 10 + 8 \times 1$

2. Write down the value of the digit 8 in each number.
(a)   340 918   (b)   871 903

Solution
(a)   In 340 918, the value of the digit 8 is 8 ones.

(b)   In 871 903, the value of the digit 8 is 800 000.

3. (a)   Which of these represents seven million, fifty-one thousand and twenty-four?
7 051 024   7 051 240   7 510 240   7 510 024
(b)   Which digit in your answer to **(a)** has the lowest value? What is its value?

Solution
(a)   7 051 024

(b)   The digit 4 has the lowest value. Its value is 4 ones.

4. Round each number to the nearest 10.
(a)   1356   (b)   382 621

Solution

(a) $1356 = 1360$ (to the nearest 10)

(b) $382\,621 = 382\,620$ (to the nearest 10)

5. Round each number to the nearest 100.
   (a) 971   (b) 416 725

Solution

(a) $971 = 1000$ (to the nearest 100)

(b) $416\,725 = 416\,700$ (to the nearest 100)

6. Round each number to the nearest 1000.
   (a) 892 549   (b) 3671 283

Solution

(a) $892\,549 = 893\,000$ (to the nearest 1000)

(b) $3671\,283 = 3671\,000$ (to the nearest 1000)

Level 2   GCSE Grade 1⁺ / 2⁻

7. The mid-year estimate for the population of Scotland in 2015 was 5373 000.
   (a) Write the population in words.
   (b) What is the place value of the digit 5?

Solution

(a) The number 5373 000 is written as: five million, three hundred and seventy-three thousand.

(b) The place value of the digit 5 is 1000 000.

8. The price of a flat is £321 495.
   (a) Which digit has the highest value? What is its value?
   (b) Round the price to the nearest £1000.

Solution

(a) The digit 3 has the highest value. Its value is 300 000.

(b) £321 495 = £321 000 (to the nearest £1000)

9. The London Eye is 135 m high.
   (a) Which digit has the lowest value? What is its value?
   (b) Round the height to the nearest 10 m.

Solution

(a) The digit 5 has the lowest value. Its value is 5 ones.

(b) Height = 135 m
    = 140 m (to the nearest 10 m)

10. The volume of water in an aquarium tank is $64\,813\,cm^3$.
    (a) What is the value of the digit 4?
    (b) Round the volume to the nearest $1000\,cm^3$.

Solution

(a) The value of the digit 4 is 4000.

(b) Volume = $64\,813\,cm^3$
            = $65\,000\,cm^3$ (to the nearest $1000\,cm^3$)

Level 3   GCSE Grade 2 / 3⁻

11. The Henry Willis organ in the Royal Albert Hall was built in 1871. It has 9999 pipes. Round the number of pipes to
    (a) the nearest 100,   (b) the nearest 1000.

Solution

Number of pipes = 9999

(a) 10 000 (to the nearest 100)

(b) 10 000 (to the nearest 1000)

12. 321 459 people applied to run the Tokyo Marathon in 2017.
    (a) Write the number in expanded form.
    (b) What is the value of the digit 2 in the number?
    (c) Round the number to the nearest 1000.

Solution

(a) $321\,459 = 3 \times 100\,000 + 2 \times 10\,000 + 1 \times 1000$
    $+ 4 \times 100 + 5 \times 10 + 9 \times 1$

(b) The value of the digit 2 in the number is 20 000.

(c) $321\,459 = 321\,000$ (to the nearest 1000)

13. Write two numbers which can be rounded to 3059 000 to the nearest 1000. One of the numbers should be smaller than 3059 000 and the other greater than 3059 000.

Solution

Numbers smaller than 3059 000 that can be rounded to 3059 000 to the nearest 1000:
    3058 500,
    3058 678,
    3058 912.
Numbers greater than 3059 000 that can be rounded to 3059000 to the nearest 1000:
    3059 099,
    3059 321,
    3059 495.
The numbers should be selected such that
$3058\,500 \leq$ number $< 3059\,500$.

14. Fred rounds the price of an antique clock to the nearest £100 and gets £260 000. The price of the clock contains only even digits. Write down two possible prices of the clock.
    Hint: 0 is an even digit.

Solution

From the rounded value, possible prices are such that $259\,950 \le$ price $< 260\,050$.
But all the digits are even so
$260\,000 \le$ price $\le 260\,048$.
Two possible prices are
£260 020 and £260 044.

Exercise 1.2

Level 1   GCSE Grade 1⁺

1. Evaluate these sums.
   (a) $439 + 561$
   (b) $817 + 9216$
   (c) $73246 + 81759$
   (d) $432829 + 271$

   Solution

   (a)
   $$\begin{array}{r} 439 \\ +\ 561 \\ \hline 1000 \\ \tiny 1\ 1 \end{array}$$

   (b)
   $$\begin{array}{r} 817 \\ +\ 9216 \\ \hline 10\,033 \\ \tiny 1\ \ 1 \end{array}$$

   $\therefore 439 + 561 = 1000$ $\therefore 817 + 9216 = 10\,033$

   (c)
   $$\begin{array}{r} 73246 \\ +\ 81759 \\ \hline 155\,005 \\ \tiny 1\ 1\ 1 \end{array}$$

   (d)
   $$\begin{array}{r} 432\,829 \\ +\ \ \ 271 \\ \hline 433\,100 \\ \tiny 1\ 1\ 1 \end{array}$$

   $\therefore 73\,246 + 81\,759$ $\therefore 432\,829 + 271$
   $= 155\,005$ $= 433\,100$

2. Calculate these sums mentally.
   (a) $36 + 45 + 24$ (b) $17 + 28 + 22 + 53$
   (c) $165 + 48 + 235$ (d) $741 + 123 + 259$
   Note: Calculate mentally means work out the sums in your head without written working.

   Solution

   (a) $36 + 45 + 24$
   $= 36 + 24 + 45$
   $= 60 + 45$
   $= 105$

   (b) $17 + 28 + 22 + 53$
   $= 17 + 53 + 28 + 22$
   $= 70 + 50$
   $= 120$

   (c) $165 + 48 + 235$
   $= 165 + 235 + 48$
   $= 400 + 48$
   $= 448$

   (d) $741 + 123 + 259$
   $= 741 + 259 + 123$
   $= 1\,000 + 123$
   $= 1123$

Level 2   GCSE Grade 2⁻/2

3. The price of a washing machine is £1398 and the price of an oven is £1350. Find the total price of these two items.

   Solution

   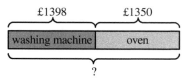

   Total price
   $= £(1398 + 1350)$
   $= £2748$

   $$\begin{array}{r} 1398 \\ +1350 \\ \hline 2748 \\ \tiny 1 \end{array}$$

4. The volume of water in a tank is $43\,825$ cm³. If 2956 cm³ of water is poured into the tank, find the new volume of water in the tank.

   Solution

   $$\begin{array}{r} 43\,825 \\ +\ 2956 \\ \hline 46\,781 \\ \tiny 1\ 1 \end{array}$$

   New volume of water $= 43\,825 + 2956 = 46\,781$ cm³

5. The annual sales of a mathematics book are $83\,549$ copies. The annual sales of a physics book are $45\,763$ copies. Find the total annual sales of these two books.

   Solution

   $$\begin{array}{r} 83549 \\ +\ 45763 \\ \hline 129312 \\ \tiny 1\ 1\ 1 \end{array}$$

   Total annual sales $= 83\,549 + 45\,763 = 129\,312$ copies

6. A lorry carries three cars of masses 1327 kg, 1475 kg and 1573 kg. What is the total mass of the cars?

   Solution

   Total mass of the cars
   $= 1327 + 1475 + 1573$
   $= 1327 + 1573 + 1475$
   $= 4375$ kg

   $$\begin{array}{r} 1327 \\ 1475 \\ +1573 \\ \hline 4375 \\ \tiny 1\ 1\ 1 \end{array}$$

GCSE Grade 2/2⁺

7. The area of Hyde Park is 142 hectares. The area of Kensington Gardens is 111 hectares.
   (a) Find their total area.
   (b) Round the result in (a) to the nearest 10 hectares.

Solution
   (a) Total area $\qquad$ 142
       $= 142 + 111$ $\qquad$ $+111$
       $= 253$ hectares $\qquad$ $\overline{253}$

   (b) 253 hectares $= 250$ hectares
       (to the nearest 10 hectares)

8. Emily orders a burger, some French fries and a hot chocolate for her lunch. Their energy contents are 3070 kJ, 1070 kJ and 450 kJ respectively.
   (a) What is the total energy content of her lunch?
   (b) Round the result in (a) to the nearest 100 kJ.

Solution
   (a) Total energy content
       $= 3070 + 1070 + 450$
       $= 3000 + 70 + 1000 + 70 + 450$
       $= 3000 + 1000 + 70 + 20 + 50 + 450$
       $= 4000 + 90 + 500$
       $= 4000 + 590$
       $= 4590$ kJ
       Alternatively,

       $\qquad$ 3070
       $\qquad$ 1070
       $\qquad$ $+\ 450$
       $\qquad$ $\overline{4590}$
       $\qquad\qquad$ 1

   (b) 4590 kJ $= 4600$ kJ
       (to the nearest 100 kJ)

9. The areas of Asia, Europe and North America are $43\,820\,000\,\text{km}^2$, $10\,180\,000\,\text{km}^2$ and $24\,490\,000\,\text{km}^2$ respectively.
   (a) Arrange these three continents in ascending order of their areas.
   (b) Find the total area of these three continents.

Solution
   (a) $10\,180\,000 < 24\,490\,000 < 43\,820\,000$ so in ascending order of size: Europe, North America, Asia.

   (b) $\qquad$ $43\,820\,000$
       $\qquad$ $10\,180\,000$
       $\qquad$ $+\ 24\,490\,000$
       $\qquad$ $\overline{78\,490\,000}$
       $\qquad\qquad$ 1 1

       The total area of the three continents is $78\,490\,000\,\text{km}^2$.

10. The number of students of ages 12, 13, 14 and 15 in the UK in 2016 were 554 237, 534 482, 537 277 and 540 947 respectively.
    (a) Find the total number of these students.
    (b) How many students were there of ages 12 to 15 in the UK in 2016 to the nearest 100?

Solution
    (a) $\qquad$ 554 237
        $\qquad$ 534 482
        $\qquad$ 537 277
        $\qquad$ $+\ 540\,947$
        $\qquad$ $\overline{2\,166\,943}$
        $\qquad\qquad$ 1 1 1 2 2

        The total number of students was 2 166 943.

    (b) To the nearest 100 the number of students was 2 166 900.

11. Find the missing digits in this calculation.

    $$\begin{array}{r} \Box\,2\,6\,\Box \\ +\ 7\,\Box\,5\,9 \\ \hline 1\ 1\ 1\ 2\ 3 \end{array}$$

Solution

    $$\begin{array}{r} \boxed{3}\,2\,6\,\boxed{4} \\ +\ 7\,\boxed{8}\,5\,9 \\ \hline 1\ 1\ 1\ 2\ 3 \end{array}$$

12. There is a red bar, a white bar and a blue bar. The sum of the lengths of the red bar and the white bar is 123 cm. The sum of the lengths of the red bar and the blue bar is 139 cm. The sum of the lengths of the white bar and the blue bar is 106 cm. Find
    (a) the total length of the three bars,
    (b) the length of the red bar.
    Hint: A bar model may help you understand the problem.

Solution
A bar model drawn to represent the problem may be helpful.

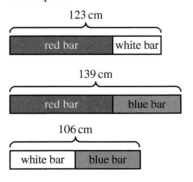

(a) If you add up all three sums of lengths above, you get length of 2 red bars, 2 blue bars and 2 white bars

$$= 123 + 139 + 106$$
$$= 368\,cm$$

Hence, the total length of 1 red bar, 1 blue bar and 1 white bar $= 368 \div 2$
$$= 184\,cm$$

(b) Length of the red bar
= total length of the three bars − length of the white bar and the blue bar
$$= 184 − 106$$
$$= 78\,cm$$

13. The missing digits in this calculation are all odd digits. Find them.

```
  1 ☐ ☐ 5
  ☐ 8 9 ☐
+ 4 ☐ ☐ 8
─────────
  1 3 5 2 6
```

Solution

```
  1 ③ ① 5
  ⑦ 8 9 ③
+ 4 ③ ① 8
─────────
  1 3 5 2 6
```

Other solutions: 1515 + 7893 + 4118 or 1115 + 7893 + 4518.

Exercise 1.3

Level 1   GCSE Grade 1⁺/2⁻

1. Calculate these expressions.
(a) 634 − 175   **(b)** 926 − 837
(c) 4371 − 2436   **(d)** 7625 − 6549

Solution

(a)
```
   ⁵¹²¹
   634
  −175
  ────
   459
```
∴ 634 − 175 = 459

(b)
```
   ⁸¹¹¹
   926
  −837
  ────
    89
```
∴ 926 − 837 = 89

(c)
```
   ³¹⁶¹
   4371
  −2436
  ─────
   1935
```
∴ 4371 − 2436 = 1935

(d)
```
   ⁵¹¹¹
   7625
  −6549
  ─────
   1076
```
∴ 7625 − 6549 = 1076

2. Calculate these expressions mentally.
(a) 426 − 99   **(b)** 532 − 198
(c) 6241 − 397   **(d)** 4875 − 501

Note: Calculate mentally means work out the expressions in your head without written working.

Solution

(a) 426 − 99
= 426 − 100 + 1
= 326 + 1
= 327

(b) 532 − 198
= 532 − 200 + 2
= 332 + 2
= 334

(c) 6241 − 397
= 6241 − 400 + 3
= 5841 + 3
= 5844

(d) 4875 − 501
= 4875 − 500 − 1
= 4375 − 1
= 4374

3. Work out the values of these expressions mentally.
(a) 89 − 24 − 39
(b) 657 − 138 − 457
(c) 326 − 215 + 174
(d) 784 + 237 − 384

Solution

(a) 89 − 24 − 39
= 89 − 39 − 24
= 50 − 24
= 50 − 20 − 4
= 30 − 4
= 26

(b) 657 − 138 − 457
= 657 − 457 − 138
= 200 − 100 − 38
= 62

(c) 326 − 215 + 174
= 326 + 174 − 215
= 500 − 200 − 15
= 300 − 15
= 285

(d) 784 + 237 − 384
= 784 − 384 + 237
= 400 + 237
= 637

Level 2   GCSE Grade 2

4. Calculate these expressions.
(a) 821 − 625 − 99
(b) 734 − 92 − 531
(c) 432 + 756 − 561
(d) 293 − 184 + 610

Solution

Students may do the calculations using the column method or mental calculation or a combination of both.

(a)
```
  ⁷¹¹¹        ⁰¹⁸¹
  821         196
 −625        − 99
 ────        ────
  196          97
```
∴ 821 − 625 − 99 = 97

(b)
$$\overset{\scriptscriptstyle 6\;1}{734} \quad\quad\overset{\nearrow}{642}$$
$$\underline{-92}\quad/\quad\underline{-531}$$
$$642\nearrow\quad\quad 111$$

$$\therefore 734 - 92 - 531 = 111$$

(c)
$$\begin{array}{r} 432 \\ +\;756 \\ \hline 1188 \\ -\;561 \\ \hline 627 \end{array}$$

$$\therefore 432 + 756 - 561 = 627$$

(d)
$$\begin{array}{r} \overset{\scriptscriptstyle 8\;1}{293} \\ -184 \\ \hline 109 \\ +610 \\ \hline 719 \end{array}$$

$$\therefore 293 - 184 + 610 = 719$$

5. Find the missing number in each expression.
  (a) $57 + \boxed{} = 91$
  (b) $\square + 256 = 820$
  (c) $846 - \triangle = 135$
  (d) $\bigcirc - 721 = 459$

Solution
  (a) $57 + \boxed{} = 91$
$$\boxed{} = 91 - 57 \qquad \overset{\scriptscriptstyle 8\;1}{91}$$
$$\boxed{} = 34 \qquad\quad \underline{-57}$$
$$\qquad\qquad\qquad\quad 34$$

  (b) $\square + 256 = 820$
$$\square = 820 - 256 \qquad \overset{\scriptscriptstyle 7\;11\;1}{820}$$
$$\quad= 564 \qquad\qquad \underline{-256}$$
$$\qquad\qquad\qquad\quad 564$$

  (c) $846 - \triangle = 135$
$$\triangle = 846 - 135 \qquad \begin{array}{r}846\\ -135\\ \hline 711\end{array}$$
$$\quad= 711$$

  (d) $\bigcirc - 721 = 459$
$$\bigcirc = 459 + 721$$
$$\quad= 459 + 21 + 700$$
$$\quad= 480 + 700$$
$$\quad= 1180$$

6. The price of a TV set is £1853. The price of a dishwasher is £754 cheaper. Find the price of the dishwasher.

Solution
Price of the dishwasher
$$= £(1853 - 754) \qquad \overset{\scriptscriptstyle 7\;14\;1}{1853}$$
$$= £1099 \qquad\qquad \underline{-754}$$
$$\qquad\qquad\qquad\quad 1099$$

7. The area of Gem Glacier in Glacier National Park (USA) reduced from $28\,135\,\text{m}^2$ in 1966 to $20\,379\,\text{m}^2$ in 2005. Find the reduction in area.

Solution
Reduction in area
$$= 28\,135 - 20\,379 \qquad \overset{\scriptscriptstyle 7\;10\;12\;1}{28135}$$
$$= 7756\,\text{m}^2 \qquad\qquad \underline{-20379}$$
$$\qquad\qquad\qquad\qquad 7756$$

8. The area of England is $130\,395\,\text{km}^2$. The area of Scotland is $80\,077\,\text{km}^2$. Find
  (a) the total area of England and Scotland,
  (b) the difference in area between England and Scotland.

Solution
  (a) Total area of England and Scotland
$$\qquad\qquad\qquad\qquad\qquad\qquad 130395$$
$$= 130\,395 + 80\,077 \qquad\quad \underline{+\;80077}$$
$$= 210\,472\,\text{km}^2 \qquad\qquad\quad 210472$$
$$\qquad\qquad\qquad\qquad\qquad\;\; {\scriptscriptstyle 1\quad\; 1\;1}$$

  (b) Difference in their areas
$$\qquad\qquad\qquad\qquad\qquad \overset{\scriptscriptstyle 0\;1\quad\; 8\;1}{130395}$$
$$= 130\,395 - 80\,077 \qquad\quad \underline{-\;80077}$$
$$= 50\,318\,\text{km}^2 \qquad\qquad\quad\;\; 50318$$

9. An exam paper has three sections, A, B and C. The time allowed for the paper is 150 minutes. Erica uses 36 minutes to finish Section A and 53 minutes to finish Section B. How much time does she leave for Section C?

Solution
Time left for Section C
$$= 150 - 36 - 53$$
$$= 150 - 53 - 36$$
$$= 150 - 50 - 3 - 30 - 6$$
$$= 100 - 30 - 3 - 6$$
$$= 70 - 9$$
$$= 61 \text{ minutes}$$

10. Mr Smith has a net annual income of £68 500. He has to use £22 983 for his home loan and £16 400 for food and utility bills. How much is left for other expenses?
  Note: Net annual income means the income in a year after deducting income tax.

Solution
Amount left for other expenses
$$\qquad\qquad\qquad\qquad\qquad\quad \overset{\scriptscriptstyle 4\;11\;10\;9\;1}{52100}$$
$$= £(68\,500 - 22\,983 - 16\,400) \quad \underline{-22983}$$
$$= £(68\,500 - 16\,400 - 22\,983) \qquad 29117$$
$$= £(52\,100 - 22\,983)$$
$$= £29\,117$$

11. **(a)** The lengths of the Central line, District line, Northern line and Piccadilly line of the London Underground are 74 km, 64 km, 58 km and 71 km respectively. Find the total length of these four lines.

(b) There are seven other London Underground lines. The total length of all 11 lines is 402 km. Find the total length of the remaining seven lines.

Solution
(a)
```
    74
    64
    58
+   71
   267
     1
```

Total length of the four lines = 267 km.

(b)
```
   3 9 1
   402
 − 267
   135
```

Total length of the remaining seven lines
= 135 km.

12. Victoria's bank account has £3285. She withdraws £2490 from it. After paying her monthly salary into the account, the balance of the account becomes £6038. Find her monthly salary.

Solution
Amount after withdrawal (£)
= 3285 − 2490
= 795
Amount after withdrawal + monthly salary = 6038
Monthly salary
= 6038 − 795
= 6038 − 800 + 5
= 5238 + 5
= 5243

Monthly salary = £5243.

13. Find the missing numbers in the diagrams.

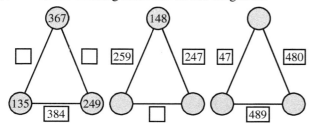

Solution

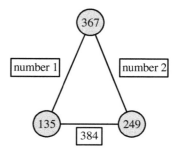

From the given information, you have
135 + 249 = 384
Hence,
number 1 = 367 + 135
= 502
number 2 = 367 + 249
= 616

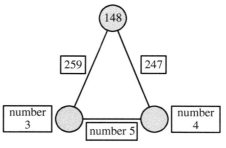

Following the operation in the first diagram, you have
number 3 + 148 = 259
number 3 = 259 − 148
= 111
number 4 + 148 = 247
number 4 = 247 − 148
= 99
∴ number 5 = 111 + 99
= 210

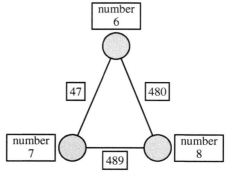

Following the earlier operation, you have
number 6 + number 7 = 47   (A)
number 6 + number 8 = 480 (B)
number 7 + number 8 = 489 (C)
Add (A), (B) and (C) to get
number 6 + number 6 + number 7 + number 7 + number 8 + number 8
= 47 + 480 + 489
= 1016
∴ number 6 + number 7 + number 8 = 508

number 6 + (number 7 + number 8) = 508
number 6 + 489 = 508   from (C) above
number 6 = 508 − 489
        = 19
Similarly,
number 7 + (number 6 + number 8) = 508
number 7 + 480 = 508   from (B) above
number 7 = 508 − 480
        = 28
number 8 + (number 6 + number 7) = 508
number 8 + 47 = 508   from (A) above
number 8 = 508 − 47
        = 461

14. A commercial printer contains 6150 sheets of paper. It is used to print two batches of documents. Write down the possible number of sheets in each batch so that the remaining number of sheets in the printer is 1380 to the nearest 10.

Solution
If the remaining number of sheets is 1380 to the nearest 10, there must be greater than or equal to 1375 sheets left and less than 1385 sheets.

So the total number of sheets used must be less than or equal to (6150 − 1375) and greater than (6150 − 1385).

6150 − 1375 = 4775
6150 − 1385 = 4765
Hence, 4765 < total of two numbers required ≤ 4775.

Some examples are: 2000 and 2770; 2400 and 2366; 1000 and 3775.

Exercise 1.4

Level 1   GCSE Grade $1^+ / 2^-$

1. Calculate these products.
   (a) 1024 × 7   (b) 6381 × 9

Solution
Students may work out the products using the grid method or the column method.

(a) Grid Method

×	1000	0	20	4
7	7000	0	140	28

7 000
   0
 140
+ 28
7168

∴ 1024 × 7 = 7168

Column Method

  1024
×   7
 7168
  1 2

∴ 1024 × 7 = 7168

(b) Grid Method

×	6000	300	80	1
9	54 000	2700	720	9

54 000
 2 700
   720
+   9
57 429
    1

∴ 6381 × 9 = 57 429

Column Method

  6381
×   9
57 429
  3 7

∴ 6381 × 9 = 57 429

2. Work out each product.
   (a) (i) 62 × 36   (ii) 62 × 37
   (b) (i) 48 × 13   (ii) 48 × 31

Solution
Students may work out the products using the grid method or the column method.

(a) (i) Grid Method

×	60	2
30	1800	60
6	360	12

1800
  60
 360
+ 12
2232
 11

∴ 62 × 36 = 2232

Column Method

   62
× 36
  372
 1860
 2232
  1 1

∴ 62 × 36 = 2232

(ii) 62×37

$= 62 \times (36 + 1)$ using result in **(a)(i)**

$= 62 \times 36 + 62 \times 1$

$= 2232 + 62$

$= 2294$

Grid Method

×	60	2
30	1800	60
7	420	14

$1800 + 60 + 420 + 14$

$= 2294$

Column Method

$$
\begin{array}{r}
62 \\
\times\ 37 \\
\hline
434 \\
1860 \\
\hline
2294 \\
\hline
\end{array}
$$
$_1$

$\therefore\ 62 \times 37 = 2294$

(b) **(i)** Grid Method

×	40	8
10	400	80
3	120	24

$$
\begin{array}{r}
400 \\
80 \\
120 \\
+\ \ 24 \\
\hline
624 \\
\hline
\end{array}
$$
$_1$

$\therefore\ 48 \times 13 = 624$

Column Method

$$
\begin{array}{r}
48 \\
\times\ 13 \\
\hline
144 \\
480 \\
\hline
624 \\
\hline
\end{array}
$$
$_1$

$\therefore\ 48 \times 13 = 624$

(ii) Mental Method

48×31

$= 48 \times 30 + 48 \times 1$

$= 1440 + 48$

$= 1488$

$$
\begin{array}{r}
48 \\
\times\ 30 \\
\hline
1440 \\
\hline
\end{array}
$$
$_2$

Grid Method

×	40	8
30	1200	240
1	40	8

$$
\begin{array}{r}
1200 \\
240 \\
40 \\
+\ \ 8 \\
\hline
1488 \\
\hline
\end{array}
$$

$\therefore\ 48 \times 31 = 1488$

Column Method

$$
\begin{array}{r}
48 \\
\times\ 31 \\
\hline
48 \\
1440 \\
\hline
1488 \\
\hline
\end{array}
$$

$\therefore\ 48 \times 31 = 1488$

3. Evaluate these products.

(a) **(i)** 58×30 **(ii)** 58×60

(b) **(i)** 96×100 **(ii)** 96×400

Solution

(a) **(i)** 58×30

$= 58 \times 3 \times 10$

$= 174 \times 10$

$= 1740$

(ii) 58×60

$= 58 \times 6 \times 10$

$= 348 \times 10$

$= 3480$

$$
\begin{array}{r}
58 \\
\times\ 6 \\
\hline
348 \\
\hline
\end{array}
$$

Alternatively, you can use the results from **(a)(i)**.

58×60

$= 58 \times 30 \times 2$

$= 1740 \times 2$

$= 3480$

(b) **(i)** $96 \times 100 = 9600$

(ii) 96×400

$= 96 \times 100 \times 4$

$= 9600 \times 4$

$= 38\,400$

$$
\begin{array}{r}
9600 \\
\times\ \ 4 \\
\hline
38\,400 \\
\hline
\end{array}
$$
$_2$

Alternatively,

96×400

$= 96 \times 4 \times 100$

$= 384 \times 100$

$= 38\,400$

$$
\begin{array}{r}
96 \\
\times\ 4 \\
\hline
384 \\
\hline
\end{array}
$$
$_2$

4. Work out these products.

    (a) 708×12 **(b)** 342×45

    (d) 26×409 **(d)** 25×368

Solution

Students may work out the products using the grid method or the column method.

(a)   Grid Method

×	**700**	**0**	**8**
12	8400	0	96

$8400 + 0 + 96 = 8496$
$\therefore 708 \times 12 = 8496$

Column Method

```
  708
× 12
8496
   9
```

$\therefore 708 \times 12 = 8496$

(b)   Grid Method

×	**300**	**40**	**2**
40	12 000	1600	80
5	1500	200	10

```
  12 000
   1 600
      80
   1 500
     200
+     10
  15 390
      1
```

$\therefore 342 \times 45 = 15\,390$

Column Method

```
    342
×    45
  1710
 13680
 15390
     1
```

$\therefore 342 \times 45 = 15\,390$

(c)   Grid Method

×	**20**	**6**
400	8000	2400
0	0	0
9	180	54

```
  8 000
  2 400
    180
+    54
 10 634
     1
```

$\therefore 26 \times 409 = 10\,634$

Column Method

```
    26
× 409
   234
   000
 10 400
 10 634
```

$\therefore 26 \times 409 = 10\,634$

(d)   Grid Method

×	**20**	**5**
300	6000	1500
60	1200	300
8	160	40

```
  6 000
  1 500
  1 200
    300
    160
+    40
  9 200
    1 1
```

$\therefore 25 \times 368 = 9200$

Column Method

```
    25
× 368
   200
 1 500
 7 500
 9 200
     1
```

$\therefore 25 \times 368 = 9200$

5. Calculate these products mentally.

    (a) 135×4 **(b)** 135×8

    (c) $5 \times 981 \times 2$ **(d)** $4 \times 36 \times 25$

    (e) $50 \times 49 \times 2$ **(f)** $8 \times 67 \times 125$

Note: Calculate mentally means work out the products in your head without written working.

Solution

(a) 135×4
$= 135 \times 2 \times 2$
$= 270 \times 2$
$= 540$

(b) 135×8
$= 135 \times 2 \times 2 \times 2$
$= 270 \times 2 \times 2$
$= 540 \times 2$
$= 1080$

(c) $5 \times 981 \times 2$
$= 981 \times 5 \times 2$
$= 981 \times 10$
$= 9810$

(d) $4 \times 36 \times 25$
$= 36 \times 4 \times 25$
$= 36 \times 100$
$= 3600$

(e) $50 \times 49 \times 2$
$= 49 \times 50 \times 2$
$= 49 \times 100$
$= 4900$

(f) $8 \times 67 \times 125$
$= 67 \times 8 \times 125$
$= 67 \times 1000$
$= 67\,000$

6. Calculate these expressions mentally.
   (a) $6 \times 123 + 4 \times 123$
   (b) $23 \times 54 + 77 \times 54$
   (c) $821 \times 732 + 179 \times 732$
   (d) $87 \times 39 - 77 \times 39$
   (e) 704×11
   (f) 823×99

Solution

(a) $6 \times 123 + 4 \times 123$
$= (6 + 4) \times 123$
$= 10 \times 123$
$= 1230$

(b) $23 \times 54 + 77 \times 54$
$= (23 + 77) \times 54$
$= 100 \times 54$
$= 5400$

(c) $821 \times 732 + 179 \times 732$
$= (821 + 179) \times 732$
$= 1000 \times 732$
$= 732\,000$

(d) $87 \times 39 - 77 \times 39$
$= (87 - 77) \times 39$
$= 10 \times 39$
$= 390$

(e) 704×11
$= 704 \times (10 + 1)$
$= 704 \times 10 + 704 \times 1$
$= 7040 + 704$
$= 7744$

$$\begin{array}{r} 7040 \\ +\ 704 \\ \hline 7744 \end{array}$$

(f) 823×99
$= 823 \times (100 - 1)$
$= 823 \times 100 - 823 \times 1$
$= 82\,300 - 823$
$= 81\,477$

$$\begin{array}{r} {}^{1\,12\,9\,\,1} \\ 82\,300 \\ 823 \\ \hline 81\,477 \end{array}$$

7. Calculate these products.
   (a) $8 \times 37 \times 25$
   (b) $50 \times 76 \times 8$
   (c) $250 \times 83 \times 4$
   (d) $16 \times 36 \times 125$

Solution

(a) $8 \times 37 \times 25$
$= 2 \times 4 \times 37 \times 25$
$= 2 \times 37 \times 4 \times 25$
$= 74 \times 100$
$= 7400$

(b) $50 \times 76 \times 8$
$= 50 \times 76 \times 2 \times 4$
$= 50 \times 2 \times 76 \times 4$
$= 100 \times 76 \times 2 \times 2$
$= 100 \times 152 \times 2$
$= 100 \times 304$
$= 30\,400$

(c) $250 \times 83 \times 4$
$= 83 \times 250 \times 4$
$= 83 \times 1000$
$= 83\,000$

(d) $16 \times 36 \times 125$
$= 8 \times 2 \times 36 \times 125$
$= 8 \times 125 \times 2 \times 36$
$= 1000 \times 72$
$= 72\,000$

8. Each box contains 36 cookies. Find the total number of cookies in 256 boxes.

Solution
Total number of cookies
$= 256 \times 36$
$= 9216$

$$\begin{array}{r} 256 \\ \times\ 36 \\ \hline 1536 \\ 7680 \\ \hline 9216 \\ \hline {}^{1\,1} \end{array}$$

9. The price of a ticket for a show is £29. Mr Thomas buys 27 tickets for his staff to watch the show. How much does he pay for the tickets?

Solution
Amount paid
$= £29 \times 27$
$= £783$

$$\begin{array}{r} 29 \\ \times\ 27 \\ \hline 203 \\ 580 \\ \hline 783 \end{array}$$

10. A jug of milk can fill nine cups each holding $196\,\text{cm}^3$ with $136\,\text{cm}^3$ left in the jug. Find
    (a) the total volume of milk in the cups,
    (b) the original volume of milk in the jug.

Solution

(a)   Total volume of milk in the cups

$$= 196 \times 9$$
$$= 1764 \, cm^3$$

$$\begin{array}{r} 196 \\ \times \quad 9 \\ \hline 1764 \\ \scriptstyle 8\,5 \end{array}$$

(b)   Original volume of milk in the jug

$$= 196 \times 9 + 136$$
$$= 1764 + 136$$
$$= 1700 + 64 + 136$$
$$= 1700 + 200$$
$$= 1900 \, cm^3$$

Level 3   GCSE Grade 2⁺/3⁻

11.   Find each missing digit in this calculation.

$$\begin{array}{r} 3\,\square \\ \times \quad \square\,2 \\ \hline 7\ 6 \\ 2\ 2\ 8\ 0 \\ \hline 2\,\square\ 5\ 6 \end{array}$$

Solution

$$\begin{array}{r} 3\square \\ \times \square 2 \\ \hline 76 \\ 2280 \\ \hline 2\blacksquare56 \end{array} \quad \begin{array}{l} \rightarrow 3\square \times 2 = 76 \\ \rightarrow 3\square \times \square 0 = 2280 \\ \rightarrow 76 + 2280 = 2\blacksquare56 \end{array}$$

$$3\,\square \times 2 = 76$$
$$3\,\square = 76 \div 2$$
$$3\,\square = 38$$

Hence, $\square = 8$

So, you have

$$38 \times \square 0 = 2280$$
$$\square 0 = 2280 \div 38$$
$$\square 0 = 60$$
$$\therefore \quad \square = 6$$

$$76 + 2280 = 2\,\blacksquare\,56$$

$$\begin{array}{r} 76 \\ 2280 \\ \hline 2356 \\ \scriptstyle 1 \end{array}$$

$$\therefore \blacksquare = 3$$

12.   A train has eight coaches and each coach can carry 76 passengers.
  (a)   Find the total passenger capacity of the train.
  (b)   If the train is full and each passenger pays £25 for a trip, what is the total train fare collected for the trip?

Solution

(a)   Total passenger capacity of the train

$$= 76 \times 8$$
$$= 608$$

$$\begin{array}{r} 76 \\ \times \quad 8 \\ \hline 608 \\ \scriptstyle 4 \end{array}$$

(b)   Total train fare collected

$$= 608 \times 25$$
$$= £15\,200$$

$$\begin{array}{r} 608 \\ \times \quad 25 \\ \hline 3040 \\ 12160 \\ \hline 15\,200 \\ \scriptstyle 1 \end{array}$$

13.   A book has 256 pages. Find the total number of pages in 190 copies of this book.

Solution

Total number of pages

$$= 256 \times 190$$
$$= 256 \times (200 - 10)$$
$$= 256 \times 200 - 256 \times 10$$
$$= 256 \times 2 \times 100 - 2560$$
$$= 512 \times 100 \; - 2560$$
$$= 51\,200 - 2560$$
$$= 48\,640$$

$$\begin{array}{r} \scriptstyle 4\,10\ 11\,1 \\ 51\,2\,0\,0 \\ 2\,5\,6\,0 \\ \hline 48\,6\,4\,0 \end{array}$$

14.   A high-definition TV set has a resolution of 1920×1080 pixels on a screen. This means the width is 1920 pixels and the height is 1080 pixels. What is the total number of pixels on the screen?

Solution

Total number of pixels

$$= 1920 \times 1080$$
$$= 1920 \times (1000 + 80)$$
$$= 1920 \times 1000 + 1920 \times 80$$
$$= 1920\,000 + 1920 \times 8 \times 10$$
$$= 1920\,000 + 15\,360 \times 10$$
$$= 1920\,000 + 153\,600$$
$$= 2073\,600$$

$$\begin{array}{r} 1920000 \\ + \ 153600 \\ \hline 2073600 \end{array}$$

15.   A chain of shops has 198 outlets. Each outlet has eight executives and one manager. The monthly salary of each executive is £2500 and the monthly salary of each manager is £3600. Work out the total monthly salaries of all the staff in these outlets.

Solution

Total monthly salaries (£)

$$= (8 \times 2500 + 1 \times 3600) \times 198$$
$$= (20\,000 + 3600) \times (200 - 2)$$
$$= 23\,600 \times 200 - 23\,600 \times 2$$
$$= 4720\,000 - 47\,200$$
$$= £4672\,800$$

16.   The ages of two brothers are consecutive numbers. The product of their ages is 1260. Find their ages.

Solution

If $\square$ is the age of the younger brother, then the older brother must be $\square + 1$.

$\square \times (\square + 1) = 1260$. You know that $30 \times 30 = 900$ and $40 \times 40 = 1600$, so you could estimate $\square$ to be somewhere between 30 and 40. By trial and error, trying □ = 35 gives 35 × 36 = 1260.

$$\begin{array}{r} 35 \\ \times\ 36 \\ \hline 210 \\ 1050 \\ \hline 1260 \end{array}$$

Their ages are 35 and 36.

Exercise 1.5

Level 1   GCSE Grade 1^{+} / 2^{-}

1. Find each quotient.
    (a)   375 ÷ 5
    (b)   720 ÷ 6
    (c)   1617 ÷ 7
    (d)   1638 ÷ 9

    Solution

    (a)
    $$\begin{array}{r} 75 \\ 5\overline{)375} \\ 35 \\ \hline 25 \\ 25 \\ \hline 0 \end{array}$$
    ∴ 375 ÷ 5 = 75

    (b)
    $$\begin{array}{r} 120 \\ 6\overline{)720} \\ 72 \\ \hline 00 \\ 0 \\ \hline 0 \end{array}$$
    ∴ 720 ÷ 6 = 120

    (c)
    $$\begin{array}{r} 231 \\ 7\overline{)1617} \\ 14 \\ \hline 21 \\ 21 \\ \hline 07 \\ 7 \\ \hline 0 \end{array}$$
    ∴ 1617 ÷ 7 = 231

    (d)
    $$\begin{array}{r} 182 \\ 9\overline{)1638} \\ 9 \\ \hline 73 \\ 72 \\ \hline 18 \\ 18 \\ \hline 0 \end{array}$$
    ∴ 1638 ÷ 9 = 182

2. Evaluate each division.
    (a) $\frac{132}{11}$
    (b) $\frac{216}{12}$
    (c) $\frac{611}{13}$
    (d) $\frac{558}{18}$
    (e) $\frac{1173}{29}$
    (f) $\frac{2294}{37}$

    Solution

    (a) $\frac{132}{11} = 132 \div 11$
    $$\begin{array}{r} 12 \\ 11\overline{)132} \\ 11 \\ \hline 22 \\ 22 \\ \hline 0 \end{array}$$
    ∴ $\frac{132}{11} = 12$

    (b)
    $$\begin{array}{r} 18 \\ 12\overline{)216} \\ 12 \\ \hline 96 \\ 96 \\ \hline 0 \end{array}$$
    ∴ $\frac{216}{12} = 18$

    (c)
    $$\begin{array}{r} 47 \\ 13\overline{)611} \\ 52 \\ \hline 91 \\ 91 \\ \hline 0 \end{array}$$

    (d)
    $$\begin{array}{r} 31 \\ 18\overline{)558} \\ 54 \\ \hline 18 \\ 18 \\ \hline 0 \end{array}$$

∴ $\frac{611}{13} = 47$ ∴ $\frac{558}{18} = 31$

(e)
$$\begin{array}{r} 40 \\ 29\overline{)1173} \\ 116 \\ \hline 13 \\ 0 \\ \hline 13 \end{array}$$

(f)
$$\begin{array}{r} 62 \\ 37\overline{)2294} \\ 222 \\ \hline 74 \\ 74 \\ \hline 0 \end{array}$$

∴ $\frac{1173}{29} = 40$, r 13   ∴ $\frac{2294}{37} = 62$

3. Find the quotient and remainder of each division.
    (a)   237 ÷ 9
    (b)   326 ÷ 7
    (c)   418 ÷ 11
    (d)   529 ÷ 17

    Solution

    (a)
    $$\begin{array}{r} 26 \\ 9\overline{)237} \\ 18 \\ \hline 57 \\ 54 \\ \hline 3 \end{array}$$
    ∴ 237 ÷ 9 = 26, r 3
    Hence, the quotient is 26 and the remainder is 3.

    (b)
    $$\begin{array}{r} 46 \\ 7\overline{)326} \\ 28 \\ \hline 46 \\ 42 \\ \hline 4 \end{array}$$
    ∴ 326 ÷ 7 = 46, r 4
    Hence, the quotient is 46 and the remainder is 4.

    (c)
    $$\begin{array}{r} 38 \\ 11\overline{)418} \\ 33 \\ \hline 88 \\ 88 \\ \hline 0 \end{array}$$
    ∴ 418 ÷ 11 = 38
    Hence, the quotient is 38 and the remainder is 0.

    (d)
    $$\begin{array}{r} 31 \\ 17\overline{)529} \\ 51 \\ \hline 19 \\ 17 \\ \hline 2 \end{array}$$
    ∴ 529 ÷ 17 = 31, r 2
    Hence, the quotient is 31 and the remainder is 2.

4. Calculate each division mentally.
    (a)   84 ÷ 2
    (b)   136 ÷ 4
    (c)   352 ÷ 8
    (d)   632 ÷ 16
    Note: Calculate mentally means work out the division in your head without written working.

Solution

(a) $84 \div 2 = 42$

(b) $136 \div 4$
$= 136 \div 2 \div 2$
$= 68 \div 2$
$= 34$

(c) $352 \div 8$
$= 352 \div 2 \div 2 \div 2$
$= 176 \div 2 \div 2$
$= 88 \div 2$
$= 44$

(d) $632 \div 16$
$= 632 \div 2 \div 2 \div 2 \div 2$
$= 316 \div 2 \div 2 \div 2$
$= 158 \div 2 \div 2$
$= 79 \div 2$
$= 39.5$

5. Work out each division mentally.
   (a) $840 \div 20$ (b) $1950 \div 50$
   (c) $624 \div 12$ (d) $1680 \div 35$

Solution

(a) $840 \div 20$
$= 840 \div 10 \div 2$
$= 84 \div 2$
$= 42$

(b) $1950 \div 50$
$= 1950 \div 10 \div 5$
$= 195 \div 5$
$= 39$

(c) $624 \div 12$
$= 624 \div 2 \div 6$
$= 312 \div 6$
$= 52$

(d) $1680 \div 35$
$= 1680 \div 7 \div 5$
$= 240 \div 5$
$= 48$

6. Evaluate these expressions mentally.
   (a) 599×5 (b) 72×25
   (c) 423×25 (d) 389×50

Solution

(a) 599×5
$= 599 \times 10 \div 2$
$= 5990 \div 2$
$= 2995$

(b) 72×25
$= 72 \times 100 \div 4$
$= 72 \times 100 \div 2 \div 2$
$= 7200 \div 2 \div 2$
$= 3600 \div 2$
$= 1800$

(c) 423×25
$= 423 \times 100 \div 4$
$= 42\,300 \div 2 \div 2$
$= 21\,150 \div 2$
$= 10\,575$

(d) 389×50
$= 389 \times 100 \div 2$
$= 38\,900 \div 2$
$= 19\,450$

Level 2   GCSE Grade **2 / 2⁺**

7. Find the missing number in each expression.
   (a) $315 \div \square = 9$
   (b) $\bigcirc \div 7 = 45$
   (c) $21 \times \bigcirc = 819$
   (d) $\triangle \times 11 = 1034$

Solution

(a) $315 \div \square = 9$
$\square = 315 \div 9$
$\therefore \quad \square = 35$

(b) $\bigcirc \div 7 = 45$
$\bigcirc = 45 \times 7$
$\therefore \quad \bigcirc = 315$

(c) $21 \times \bigcirc = 819$
$\bigcirc = 819 \div 21$
$\bigcirc = 819 \div 3 \div 7$
$\bigcirc = 273 \div 7$
$\therefore \quad \bigcirc = 39$

(d) $\triangle \times 11 = 1034$
$\triangle = 1034 \div 11$
$\therefore \quad \triangle = 94$

8. A carpenter has 635 table legs. If each table requires four legs, how many complete tables can she make?

Solution
First, find $635 \div 4$.

$$\begin{array}{r} 158 \\ 4\overline{)635} \\ \underline{4} \\ 23 \\ \underline{20} \\ 35 \\ \underline{32} \\ 3 \end{array}$$

$635 \div 4 = 158$, r 3
Hence, 158 complete tables can be made.

9. A charity distributes 400 cans of fish equally among 97 people. How many cans
   (a) does each person get,
   (b) are left over?

Solution
First, find $400 \div 97$.

$$\begin{array}{r} 4 \\ 97\overline{)400} \\ \underline{388} \\ 12 \end{array}$$

(a) Hence, each person gets 4 cans.

(b) There are 12 cans left over.

Level 3   GCSE Grade **2⁺ / 3⁻**

10. The price of an oven is £1332. It can be purchased by 12 equal monthly instalments. How much is each instalment?

Solution
Each instalment is
£$(1332 \div 12)$
$=$ £111

$$\begin{array}{r} 111 \\ 12\overline{)1332} \\ \underline{12} \\ 13 \\ \underline{12} \\ 12 \\ \underline{12} \\ 0 \end{array}$$

11. A man needs 56 grams of protein from food daily. If an egg contains 6 grams of protein, how many eggs would a man need to eat if he got all of his day's protein from eggs?

Solution

$56 \div 6 = 9$, r 2

If a man eats 9 eggs, it will only provide him with $9 \times 6 = 54$ grams of proteins.

Hence, to meet the daily nutrition requirement of 56 grams of protein, a man would need to eat 10 eggs in a day.

12. A black cab carries five passengers. If there are 117 people in the queue at a taxi rank, what is the least number of taxis required to transport all the people?

Solution

First, find $117 \div 5$.

```
    23
5)117
   10
   --
   17
   15
   --
    2
```

$\therefore 117 \div 5 = 23$, r 2

Check: $23 \times 5 = 115$

23 taxis will only carry 115 people.

$\therefore$ the least number of taxis required to take all 117 people is 24.

13. At a party, guests are seated at tables of eight. There are 27 full tables and a table with only five guests.

(a) How many guests are there?

(b) 20 extra guests arrive at the party. How many full tables are there now?

Solution

(a) Number of guests
$= 27 \times 8 + 5$
$= 216 + 5$
$= 221$

(b) $221 + 20 = 241$
$241 \div 8 = 30$, r 1
There are 30 full tables now.

14. Five senior staff and fifteen junior staff at a company share a £10 950 bonus. Each senior staff member gets £780. Each junior staff member gets has an equal amount. How much bonus does each junior staff member get?

Solution

$10\,950 = 5 \times 780 + 15 \times$ junior bonus
$10\,950 = 3900 + 15 \times$ junior bonus
Hence, $15 \times$ junior bonus $= 10\,950 - 3900$
$\qquad\qquad\qquad\qquad = 7050$

Junior bonus $= 7050 \div 15$
$\qquad\qquad = 7050 \div 5 \div 3$
$\qquad\qquad = 1410 \div 3$
$\qquad\qquad = 470$

Each junior staff member gets a bonus of £470.

15. Find two 2-digit numbers whose product is 2772.

Solution

$2772 \div 2 = 1386$
$1386 \div 2 = 693$, so 2772 is divisible by $2 \times 2 = 4$.
$2772 \div 9 = 308$, so 2772 is divisible by 9.
$2772 \div 36 = 2772 \div 9 \div 4$
$\qquad\qquad = 308 \div 4$
$\qquad\qquad = 77$

One pair of numbers: $36 \times 77 = 2772$.

Other possible answers: 99×28, 44×63, 66×42, 33×84.

Exercise 1.6

Level 1　　GCSE Grade **1⁺**

1. Work out these square numbers without using a calculator.

(a) 13^2　　　　　　　　(b) 15^2

Solution

(a) $13^2 = 13 \times 13$　　　(b) $15^2 = 15 \times 15$
$\qquad = 169$　　　　　　　　$\qquad = 225$

2. Calculate these cube numbers without using a calculator.

(a) 9^3　　　　　　　　(b) 12^3

Solution

(a) $9^3 = 9 \times 9 \times 9$　　(b) $12^3 = 12 \times 12 \times 12$
$\qquad = 729$　　　　　　　　$\qquad = 1728$

3. Work out these values without using a calculator.

(a) 4^4　　(b) 5^5　　(c) 3^6　　(d) 2^7

Solution

(a) $4^4 = 4 \times 4 \times 4 \times 4$
$\qquad = 256$

(b) $5^5 = 5 \times 5 \times 5 \times 5 \times 5$
$\qquad = 3125$

(c) $3^6 = 3 \times 3 \times 3 \times 3 \times 3 \times 3$
$\qquad = 729$

(d) $2^7 = 2 \times 2 \times 2 \times 2 \times 2 \times 2 \times 2$
$\qquad = 128$

4. Find these values without using a calculator.

(a) $\sqrt{121}$　　　　　　(b) $\sqrt{196}$

Solution

(a) $11 \times 11 = 121$
$\therefore \sqrt{121} = 11$

(b) $14 \times 14 = 196$
$\therefore \sqrt{196} = 14$

5. Find these values without using a calculator.

(a) $\sqrt[3]{729}$

(b) $\sqrt[3]{1331}$

Solution

(a) $9 \times 9 \times 9 = 729$
$\therefore \sqrt[3]{729} = 9$

(b) $11 \times 11 \times 11 = 1331$
$\therefore \sqrt[3]{1331} = 11$

Level 2   GCSE Grade 2^- / 2

6. Find the two consecutive integers that the given number lies between.

(a) $\sqrt{50}$

(b) $\sqrt{130}$

Solution

(a) $7 \times 7 = 49$ and $8 \times 8 = 64$
$\therefore \sqrt{49} < \sqrt{50} < \sqrt{64}$
i.e. $7 < \sqrt{50} < 8$

Hence, $\sqrt{50}$ lies between the two consecutive integers, 7 and 8.

(b) $11 \times 11 = 121$ and $12 \times 12 = 144$
$\therefore \sqrt{121} < \sqrt{130} < \sqrt{144}$
i.e. $11 < \sqrt{130} < 12$

$\sqrt{130}$ lies between the two consecutive integers, 11 and 12.

7. Find the two consecutive integers that the given number lies between.

(a) $\sqrt[3]{240}$

(b) $\sqrt[3]{321}$

Solution

(a) $6 \times 6 \times 6 = 216$ and $7 \times 7 \times 7 = 343$
$\therefore \sqrt[3]{216} < \sqrt[3]{240} < \sqrt[3]{343}$
i.e. $6 < \sqrt[3]{240} < 7$

$\sqrt[3]{200}$ lies between the two consecutive integers, 6 and 7.

(b) $6 \times 6 \times 6 = 216$ and $7 \times 7 \times 7 = 343$
$\therefore \sqrt[3]{216} < \sqrt[3]{321} < \sqrt[3]{343}$
i.e. $6 < \sqrt[3]{321} < 7$

$\sqrt[3]{321}$ lies between the two consecutive integers, 6 and 7.

Level 3   GCSE Grade 2^+ / 3^-

8. (a) Write down the first five squares of even integers.
   (b) What do you notice?

Solution

(a) First five even integers: 2, 4, 6, 8, 10.
Squares of these even integers are 4, 16, 36, 64, 100.

(b) The squares of these even integers are also even.

9. (a) Write down the first five squares of odd integers.
   (b) What do you notice about the last digits?

Solution

(a) First five odd integers: 1, 3, 5, 7, 9.
Squares of these odd integers are 1, 9, 25, 49, 81.

(b) The last digits of these squares are 1, 5 and 9.

10. I am thinking of a number. Its square is the same as its cube. Its square root and cube root are the same as the number itself. What number am I thinking of?

Solution

1 or 0

11. Write a number whose square root is between 13 and 14.

Solution

$13 \times 13 = 169$ and $14 \times 14 = 196$
Hence, any number between 169 and 196 would have a square root between 13 and 14.

12. In biological cell division, a cell splits into two cells every hour. If there is one cell at the beginning, find the number of cells after eight hours. Explain how you worked this out.

Solution

At the start, the number of cells $= 1$,
after 1 hour, the number of cells $= 2$,
after 2 hours, the number of cells $= 2 \times 2$,
after 3 hours, the number of cells $= 2 \times 2 \times 2 = 2^3$,
after 4 hours, the number of cells $= 2 \times 2 \times 2 \times 2 = 2^4$,
… and after 8 hours the number of cells $= 2^8$
$= 2 \times 2 \times 2 \times 2 \times 2 \times 2 \times 2 \times 2 = 256$.

Exercise 1.7

Level 1   GCSE Grade 1^+ / 2^-

1. Work out the values of these expressions without using a calculator.
   (a) $5 + 8 \times 2$
   (b) $17 - 5 \times 3$
   (c) $83 + 28 + 4$
   (d) $56 - 95 + 19$

Solution

(a) $5 + 8 \times 2$
$= 5 + 16$
$= 21$

(b) $17 - 5 \times 3$
$= 17 - 15$
$= 2$

(c) $83 + 28 \div 4$
$= 83 + 7$
$= 90$

(d) $56 - 95 \div 19$
$= 56 - 5$
$= 51$

2. Calculate these expressions without using a calculator.

(a) $7 \times 4 + 3 \times 6$

(b) $75 \div 5 - 36 \div 4$

(c) $15 \times 6 - 49 \div 7$

(d) $42 \div 3 + 11 \times 5$

Solution

(a) $7 \times 4 + 3 \times 6$
$= 28 + 18$
$= 46$

(b) $75 \div 5 - 36 \div 4$
$= 15 - 9$
$= 6$

(c) $15 \times 6 - 49 \div 7$
$= 90 - 7$
$= 83$

(d) $42 \div 3 + 11 \times 5$
$= 14 + 55$
$= 69$

3. Calculate these expressions without using a calculator.

(a) $19 + 3 \times 5 - 29$

(b) $62 - 72 \div 9 \times 3$

(c) $28 - 17 + 6 \times 5$

(d) $39 \div 3 + 54 - 7 \times 8$

Solution

(a) $19 + 3 \times 5 - 29$
$= 19 + 15 - 29$
$= 34 - 29$
$= 5$

(b) $62 - 72 \div 9 \times 3$
$= 62 - 8 \times 3$
$= 62 - 24$
$= 38$

(c) $28 - 17 + 6 \times 5$
$= 28 - 17 + 30$
$= 11 + 30$
$= 41$

(d) $39 \div 3 + 54 - 7 \times 8$
$= 13 + 54 - 56$
$= 67 - 56$
$= 11$

4. Evaluate these expressions without using a calculator.

(a) $9 + 2 \times 5^2$

(b) $50 - 3 \times 4^2$

(c) $3 \times 5 + 8^3$

(d) $11 - 32 \div 2^4$

Solution

(a) $9 + 2 \times 5^2$
$= 9 + 2 \times 25$
$= 9 + 50$
$= 59$

(b) $50 - 3 \times 4^2$
$= 50 - 3 \times 16$
$= 50 - 48$
$= 2$

(c) $3 \times 5 + 8^3$
$= 3 \times 5 + 512$
$= 15 + 512$
$= 527$

(d) $11 - 32 \div 2^4$
$= 11 - 32 \div 16$
$= 11 - 2$
$= 9$

5. Work out the values of these expressions without using a calculator.

(a) $38 - (27 - 15)$

(b) $49 - (28 + 17)$

(c) $(42 + 3) \div 9$

(d) $(11 + 3) \times (2 + 8)$

Solution

(a) $38 - (27 - 15)$
$= 38 - 12$
$= 26$

(b) $49 - (28 + 17)$
$= 49 - 45$
$= 4$

(c) $(42 + 3) \div 9$
$= 45 \div 9$
$= 5$

(d) $(11 + 3) \times (2 + 8)$
$= 14 \times 10$
$= 140$

Level 2 GCSE Grade **2**

6. Calculate these expressions without using a calculator.

(a) $21 + 8 \times 5 - 4$

(b) $(21 + 8) \times 5 - 4$

(c) $21 + (8 \times 5 - 4)$

(d) $21 + 8 \times (5 - 4)$

Solution

(a) $21 + 8 \times 5 - 4$
$= 21 + 40 - 4$
$= 61 - 4$
$= 57$

(b) $(21 + 8) \times 5 - 4$
$= 29 \times 5 - 4$
$= 145 - 4$
$= 141$

(c) $21 + (8 \times 5 - 4)$
$= 21 + (40 - 4)$
$= 21 + 36$
$= 57$

(d) $21 + 8 \times (5 - 4)$
$= 21 + 8 \times 1$
$= 21 + 8$
$= 29$

7. Work out the values of these expressions without using a calculator.

(a) $79 - 2 \times 3^3 + 6$

(b) $79 - (2 \times 3^3 + 6)$

(c) $8 \times 5 + (7^2 - 10) \times 3$

(d) $8 \times 5 + (7^2 - 10 \times 3)$

Solution

(a) $79 - 2 \times 3^3 + 6$
$= 79 - 2 \times 27 + 6$
$= 79 - 54 + 6$
$= 25 + 6$
$= 31$

(b) $79 - (2 \times 3^3 + 6)$
$= 79 - (2 \times 27 + 6)$
$= 79 - (54 + 6)$
$= 79 - 60$
$= 19$

(c) $8 \times 5 + (7^2 - 10) \times 3$
$= 40 + (49 - 10) \times 3$
$= 40 + 39 \times 3$
$= 40 + 117$
$= 157$

(d) $8 \times 5 + (7^2 - 10 \times 3)$
$= 40 + (49 - 30)$
$= 40 + 19$
$= 59$

8. Evaluate these expressions without using a calculator.
   (a) $26 + [4 + (7 - 6)]$
   (b) $26 + [(4 + 7) - 6]$
   (c) $18 - 2 \times [10 - (7 - 2)]$
   (d) $18 - 2 \times [(10 - 7) - 2]$
   (e) $[12 - (7 + 3)] \div 2 + 2^5$
   (f) $[(12 - 7) + 3] \div 2 + 2^5$

   Solution
   (a) $26 + [4 + (7 - 6)]$
   $= 26 + [4 + 1]$
   $= 26 + 5$
   $= 31$

   (b) $26 + [(4 + 7) - 6]$
   $= 26 + [11 - 6]$
   $= 26 + 5$
   $= 31$

   (c) $18 - 2 \times [10 - (7 - 2)]$
   $= 18 - 2 \times [10 - 5]$
   $= 18 - 2 \times 5$
   $= 18 - 10$
   $= 8$

   (d) $18 - 2 \times [(10 - 7) - 2]$
   $= 18 - 2 \times [3 - 2]$
   $= 18 - 2 \times 1$
   $= 18 - 2$
   $= 16$

   (e) $[12 - (7 + 3)] \div 2 + 2^5$
   $= [12 - 10] \div 2 + 32$
   $= 2 \div 2 + 32$
   $= 1 + 32$
   $= 33$

   (f) $[(12 - 7) + 3] \div 2 + 2^5$
   $= [5 + 3] \div 2 + 32$
   $= 8 \div 2 + 32$
   $= 4 + 32$
   $= 36$

9. There are eight banknotes in a wallet, six of them are £10 notes and the rest are £50 notes. What is the total amount of money in the wallet?
   Hint: Draw a picture to help you visualise the problem.

   Solution
   Total amount of money
   $= 10 \times 6 + 50 \times (8 - 6)$
   $= 10 \times 6 + 50 \times 2$
   $= 60 + 100$
   $= £160$

10. The mass of a bottle of honey is 450 grams. If the mass of the bottle itself is 80 grams, find the total mass of honey in seven bottles.

Solution
Mass of honey in one bottle $= (450 - 80)\,\text{g}$
$\therefore$ the total mass of honey in 7 bottles
$= 7 \times (450 - 80)$
$= 7 \times 370$
$= 2590$ grams

Level 3 GCSE Grade **2⁺ / 3⁻**

11. Concrete for making six piles is formed by mixing 130 kg of cement, 260 kg of sand and 390 kg of aggregate. Find the mass of concrete in each pile.

   Solution
   Mass of concrete in 6 piles
   $= (130 + 260 + 390)\,\text{kg}$
   $\therefore$ mass of concrete in each pile
   $= (130 + 260 + 390) \div 6$
   $= 780 \div 6$
   $= 130\,\text{kg}$

12. The price of a bottle of vitamins is £28. There is a discount of £10 for each bottle when purchasing online. A customer orders five bottles online and the postage for the order is £3. Write a single expression that shows what calculation you need to do to find the cost of this order. How much does the customer pay?

   Solution
   Price of a bottle of vitamins when purchased online
   $= £(28 - 10)$
   Total amount paid for an online purchase of 5 bottles inclusive of postage
   $= 5 \times (28 - 10) + 3$
   $= 5 \times 18 + 3$
   $= 90 + 3$
   $= £93$

13. A train on the Piccadilly line of the London Underground has six carriages. Each carriage has space for 38 sitting passengers and 95 standing passengers. Write a single expression that shows what calculation you need to do to find the total capacity of the train. Find the total number of passengers the train can hold.

   Solution
   Total number of passengers
   $= (38 + 95) \times 6$
   $= 133 \times 6$
   $= 798$

14. A wall is clad with 11 rows of tiles and there are 18 tiles in each row. It consists of 40 decorative tiles, costing £8 each. The remaining plain tiles cost £3 each. Find the total cost of the tiles.

Solution

Number of tiles = $11 \times 18 = 198$
Number of plain tiles = $198 - 40 = 158$
Total cost = $158 \times 3 + 40 \times 8$
= $474 + 320$
= 794
Total cost of the tiles is £794.

Exercise 1.8

Level 1 GCSE Grade **1⁺** / **2⁻**

1. Find all the factors of these numbers.
   (a) 36 **(b)** 37
   (c) 45 **(d)** 59

Solution

(a) $36 = 1 \times 36$
$= 2 \times 18$
$= 3 \times 12$
$= 4 \times 9$
$= 6 \times 6$
∴ the factors of 36 are 1, 2, 3, 4, 6, 9, 12, 18, 36.

(b) $37 = 1 \times 37$
∴ the factors of 37 are 1 and 37.

(c) $45 = 1 \times 45$
$= 3 \times 15$
$= 5 \times 9$
∴ the factors of 45 are 1, 3, 5, 9, 15, 45.

(d) $59 = 1 \times 59$
∴ the factors of 59 are 1 and 59.

2. Determine whether the second number is a factor of the first number.
   (a) 35, 7 **(b)** 42, 4
   (c) 139, 9 **(d)** 144, 6

Solution

(a) Since $35 \div 7 = 5$,
35 is divisible by 7.
∴ 7 is a factor of 35.

(b) Divide 42 by 4 to see if 42 is divisible by 4.
$42 \div 4 = 10$, r 2
Since the remainder
is non-zero, 42 is not
divisible by 4.
∴ 4 is not a factor of 42.

$$\begin{array}{r} 10 \\ 4\overline{\smash)42} \\ \underline{4} \\ 02 \\ \underline{0} \\ 2 \end{array}$$

(c) $139 \div 9 = 15$, r 4
Since the remainder is non-zero,
139 is not divisible by 9.
∴ 9 is not a factor of 139.

$$\begin{array}{r} 15 \\ 9\overline{\smash)139} \\ \underline{9} \\ 49 \\ \underline{45} \\ 4 \end{array}$$

(d) $144 \div 6 = 24$
Since the remainder is zero,
144 is divisible by 6.
∴ 6 is a factor of 144.

$$\begin{array}{r} 24 \\ 6\overline{\smash)144} \\ \underline{12} \\ 24 \\ \underline{24} \\ 0 \end{array}$$

3. Write down the first five multiples of these numbers.
   (a) 6 **(b)** 12
   (c) 8 **(d)** 11

Solution

(a) The first five multiples of 6 are
$1 \times 6, 2 \times 6, 3 \times 6, 4 \times 6, 5 \times 6$,
i.e. 6, 12, 18, 24, 30.

(b) The first five multiples of 12 are
12, 24, 36, 48, 60.

(c) The first five multiples of 8 are
8, 16, 24, 32, 40.

(d) The first five multiples of 11 are
11, 22, 33, 44, 55.

4. Determine whether the first number is a multiple of the second number.
   (a) 23, 2 **(b)** 36, 4
   (c) 95, 5 **(d)** 91, 7
   (e) 108, 3 **(f)** 156, 11

Solution

(a) To determine if the first number is a multiple of the second number, divide the first number by the second number.
$23 \div 2 = 11$, r 1
Since the remainder is non-zero,
23 is not divisible by 2.
∴ 23 is not a multiple of 2.

$$\begin{array}{r} 11 \\ 2\overline{\smash)23} \\ \underline{2} \\ 03 \\ \underline{2} \\ 1 \end{array}$$

(b) $36 \div 4 = 9$
i.e. $36 = 4 \times 9$
∴ 36 is a multiple of 4.

(c) $95 \div 5 = 19$
i.e. $95 = 5 \times 19$

∴ 95 is a multiple of 5.

$$\begin{array}{r} 19 \\ 5\overline{\smash)95} \\ \underline{5} \\ 45 \\ \underline{45} \\ 0 \end{array}$$

(d) $91 \div 7 = 13$
i.e. $91 = 7 \times 13$

∴ 91 is a multiple of 7.

$$\begin{array}{r} 13 \\ 7\overline{\smash)91} \\ \underline{7} \\ 21 \\ \underline{21} \\ 0 \end{array}$$

(e) $108 \div 3 = 36$
i.e. $108 = 3 \times 36$

∴ 108 is a multiple of 3.

$$\begin{array}{r} 36 \\ 3\overline{\smash)108} \\ \underline{9} \\ 18 \\ \underline{18} \\ 0 \end{array}$$

(f) $156 \div 11 = 14$, r 2
Since the remainder is non-zero, 156 is not divisible by 11.

$$\begin{array}{r} 14 \\ 11\overline{)156} \\ \underline{11} \\ 46 \\ \underline{44} \\ 2 \end{array}$$

∴ 156 is not a multiple of 11.

Level 2   GCSE Grade 2 / 2⁺

5. Write down all the factors of 100 which are less than 20.

Solution
$100 = 1 \times 100$
$ = 2 \times 50$
$ = 4 \times 25$
$ = 5 \times 20$
$ = 10 \times 10$
The factors of 100 are 1, 2, 4, 5, 10, 20, 25, 50, 100.
∴ the factors of 100 which are less than 20 are 1, 2, 4, 5, 10.

6. List all the factors of 72 which are greater than 10.

Solution
$72 = 1 \times 72$
$ = 2 \times 36$
$ = 3 \times 24$
$ = 4 \times 18$
$ = 6 \times 12$
$ = 8 \times 9$
∴ the factors of 72 which are greater than 10 are 12, 18, 24, 36, 72.

7. Write down all the common factors of 45 and 75.

Solution
$45 = 1 \times 45$
$ = 3 \times 15$
$ = 5 \times 9$
$75 = 1 \times 75$
$ = 3 \times 24$
$ = 5 \times 15$
The common factors of 45 and 75 are 1, 3, 5 and 15.

8. Find all the multiples of 4 which are less than 20.

Solution
The multiples of 4 which are less than 20 are 4, 8, 12, 16.

9. List all the multiples of 3 which are between 20 and 30.

Solution
The multiples of 3 which are between 20 and 30 are 21, 24, 27.

10. Find the smallest common multiple of 10 and 15.

Solution
First, list some multiples of the numbers and see whether you can find their common multiples.
The first ten multiples of 10 are
10, 20, 30, 40, 50, 60, 70, 80, 90, 100.
The first ten multiples of 15 are
15, 30, 45, 60, 75, 90, 105, 120, 135, 150.
In the above two lists, 30, 60 and 90 are their common multiples.
∴ the smallest common multiple of 10 and 15 is 30.

11. Find the first two common multiples of 4 and 7.

Solution
The first fifteen multiples of 4 are
4, 8, 12, 16, 20, 24, 28, 32, 36, 40, 44, 48, 52, 56, 60.
The first ten multiples of 7 are
7, 14, 21, 28, 35, 42, 49, 56, 63, 70.
∴ the first two common multiples of 4 and 7 are 28 and 56.

Level 3   GCSE Grade 3⁻ / 3

12. **(a)** Which of these numbers has 5 as a factor?
20, 24, 25, 39, 60, 73, 75, 81
(b) What is the last digit of a number with 5 as a factor? Explain your answer.

Solution
(a) Numbers which have 5 as a factor are 20, 25, 60, 75.

(b) The last digit of a number with 5 as a factor is either 0 or 5.
Only numbers ending with the digit 0 or 5 are divisible by 5. Hence, they have 5 as a factor.

13. A ribbon is 134 cm long. Can it be cut into an exact number of pieces each of length 8 cm? Explain your answer.

Solution
Divide 134 by 8 to see whether 134 is divisible by 8.
$134 \div 8 = 16$, r 6
Since the remainder is non-zero, 134 is not divisible by 8.
Hence, the ribbon cannot be cut into an exact number of 8-cm pieces.

$$\begin{array}{r} 16 \\ 8\overline{)134} \\ \underline{8} \\ 54 \\ \underline{48} \\ 6 \end{array}$$

14. A side of a car park is 121 m long. Can it be marked into an exact number of car spaces each of length 6 m? Explain your answer.

Solution

Divide 121 by 6 to see whether 121 is divisible by 6.
121 ÷ 6 = 20, r 1
Since the remainder is non-zero, 121 is not divisible by 6.
Hence, the side of the car park which is 121 m long cannot be marked into an exact number of 6-m car spaces.

$$\begin{array}{r} 20 \\ 6\overline{\smash{\big)}\,121} \\ \underline{12} \\ 01 \\ \underline{0} \\ 1 \end{array}$$

15. 28 square tiles are put together to form a rectangle. How many tiles can form the width of the rectangle?

Solution

The different rectangles that can be formed are 1×28, 2×14, and 4×7. Hence, the width could be 1, 2 or 4 tiles.

16. Two bus services A and B start at the same bus terminal. The schedule time of A is every 15 minutes and the schedule time of B is every 25 minutes. If the two services leave the terminal together at their common schedule time of 6 am, what is their next common schedule time?

Hint: Write a list of the departure times of each bus after 6 am.

Solution

The schedule time of A is every 15 minutes, that is, from a particular time, A will leave after 15, 30, 45, 60, 75, 90, ... minutes. The schedule time of B is every 25 minutes, that is, from a particular time, B will leave after 25, 50, 75, 100, ... minutes.
From the two lists above, you know that the two services will leave the terminal together after 75 minutes, i.e. 1 hour 15 minutes.
∴ their next common schedule time after 6.00 am is
6.00 + 1.15 = 7.15 am.

17. David has some coins. If he has three more coins, he can stack the coins with 12 coins in a pile or 15 coins in a pile. Find the least number of coins that David has.

Solution

The number of coins David has plus another 3 is a multiple of 12 and 15.
First few multiples of 12 are: 12, 24, 36, 48, 60, 72.
First few multiples of 15 are: 15, 30, 45, 60, 75.
The first common number in both lists is 60 so the least number of coins David has
= 60 − 3
= 57 coins

18. There is a box of mangoes. If the mangoes are divided into groups of 7, four mangoes will be left. If the mangoes are divided into groups of 11, five mangoes will be left. Find the smallest number of mangoes in the box.

Solution

The number of mangoes is a multiple of 7 plus 4.
The number of mangoes is one of:
7 + 4, 14 + 4, 21 + 4, 28 + 4, 35 + 4, 42 + 4, 49 + 4, 56 + 4, 63 + 4, ...
i.e. one of: 11, 18, 25, 32, 39, 46, 53, 60, 67, ...

Also, the number of mangoes is a multiple of 11 plus 5.
The number of mangoes is one of:
11 + 5, 22 + 5, 33 + 5, 44 + 5, 55 + 5, 66 + 5, ...
i.e. one of: 16, 27, 38, 49, 60, 71, ...

The number of mangoes in the box is the smallest number common to both lists, i.e. 60.

Revision Exercise 1

1. Round the numbers to the required degree of accuracy.

GCSE Grade 1⁺

(a) 6792, to the nearest 10
(b) 34 751, to the nearest 100
(c) 632 499, to the nearest 1000

Solution

(a) 6792 = 6790 (to the nearest 10)

(b) 34 751 = 34 800 (to the nearest 100)

(c) 632 499 = 632 000 (to the nearest 1000)

2. The number of spectators at a football match is 34 146.

GCSE Grade 2⁻

(a) What is the place value of the digit 3?
(b) Round the number to the nearest 1000.
(c) If 28 189 spectators are male, what is the number of female spectators?

Solution

(a) The place value of the digit 3 is 10 000.

(b) 34 146 = 34 000 (to the nearest 1000)

(c) Number of female spectators
= 34 146 − 28 189
= 5957

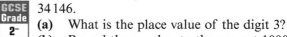

$$\begin{array}{r} {}^{2\,13\,10\,13\,1} \\ 34146 \\ -28189 \\ \hline 5957 \end{array}$$

3. Calculate these expressions.

(a) $36\,742 + 6959$ **(b)** $9816 - 2477$

(c) 175×36 **(d)** $3982 \div 16$

Solution

(a)
$$\begin{array}{r} 36\,742 \\ +\ 6959 \\ \hline 43\,701 \\ \hline {\scriptstyle 1\ 1\ 1\ 1} \end{array}$$

∴ $36\,742 + 6959 = 43\,701$

(b)
$$\begin{array}{r} 9\overset{7\ 10\ 1}{8\,1\,6} \\ -2\,477 \\ \hline 7\,339 \end{array}$$

∴ $9816 - 2477 = 7339$

(c)
$$\begin{array}{r} 175 \\ \times\ 36 \\ \hline 1050 \\ 5250 \\ \hline 6300 \\ \hline {\scriptstyle 1} \end{array}$$

∴ $175 \times 36 = 6300$

(d)
$$\begin{array}{r} 248 \\ 16\overline{\smash{\big)}\,3982} \\ \underline{32} \\ 78 \\ \underline{64} \\ 142 \\ \underline{128} \\ 14 \end{array}$$

∴ $3982 \div 16 = 248$, r 14

4. Evaluate these expressions.

(a) 14^2 **(b)** 10^4

(c) $\sqrt{225}$ **(d)** $\sqrt[3]{343}$

Solution

(a) $14^2 = 14 \times 14$
$= 196$

(b) $10^4 = 10 \times 10 \times 10 \times 10$
$= 10\,000$

(c) $15 \times 15 = 225$
∴ $\sqrt{225} = 15$

(d) $7 \times 7 \times 7 = 343$
∴ $\sqrt[3]{343} = 7$

5. Work out the values of these expressions.

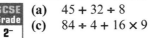

(a) $45 + 32 \div 8$ **(b)** $21 \times 3 - 7^2$

(c) $84 \div 4 + 16 \times 9$ **(d)** $6 \times 4^2 - 3 \times 2^5 + 31$

Solution

(a) $45 + 32 \div 8$
$= 45 + 4$
$= 49$

(b) $21 \times 3 - 7^2$
$= 63 - 49$
$= 14$

(c) $84 \div 4 + 16 \times 9$
$= 21 + 144$
$= 165$

(d) $6 \times 4^2 - 3 \times 2^5 + 31$
$= 6 \times 16 - 3 \times 32 + 31$
$= 96 - 96 + 31$
$= 31$

6. Calculate these expressions mentally.

(a) $39 + 47 + 161$ **(b)** $4 \times 93 \times 25$

(c) $37 \times 15 + 63 \times 15$ **(d)** 42×98

Solution

(a) $39 + 47 + 161$
$= 39 + 161 + 47$
$= 200 + 47$
$= 247$

(b) $4 \times 93 \times 25$
$= 4 \times 25 \times 93$
$= 100 \times 93$
$= 9300$

(c) $37 \times 15 + 63 \times 15$
$= (37 + 63) \times 15$
$= 100 \times 15$
$= 1500$

(d) 42×98
$= 42 \times (100 - 2)$
$42 \times 100 - 42 \times 2$
$= 4200 - 84$
$= 4116$

$$\begin{array}{r} \overset{1\ 9\ 1}{4\,200} \\ -\ \ 84 \\ \hline 4116 \end{array}$$

7. Work out the values of these expressions.

(a) $256 - (74 + 18)$
(b) $8^2 + 4 \times (28 - 11)$
(c) $69 \div (7 - 4) - 6^2 + 12$
(d) $5^3 - [7^2 - (19 - 15)]$

Solution

(a) $256 - (74 + 18)$
$= 256 - 92$
$= 164$

$$\begin{array}{r} \overset{1\ 1}{256} \\ -\ 92 \\ \hline 164 \end{array}$$

(b) $8^2 + 4 \times (28 - 11)$
$= 64 + 4 \times 17$
$= 64 + 68$
$= 132$

(c) $69 \div (7 - 4) - 6^2 + 12$
$= 69 \div 3 - 36 + 12$
$= 23 - 3$
$= 20$

(d) $5^3 - [7^2 - (19 - 15)]$
$= 125 - [49 - 4]$
$= 125 - 45$
$= 80$

8. **(a)** Find the factors of 96.

(b) If a rod of length 96 cm is cut into equal parts, can the length of each part be exactly 7 cm? Explain your answer.

Solution

(a) $96 = 1 \times 96$
$= 2 \times 48$
$= 3 \times 32$
$= 4 \times 24$
$= 6 \times 16$
$= 8 \times 12$
∴ the factors of 96 are 1, 2, 3, 4, 6, 8, 12, 16, 24, 32, 48, 96.

(b) No, the length of each part cannot be exactly 7 cm as 7 is not a factor of 96, that is, 96 is not divisible by 7.

9. In 2011, the M74 motorway in Glasgow was extended by 8000 metres. The construction cost was £692 000 000.

(a) Find the construction cost of a metre of the extension.
(b) Round the answer in **(a)** to the nearest £1000.

Solution

(a) Construction cost of a metre of the extension
$= £692\,000\,000 \div 8000$
$= £692\,000\,000 \div 1000 \div 8$
$= £692\,000 \div 8$
$= £86\,500$

```
        86500
     8 )692000
        64
        52
        48
         40
         40
         00
          0
          00
           0
           0
```

(b) $£86\,500 = £87\,000$
(to the nearest 1000)

10. Building a rectangular cage requires four beams each of length 3 m and eight beams each of length 2 m. A beam costs £15 a metre.
(a) Write a single calculation to find the total length of the beams.
(b) Find the total length of the beams.
(c) Find the total cost for the beams.

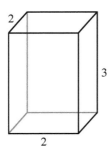

Solution

(a) Total length of the beams
$= 3 \times 4 + 2 \times 8$

(b) $3 \times 4 + 2 \times 8 = 12 + 16$
$= 28 \, \text{m}$

(c) Total cost of the beams
$= £15 \times 28$
$= £420$

```
      15
    × 28
    120
    300
    420
```

11. A theatre has 25 rows of seats with 22 seats in each row. The price for constructing each seat is £103. Find
(a) the number of seats in the theatre,
(b) the total price for constructing these seats.

Solution

(a) Number of seats
$= 25 \times 22$
$= 550$

```
      25
    × 22
      50
    500
    550
```

(b) Total price for constructing the seats
$= £103 \times 550$
$= £56\,650$

```
      103
    × 550
     5150
    51500
    56650
```

12. There are 628 cm³ of solution in a beaker. The solution is poured into 13 test tubes so that each test tube contains 45 cm³ of solution. Find
(a) the total volume of the solution in the test tubes,
(b) the remaining volume of the solution in the beaker.

Solution

(a) Total volume of solution in the test tubes
$= 45 \times 13$
$= 585 \, \text{cm}^3$

```
      45
    × 13
     135
     450
     585
```

(b) Remaining volume of solution in the beaker
$= 628 - (45 \times 13)$
$= 628 - 585$
$= 43 \, \text{cm}^3$

```
     51
     628
   − 585
      43
```

13. **(a)** Find the first two common multiples of 6 and 8.

(b) If a number is a common multiple of 6 and 8, will it be divisible by 12? Explain your answer.

Solution

(a) The first ten multiples of 6 are 6, 12, 18, 24, 30, 36, 42, 48, 54, 60.
The first ten multiples of 8 are 8, 16, 24, 32, 40, 48, 56, 64, 72, 80.
In the above two lists, 24 and 48 are their common multiples.
∴ the first two common multiples of 6 and 8 are 24 and 48.

(b) If you continue listing more multiples of 6 and 8, you will see more of their common multiples
24, 48, 72, 96, ...
= 1 × 24, 2 × 24, 3 × 24, 4 × 24
They are multiples of 24. Since 24 is divisible by 12, a number which is a common multiple of 6 and 8 will be divisible by 12.

14. Three boys form a band and sell their own album. The price of each album is £12 and they sell 265 copies. The total cost of producing these albums is £960. They share the profit equally. How much profit does each boy get?

Solution

Amount of money collected from sale of albums
= 265 × 12
= £3180

$$\begin{array}{r} 265 \\ \times\ 12 \\ \hline 3180 \\ {\scriptstyle 76} \end{array}$$

Profit earned
= £3180 − £960
= £2220

$$\begin{array}{r} 3180 \\ -\ 960 \\ \hline 2220 \end{array}$$

∴ the amount of profit each boy gets
= £2220 ÷ 3
= £740

$$\begin{array}{r} 740 \\ 3\overline{)2220} \\ \underline{21} \\ 12 \\ \underline{12} \\ 00 \\ \underline{0} \\ 0 \end{array}$$

Note: More able students may be able to handle the whole problem as (265 × 12 − 960) ÷ 3.

15. David divides 1800 apples into equal groups such that each group has more than five apples but fewer than 10 apples. How many groups are possible?

Solution

The number of groups is a factor of 1800. First find the factors of 1800:

$$\begin{array}{l} 1800 = 1 \times 1800 \\ \ 2 \times 900 \\ \ 3 \times 600 \\ \ 4 \times 450 \\ \ 5 \times 360 \\ \ 6 \times 300 \\ \ 8 \times 225 \\ \ 9 \times 200... \end{array}$$

Each group has more than 5 but fewer than 10 apples so the possible number of apples in each group from the above list is 6, 8 or 9. The corresponding number of groups is 300, 225 or 200.

2 Negative Real Numbers

Class Activity 1

Objective: To identify the use of negative numbers in the real world.

Task

Take a look at your surroundings. Where can you find the use of negative numbers? You may take photos of such scenarios. Show and discuss with your classmates what the '−' sign means in these scenarios you have captured.

Suggested answers:

- Time zone
- Temperature
- Hockey scores
- Golf scores
- Music chart
- Stock market
- Timeline
- Altitude
- Credit card balances
- Latitudes
- Polarities in electricity

Class Activity 2

Objective: To perform addition of integers using algebra discs.

Tasks

1. **Adding two integers with the same sign**
   For example, evaluate $(-3) + (-2)$.

    Place three -1 discs in the first row.

   Place two -1 discs in the second row.

   $\therefore (-3) + (-2) = -5$ Count the total number of -1 discs.

   In fact, you can also write $(-3) + (-2)$ $\begin{aligned} &= -3 - 2 \\ &= -5 \end{aligned}$ or $\begin{aligned} (-3) + (-2) &= (-2) + (-3) \\ &= -2 - 3 \\ &= -5 \end{aligned}$

   Here, when adding two negative numbers, the answer is negative.

   Evaluate these expressions.
   (a) $2 + 4$

   Place two 1 discs in the first row.

   Place four 1 discs in the second row.

   $\therefore 2 + 4 = 6$ Count the total number of 1 discs.

(b) $3 + 5$

Place three discs in the first row.

Place five disc in the second row.

∴ $3 + 5 = 8$

Count the total number of discs.

(c) $(-2) + (-4)$

Place two discs in the first row.

Place four discs in the second row.

∴ $(-2) + (-4) = -6$

Count the total number of discs.

(d) $(-3) + (-5)$

Place three discs in the first row.

Place five discs in the second row.

∴ $(-3) + (-5) = -8$

Count the total number of discs.

---

2. **Adding two integers with different signs**
For example, evaluate $(-5) + 2$.

Place five discs in the first row.

Place two discs in the second row.

zero pairs

∴ $(-5) + 2 = -3$ Count the discs left after taking away the zero pairs.

You can also write $(-5) + 2 = -5 + 2$ or $(-5) + 2 = 2 + (-5)$
$$= -3$$ $$= 2 - 5$$
$$= -3$$

Here, you add a positive number and a negative number together. Since there are more discs than discs, the answer is negative.

Evaluate these expressions.
(a) $7 + (-3)$

Place seven discs in the first row.

Place three discs in the second row.

zero pairs

∴ $7 + (-3) = 4$ Count the discs left after taking away the zero pairs.

(b) $(-4) + 6$

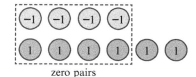

Place four $\boxed{-1}$ discs in the first row.

Place six $\boxed{1}$ discs in the second row.

zero pairs

∴ $(-4) + 6 = 2$

Count the discs left after taking away the zero pairs.

(c) $3 + (-5)$

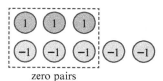

Place three $\boxed{1}$ discs in the first row.

Place five $\boxed{-1}$ discs in the second row.

zero pairs

∴ $3 + (-5) = -2$

Count the discs left after taking away the zero pairs.

(d) $(-8) + 2$

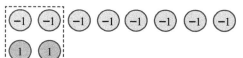

Place eight $\boxed{-1}$ discs in the first row.

Place two $\boxed{1}$ discs in the second row.

zero pairs

∴ $(-8) + 2 = -6$

Count the discs left after taking away the zero pairs.

3. (a) Think of two integers $\triangle$ and $\square$ (including negative integers). Calculate both $\triangle + \square$ and $\square + \triangle$.

(b) Repeat **(a)** with two different integers. Do this two more times.

Suggested answer for (a) and (b):

Consider two integers a and b where $a < 0$ and $b > 0$.

Case	$\triangle + \square$	$\square + \triangle$
1	$(+a) + (+b) = a + b$	$(+b) + (+a) = b + a$
2	$(-a) + (-b) = -a - b$	$(-b) + (-a) = -b - a$
3	$(+a) + (-b) = a - b$	$(-b) + (+a) = -b + a$
4	$(-a) + (+b) = -a + b$	$(+b) + (-a) = b - a$
5	$(+a) + 0 = a$	$0 + (+a) = a$
6	$(-a) + 0 = -a$	$0 + (-a) = -a$

(c) From **(a)** and **(b)**, what do you observe?

The results are always the same. The order of addition does not affect the result.

Class Activity 3

Objective: To perform subtraction of integers using algebra discs.

Tasks

1. **Subtracting a positive integer**

   For example, evaluate 3 − 7.

   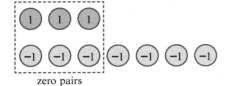

   zero pairs

   Place three ① discs in the first row.

   Place seven ⊖ discs in the second row.

   ∴ 3 − 7 = −4

   Count the discs left after taking away the zero pairs.

   Here, you add a positive number and a negative number together. Since there are more ⊖ discs than ① discs, the answer is negative.

   Evaluate −2 − 4.

   Place two ⊖ discs in the first row.

   Place four ⊖ discs in the second row.

   ∴ −2 − 4 = −6

   Count the total number of ⊖ discs.

   Here, when adding two negative numbers, the answer is negative.

   Evaluate these expressions.

   (a) 5 − 2

   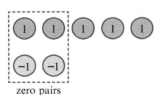

   zero pairs

   Place five ① discs in the first row.

   Place two ⊖ discs in the second row.

   ∴ 5 − 2 = 3

   Count the discs left after taking away the zero pairs.

   (b) 3 − 4

   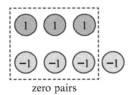

   zero pairs

   Place three ① discs in the first row.

   Place four ⊖ discs in the second row.

   ∴ 3 − 4 = −1

   Count the discs left after taking away the zero pairs.

(c) −3 − 1

Place three discs in the first row.

Place one (−1) disc in the second row.

∴ −3 − 1 = −4   Count the total number of discs.

(d) −6 − 3

Place six (−1) discs in the first row.

Place three (−1) discs in the second row.

∴ −6 − 3 = −9   Count the total number of discs.

When you subtract a positive number from another positive number and get more (1) discs than (−1) discs, is your answer positive or negative?

The answer is positive.

2. **Subtracting a negative integer**
For example, evaluate 5 − (−2).

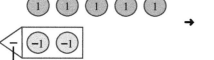

→

This means flipping over all the discs inside the box.

Get the negative of −2.

∴ 5 − (−2) = 7

You can also write 5 − (−2) = 5 + 2 Change signs as the discs are flipped.
        = 7

Here, when adding two positive numbers, the answer is positive.
Note that subtracting a negative number is the same as adding a positive number.

For example, evaluate (−3) − (−8).

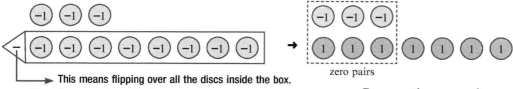

→

This means flipping over all the discs inside the box.

Get the negative of −8.   Remove the zero pairs.

zero pairs

→

∴ (−3) − (−8) = 5

You can also write (−3) $\boxed{- (−8)}$ = (−3) $\boxed{+ 8}$ Change signs as the discs are flipped.
= −3 + 8
= 5

Here, you add a negative number and a positive number together. Since there are more ① discs than ⑴ discs, the answer is positive.

Evaluate these expressions.

(a) 6 − (−3)

Get the negative of −3. (Flip over the discs inside the box.)

∴ 6 − (−3) = 6 + 3 = 9   Change signs as the discs are flipped.

(b) 3 − (−4)

Get the negative of −4.

∴ 3 − (−4) = 3 + 4 = 7   Change signs as the discs are flipped.

(c) −4 − (−7)

Get the negative of −7.   Remove the zero pairs.

∴ −4 − (−7) = −4 + 7 = 3   Change signs as the discs are flipped.

(d) −7 − (−5)

Get the negative of −5.   Remove the zero pairs.

∴ −7 − (−5) = −7 + 5 = −2   Change signs as the discs are flipped.

3. **(a)** Think of two integers △ and □ (including negative integers). Calculate both △ − □ and □ − △.
   (b) Repeat **(a)** with two different integers. Do this two more times.

   Suggested answer for (a) and (b):

   Consider two integers a and b where $a > 0$ and $b > 0$.

Case	△ − □	△ − □
1	$(+a) - (+b) = a - b$	$(+b) - (+a) = b - a$
2	$(-a) - (-b) = -a + b$	$(-b) - (-a) = -b + a$
3	$(+a) - (-b) = a + b$	$(-b) - (+a) = -b - a$
4	$(-a) - (+b) = -a - b$	$(+b) - (-a) = b + a$
5	$(+a) - 0 = a$	$0 - (+a) = -a$
6	$(-a) - 0 = -a$	$0 - (-a) = a$

   (c) From **(a)** and **(b)**, what do you observe?

   The results are not the same. The order of subtraction does affect the result.

Class Activity 4

Objective: To perform multiplication of integers using algebra discs.

Tasks

1. **Multiplying a positive integer by an integer**
   For example, evaluate $2 \times (-5)$.

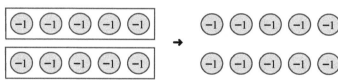

   Get 2 groups of −5.   Ungroup the discs.

   ∴ $2 \times (-5) = -10$ Observe that the answer is negative. Here, you multiply a positive number by a negative number.

   Evaluate these expressions.
   (a) 2×4

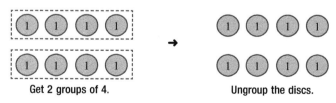

   Get 2 groups of 4.   Ungroup the discs.

   $2 \times 4 = 8$

105

(b) 3×6

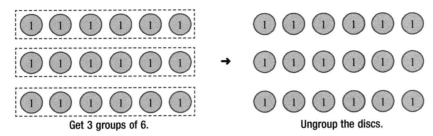

Get 3 groups of 6.   Ungroup the discs.

$3 \times 6 = 18$

(c) $3 \times (-4)$

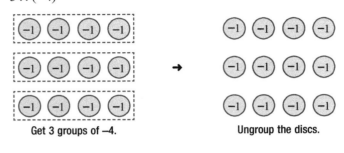

Get 3 groups of −4.   Ungroup the discs.

$3 \times (-4) = -12$

(d) $4 \times (-5)$

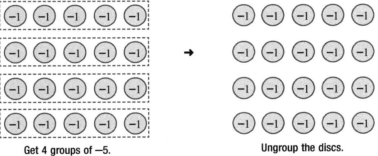

Get 4 groups of −5.   Ungroup the discs.

$4 \times (-5) = -20$

If you multiply a positive number by a positive number, is your answer positive or negative?

The answer is positive.

---

2. **Multiplying a negative integer by an integer**

For example, evaluate $(-3) \times 4$.

$(-3) \times 4$ is the same as $4 \times (-3)$, so you can write $(-3) \times 4 = 4 \times (-3)$.

Get 4 groups of –3.   Ungroup the discs.

$\therefore (-3) \times 4 = 4 \times (-3)$
$\qquad\qquad\quad = -12$

Observe that the answer is negative. Here, you multiply a negative number by a positive number.

Evaluate these expressions.

(a) $(-1) \times 5$

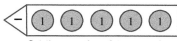

Get the negative of 1 group of 5.   Ungroup the discs.

$(-1) \times 5 = -5$

(b) $(-2) \times 3$

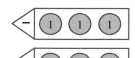

Get the negative of 2 groups of 3.   Ungroup the discs.

$(-2) \times 3 = -6$

3. **Multiplying two negative integers**

For example, evaluate $(-2) \times (-3)$.

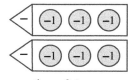

Get the negative of 2 groups of –3.   Ungroup the discs.
(Flip over the discs of each group.)

$\therefore (-2) \times (-3) = 6$

Observe that the answer is positive. Here, you multiply a negative number by a negative number.

$(-2) \times (-3) = -[2 \times (-3)]$

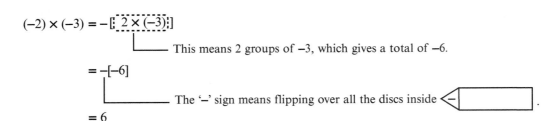

This means 2 groups of –3, which gives a total of –6.

$= -[-6]$

The '–' sign means flipping over all the discs inside .

$= 6$

In fact, you can also write $(-2) \times (-3) = (-3) \times (-2)$

$$= -[3 \times (-2)]$$
$$= -[-6]$$
$$= 6 \quad \text{Observe that the answer is the same as above.}$$

Evaluate these expressions.

(a) $(-3) \times (-4)$

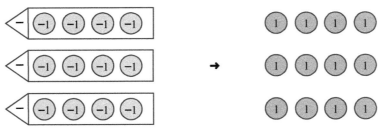

Get the negative of 3 groups of –4.   Ungroup the discs.

$(-3) \times (-4) = 12$

(b) $(-4) \times (-2)$

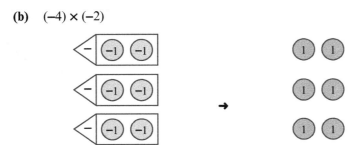

Get the negative of 4 groups of –2.   Ungroup the discs.

$(-4) \times (-2) = 8$

4. (a) Think of two integers △ and □ (including negative integers). Calculate both △ × □ and □ × △.
(b) Repeat **(a)** with two different integers. Do this two more times.

Suggested answer for (a) and (b):

Consider two integers a and b where $a > 0$ and $b > 0$.

Case	△ × □	△ × □
1	$(+a) \times (+b) = ab$	$(+b) \times (+a) = ab$
2	$(-a) \times (-b) = ab$	$(-b) \times (-a) = ab$
3	$(+a) \times (-b) = -ab$	$(-b) \times (+a) = -ab$
4	$(-a) \times (+b) = -ab$	$(+b) \times (-a) = -ab$
5	$(+a) \times 0 = 0$	$0 \times (+a) = 0$
6	$(-a) \times 0 = 0$	$0 \times (-a) = 0$

(c) From **(a)** and **(b)**, what do you observe?

The results are always the same. The order of multiplication does not affect the result.

Try It!

Section 2.1

1. An aeroplane is 1320 m above sea level and a submarine is 56 m below sea level. Represent their altitudes using positive and negative numbers.

Solution
Suppose the altitude above sea level is positive.
Altitude of the aeroplane = 1320 m
Altitude of the submarine = −56 m

2. (a) Represent the numbers −1, −3.5 and $2\frac{1}{2}$ on a number line.
(b) Arrange the given numbers in descending order.

Solution
(a) The representation of the numbers −1, −3.5 and $2\frac{1}{2}$ is shown below.

(b) The descending order of the numbers is $2\frac{1}{2}$, −1, −3.5.

3. (a) List three numbers that are greater than −27. Express the relationships using the inequality sign '>'.
(b) List three numbers that are less than −11. Express the relationships using the inequality sign '<'.

Solution
(a) For example, $42 > -\frac{4}{3} > -26$.
(b) For example, $-100.1 < -12\frac{1}{3} < -12$.

Section 2.2

4. For each of these expressions, guess whether the answer is positive or negative before evaluating it. Show your steps in getting the answers.
(a) $(-6) + (-14)$ **(b)** $17 + (-9)$
(c) $(-23) + 12$ **(d)** $0 + (+5)$

Solution
(a) $(-6) + (-14)$
Since both numbers are negative, the answer is negative.
$(-6) + (-14) = -6 - 14$
$= -20$

(b) $17 + (-9)$
Since there are more positive ones than negative ones, the answer is positive.
$17 + (-9) = 17 - 9$
$= 8$

(c) $(-23) + 12$
Since there are more negative ones than positive ones, the answer is negative.
$(-23) + 12 = -23 + 12$
$= -11$

(d) $0 + (+5)$
Since the sum is zero and positive ones, the answer is positive.
$0 + (+5) = 0 + 5$
$= 5$

5. Evaluate these expressions. Guess whether the answer is positive or negative before evaluating it. Show your steps in getting the answers.
   (a) $13 - (-21)$ (b) $-9 - (-4)$
   (c) $0 - (-6)$ (d) $7 + (-3)$
   (e) $-4 + (-10)$ (f) $-11 + (-5)$

Solution

(a) $13 - (-21) = 13 + 21$
                $= 34$
      Since the sum is positive ones, the answer is positive.

(b) $-9 - (-4) = -9 + 4$
                $= -5$
      Since there are more negative ones than positive ones, the answer is negative.

(c) $0 - (-6) = 0 + 6$
                $= 6$
      Since the sum is zero and positive ones, the answer is positive.

(d) $7 + (-3) = 7 - 3$
                $= 4$
      Since there are more positive ones than negative ones, the answer is positive.

(e) $-4 + (-10) = -4 - 10$
                $= -14$
      Since the sum is negative ones, the answer is negative.

(f) $-11 + (-5) = -11 - 5$
                $= -16$
      Since the sum is negative ones, the answer is negative.

6. In July, the time zone in Sydney is GMT+10 and the time zone in Vancouver is GMT−8.
   (a)   By how many hours is the local time in Vancouver behind the local time in Sydney?
   (b)   When it is 4 pm on 3 July in Vancouver, what is the date and the local time in Sydney?

Solution

(a)   The required hours $= 10 - (-8)$
                       $= 18$ hours

(b)

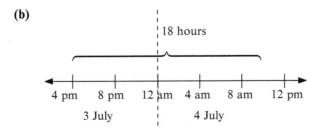

By counting forward 18 hours from 4 pm on 3 July, in Sydney it is 10 am on 4 July.

7. A submarine descended $23\,\text{m}$. It then ascended $47\,\text{m}$. Finally, it descended $35\,\text{m}$. Find the overall change in its level.

Solution

Overall change in position $= (-23) + 47 + (-35)$
                         $= -23 + 47 - 35$
                         $= -11$
Overall change in its level is $-11\,\text{m}$.

Section 2.3

8. Find the values of these expressions.
   (a) $8 \times (-12)$
   (b) $(-3) \times (-6)$
   (c) $(-5) \times 6 \times (-4)$

Solution

(a) $8 \times (-12) = -(8 \times 12)$
                     $= -96$

(b) $(-3) \times (-6) = 3 \times 6$
                       $= 18$

(c) $(-5) \times 6 \times (-4) = -(5 \times 6) \times (-4)$
                               $= 30 \times 4$
                               $= 120$

9. Find the values of these expressions.
   (a) $(+16) \div (+2)$ (b) $(-75) \div (-5)$
   (c) $(+63) \div (-7)$ (d) $(-54) \div 6$

Solution

(a) $(+16) \div (+2) = \dfrac{16}{2}$ (b) $(-75) \div (-5) = \dfrac{75}{5}$
                      $= 8$ $= 15$

(c) $(+63) \div (-7) = -\dfrac{63}{7}$ (d) $(-54) \div 6 = -\dfrac{54}{6}$
                      $= -9$ $= -9$

10. Find the values of these expressions.
    (a) $32 \div (-4) \times (-7)$
    (b) $(-8) - (-2) + (-28) \div 4$
    (c) $(-8) \times (-5) - (-36) \div 9$

Solution

(a) $32 \div (-4) \times (-7) = (-8) \times (-7)$
                               $= 56$

(b) $(-8) - (-2) + (-28) \div 4$
      $= (-8) - (-2) + (-7)$
      $= -8 + 2 - 7$
      $= -13$

(c) $(-8) \times (-5) - (-36) \div 9$
$= 40 + 36 \div 9$
$= 40 + 4$
$= 44$

11. Evaluate these expressions.
    (a) $(-6)^3 + (-12) + [(-8) - (-3)]^2 \times (-2)$
    (b) $(5 - 9)^2 + [(-5) - (-3)]^3 - (-7) \times (-6) + (-20)$

Solution
(a) $(-6)^3 + (-12) + [(-8) - (-3)]^2 \times (-2)$
$= (-6)^3 + (-12) + (-5)^2 \times (-2)$
$= (-216) + (-12) + 25 \times (-2)$
$= 18 + (-50)$
$= -32$

(b) $(5 - 9)^2 + [(-5) - (-3)]^3 - (-7) \times (-6) + (-20)$
$= (-4)^2 + (-2)^3 - 42 - 20$
$= 16 + (-8) - 62$
$= -2 - 62$
$= -64$

Exercise 2.1

Level 1 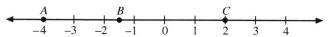 GCSE Grade 1⁺/2⁻

1. If $-7\,°C$ denotes a temperature drop of $7\,°C$, what does $5\,°C$ denote?

Solution
$5\,°C$ denotes a temperature rise of $5\,°C$.

2. **(a)** If $-4\,km/h$ means $4\,km/h$ below the speed limit, what does $12\,km/h$ mean?
    (b) If $-3\,km$ denotes a distance of $3\,km$ due south, what is the meaning of $+5\,km$?

Solution
    (a) $12\,km/h$ means $12\,km/h$ above the speed limit.

    (b) $+5\,km$ denotes a distance of $5\,km$ due north.

3. If $-£2800$ denotes a withdrawal of £2800 from a bank account, what does £1650 mean?

Solution
£1650 means a deposit of £1650.

4. Consider a gain in mass to be positive. Write down the following changes in mass using positive and negative numbers.
    (a) The mass of a crystal is increased by 2 grams after an experiment.
    (b) The mass of an ice cube is reduced by 13 grams as it melts.

Solution
    (a) Change in crystal's mass $= 2\,g$

    (b) Change in mass of ice cube $= -13\,g$

5. State the numbers represented by the points A, B and C on the number line below.

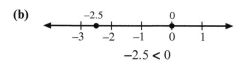

Solution
The numbers represented by A, B and C are -4, -1.5 and 2 respectively.

6. Represent each pair of numbers on a number line and write down their relationship using the '<' sign.
    (a) 0, 4   **(b)** $-2.5, 0$

Solution
(a)

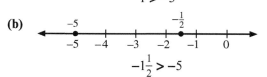

$0 < 4$

(b)

$-2.5 < 0$

7. Represent each pair of numbers on a number line and write down their relationship using the '>' sign.
    (a) $-3, 1$ **(b)** $-5, -1\frac{1}{2}$

Solution
(a)

$1 > -3$

(b)

$-1\frac{1}{2} > -5$

8. Copy and fill in the blanks with '<' or '>'.
    (a) 2 _____ 7   **(b)** -3 _____ -10
    (c) 3 _____ -2 **(d)** -14 _____ 27
    (e) -5 _____ 0   **(f)** -11 _____ -6

Solution
    (a) $2 < 7$ **(b)** $-3 > -10$

    (c) $3 > -2$ **(d)** $-14 < 27$

    (e) $-5 < 0$ **(f)** $-11 < -6$

Level 2 GCSE Grade 2/2⁺

Describe the meaning of each quantity in Questions **9** to **11**.

9. The adjustment of the hourly wage of a worker is $-£5$.

Solution
The hourly wage decreases by £5.

10. The movement of a lift is +2 levels.

    Solution
    The lift moves up by 2 levels.

11. The change in the volume of water in a tank is −1 litre.

    Solution
    The volume of water in the tank has reduced by 1 litre.

12. (a) Represent the numbers −2.7, $1\frac{1}{3}$ and −0.4 on a number line.
    (b) Arrange the given numbers in ascending order.

    Solution
    (a) The representation is shown below.

    (b) The numbers in ascending order are −2.7, −0.4, $1\frac{1}{3}$.

13. (a) Represent the numbers 5, $-3\frac{1}{2}$ and 0.5 on a number line.
    (b) Arrange the given numbers in descending order.

    Solution
    (a) The representation is shown below.

    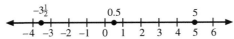

    (b) The numbers in descending order are 5, 0.5, $-3\frac{1}{2}$.

14. Arrange the numbers −50, 210, 0 and −300 in ascending order.

    Solution
    The numbers in ascending order are −300, −50, 0, 210.

15. Arrange the numbers −22, 4, 7 and −9 in descending order.

    Solution
    The numbers in descending order are 7, 4, −9, −22.

Level 3 **GCSE Grade 3⁻ / 3**

16. The table below shows the maximum temperatures in four cities on 1 January 2017.

City	Beijing	London	Singapore	Winnipeg
Maximum temperature (°C)	−2	9	32	−7

    Arrange these cities in ascending order of their temperatures.

    Solution
    The required order of the cities is Winnipeg, Beijing, London, Singapore.

17. The bank account balances of Rahim, Kelly and Sammy are −£3250, £760 and −£2180 respectively. Based on these figures, who has the
    (a) most money,
    (b) least money?

    Solution
    (a) Kelly has the most money.
    (b) Rahim has the least money.

18. The following table shows a list of transactions for a savings account.

Date	Deposit	Withdrawal	Balance
3 JAN 2018	£3000.00		£3000.00
5 JAN 2018		£200.00	£2800.00
11 JAN 2018	£150.00		£2950.00
18 JAN 2018		£400.00	£2550.00

    Design a page that shows the deposits and withdrawals under the same column.

    Solution

Date	Deposit/ Withdrawal	Balance
3 JAN 2018	£3000.00	£3000.00
5 JAN 2018	−£200.00	£2800.00
11 JAN 2018	£150.00	£2950.00
18 JAN 2018	−£400.00	£2550.00

    In the table, '+' means deposit and '−' means withdrawal.

19. The following information lists the altitudes of some places.
    Death Valley, USA: −86 m,
    Mount Fuji, Japan: 3376 m,
    Snowdon, UK: 1085 m,
    Turfan Depression, China: −154 m.
    Arrange these places in ascending order of their altitudes.

Solution

$-154 < -86 < 1085 < 3376$

The places in ascending order of their altitudes are Turfan Depression, Death Valley, Snowdon and Mount Fuji.

20. Ryan is one of the finalists in the men's 400 m run at an athletics meet. The results of the other six runners in the race compared to Ryan's are shown below.

Harry: 1.74 s faster than Ryan
AJ: 3.91 s slower than Ryan
Diego: 7.55 s slower than Ryan
Marcin: 1.35 s slower than Ryan
Dan: 0.25 s faster than Ryan
Lucas: 1.92 s faster than Ryan

(a) If −1 s means 1 second faster than Ryan, represent the results of the above six runners using positive or negative numbers.

(b) Who was the winner of the race?

(c) Who finished last in the race?

(d) In what position did Ryan come?

(e) If Ryan's time was 50.45 s, find the winner's time.

Solution

(a) Harry: −1.74 s
AJ: +3.91 s
Diego: +7.55 s
Marcin: +1.35 s
Dan: −0.25 s
Lucas: −1.92 s

(b) The winner was Lucas.

(c) Diego finished last in the race.

(d) Ryan was slower than Harry, Dan and Lucas.
∴ Ryan came 4th in the race.

(e) The winner's time = 50.45 − 1.92
= 48.53 s

21. Discuss whether these numbers exist. If they do, write down their values.
(a) The largest positive integer
(b) The smallest positive integer
(c) The largest negative integer
(d) The smallest negative integer

Solution

(a) No, you can always add 1 to any positive integer to make a larger positive integer.

(b) Yes, 1.

(c) Yes, −1.

(d) No, you can always subtract 1 from any negative integer to make a smaller negative integer.

22. Is it possible to draw a vertical number line? If so, draw a vertical number line. Are there examples in the real world where vertical number lines can be used? Discuss.

Solution

Yes, it is possible to draw a vertical number line as shown below.

A thermometer is an example.

Exercise 2.2

Level 1 GCSE Grade 2⁺

1. Evaluate these expressions.
(a) $3 + 5$ (b) $(-2) + (-7)$
(c) $(-4) + 8$ (d) $6 + (-11)$
(e) $0 + (-2)$ (f) $(-5) + 17$
(g) $(-12) + (-25)$ (h) $24 + (-30)$

Solution

(a) $3 + 5 = 8$ (b) $(-2) + (-7) = -9$

(c) $(-4) + 8 = 4$ (d) $6 + (-11) = -5$

(e) $0 + (-2) = -2$ (f) $(-5) + 17 = 12$

(g) $(-12) + (-25) = -37$ (h) $24 + (-30) = -6$

2. Evaluate these expressions.
(a) $13 - 6$ (b) $(-17) - 8$
(c) $9 - (-7)$ (d) $-3 - (-2)$
(e) $-5 - (-5)$ (f) $(-18) - 6$
(g) $(-9) - (-3)$ (h) $11 - (-24)$

Solution

(a) $13 - 6 = 7$ (b) $(-17) - 8 = -25$

(c) $9 - (-7) = 16$ (d) $-3 - (-2) = -1$

(e) $-5 - (-5) = 0$ (f) $(-18) - 6 = -24$

(g) $(-9) - (-3) = -6$ (h) $11 - (-24) = 35$

Level 2 GCSE Grade 2⁺ / 3⁻

3. Evaluate these expressions.
(a) $3 - (-8) + (-4)$ (b) $(-2) + 5 + (-3)$
(c) $(-9) + (-2) - (-7)$ (d) $4 - (-2) - 4$
(e) $7 + (-12) - 6$ (f) $-19 - (-15) + 10$

Solution
(a) $3 - (-8) + (-4) = 7$ (b) $(-2) + 5 + (-3) = 0$

(c) $(-9) + (-2) - (-7) = -4$ (d) $4 - (-2) - 4 = 2$

(e) $7 + (-12) - 6 = -11$ (f) $-19 - (-15) + 10 = 6$

4. Find the missing numbers.
   (a) $7 + (\ ) = 3$ (b) $11 + (\ ) = -5$
   (c) $-9 - (\ ) = -13$ (d) $-8 - (\ ) = 10$
   (e) $-8 + (\ ) = 6$ (f) $4 - (\ ) = 7$

Solution
(a) $7 + (-4) = 3$ (b) $11 + (-16) = -5$

(c) $-9 - (4) = -13$ (d) $-8 - (-18) = 10$

(e) $-8 + (14) = 6$ (f) $4 - (-3) = 7$

Level 3   **GCSE Grade** 3^- / 3

5. A helicopter flying 120 m above sea level detects a submarine. If the submarine is 39 m below sea level, what is the vertical distance between the helicopter and the submarine?

Solution
The required vertical distance $= [120 - (-39)]$
$$= 159\,\text{m}$$

6. The bank account of a company has an overdraft facility. The balance yesterday was −£390. The company deposits £600 into the account today and it will withdraw £450 tomorrow. Find the balance in the account
   (a) today,
   (b) tomorrow.

Solution
(a) Balance today $= £[(-390) + 600]$
$$= £210$$

(b) Balance tomorrow $=$ balance today $- £450$
$$= £210 - £450$$
$$= -£240$$

7. A car travels 16 km due south, 33 km due north and then 12 km due south. What is its final position from the starting point?

Solution
Taking the north direction to be positive, from its starting point the car travels
$= (-16) + 33 + (-12)$
$= 5$
Final position is 5 km north of the starting point.

8. The following table records the maximum and minimum daily temperatures of a city on five consecutive days.

Day	Mon	Tue	Wed	Thu	Fri
Maximum temperature (°C)	−2	6	0	−1	10
Minimum temperature (°C)	−10	−4	−3	−5	3

   (a) Which day shows the greatest temperature difference?
   (b) Which day shows the least temperature difference?

Solution

Day	Temperature difference (°C)
Mon	$-2 - (-10) = 8$
Tue	$6 - (-4) = 10$
Wed	$0 - (-3) = 3$
Thu	$-1 - (-5) = 4$
Fri	$10 - 3 = 7$

   (a) Tuesday has the greatest temperature difference.
   (b) Wednesday has the least temperature difference.

9. A lift, initially at the 11th floor, goes up seven floors and then goes down 10 floors. Find the level it finally stops at.

Solution
The required level $= 11 + 7 + (-10)$
$$= 8\text{th floor}$$

10. Ali has been running a small business for four years. The following table shows her profits (positive) and losses (negative) in these years.

Year	Profit/Loss
1	−£31 000
2	−£600
3	£9000
4	£17 000

   (a) Find her total profit or loss in these four years.
   (b) If her target total profit is £18 000 in the first five years, what should her profit be in the 5th year?

Solution
(a) Total
$$= (-£31\,000) + (-£6000) + £9000 + £17\,000$$
$$= -£5600$$
Her total loss is £5600.

(b) $£18\,000 - (-£5600) = £23\,600$
Her profit should be £23 600.

11. **(a)** Copy and fill in the same shapes with the same integers in the following table.

Left side	Right side
□ + ○	○ + □
(□ + ○) + ⬡	□ + (○ + ⬡)
□ − ○	○ − □
(□ − ○) − ⬡	□ − (○ − ⬡)

(b) Evaluate each expression and compare the results on the left side with those on the right side. What do you notice?

(c) Compare results with your classmates. What can you conclude?

Solution

(a)

Left side	Right side
3 + (−5)	(−5) + 3
[3 + (−5)] + 6	3 + [(−5) + 6]
3 − (−5)	(−5) − 3
[3 − (−5)] − 6	3 − [(−5) − 6]

(b) The results are as follows:

Left side	Right side
−2	−2
4	4
8	−8
2	14

The values on the left side are equal to those on the right side for the first two rows.
Left side = −Right side for the third row.
Left side ≠ Right side for the fourth row.

(c) For any three integers a, b and c,
(i) $a + b = b + a$
(ii) $(a + b) + c = a + (b + c)$
(iii) $a − b = −(b − a)$
(iv) $(a − b) − c \neq a − (b − c)$

Exercise 2.3

Level 1   GCSE Grade 2⁺

1. Evaluate these expressions.
   (a) $8 \times (−9)$
   (b) $(−5) \times (−4)$
   (c) $(−6) \times 7$
   (d) 3×17
   (e) $(−12)^2$
   (f) $(−4)^3$
   (g) $(−3)^2 \times 5$
   (h) $(−2)^3 \times (−9)$

Solution
   (a) $8 \times (−9) = −72$
   (b) $(−5) \times (−4) = 20$
   (c) $(−6) \times 7 = −42$
   (d) $3 \times 17 = 51$

   (e) $(−12)^2 = 144$
   (f) $(−4)^3 = −64$
   (g) $(−3)^2 \times 5 = 9 \times 5 = 45$
   (h) $(−2)^3 \times (−9)$
       $= (−8) \times (−9) = 72$

2. Evaluate these expressions.
   (a) $(−38) \div (−2)$
   (b) $132 \div (−11)$
   (c) $65 \div 5$
   (d) $(−57) \div 3$
   (e) $\dfrac{0}{−7}$
   (f) $(−144) \div (−9)$
   (g) $(−6)^3$
   (h) $\dfrac{162}{(−3)^3}$

Solution
   (a) $(−38) \div (−2) = 19$
   (b) $132 \div (−11) = −12$
   (c) $65 \div 5 = 13$
   (d) $(−57) \div 3 = −19$
   (e) $\dfrac{0}{−7} = 0$
   (f) $(−144) \div (−9) = 16$
   (g) $(−6)^3 = −216$
   (h) $\dfrac{162}{(−3)^3} = \dfrac{162}{−27} = −6$

Level 2   GCSE Grade 3⁻

3. Evaluate these expressions.
   (a) $(−6) \times 3 \times (−1)$
   (b) $(−84) \div 7 \times 5$
   (c) $(−37) \times 0 − (−8)$
   (d) $63 \div (−9) + (−2) \times (−10)$
   (e) $(−47) − 33 \div (−3) − 3 \times (−7)$
   (f) $196 \div [(−8) + (−6)] \times (−2)$
   (g) $[(−23) + 14] \times (−2)^2$
   (h) $(−45) \times 6 \div (−3)^3$
   (i) $(−7) \times (−8) \times 0 \times 34 − 4 \times (−5)^2$
   (j) $(−6)^3 \div 3^2 + [−9 − (−8)]^3$

Solution
   (a) $(−6) \times 3 \times (−1) = (−18) \times (−1) = 18$

   (b) $(−84) \div 7 \times 5 = (−12) \times 5 = −60$

   (c) $(−37) \times 0 − (−8) = 0 + 8 = 8$

   (d) $63 \div (−9) + (−2) \times (−10) = (−7) + 20 = 13$

   (e) $(−47) − 33 \div (−3) − 3 \times (−7) = −47 + 11 + 21$
       $= −15$

   (f) $196 \div [(−8) + (−6)] \times (−2) = 196 \div (−14) \times (−2)$
       $= −14 \times (−2) = 28$

   (g) $[(−23) + 14] \times (−2)^2 = (−9) \times 4 = −36$

   (h) $(−45) \times 6 \div (0−3)^3 = (−270) \div (−27) = 10$

   (i) $(−7) \times (−8) \times 0 \times 34 − 4 \times (−5)^2 = 0 − 4 \times 25$
       $= −100$

   (j) $(−6)^3 \div 3^2 + [−9 − (−8)]^3 = (−216) \div 9 + (−1)^3$
       $= (−24) + (−1) = 24$

Level 3   GCSE Grade 3 / 3⁺

4. The depth of water in a beaker decreases by 2 mm every day due to evaporation.
   (a) Find the change in the depth of water after three days.

(b) If the original depth of water is 65 mm, find the depth after three days.

Solution

(a) Change in depth $= (-2) \times 3$
$$= -6 \text{ mm}$$

(b) Depth after three days
$$= 65 + (-6)$$
$$= 59 \text{ mm}$$

5. A shop sells four mobile phones at a loss. If the loss per phone is £40, what is the total loss incurred?

Solution

Total loss $= £40 \times 4$
$$= £160$$

6. The number of bacteria in a petri dish doubles every 10 seconds. If there are 15 bacteria to begin with, how many bacteria are there after 30 seconds?

Solution

Number of bacteria $= 15 \times 2 \times 2 \times 2 = 120$

7. At cruising altitude, the outside air temperature of an aircraft is −57 °C.
   (a) If the inside air temperature of the aircraft is 23 °C, find the difference between the outside air temperature and the inside air temperature of the aircraft.
   (b) If the ground temperature is −4 °C, what is the difference between the outside air temperature and the ground temperature?

Solution

(a) Outside air temperature − inside air temperature $= (-57) - 23$
$$= -80$$
Temperature difference is 80 °C.

(b) Outside air temperature − ground temperature
$$= (-57) - (-4)$$
$$= -57 + 4$$
$$= -53$$
Temperature difference is 53 °C.

8. Tom borrowed a sum of money from his father seven months ago. He returned £400 per month to his father. Currently, he owes his father £2500.
   (a) How much will he owe his father three months from now?
   (b) How much money did he borrow from his father?

Solution

(a) Amount owed $= £(2500 - 400 \times 3) = £1300$

(b) Amount borrowed $= £[2500 + (-400) \times (-7)]$
$$= £(2500 + 2800)$$
$$= £5300$$

9. Mrs Clarke has 400 shares of Stock A and 500 shares of Stock B. She gains £3 per share from Stock A and loses £2 per share from Stock B. How much does she gain or lose from these two stocks taken together?

Solution

Amount $= 400 \times 3 + 500 \times (-2)$
$$= 1200 - 1000$$
$$= 200$$
Mrs Clarke gains £200.

10. Henry is playing a card game. He starts with 100 points. If Henry wins a round, he gains 10 points and if he loses a round, he loses 4 points. In playing 10 rounds, Henry wins three and loses seven. How many points does Henry have now?

Solution

Total points $= 100 + 10 \times 3 - 4 \times 7$
$$= 100 + 30 - 28$$
$$= 102$$

11. A skyscraper in a city is 164 m above ground level. At a nearby site, the base of a quarry is 132 m below ground level.
    (a) Find the vertical distance between the top of the skyscraper and the base of the quarry.
    (b) How high is an office building above ground level if its top is vertically midway between the top of the skyscraper and the base of the quarry?

Solution

(a) Distance $= 164 - (-132)$
$$= 164 + 132$$
$$= 296$$
The vertical distance between the top of the skyscraper and the base of the quarry is 296 m.

(b) Height above the base of the quarry
$$= \frac{1}{2} \times \text{vertical distance between the two}$$
$$= \frac{1}{2} \times 296$$
$$= 148$$
Height above ground level $= (148 - 132) \text{ m}$
The building is 16 m high.

12. A mathematics quiz consists of five 'true/false' questions. The mark scheme awards 3 marks for every correct answer and −2 marks for every incorrect answer and 0 marks for every question not answered.
    (a) What is the maximum score of the quiz?
    (b) What is the minimum score of the quiz?

(c) Write about a situation where a student scores 3 marks for the quiz.

(d) Write about a situation where a student scores −3 marks for the quiz.

Solution

(a) The maximum score $= 3 \times 5 = 15$ marks

(b) The minimum score $= (-2) \times 5 = -10$ marks

(c) The score is 3 marks if there is 1 correct answer and 4 unanswered questions.

(d) The score is −3 marks if there are 3 incorrect answers, 1 correct answer and 1 unanswered question.

13. **(a)** Copy and fill in the same shapes with the same integers in the following table.

Left side	Right side
$\square \times \bigcirc$	$\bigcirc \times \square$
$(\square \times \bigcirc) \times \hexagon$	$\square \times (\bigcirc \times \hexagon)$
$\square \div \bigcirc$	$\bigcirc \div \square$
$(\square \div \bigcirc) \div \hexagon$	$\square \div (\bigcirc \div \hexagon)$

(b) Evaluate each expression and compare the results on the left side with those on the right side. What do you notice?

(c) Compare results with those of your classmates. What can you conclude?

Solution

(a)

Left side	Right side
$4 \times (-12)$	$(-12) \times 4$
$[4 \times (-12)] \times 6$	$4 \times [(-12) \times 6]$
$4 \div (-12)$	$(-12) \div 4$
$[4 \div (-12)] \div 6$	$4 \div [(-12) \div 6]$

(b) The results are as follows.

Left side	Right side
−48	−48
−288	−288
$-\dfrac{1}{3}$	−3
$-\dfrac{1}{18}$	−2

Left side = Right side for the first two rows.

Left side $= \dfrac{1}{\text{Right side}}$ for the third row.

Left side $\neq$ Right side for the fourth row.

(c) For any three integers a, b and c,
(i) $a \times b = b \times a$
(ii) $(a \times b) \times c = a \times (b \times c)$
(iii) $a \div b = \dfrac{1}{b \div a}$ provided $a \neq 0$ and $b \neq 0$.
(iv) $(a \div b) \div c \neq a \div (b \div c)$ provided $b \neq 0$ and $c \neq 0$.

Revision Exercise 2

1. The world is divided into 24 standard time zones. Relative to the UK in April, Sydney's time is +11 hours, New York's time is −5 hours and Honolulu's time is −11 hours. If it is Tuesday, 12 April, 9 am in the UK, find the local time in
(a) Sydney, **(b)** New York, **(c)** Honolulu.

[GCSE Grade 2+]

Solution

(a) $9 + 11 = 20$
The local time in Sydney is Tuesday, 12 April, 8 pm.

(b) $9 - 5 = 4$
The local time in New York is Tuesday, 12 April, 4 am.

(c) $9 - 11 = -2$
The local time in Honolulu is Monday, 11 April, 10 pm.

2. Copy and complete the following addition table in which the number in each cell is the sum of the number on its row header and the number on its column header.

[GCSE Grade 3−]

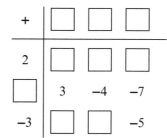

Solution

Let a to i represent the missing values in the table.

+	a	b	c
2	d	e	f
g	3	−4	−7
−3	h	i	−5

$c + (-3) = -5$
$\therefore \quad c = -2$

$f = c + 2$
$\quad = (-2) + 2$
$\quad = 0$

$-7 = c + g$
$\therefore \quad g = -7 - c$
$\quad = -7 - (-2)$
$\quad = -5$

$$a + g = 3$$
$$\therefore \quad a = 3 - g$$
$$= 3 - (-5)$$
$$= 8$$

$$b + g = -4$$
$$\therefore \quad b = -4 - g$$
$$= -4 - (-5)$$
$$= 1$$

$$d = a + 2$$
$$= 8 + 2$$
$$= 10$$

$$e = b + 2$$
$$= 1 + 2$$
$$= 3$$

$$h = a + (-3)$$
$$= 8 - 3$$
$$= 5$$

$$i = b + (-3)$$
$$= 1 - 3$$
$$= -2$$

The values in the table are as shown.

+	8	1	−2
2	10	3	0
−5	3	−4	−7
−3	5	−2	−5

3. Copy and complete the following multiplication table in which the number in each cell is the product of the number on its row header and the number on its column header.

Solution

Let a to i represent the missing values in the table.

×	−3	a	b
c	15	d	e
−2	f	8	g
7	h	i	−42

$$c \times (-3) = 15$$
$$\therefore \quad c = -5$$

$$f = (-3) \times (-2)$$
$$= 6$$

$$h = (-3) \times 7$$
$$= -21$$

$$a \times (-2) = 8$$
$$\therefore \quad a = -4$$

$$d = a \times c$$
$$= (-4) \times (-5)$$
$$= 20$$

$$i = a \times 7$$
$$= (-4) \times 7$$
$$= -28$$

$$b \times 7 = -42$$
$$\therefore \quad b = -6$$

$$e = b \times c$$
$$= (-6) \times (-5)$$
$$= 30$$

$$g = (-2) \times b$$
$$= (-2) \times (-6)$$
$$= 12$$

The values in the table are as shown.

×	−3	−4	−6
−5	15	20	30
−2	6	8	12
7	−21	−28	−42

4. **(a)** Find the values of 2^2 and $(-3)^2$.

(b) Represent 2, 2^2, −3 and $(-3)^2$ on a number line.

(c) Write down an inequality connecting 2 and −3.

(d) Write down an inequality connecting 2^2 and $(-3)^2$.

Solution

(a) $(-2)^2 = 4$
$(-3)^2 = 9$

(b)

```
        -3              2   2²          (-3)²
   <─●──┼──┼──┼──┼──●──●──┼──┼──●──>
    -3 -2 -1  0  1  2  3  4  5  6  7  8  9
```

(c) $-3 < 2$

(d) $2^2 < (-3)^2$

5. Evaluate these expressions.

(a) $(-16) \times (-3) - (-8) \times 5$ **(b)** $[-2 + (-7)]^3$

Solution

(a) $(-16) \times (-3) - (-8) \times 5 = 48 + 40$
$$= 88$$

(b) $[-2 + (-7)]^3 = (-9)^3$
$$= -729$$

6. The temperatures in five cities at noon on a
particular day are given as in the table.

Beijing	Hong Kong	Singapore	Stockholm	Toronto
–7°C	16°C	28°C	T°C	–2°C

(a) Find the difference between the temperatures
in Singapore and Toronto.
(b) The temperature in Stockholm is 26°C lower
than that in Hong Kong.
  (i) Find the temperature in Stockholm.
  (ii) Determine whether the temperature
    in Beijing is higher or lower than
    the temperature in Stockholm.
    What is the difference between their
    temperatures?

Solution
(a) The required difference
  = 28 – (–2)
  = 30°C

(b) (i) Temperature in Stockholm
    = 16 – 26
    = –10°C
  (ii) –10 < –7
    and –7 – (–10) = 3
    The temperature in Beijing is higher than
    the temperature in Stockholm.
    Their difference is 3°C.

7. Liquid air consists of a mixture of liquid
nitrogen and liquid oxygen. The boiling point
of nitrogen is –196°C and that of oxygen is
–183°C. When liquid air heats up, which
element will evaporate first? Explain
your answer.
Note: This property is used for the production
of oxygen using a method called fractional
distillation.

Solution
–196 < –183
When liquid air heats up, it will reach the
temperature –196°C first. Hence, nitrogen will
evaporate first.

8. (a) A duck flying 324 m above sea level drops a
shell which hits the sea bed at 58 m below sea
level. Find the vertical distance travelled by
the shell.
(b) If a gull is flying midway between the duck
and the sea bed, how high is the gull above sea
level?

Solution
(a) Vertical distance travelled = 324 – (–58)
  = 382 m

(b) Distance of gull below the duck = $\frac{1}{2}$ × 382
  = 191
Distance above sea level = 324 – 191
  = 133 m

9. A quality control supervisor measures the actual
volumes of six packets of fruit juice. Each packet
of fruit juice is supposed to contain 375 ml of juice.
The table shows the inspection results.

Packet	Amount below or above the required volume (ml)
1	–5
2	+12
3	–6
4	–9
5	+7
6	–2

(a) Find the actual volumes of juice in packet 1
and packet 2.
(b) Find the total volume of juice in the six
packets.

Solution
(a) Volume of juice in packet 1 = (375 – 5)
  = 370 ml
  Volume of juice in packet 2 = (375 + 12)
  = 387 ml

(b) (–5) + (+12) + (–6) + (–9) + (+7) + (–2)
  = –5 + 12 – 6 – 9 + 7 – 2
  = –3
  Total volume of juice = [375 × 6 + (–3)]
  = 2247 ml

10. Four people participated in a golf tournament.
Their scores (which are the numbers of strokes
below or above a standard value) in three rounds
are shown in the following table.

	Ali	Ben	Chris	Dan
Round 1	–5	+3	+10	–3
Round 2	–1	–2	+2	–4
Round 3	–2	–1	–3	+5

(a) Who had the lowest score in round 1?
(b) Find the total score of each person for the
three rounds.

(c) The winner in the tournament was the person with the lowest total score. Who was the winner?

Solution

(a) $-5 < -3 < 3 < 10$

∴ Ali had the lowest score in round 1.

(b)   Ali's total score $= (-5) + (-1) + (-2)$
$= -8$

Ben's total score $= (+3) + (-2) + (-1)$
$= 0$

Chris's total score $= (+10) + (+2) + (-3)$
$= 9$

Dan's total score $= (-3) + (-4) + (+5)$
$= -2$

(c)   The winner was Ali.

11. A lift in a commercial building is initially $108\,\text{m}$ above ground level. It descends $6\,\text{m}$ per second for 12 seconds. Then it rises $65\,\text{m}$ in 13 seconds. Find

(a)   the distance it travelled during the descent,

(b)   the distance it travelled in one second during the rise,

(c)   its final position above ground level.

Solution

(a)   Distance travelled during the descent $= 6 \times 12$
$= 72\,\text{m}$

(b)   Distance in one second when rising $= 65 \div 13$
$= 5\,\text{m}$

(c)   Final position above ground $= 108 - 72 + 65$
$= 101\,\text{m}$

12. A glassware shop sells three vases at a loss of £18 each, and two bowls at a gain of £7 each.

(a)   Find the overall gain or loss in selling these vases and bowls.

(b)   The shop sells five plates such that the overall gain or loss in selling these vases, bowls and plates is zero. What is the gain or loss of each plate?

Solution

(a)   Overall gain or loss $= 3 \times (-18) + 2 \times 7$
$= -54 + 14$
$= -40$

The overall loss was £40.

(b)   Gain or loss from one plate $\times$ 5 + overall gain or loss from vases and bowls from **(a)** $= 0$

∴ gain or loss from one plate $\times 5 - 40 = 0$

∴ gain or loss from one plate $= 40 \div 5$
$= 8$

The gain from each plate was £8.

Introduction to Algebra

Class Activity 1

Objective: To compare the algebraic expressions $3 + n$, $3n$, $(3n)^2$, $3n^2$, $9n^2$, $(5n)^3$ and $5n^3$.

Task

	A	B	C	D	E	F	G	H
1	Algebraic Expressions							
2								
3	n	3 + n	3n	(3n)^2	3n^2	9n^2	(5n)^3	5n^3
4	−3	0	−9	81	27	81	−3375	−135
5	−2	1	−6	36	12	36	−1000	−40
6	−1	2	−3	9	3	9	−125	−5
7	0	3	0	0	0	0	0	0
8	1	4	3	9	3	9	125	5
9	2	5	6	36	12	36	1000	40
10	3	6	9	81	27	81	3375	135

1. In a spreadsheet, enter the headings (row 1 and row 3) and the first column as shown.
2. Generate the values of other columns using formulae in the spreadsheet. You may use the copy and paste buttons to copy the formulae from one row to the other rows.
   Note: In a spreadsheet, * stands for multiplication and ^ stands for the index.

Questions

1. Look at the values under the columns $3 + n$ and $3n$. Can you say that $3 + n = 3n$? Explain your answer.

   The values are different. $3 + n$ and $3n$ are not equal, that is, $3 + n \neq 3n$.

2. Compare the columns of $(3n)^2$, $3n^2$ and $9n^2$. What are the relationships between these three expressions? Explain your answer.

   The values of $(3n)^2$ are equal to the values of $9n^2$. You say that $(3n)^2 = 9n^2$.

   The values of $(3n)^2$ are three times the values of $3n^2$. You say that $(3n)^2 = 3(3n^2)$.

   The values of $9n^2$ are three times the values of $3n^2$. You say that $9n^2 = 3(3n^2)$.

3. Compare the columns of $(5n)^3$ and $5n^3$. What is the relationship between these two expressions? Explain your answer.

   The values of $(5n)^3$ are 25 times the values of $5n^3$. $(5n)^3 = 5^3 \times n^3 = 25 \times (5n^3)$.

Class Activity 2

Objective: To apply the process of collecting like terms using algebra discs.

As well as number discs, you have x-discs and y-discs.

    front   back   front   back   front   back

Each disc has two sides. You can flip a disc to show either the front or the back. Just like 1 and −1, x and −x and y and −y form **zero pairs**. That is, $1 + (-1) = 0$, $x + (-x) = 0$ and $y + (-y) = 0$. Examples of zero pairs are:

(a) $2x + (-2x) = 2x - 2x = 0$

zero pairs

(b) $(-3y) + 3y = -3y + 3y = 0$

zero pairs

Some algebraic expressions can be represented by a set of algebra discs. For example,

(a) $2x + 3$:   This set of algebra discs can also represent $3 + 2x$.

(b) $y - 4$:   This set of algebra discs can also represent $-4 + y$.

(c) $-x + 3y - 2$:   This set of algebra discs can also represent $-2 + 3y - x$, $-2 - x + 3y$, $3y - x - 2$, $3y - 2 - x$ and $-x - 2 + 3y$.

Terms involving x and y can be simplified by collecting like terms as illustrated below.

$2x + 3y - 5x + y$

Collect the like terms.
$2x + 3y \boxed{- 5x} + y$

$= 2x \boxed{- 5x} + 3y + y$
   $\underbrace{}_{-3x}$ $\underbrace{}_{4y}$

$-3x + 4y$

$2x + 3y - 5x + y = 2x - 5x + 3y + y$
                   $= -3x + 4y$

Tasks

1. Represent these algebraic expressions using the algebra discs.
   (a) $3x + 2$

   (b) $x + 4y$

   (c) $-2x - 3y + 4$

2. Simplify these expressions. Use algebra discs to help you.
   (a) $2x + 5x$

   $\therefore 2x + 5x = 7x$

(b) $2x - 5x$

zero pairs

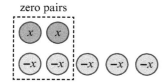

∴ $2x - 5x = -3x$

(c) $-2x + 5x$

zero pairs

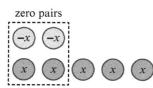

∴ $-2x + 5x = 3x$

(d) $-2x - 5x$

∴ $-2x - 5x = -7x$

(e) $3y + 1 + 4y + 3$

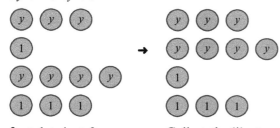

$3y + 1 + 4y + 3$ Collect the like terms.
$3y + 4y + 1 + 3$

∴ $3y + 1 + 4y + 3 = 3y + 4y + 1 + 3$
$= 7y + 4$

(f) $3y + 1 - 4y - 3$

zero pairs

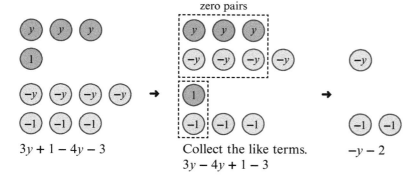

$3y + 1 - 4y - 3$ Collect the like terms. $-y - 2$
$3y - 4y + 1 - 3$

∴ $3y + 1 - 4y - 3 = 3y - 4y + 1 - 3$
$= -y - 2$

123

(g) $-3y - 1 + 4y + 3$

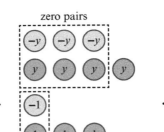

zero pairs

$-3y - 1 + 4y + 3$

Collect the like terms.
$-3y + 4y - 1 + 3$

$y + 2$

$\therefore -3y - 1 + 4y + 3 = -3y + 4y - 1 + 3$
$\qquad\qquad\qquad\quad = y + 2$

(h) $-3y - 1 - 4y - 3$

$-3y - 1 - 4y - 3$

Collect the like terms.
$-3y - 4y - 1 - 3$

$\therefore -3y - 1 - 4y - 3 = -3y - 4y - 1 - 3$
$\qquad\qquad\qquad\quad = -7y - 4$

(i) $4x - 5y + x + 2y - 1$

$4x - 5y + x + 2y - 1$

zero pairs

Collect the like terms.
$4x + x - 5y + 2y - 1$

$5x - 3y - 1$

$\therefore 4x - 5y + x + 2y - 1$
$\quad = 4x + x - 5y + 2y - 1$
$\quad = 5x - 3y - 1$

(j) $-3x + 2y - 4 - x + y + 1$

$-3x + 2y - 4 - x + y + 1$ Collect the like terms. $-4x + 3y - 3$
$-4x + 3y - 4 + 1$

$\therefore -3x + 2y - 4 - x + y + 1 = -4x + 3y - 4 + 1$
$= -4x + 3y - 3$

Questions

1. Explain how you would simplify $ax + bx$, where a and b are given integers. You may substitute a and b with different integers to help you illustrate your explanation.

   $ax + bx = (a + b)x$

2. Can you write $3x + 4y$ as $7xy$? You may substitute x and y with numbers to help you illustrate your explanation.

   No, $3x + 4y \neq 7xy$. $3x$ and $4y$ are unlike terms. Therefore, $3x + 4y$ cannot be simplified.

Class Activity 3

Objective: To perform the addition and subtraction of linear expressions using algebra discs.

Tasks

1. To obtain the negative of an expression, you flip the discs that represent the expression. For example, simplify $-(3x - 2)$.

    ⟶ This means flipping over all the discs inside the box.

$\therefore -(3x - 2) = -3x + 2$

    ⟶ This means changing the sign of all the terms inside the brackets. Thus, $3x$ becomes $-3x$ and -2 becomes 2.

Simplify these expressions. Use algebra discs to help you.
(a) $-(2x + 4)$

$\therefore -(2x + 4) = -2x - 4$

(b) $-(y - 3)$

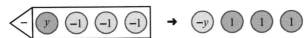

$\therefore -(y - 3) = -y + 3$

(c) $-(-3x + 2y)$

$\therefore -(-3x + 2y) = 3x - 2y$

(d) $-(x - 4y + 2)$

$\therefore -(x - 4y + 2) = -x + 4y - 2$

2. To add two expressions, you remove the brackets and collect the like terms.
For example, simplify $(2x - 3y) + (-3x + y)$.

zero pairs

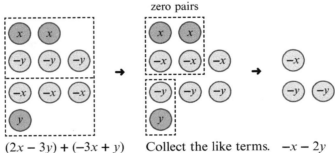

$(2x - 3y) + (-3x + y)$ Collect the like terms. $-x - 2y$

$(2x - 3y) \boxed{+ (-3x + y)}$

$= 2x - 3y \boxed{- 3x + y}$ **The signs of all terms in the brackets remain unchanged.**

$= 2x - 3x - 3y + y$

$= -x - 2y$

Simplify these expressions. Use algebra discs to help you.

(a) $(3x + 1) + (-x + 2)$

zero pair

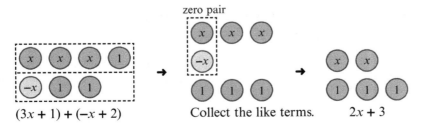

$(3x + 1) + (-x + 2)$ Collect the like terms. $2x + 3$

$\therefore (3x + 1) + (-x + 2) = 3x + 1 - x + 2$

$= 3x - x + 1 + 2$

$= 2x + 3$

(b) $(-2x + y) + (-3x - y)$

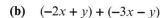
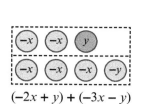

zero pair

$(-2x + y) + (-3x - y)$ Collect the like terms. $-5x$

$\therefore (-2x + y) + (-3x - y) = -2x + y - 3x - y$
$= -2x - 3x + y - y$
$= -5x$

(c) $(4y - 3) + (y - 1)$

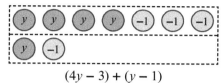

$(4y - 3) + (y - 1)$ Collect the like terms.

$\therefore (4y - 3) + (y - 1) = 4y - 3 + y - 1$
$= 4y + y - 3 - 1$
$= 5y - 4$

(d) $(-3x - y + 1) + (-2x + 3y + 4)$

zero pair

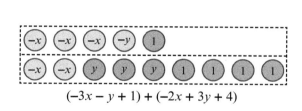

$(-3x - y + 1) + (-2x + 3y + 4)$ Collect the like terms.

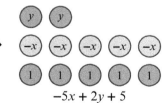

$-5x + 2y + 5$

$\therefore (-3x - y + 1) + (-2x + 3y + 4) = -3x - y + 1 - 2x + 3y + 4$
$= -5x + 2y + 5$

127

3. Subtracting an expression is the same as adding the negative of that expression.
For example, simplify $(2x - 3y) - (-3x + y)$.

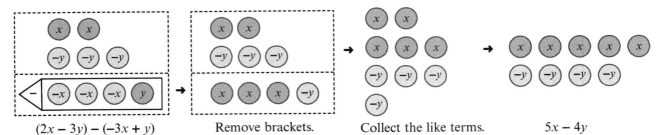

| $(2x - 3y) - (-3x + y)$ | Remove brackets. | Collect the like terms. | $5x - 4y$ |

$(2x - 3y) \boxed{- (-3x + y)}$

$= 2x - 3y \boxed{+ 3x - y}$ Observe that all the terms inside the brackets change sign when the brackets are removed.

$= 2x + 3x - 3y - y$

$= 5x - 4y$

Simplify these expressions. Use algebra discs to help you.

(a) $3x - (-5x)$

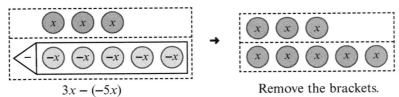

| $3x - (-5x)$ | Remove the brackets. |

$\therefore 3x - (-5x) = 3x + 5x$

$\qquad\qquad\quad = 8x$

(b) $(2x - 1) - (3x + 2)$

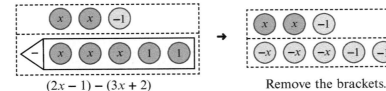

| $(2x - 1) - (3x + 2)$ | Remove the brackets. |

$\therefore (2x - 1) - (3x + 2) = 2x - 1 - 3x - 2$

$\qquad\qquad\qquad\qquad\quad = -x - 3$

(c) $(-2x + 3y) - (x - 2y)$

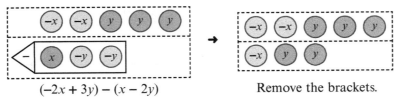

| $(-2x + 3y) - (x - 2y)$ | Remove the brackets. |

$\therefore (-2x + 3y) - (x - 2y) = -2x + 3y - x + 2y$

$\qquad\qquad\qquad\qquad\qquad = -3x + 5y$

(d) $(-3x - y + 4) - (-2x + y - 1)$

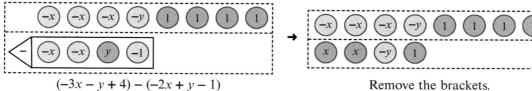

$(-3x - y + 4) - (-2x + y - 1)$ Remove the brackets.

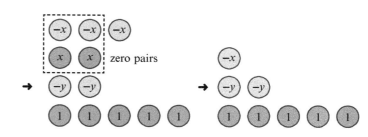

$\therefore\ (-3x - y + 4) - (-2x + y - 1) = -3x - y + 4 + 2x - y + 1$
$$= -x - 2y + 5$$

Class Activity 4

Objective: To rewrite expressions with brackets as expressions without brackets.

1. $2(3x)$ can be considered as 2 groups of $3x$.

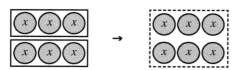

You can ungroup all of the groups to get $6x$. That is,

$2(3x) = 2$ groups of $3x$
$\qquad = 2 \times 3x$
$\qquad = 6x$

$2(-3x)$ can be considered as 2 groups of $-3x$.

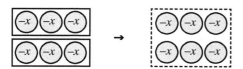

Ungrouping all of the groups, you get $-6x$. That is

$2(-3x) = 2$ groups of $-3x$
$\qquad = 2 \times (-3x)$
$\qquad = -6x$

$-2(3x)$ can be considered as the negative of 2 groups of $3x$.

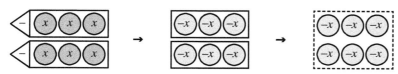

$-2(3x) =$ negative of 2 groups of $3x$
$\qquad =$ two groups of $-3x$ **Flipping the discs.**
$\qquad = 2 \times (-3x)$
$\qquad = -6x$

−2(−3x) can be considered as the negative of 2 groups of −3x.

 → →

−2(−3x) = negative of 2 groups of −3x
     = 2 groups of 3x   **Flipping the discs.**
     = 2 × 3x
     = 6x

Expand the brackets in these expressions using algebra discs to help you.

(a)   3(2x)

 →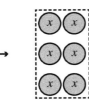

3(2x) can be considered as 3 groups of 2x.
You can ungroup all of the groups to get 6x. That is,
3(2x) = 3 groups of 2x
     = 3 × 2x
     = 6x

(b)   3(−2x)

 →

3(−2x) can be considered as 3 groups of −2x.
3(−2x) = 3 groups of −2x
     = 3 × (−2x)
     = −6x

(c)   −4(5x)

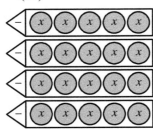 → 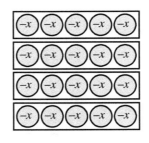 →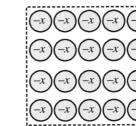

−4(5x) can be considered as the negative of 4 groups of 5x.
−4(5x) = negative of 4 groups of 5x
     = 4 groups of −5x
     = 4 × (−5x)
     = −20x

(d) $-4(-5x)$

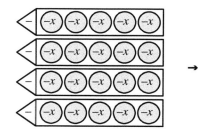 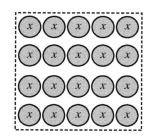

$-4(-5x)$ can be considered as the negative of 4 groups of $-5x$.

$-4(-5x)$ = negative of 4 groups of $-5x$

 = 4 groups of $5x$

 = $4 \times 5x$

 = $20x$

2. The brackets in $2(3x + 2)$ and $-3(x - 3y)$ can be expanded in a similar way.

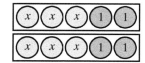 →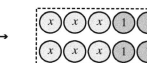

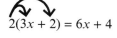

$2(3x + 2)$ = 2 groups of $(3x + 2)$ $\qquad$ $2(3x + 2) = 6x + 4$

 = $6x + 4$ $\qquad$ **Ungrouping.**

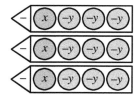 → 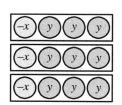 →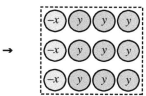

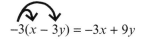

$-3(x - 3y)$ = 3 groups of the negative of $(x - 3y)$ $\qquad$ $-3(x - 3y) = -3x + 9y$

 = 3 groups of $(-x + 3y)$

 = $-3x + 9y$

Remove the brackets in these expressions using algebra discs.

(a) $3(x + 2)$

 →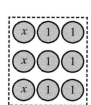

$3(x + 2)$ = 3 groups of $(x + 2)$

 = $3x + 6$

131

(b) $4(2x - 1)$

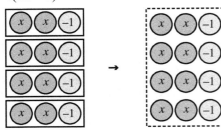

$4(2x - 1) = 4$ groups of $(2x - 1)$
$= 8x - 4$

(c) $-2(3x + y)$

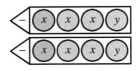 → 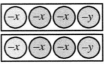 →

$-2(3x + y) = 2$ groups of the negative of $(3x + y)$
$= 2$ groups of $(-3x - y)$
$= -6x - 2y$

(d) $-5(x - 2y)$

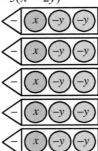 → 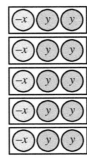 →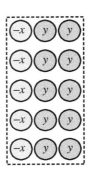

$-5(x - 2y) = 5$ groups of the negative of $(x - 2y)$
$= 5$ groups of $(-x + 2y)$
$= -5x + 10y$

3. Rewrite $a(bx)$, where a and b are numbers, without brackets.

$a(bx)$ can be considered as a groups of bx
$a(bx) = a \times (bx)$
$= abx$

4. Rewrite $a(x + y)$ and $a(x - y)$, where a is a number, without brackets.

$a(x + y) = a$ groups of $(x + y)$
$= a$ groups of x and a groups of y
$= ax + ay$

$a(x - y) = a$ groups of $(x - y)$
$= a$ groups of x and a groups of $(-y)$
$= ax - ay$

Try It!

Section 3.1

1. Paul's pocket money is £8 less than Lucy's pocket money. Find Paul's pocket money if Lucy's is
   (a) £20,   (b) £p.

   Solution
   Paul's pocket money = Lucy's − £8

   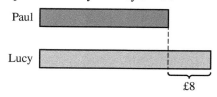

   (a) When Lucy's pocket money is £20,

   $$\text{Paul's} = £20 - £8$$
   $$= £12$$

   (b) When Lucy's pocket money is £p,
   Paul's = £(p − 8)

2. The time Henry takes to complete a quiz is twice the time Rose takes. Find the time Henry takes to complete the quiz if the time Rose takes is
   (a) 20 minutes,   (b) t minutes.

   Solution
   Time Henry takes = twice the time Rose takes

   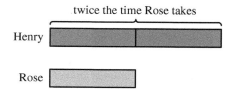

   (a) If Rose takes 20 minutes, the time Henry takes
   $$= 2 \times 20$$
   $$= 40 \text{ minutes}$$

   (b) If Rose takes t minutes, the time Henry takes
   $$= 2 \times t$$
   $$= 2t \text{ minutes}$$

3. Erica takes half the time that Harry takes to finish a mathematics assignment. Find the time Erica takes if Harry takes
   (a) 50 minutes,   (b) T hours.

   Solution
   Time Erica takes = $\frac{1}{2}$ × time Harry takes

   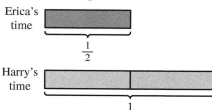

   (a) If Harry takes 50 minutes, the time Erica takes
   $$= \frac{1}{2} \times 50$$
   $$= 25 \text{ minutes}$$

   (b) If Harry takes T hours, the time Erica takes
   $$= \frac{1}{2} \times T$$
   $$= \frac{T}{2} \text{ hours}$$

4. The price for a chocolate bar is £1 and the price for a pizza is £5. Find the total price for
   (a) three chocolate bars and two pizzas,
   (b) m chocolate bars and n pizzas in terms of m and n.

   Solution
   (a) Price of three chocolate bars
   $$= £1 \times 3$$
   $$= £3$$
   Price of two pizzas
   $$= £5 \times 2$$
   $$= £10$$
   ∴ total price = £3 + £10
   $$= £13$$

   (b) Price of m chocolate bars
   $$= £1 \times m$$
   $$= £m$$
   Price of n pizzas
   $$= £5 \times n$$
   $$= £5n$$
   ∴ total price = £m + £5n
   $$= £(m + 5n)$$

5. Write these statements as algebraic expressions.
   (a) Add y to 3x.
   (b) Subtract 7p from 3q.
   (c) Multiply 4m and n.
   (d) Divide (4a + 3b) by 9.

   Solution
   (a) $3x + y$

   (b) $3q - 7p$

   (c) $4m \times n = 4mn$

   (d) $(4a + 3b) \div 9$
   $$= \frac{4a + 3b}{9}$$

6. Simplify these expressions.
   (a) $c \times 3 \times d \times 2$
   (b) $h \times 7 \times h$
   (c) $r \times r \times 5 \times r$

Solution

(a) $c \times 3 \times d \times 2$
$= 3 \times 2 \times c \times d$
$= 6 \times cd$
$= 6cd$

(b) $h \times 7 \times h$
$= 7 \times h \times h$
$= 7 \times h^2$
$= 7h^2$

(c) $r \times r \times 5 \times r$
$= 5 \times r \times r \times r$
$= 5 \times r^3$
$= 5r^3$

7. Determine whether $5y^2$ and $(5y)^2$ are equal.

Solution

$5y^2 = 5 \times y \times y$
$(5y)^2 = 5y \times 5y$
$= 5 \times y \times 5 \times y$
$= 5 \times 5 \times y \times y$
$= 25y^2$
$\therefore 5y^2 \neq (5y)^2$

Section 3.2

8. When $p = 6$, find the value of
   (a) $5p$,
   (b) $20 - 3p$.

Solution

(a) $5p = 5 \times 6$
$= 30$

(b) $20 - 3p = 20 - 3 \times 6$
$= 20 - 18$
$= 2$

9. The height of a candle is $(21 - 4t)$ cm after burning for t hours. Find the height of the candle after burning for three hours.

Solution

Height $= (21 - 4t)$ cm
When $t = 3$,
height $= 21 - 4 \times 3$
$= 9$ cm

10. When $m = 3$ and $n = -2$, work out the values of these expressions.
    (a) $12mn$
    (b) $7m - 2n$

Solution

(a) $12mn = 12 \times 3 \times (-2)$
$= -72$

(b) $7m - 2n = 7 \times 3 - 2 \times (-2)$
$= 21 + 4$
$= 25$

11. The total length of x red rods and y blue rods in a model kit is $(8x + 15y)$ cm. Find the total length of six red rods and three blue rods.

Solution

Total length $= (8x + 15y)$ cm
When $x = 6$ and $y = 3$,
total length $= 8 \times 6 + 15 \times 3$
$= 48 + 45$
$= 93$ cm

12. Given the formula $S = 8 + 3p$, find the value of S when
    (a) $p = 9$,
    (b) $p = -4$.

Solution

(a) $S = 8 + 3p$
When $p = 9$,
$S = 8 + 3 \times 9$
$= 8 + 27$
$= 35$

(b) When $p = -4$,
$S = 8 + 3 \times (-4)$
$= 8 - 12$
$= -4$

13. Given the formula $w = 8 + 3n^4$, find the value of w when $n = 2$.

Solution

$w = 8 + 3n^4$
When $n = 2$,
$w = 8 + 3 \times 2^4$
$= 8 + 3 \times 16$
$= 8 + 48$
$= 56$

14. For a rectangle of length L cm and width W cm, its area A cm^2 is given by the formula $A = LW$. Using the formula, find the area of a rectangle of length 9 cm and width 5 cm.

Solution

$A = LW$
When $L = 9$ and $W = 5$,
$A = 9 \times 5$
$= 45$
The required area is 45 cm^2.

Section 3.3

15. In a shot-put event, Ada's putting distance was 3 metres longer than Janet's.
    (a) Let x metres be Janet's putting distance. Express Ada's putting distance in terms of x.
    (b) Let y metres be Ada's putting distance. Write a formula connecting x and y.

Solution

(a) Ada's putting distance = 3 + Janet's putting distance
$= (3 + x)$ metres

(b) Formula connecting x and y is
$y = 3 + x$

16. The capacity of a cup is one-fifth the capacity of a bowl.
  (a) Let b ml be the capacity of the bowl. Express the capacity of the cup in terms of b.
  (b) Let c ml be the capacity of the cup. Write a formula connecting b and c.

Solution
(a) Capacity of a cup $= \dfrac{1}{5} \times$ capacity of a bowl

$$= \dfrac{1}{5} \times b$$

$$= \dfrac{b}{5} \text{ ml}$$

(b) The formula is

$$c = \dfrac{b}{5}$$

17. There are p bicycles and q tricycles in a shop. Let W be the total number of their wheels.
  (a) Write a formula connecting p, q and W.
  (b) If there are five bicycles and seven tricycles, find the total number of wheels.

Solution
(a) Each bicycle has 2 wheels.
      Number of wheels on p bicycles $= 2p$
      Each tricycle has 3 wheels.
      Number of wheels on q tricycles $= 3q$
      Total number of wheels, $W = 2p + 3q$

(b) When $p = 5$ and $q = 7$,
$$W = 2 \times 5 + 3 \times 7$$
$$= 10 + 21$$
$$= 31$$
The total number of wheels is 31.

Section 3.4

18. Given the expression $-9mn + n - 6$, state
  (a) the numbers of terms in the expression,
  (b) the coefficient of n,
  (c) the coefficient of mn,
  (d) the constant term.

Solution
Expression: $-9mn + n - 6$.
(a) There are 3 terms in the expression: $-9mn$, n and -6.

(b) The coefficient of n is 1.

(c) The coefficient of mn is -9.

(d) The constant term is -6.

19. Simplify these expressions.
  (a) $5t + 6t - 7t$ **(b)** $-4z - 3z + 5z$

Solution
(a) $5t + 6t - 7t = 11t - 7t$
$$= 4t$$

(b) $-4z - 3z + 5z = -7z + 5z$
$$= -2z$$

20. Simplify these expressions.
  (a) $5c - 4d - 3c - d$
  (b) $2t - 7x + 3 + t - 2x - 1$

Solution
(a) $5c - 4d - 3c - d$
$$= 5c - 3c - 4d - d$$
$$= (5 - 3)c + (-4 - 1)d$$
$$= 2c - 5d$$

(b) $2t - 7x + 3 + t - 2x - 1$
$$= 2t + t - 7x - 2x + 3 - 1$$
$$= (2 + 1)t + (-7 - 2)x + (3 - 1)$$
$$= 3t - 9x + 2$$

21. The total value of four stacks of coins is £$(10m + 4n + 7m + 5n)$.

  (a) Simplify the expression $10m + 4n + 7m + 5n$.
  (b) Find the total value if $m = 1$ and $n = 2$.

Solution
(a) $10m + 4n + 7m + 5n$
$$= 10m + 7m + 4n + 5n$$
$$= 17m + 9n$$

(b) When $m = 1$ and $n = 2$, total value
$$= £[17(1) + 9(2)]$$
$$= £35$$

Section 3.5

22. Simplify $(4a + b) + (3a - 6b)$.

Solution
$(4a + b) + (3a - 6b)$
$$= 4a + b + 3a - 6b$$
$$= 4a + 3a + b - 6b$$
$$= 7a - 5b$$

23. Find the sum of $5p - 4q + 7$ and $-3p - q + 2$.

Solution
$(5p - 4q + 7) + (-3p - q + 2)$
$$= 5p - 4q + 7 - 3p - q + 2$$
$$= 5p - 3p - 4q - q + 7 + 2$$
$$= 2p - 5q + 9$$

24. Simplify $(7y - 2) - (4y - 9)$.

Solution
$(7y - 2) - (4y - 9)$
$= 7y - 2 - 4y + 9$
$= 7y - 4y - 2 + 9$
$= 3y + 7$

25. There are two consecutive even integers. If the smaller integer is $2n$, find the sum of the two integers in terms of n.

Solution
Since the smaller integer $= 2n$,
    the larger integer $= 2n + 2$
Their sum $= 2n + (2n + 2)$
          $= 2n + 2n + 2$
          $= 4n + 2$

26. A lift goes up $(7x + 3)$ metres, then goes down $(4x - 6)$ metres, and finally goes up $(2x - 1)$ metres. How high is the lift above its starting point?

Solution
Height of the lift above its starting point
$= (7x + 3) - (4x - 6) + (2x - 1)$
$= 7x + 3 - 4x + 6 + 2x - 1$
$= 7x - 4x + 2x + 3 + 6 - 1$
$= (5x + 8)$ metres

27. Expand these expressions.

(a) $2(8p)$ **(b)** $-6(5q)$

Solution
(a) $2(8p) = 2 \times 8p$
            $= 16p$

(b) $-6(5q) = -6 \times 5q$
              $= -30q$

28. Expand these expressions.

(a) $4(3b + 8)$ **(b)** $-5(2 - n)$

Solution
(a) $4(3b + 8) = 4 \times 3b + 4 \times 8$
                  $= 12b + 32$

(b) $-5(2 - n) = -5 \times 2 - 5 \times (-n)$
                  $= -10 + 5n$

Exercise 3.1
Level 1

GCSE Grade **2⁻/ 2**

1. Frankie is 13 years old. Find her age after
(a) 4 years,   **(b)** t years.

Solution
(a) Frankie's age after 4 years $= 13 + 4 = 17$ years

(b) Frankie's age after t years $= (13 + t)$ years

2. Anna is 6 cm shorter than Fred. Find Anna's height if Fred's height is
(a) 163 cm,   **(b)** H cm.

Solution
Anna's height = Fred's height − 6 cm

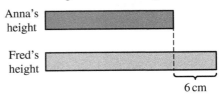

(a) If Fred's height is 163 cm,
Anna's height $= 163 - 6$
              $= 157$ cm

(b) If Fred's height is H cm,
Anna's height is $(H - 6)$ cm

3. The capacity of a small bottle is one-third that of a large bottle. Find the capacity of the small bottle if the capacity of the large bottle is
(a) 600 ml,   **(b)** p ml.

Solution
Capacity of a small bottle $= \frac{1}{3} \times$ capacity of a large bottle

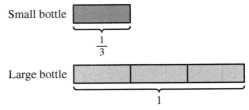

(a) Capacity of the small bottle $= \frac{1}{3} \times 600$
                                    $= 200$ ml

(b) Capacity of the small bottle $= \frac{1}{3} \times p$
                                    $= \frac{p}{3}$ ml

4. Some students share 360 jelly beans equally. Find the number of jelly beans each student gets if there are
(a) nine students,   **(b)** m students.

Solution
(a) Share of each student $= 360 \div 9$
                              $= 40$ jelly beans
(b) Share of each student $= 360 \div m$
                              $= \frac{360}{m}$ jelly beans

5. Find the number of wheels in
    (a) eight tricycles,
    (b) N tricycles.

Solution
    (a) Number of wheels in 8 tricycles $= 3 \times 8$
                                          $= 24$

    (b) Number of wheels in N tricycles $= 3 \times N$
                                            $= 3N$

6. Simplify these expressions.
    (a) $a \times 3$ **(b)** $b \times 4 \times c$
    (c) $d \times d$ **(d)** $h \times 7h$
    (e) $2m \times 6n$ **(f)** $3p \div 5q$

Solution
    (a) $a \times 3 = 3a$

    (b) $b \times 4 \times c = 4bc$

    (c) $d \times d = d^2$

    (d) $h \times 7h = 7h^2$

    (e) $2m \times 6n = 12mn$

    (f) $3p \div 5q = \dfrac{3p}{5q}$

7. Write these statements as algebraic expressions.
    (a) Add 5 to $3a$.
    (b) Take away $4c$ from 15.
    (c) The product of $2d$ and $3d$.
    (d) Divide m by $12n$.
    (e) Subtract 13 from the cube of r.
    (f) The sum of a to the power of 4 and $4b$.

Solution
    (a) Expression: $3a + 5$

    (b) Expression: $15 - 4c$

    (c) Expression: $2d \times 3d = 6d^2$

    (d) Expression: $m \div 12n = \dfrac{m}{12n}$

    (e) Expression: $r^3 - 13$

    (f) Expression: $a^4 + 4b$

Level 2   **GCSE Grade** $\boxed{2^+}$

8. Simplify these expressions.
    (a) $r \times 4r \times r$ **(b)** $2s \times 3t \times s$
    (c) $4u \div v \times u$ **(d)** $3x \times 8y \div 9$

Solution
    (a) $r \times 4r \times r = 4r^3$

    (b) $2s \times 3t \times s = 6s^2t$

    (c) $4u \div v \times u = \dfrac{4u}{v} \times u$
                                $= \dfrac{4u^2}{v}$

    (d) $3x \times 8y \div 9 = 3x \times \dfrac{8y}{9}$
                                  $= \dfrac{24xy}{9}$

9. 400 gram tins of baked beans are placed in a box of mass 250 grams. Find the total mass of the box which contains
    (a) five tins of baked beans,
    (b) n tins of baked beans in terms of n.

Solution
    (a) Mass of 5 tins of baked beans $= 400 \times 5$
                                          $= 2000\,\text{g}$
        Total mass of the box with 5 tins of baked beans $= 2000 + 250$
                                       $= 2250\,\text{grams}$

    (b) Mass of n tins of baked beans $= 400 \times n$
                                          $= 400n\,\text{grams}$
        Total mass of the box with n tins of baked beans $= (400n + 250)\,\text{grams}$

10. The price of a calculator is £10 and the price of a pen is £2. Find the total price of
    (a) three calculators and four pens,
    (b) p calculators and q pens in terms of p and q.

Solution
    (a) Total price $= £(10 \times 3 + 2 \times 4)$
                               $= £38$

    (b) Total price $= £(10 \times p + 2 \times q)$
                               $= £(10p + 2q)$

11. A rod of length 120 cm is cut into three pieces, A, B and C.
    (a) If the length of A is 47 cm and the length of B is 52 cm, find the length of C.
    (b) If the length of A is x cm and the length of B is y cm, find the length of C in terms of x and y.
    Hint: You may draw a bar model to help.

Solution
    (a) Length of C $=$ length of rod $-$ length of A $-$ length of B
                                $= 120 - 47 - 52$
                                $= 21\,\text{cm}$

    (b) Length of C $= (120 - x - y)\,\text{cm}$

12. Find an expression for the total value of
    (a) six £1 coins and m £2 coins,
    (b) h £1 coins and k £2 coins.

Solution
    (a) Total value $= £(1 \times 6 + 2 \times m)$
                                $= £(6 + 2m)$

    (b) Total value $= £(1 \times h + 2 \times k)$
                                $= £(h + 2k)$

13. A history book is 2 cm thick and a science book is 3 cm thick. If m history books and n science books are placed in a stack, find, in terms of m and n,
(a) the number of books in the stack,
(b) the height of the stack.

Solution
(a) Number of books $= m + n$

(b) Height of the stack $= 2 \times m + 3 \times n$
$= (2m + 3n)\,\text{cm}$

14. There is one £5 note, x £10 notes and y £50 notes in a wallet. Express, in terms of x and y,
(a) the number of bank notes in the wallet,
(b) the total value of the bank notes in the wallet.

Solution
(a) Number of bank notes $= 1 + x + y$

(b) Total value of the bank notes
$= £(5 \times 1 + 10 \times x + 50 \times y)$
$= £(5 + 10x + 50y)$

15. A boy is N years old. His father is four times as old as him. His mother is three years younger than his father. Express, in terms of N, the age of
(a) his father,
(b) his mother.
Hint: You may draw a bar model to help.

Solution
(a) Age of father $= 4 \times N = 4N$ years

(b) Age of mother $= (4N - 3)$ years

16. Alice got m marks in a test. Bob's score was 15 more than Alice's score. Carol's score was half of Bob's score. Express, in terms of m,
(a) Bob's score,
(b) Carol's score.

Solution
(a) Bob's score $= m + 15$

(b) Carol's score $= \dfrac{m+15}{2}$

17. Describe a real-life situation that could be represented by the expression $2x + 3y$.

Solution
For example, the total amount of money raised at a bake sale if x number of cookies are sold for £2 each and y number of cakes at £3 each.

Exercise 3.2

1. Find the value of $2x + 1$ when
(a) $x = 7$,
(b) $x = -1$.

Solution
(a) When $x = 7$,
$2x + 1 = 2(7) + 1$
$= 14 + 1$
$= 15$

(b) When $x = -1$,
$2x + 1 = 2(-1) + 1$
$= -2 + 1$
$= -1$

2. Find the value of $9 - y$ when
(a) $y = 5$,
(b) $y = -4$.

Solution
(a) When $y = 5$,
$9 - y = 9 - 5$
$= 4$

(b) When $y = -4$,
$9 - y = 9 - (-4)$
$= 9 + 4$
$= 13$

3. Find the value of $\dfrac{z}{6}$ when
(a) $z = 2$,
(b) $z = -18$.

Solution
(a) When $z = 2$,
$\dfrac{z}{6} = \dfrac{2}{6}$
$= \dfrac{1}{3}$

(b) When $z = -18$,
$\dfrac{z}{6} = \dfrac{-18}{6}$
$= -3$

4. Find the value of $3b + c$ when
(a) $b = 2$ and $c = 5$,
(b) $b = -1$ and $c = -4$.

Solution
(a) When $b = 2$ and $c = 5$,
$3b + c = 3(2) + 5$
$= 6 + 5$
$= 11$

(b) When $b = -1$ and $c = -4$,
$3b + c = 3(-1) + (-4)$
$= -3 - 4$
$= -7$

5. Find the value of $8 - 2h + 3k$ when
(a) $h = 7$ and $k = 5$,
(b) $h = -2$ and $k = 4$.

Solution

(a) When $h = 7$ and $k = 5$,
$$8 - 2h + 3k = 8 - 2(7) + 3(5)$$
$$= 8 - 14 + 15$$
$$= 9$$

(b) When $h = -2$ and $k = 4$,
$$8 - 2h + 3k = 8 - 2(-2) + 3(4)$$
$$= 8 + 4 + 12$$
$$= 24$$

6. Given that $y = 1 - 3x$, find the value of y when
(a) $x = 4$, **(b)** $x = 0$.

Solution

(a) $y = 1 - 3x$
When $x = 4$,
$$y = 1 - 3(4)$$
$$= 1 - 12$$
$$= -11$$

(b) When $x = 0$,
$$y = 1 - 3(0)$$
$$= 1 - 0$$
$$= 1$$

7. Given that $s = \frac{3t}{4}$, find the value of s when
(a) $t = 24$, **(b)** $t = -8$.

Solution

(a) $s = \frac{3t}{4}$
When $t = 24$,
$$s = \frac{3(24)}{4}$$
$$= \frac{72}{4}$$
$$= 18$$

(b) When $t = -8$,
$$s = \frac{3(-8)}{4}$$
$$= \frac{-24}{4}$$
$$= -6$$

8. Given that $w = 2u - 3v - 7$, find the value of w when
(a) $u = 5$ and $v = 4$,
(b) $u = -4$ and $v = -1$.

Solution

(a) $w = 2u - 3v - 7$
When $u = 5$ and $v = 4$,
$$w = 2(5) - 3(4) - 7$$
$$= 10 - 12 - 7$$
$$= -2 - 7$$
$$= -9$$

(b) When $u = -4$ and $v = -1$,
$$w = 2(-4) - 3(-1) - 7$$
$$= -8 + 3 - 7$$
$$= -5 - 7$$
$$= -12$$

9. Given that $A = bh$, find the value of A when
(a) $b = 4$ and $h = 3$,
(b) $b = 7$ and $h = -8$.

Solution

(a) $A = bh$
When $b = 4$ and $h = 3$,
$$A = 4 \times 3$$
$$= 12$$

(b) When $b = 7$ and $h = -8$,
$$A = 7 \times (-8)$$
$$= -56$$

Level 2 | **GCSE Grade** 3^- / 3

10. Find the value of $3x - 24$ when
(a) $x = 0$, **(b)** $x = -2$.

Solution

(a) When $x = 0$,
$$3x - 24 = 3(0) - 24$$
$$= 0 - 24$$
$$= -24$$

(b) When $x = -2$,
$$3x - 24 = 3(-2) - 24$$
$$= -6 - 24$$
$$= -30$$

11. Given the formula $m = \frac{a + b}{2}$, find the value of m when
(a) $a = 4$ and $b = 18$, **(b)** $a = -3$ and $b = 7$.

Solution

(a) $m = \frac{a + b}{2}$
When $a = 4$ and $b = 18$,
$$m = \frac{4 + 18}{2}$$
$$= \frac{22}{2}$$
$$= 11$$

(b) When $a = -3$ and $b = 7$,
$$m = \frac{-3 + 7}{2}$$
$$= \frac{4}{2}$$
$$= 2$$

12. Given the formula $y = 1 - 2x^2$, find the value of y when
(a) $x = 0$, **(b)** $x = 3$.

Solution

(a) $y = 1 - 2x^2$
When $x = 0$,
$$y = 1 - 2(0)^2$$
$$= 1 - 2 \times 0$$
$$= 1$$

(b) When $x = 3$,
$$y = 1 - 2(3)^2$$
$$= 1 - 2 \times 9$$
$$= 1 - 18$$
$$= -17$$

13. Given the formula $P = 30 \times (1 + rt)$, find the value of P when
    (a) $r = 2$ and $t = 1$,   (b) $r = -3$ and $t = -4$.

    Solution
    (a) $P = 30 \times (1 + rt)$
        When $r = 2$ and $t = 1$,
        $P = 30 \times (1 + 2 \times 1)$
        $= 30 \times (1 + 2)$
        $= 30 \times 3$
        $= 90$

    (b) When $r = -3$ and $t = -4$,
        $P = 30 \times [1 + (-3)(-4)]$
        $= 30 \times [1 + 12]$
        $= 30 \times 13$
        $= 390$

14. Given the formula $S = 6 + n^3$, find the value of S when $n = 5$.

    Solution
    $S = 6 + n^3$
    When $n = 5$,
    $S = 6 + 5^3$
    $= 6 + 125$
    $= 131$

15. Given the formula $T = \frac{3q^4}{4}$, find the value of T when $q = 2$.

    Solution

    $T = \frac{3q^4}{4}$
    When $q = 2$,

    $T = \frac{3 \times 2^4}{4}$

    $= \frac{3 \times 16}{4}$

    $= \frac{48}{4}$

    $= 12$

Level 3   GCSE Grade 3 / 3+

16. Erica is a part-time clerk. Her weekly wage is £14h, where h is the number of hours she works in a week.
    (a) If Erica works 30 hours in a week, find her weekly wage.
    (b) What do you think the number 14 in the expression 14h stands for?

Solution
(a) When $t = 30$,
    Erica's weekly wage = £(14×30)
    $= £420$

(b) The number 14 stands for the hourly wage in £.

17. The total price for m burgers and n cups of coffee is £$(3m + 2n)$.
    (a) Find the total price for five burgers and four cups of coffee.
    (b) What do you think the numbers 3 and 2 in the expression $3m + 2n$ stand for?

Solution
(a) When $m = 5$ and $n = 4$,
    the total price = £$(3 \times 5 + 2 \times 4)$
    $= £23$

(b) In the expression $3m + 2n$, the number 3 is the price of a burger and 2 is the price of a cup of coffee in £.

18. The conversion of $x\,°C$ (Celsius) to $y\,°F$ (Fahrenheit) is given by the formula $y = \frac{9}{5}x + 32$.
    (a) The freezing point of water is $0\,°C$. Work out the freezing point in Fahrenheit.
    (b) The boiling point of water is $100\,°C$. Work out the boiling point in Fahrenheit.

Solution
(a) $y = \frac{9}{5}x + 32$
    When $x = 0$,
    $y = \frac{9}{5}(0) + 32$
    $= 32$
    The freezing point of water is $32\,°F$.

(b) When $x = 100$,
    $y = \frac{9}{5}(100) + 32$
    $= 212$
    The boiling point of water is $212\,°F$.

19. The cost, £C, of making a square glass frame of side length $x\,$m is given by the formula
    $$C = 12x + 30x^2.$$
    How much more is the cost of making a square glass frame of side length $3\,$m than that of side length $2\,$m?

Solution
$C = 12x + 30x^2$
When $x = 3$,
$C = 12 \times 3 + 30 \times 3^2$
$= 36 + 30 \times 9$
$= 306$

When $x = 2$,
$C = 12 \times 2 + 30 \times 2^2$
$\quad = 24 + 30 \times 4$
$\quad = 144$
$\therefore$ extra cost of making a frame of side length $3\,\mathrm{m}$ rather than $2\,\mathrm{m}$
$\quad = £\,(306 - 144)$
$\quad = £162$

20. The mass, M grams, of a glass cube of side length x cm is given by the formula $M = \dfrac{5x^3}{2}$. The mass, N grams, of an iron pyrite cube of side length y cm is given by the formula $N = 5y^3$. Find the total mass of two glass cubes of side length 4 cm and seven iron pyrite cubes of side length 2 cm.

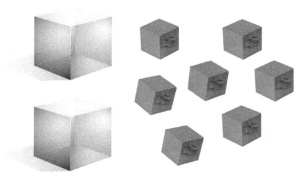

Solution

$M = \dfrac{5x^3}{2}$ and $N = 5y^3$
Total mass $= 2M + 7N$
When $x = 4$ and $y = 2$,

total mass $= 2 \times \dfrac{5 \times 4^3}{2} + 7 \times (5 \times 2^3)$

$\quad = 2 \times \dfrac{5 \times 64}{2} + 7 \times 5 \times 8$

$\quad = 320 + 280$

$\quad = 600$

Total mass of the 2 glass cubes and 7 iron cubes is 600 g.

21. Create a formula connecting x and y such that $y = 5$ when $x = 3$.

Solution
For example,
$y = x + 2$
$y = x^2 - 4$
$y = \dfrac{30}{x} - 5$

22. Create a formula connecting s and t such that
(a) $s = 64$ when $t = 2$,
(b) $s = 61$ when $t = 2$.
Hint: You may use indices.

Solution
(a) For example, $s = 8^t$.

(b) For example, $s = 8^t - 3$.

Exercise 3.3

Level 1 GCSE Grade 2⁺

1. The mass of Jim is $p\,\mathrm{kg}$ and the mass of Lily is $q\,\mathrm{kg}$.
(a) Express x in the bar model in terms of p and q.
(b) What does x represent?

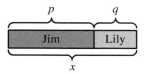

Solution
(a) $x = p + q$

(b) x represents the combined masses of Jim and Lily.

2. Tom's long jump distance is x metres. Shaun's long jump distance is y metres.
(a) Express z in the bar model in terms of x and y.
(b) What does z represent?

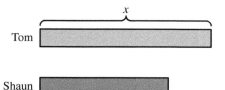

Solution
(a) $z = x - y$

(b) z represents how much further Tom's long jump distance is than Shaun's.

3. Richard is m years old and Susan is n years old. The bar model represents their ages.
(a) Express n in terms of m.
(b) What can you say about the relationship between their ages?

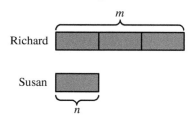

Solution

(a) $n = \dfrac{m}{3}$

(b) Susan's age is one third of Richard's age, or Richard is three times as old as Susan.

4. Tom's age is four times the age of his son. If the age of his son is x years, express Tom's age in terms of x.

Solution

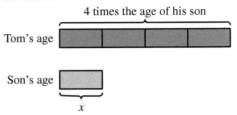

4 times the age of his son

Tom's age

Son's age

x

Hence, Tom's age is $4x$ years.

5. Mandy spends one-quarter of her weekly salary on a pair of sports shoes. If her weekly salary is £w, express the price of the pair of sports shoes in terms of w.

Solution

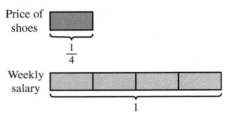

Price of shoes

$\dfrac{1}{4}$

Weekly salary

1

If the weekly salary is £w, the price of the sports shoes is $£\left(\dfrac{1}{4}w\right) = £\left(\dfrac{w}{4}\right)$.

Level 2   GCSE Grade **3⁻**

6. The initial temperature of a cup of water is $x\,°C$. The temperature drops $23\,°C$ after an hour and reaches $y\,°C$. Write down a formula connecting x and y.

Solution

The formula is $y = x - 23$.

7. The thickness of a dictionary is twice the thickness of another book. Let $d\,cm$ and $b\,cm$ be the thicknesses of the dictionary and the book respectively. Express d in terms of b.

Solution

The formula is $d = 2b$.

8. The height of a London Eye souvenir is one-thousandth of the actual height of the London Eye. Let $h\,cm$ and $H\,cm$ be the heights of the souvenir and the London Eye respectively. Express h in terms of H.

Solution

The formula is $h = \dfrac{H}{1000}$ or
$$h = 0.001H$$

9. The length of a folk song is x minutes. The length of a pop song is y minutes. The length of the pop song is half the length of the folk song.
   (a) Express y in terms of x.
   (b) If the length of the folk song is 4 minutes, find the length of the pop song.

Solution

(a) $y = \dfrac{x}{2}$

(b) If $x = 4$, $y = \dfrac{4}{2} = 2$

The length of the pop song is 2 minutes.

10. The area of Paul's flat is $p\,m^2$ and the area of Queenie's flat is $q\,m^2$. Paul's flat is $15\,m^2$ more than Queenie's flat.
    (a) Express p in terms of q.
    (b) If Queenie's flat is $90\,m^2$, find the area of Paul's flat.

Solution

(a) $p = q + 15$

(b) If $q = 90$,
$p = 90 + 15$
$= 105$
The area of Paul's flat is $105\,m^2$.

Level 3   GCSE Grade **3 / 3⁺**

11. Mrs Atkins gives a money box with £9 in it to her son. She asks her son to put £2 into the money box each week.
    (a) Express the amount in the money box after n weeks in terms of n.
    (b) Find the amount in the money box after 10 weeks.

Solution

(a) Amount put into money box after n weeks
$= £(2 \times n)$
$= £(2n)$
Total amount in the money box after n weeks
$= £(9 + 2n)$

(b) When $n = 10$,
$9 + 2n = 9 + 2(10)$
$= 29$
The amount in the money box after 10 weeks is £29.

12. In an exam, Emily's science mark is 17 higher than her mathematics mark. Let x be her mark in mathematics.
    (a) Express Emily's science mark in terms of x.
    (b) Let T be the sum of the science and mathematics marks. Write a formula connecting x and T.
    (c) If Emily gets 63 marks in mathematics, find the sum of the science and mathematics marks.

Solution
    (a) Science mark = $x + 17$
    (b) $T = (x + 17) + x$
        $= 2x + 17$
    (c) When $x = 63$,
        $T = 2 \times 63 + 17$
        $= 126 + 17$
        $= 143$

The sum of Emily's marks is 143.

13. There are two consecutive even numbers. Let n be the smaller number.
    (a) Express the greater number in terms of n.
    (b) Let P be the product of these two numbers. Write a formula connecting n and P.
    (c) Find the product of the two numbers when $n = 6$.
    (d) What are the two original consecutive even numbers in (c)? Check whether their product is equal to the answer you gave to (c).

Solution
    (a) The greater number = $n + 2$
    (b) $P = n \times (n + 2)$
    (c) When $n = 6$,
        $P = 6 \times (6 + 2)$
        $= 6 \times 8$
        $= 48$
    (d) The two consecutive even numbers are n and $(n + 2)$. When $n = 6$, the two numbers are 6 and 8. $6 \times 8 = 48$, which is the same answer as in (c).

14. Frank has two part-time jobs. The weekly salary of the second job is three times the weekly salary of the first job. Let £m be the weekly salary of the first job.
    (a) Express the weekly salary of the second job in terms of m.
    (b) Let £T be the total weekly salary of Frank's part-time jobs. Write a formula connecting m and T.
    (c) If the weekly salary of the first job is £130, find the total weekly salary of Frank's part-time jobs.

Solution
    (a) The weekly salary of the second job = £$(3 \times m)$
        $= £(3m)$
    (b) Total weekly salary = £m + £$(3m)$
        $= £(4m)$
        The formula is $T = 4m$.
    (c) If $m = 130$,
        $T = 4 \times 130$
        $= 520$
        The total weekly salary of Frank's two jobs is £520.

15. Carbon and hydrogen form a compound. The number of hydrogen atoms in the compound is twice the number of carbon atoms.
    (a) If there are n carbon atoms, express, in terms of n,
        (i) the number of hydrogen atoms,
        (ii) the total number of atoms in the compound.
    (b) If the compound has three carbon atoms, find the total number of atoms in the compound.
    Note: Propene, whose molecular formula is C_3H_6, is an example of this type of compound.

Solution
    (a) (i) Number of hydrogen atoms = $2n$
        (ii) Total number of atoms = $n + 2n$
             $= 3n$
    (b) If $n = 3$,
        the total number of atoms = $3 \times 3 = 9$

16. Create a situation that forms a formula connecting variables M, x and y such that $M = 52$ when $x = 4$ and $y = 7$.

Solution
One possible formula connecting M, x and y is $M = 9.5x + 2y$.

The mass of a bag of charcoal is $9.5\,kg$ and the mass of a bag of potatoes is $2\,kg$.
Let $M\,kg$ be the total mass of x bags of charcoal and y bags of potatoes.
Hence, $M = 9.5x + 2y$.
If $x = 4$ and $y = 7$,
$M = 9.5(4) + 2(7)$
    $= 38 + 14$
    $= 52$ (checked)
Hint: First, think of some possible formulae connecting M, x and y such that $M = 52$ when $x = 4$ and $y = 7$. Next, create a situation for the formula you have written.

Exercise 3.4

Level 1   GCSE Grade 2 / 2⁺

1. State the number of terms and the constant term in each of these expressions.
   - (a) $2a - 3b - 1$
   - (b) $7x + 6 - 4y + 5z$

   Solution
   - (a) $2a - 3b - 1$
     There are 3 terms.
     The constant term is -1.

   - (b) $7x + 6 - 4y + 5z$
     There are 4 terms.
     The constant term is 6.

2. Write down the coefficients of x and y in each of these expressions.
   - (a) $3x - 4y + 6$
   - (b) $x^2 - x + y + 8$

   Solution
   - (a) $3x - 4y + 6$
     The coefficient of x is 3.
     The coefficient of y is -4.

   - (b) $x^2 - x + y + 8$
     The coefficient of x is -1.
     The coefficient of y is 1.

3. Simplify these expressions.
   - (a) $7a + 2a$
   - (b) $5b - 8b$
   - (c) $-4x + 6x$
   - (d) $-2y - 3y$
   - (e) $c + c + c$
   - (f) $d + 2d - 9d$
   - (g) $-3p + p + 4p$
   - (h) $4y - 9y + 5y$
   - (i) $-4m - 2m + 5m - m$

   Solution
   - (a) $7a + 2a = 9a$

   - (b) $5b - 8b = -3b$

   - (c) $-4x + 6x = 2x$

   - (d) $-2y - 3y = -5y$

   - (e) $c + c + c = 3c$

   - (f) $d + 2d - 9d = (1 + 2 - 9)d$
     $= -6d$

   - (g) $-3p + p + 4p = (-3 + 1 + 4)p$
     $= 2p$

   - (h) $4y - 9y + 5y = (4 - 9 + 5)y$
     $= 0$

   - (i) $-4m - 2m + 5m - m = (-4 - 2 + 5 - 1)m$
     $= -2m$

Level 2   GCSE Grade 3⁻

4. Simplify these expressions.
   - (a) $3n + 10 - 4n - 11$
   - (b) $-6 + 3k - 4k + 7$
   - (c) $3m + 4n - 2n + 5m$
   - (d) $-7x - 3y - 2x + 3y$
   - (e) $3p - 4q + 6p - q$
   - (f) $7t + 4av - 5t + av$

   Solution
   - (a) $3n + 10 - 4n - 11$
     $= 3n - 4n + 10 - 11$
     $= -n - 1$

   - (b) $-6 + 3k - 4k + 7$
     $= 3k - 4k + 7 - 6$
     $= -k + 1$

   - (c) $3m + 4n - 2n + 5m$
     $= 3m + 5m + 4n - 2n$
     $= 8m + 2n$

   - (d) $-7x - 3y - 2x + 3y$
     $= -7x - 2x - 3y + 3y$
     $= -9x$

   - (e) $3p - 4q + 6p - q$
     $= 3p + 6p - 4q - q$
     $= 9p - 5q$

   - (f) $7t + 4av - 5t + av$
     $= 7t - 5t + 4av + av$
     $= 2t + 5av$

5. (a) Simplify the expression $-4 - 2x + 5 + x$.
   (b) Find the value of the expression when $x = 2$.

   Solution
   - (a) $-4 - 2x + 5 + x = -4 + 5 - 2x + x$
     $= 1 - x$
   - (b) When $x = 2$,
     $-4 - 2x + 5 + x = 1 - x$
     $= 1 - 2$
     $= -1$

6. (a) Simplify the expression $7a - 2b + 5b - a - 3$.
   (b) Find the value of the expression when $a = -1$ and $b = 2$.

   Solution
   - (a) $7a - 2b + 5b - a - 3 = 7a - a - 2b + 5b - 3$
     $= 6a + 3b - 3$

   - (b) When $a = -1$ and $b = 2$,
     $6a + 3b - 3 = 6(-1) + 3(2) - 3$
     $= -6 + 6 - 3$
     $= -3$

7. **(a)** Simplify the expression $3x - 2 - y + 1 - x$.
  (b) Find the value of the expression when $x = -2$ and $y = -6$.

Solution
(a) $3x - 2 - y + 1 - x = 3x - x - y - 2 + 1$
$$= 2x - y - 1$$

(b) When $x = -2$ and $y = -6$,
$2x - y - 1 = 2(-2) - (-6) - 1$
$$= -4 + 6 - 1$$
$$= 1$$

Level 3   **GCSE Grade 3**

8. The total number of atoms in the compound C_nH_{2n+2} is $n + 2n + 2$.
  (a) Simplify $n + 2n + 2$.
  (b) Find the total number of atoms if $n = 10$.

Solution
(a) $n + 2n + 2 = 3n + 2$

(b) When $n = 10$,
$3n + 2 = 3(10) + 2$
$$= 32$$

9. The total price of a student ticket, an ordinary ticket and a VIP ticket for a concert is given by £$(p + 50 + p + 2p - 30)$.
  (a) Simplify $p + 50 + p + 2p - 30$.
  (b) Find the total price if $p = 90$.

Solution
(a) $p + 50 + p + 2p - 30$
$= p + p + 2p + 50 - 30$
$= 4p + 20$

(b) When $p = 90$,
$4p + 20 = 4(90) + 20$
$$= 380$$
The total price is £380.

10. The height of a stack of 10 books is given by $(2x + 3y + 4x + y)$ cm.
  (a) Simplify the expression $2x + 3y + 4x + y$.
  (b) Find the height of the stack if $x = 2$ and $y = 3$.

Solution
(a) $2x + 3y + 4x + y$
$= 2x + 4x + 3y + y$
$= 6x + 4y$

(b) When $x = 2$ and $y = 3$,
$6x + 4y = 6(2) + 4(3)$
$$= 24$$
The height of the stack is 24 cm.

11. The lengths of the sides of a triangle are $2x$ cm, $4y$ cm and $3x$ cm. Express the perimeter of the triangle in terms of x and y.

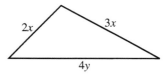

Solution
Perimeter of the triangle $= (2x + 4y + 3x)$
$$= (5x + 4y) \text{ cm}$$

12. A rectangle is $3p$ cm long and $2p$ cm wide.

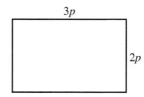

  (a) Express the perimeter of the rectangle in terms of p.
  (b) When $p = 12$, find the perimeter of the rectangle.

Solution
(a) Perimeter of the rectangle $= 2(3p) + 2(2p)$
$$= 10p \text{ cm}$$
(b) When $p = 12$,
perimeter of the rectangle $= 10(12)$
$$= 120 \text{ cm}$$

13. A woman works $2t$ hours each day from Monday to Friday. She works $(2t - y)$ hours on Saturdays. She does not work on Sundays.
  (a) Express her working hours in a week in terms of t and y.
  (b) How many hours does she work each week when $t = 4$ and $y = 3$?

Solution
(a) Working hours in a week $= [2t \times 5 + (2t - y)]$
$$= [10t + 2t - y]$$
$$= [12t - y] \text{ hours}$$

(b) When $t = 4$ and $y = 3$,
working hours in a week $= [12(4) - 3]$
$$= 45 \text{ hours}$$
She works 45 hours each week when $t = 4$ and $y = 3$.

14. Write an algebraic expression that has three terms involving the variables p and q.

Solution
For example,
$10p - q + 25$
$p^2 + 2pq + q^2$.

15. Create a problem with an answer that can be simplified to $7x$.

Solution

For example, a student spends x hours on the internet on Sundays. He spends $(x - 1)$ hours online each day from Monday to Thursday. On Fridays and Saturdays, he spends $(x + 2)$ hours on the internet each day.

The total time spent on the internet in a week by the student is
$x + (x - 1) + (x - 1) + (x - 1) + (x - 1) + (x + 2)$
$+ (x + 2)$
$= 7x - 4 + 4$
$= 7x$

Exercise 3.5

Level 1   GCSE Grade 2⁺

1. Simplify these expressions.
   (a) $-(2x + 1)$
   (b) $-(-3x + 6)$
   (c) $-(4y - 9)$
   (d) $-(-5x + 8y - 7)$

Solution
   (a) $-(2x + 1) = -2x - 1$

   (b) $-(-3x + 6) = 3x - 6$

   (c) $-(4y - 9) = -4y + 9$

   (d) $-(-5x + 8y - 7) = 5x - 8y + 7$

2. Simplify these expressions.
   (a) $(2a + 3) + (a - 4)$
   (b) $(-2b - 5) + (3b - 1)$
   (c) $(-4c + 2d) + (-3c + d)$
   (d) $(8m - 7n) + (-5m - 2n)$

Solution
   (a) $(2a + 3) + (a - 4) = 2a + 3 + a - 4$
                     $= 2a + a + 3 - 4$
                     $= 3a - 1$

   (b) $(-2b - 5) + (3b - 1) = -2b - 5 + 3b - 1$
                         $= -2b + 3b - 5 - 1$
                         $= b - 6$

   (c) $(-4c + 2d) + (-3c + d) = -4c + 2d - 3c + d$
                            $= -4c - 3c + 2d + d$
                            $= -7c + 3d$

   (d) $(8m - 7n) + (-5m - 2n) = 8m - 7n - 5m - 2n$
                            $= 8m - 5m - 7n - 2n$
                            $= 3m - 9n$

3. Simplify these expressions.
   (a) $(6p + 7) - (3p + q)$
   (b) $-4 - (6x - 3)$
   (c) $(-2s - t) - (3s + t)$
   (d) $(-4x + 5y) - (3x - 6y)$

Solution
   (a) $(6p + 7) - (3p + q) = 6p + 7 - 3p - q$
                         $= 6p - 3p - q + 7$
                         $= 3p - q + 7$

   (b) $-4 - (6x - 3) = -4 - 6x + 3$
                     $= -6x - 4 + 3$
                     $= -6x - 1$

   (c) $(-2s - t) - (3s + t) = -2s - t - 3s - t$
                       $= -2s - 3s - t - t$
                       $= -5s - 2t$

   (d) $(-4x + 5y) - (3x - 6y) = -4x + 5y - 3x + 6y$
                            $= -4x - 3x + 5y + 6y$
                            $= -7x + 11y$

Level 2   GCSE Grade 3⁻

4. Simplify these expressions.
   (a) $(2h - 3k + 6) + (8h - 5k - 2)$
   (b) $(-m - 8n + 1) + (-7m + 6n + 3)$
   (c) $(7x + 2y) + (4x - 6) - (-3 + 2y)$
   (d) $(2t - 3z) - (9 - 4z) + (2z + t - 5)$

Solution
   (a) $(2h - 3k + 6) + (8h - 5k - 2)$
        $= 2h - 3k + 6 + 8h - 5k - 2$
        $= 10h - 8k + 4$

   (b) $(-m - 8n + 1) + (-7m + 6n + 3)$
        $= -m - 8n + 1 - 7m + 6n + 3$
        $= -8m - 2n + 4$

   (c) $(7x + 2y) + (4x - 6) - (-3 + 2y)$
        $= 7x + 2y + 4x - 6 + 3 - 2y$
        $= 11x - 3$

   (d) $(2t - 3z) - (9 - 4z) + (2z + t - 5)$
        $= 2t - 3z - 9 + 4z + 2z + t - 5$
        $= 3t + 3z - 14$

5. Add $7x - 2y - 4z$ to $-2x + 3y - 5z$.

Solution
$(-2x + 3y - 5z) + (7x - 2y - 4z)$
$= -2x + 3y - 5z + 7x - 2y - 4z$
$= 5x + y - 9z$

6. Find the sum of $5a - 3b$, $7b - 3c$ and $9c - a$.

Solution
$(5a - 3b) + (7b - 3c) + (9c - a)$
$= 5a - 3b + 7b - 3c + 9c - a$
$= 4a + 4b + 6c$

7. Subtract $a - 4b - 3c$ from $a + 2b - 6c$.

Solution
$(a + 2b - 6c) - (a - 4b - 3c)$
$= a + 2b - 6c - a + 4b + 3c$
$= 6b - 3c$

8. Subtract $t - 3v$ from the sum of $7t - 2u - 3v$ and $3t + 5u - 8v$.

Solution
$(7t - 2u - 3v + 3t + 5u - 8v) - (t - 3v)$
$= 7t - 2u - 3v + 3t + 5u - 8v - t + 3v$
$= 9t + 3u - 8v$

Level 3   GCSE Grade 3

9. There are three consecutive integers. If the smallest one is n, find the sum of these three integers in terms of n.
Hint: For consecutive numbers, the difference between one number and the next number is 1.

Solution
The three integers are n, $n + 1$ and $n + 2$.
Their sum $= n + (n + 1) + (n + 2)$
$\quad\quad\quad\quad = n + n + 1 + n + 2$
$\quad\quad\quad\quad = 3n + 3$

10. The masses of three boxes of chocolates are $(3p + 4q + 2)$ grams, $(4p + 6q + 5)$ grams and $(p + 7q + 9)$ grams.
(a) Find their total mass in terms of p and q.
(b) If $p = 10$ and $q = 30$, find the total mass.

Solution
(a) Total mass
$= (3p + 4q + 2) + (4p + 6q + 5) + (p + 7q + 9)$
$= 3p + 4q + 2 + 4p + 6q + 5 + p + 7q + 9$
$= 3p + 4p + p + 4q + 6q + 7q + 2 + 5 + 9$
$= (8p + 17q + 16)$ grams

(b) When $p = 10$ and $q = 30$,
total mass $= 8p + 17q + 16$
$\quad\quad\quad\quad = 8(10) + 17(30) + 16$
$\quad\quad\quad\quad = 606$ grams

11. The perimeter of a triangle is $(7x - 3y + 6)$ cm. The lengths of two sides of the triangle are $(2x + y - 1)$ cm and $(x - 2y + 10)$ cm.
(a) Find the length of the third side in terms of x and y.
(b) If $x = 5$ and $y = -1$, find the length of the third side.

Solution
(a) Length of the third side
$= (7x - 3y + 6) - (2x + y - 1) - (x - 2y + 10)$
$= 7x - 3y + 6 - 2x - y + 1 - x + 2y - 10$
$= 7x - 2x - x - 3y - y + 2y + 6 + 1 - 10$
$= (4x - 2y - 3)$ cm

(b) When $x = 5$ and $y = -1$,
length of the third side $= 4x - 2y - 3$
$\quad\quad\quad\quad\quad\quad = 4(5) - 2(-1) - 3$
$\quad\quad\quad\quad\quad\quad = 19$ cm

12. Peter's mother is four times as old as Peter. Peter's sister is three years younger than Peter. Let n years be the age of Peter. Express, in terms of n,
(a) the age of Peter's mother,
(b) the age of Peter's sister,
(c) the sum of the ages of Peter, his mother and his sister.

Solution
(a) Age of Peter's mother $= 4n$ years

(b) Age of Peter's sister $= (n - 3)$ years

(c) Sum of the ages $= n + 4n + n - 3$
$\quad\quad\quad\quad\quad\quad = (6n - 3)$ years

13. In an experiment, the original temperature of a beaker of pure water is $(t + 20)\,°C$ under standard pressure. It is heated up by $(3t + 15)\,°C$ and then cools down by $(2t - 10)\,°C$.
(a) Find the final temperature in terms of t.
(b) If $t = 11$, find the final temperature.
(c) Is it possible that $t = 25$? Explain briefly.

Solution
(a) Final temperature
$= (t + 20) + (3t + 15) - (2t - 10)$
$= t + 20 + 3t + 15 - 2t + 10$
$= t + 3t - 2t + 20 + 15 + 10$
$= (2t + 45)\,°C$

(b) When $t = 11$,
final temperature $= 2t + 45$
$\quad\quad\quad\quad\quad\quad = 2(11) + 45$
$\quad\quad\quad\quad\quad\quad = 67\,°C$

(c) When $t = 25$,
initial temperature $= t + 20$
$\quad\quad\quad\quad\quad\quad = 25 + 20$
$\quad\quad\quad\quad\quad\quad = 45\,°C$
rise in temperature $= 3t + 15$
$\quad\quad\quad\quad\quad\quad = 3(25) + 15$
$\quad\quad\quad\quad\quad\quad = 90\,°C$
However $45\,°C + 90\,°C = 135\,°C$, which exceeds the boiling point, $100\,°C$, of pure water.
Hence, it is not possible that $t = 25$.

14.

Sun	Mon	Tue	Wed	Thu	Fri	Sat
		1	2	3	4	5
6	7	8	9	10	11	12
13	14	15	16	17	18	19
20	21	22	23	24	25	26
27	28	29	30	31		

Suppose nine dates in a certain month are enclosed by a rectangle as shown above.
(a) Explain a quick way to calculate the sum of the nine numbers.

(b) Let n be the number at the top left-hand corner of the rectangle. Express the sum of the nine numbers in terms of n.

(c) Let m be the middle number in the rectangle. Express the sum of the nine numbers in terms of m.

(d) If '13' falls on a Friday, on which day will the first of the month be?

(e) Describe some other interesting properties about the numbers within the rectangle.
   Hint: Observe the sum of the three numbers on each diagonal.

Solution

(a) A quick way to calculate the sum of the nine numbers is to
   (i) add the two numbers on the opposite ends of each diagonal, that is $(7 + 23) + (9 + 21)$,
   (ii) add the two numbers on the opposite side of the rectangle, that is $(8 + 22) + (14 + 16)$,
   (iii) add the middle number 15 to **(i)** and **(ii)**.
   Hence the sum $= (7 + 23) + (9 + 21) + (8 + 22) +$
   $$(14 + 16) + 15$$
   $$= 30 + 30 + 30 + 30 + 15$$
   $$= 135$$

(b) If the number at the top left-hand corner of the rectangle is n, you have

n	$n + 1$	$n + 2$
$n + 7$	$n + 8$	$n + 9$
$n + 14$	$n + 15$	$n + 16$

Using the method in **(a)**, the sum of the nine numbers
$$= (n + n + 16) + (n + 2 + n + 14) +$$
$$(n + 1 + n + 15) + (n + 7 + n + 9) + n + 8$$
$$= (2n + 16) + (2n + 16) + (2n + 16) + (2n + 16) +$$
$$n + 8$$
$$= 9n + 72$$

(c) If the middle number in the rectangle is m, you have

$m - 8$	$m - 7$	$m - 6$
$m - 1$	m	$m + 1$
$m + 6$	$m + 7$	$m + 8$

Using the method in **(a)**, the sum of the nine numbers
$$= (m - 8 + m + 8) + (m - 6 + m + 6) + (m - 7 +$$
$$m + 7) + (m - 1 + m + 1) + m$$
$$= 2m + 2m + 2m + 2m + n$$
$$= 9m$$

(d) If '13' falls on a Friday, the first of the month will be on a Sunday.

(e) Some other properties are:
   (i) The sum of the three numbers on each diagonal is the same.
   $$7 + 15 + 23 = 45$$
   $$9 + 15 + 21 = 45$$
   (ii) The sum of the three numbers across the opposite sides of the rectangle is the same.
   $$8 + 15 + 22 = 45$$
   $$14 + 15 + 16 = 45$$

Exercise 3.6

Level 1   GCSE Grade **2⁺**

1. Expand these expressions.
   (a) $4(6a)$ **(b)** $6(4a)$
   (c) $4(-6a)$ **(d)** $-4(-6a)$

   Solution
   (a) $4(6a) = 4 \times 6a$
   $$= 24a$$

   (b) $6(4a) = 6 \times 4a$
   $$= 24a$$

   (c) $4(-6a) = 4 \times (-6)a$
   $$= -24a$$

   (d) $-4(-6a) = -4 \times (-6)a$
   $$= 24a$$

2. Expand these expressions.
   (a) $2(c + 3)$ **(b)** $2(c - 3)$
   (c) $2(-c + 3)$ **(d)** $-2(c + 3)$
   (e) $-2(-c + 3)$ **(f)** $-2(-c - 3)$

   Solution
   (a) $2(c + 3) = 2c + 6$
   (b) $2(c - 3) = 2c - 6$
   (c) $2(-c + 3) = -2c + 6$
   (d) $-2(c + 3) = -2c - 6$
   (e) $-2(-c + 3) = 2c - 6$
   (f) $-2(-c - 3) = 2c + 6$

Level 2   GCSE Grade **3⁻**

3. Remove the brackets in these expressions.
   (a) $4(m + 2)$ **(b)** $5(7p + 1)$
   (c) $3(8 - 9s)$ **(d)** $6(-5u - 7)$

   Solution
   (a) $4(m + 2) = 4m + 8$
   (b) $5(7p + 1) = 35p + 5$
   (c) $3(8 - 9s) = 24 - 27s$
   (d) $6(-5u - 7) = -30u - 42$

4. Expand these expressions.

(a) $-2(4a + 1)$ (b) $-5(1 - 7b)$

(c) $-8(6c - 5)$ (d) $-9(-2 - 3d)$

Solution

(a) $-2(4a + 1) = -8a - 2$

(b) $-5(1 - 7b) = -5 + 35b$

(c) $-8(6c - 5) = -48c + 40$

(d) $-9(-2 - 3d) = 18 + 27d$

Level 3

 GCSE Grade 3 / 3+

5. Find the expression in each rectangle.

(a) $3(\boxed{}) = 12x$ (b) $(5y) = -20y$

(c) $2(\boxed{}) = 10a + 6$ (d) $-7(\boxed{}) = 21c - 28$

Solution

(a) $3(\boxed{}) = 12x$
$$= 3 \times 4x$$
$$\therefore \boxed{} = 4x$$

(b) $\boxed{}(5y) = -20y$
$$= -4 \times 5y$$
$$\therefore \boxed{} = -4$$

(c) $2(\boxed{}) = 10a + 6$
$$= 2 \times 5a + 2 \times 3$$
$$= 2(5a + 3)$$
$$\therefore \boxed{} = 5a + 3$$

(d) $-7(\boxed{}) = 21c - 28$
$$= -7 \times (-3c) - 7 \times 4$$
$$= -7(-3c + 4)$$
$$\therefore \boxed{} = -3c + 4$$

6. Write two expressions using brackets which simplify to give the answer $12x - 3$.

Solution

For example,
$12x - 3 = 3(4x - 1)$
$12x - 3 = 4(4x - 2) - (4x - 5)$

Revision Exercise 3

1. Simplify these expressions.

 GCSE Grade 2+

(a) $2 \times x \times 5$ (b) $2 \times x \times 5 \times y$

(c) $3 + 2 \times x$ (d) $3 + 2 \times x - 4 \times y$

Solution

(a) $2 \times x \times 5$
$$= 2 \times 5 \times x$$
$$= 10x$$

(b) $2 \times x \times 5 \times y$
$$= 2 \times 5 \times x \times y$$
$$= 10xy$$

(c) $3 + 2 \times x$
$$= 3 + 2x$$

(d) $3 + 2 \times x - 4 \times y$
$$= 3 + 2x - 4y$$

2. Simplify these expressions.

 GCSE Grade 2+

(a) $p \times 7 \times p$ (b) $p \times 7 \times p \times p$

(c) $p \times p \times p \div q$

Solution

(a) $p \times 7 \times p$
$$= 7 \times p \times p$$
$$= 7p^2$$

(b) $p \times 7 \times p \times p$
$$= 7 \times p \times p \times p$$
$$= 7p^3$$

(c) $p \times p \times p \div q$
$$= p^3 \div q$$
$$= \frac{p^3}{q}$$

3. Write these statements as algebraic expressions.

 GCSE Grade 2+

(a) Add c squared to $3d$.

(b) Subtract $2 \times h$ from k.

(c) Multiply $p \times q$ and $p \times 3$.

(d) Divide x cubed by 7.

Solution

(a) $3d + c^2$

(b) $k - (2 \times h) = k - 2h$

(c) $(p \times q) \times (p \times 3)$
$$= 3 \times p \times p \times q$$
$$= 3p^2q$$

(d) $x^3 \div 7 = \frac{x^3}{7}$

4. Find the values of these expressions when $n = 4$.

 GCSE Grade 2+

(a) $2n + 5$ (b) $5n - 2$

(c) $7(1 - 3n)$

Solution

(a) When $n = 4$,
$2n + 5 = 2(4) + 5$
$$= 13$$

(b) When $n = 4$,
$5n - 2 = 5(4) - 2$
$$= 18$$

(c) When $n = 4$,
$7(1 - 3n) = 7(1 - 3 \times 4)$
$$= 7(1 - 12)$$
$$= 7(-11)$$
$$= -77$$

5. When $a = 3$ and $b = -2$, find the values of

 GCSE Grade 3

(a) a^4,

(b) b^3,

(c) $-5b^3$,

(d) $a^4 - 5b^3$.

Solution

When $a = 3$ and $b = -2$,

(a) $a^4 = 3^4$
$$= 81$$

(b) $b^3 = (-2)^3$
$$= -8$$

(c) $-5b^3 = -5 \times (-8)$ (using the result from **(b)**)
$$= 40$$

(d) $a^4 - 5b^3 = 81 - 40$ (using the results from
$$= 41 \qquad \text{(a) and (c))}$$

6. Find the value of the expression $g^3 + 7h^2$ when $g = 5$ and $h = -4$.

 GCSE Grade 3

Solution

When $g = 5$ and $h = -4$,
$$g^3 + 7h^2 = 5^3 + 7 \times (-4)^2$$
$$= 125 + 7 \times 16$$
$$= 125 + 112$$
$$= 237$$

7. Given the formula $E = \frac{1}{2}mv^2$, find the value of E when $m = 3$ and $v = 2$.

 GCSE Grade 3

Solution

When $m = 3$ and $v = 2$,
$$E = \frac{1}{2}mv^2$$
$$= \frac{1}{2} \times 3 \times 2^2$$
$$= 6$$

8. Simplify these expressions.

GCSE Grade 3⁻

(a) $3 + 4n - 2 + 5n$
(b) $2a - 3b - 4a - b$
(c) $-3p + 5 + 2q - 6p$
(d) $3x - 7y + 8 - x - 2y$

Solution

(a) $3 + 4n - 2 + 5n$
$= 3 - 2 + 4n + 5n$
$= 1 + 9n$

(b) $2a - 3b - 4a - b$
$= 2a - 4a - 3b - b$
$= -2a - 4b$

(c) $-3p + 5 + 2q - 6p$
$= -3p - 6p + 2q + 5$
$= -9p + 2q + 5$

(d) $3x - 7y + 8 - x - 2y$
$= 3x - x - 7y - 2y + 8$
$= 2x - 9y + 8$

9. Simplify these expressions.

 GCSE Grade 2⁺

(a) $(1 + 5a) + (3 + 4a)$
(b) $(2c - 7d) + (-d - 5c)$
(c) $(-3m + n) - (2m + n)$
(d) $(5x - 6y) - (-7y + 2x)$

Solution

(a) $(1 + 5a) + (3 + 4a)$
$= 1 + 5a + 3 + 4a$
$= 1 + 3 + 5a + 4a$
$= 4 + 9a$

(b) $(2c - 7d) + (-d - 5c)$
$= 2c - 7d - d - 5c$
$= 2c - 5c - 7d - d$
$= -3c - 8d$

(c) $(-3m + n) - (2m + n)$
$= -3m + n - 2m - n$
$= -3m - 2m + n - n$
$= -5m$

(d) $(5x - 6y) - (-7y + 2x)$
$= 5x - 6y + 7y - 2x$
$= 5x - 2x - 6y + 7y$
$= 3x + y$

10. Expand these expressions.

GCSE Grade 3⁻

(a) $4(9x)$
(b) $-7(5y)$
(c) $5(3a + 8)$
(d) $-6(-4 + 7q)$

Solution

(a) $4(9x) = 36x$

(b) $-7(5y) = -35y$

(c) $5(3a + 8) = 5 \times 3a + 5 \times 8$
$= 15a + 40$

(d) $-6(-4 + 7q) = -6 \times (-4) - 6 \times 7q$
$= 24 - 42q$

11. The price, £P, of planting a square flowerbed of side x metres is given by the formula
$$P = 8x + 20x^2.$$
Find the price of planting a square flowerbed of side 3 metres.

 GCSE Grade 3

Solution

$P = 8x + 20x^2$
When $x = 3$,
$P = 8(3) + 20(3^2)$
$= 204$
The price of planting a square flowerbed of side 3 metres is £204.

12. The temperature of an iron bar is 17 °C. When it is heated, the temperature rises by 20 °C every minute.

GCSE Grade 2⁺

(a) Find the temperature of the iron bar after 3 minutes.
(b) If the temperature of the iron bar after t minutes is T °C, express T in terms of t.
(c) Find the temperature of the iron bar after 9 minutes.

Solution

(a) Rise in temperature after 3 minutes
$= 20 \times 3$
$= 60\,°C$
Temperature of the iron bar after 3 minutes
$= 17 + 60$
$= 77\,°C$

(b) $T = 17 + 20 \times t$
$\therefore T = 17 + 20t$

(c) When $t = 9$
$$T = 17 + 20(9)$$
$$= 197 \, °C$$
The temperature of the iron bar after 9 minutes is $197 \, °C$.

13. There are three consecutive odd numbers. The smallest number is n.

(a) Express the other two numbers in terms of n.
(b) Let S be the sum of these three numbers. Write a formula connecting n and S.
(c) Hence find the value of S when the smallest number is 13.

Solution

(a) The next two odd numbers are $n + 2$ and $n + 4$.

(b) $S = n + n + 2 + n + 4$
$\quad = 3n + 6$

(c) When $n = 13$, $S = 3(13) + 6$
$\qquad\qquad\qquad\quad = 45$

14. The price for a bag of pasta is £2 and the price for a pack of sausages is £3. Mrs Stocks buys m bags of pasta and n packs of sausages.

(a) Express the total price of the items in terms of m and n.
(b) Mrs Stocks pays with a £50 note at the counter and she gets £C change. Write a formula connecting m, n and C.
(c) Find the change that Mrs Stocks receives if she buys four bags of pasta and two packs of sausages.

Solution

(a) Total price of the items $= 2m + 3n$

(b) $C = 50 - (2m + 3n)$
$\therefore C = 50 - 2m - 3n$

(c) When $m = 4$ and $n = 2$,
$C = 50 - 2(4) - 3(2)$
$\quad = 36$
Mrs Stocks receives £36 change.

15. The mass of three apples is $3x$ grams. The mass of four apples and a basket is $(4x + 120)$ grams.

(a) Express the total mass of these seven apples and the basket in terms of x.
(b) Find the total mass of these seven apples and the basket when $x = 150$.

Solution

(a) Total mass of the seven apples and the basket
$= 3x + (4x + 120)$
$= 3x + 4x + 120$
$= (7x + 120)$ grams

(b) When $x = 150$,
the total mass $= 7(150) + 120$
$\qquad\qquad\qquad = 1170$ grams

16. In the Leeds Triathlon, an athlete's swimming time is t minutes. Her cycling time is three times the swimming time. Her running time is 20 minutes more than the swimming time.

(a) Express her cycling time and running time in terms of t.
(b) Let T minutes be the time taken by the athlete in the race. Write a formula connecting t and T.
(c) If the athlete's swimming time is 25 minutes, find her time taken, in hours, to complete the race.

Solution

(a) Cycling time $= 3t$ minutes
Running time $= (t + 20)$ minutes

(b) $T = t + 3t + t + 20$
$\therefore T = 5t + 20$

(c) When $t = 25$,
$T = 5(25) + 20$
$\quad = 145$
The athlete takes 145 minutes to complete the race.
Hence, the time taken, in hours, to complete the race is $\frac{145}{60} = 2$ hours 25 minutes.

17. A rectangular lawn is $(2x + 3y)$ metres long and $(6y - x)$ metres wide.

(a) Let P metres be the perimeter of the lawn. Find a formula connecting P, x and y.

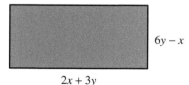

$6y - x$

$2x + 3y$

(b) The cost of making the fence around the lawn is £3 per metre. Find the cost of making the fence when $x = 5$ and $y = 2$.

Solution

(a) Perimeter $= 2x + 3y + 2x + 3y + 6y - x + 6y - x$
$= 2x + 2x - x - x + 3y + 3y + 6y + 6y$
$= 2x + 18y$
The formula is $P = 2x + 18y$.

(b) When $x = 5$ and $y = 2$,
$P = 2 \times 5 + 18 \times 2$
$\quad = 46$
The perimeter of the lawn is 46 metres.
$\therefore$ the cost of making the fence $= 46 \times 3$
$\qquad\qquad\qquad\qquad\qquad\quad = £138$

18. A bottle contains 90 tablets of vitamin C. Each tablet provides 500 mg of vitamin C. David takes two tablets per day.

(a) Express David's intake of vitamin C from the tablets in

    (i) seven days,

    (ii) n days in terms of n.

(b) Find the number of tablets in the bottle after seven days.

(c) Let y be the number of tablets in the bottle after n days. Write a formula connecting n and y.

(d) Find the number of tablets in the bottle after 17 days.

    Hint: You may draw a picture to help you understand the situation.

Solution

(a) (i) David's intake in 7 days in mg
$$= 7 \times \text{number of tablets per day} \times 500$$
$$= 7 \times 2 \times 500$$
$$= 7000$$
David's intake in 7 days is 7000 mg or 7 g.

(ii) David's intake in n days in mg $= n \times 2 \times 500$
$$= 1000n$$
David's intake in n days is $1000n$ mg or n g.

(b) Number of tablets left in the bottle after 7 days $= 90 - 2 \times 7$
$$= 90 - 14$$
$$= 76$$

(c) $y = 90 - 2n$

(d) When $n = 17$, $y = 90 - 2 \times 17$
$$= 90 - 34$$
$$= 56$$

After 17 days, there are 56 tablets in the bottle.

19. The production cost of a shirt in a garment factory is £x. A retailer purchases 20 shirts and her purchase price of each shirt is £4 more than the production cost. The retailer marks the price of each shirt to be three times her purchase price. She sells 16 shirts at the marked price and the remaining shirts at half of the marked price.

(a) Express, in terms of x,

    (i) the retailer's purchase price of each shirt,

    (ii) the retailer's marked price of each shirt.

(b) Let £P be the retailer's profit from selling the shirts.

    (i) Write a formula connecting x and P.

    (ii) Find the profit of the retailer when $x = 9$.

Solution

(a) (i) Retailer's purchase price of each shirt
$$= £(x + 4)$$

(ii) Retailer's marked price for each shirt
$$= £[3(x + 4)]$$
$$= £(3x + 12)$$

(b) (i) Profit in £ = marked price × number sold at marked price + (marked price ÷ 2) × number sold at reduced price less − purchase price per shirt × total number of shirts

$$P = 3(x + 4) \times 16 + 3(x + 4) \div 2$$
$$\times (20 - 16) - (x + 4) \times 20$$
$$= (x + 4) \times (3 \times 16 + 3 \div 2 \times 4 - 20)$$
$$= (x + 4) \times (48 + 6 - 20)$$
$$= 34(x + 4)$$

(ii) When $x = 9$, $P = 34(9 + 4)$
$$= 34 \times 13$$
$$= 442$$

When $x = 9$, the profit of the retailer is £442.

Simple Equations

Class Activity 1

Objective: To explore how to solve an equation.

Tasks

In each question, you will explore two possible methods for finding the solution. In part A, you will use a bar model and in part B, you will use balancing scales. For each part, copy and complete the diagram and equation.

1. Solve the equation $2x + 3 = 7$.
    A. *Using a Bar Model*
    1. Represent the equation using a bar model.

    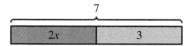

    $2x + 3 = 7$

    2. Take away 3. Copy and fill in the diagram and the equation.

    $2x = \boxed{4}$

    3. Divide the bar into two equal parts. Each part is x. Copy and fill in the diagram and the equation.

    $x = \boxed{2}$

    B. *Using Balancing Scales*
    Both the left-hand side (LHS) and the right-hand side (RHS) of the scales must be equal in value to keep the supporting beam of the two sides in a level position.
    1. Place the corresponding discs on the LHS and RHS of the scales.

    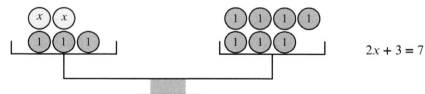

    $2x + 3 = 7$

    2. To remove 3 from the LHS, you add −3 to both sides. Copy and complete the equation.

    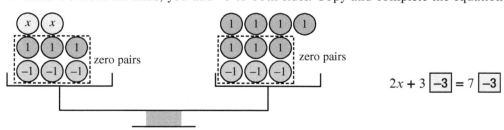

    $2x + 3 \boxed{-3} = 7 \boxed{-3}$

3. Group the numbers on each side of the scales. Copy and complete the balancing scales and the equation.

$2x = \boxed{4}$

4. Divide both sides into two equal parts. Copy and complete the balancing scales and the equation.

$x = \boxed{2}$

2. Solve the equation $4x - 3 = 5$.
   A. *Using a Bar Model*
     1. Represent the equation using a bar model. A bar representing $4x$ is drawn. If you subtract 3 from it, the remaining part is 5.

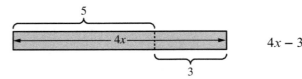

$4x - 3 = 5$

     2. The full bar is $5 + 3$. Copy and fill in the diagram and the equation.

$4x = \boxed{8}$

     3. Divide the bar into four equal parts. Copy and fill in the diagram and the equation.

$x = \boxed{2}$

   B. *Using Balancing Scales*
     1. Place the corresponding discs on the LHS and RHS of the scales.

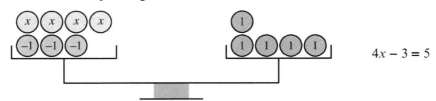

$4x - 3 = 5$

     2. To remove -3 from the LHS, you add 3 to both sides. Copy and complete the equation.

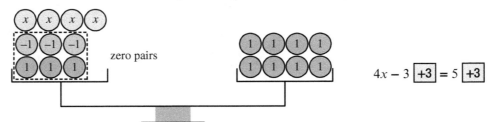

zero pairs

$4x - 3 \boxed{+3} = 5 \boxed{+3}$

3. Group the numbers on each side of the scales. Copy and complete the balancing scales and the equation.

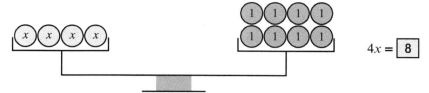

$4x = \boxed{8}$

4. Divide both sides into four equal parts. Copy and complete the balancing scales and the equation.

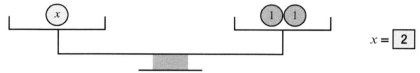

$x = \boxed{2}$

3. Solve the equation $\dfrac{x}{3} = 4$.

   A. *Using a Bar Model*

      1. Represent the equation using a bar model.

$\dfrac{x}{3} = 4$

      2. Multiply the bar by 3 to make a bar of x. Copy and fill in the diagram and the equation.

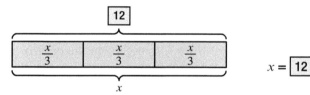

$x = \boxed{12}$

   B. *Using Balancing Scales*

      1. Place the corresponding discs on each side of the scales.

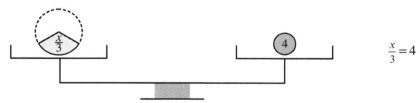

$\dfrac{x}{3} = 4$

      2. Multiply both sides by 3. Copy and complete the balancing scales and the equation.

$x = \boxed{12}$

4. By observing the process of solving equations in the previous three questions, suggest some rules for solving an equation.

When both sides of an equation are added, subtracted, multiplied or divided by the same number, the equation remains balanced.

Class Activity 2

Objective: To write equations to solve problems.

1. Noah is 8 cm taller than Mia. The total height of Noah and Mia is 338 cm. Find Mia's height.
   (a) Let x cm be Mia's height. Copy and fill in the empty boxes in this bar model.

   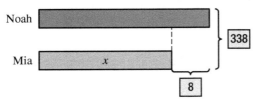

   Answer these questions.

   (b) Express Noah's height in terms of x.

   Noah's height $= (x + 8)$ cm

   (c) As the total height of Noah and Mia is 338 cm, write an equation in x.

   $(x + 8) + x = 338$

   (d) Solve the equation and hence write down Mia's height.

   $(x + 8) + x = 338$
   $2x + 8 = 338$
   $2x = 330$
   $x = 165$
   Mia's height is 165 cm.

2. A dress costs three times as much as a T-shirt. The price of the dress is £30 more than the price of the T-shirt. Find the price of the T-shirt.
   (a) Let £x be the price of the T-shirt. Copy and fill in the empty boxes in this bar model.

   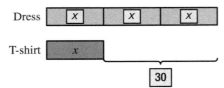

   Answer these questions.
   (b) Express the price of the dress in terms of x.

   Price of the dress $= 3x$

   (c) As the price of the dress is £30 more than the price of the T-shirt, write an equation in x.

   $3x - x = 30$

   (d) Solve the equation and hence write down the price of the T-shirt.

   $3x - x = 30$
   $2x = 30$
   $x = 15$
   The price of the T-shirt is £15.

Try It!

Section 4.1

1. Solve the equation $x - 4 = 5$.

    Solution
    $$x - 4 = 5$$
    $$x - 4 + 4 = 5 + 4$$
    $$x = 9$$

2. Solve the equation $y + 2 = -7$.

    Solution
    $$y + 2 = -7$$
    $$y + 2 - 2 = -7 - 2$$
    $$y = -9$$

3. Solve the equation $\frac{z}{2} = 9$.

    Solution
    $$\frac{z}{2} = 9$$
    $$\frac{z}{2} \times 2 = 9 \times 2$$
    $$z = 18$$

4. Solve the equation $5x = -35$.

    Solution
    $$5x = -35$$
    $$\frac{5x}{5} = \frac{-35}{5}$$
    $$x = -7$$

5. Solve the equation $2 - 3x = -2$.

    Solution
    $$2 - 3x = -2$$
    $$2 - 3x - 2 = -2 - 2$$
    $$-3x = -4$$
    $$\frac{-3x}{-3} = \frac{-4}{-3}$$
    $$x = \frac{4}{3}$$

    Check: When $x = \frac{4}{3}$, LHS $= 2 - 3 \times \frac{4}{3}$
    $$= 2 - 4$$
    $$= -2$$
    $$= \text{RHS}$$

6. Solve the equation $5x - 9 = 4x + 10$.

    Solution
    $$5x - 9 = 4x + 10$$
    $$5x - 9 - 4x = 4x + 10 - 4x$$
    $$x - 9 = 10$$
    $$x - 9 + 9 = 10 + 9$$
    $$x = 19$$

    Check: When $x = 19$, LHS $= 5 \times 19 - 9$
    $$= 95 - 9$$
    $$= 86$$
    RHS $= 4 \times 19 + 10$
    $$= 76 + 10$$
    $$= 86$$
    $$\therefore \text{LHS} = \text{RHS}$$

Section 4.2

7. Solve the equation $3(x - 1) = 15$.

    Solution
    $$3(x - 1) = 15$$
    $$3x - 3 = 15$$
    $$3x - 3 + 3 = 15 + 3$$
    $$3x = 18$$
    $$\frac{3x}{3} = \frac{18}{3}$$
    $$x = 6$$

8. Find the root of the equation $7 = 2(t + 3)$.

    Solution
    $$7 = 2(t + 3)$$
    $$7 = 2t + 6$$
    $$7 - 6 = 2t$$
    $$1 = 2t$$
    $$\frac{1}{2} = \frac{2t}{2}$$
    $$t = \frac{1}{2}$$

9. What is the solution of the equation $2(3x) = 5(x - 4)$?

    Solution
    $$2(3x) = 5(x - 4)$$
    $$6x = 5x - 20$$
    $$6x - 5x = 5x - 20 - 5x$$
    $$x = -20$$

10. Find the value of w that satisfies the equation $2(4w - 1) = 7(w + 4)$.

    Solution
    $$2(4w - 1) = 7(w + 4)$$
    $$8w - 2 = 7w + 28$$
    $$8w - 2 - 7w = 7w + 28 - 7w$$
    $$w - 2 = 28$$
    $$w - 2 + 2 = 28 + 2$$
    $$w = 30$$

Section 4.3

11. The sum of two consecutive odd numbers is 96. Find the numbers.

Solution

Let x be the smaller odd number.
This problem can be represented with a bar model.

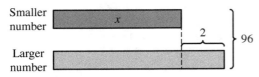

Larger odd number $= x + 2$
Sum of the two numbers $= 96$
$x + (x + 2) = 96$
$x + x + 2 = 96$
$2x + 2 = 96$
$2x = 94$
$x = \dfrac{94}{2}$
$x = 47$

The two consecutive odd numbers are 47 and 49.

12. A committee has a total of 57 members. If there are 11 fewer male members than female members, find the number of female members.

Solution

Let x be the number of male members. This problem can be represented by the following bar model.

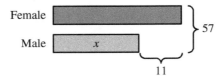

Number of female members $= x + 11$
Total number of members $= 57$
$\therefore\ x + (x + 11) = 57$
$x + x + 11 = 57$
$2x = 57 - 11$
$2x = 46$
$x = 23$
When $x = 23$,
$x + 11 = 23 + 11$
$= 34$
$\therefore$ the number of female members is 34.

13. David is four times as old as his son. The difference in their ages is 33 years. Find David's age.

Solution

Let x years be the age of David's son.
This problem can be represented by a bar model.

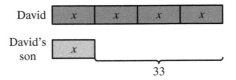

David's age $= 4x$ years
Difference of their ages $= 33$
$\therefore\qquad 4x - x = 33$
$3x = 33$
$x = \dfrac{33}{3}$
$x = 11$
$\therefore\qquad$ David's age $= 4x$
$= 4 \times 11$
$= 44$ years

14. A bottle of medicine contains 100 ml. After taking five equal doses, the remaining volume is 60 ml. Find the volume of each dose.

Solution

Let x ml be the volume of each doses.
The bar model can be drawn as shown.

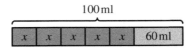

Volume of the 5 doses + remaining volume = original volume
$\therefore\ 5x + 60 = 100$
$5x = 100 - 60$
$5x = 40$
$x = \dfrac{40}{5}$
$x = 8$

Hence, the volume of each dose is 8 ml.

Exercise 4.1

Level 1 | **GCSE Grade 2⁺**

1. Solve these equations.
   (a) $a + 8 = 13$ (b) $c - 6 = 2$
   (c) $3 + f = -10$ (d) $g - 9 = -5$

Solution

(a) $a + 8 = 13$ (b) $c - 6 = 2$
$a + 8 - 8 = 13 - 8$ $c - 6 + 6 = 2 + 6$
$a = 5$ $c = 8$

(c) $3 + f = -10$ (d) $g - 9 = -5$
$3 + f - 3 = -10 - 3$ $g - 9 + 9 = -5 + 9$
$f = -13$ $g = 4$

2. Solve these equations.
  (a) $3n = 18$ **(b)** $5q = 2$
  (c) $-2r = 6$ **(d)** $-7u = -4$

Solution
  (a) $3n = 18$ **(b)** $5q = 2$
  $\dfrac{3n}{3} = \dfrac{18}{3}$ $\dfrac{5q}{5} = \dfrac{2}{5}$
  $n = 6$ $q = \dfrac{2}{5}$

  (c) $-2r = 6$ **(d)** $-7u = -4$
  $\dfrac{-2r}{-2} = \dfrac{6}{-2}$ $\dfrac{-7u}{-7} = \dfrac{-4}{-7}$
  $r = -3$ $u = \dfrac{4}{7}$

3. Solve these equations.
  (a) $\dfrac{v}{2} = 7$ **(b)** $\dfrac{w}{3} = 5$
  (c) $\dfrac{x}{4} = -6$ **(d)** $\dfrac{y}{5} = -4$
  (e) $\dfrac{z}{-2} = 7$ **(f)** $\dfrac{x}{-3} = -5$

Solution
  (a) $\dfrac{v}{2} = 7$ **(b)** $\dfrac{w}{3} = 5$
  $\dfrac{v}{2} \times 2 = 7 \times 2$ $\dfrac{w}{3} \times 3 = 5 \times 3$
  $v = 14$ $w = 15$

  (c) $\dfrac{x}{4} = -6$ **(d)** $\dfrac{y}{5} = -4$
  $\dfrac{x}{4} \times 4 = -6 \times 4$ $\dfrac{y}{5} \times 5 = -4 \times 5$
  $x = -24$ $y = -20$

  (e) $\dfrac{z}{-2} = 7$ **(f)** $\dfrac{x}{-3} = 5$
  $\dfrac{z}{-2} \times (-2) = 7 \times (-2)$ $\dfrac{x}{-3} \times (-3) = -5 \times (-3)$
  $z = -14$ $x = 15$

Level 2 GCSE Grade **3⁻ / 3**

4. Write an equation represented by each of these bar models and solve it.

  (a)
  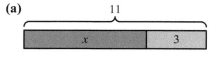

  (b)
  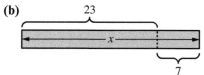

Solution
  (a) The equation is $x + 3 = 11$.
  $x + 3 = 11$
  $x + 3 - 3 = 11 - 3$
  $x = 8$

(b) The equation is $x - 7 = 23$.
  $x - 7 = 23$
  $x - 7 + 7 = 23 + 7$
  $x = 30$

5. Solve these equations.
  (a) $-17 = 6 - q$ **(b)** $-\dfrac{x}{4} = 6$
  (c) $-\dfrac{y}{7} = -5$ **(d)** $-9 - z = -8$

Solution
  (a) $-17 = 6 - q$ **(b)** $-\dfrac{x}{4} = 6$
  $-17 - 6 = 6 - q - 6$ $-\dfrac{x}{4} \times (-4) = 6 \times (-4)$
  $-23 = -q$ $x = -24$
  $\dfrac{-23}{-1} = \dfrac{-q}{-1}$
  $23 = q$
  $q = 23$

  (c) $-\dfrac{y}{7} = -5$ **(d)** $-9 - z = -8$
  $-\dfrac{y}{7} \times (-7) = -5 \times (-7)$ $-9 - z + 9 = -8 + 9$
  $y = 35$ $-z = 1$
            $z = -1$

6. Find the value of the letter in each equation.
  (a) $2x + 1 = 7$ **(b)** $3x + 5 = -13$
  (c) $4x - 2 = 3$ **(d)** $5x - 6 = -2$

Solution
  (a) $2x + 1 = 7$ **(b)** $3x + 5 = -13$
  $2x + 1 - 1 = 7 - 1$ $3x + 5 - 5 = -13 - 5$
  $2x = 6$ $3x = -18$
  $\dfrac{2x}{2} = \dfrac{6}{2}$ $\dfrac{3x}{3} = \dfrac{-18}{3}$
  $x = 3$ $x = -6$

  (c) $4x - 2 = 3$ **(d)** $5x - 6 = -2$
  $4x - 2 + 2 = 3 + 2$ $5x - 6 + 6 = -2 + 6$
  $4x = 5$ $5x = 4$
  $\dfrac{4x}{4} = \dfrac{5}{4}$ $\dfrac{5x}{5} = \dfrac{4}{5}$
  $x = \dfrac{5}{4}$ $x = \dfrac{4}{5}$

7. Solve these equations.
  (a) $3x = 2x + 8$ **(b)** $4x - 12 = 5x$
  (c) $4x - 3 = x$ **(d)** $2x = 8x - 7$

Solution
  (a) $3x = 2x + 8$
  $3x - 2x = 2x + 8 - 2x$
  $x = 8$

  (b) $4x - 12 = 5x$
  $4x - 12 - 4x = 5x - 4x$
  $-12 = x$
  $x = -12$

(c)
$$4x - 3 = x$$
$$4x - 3 - 4x = x - 4x$$
$$-3 = -3x$$
$$\frac{-3}{-3} = \frac{-3x}{-3}$$
$$x = 1$$

(d)
$$2x = 8x - 7$$
$$2x - 8x = 8x - 7 - 8x$$
$$-6x = -7$$
$$\frac{-6x}{-6} = \frac{-7}{-6}$$
$$x = \frac{7}{6}$$

8. Write an equation represented by each of these bar models and solve it.

(a)

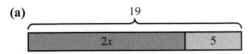

(b)

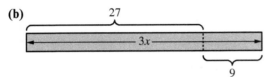

Solution

(a) The equation is $2x + 5 = 19$.
$$2x + 5 = 19$$
$$2x + 5 - 5 = 19 - 5$$
$$2x = 14$$
$$\frac{2x}{2} = \frac{14}{2}$$
$$x = 7$$

(b) The equation is $3x - 9 = 27$.
$$3x - 9 = 27$$
$$3x - 9 + 9 = 27 + 9$$
$$3x = 36$$
$$\frac{3x}{3} = \frac{36}{3}$$
$$x = 12$$

Level 3   **GCSE Grade 3 / 3⁺**

9. Solve these equations.
(a) $1 - 2m = 9$ **(b)** $-6 = 8 - 7n$
(c) $-5 - 3p = 10$ **(d)** $-8q - 1 = -4$

Solution

(a)
$$1 - 2m = 9$$
$$1 - 2m - 1 = 9 - 1$$
$$-2m = 8$$
$$\frac{-2m}{-2} = \frac{8}{-2}$$
$$m = -4$$

(b)
$$-6 = 8 - 7n$$
$$-6 - 8 = 8 - 7n - 8$$
$$-14 = -7n$$
$$\frac{-14}{-7} = \frac{-7n}{-7}$$
$$2 = n$$
$$n = 2$$

(c)
$$-5 - 3p = 10$$
$$-5 - 3p + 5 = 10 + 5$$
$$-3p = 15$$
$$\frac{-3p}{-3} = \frac{15}{-3}$$
$$p = -5$$

(d)
$$-8q - 1 = -4$$
$$-8q - 1 + 1 = -4 + 1$$
$$-8q = -3$$
$$\frac{-8q}{-8} = \frac{-3}{-8}$$
$$q = \frac{3}{8}$$

10. Solve these equations.
(a) $5t = 2t - 12$ **(b)** $3x = -2x + 30$
(c) $-5 - 3y = -2y$ **(d)** $-12y = -7 - 3y$

Solution

(a)
$$5t = 2t - 12$$
$$5t - 2t = 2t - 12 - 2t$$
$$3t = -12$$
$$\frac{3t}{3} = \frac{-12}{3}$$
$$t = -4$$

(b)
$$3x = -2x + 30$$
$$3x + 2x = -2x + 30 + 2x$$
$$5x = 30$$
$$\frac{5x}{5} = \frac{30}{5}$$
$$x = 6$$

(c)
$$-5 - 3y = -2y$$
$$-5 - 3y + 3y = -2y + 3y$$
$$-5 = y$$
$$y = -5$$

(d)
$$-12y = -7 - 3y$$
$$-12y + 3y = -7 - 3y + 3y$$
$$-9y = -7$$
$$\frac{-9y}{-9} = \frac{-7}{-9}$$
$$y = \frac{7}{9}$$

11. Write down a value for a, a value for b and a value for c such that the solution to the equation $ax + b = c$ is $x = -3$.

Solution
A possible equation is
$2x + 1 = -5$, where $a = 2$, $b = 1$ and $c = -5$.

12. Find the value of x in each equation.
(a) $3x + 5 = 2x + 9$ **(b)** $5x - 4 = 4x + 11$
(c) $6x + 8 = 7x - 13$ **(d)** $7 - 8x = 15 - 9x$

Solution

(a)
$$3x + 5 = 2x + 9$$
$$3x + 5 - 2x = 2x + 9 - 2x$$
$$x + 5 = 9$$
$$x + 5 - 5 = 9 - 5$$
$$x = 4$$

(b)
$$5x - 4 = 4x + 11$$
$$5x - 4 - 4x = 4x + 11 - 4x$$
$$x - 4 = 11$$
$$x - 4 + 4 = 11 + 4$$
$$x = 15$$

(c)
$$6x + 8 = 7x - 13$$
$$6x + 8 - 6x = 7x - 13 - 6x$$
$$8 = x - 13$$
$$8 + 13 = x - 13 + 13$$
$$x = 21$$

(d)
$$7 - 8x = 15 - 9x$$
$$7 - 8x + 9x = 15 - 9x + 9x$$
$$7 + x = 15$$
$$7 + x - 7 = 15 - 7$$
$$x = 8$$

13. (a) Mary's year of birth is the solution to the equation $13x + 927 = 14x - 1065$. What is her year of birth?

(b) Copy and complete this sentence 'In part **(a)**, the letter x represents …'.

Solution

(a)
$$13x + 927 = 14x - 1065$$
$$13x + 927 - 13x = 14x - 1065 - 13x$$
$$927 = x - 1065$$
$$927 + 1065 = x - 1065 + 1065$$
$$x = 1992$$
Mary's year of birth is 1992.

(b) In part **(a)**, the letter x represents Mary's year of birth.

Exercise 4.2

Level 1

1. Solve these equations.
(a) $3(x + 1) = 15$ **(b)** $2(x + 4) = -10$
(c) $4(x - 9) = 8$ **(d)** $-3(x - 1) = -12$

Solution

(a)
$$3(x + 1) = 15$$
$$3x + 3 = 15$$
$$3x + 3 - 3 = 15 - 3$$
$$3x = 12$$
$$\frac{3x}{3} = \frac{12}{3}$$
$$x = 4$$

(b)
$$2(x + 4) = -10$$
$$2x + 8 = -10$$
$$2x + 8 - 8 = -10 - 8$$
$$2x = -18$$
$$\frac{2x}{2} = \frac{-18}{2}$$
$$x = -9$$

(c)
$$4(x - 9) = 8$$
$$4x - 36 = 8$$
$$4x - 36 + 36 = 8 + 36$$
$$4x = 44$$
$$\frac{4x}{4} = \frac{44}{4}$$
$$x = 11$$

(d)
$$-3(x - 1) = -12$$
$$-3x + 3 = -12$$
$$-3x + 3 - 3 = -12 - 3$$
$$-3x = -15$$
$$\frac{-3x}{-3} = \frac{-15}{-3}$$
$$x = 5$$

2. Find the roots of these equations.
(a) $3(2y + 1) = 21$ **(b)** $5(3y - 4) = 25$
(c) $2(9 - y) = 8$ **(d)** $3(7 - 4y) = 15$

Solution

(a)
$$3(2y + 1) = 21$$
$$\frac{3(2y + 1)}{3} = \frac{21}{3}$$
$$2y + 1 = 7$$
$$2y + 1 - 1 = 7 - 1$$
$$2y = 6$$
$$\frac{2y}{2} = \frac{6}{2}$$
$$y = 3$$

(b)
$$5(3y - 4) = 25$$
$$\frac{5(3y - 4)}{5} = \frac{25}{5}$$
$$3y - 4 = 5$$
$$3y - 4 + 4 = 5 + 4$$
$$3y = 9$$
$$\frac{3y}{3} = \frac{9}{3}$$
$$y = 3$$

(c)
$$2(9 - y) = 8$$
$$\frac{2(9 - y)}{2} = \frac{8}{2}$$
$$9 - y = 4$$
$$9 - y - 9 = 4 - 9$$
$$-y = -5$$
$$y = 5$$

(d)
$$3(7 - 4y) = 15$$
$$\frac{3(7 - 4y)}{3} = \frac{15}{3}$$
$$7 - 4y = 5$$
$$7 - 4y - 7 = 5 - 7$$
$$-4y = -2$$
$$\frac{-4y}{-4} = \frac{-2}{-4}$$
$$y = \frac{1}{2}$$

3. Find the roots of these equations.
(a) $3(2x) = 12$ **(b)** $2(3x) = 42$
(c) $5(3x) = 60$ **(d)** $45 = 3(5x)$

Solution

(a)
$$3(2x) = 12$$
$$6x = 12$$
$$\frac{6x}{6} = \frac{12}{6}$$
$$x = 2$$

(b)
$$2(3x) = 42$$
$$\frac{6x}{6} = \frac{42}{6}$$
$$x = 7$$

(c)
$$5(3x) = 60$$
$$\frac{5(3x)}{5} = \frac{60}{5}$$
$$3x = 12$$
$$\frac{3x}{3} = \frac{12}{3}$$
$$x = 4$$

(d)
$$45 = 3(5x)$$
$$45 = 15x$$
$$\frac{45}{15} = \frac{15x}{15}$$
$$x = 3$$

Level 2

4. Find the solutions of these equations.

   (a) $10 = 5(z - 4)$ **(b)** $-63 = 9(2z + 1)$

   (c) $7 = 4(1 - z)$ **(d)** $-1 = 2(-4 + 3z)$

Solution

(a)
$$10 = 5(z - 4)$$
$$\frac{10}{5} = \frac{5(z-4)}{5}$$
$$2 = z - 4$$
$$2 + 4 = z - 4 + 4$$
$$z = 6$$

(b)
$$-63 = 9(2z + 1)$$
$$\frac{-63}{9} = \frac{9(2z+1)}{9}$$
$$-7 = 2z + 1$$
$$-7 - 1 = 2z + 1 - 1$$
$$-8 = 2z$$
$$\frac{-8}{2} = \frac{2z}{2}$$
$$z = -4$$

(c)
$$7 = 4(1 - z)$$
$$7 = 4 - 4z$$
$$7 - 4 = 4 - 4z - 4$$
$$3 = -4z$$
$$\frac{3}{-4} = \frac{-4z}{-4}$$
$$z = -\frac{3}{4}$$

(d)
$$-1 = 2(-4 + 3z)$$
$$-1 = -8 + 6z$$
$$-1 + 8 = -8 + 6z + 8$$
$$7 = 6z$$
$$\frac{7}{6} = \frac{6z}{6}$$
$$z = \frac{7}{6}$$

5. Solve these equations.

   (a) $7x = 6(x - 4)$ **(b)** $4(2x) = 7(x - 3)$

   (c) $3(-5x) = -2(7x + 6)$ **(d)** $3(-2x) = 5(4 - x)$

Solution

(a)
$$7x = 6(x - 4)$$
$$7x = 6x - 24$$
$$7x - 6x = 6x - 24 - 6x$$
$$x = -24$$

(b)
$$4(2x) = 7(x - 3)$$
$$8x = 7x - 21$$
$$8x - 7x = 7x - 21 - 7x$$
$$x = -21$$

(c)
$$3(-5x) = -2(7x + 6)$$
$$-15x = -14x + 12$$
$$-15x + 14x = -14x + 12 + 14x$$
$$-x = 12$$
$$x = -12$$

(d)
$$3(-2x) = 5(4 - x)$$
$$-6x = 20 - 5x$$
$$-6x + 5x = 20 - 5x + 5x$$
$$-x = 20$$
$$x = -20$$

6. Solve these equations.

   (a) $3(t - 4) = 2(t + 1)$

   (b) $2(2u + 9) = 3(u - 5)$

   (c) $4(2v - 1) = 9(v - 2)$

   (d) $7(3 - 2w) = 5(6 - 3w)$

Solution

(a)
$$3(t - 4) = 2(t + 1)$$
$$3t - 12 = 2t + 2$$
$$3t - 12 - 2t = 2t + 2 - 2t$$
$$t - 12 = 2$$
$$t - 12 + 12 = 2 + 12$$
$$t = 14$$

(b)
$$2(2u + 9) = 3(u - 5)$$
$$4u + 18 = 3u - 15$$
$$4u + 18 - 3u = 3u - 15 - 3u$$
$$u + 18 = -15$$
$$u + 18 - 18 = -15 - 18$$
$$u = -33$$

(c)
$$4(2v - 1) = 9(v - 2)$$
$$8v - 4 = 9v - 18$$
$$8v - 4 - 9v = 9v - 18 - 9v$$
$$-4 - v = -18$$
$$-4 - v = -18$$
$$-4 - v + 4 = -18 + 4$$
$$-v = -14$$
$$v = 14$$

(d)
$$7(3 - 2w) = 5(6 - 3w)$$
$$21 - 14w = 30 - 15w$$
$$21 - 14w + 15w = 30 - 15w + 15w$$
$$21 + w = 30$$
$$21 + w - 21 = 30 - 21$$
$$w = 9$$

Level 3

7. The total value, £T, of n £10 notes and $(n - 2)$ £20 notes is given by the formula

$$T = 10n + 20(n - 2).$$

   (a) Find the value of six £10 notes and four £20 notes.

   (b) If the total value is £110, find the value of n. Check your answer and discuss your method with your classmates.

Solution

(a)
$$T = 10(6) + 20(4)$$
$$= 60 + 80$$
$$= 140$$
The total value is £140.

(b) When $T = 110$,
$$110 = 10n + 20(n - 2)$$
$$110 = 10n + 20n - 40$$
$$110 + 40 = 30n - 40 + 40$$
$$150 = 30n$$
$$\frac{30n}{30} = \frac{150}{30}$$
$$n = 5$$
Check: $5 \times 10 + 3 \times 20 = 110$.

8. The total number, N, of legs of p cats and q dogs is given by the formula

$$N = 4(p + q).$$

(a) Find the total number of legs if there are four cats and three dogs.

(b) If there are six cats and $N = 72$, find the number of dogs.

Solution

(a) When $p = 4$ and $q = 3$,
$$N = 4(4 + 3)$$
$$= 4(7)$$
$$= 28$$
There are 28 legs.

(b) When $p = 6$ and $N = 72$,
$$72 = 4(6 + q)$$
$$\frac{72}{4} = \frac{4(6+q)}{4}$$
$$18 = 6 + q$$
$$18 - 6 = 6 + q - 6$$
$$q = 12$$
There are 12 dogs.

9. Luke is working with the equation $3(2x - 1) = k$. He wants to find a value for k such that the solution to the equation is an integer.

(a) He writes $3(2x - 1) = 9$. Does this value of k work?

(b) Find two possible values of k that work. Discuss your method with your classmates.

Hint: Integers are the numbers ..., $-3, -2, -1, 0, 1, 2, 3, ...$

Solution

(a) $3(2x - 1) = 9$
$$\frac{3(2x-1)}{3} = \frac{9}{3}$$
$$2x - 1 = 3$$
$$2x - 1 + 1 = 3 + 1$$
$$2x = 4$$
$$x = 2$$
The solution is an integer so this value of $k = 9$ works.

(b) For the general case k,
$$3(2x - 1) = k$$
$$6x - 3 = k$$
$$6x = k + 3$$
$$\frac{6x}{6} = \frac{k+3}{6}$$
$$x = \frac{k+3}{6}$$
For x to be an integer, $k + 3$ must be a multiple of 6. This means k must be a multiple of 6 minus 3.
For example, k could be $-15, -9, -3, 3, 9, 15$ (which would give values for x of $-2, -1, 0, 1, 2, 3$ respectively).

Exercise 4.3

Level 1   **GCSE Grade 2⁺**

1. In a swimming club, the number of boys is twice the number of girls.

(a) Which of these bar models illustrates the situation?

Model 1

Boys   [2   ]

Girls   [ ]

Model 2

Boys   [|]

Girls   [ ]

Model 3

Boys   [ ]

Girls   [|]

(b) If the total number of boys and girls in the club is 48, write an equation and solve it to find the number of girls.

Solution

(a) Model 2 illustrates the situation.

(b) Let x be the number of girls.
Then the number of boys $= 2x$
Total number of boys and girls $= 48$
$$\therefore 2x + x = 48$$
$$3x = 48$$
$$x = \frac{48}{3}$$
$$x = 16$$
Hence, the number of girls is 16.

2. The price of a book is £3 more than the price of a pen.

(a) Which of these bar models represents the situation?

Model 1

Book   [ ]

Pen   [ ]
3

Model 2

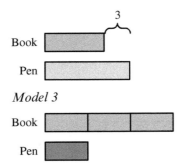

Model 3

(b) If the total price of the book and the pen is £11, write an equation and use it to find the price of the book.

Solution

(a) Model 1 represents the situation.

(b) Let £x be the price of a pen.
The price of a book = £$(x + 3)$
Total price of the book and the pen = £11
∴ $x + 3 + x = 11$
$2x + 3 = 11$
$2x = 11 - 3$
$2x = 8$
$x = \dfrac{8}{2}$
$x = 4$
The price of the book = £$(x + 3)$
= £$(4 + 3)$
= £7

3. In an aquarium tank, the number of red fish is seven more than the number of white fish. The total number of red and white fish is 47. Write an equation and solve it to find the number of white fish in the tank.

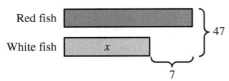

Solution

From the bar model, the number of white fish = x and the number of red fish = $x + 7$.
Total number of fish = 47
∴ $x + x + 7 = 47$
$2x + 7 = 47$
$2x = 47 - 7$
$2x = 40$
$x = \dfrac{40}{2}$
$x = 20$
∴ the number of white fish in the tank is 20.

4. The mass of a dog is four times the mass of a cat. The dog is 9 kg heavier than the cat. Write an equation and solve it to find the masses of the dog and the cat.

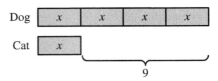

Solution

From the bar model,
$4x = x + 9$
$4x - x = 9$
$3x = 9$
$x = \dfrac{9}{3}$
$x = 3$
∴ the mass of the cat = x
= 3 kg
and the mass of the dog = $4x$
= 4×3
= 12 kg

5. A brass rod is 20 cm shorter than an iron rod. The total length of the two rods is 84 cm. Let x cm be the length of the brass rod.
   (a) Copy and complete the bar model.

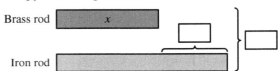

   (b) Write an equation and solve it to find the length of the iron rod.

Solution

(a)

Brass rod x
20 cm
Iron rod   } 84 cm

(b) Length of the iron rod = $(x + 20)$ cm
Total length of the two rods = 84 cm
∴ $x + (x + 20) = 84$
$x + x + 20 = 84$
$2x = 84 - 20$
$2x = 64$
$x = \dfrac{64}{2}$
$x = 32$
When $x = 32$,
$x + 20 = 32 + 20$
= 52
∴ the length of the iron rod is 52 cm.

Level 2   **GCSE Grade 3⁻**

6. A maple tree is 3 m taller than a peach tree. The total height of the two trees is 11 m. Write an equation and solve it to find the height of the peach tree.
   Hint: You may draw a bar model to help you.

   Solution
   Let x metres be the height of a peach tree.
   The situation can be represented by a bar model.

   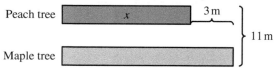

   The height of the maple tree = $(x + 3)$ m
   Total height of the two trees = 11 m
   $\therefore x + x + 3 = 11$
   $\qquad 2x + 3 = 11$
   $\qquad\qquad 2x = 11 - 3$
   $\qquad\qquad 2x = 8$
   $\qquad\qquad x = \dfrac{8}{2}$
   $\qquad\qquad x = 4$
   $\therefore$ the height of the peach tree is 4 m.

7. Peter has four times as many stamps as Ali. Their total number of stamps is 180. Write an equation and solve it to find the number of stamps Ali has.
   Hint: You may draw a bar model to help you.

   Solution
   Let x be the number of stamps Ali has.
   The bar model for the situation can be drawn as shown.

   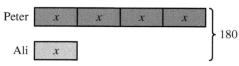

   Number of stamps Peter has = $4x$
   Total number of stamps = 180
   $\therefore 4x + x = 180$
   $\qquad\quad 5x = 180$
   $\qquad\quad\;\; x = \dfrac{180}{5}$
   $\qquad\quad\;\; x = 36$
   $\therefore$ Ali has 36 stamps.

8. The sum of two consecutive numbers is 175. Write an equation and solve it to find the two numbers.

   Solution
   Let the smaller number be n and the larger number be $n + 1$.
   The sum of the two numbers = 175
   $\therefore n + n + 1 = 175$
   $\qquad 2n + 1 = 175$
   $\qquad\quad 2n = 175 - 1$
   $\qquad\quad 2n = 174$
   $\qquad\quad\; n = \dfrac{174}{2}$
   $\qquad\quad\; n = 87$
   The two consecutive numbers are 87 and 88.

9. James has £28 in his pocket. After buying six burgers, he has £10 left in his pocket. Write an equation and solve it to find the price of a burger.

   Solution
   Let £p be the price of a burger.
   The situation can be represented by a bar model.

   £28

   | p | p | p | p | p | p | £10 |

   Price of 6 burgers + amount left = initial amount
   $\therefore 6p + 10 = 28$
   $\qquad\quad 6p = 28 - 10$
   $\qquad\quad 6p = 18$
   $\qquad\quad\; p = \dfrac{18}{6}$
   $\qquad\quad\; p = 3$
   Hence, the price of a burger is £3.

10. The total length of eight bricks is 75 cm longer than the total length of five bricks. Write an equation and solve it to find the length of each brick.

    Solution
    Let y cm be the length of each brick.
    Hence the total length of 5 bricks is $5y$ cm and the total length of 8 bricks is $8y$ cm.
    From the given information,
    $\qquad 8y = 75 + 5y$
    $8y - 5y = 75$
    $\qquad 3y = 75$
    $\qquad\;\; y = \dfrac{75}{3}$
    $\qquad\;\; y = 25$
    Hence, the length of each brick is 25 cm.

Level 3   **GCSE Grade** **3**

11. Alan has twice as many coins as Bob. If Bob had three more coins, the number of coins he had would be six fewer than the number of coins Alan had.

Original situation:

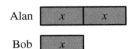

Situation after Bob has three more coins:

(a) Write down the values of a and b in the bar model.

(b) Write an equation and solve it to find the original number of coins Bob has.

Solution

(a) Bob is given 3 more coins so, in the diagram, $a = 3$.

Now Bob has 6 fewer coins than Alan so $b = 6$.

(b) From the given information,
$$2x - 6 = x + 3$$
$$x - 6 = 3$$
$$x = 3 + 6$$
$$x = 9$$

Hence, the original number of coins Bob has is 9.

12. The volume of acid in a conical flask is twice the volume of acid in a beaker. The total volume of acid in the flask and the beaker is 2 litres. Write an equation and find the volume of the acid in the beaker.

Solution

Let v be the volume of acid in the beaker.
The volume of acid in the flask is $2v$.
The total volume is 2 (litres).
$$\therefore v + 2v = 2$$
$$3v = 2$$
$$v = \frac{2}{3}$$

The volume of acid in the beaker is $\frac{2}{3}$ of a litre.

13. John has three times as much money as Ava to spend. If John spends £40, he would have twice as much money as Ava. Draw a bar model for the situation. Write an equation and solve it to find the amount of money that John had originally.

Solution

Let £x be the amount of money Ava has.
The problem can be represented by a bar model.
Original situation:

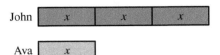

Situation after John spends £40:

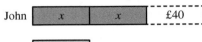

From the given information,
$$3x - 40 = 2x$$
$$3x = 2x + 40$$
$$3x - 2x = 40$$
$$x = 40$$

When $x = 40$,
$$3x = 3 \times 40$$
$$= 120$$

$\therefore$ the original amount of money John had is £120.

14. A calculator costs £4 more than a pen. The total price of a calculator and two pens is £22. Write an equation and solve it to find the price of the pen.

Solution

Let £p be the price of a pen.
Hence, the price of a calculator $=$ £$(p + 4)$.
From the given information, the total price of a calculator and two pens $=$ £22.
$$\therefore (p + 4) + 2 \times p = 22$$
$$p + 4 + 2p = 22$$
$$3p = 22 - 4$$
$$3p = 18$$
$$p = \frac{18}{3}$$
$$p = 6$$

$\therefore$ the price of a pen is £6.

15. The sum of three consecutive odd numbers is 99. Write an equation and solve it to find the smallest of these numbers.

Solution

Let n be the smallest odd number.
The next two larger odd numbers are $n + 2$ and $n + 4$.
From the given information, the sum of the three consecutive odd numbers $=$ 99.
$$\therefore n + n + 2 + n + 4 = 99$$
$$3n + 6 = 99$$
$$3n = 99 - 6$$
$$3n = 93$$
$$n = \frac{93}{3}$$
$$n = 31$$

Hence, the smallest odd number is 31.

16. In a money box, the number of £2 coins is three times as many as the number of £1 coins. The total value of all of these coins is £224. Write an equation and solve it to find the number of £1 coins.

Solution
Let c be the number of £1 coins.
The number of £2 coins $= 3c$.
From the given information,
the total value of the coins $=$ £224.
$\therefore 1 \times c + 2 \times 3c = 224$
$\qquad c + 6c = 224$
$\qquad 7c = 224$
$\qquad c = \dfrac{224}{7}$
$\qquad c = 32$
Hence, the number of £1 coins is 32.

17. The atomic number of oxygen is one more than the atomic number of nitrogen. The atomic number of sulphur is twice the atomic number of oxygen. The sum of the atomic numbers of oxygen, nitrogen and sulphur is 31. Write an equation and solve it to find the atomic number of oxygen.

Solution
Let n be the atomic number of oxygen.
Thus, the atomic number of nitrogen $= n - 1$.
The atomic number of sulphur $= 2n$.
From the given information,
the sum of the atomic numbers $= 31$.
$\therefore n + n - 1 + 2n = 31$
$\qquad 4n - 1 = 31$
$\qquad 4n = 31 + 1$
$\qquad 4n = 32$
$\qquad n = \dfrac{32}{4}$
$\qquad n = 8$
Hence, the atomic number of oxygen is 8.

18. A store has a combined total of 20 bicycles and tricycles in stock. If the total number of all of the wheels is 47, write an equation and use it to find the number of bicycles in stock.

Solution
Let x be the number of bicycles in stock.
A bicycle has 2 wheels and a tricycle has 3.
From the given information,
the total number of wheels $= 47$.
$\therefore 2 \times x + 3 \times (20 - x) = 47$
$\qquad 2x + 60 - 3x = 47$
$\qquad 60 - x = 47$
$\qquad -x = 47 - 60$
$\qquad -x = -13$
$\qquad x = 13$
Hence, the number of bicycles in stock is 13.

19. The total price of three cups and one plate is £41. The total price of three cups and three plates is £57. Find the price of a plate.

Solution
Let £x be the price of a plate.

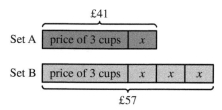

Both sets of crockery have three cups, but there are two more plates in Set B than in Set A.
$\therefore$ the price of the two plates = the price difference of the two sets.
$3x - x = 57 - 41$
$\qquad 2x = 16$
$\qquad x = \dfrac{16}{2}$
$\qquad x = 8$
Hence, the price of a plate is £8.

Revision Exercise 4

1. Solve these equations.
   (a) $x + 8 = 17$ (b) $x - 2 = -9$
   (c) $3 + x = -11$ (d) $6 - x = 5$

Solution
(a) $x + 8 = 17$ (b) $x - 2 = -9$
$\quad x = 17 - 8$ $x = -9 + 2$
$\quad x = 9$ $x = -7$

(c) $3 + x = -11$ (d) $6 - x = 5$
$\quad x = -11 - 3$ $-x = 5 - 6$
$\quad x = -14$ $-x = -1$
                $x = \dfrac{-1}{-1}$
                $x = 1$

2. Find the values of x in these equations.
   (a) $3x = 36$ (b) $2x = -14$
   (c) $-5x = -65$ (d) $-4x = 7$

Solution
(a) $3x = 36$ (b) $2x = -14$
$\quad x = \dfrac{36}{3}$ $x = \dfrac{-14}{2}$
$\quad x = 12$ $x = -7$

(c) $-5x = -65$ (d) $-4x = 7$
$\quad x = \dfrac{-65}{-5}$ $x = \dfrac{7}{-4}$
$\quad x = 13$ $x = -1\dfrac{3}{4}$

3. Find the values of x that satisfy these equations.

(a) $\dfrac{x}{3} = 7$ (b) $\dfrac{x}{4} = -5$

(c) $\dfrac{x}{-2} = 9$ (d) $\dfrac{x}{-5} = -4$

Solution

(a) $\dfrac{x}{3} = 7$ (b) $\dfrac{x}{4} = -5$

$x = 7 \times 3$ $x = -5 \times 4$

$x = 21$ $x = -20$

(c) $\dfrac{x}{-2} = 9$ (d) $\dfrac{x}{-5} = -4$

$x = 9 \times (-2)$ $x = -4 \times (-5)$

$x = -18$ $x = 20$

4. Solve to find the values of x in these equations.

(a) $2x - 7 = 9$ (b) $1 - 3x = 22$

(c) $4x + 3 = -5$ (d) $5 - 2x = -6$

Solution

(a) $2x - 7 = 9$ (b) $1 - 3x = 22$

$2x = 9 + 7$ $-3x = 22 - 1$

$2x = 16$ $-3x = 21$

$x = \dfrac{16}{2}$ $x = \dfrac{21}{-3}$

$x = 8$ $x = -7$

(c) $4x + 3 = -5$ (d) $5 - 2x = -6$

$4x = -5 - 3$ $-2x = -6 - 5$

$4x = -8$ $-2x = -11$

$x = \dfrac{-8}{4}$ $x = \dfrac{-11}{-2}$

$x = -2$ $x = 5\dfrac{1}{2}$

5. Solve these equations.

(a) $4y = -y + 15$ (b) $5t = 8t - 6$

(c) $3w + 16 = 2w + 9$ (d) $-3z - 5 = -2z + 11$

Solution

(a) $4y = -y + 15$ (b) $5t = 8t - 6$

$4y + y = 15$ $5t - 8t = -6$

$5y = 15$ $-3t = -6$

$y = \dfrac{15}{5}$ $t = \dfrac{-6}{-3}$

$y = 3$ $t = 2$

(c) $3w + 16 = 2w + 9$ (d) $-3z - 5 = -2z + 11$

$3w + 16 - 2w = 9$ $-5 = -2z + 11 + 3z$

$w + 16 = 9$ $-5 = 11 + z$

$w = 9 - 16$ $z = -5 - 11$

$w = -7$ $z = -16$

6. Find the roots of these equations.

(a) $2(5p) = -20$ (b) $6(2q + 3) = 17$

(c) $3(-2r) = 5(8 - r)$ (d) $4(2s - 5) = 7(s + 1)$

Solution

(a) $2(5p) = -20$

$p = \dfrac{-20}{10}$

$p = -2$

(b) $6(2q + 3) = 17$

$12q + 18 = 17$

$12q = 17 - 18$

$12q = -1$

$q = -\dfrac{1}{12}$

(c) $3(-2r) = 5(8 - r)$

$-6r = 40 - 5r$

$-6r + 5r = 40$

$-r = 40$

$r = -40$

(d) $4(2s - 5) = 7(s + 1)$

$8s - 20 = 7s + 7$

$8s - 20 - 7s = 7$

$s - 20 = 7$

$s = 7 + 20$

$s = 27$

7. Aria reads two more books than Ken in a month. They read 16 books altogether. Draw a bar model for the situation. Write an equation and solve it to find the number of books that Ken reads.

Solution

Let b be the number of books that Ken reads.
Aria reads $(b + 2)$ books.
A bar model for the situation can be drawn as shown.

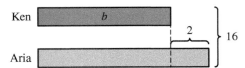

From the given information,

$b + (b + 2) = 16$

$2b = 16 - 2$

$2b = 14$

$b = \dfrac{14}{2}$

$b = 7$

∴ the number of books that Ken reads is 7.

8. A pine tree is twice as tall as a lemon tree. The total height of these two trees is 18 m. Write an equation and solve it to find the height of each tree.

Solution

Let h metres be the height of the lemon tree.
The height of the pine tree $= 2h$ metres

From the given information,
the total height of the two trees = 18 m.
∴ $h + 2h = 18$
$$3h = 18$$
$$h = \frac{18}{3}$$
$$h = 6$$
Hence, the height of the pine tree is $2 \times 6 = 12$ m
and the height of the lemon tree is 6 m.

9. An iron rod is three times as long as a copper rod. If the iron rod is 1 m longer than the copper rod, find the length of the copper rod.

Solution

Let r be the length of the copper rod.
The length of the iron rod is $3r$.
Also the length of the iron rod is $r + 1$.
∴ $3r = r + 1$
$$3r - r = 1$$
$$2r = 1$$
$$r = \frac{1}{2}$$

The copper rod is $\frac{1}{2}$ m long.

10. A flask contains three times as much solution as a beaker. The flask contains 180 ml more solution than the beaker. Draw a bar model for this situation. Write an equation and solve it to find the volume of solution in the beaker.

Solution

Let v ml be the volume of solution in the beaker.
The flask contains $3v$ ml of solution.
A bar model for the situation can be drawn as shown.

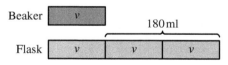

From the given information,
$3v - v = 180$
$$2v = 180$$
$$v = \frac{180}{2}$$
$$v = 90$$
∴ the volume of solution in the beaker is 90 ml.

11. Mrs Jones bought a set of paints and a jigsaw puzzle as birthday gifts for her daughter. She paid a total of £19. The jigsaw is £3 cheaper than the set of paints. Write an equation and solve it to find the prices of the set of paints and the jigsaw puzzle.

Solution

Let £p be the price of the set of paints.
The price of the jigsaw puzzle is £$(p - 3)$

From the given information,
the total payment for the two items = £19.
$p + (p - 3) = 19$
$$2p = 19 + 3$$
$$2p = 22$$
$$p = \frac{22}{2}$$
$$p = 11$$
Hence, the price of the jigsaw puzzle is £$(11 - 3) = £8$
and the price of the set of paints is £11.

12. Square tiles are paved along a side of a room. If 16 tiles are used, a length of 11 cm is left unpaved. If 17 tiles are used, 29 cm has to be cut off from a side of a tile. Find the length of the side of the room.

Solution

Let t be the side length of one of the tiles, measured in cm.
The length of the side of the room is given as $16t + 11$ and also as $17t - 29$.
∴ $16t + 11 = 17t - 29$
$$11 = 17t - 29 - 16t$$
$$11 = t - 29$$
$$t = 11 + 29$$
$$t = 40$$
Hence the room length is
$$16(40) + 11 = 640 + 11$$
$$= 651$$

The length of the side of the room is 651 cm.

13. David works the same number of hours each day, five days a week. If he works 1 hour less a day, the total number of working hours in a week is 3 hours more than his original total number of working hours in 4 days. Find his original number of working hours in a day.

Solution

Let h be David's original number of working hours in a day.
In four days he works $4h$ hours in total.
After reducing his hours, the number of hours he works in a week is $(h - 1) \times 5$.
From the information given,
$$5(h - 1) = 4h + 3$$
$$5h - 5 = 4h + 3$$
$$5h - 5 - 4h = 3$$
$$h - 5 = 3$$
$$h = 3 + 5$$
$$h = 8$$

David's original number of working hours in a day is 8.

Review Exercise 1

1. The number of spectators at a football match is 28 371.
   (a) State the place value of the digit 2.
   (b) Is the number a multiple of 3? Explain your answer.
   (c) Round the number to the nearest thousand.

Solution

(a) The place value of the digit 2 is 10 000.

(b) Divide 28 371 by 3 to see whether 28 371 is divisible by 3.

```
      9457
3 ) 28371
    27
    ──
    13
    12
    ──
    17
    15
    ──
    21
    21
    ──
     0
```
28 371 ÷ 3 = 9457
∴ 28 371 = 3 × 9457
Hence, 28 371 is a multiple of 3.

(c) 28 371 = 28 000 (to the nearest 1000)

2. The number of raffle tickets sold at a fund raising event is 16 875. The price of each ticket is £3. The total cost of the prizes for the winning tickets is £5839.
   (a) Round the number of tickets sold to the nearest hundred.
   (b) How much money is raised?

Solution

(a) 16 875 = 16 900 (to the nearest 100)

(b) The money raised is
    16 875 × 3 − 5839
    = 50 625 − 5839
    = 44 776
    The money raised is £44 786.

$$
\begin{array}{r}
16875 \\
\times 3 \\
\hline
50625 \\
{\scriptstyle 2\,2\,2\,1}
\end{array}
\qquad
\begin{array}{r}
{\scriptstyle 4\,9\,15\,11\,1} \\
50625 \\
-5839 \\
\hline
44786
\end{array}
$$

3. Calculate these expressions.
   (a) 326×99
   (b) $42 - 5^2 + 4 \times (16 + 3)$
   (c) $101 \times (43 - 24) - 3645 \div 15$
   (d) $-187 \div \left(\sqrt{144} + \sqrt[3]{125}\right)$

Solution

(a) 326×99
    $= 326 \times (100 - 1)$
    $= 326 \times 100 - 326 \times 1$
    $= 32\,600 - 326$
    $= 32\,274$

(b) $42 - 5^2 + 4 \times (16 + 3)$
    $= 42 - 25 + 4 \times 19$
    $= 42 - 25 + 76$
    $= 17 + 76$
    $= 93$

(c) $101 \times (43 - 24) - 3645 \div 15$
    $= 101 \times 19 - 243$
    $= 1919 - 243$
    $= 1919 - 219 - 24$
    $= 1700 - 24$
    $= 1676$

(d) $-187 \div \left(\sqrt{144} + \sqrt[3]{125}\right)$
    $= \dfrac{-187}{12 + 5}$
    $= -\dfrac{187}{17}$
    $= -11$

4. The balance of a bank account changes from −£135 to −£36.
   (a) Is the change an increase or a decrease? By how much? Explain your answer.
   (b) Find the common factors of the numbers 135 and 36.

Solution

(a) The change is an increase.
    Difference in balance $= -36 - (-135)$
    $= -36 + 135$
    $= 99$
    The balance has increased by £99.

(b) $135 = 1 \times 135$
    $= 3 \times 45$
    $= 5 \times 27$
    $= 9 \times 15$
    The factors of 135 are 1, 3, 5, 9, 15, 27, 45, 135.
    $36 = 1 \times 36$
    $= 2 \times 18$
    $= 3 \times 12$
    $= 4 \times 9$
    $= 6 \times 6$
    The factors of 36 are 1, 2, 3, 4, 6, 9, 12, 18, 36.
    ∴ the common factors of 135 and 36 are 1, 3 and 9.

5. Copy and complete the magic square so that the sum of each row, each column and each diagonal is equal.

-4	3	
	-1	
		2

Solution

Consider using algebraic variables for each missing entry.

-4	3	a
b	-1	c
d	e	2

The sum of the diagonal is $(-4) + (-1) + 2 = -3$. So the sum of each row, each column and each diagonal must equal -3.

$(-4) + 3 + a = -3$
$\quad a = (-3) - (-4) - 3$
$\quad\quad = -2$

$(-2) + c + 2 = -3$
$\quad c = (-3) - (-2) - 2$
$\quad c = -3$

$b + (-1) + (-3) = -3$
$\quad b = -3 - (-1) - (-3)$
$\quad b = 1$

$(-4) + 1 + d = -3$
$\quad d = (-3) - (-4) - 1$
$\quad d = 0$

$0 + e + 2 = -3$
$\quad e = (-3) - 2$
$\quad e = -5$

The complete magic square is as shown.

-4	3	-2
1	-1	-3
0	-5	2

6. Find the values of these expressions when $x = 6$ and $y = -2$.

(a) $4y - 7x + 9$
(b) $x^3 + y^2$
(c) $3x^2 - y^3$

Solution

(a) When $x = 6$ and $y = -2$,
$4y - 7x + 9 = 4(-2) - 7(6) + 9$
$\quad\quad = -8 - 42 + 9$
$\quad\quad = -50 + 9$
$\quad\quad = -41$

(b) When $x = 6$ and $y = -2$,
$x^3 + y^2 = 6^3 + (-2)^2$
$\quad\quad = 216 + 4$
$\quad\quad = 220$

(c) When $x = 6$ and $y = -2$,
$3x^2 - y^3 = 3 \times 6^2 - (-2)^3$
$\quad\quad = 3 \times 36 - (-8)$
$\quad\quad = 108 + 8$
$\quad\quad = 116$

7. Write these statements as algebraic expressions.

(a) Add $3a$ to b^2.
(b) Subtract $5h$ from k^4.
(c) The product of $7pq$ and $3p$.
(d) Divide the cube root of n by $6m$.

Solution

The algebraic expressions are

(a) $b^2 + 3a$

(b) $k^4 - 5h$

(c) $7pq \times 3p$
$\quad = 7 \times 3 \times p \times p \times q$
$\quad = 21p^2q$

(d) $\frac{\sqrt[3]{n}}{6m}$

8. Here are five expressions, A to E, in x and y.

$A \quad 2x - 3y$
$B \quad 4x - 3y$
$C \quad 3y - x$
$D \quad y - x$
$E \quad x - 3y$

(a) Which two expressions will give a sum of $3x$?
(b) Find the sum of two different expressions and challenge your partner to find the expressions you chose.

Solution

(a) $B + C = (4x - 3y) + (3y - x)$
$\quad\quad = 4x - 3y + 3y - x$
$\quad\quad = 3x$

Hence, the two expressions which give a sum of $3x$ are B and C.

(b) Student's own answers

9. Simplify these expressions.

(a) $4(3x + 1)$
(b) $-7(3 - b)$

Solution

(a) $4(3x + 1) = 12x + 4$

(b) $-7(3 - b) = -21 - 7 \times (-b)$
$\quad\quad = -21 + 7b$

10. Solve these equations.

(a) $\frac{x}{5} = 3$
(b) $3x + 7 = 1$
(c) $7 = 4(2x + 5)$

Solution

(a) $\dfrac{x}{5} = 5$

$x = 3 \times 5$

$x = 15$

(b) $3x + 7 = 1$

$3x = 1 - 7$

$3x = -6$

$x = \dfrac{-6}{3}$

$x = -2$

(c) $7 = 4(2x + 5)$

$7 = 8x + 20$

$7 - 20 = 8x$

$-13 = 8x$

$x = -\dfrac{13}{8}$

$x = -1\dfrac{5}{8}$

11. (a) Given the formula $y = \dfrac{5x^2}{k}$, find the value of y when $x = -4$ and $k = 8$.

GCSE Grade 3

(b) Given the formula $z = 6 - \dfrac{k}{x}$, find the value of z when $x = -4$ and $k = 8$.

(c) Find the smallest common multiple of the values of y and z found in (a) and (b).

Solution

(a) $y = \dfrac{5x^2}{k}$

When $x = -4$ and $k = 8$,

$y = \dfrac{5(-4)^2}{8}$

$= \dfrac{80}{8}$

$= 10$

(b) $z = 6 - \dfrac{k}{x}$

When $x = -4$ and $k = 8$,

$z = 6 - \dfrac{8}{(-4)}$

$= 6 - (-2)$

$= 8$

(c) 40

12. The amount of fuel used, V litres, by an airliner in flying d km is given by the formula

GCSE Grade 3

$V = 12d$.

(a) Find the amount of fuel used in a journey of 7500 km.

(b) The fuel capacity of the airliner is 183 384 litres. What is the longest journey it can fly? Give your answer correct to the nearest 100 km.

Solution

(a) When $d = 7500$,

$V = 12(7500)$

$= 90\,000$

The amount of fuel used is 90 000 litres.

(b) When $V = 183\,384$,

$183\,384 = 12d$

$d = 183\,384 \div 12$

$= 15\,282$

$= 15\,300$ (to the nearest 100)

The longest journey is 15 300 km, to the nearest 100 km.

```
        15282
  12)183384
        12
        63
        60
         33
         24
         98
         96
         24
         24
          0
```

13. In a silver cutlery set, the price of a knife is twice the price of a fork. The price of a fork is £3 more than the price of a spoon. Let £s be the price of a spoon.

GCSE Grade 3

(a) Express the price of a fork and the price of a knife in terms of s.

(b) Mrs Brown buys six knives, six forks and five spoons.

(i) Express the total price of the items in terms of s.

(ii) If $s = 4$, how much does Mrs Brown pay?

Solution

(a) The price of a fork is $(s + 3)$.

The price of a knife is $2(s + 3)$.

(b) (i) Total price is $6 \times [2(s + 3)] + 6 \times (s + 3) + 5s$

$= 18(s + 3) + 5s$

$= 18s + 54 + 5s$

$= 23s + 54$

(ii) When $s = 4$,

total price $= 23(4) + 54$

$= 92 + 54$

$= 146$

The total Mrs Brown pays is £146.

14. The total cost, £C, of a pot and n cups is given by the formula

GCSE Grade 3⁺

$C = 5 + 2n$.

(a) Find the total cost of a pot and four cups.

(b) Find the cost of the pot only.

(c) If the total cost is £17, how many cups are there?

Solution

(a) $C = 5 + 2n$

When $n = 4$,

$C = 5 + 2(4)$

$= 5 + 8$

$= 13$

The total cost of a pot and four cups is £13.

(b) If there are no cups, i.e. $n = 0$, $C = 5$.

The cost of the pot only is £5.

(c) If the total cost is £17,
$$17 = 5 + 2n$$
$$17 - 5 = 2n$$
$$12 = 2n$$
$$n = 12 \div 2$$
$$n = 6$$
When the total cost is £17, the number of cups is 6.

15. Nancy has 15 banknotes in her purse. Some of them are £20 notes and the rest are £50 notes. The total value of the banknotes is £570.

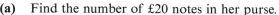

(a) Find the number of £20 notes in her purse.
(b) If Nancy gave two £50 notes to David, the amount she had left would be twice the amount that David had. Find the original amount that David had.

Solution

(a) Let the number of £20 notes Nancy has be x.
Then the number of £50 notes she has is $(15 - x)$.
The total value of the banknotes in £ is
$$20x + 50(15 - x)$$
$$= 20x + 750 - 50x$$
$$= 750 - 30x$$

The total value is given as £570.
$$\therefore \ 750 - 30x = 570$$
$$-30x = 570 - 750$$
$$-30x = -180$$
$$x = (-180) \div (-30)$$
$$x = 6$$
The number of £20 banknotes Nancy has in her purse is 6.

(b) If Nancy gave 2×50 away, the money she would have left is $570 - 2 \times 50 = 470$.
Let d be the original amount that David had.
Then the current amount David has is $(d + 100)$.
From the information given,
$$2(d + 100) = 470$$
$$2d + 200 = 470$$
$$2d = 470 - 200$$
$$2d = 270$$
$$d = 270 \div 2$$
$$d = 135$$
The original amount David had is £135.

Fractions

Class Activity 1

Objective: To explore the ways of comparing fractions.

1. In the bars below, the shaded parts represent the fractions $\frac{1}{2}$, $\frac{1}{3}$ and $\frac{1}{6}$ respectively.

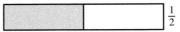

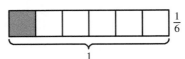

   (a) Which fraction is the smallest?

   $\frac{1}{6}$ is the smallest.

   (b) Which fraction is the greatest?

   $\frac{1}{2}$ is the greatest.

2. In the bars below, the shaded parts represent the fractions $\frac{3}{7}$ and $\frac{3}{10}$ respectively. Which fraction is smaller?

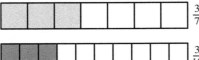
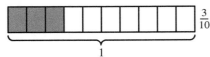

   $\frac{3}{10}$ is smaller than $\frac{3}{7}$.

3. Observing the results in Questions **1** and **2**, when two fractions have the same numerator, which fraction is greater: the one with the smaller denominator or the bigger denominator? Explain your answer.

   When two fractions have the same numerator, the one with the smaller denominator is greater. When the denominator is smaller, it means the whole

   (bar) is divided into fewer parts and so each part is larger than one that is from a bar which is divided into more parts.

4. When two fractions have the same denominator, for example $\frac{5}{9}$ and $\frac{8}{9}$, which is greater: the one with the smaller numerator or the bigger numerator? Explain your answer.

   When two fractions have the same denominator, the one with the bigger numerator is greater. When the denominators are the same, it means the

   wholes representing the fractions are divided into the same number of parts. The fraction with the bigger numerator is represented by more parts

   and thus the fraction is greater.

$\frac{5}{9}$

$\frac{8}{9}$

$\frac{8}{9} > \frac{5}{9}$

5. Explain how you would compare $\frac{3}{5}$ and $\frac{4}{7}$. Draw bars with shaded parts to help you.

To compare $\frac{3}{5}$ and $\frac{4}{7}$, you can change both fractions to equivalent fractions with the same denominator.

35 is a common multiple of 5 and 7. Change both fractions to equivalent fractions with 35 as the denominator.

$\frac{3}{5} = \frac{3 \times 7}{5 \times 7} = \frac{21}{35}$

$\frac{4}{7} = \frac{4 \times 5}{7 \times 5} = \frac{20}{35}$

Since 21 > 20, $\frac{21}{35} > \frac{20}{35}$.

Hence, $\frac{3}{5} > \frac{4}{7}$.

Alternatively, you can make the numerators of the two fractions the same and compare $\frac{3}{5}$ and $\frac{4}{7}$ as stated in Question 3.

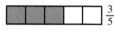 $\frac{3}{5}$

 $\frac{4}{7}$

$\frac{3}{5} > \frac{4}{7}$

Try It!

Section 5.1

1. (a) What mixed number do the shaded parts represent?

whole

(b) Express the mixed number as an improper fraction.

Solution

(a) The shaded parts
= 1 whole and 2 thirds
= $1\frac{2}{3}$

(b) $1\frac{2}{3}$ = 3 thirds + 2 thirds
= 5 thirds
= $\frac{5}{3}$

Alternatively,

$1\frac{2}{3} = \frac{1 \times 3 + 2}{3}$
$= \frac{5}{3}$

2. Express these improper fractions as mixed numbers.

(a) $\frac{11}{4}$ (b) $\frac{11}{5}$

Solution

(a) $\frac{11}{4}$ = 11 fourths
= 4 fourths + 4 fourths + 3 fourths
= $1 + 1 + \frac{3}{4}$
= $2\frac{3}{4}$

Alternatively,

$$4\overline{)11}$$
$$\underline{8}$$
$$3$$

$\therefore \frac{11}{4} = 2\frac{3}{4}$

175

(b) $\dfrac{11}{5} = 11$ fifths

$\qquad = 5$ fifths $+ 5$ fifths $+ 1$ fifth

$\qquad = 1 + 1 + \dfrac{1}{5}$

$\qquad = 2\dfrac{1}{5}$

Alternatively,

$$5\overline{)11}$$
$$\underline{10}$$
$$\;\;1$$
with quotient 2

$\therefore \dfrac{11}{5} = 2\dfrac{1}{5}$

3. There are seven mathematics books and five science books on a table. Express the number of mathematics books as a fraction of
   (a) the total number of books,
   (b) the number of science books.

Solution
(a) Total number of books
$\qquad = 7 + 5$
$\qquad = 12$
The required fraction
$\qquad = \dfrac{\text{Number of maths books}}{\text{Total number of books}}$
$\qquad = \dfrac{7}{12}$

(b) The required fraction
$\qquad = \dfrac{\text{Number of maths books}}{\text{Number of science books}}$
$\qquad = \dfrac{7}{5}$

Section 5.2

4. Express $\dfrac{36}{42}$ in its simplest form.

Solution
$\dfrac{36}{42} = \dfrac{36 \div 6}{42 \div 6}$
$\qquad = \dfrac{6}{7}$

5. If the fractions $\dfrac{7}{8}$ and $\dfrac{x}{24}$ are equivalent, find the value of x.

Solution
Since $24 = 8 \times 3$, you have
$\dfrac{7}{8} = \dfrac{7 \times 3}{8 \times 3}$
$\quad = \dfrac{21}{24}$
So, $x = 21$.

6. Which fraction is greater, $\dfrac{4}{5}$ or $\dfrac{7}{9}$?

Solution
45 is a common multiple of 5 and 9.
$\dfrac{4}{5} = \dfrac{4 \times 9}{5 \times 9} = \dfrac{36}{45}$
$\dfrac{7}{9} = \dfrac{7 \times 5}{9 \times 5} = \dfrac{35}{45}$
As $\qquad \dfrac{36}{45} > \dfrac{35}{45}$,
you know $\dfrac{4}{5} > \dfrac{7}{9}$.

Hence, $\dfrac{4}{5}$ is greater.

7. Which fraction is smaller, $-\dfrac{7}{8}$ or $-\dfrac{3}{4}$?

Solution
Change the fraction $-\dfrac{3}{4}$ to an equivalent fraction with 8 as the denominator.
$-\dfrac{3}{4} = -\dfrac{3 \times 2}{4 \times 2}$
$\qquad = -\dfrac{6}{8}$
Since $-7 < -6$, $-\dfrac{7}{8} < -\dfrac{6}{8}$.

Hence, $-\dfrac{7}{8}$ is smaller.
A number line can also be drawn to compare the fractions.

Since $-\dfrac{7}{8}$ is on the left of $-\dfrac{6}{8}$ on the number line, $-\dfrac{7}{8}$ is smaller.

8. Which number is smaller, $-\dfrac{11}{4}$ or $-2\dfrac{2}{3}$?

Solution
To compare the two numbers, you can express both numbers as improper fractions with the same denominator.
$-\dfrac{11}{4} = -\dfrac{11 \times 3}{4 \times 3} = -\dfrac{33}{12}$
$-2\dfrac{2}{3} = -\dfrac{2 \times 3 + 2}{3}$
$\qquad = -\dfrac{8}{3}$
$\qquad = -\dfrac{8 \times 4}{3 \times 4}$
$\qquad = -\dfrac{32}{12}$
Since $-33 < -32$,
$-\dfrac{33}{12} < -\dfrac{32}{12}$.

Hence, $-\dfrac{11}{4}$ is smaller.

Section 5.3

9. Calculate these values and give your answers as fractions in their simplest form.

(a) $\frac{1}{6} + \frac{3}{6}$

(b) $\frac{7}{8} - \frac{3}{8}$

Solution

(a) $\frac{1}{6} + \frac{3}{6} = \frac{1+3}{6}$

$= \frac{4}{6}$

$= \frac{2}{3}$

(b) $\frac{7}{8} - \frac{3}{8} = \frac{7-3}{8}$

$= \frac{4}{8}$

$= \frac{1}{2}$

10. Work out these values and give your answers as fractions in their simplest form.

(a) Add $\frac{2}{3}$ and $\frac{5}{6}$.

(b) Subtract $\frac{5}{7}$ from $\frac{3}{4}$.

Solution

(a) $\frac{2}{3} + \frac{5}{6} = \frac{4}{6} + \frac{5}{6}$

$= \frac{9}{6}$

$= \frac{3}{2}$

$= 1\frac{1}{2}$

(b) $\frac{3}{4} - \frac{5}{7} = \frac{21}{28} - \frac{20}{28}$

$= \frac{1}{28}$

11. Calculate $2\frac{1}{3} + 7\frac{5}{6}$.

Solution

Method 1

$2\frac{1}{3} + 7\frac{5}{6}$

$= 2 + \frac{1}{3} + 7 + \frac{5}{6}$

$= (2 + 7) + \left(\frac{1}{3} + \frac{5}{6}\right)$

$= 9 + \left(\frac{2}{6} + \frac{5}{6}\right)$

$= 9 + \frac{7}{6}$

$= 9 + 1\frac{1}{6}$

$= 10\frac{1}{6}$

Method 2

$2\frac{1}{3} + 7\frac{5}{6}$

$= \frac{7}{3} + \frac{47}{6}$

$= \frac{14}{6} + \frac{47}{6}$

$= \frac{61}{6}$

$= 10\frac{1}{6}$

12. Calculate $5\frac{1}{2} - 3\frac{2}{3}$.

Solution

Method 1

$5\frac{1}{2} - 3\frac{2}{3}$

$= (5 - 3) + \left(\frac{1}{2} - \frac{2}{3}\right)$

$= 2 + \left(\frac{3}{6} - \frac{4}{6}\right)$

$= 2 + \left(-\frac{1}{6}\right)$

$= 2 - \frac{1}{6}$

$= 1\frac{5}{6}$

Method 2

$5\frac{1}{2} - 3\frac{2}{3}$

$= \frac{11}{2} - \frac{11}{3}$

$= \frac{33}{6} - \frac{22}{6}$

$= \frac{11}{6}$

$= 1\frac{5}{6}$

13. Evan has 2 litres of orange juice, $1\frac{1}{3}$ litres of apple juice and $\frac{3}{8}$ litres of grapefruit juice in the refrigerator. Find the total volume of the juices.

Solution

The total volume of the juices

$= 2 + 1\frac{1}{3} + \frac{3}{8}$

$= 2 + \frac{4}{3} + \frac{3}{8}$

$= \frac{48}{24} + \frac{32}{24} + \frac{9}{24}$

$= \frac{48 + 32 + 9}{24}$

$= \frac{89}{24}$

$= 3\frac{17}{24}$ litres

Section 5.4

14. A girl has £45. She uses $\frac{2}{9}$ of it to buy a calculator. Find the price of the calculator.

Solution

Price of the calculator

$= \frac{2}{9}$ of £45

$= \frac{2}{\cancel{9}_1} \times £\cancel{45}^{5}$

$= 2 \times £5$

$= £10$

15. Find the number of days in $\frac{4}{5}$ of the days in April.

Solution

There are 30 days in the month of April.

$\frac{4}{5}$ of the days in April

$= \frac{4}{\cancel{5}_1} \times \cancel{30}^{6}$

$= 4 \times 6$

$= 24$ days

16. Calculate

    (a) $\dfrac{5}{12} \times \dfrac{4}{7}$,   (b) $2\dfrac{2}{5} \times 1\dfrac{7}{8}$.

    Solution

    (a) $\dfrac{5}{12} \times \dfrac{4}{7}$

    $= \dfrac{5}{\cancel{12}_3} \times \dfrac{\cancel{4}^1}{7}$

    $= \dfrac{5 \times 1}{3 \times 7}$

    $= \dfrac{5}{21}$

    (b) $2\dfrac{2}{5} \times 1\dfrac{7}{8}$

    $= \dfrac{\cancel{12}^3}{\cancel{5}_1} \times \dfrac{\cancel{15}^3}{\cancel{8}_2}$

    $= \dfrac{3 \times 3}{1 \times 2}$

    $= \dfrac{9}{2}$

    $= 4\dfrac{1}{2}$

17. Calculate $3\dfrac{1}{2} \times 4\dfrac{3}{7}$ using the grid method.

    Solution

×	4	$\dfrac{3}{7}$
3	12	$\dfrac{9}{7}$
$\dfrac{1}{2}$	2	$\dfrac{3}{14}$

    $3\dfrac{1}{2} \times 4\dfrac{3}{7} = 12 + \dfrac{9}{7} + 2 + \dfrac{3}{14}$

    $= 12 + \dfrac{18}{14} + 2 + \dfrac{3}{14}$

    $= 14 + \dfrac{21}{14}$

    $= 14 + 1\dfrac{7}{14}$

    $= 15\dfrac{1}{2}$

18. The area of a living room floor is $18\dfrac{1}{3}\,\text{m}^2$. If $\dfrac{6}{11}$ of the living room is covered with carpet, find the area of the carpet.

    Solution
    Area of the carpet
    $= \dfrac{6}{11} \times 18\dfrac{1}{3}$
    $= \dfrac{\cancel{6}^2}{\cancel{11}_1} \times \dfrac{\cancel{55}^5}{\cancel{3}_1}$
    $= 2 \times 5$
    $= 10\,\text{m}^2$

Section 5.5

19. If $\dfrac{3}{8}$ kg of sugar is divided into six equal bowls, how much sugar is in each bowl?

Solution
Amount of sugar in each bowl
$= \dfrac{3}{8} \div 6$

$= \dfrac{\cancel{3}^1}{8} \times \dfrac{1}{\cancel{6}_2}$

$= \dfrac{1 \times 1}{8 \times 2}$

$= \dfrac{1}{16}\,\text{kg}$

20. Calculate these values.

    (a) $\dfrac{8}{21} \div \dfrac{12}{35}$ (b) $\left(-4\dfrac{1}{2}\right) \div 3\dfrac{3}{8}$

    Solution

    (a) $\dfrac{8}{21} \div \dfrac{12}{35}$

    $= \dfrac{\cancel{8}^2}{\cancel{21}_3} \times \dfrac{\cancel{35}^5}{\cancel{12}_3}$

    $= \dfrac{2 \times 5}{3 \times 3}$

    $= \dfrac{10}{9}$

    $= 1\dfrac{1}{9}$

    (b) $\left(-4\dfrac{1}{2}\right) \div 3\dfrac{3}{8}$

    $= \left(-\dfrac{9}{2}\right) \div \dfrac{27}{8}$

    $= -\dfrac{\cancel{9}^1}{\cancel{2}_1} \times \dfrac{\cancel{8}^4}{\cancel{27}_3}$

    $= -\dfrac{1 \times 4}{1 \times 3}$

    $= -\dfrac{4}{3}$

    $= -1\dfrac{1}{3}$

21. Calculate $6\dfrac{3}{7} \div \dfrac{10}{21} \div \dfrac{9}{16}$.

    Solution
    $6\dfrac{3}{7} \div \dfrac{10}{21} \div \dfrac{9}{16}$
    $= \dfrac{45}{7} \times \dfrac{21}{10} \div \dfrac{9}{16}$
    $= \dfrac{9 \times 3}{1 \times 2} \div \dfrac{9}{16}$
    $= \dfrac{27}{2} \times \dfrac{16}{9}$
    $= 3 \times 8$
    $= 24$

22. Olivia has $4\dfrac{1}{2}$ litres of orange juice. She pours the juice into bottles that can each contain $\dfrac{3}{5}$ litres of juice.
    (a) How many complete bottles can be filled?
    (b) How much juice will be left over?

    Solution
    (a) $4\dfrac{1}{2} \div \dfrac{3}{5}$

    $= \dfrac{9}{2} \times \dfrac{5}{3}$

    $= \dfrac{3 \times 5}{2 \times 1}$

    $= \dfrac{15}{2}$

    $= 7\dfrac{1}{2}$

    $\therefore$ 7 complete bottles can be filled.

(b) Volume of juice that remains

= volume of $\frac{1}{2}$ a bottle

$= \frac{1}{2} \times \frac{3}{5}$

$= \frac{3}{10}$ litres

Alternatively,

$4\frac{1}{2} - \left(7 \times \frac{3}{5}\right)$

$= 4\frac{1}{2} - \frac{21}{5}$

$= \frac{9}{2} - \frac{21}{5}$

$= \frac{45}{10} - \frac{42}{10}$

$= \frac{3}{10}$ litres

Section 5.6

23. Mrs Smith paints a flag pole which is $3\frac{3}{4}$ m long. She paints $\frac{3}{5}$ red and $\frac{1}{6}$ blue. How much longer is the red part than the blue part?

Solution

The red part is longer than the blue part by

$\left(\frac{3}{5} - \frac{1}{6}\right) \times 3\frac{3}{4}$

$= \left(\frac{18}{30} - \frac{5}{30}\right) \times \frac{15}{4}$

$= \frac{13}{30} \times \frac{15}{4}$

$= \frac{13 \times 1}{2 \times 4}$

$= \frac{13}{8}$

$= 1\frac{5}{8}$ m

Exercise 5.1

Level 1

 GCSE Grade 2^{-} / 2

1. What fraction of the whole is represented by the shaded parts?

(a) 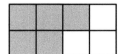 **(b)**

Solution

The fraction of the whole that has been shaded is

(a) $\frac{5}{8}$ **(b)** $\frac{5}{8}$

2. Write the mixed number and the improper fraction that are represented by the shaded parts.

(a)

whole   whole

(b)

whole   whole   whole

Solution

(a) The shaded parts = 2 wholes and 5 sixths

$= 2\frac{5}{6}$ (mixed number)

$= \frac{17}{6}$ (improper fraction)

(b) The shaded parts = 3 wholes and 2 quarters

$= 3\frac{2}{4}$ (mixed number)

$= \frac{14}{4}$ (improper fraction)

Some students should be able to see that the shaded parts = 3 wholes and 1 half

$= 3\frac{1}{2}$ (mixed number)

$= \frac{7}{2}$ (improper fraction)

Level 2

GCSE Grade 2 / 2^{+}

3. A class has 13 boys and 17 girls. What is the fraction of boys in the class?

Solution

Total number of students in the class = 13 + 17

= 30

The fraction of boys in the class $= \frac{13}{30}$

4. Saraka has seven yellow ribbons and two blue ribbons. Express the number of blue ribbons as a fraction of the total number of ribbons.

Solution

The required fraction $= \dfrac{\text{Number of blue ribbons}}{\text{Total number of ribbons}}$

$= \frac{2}{7+2}$

$= \frac{2}{9}$

5. Express each mixed number as an improper fraction.

(a) $1\frac{1}{2}$ **(b)** $2\frac{1}{2}$

(c) $3\frac{3}{5}$ **(d)** $3\frac{4}{5}$

(e) $4\frac{2}{7}$ **(f)** $4\frac{2}{9}$

Solution

Two methods are shown below. Students can use either method.

(a) Method 1

$$1\frac{1}{2} = 1 \text{ whole} + 1 \text{ half}$$
$$= 2 \text{ halves} + 1 \text{ half}$$
$$= 3 \text{ halves}$$
$$= \frac{3}{2}$$

Method 2

$$1\frac{1}{2} = \frac{1 \times 2 + 1}{2}$$
$$= \frac{3}{2}$$

(b) Method 1

$$2\frac{1}{2} = 2 \text{ halves} + 2 \text{ halves} + 1 \text{ half}$$
$$= 5 \text{ halves}$$
$$= \frac{5}{2}$$

Method 2

$$2\frac{1}{2} = \frac{2 \times 2 + 1}{2}$$
$$= \frac{5}{2}$$

(c) Method 1

$$3\frac{3}{5} = 5 \text{ fifths} + 5 \text{ fifths} + 5 \text{ fifths} + 3 \text{ fifths}$$
$$= 18 \text{ fifths}$$
$$= \frac{18}{5}$$

Method 2

$$3\frac{3}{5} = \frac{3 \times 5 + 3}{5}$$
$$= \frac{18}{5}$$

(d) Method 1

$$3\frac{4}{5} = 5 \text{ fifths} + 5 \text{ fifths} + 5 \text{ fifths} + 4 \text{ fifths}$$
$$= 19 \text{ fifths}$$
$$= \frac{19}{5}$$

Method 2

$$3\frac{4}{5} = \frac{3 \times 5 + 4}{5}$$
$$= \frac{19}{5}$$

(e) Method 1

$$4\frac{2}{7} = 7 \text{ sevenths} + 7 \text{ sevenths} + 7 \text{ sevenths} +$$
$$7 \text{ sevenths} + 2 \text{ sevenths}$$
$$= 30 \text{ sevenths}$$
$$= \frac{30}{7}$$

Method 2

$$4\frac{2}{7} = \frac{4 \times 7 + 2}{7}$$
$$= \frac{30}{7}$$

(f) Method 1

$$4\frac{2}{9} = 9 \text{ ninths} + 9 \text{ ninths} + 9 \text{ ninths}$$
$$+ 2 \text{ ninths}$$
$$= 38 \text{ ninths}$$
$$= \frac{38}{9}$$

Method 2

$$4\frac{2}{9} = \frac{4 \times 9 + 2}{9}$$
$$= \frac{38}{9}$$

6. Find the missing numbers.

   (a) $5 = \dfrac{\square}{3}$

   (b) $7 = \dfrac{\square}{4}$

Solution

(a)
$$5 = \frac{\square}{3}$$
$$5 \times 3 = \square$$
$$\square = 15$$

(b)
$$7 = \frac{\square}{4}$$
$$7 \times 4 = \square$$
$$\square = 28$$

7. Express each improper fraction as a mixed number or whole number.

   (a) $\dfrac{5}{2}$ **(b)** $\dfrac{7}{2}$

   (c) $\dfrac{8}{3}$ **(d)** $\dfrac{8}{5}$

   (e) $\dfrac{9}{6}$ **(f)** $\dfrac{12}{6}$

Solution

Two methods are shown below. Students can use either method.

(a) Method 1

$$\frac{5}{2} = 5 \text{ halves}$$
$$= 2 \text{ halves} + 2 \text{ halves} + 1 \text{ half}$$
$$= 1 + 1 + \frac{1}{2}$$
$$= 2\frac{1}{2}$$

Method 2

$$\begin{array}{r} 2 \\ 2\overline{)5} \\ 4 \\ \hline 1 \end{array}$$

$$\therefore \frac{5}{2} = 2\frac{1}{2}$$

(b) Method 1

$\frac{7}{2} = 7$ halves

$= 2$ halves $+ 2$ halves $+ 2$ halves $+ 1$ half

$= 1 + 1 + 1 + \frac{1}{2}$

$= 3\frac{1}{2}$

Method 2

$$2\overline{\smash{\big)}\,7} \\ \quad\frac{6}{1}$$

$\therefore \frac{7}{2} = 3\frac{1}{2}$

(c) Method 1

$\frac{8}{3} = 8$ thirds $= 3$ thirds $+ 3$ thirds $+ 2$ thirds

$= 1 + 1 + \frac{2}{3}$

$= 2\frac{2}{3}$

Method 2

$$3\overline{\smash{\big)}\,8} \\ \quad\frac{6}{2}$$

$\therefore \frac{8}{3} = 2\frac{2}{3}$

(d) Method 1

$\frac{8}{5} = 8$ fifths

$= 5$ fifths $+ 3$ fifths

$= 1 + \frac{3}{5}$

$= 1\frac{3}{5}$

Method 2

$$5\overline{\smash{\big)}\,8} \\ \quad\frac{5}{3}$$

$\therefore \frac{8}{5} = 1\frac{3}{5}$

(e) Method 1

$\frac{9}{6} = 9$ sixths

$= 6$ sixths $+ 3$ sixths

$= 1 + \frac{3}{6}$

$= 1\frac{1}{2}$

Method 2

$$6\overline{\smash{\big)}\,9} \\ \quad\frac{6}{3}$$

$\therefore \frac{9}{6} = 1\frac{3}{6} = 1\frac{1}{2}$

(f) Method 1

$\frac{12}{6} = 12$ sixths

$= 6$ sixths $+ 6$ sixths

$= 1 + 1$

$= 2$

Method 2

$$6\overline{\smash{\big)}\,12} \\ \quad\frac{12}{0}$$

$\therefore \frac{12}{6} = 2$

Level 3 GCSE Grade **3⁻ / 3**

8. A bouquet consists of two white roses, six red roses and three yellow roses. Find the fraction of
   (a) white roses,
   (b) red roses.

   Solution
   (a) Total number of roses
   $= 2 + 6 + 3$
   $= 11$
   Fraction of white roses
   $= \frac{2}{11}$
   (b) Fraction of red roses $= \frac{6}{11}$

9. It takes $\frac{11}{4}$ tins of paint to cover a fence. How many whole tins of paint should be bought?

   Solution
   $\frac{11}{4} = 2\frac{3}{4}$ $\qquad 4\overline{\smash{\big)}\,11}$
   $\qquad\qquad\qquad\qquad \frac{8}{3}$

   3 tins of paints should be bought.

10. A mathematics project takes 187 minutes to finish. Express the time taken as a mixed number of hours.
    Hint: 1 hour $= 60$ minutes.

    Solution
    187 minutes
    $= \frac{187}{60}$ hours $\qquad 60\overline{\smash{\big)}\,187}$
    $\qquad\qquad\qquad\qquad \frac{180}{7}$
    $= 3\frac{7}{60}$ hours
    So, the time taken is $3\frac{7}{60}$ hours.

11. There are $\frac{100}{13}$ litres of acid and $7\frac{4}{13}$ litres of alkali in a laboratory. Which liquid has a greater volume? Explain your answer.

Solution

The volume of acid in litres is

$\frac{100}{13} = 7\frac{9}{13}$

$\begin{array}{r} 7 \\ 13\overline{\smash{)}100} \\ \underline{91} \\ 9 \end{array}$

Since $7\frac{9}{13} > 7\frac{4}{13}$, the acid has the greater volume.

12. **(a)** Create a mixed number using each of the digits 3, 5 and 7 once.
(b) Express your mixed number as an improper fraction.
(c) How many different mixed numbers can be created?

Solution

(a) $3\frac{5}{7}$ or $5\frac{3}{7}$ or $7\frac{3}{5}$

(b) $3\frac{5}{7} = \frac{3 \times 7 + 5}{7}$

$= \frac{26}{7}$

(c) Other mixed numbers that can be created using each of the digits 3, 5 and 7 once are $5\frac{3}{7}$ and $7\frac{3}{5}$. A total of three different mixed numbers can be created.

13. Write down an improper fraction which is greater than 2.

Solution

One way of generating examples is to first write down any mixed number greater than 2 and then convert it to an improper fraction.

For example, $10\frac{1}{3}$.

$10\frac{1}{3} = (10 \times 3 + 1) \div 3$

$= \frac{31}{3}$

Exercise 5.2

Level 1

GCSE Grade 2^- / 2

1. Express each fraction in its simplest form.
(a) $\frac{5}{15}$ **(b)** $\frac{7}{56}$

(c) $\frac{12}{20}$ **(d)** $\frac{18}{45}$

Solution

(a) $\frac{5}{15} = \frac{5 \div 5}{15 \div 5}$ **(b)** $\frac{7}{56} = \frac{7 \div 7}{56 \div 7}$

     $= \frac{1}{3}$ $= \frac{1}{8}$

(c) $\frac{12}{20} = \frac{12 \div 4}{20 \div 4}$ **(d)** $\frac{18}{45} = \frac{18 \div 9}{45 \div 9}$

     $= \frac{3}{5}$ $= \frac{2}{5}$

2. Express each fraction in its lowest terms.
(a) $-\frac{6}{9}$ **(b)** $-\frac{18}{21}$

(c) $-\frac{24}{36}$ **(d)** $-\frac{4}{16}$

Solution

(a) $-\frac{6}{9} = -\frac{6 \div 3}{9 \div 3}$ **(b)** $-\frac{18}{21} = -\frac{18 \div 3}{21 \div 3}$

     $= -\frac{2}{3}$ $= -\frac{6}{7}$

(c) $-\frac{24}{36} = -\frac{24 \div 12}{36 \div 12}$ **(d)** $-\frac{4}{16} = -\frac{4 \div 4}{16 \div 4}$

     $= -\frac{2}{3}$ $= -\frac{1}{4}$

3. Find the value of x if each pair of fractions is equivalent.
(a) $\frac{2}{3}, \frac{x}{12}$ **(b)** $\frac{4}{7}, \frac{20}{x}$

(c) $-\frac{x}{8}, -\frac{3}{4}$ **(d)** $-\frac{6}{x}, -\frac{30}{40}$

Solution

(a) Since $12 = 3 \times 4$, you have $\frac{2}{3} = \frac{2 \times 4}{3 \times 4} = \frac{8}{12}$. Hence, $x = 8$.

(b) Since $20 = 4 \times 5$, you have $\frac{4}{7} = \frac{4 \times 5}{7 \times 5} = \frac{20}{35}$. Hence, $x = 35$.

(c) Since $8 = 4 \times 2$, you have $-\frac{3}{4} = -\frac{3 \times 2}{4 \times 2} = -\frac{6}{8}$. Hence, $x = 6$.

(d) Since $-6 = -30 \div 5$, you have $-\frac{30}{40} = -\frac{30 \div 5}{40 \div 5} = -\frac{6}{8}$. Hence, $x = 8$.

4. Identify the smaller fraction in each pair.
(a) $\frac{1}{6}, \frac{1}{7}$ **(b)** $\frac{4}{11}, \frac{4}{9}$

(c) $\frac{5}{12}, \frac{7}{12}$ **(d)** $-\frac{3}{8}, -\frac{5}{8}$

Solution

(a) When the numerators of the two fractions are the same, the fraction with the bigger denominator is smaller.

Hence, $\frac{1}{7}$ is the smaller fraction.

(b) With the same reasoning as **(a)**, $\frac{4}{11}$ is the smaller fraction.

(c) When two fractions have the same denominator, the one with the smaller numerator is smaller.

Hence, $\frac{5}{12}$ is the smaller fraction.

(d) Since $-5 < -3$, $-\frac{5}{8} < -\frac{3}{8}$.

Hence, $-\frac{5}{8}$ is the smaller fraction.

Level 2 GCSE Grade **2⁺/3⁻**

5. Express each improper fraction as a mixed number in its simplest form.

(a) $\frac{14}{6}$ **(b)** $\frac{125}{60}$

(c) $-\frac{80}{25}$ **(d)** $-\frac{48}{18}$

Solution

(a) $\frac{14}{6} = \frac{14 \div 2}{6 \div 2}$

$= \frac{7}{3}$

$= 2\frac{1}{3}$

$$3 \overline{\smash{\big)}\, 7} \\ \,6 \\ \,1$$

Alternatively, $\frac{14}{6} = \frac{7}{3} = 7$ thirds

$= 3$ thirds $+ 3$ thirds $+ 1$ third

$= 1 + 1 + \frac{1}{3}$

$= 2\frac{1}{3}$

(b) $\frac{125}{60} = \frac{125 \div 5}{60 \div 5}$

$= \frac{25}{12}$

$= 2\frac{1}{12}$

$$12 \overline{\smash{\big)}\, 25} \\ \,24 \\ \,1$$

(c) $-\frac{80}{25} = -\frac{80 \div 5}{25 \div 5}$

$= -\frac{16}{5}$

$= -3\frac{1}{5}$

$$5 \overline{\smash{\big)}\, 16} \\ \,15 \\ \,1$$

(d) $-\frac{48}{18} = -\frac{48 \div 6}{18 \div 6}$

$= -\frac{8}{3}$

$= -2\frac{2}{3}$

$$3 \overline{\smash{\big)}\, 8} \\ \,6 \\ \,2$$

6. Express each mixed number as an improper fraction in its lowest terms.

(a) $1\frac{6}{8}$ **(b)** $4\frac{6}{10}$

(c) $-3\frac{6}{12}$ **(d)** $-2\frac{14}{21}$

Solution

(a) $1\frac{6}{8} = \frac{1 \times 8 + 6}{8}$

$= \frac{14}{8}$

$= \frac{14 \div 2}{8 \div 2}$

$= \frac{7}{4}$

(b) $4\frac{6}{10} = \frac{4 \times 10 + 6}{10}$

$= \frac{46}{10}$

$= \frac{46 \div 2}{10 \div 2}$

$= \frac{23}{5}$

(c) $-3\frac{6}{12} = -\frac{3 \times 12 + 6}{12}$

$= -\frac{42}{12}$

$= -\frac{42 \div 6}{12 \div 6}$

$= -\frac{7}{2}$

(d) $-2\frac{14}{21} = -\frac{2 \times 21 + 14}{21}$

$= -\frac{56}{21}$

$= -\frac{56 \div 7}{21 \div 7}$

$= -\frac{8}{3}$

7. Identify the smaller number in each pair.

(a) $1\frac{3}{7}$, $1\frac{3}{5}$ **(b)** $2\frac{1}{4}$, $2\frac{2}{9}$

(c) $-3\frac{5}{8}$, $-3\frac{1}{6}$ **(d)** $-2\frac{1}{5}$, $1\frac{5}{6}$

Solution

(a) The whole numbers of both mixed numbers are the same. You need to compare the proper fraction parts. Since the fraction parts have the same numerator, the one with the bigger denominator is smaller.

Hence, $1\frac{3}{7}$ is the smaller number.

(b) Both mixed numbers have the same whole number parts.

$\frac{1}{4} = \frac{1 \times 9}{4 \times 9} = \frac{9}{36}$

$\frac{2}{9} = \frac{2 \times 4}{9 \times 4} = \frac{8}{36}$

As $\frac{8}{36} < \frac{9}{36}$,

you have $\frac{2}{9} < \frac{1}{4}$

and $2\frac{2}{9} < 2\frac{1}{4}$.

Hence, $2\frac{2}{9}$ is the smaller number.

(c) Both mixed numbers have the same whole number parts.

$\frac{5}{8} = \frac{5 \times 3}{8 \times 3} = \frac{15}{24}$

$\frac{1}{6} = \frac{1 \times 4}{6 \times 4} = \frac{4}{24}$

That is,

$-3\frac{5}{8} = -3\frac{15}{24}$ and

$-3\frac{1}{6} = -3\frac{4}{24}$.

As $-15 < -4$,

you have $-3\frac{15}{24} < -3\frac{4}{24}$.

and $-3\frac{5}{8} < -3\frac{1}{6}$.

Hence, $-3\frac{5}{8}$ is the smaller number.

(d) Comparing the whole number parts,
$-2 < 1$.
$\therefore -2\frac{1}{5} < 1\frac{5}{6}$.
Hence, $-2\frac{1}{5}$ is the smaller number.

8. Peter took $1\frac{1}{3}$ hours to complete his homework. Ann took $1\frac{2}{5}$ hours to complete the same homework. Who was faster?

Solution

$1\frac{1}{3} = \frac{4}{3}$

$\quad = \frac{4 \times 5}{3 \times 5}$

$\quad = \frac{20}{15}$

$1\frac{2}{5} = \frac{7}{5}$

$\quad = \frac{7 \times 3}{5 \times 3}$

$\quad = \frac{21}{15}$

i.e. Peter took $\frac{20}{15}$ hours and Ann took $\frac{21}{15}$ hours. As $\frac{20}{15} < \frac{21}{15}$, Peter was faster.

9. A green bottle contains $\frac{12}{16}$ litres of water. A blue bottle contains $\frac{15}{20}$ litres of water. Compare the volumes of water in the two bottles.

Solution

$\frac{12}{16} = \frac{12 \div 4}{16 \div 4}$

$\quad = \frac{3}{4}$

$\frac{15}{20} = \frac{15 \div 5}{20 \div 5}$

$\quad = \frac{3}{4}$

You have $\frac{12}{16} = \frac{15}{20} = \frac{3}{4}$.

The volumes of water in the two bottles are equal.

10. Write these fractions in order from smallest to largest.
$\frac{2}{3}, \frac{5}{12}, -\frac{2}{5}, \frac{3}{4}, \frac{5}{8}, -\frac{3}{10}$

Hint: Find equivalent fractions for the negative fractions so they share the same denominator, then compare. Do the same for the positive fractions, then write your list.

Solution

First compare the two negative fractions by converting to fractions with the same denominator (in this case, 10).

$\frac{2}{5} = \frac{2 \times 2}{5 \times 2} = \frac{4}{10}$

Since $-4 < -3$,

$-\frac{2}{5} = -\frac{4}{10} < -\frac{3}{10}$

For the positive fractions, a common multiple of the denominators (3, 12, 4 and 8) is 24, so convert the fractions to equivalent fractions with 24 as a denominator to compare them.

$\frac{2}{3} = \frac{2 \times 8}{3 \times 8} = \frac{16}{24}$

$\frac{5}{12} = \frac{5 \times 2}{12 \times 2} = \frac{10}{24}$

$\frac{3}{4} = \frac{3 \times 6}{4 \times 6} = \frac{18}{24}$

$\frac{5}{8} = \frac{5 \times 3}{8 \times 3} = \frac{15}{24}$

Ordering these by the size of the numerator and including the negative fractions gives the whole list, from smallest to largest.

$-\frac{2}{5}, -\frac{3}{10}, \frac{5}{12}, \frac{5}{8}, \frac{2}{3}, \frac{3}{4}$

Level 3   GCSE Grade **3 / 3⁺**

11. Find two equivalent fractions for $\frac{4}{7}$.

Solution

Two equivalent fractions for $\frac{4}{7}$ are $\frac{8}{14}$ and $\frac{12}{21}$.
(Equivalent fractions can be found by multiplying or dividing both the numerator and the denominator by the same number.)

12. Find a fraction which lies between $\frac{3}{4}$ and $\frac{4}{5}$.

Solution

Change the two fractions, $\frac{3}{4}$ and $\frac{4}{5}$, to equivalent fractions with the same denominator.
40 is a common multiple of 4 and 5.

$\frac{3}{4} = \frac{3 \times 10}{4 \times 10} = \frac{30}{40}$

$\frac{4}{5} = \frac{4 \times 8}{5 \times 8} = \frac{32}{40}$

A fraction which lies between $\frac{3}{4}$ and $\frac{4}{5}$ is $\frac{31}{40}$.

Students can also try other common multiples of 4 and 5, like 60, 80 or 100, for the denominator.

13. Solution A has 50 grams of salt dissolved in 150 grams of water. Solution B has 24 grams of salt dissolved in 60 grams of water. Which solution has a higher fraction of salt?

Solution
Change the two fractions to equivalent fractions with the same denominator.

$$\frac{50}{150} = \frac{50 \div 10}{150 \div 10} = \frac{5}{15}$$

$$\frac{24}{60} = \frac{24 \div 4}{60 \div 4} = \frac{6}{15}$$

Since $\frac{6}{15} > \frac{5}{15}$, you have $\frac{24}{60} > \frac{50}{150}$.

Solution B has the higher fraction of salt.

14. The compound glucose $C_6H_{12}O_6$ has six atoms of carbon, 12 atoms of hydrogen and six atoms of oxygen. The compound ethanol C_2H_5OH has two atoms of carbon, six atoms of hydrogen and one atom of oxygen.
    (a) Find the fraction of the number of atoms of hydrogen in glucose.
    (b) Find the fraction of the number of atoms of hydrogen in ethanol.
    (c) Which compound has a greater fraction of atoms of hydrogen?

Solution
(a) Fraction of atoms of H in glucose $= \frac{12}{6+12+6}$

$$= \frac{12}{24}$$

$$= \frac{1}{2}$$

(b) Fraction of atoms of H in ethanol $= \frac{5+1}{2+5+1+1}$

$$= \frac{6}{9}$$

$$= \frac{2}{3}$$

(c) $\frac{1}{2} = \frac{1 \times 3}{2 \times 3} = \frac{3}{6}$

$\frac{2}{3} = \frac{2 \times 2}{3 \times 2} = \frac{4}{6}$

As $\frac{4}{6} > \frac{3}{6}$,

you have $\frac{2}{3} > \frac{1}{2}$.

Hence, ethanol has a greater fraction of atoms of hydrogen.

15. Arrange the fractions $\frac{m}{n}$, $\frac{m+1}{n}$ and $\frac{m}{n+1}$ in ascending order, where m and n are positive integers. Explain your answer.
    Hint: Try substituting numbers for m and n. You can choose any numbers.

Solution
m and n are positive integers.
Looking at the first two fractions,
$$m < m + 1$$
$$\therefore \frac{m}{n} < \frac{m+1}{n}$$
In other words, for fractions with the same denominator, the larger fraction is the one with the larger numerator.

Looking at the first and third fractions,
$$n + 1 > n$$
$$\therefore \frac{1}{n+1} < \frac{1}{n}$$
$$\therefore \frac{m}{n+1} < \frac{m}{n}$$

In other words, for fractions with the same numerator, the larger fraction is the one with the smaller denominator.

Using these two inequalities the fractions in ascending order are
$$\frac{m}{n+1}, \frac{m}{n}, \frac{m+1}{n}.$$

Exercise 5.3

In this exercise, write your answers as proper fractions in their simplest form or mixed numbers where appropriate.

Level 1 GCSE Grade **3⁻**

1. Find these sums.
   (a) $\frac{2}{3} + \frac{1}{6}$
   (b) $2\frac{1}{6} + 4\frac{5}{6}$
   (c) $3\frac{2}{5} + \frac{3}{10}$
   (d) $6\frac{3}{4} + 2\frac{1}{2}$

   Solution
   (a) $\frac{2}{3} + \frac{1}{6} = \frac{4}{6} + \frac{1}{6}$

   $$= \frac{5}{6}$$

   (b) $2\frac{1}{6} + 4\frac{5}{6} = 6\frac{6}{6}$

   $$= 7$$

   (c) $3\frac{2}{5} + \frac{3}{10} = 3 + \frac{4}{10} + \frac{3}{10}$

   $$= 3\frac{7}{10}$$

   (d) $6\frac{3}{4} + 2\frac{1}{2} = 8 + \frac{3}{4} + \frac{2}{4}$

   $$= 8\frac{5}{4}$$

   $$= 9\frac{1}{4}$$

2. Find these subtractions.
   (a) $\frac{7}{9} - \frac{5}{9}$
   (b) $\frac{5}{9} - \frac{7}{9}$
   (c) $2\frac{1}{6} - \frac{5}{6}$
   (d) $\frac{3}{4} - \frac{1}{8}$
   (e) $\frac{2}{5} - \frac{7}{10}$
   (f) $1\frac{5}{14} - 2\frac{5}{7}$

Solution

(a) $\frac{7}{9} - \frac{5}{9} = \frac{2}{9}$

(b) $\frac{5}{9} - \frac{7}{9} = -\frac{2}{9}$

(c) $2\frac{1}{6} - \frac{5}{6} = \frac{13}{6} - \frac{5}{6}$
$= \frac{8}{6}$
$= \frac{4}{3} = 1\frac{1}{3}$

(d) $\frac{3}{4} - \frac{1}{8} = \frac{6}{8} - \frac{1}{8}$
$= \frac{5}{8}$

(e) $\frac{2}{5} - \frac{7}{10} = \frac{4}{10} - \frac{7}{10}$
$= -\frac{3}{10}$

(f) $1\frac{5}{14} - 2\frac{5}{7} = \frac{19}{14} - \frac{19}{7}$
$= \frac{19}{14} - \frac{38}{14}$
$= -\frac{19}{14} = -1\frac{5}{14}$

Level 2

GCSE Grade 3

3. Find these sums.

(a) $\frac{2}{7} + \frac{3}{5}$

(b) $\frac{3}{4} + \frac{5}{6}$

(c) $5\frac{1}{6} + \frac{7}{8}$

(d) $-8\frac{3}{4} + 3\frac{7}{10}$

Solution

(a) $\frac{2}{7} + \frac{3}{5} = \frac{10}{35} + \frac{21}{35}$
$= \frac{31}{35}$

(b) $\frac{3}{4} + \frac{5}{6} = \frac{9}{12} + \frac{10}{12}$
$= \frac{19}{12}$
$= 1\frac{7}{12}$

(c) $5\frac{1}{6} + \frac{7}{8}$
$= 5 + \frac{1}{6} + \frac{7}{8}$
$= 5 + \frac{4}{24} + \frac{21}{24}$
$= 5 + \frac{25}{24}$
$= 5 + 1\frac{1}{24}$
$= 6\frac{1}{24}$

(d) $-8\frac{3}{4} + 3\frac{7}{10}$
$= -8 - \frac{3}{4} + 3 + \frac{7}{10}$
$= (-8 + 3) + \left(-\frac{3}{4} + \frac{7}{10}\right)$
$= -5 + \left(-\frac{15}{20} + \frac{14}{20}\right)$
$= -5 - \frac{1}{20}$
$= -5\frac{1}{20}$

4. Calculate these values.

(a) $\frac{6}{7} - \frac{3}{4}$

(b) $\frac{1}{2} - \frac{2}{3}$

(c) $6\frac{1}{3} - 7\frac{1}{5}$

(d) $5\frac{2}{9} - 4\frac{5}{6}$

Solution

(a) $\frac{6}{7} - \frac{3}{4} = \frac{24}{28} - \frac{21}{28}$
$= \frac{3}{28}$

(b) $\frac{1}{2} - \frac{2}{3} = \frac{3}{6} - \frac{4}{6}$
$= -\frac{1}{6}$

(c) $6\frac{1}{3} - 7\frac{1}{5} = \frac{19}{3} - \frac{36}{5}$
$= \frac{95}{15} - \frac{108}{15}$
$= -\frac{13}{15}$

(d) $5\frac{2}{9} - 4\frac{5}{6} = \frac{47}{9} - \frac{29}{6}$
$= \frac{94}{18} - \frac{87}{18}$
$= \frac{7}{18}$

5. Find these values.

(a) $\frac{1}{2} + \frac{1}{4} + \frac{3}{8}$

(b) $\frac{2}{3} + \frac{1}{6} + \frac{7}{9}$

(c) $\frac{3}{4} + \frac{1}{8} + 5$

(d) $\frac{1}{3} + 2\frac{1}{2} + \frac{5}{12}$

Solution

(a) $\frac{1}{2} + \frac{1}{4} + \frac{3}{8}$
$= \frac{4}{8} + \frac{2}{8} + \frac{3}{8}$
$= \frac{9}{8}$
$= 1\frac{1}{8}$

(b) $\frac{2}{3} + \frac{1}{6} + \frac{7}{9}$
$= \frac{12}{18} + \frac{3}{18} + \frac{14}{18}$
$= \frac{29}{18}$
$= 1\frac{11}{18}$

(c) $\frac{3}{4} + \frac{1}{8} + 5$
$= \frac{6}{8} + \frac{1}{8} + 5$
$= \frac{7}{8} + 5$
$= 5\frac{7}{8}$

(d) $\frac{1}{3} + 2\frac{1}{2} + \frac{5}{12}$
$= \frac{4}{12} + 2\frac{6}{12} + \frac{5}{12}$
$= 2 + \left(\frac{4}{12} + \frac{6}{12} + \frac{5}{12}\right)$
$= 2 + \frac{15}{12}$
$= 2 + \frac{5}{4}$
$= 2 + 1\frac{1}{4}$
$= 3\frac{1}{4}$

6. Work out these values.

(a) $7 - \frac{2}{3} - \frac{1}{15}$

(b) $\frac{11}{12} - \frac{1}{4} - \frac{1}{2}$

(c) $\frac{17}{18} - \frac{1}{6} - \frac{2}{3}$

(d) $6\frac{3}{5} - 4 - 1\frac{1}{10}$

Solution

(a) $7 - \frac{2}{3} - \frac{1}{15}$
$= 6\frac{1}{3} - \frac{1}{15}$
$= 6\frac{5}{15} - \frac{1}{15}$
$= 6\frac{4}{15}$

(b) $\frac{11}{12} - \frac{1}{4} - \frac{1}{2}$
$= \frac{11}{12} - \frac{3}{12} - \frac{6}{12}$
$= \frac{2}{12}$
$= \frac{1}{6}$

(c) $\frac{17}{18} - \frac{1}{6} - \frac{2}{3}$
$= \frac{17}{18} - \frac{3}{18} - \frac{12}{18}$
$= \frac{2}{18}$
$= \frac{1}{9}$

(d) $6\frac{3}{5} - 4 - 1\frac{1}{10}$

$= 2\frac{3}{5} - 1\frac{1}{10}$

$= (2 - 1) + \left(\frac{3}{5} - \frac{1}{10}\right)$

$= 1 + \left(\frac{6}{10} - \frac{1}{10}\right)$

$= 1 + \frac{5}{10}$

$= 1 + \frac{1}{2}$

$= 1\frac{1}{2}$

Alternatively,

$2\frac{3}{5} - 1\frac{1}{10}$

$= \frac{13}{5} - \frac{11}{10}$

$= \frac{26}{10} - \frac{11}{10}$

$= \frac{15}{10}$

$= \frac{3}{2}$

$= 1\frac{1}{2}$

Level 3 **GCSE Grade 3⁺**

7. Track A is $2\frac{3}{4}$ km long. Track B is $4\frac{1}{3}$ km long. What is the total length of the two tracks?

Solution
Total length of the two tracks

$= 2\frac{3}{4} + 4\frac{1}{3}$

$= (2 + 4) + \left(\frac{3}{4} + \frac{1}{3}\right)$

$= 6 + \left(\frac{9}{12} + \frac{4}{12}\right)$

$= 6 + \frac{13}{12}$

$= 6 + 1\frac{1}{12}$

$= 7\frac{1}{12}$ km

8. A jug contains $1\frac{3}{8}$ litres of milk. If $\frac{5}{6}$ litres are used to make a milkshake, how much milk will be left in the jug?

Solution
Amount of milk left in the jug

$= 1\frac{3}{8} - \frac{5}{6}$

$= \frac{11}{8} - \frac{5}{6}$

$= \frac{33}{24} - \frac{20}{24}$

$= \frac{13}{24}$ litres

9. Find these values.
(a) $3\frac{1}{2} + 2\frac{3}{4} + 1\frac{5}{12}$ **(b)** $5\frac{1}{2} + 3\frac{4}{5} + 6\frac{3}{4}$
(c) $8\frac{1}{3} - 5\frac{5}{12} - 2\frac{3}{4}$ **(d)** $7\frac{1}{6} - 3\frac{5}{8} - 4\frac{2}{3}$

Solution

(a) $3\frac{1}{2} + 2\frac{3}{4} + 1\frac{5}{12}$

$= (3 + 2 + 1) + \left(\frac{1}{2} + \frac{3}{4} + \frac{5}{12}\right)$

$= 6 + \left(\frac{6}{12} + \frac{9}{12} + \frac{5}{12}\right)$

$= 6 + \frac{20}{12}$

$= 6 + \frac{5}{3}$

$= 6 + 1\frac{2}{3}$

$= 7\frac{2}{3}$

(b) $5\frac{1}{2} + 3\frac{4}{5} + 6\frac{3}{4}$

$= (5 + 3 + 6) + \left(\frac{1}{2} + \frac{4}{5} + \frac{3}{4}\right)$

$= 14 + \left(\frac{10}{20} + \frac{16}{20} + \frac{15}{20}\right)$

$= 14 + \frac{41}{20}$

$= 14 + 2\frac{1}{20}$

$= 16\frac{1}{20}$

(c) $8\frac{1}{3} - 5\frac{5}{12} - 2\frac{3}{4}$

$= (8 - 5 - 2) + \left(\frac{1}{3} - \frac{5}{12} - \frac{3}{4}\right)$

$= 1 + \left(\frac{4}{12} - \frac{5}{12} - \frac{9}{12}\right)$

$= 1 + \left(-\frac{10}{12}\right)$

$= \frac{12}{12} - \frac{10}{12}$

$= \frac{2}{12}$

$= \frac{1}{6}$

(d) $7\frac{1}{6} - 3\frac{5}{8} - 4\frac{2}{3}$

$= (7 - 3 - 4) + \left(\frac{1}{6} - \frac{5}{8} - \frac{2}{3}\right)$

$= 0 + \left(\frac{4}{24} - \frac{15}{24} - \frac{16}{24}\right)$

$= -\frac{27}{24}$

$= -\frac{9}{8}$

$= -1\frac{1}{8}$

10. Work out these values.
(a) $2 - \left(\frac{1}{3} + \frac{1}{6}\right)$ **(b)** $3\frac{1}{2} - \left(2\frac{3}{4} + 1\frac{1}{6}\right)$
(c) $\frac{1}{6} - \left(1\frac{1}{5} - \frac{2}{3}\right)$ **(d)** $1\frac{1}{3} - \left(4\frac{1}{6} - 3\frac{5}{7}\right)$

Solution

(a) $2 - \left(\frac{1}{3} + \frac{1}{6}\right)$

$= 2 - \left(\frac{2}{6} + \frac{1}{6}\right)$

$= 2 - \frac{3}{6}$

$= 2 - \frac{1}{2}$

$= 1\frac{1}{2}$

(b) $3\frac{1}{2} - \left(2\frac{3}{4} + 1\frac{1}{6}\right)$

$= 3\frac{1}{2} - \left(2 + 1 + \frac{3}{4} + \frac{1}{6}\right)$

$= 3\frac{1}{2} - \left(3 + \frac{9}{12} + \frac{2}{12}\right)$

$= 3\frac{1}{2} - 3\frac{11}{12}$

$= (3 - 3) + \left(\frac{1}{2} - \frac{11}{12}\right)$

$= 0 + \left(\frac{6}{12} - \frac{11}{12}\right)$

$= -\frac{5}{12}$

(c) $\frac{1}{6} - \left(1\frac{1}{5} - \frac{2}{3}\right)$

$= \frac{1}{6} - \left(\frac{6}{5} - \frac{2}{3}\right)$

$= \frac{5}{30} - \left(\frac{36}{30} - \frac{20}{30}\right)$

$= \frac{5}{30} - \frac{16}{30}$

$= -\frac{11}{30}$

(d) $1\frac{1}{3} - \left(4\frac{1}{6} - 3\frac{5}{7}\right)$

$= \frac{4}{3} - \left(\frac{25}{6} - \frac{26}{7}\right)$

$= \frac{56}{42} - \left(\frac{175}{42} - \frac{156}{42}\right)$

$= \frac{56}{42} - \frac{19}{42}$

$= \frac{37}{42}$

11. Mrs Brown bought $3\,$kg of oranges, $1\frac{1}{4}\,$kg of apples and $\frac{7}{8}\,$kg of plums from a supermarket. What is the total mass of the fruit she bought?

Solution
Total mass of fruits bought

$= 3 + 1\frac{1}{4} + \frac{7}{8}$

$= 3 + 1 + \frac{1}{4} + \frac{7}{8}$

$= 4 + \frac{2}{8} + \frac{7}{8}$

$= 4 + 1\frac{1}{8}$

$= 5\frac{1}{8}\,$kg

12. An examination paper has three sections, A, B and C. The time allowed for the paper is $2\frac{1}{2}$ hours. Tariq spent $\frac{1}{3}$ hours on Section A and $1\frac{1}{6}$ hours on Section B. How much time did he spend on Section C?

Solution
Time left for Section C

$= 2\frac{1}{2} - \frac{1}{3} - 1\frac{1}{6}$

$= \frac{5}{2} - \frac{1}{3} - \frac{7}{6}$

$= \frac{15}{6} - \frac{2}{6} - \frac{7}{6}$

$= \frac{6}{6}$

$= 1\,$hour

13. There are $12\frac{5}{9}\,$m of ribbon on a roll. If Anna uses $4\frac{2}{3}\,$m for decorations and Sara uses $\frac{4}{5}\,$m for wrapping a gift, how many metres of ribbon will be left?

Solution
Length of ribbon left

$= 12\frac{5}{9} - 4\frac{2}{3} - \frac{4}{5}$

$= (12 - 4) + \left(\frac{5}{9} - \frac{2}{3} - \frac{4}{5}\right)$

$= 8 + \left(\frac{25}{45} - \frac{30}{45} - \frac{36}{45}\right)$

$= 8 + \left(-\frac{41}{45}\right)$

$= 7 + 1 - \frac{41}{45} \qquad \left(1 = \frac{45}{45}\right)$

$= 7 + \frac{4}{45}$

$= 7\frac{4}{45}\,$m

14. There are four rooms, A, B, C and D, in a flat. The total area of rooms A and B is equal to the total area of rooms C and D. If the areas of rooms A, B and C are $10\frac{1}{2}\,$m^2, $24\frac{2}{3}\,$m^2 and $18\frac{5}{6}\,$m^2 respectively, find the area of room D.

Solution
The area of room D is

$10\frac{1}{2} + 24\frac{2}{3} - 18\frac{5}{6}$

$= (10 + 24 - 18) + \frac{1}{2} + \frac{2}{3} - \frac{5}{6}$

$= 16 + \frac{3}{6} + \frac{4}{6} - \frac{5}{6}$

$= 16\frac{2}{6}$

$= 16\frac{1}{3}$

The area of room D is $16\frac{1}{3}\,$m^2.

15. Find two possible proper fractions such that their sum is $1\frac{1}{2}$.

Solution
Possible proper fractions such that their sum is $1\frac{1}{2}$ could be

(i) $\frac{4}{5}$ and $\frac{7}{10}$,

(ii) $\frac{5}{6}$ and $\frac{2}{3}$,

(iii) $\frac{6}{7}$ and $\frac{9}{14}$.

One possible method for finding two proper fractions is to first find equivalent fractions of $\frac{3}{2}$ $\left(1\frac{1}{2}\right)$ with a larger denominator so that it is easier to split into two proper fractions such that their sum is $1\frac{1}{2}$.

In **(i)**, the equivalent fraction of $\frac{3}{2}$ used is $\frac{15}{10}$.

Since $\frac{8}{10}+\frac{7}{10}=\frac{15}{10}$, you have $\frac{4}{5}+\frac{7}{10}=\frac{15}{10}$.

So two possible proper fractions are $\frac{4}{5}$ and $\frac{7}{10}$.

16. Find two possible mixed numbers such that their difference is $2\frac{1}{3}$.

Solution
Possible mixed numbers such that their difference is $2\frac{1}{3}$ could be

(i) $3\frac{1}{2}$ and $1\frac{1}{6}$,

(ii) $3\frac{2}{3}$ and $1\frac{1}{3}$,

(iii) $3\frac{5}{6}$ and $1\frac{1}{2}$.

Similar to Question **15**, equivalent fractions can be used. In these three sets of possible mixed numbers, the equivalent fraction of $\frac{7}{3}$ $\left(2\frac{1}{3}\right)$ used is $\frac{14}{6}$.

In **(i)**, since $\frac{21}{6}-\frac{7}{6}=\frac{14}{6}$, you have $3\frac{1}{2}-1\frac{1}{6}=2\frac{1}{3}$.

In **(ii)**, since $\frac{22}{6}-\frac{8}{6}=\frac{14}{6}$, you have $3\frac{2}{3}-1\frac{1}{3}=2\frac{1}{3}$.

In **(iii)**, since $\frac{23}{6}-\frac{9}{6}=\frac{14}{6}$, you have $3\frac{5}{6}-1\frac{1}{2}=2\frac{1}{3}$.

You can also use the inverse relationship between addition and subtraction of numbers to work out this problem.

number 1 − number 2 = difference

The difference given is $2\frac{1}{3}$. You can pick any mixed number of your choice to be number 2.

For instance, you could choose $2\frac{3}{4}$ to be number 2.

Then number $1=2\frac{1}{3}+2\frac{3}{4}$

$=5\frac{1}{12}$

i.e. the two possible mixed numbers with a difference of $2\frac{1}{3}$ are $5\frac{1}{12}$ and $2\frac{3}{4}$.

Exercise 5.4

In this exercise, express your answers as proper fractions in their simplest form or mixed numbers where appropriate.

Level 1   GCSE Grade 3^- / 3

1. Find these values.

(a) $\frac{2}{5}\times30$ **(b)** $18\times\frac{4}{9}$

(c) $\frac{1}{2}\times\frac{2}{3}$ **(d)** $\frac{1}{6}\times\frac{4}{5}$

(e) $\frac{4}{15}\times\left(-\frac{5}{8}\right)$ **(f)** $\left(-\frac{21}{40}\right)\times\left(-\frac{12}{35}\right)$

Hint: positive × negative = negative and negative × negative = positive.

Solution

(a) $\frac{2}{5}\times30=\frac{2}{\cancel{5}_1}\times\cancel{30}^6$
$=2\times6$
$=12$

(b) $18\times\frac{4}{9}=\,^2\cancel{18}\times\frac{4}{\cancel{9}_1}$
$=2\times4$
$=8$

(c) $\frac{1}{2}\times\frac{2}{3}=\frac{1}{\cancel{2}_1}\times\frac{\cancel{2}^1}{3}$
$=\frac{1\times1}{1\times3}$
$=\frac{1}{3}$

(d) $\frac{1}{6}\times\frac{4}{5}=\frac{1}{_3\cancel{6}}\times\frac{\cancel{4}^2}{5}$
$=\frac{1\times2}{3\times5}$
$=\frac{2}{15}$

(e) $\frac{4}{15}\times\left(-\frac{5}{8}\right)=\frac{^1\cancel{4}}{_3\cancel{15}}\times\left(-\frac{\cancel{5}^1}{\cancel{8}_2}\right)$
$=-\frac{1\times1}{3\times2}$
$=-\frac{1}{6}$

(f) $\left(-\frac{21}{40}\right)\times\left(-\frac{12}{35}\right)=\frac{^3\cancel{21}}{_{10}\cancel{40}}\times\frac{\cancel{12}^3}{\cancel{35}_5}$
$=\frac{3\times3}{10\times5}$
$=\frac{9}{50}$

2. Calculate these values.

(a) $1\frac{4}{5}\times\frac{1}{6}$ **(b)** $\frac{7}{9}\times3\frac{3}{8}$

(c) $\frac{14}{15}\times1\frac{3}{7}$ **(d)** $1\frac{5}{27}\times\frac{9}{16}$

Solution

(a) $1\frac{4}{5} \times \frac{1}{6}$

$= \frac{9}{5} \times \frac{1}{6}$

$= \frac{3 \times 1}{5 \times 2}$

$= \frac{3}{10}$

(b) $\frac{7}{9} \times 3\frac{3}{8}$

$= \frac{7}{9} \times \frac{27}{8}$

$= \frac{7 \times 3}{1 \times 8}$

$= \frac{21}{8}$

$= 2\frac{5}{8}$

(c) $\frac{14}{15} \times 1\frac{3}{7}$

$= \frac{14}{15} \times \frac{10}{7}$

$= \frac{2 \times 2}{3 \times 1}$

$= \frac{4}{3}$

$= 1\frac{1}{3}$

(d) $1\frac{5}{27} \times \frac{9}{16}$

$= \frac{32}{27} \times \frac{9}{16}$

$= \frac{2 \times 1}{3 \times 1}$

$= \frac{2}{3}$

3. Work out these products using the grid method.

(a) $1\frac{1}{2} \times 2\frac{1}{3}$

(b) $2\frac{3}{4} \times 1\frac{1}{5}$

(c) $3\frac{3}{7} \times 1\frac{1}{6}$

(d) $-2\frac{2}{5} \times 4\frac{3}{8}$

Hint: When a product involves negative numbers, first work out the product by ignoring the signs. Then determine the sign of the product and place it at the front.

Solution

(a)

×	2	$\frac{1}{3}$
1	2	$\frac{1}{3}$
$\frac{1}{2}$	1	$\frac{1}{6}$

$1\frac{1}{2} \times 2\frac{1}{3} = 2 + \frac{1}{3} + 1 + \frac{1}{6}$

$= 2 + \frac{2}{6} + 1 + \frac{1}{6}$

$= 3 + \frac{3}{6}$

$= 3\frac{1}{2}$

(b)

×	1	$\frac{1}{5}$
2	2	$\frac{2}{5}$
$\frac{3}{4}$	$\frac{3}{4}$	$\frac{3}{20}$

$2\frac{3}{4} \times 1\frac{1}{5} = 2 + \frac{2}{5} + \frac{3}{4} + \frac{3}{20}$

$= 2 + \frac{8}{20} + \frac{15}{20} + \frac{3}{20}$

$= 2 + \frac{26}{20}$

$= 2 + 1\frac{6}{20}$

$= 3\frac{3}{10}$

(c)

×	1	$\frac{1}{6}$
3	3	$\frac{1}{2}$
$\frac{3}{7}$	$\frac{3}{7}$	$\frac{1}{14}$

$3\frac{3}{7} \times 1\frac{1}{6} = 3 + \frac{1}{2} + \frac{3}{7} + \frac{1}{14}$

$= 3 + \frac{7}{14} + \frac{6}{14} + \frac{1}{14}$

$= 3 + \frac{14}{14}$

$= 4$

(d)

×	4	$\frac{3}{8}$
2	8	$\frac{3}{4}$
$\frac{2}{5}$	$\frac{8}{5}$	$\frac{3}{20}$

$2\frac{2}{5} \times 4\frac{3}{8} = 8 + \frac{3}{4} + \frac{8}{5} + \frac{3}{20}$

$= 8 + \frac{15}{20} + \frac{32}{20} + \frac{3}{20}$

$= 8 + \frac{50}{20}$

$= 8 + 2\frac{10}{20}$

$= 10\frac{1}{2}$

In the calculation $-2\frac{2}{5} \times 4\frac{3}{8}$, you are multiplying a negative and a positive together.

Hence, the answer is negative.

$-2\frac{2}{5} \times 4\frac{3}{8} = -10\frac{1}{2}$

4. Find these values.

(a) $\frac{2}{5}$ of £15

(b) $\frac{3}{7}$ of 28 cm

(c) $\frac{4}{11}$ of $3\frac{1}{7}$ kg

(d) $1\frac{3}{4}$ of $4\frac{4}{5}$ litres

Solution

(a) $\frac{2}{5}$ of £15

$= \frac{2}{5} \times £15$

$= £(2 \times 3)$

$= £6$

(b) $\frac{3}{7}$ of 28 cm

$= \frac{3}{7} \times 28$ cm

$= 3 \times 4$ cm

$= 12$ cm

(c) $\dfrac{4}{11}$ of $3\dfrac{1}{7}$ kg

$= \dfrac{4}{11} \times \dfrac{22}{7}$ kg

$= \dfrac{4 \times 2}{1 \times 7}$ kg

$= \dfrac{8}{7}$ kg

$= 1\dfrac{1}{7}$ kg

(d) $1\dfrac{3}{4}$ of $4\dfrac{4}{5}$ litres

$= \dfrac{7}{4} \times \dfrac{24}{5}$ litres

$= \dfrac{7 \times 6}{1 \times 5}$ litres

$= \dfrac{42}{5}$ litres

$= 8\dfrac{2}{5}$ litres

Level 2   **GCSE Grade 3 / 3⁺**

5. Work out these values.

   (a) $1\dfrac{8}{9} \times \left(-\dfrac{15}{34}\right)$ **(b)** $\left(-\dfrac{24}{25}\right) \times \left(-3\dfrac{1}{3}\right)$

   (c) $\left(-1\dfrac{15}{18}\right) \times 2\dfrac{1}{22}$ **(d)** $4\dfrac{2}{7} \times \left(-2\dfrac{1}{10}\right)$

Solution

(a) $1\dfrac{8}{9} \times \left(-\dfrac{15}{34}\right)$

$= \dfrac{17}{9} \times \left(-\dfrac{15}{34}\right)$

$= -\dfrac{1 \times 5}{3 \times 2}$

$= -\dfrac{5}{6}$

(b) $\left(-\dfrac{24}{25}\right) \times \left(-3\dfrac{1}{3}\right)$

$= \dfrac{24}{25} \times \dfrac{10}{3}$

$= \dfrac{8 \times 2}{5 \times 1}$

$= \dfrac{16}{5}$

$= 3\dfrac{1}{5}$

(c) $\left(-1\dfrac{15}{18}\right) \times 2\dfrac{1}{22}$

$= -\dfrac{33}{18} \times \dfrac{45}{22}$

$= -\dfrac{3 \times 5}{2 \times 2}$

$= -\dfrac{15}{4}$

$= -3\dfrac{3}{4}$

(d) $4\dfrac{2}{7} \times \left(-2\dfrac{1}{10}\right)$

$= \dfrac{30}{7} \times \left(-\dfrac{21}{10}\right)$

$= -\dfrac{3 \times 3}{1 \times 1}$

$= -9$

6. Find these values.

   (a) $\dfrac{7}{11} \times 6 \times \dfrac{11}{18}$ **(b)** $2 \times \dfrac{5}{8} \times \dfrac{4}{15}$

   (c) $2 - \dfrac{7}{10} \times 1\dfrac{5}{7}$ **(d)** $3\dfrac{1}{5} \times 2\dfrac{4}{13} - 6$

Hint: Remember the order of operations.

Solution

(a) $\dfrac{7}{11} \times 6 \times \dfrac{11}{18}$

$= \dfrac{7 \times 1 \times 1}{1 \times 3}$

$= \dfrac{7}{3}$

$= 2\dfrac{1}{3}$

(b) $2 \times \dfrac{5}{8} \times \dfrac{4}{15}$

$= \dfrac{1}{3}$

(c) $2 - \dfrac{7}{10} \times 1\dfrac{5}{7}$

$= 2 - \dfrac{7}{10} \times \dfrac{12}{7}$

$= 2 - \dfrac{6}{5}$

$= 2 - 1\dfrac{1}{5}$

$= \dfrac{4}{5}$

(d) $3\dfrac{1}{5} \times 2\dfrac{4}{13} - 6$

$= \dfrac{16}{5} \times \dfrac{30}{13} - 6$

$= \dfrac{16 \times 6}{1 \times 13} - 6$

$= \dfrac{96}{13} - 6$

$= 7\dfrac{5}{13} - 6$

$= 1\dfrac{5}{13}$

7. A choir has 45 students. If $\dfrac{5}{9}$ of the students are girls, find the number of girls in the choir.

Solution

Number of girls in the choir

$= \dfrac{5}{9} \times 45$

$= 5 \times 5$

$= 25$

8. A cake mix has mass $2\dfrac{1}{2}$ kg. If $\dfrac{2}{5}$ of the mix is flour, find the mass of flour in the cake mix.

Solution

Mass of flour in the cake mix

$= \dfrac{2}{5} \times 2\dfrac{1}{2}$ kg

$= \dfrac{2}{5} \times \dfrac{5}{2}$ kg

$= 1$ kg

Level 3   **GCSE Grade 3⁺ / 4⁻**

9. Calculate these values.

   (a) $\dfrac{3}{4} \times \dfrac{5}{9} + \dfrac{7}{24}$ **(b)** $1\dfrac{2}{3} + \dfrac{4}{7} \times \left(-2\dfrac{4}{5}\right)$

   (c) $3\dfrac{1}{4} \times 1\dfrac{5}{13} - 2\dfrac{1}{2}$ **(d)** $\left(-5\dfrac{3}{8}\right) - 1\dfrac{1}{3} \times 2\dfrac{1}{4}$

   (e) $\left(\dfrac{2}{3} + \dfrac{5}{6}\right) \times 4\dfrac{2}{7}$ **(f)** $3\dfrac{3}{5} \times \left(6\dfrac{1}{2} - 4\dfrac{5}{9}\right)$

Hint: Remember the order of operations.

Solution

(a) $\dfrac{3}{4} \times \dfrac{5}{9} + \dfrac{7}{24}$

$= \dfrac{1 \times 5}{4 \times 3} + \dfrac{7}{24}$

$= \dfrac{5}{12} + \dfrac{7}{24}$

$= \dfrac{10}{24} + \dfrac{7}{24}$

$= \dfrac{17}{24}$

(b) $1\dfrac{2}{3} + \dfrac{4}{7} \times \left(-2\dfrac{4}{5}\right)$

$= 1\dfrac{2}{3} + \dfrac{4}{7} \times \left(-\dfrac{14}{5}\right)$

$= 1\dfrac{2}{3} + \left(-\dfrac{4 \times 2}{1 \times 5}\right)$

$= 1\dfrac{2}{3} - \dfrac{8}{5}$

$= \dfrac{5}{3} - \dfrac{8}{5}$

$= \dfrac{25}{15} - \dfrac{24}{15}$

$= \dfrac{1}{15}$

(c) $3\frac{1}{4} \times 1\frac{5}{13} - 2\frac{1}{2}$

$= \frac{13}{4} \times \frac{18}{13} - 2\frac{1}{2}$

$= \frac{9}{2} - 2\frac{1}{2}$

$= 4\frac{1}{2} - 2\frac{1}{2}$

$= 2$

(d) $\left(-5\frac{3}{8}\right) - 1\frac{1}{3} \times 2\frac{1}{4}$

$= \left(-5\frac{3}{8}\right) - \frac{4}{3} \times \frac{9}{4}$

$= \left(-5\frac{3}{8}\right) - 3$

$= -5\frac{3}{8} - 3$

$= -8\frac{3}{8}$

(e) $\left(\frac{2}{3} + \frac{5}{6}\right) \times 4\frac{2}{7}$

$= \left(\frac{4}{6} + \frac{5}{6}\right) \times \frac{30}{7}$

$= \frac{9}{6} \times \frac{30}{7}$

$= \frac{9 \times 5}{1 \times 7}$

$= \frac{45}{7}$

$= 6\frac{3}{7}$

(f) $3\frac{3}{5} \times \left(6\frac{1}{2} - 4\frac{5}{9}\right)$

$= \frac{18}{5} \times \left(\frac{13}{2} - \frac{41}{9}\right)$

$= \frac{18}{5} \times \left(\frac{117}{18} - \frac{82}{18}\right)$

$= \frac{18}{5} \times \frac{35}{18}$

$= 7$

10. A company has 40 staff. If $\frac{1}{5}$ of the staff are in the accounting department and $\frac{3}{4}$ of the accounting staff are female, find the number of female accounting staff in the company.

Solution
Number of accounting staff

$= \frac{1}{5} \times 40$

$= 8$

Number of female accounting staff

$= \frac{3}{4} \times 8$

$= 3 \times 2$

$= 6$

11. A prize of £1400 is shared among three winners. The first winner gets $\frac{4}{7}$ of the prize. The second winner gets $\frac{3}{10}$ of the prize. Find the value of the prize that the third winner gets.

Solution
Method 1
Value of prize that the first winner gets

$= \frac{4}{7} \times £1400$

$= 4 \times £200$

$= £800$

Value of prize that the second winner gets

$= \frac{3}{10} \times £1400$

$= 3 \times £140$

$= £420$

Hence, the third winner gets £1400 − £800 − £420
= £180

Method 2
Fraction of the prize that the third winner gets

$= 1 - \frac{4}{7} - \frac{3}{10}$

$= \frac{70}{70} - \frac{40}{70} - \frac{21}{70}$

$= \frac{9}{70}$

Value of prize that the third winner gets

$= \frac{9}{70} \times £1400$

$= 9 \times £20$

$= £180$

12. An iron rod is $3\frac{1}{4}$ m long. Seven pieces of $\frac{3}{8}$ m are cut from it. What is the remaining length of the rod?

Solution
The remaining length of the rod is

$3\frac{1}{4} - 7 \times \frac{3}{8} = \frac{13}{4} - \frac{21}{8}$

$= \frac{26}{8} - \frac{21}{8}$

$= \frac{5}{8}$

The remaining length of the rod is $\frac{5}{8}$ m.

13. Chloe spends $6\frac{2}{3}$ hours on her mobile phone in a day. If $\frac{2}{5}$ of the time is spent playing games and $\frac{1}{3}$ of the time is spent chatting with friends, how many more hours does she spend playing games than chatting with friends?

Solution
Method 1
Length of time spent playing games

$= \frac{2}{5} \times 6\frac{2}{3}$

$= \frac{2}{5} \times \frac{20}{3}$

$= \frac{2 \times 4}{1 \times 3}$

$= \frac{8}{3}$

$= 2\frac{2}{3}$ hours

Length of time spent chatting with friends

$= \frac{1}{3} \times 6\frac{2}{3}$

$= \frac{1}{3} \times \frac{20}{3}$

$= \frac{20}{9}$

$= 2\frac{2}{9}$ hours

$$2\frac{2}{3} - 2\frac{2}{9} = \frac{8}{3} - \frac{20}{9}$$
$$= \frac{24}{9} - \frac{20}{9}$$
$$= \frac{4}{9}$$

Chloe spent $\frac{4}{9}$ hours more playing games than chatting with friends.

Method 2
Fraction of time spent playing games more than chatting with friends
$$= \frac{2}{5} - \frac{1}{3}$$
$$= \frac{6}{15} - \frac{5}{15}$$
$$= \frac{1}{15}$$

Number of hours more
$$= \frac{1}{15} \times 6\frac{2}{3}$$
$$= \frac{1}{15} \times \frac{20}{3}$$
$$= \frac{1 \times 4}{3 \times 3}$$
$$= \frac{4}{9}.$$

14. Find a proper fraction and a mixed number such that their product is $1\frac{3}{5}$.

Solution
One method is to first write the product you are aiming for as an improper fraction. Then choose a proper fraction and an improper fraction which multiply to give this. You can then convert the improper fraction you've thought of to a mixed number.
$$1\frac{3}{5} = \frac{8}{5}$$
Possible pairs are
$$\frac{3}{5} \text{ and } \frac{8}{3} = 2\frac{2}{3}$$
$$\frac{12}{5} = 2\frac{2}{5} \text{ and } \frac{8}{12} = \frac{2}{3}$$

15. Find two mixed numbers such that their product is $3\frac{4}{7}$.

Solution
$$3\frac{4}{7} = \frac{25}{7}$$

Some possible improper fractions are
$$\frac{8}{7} \text{ and } \frac{25}{8}, \frac{13}{7} \text{ and } \frac{25}{13}, \frac{24}{7} \text{ and } \frac{25}{24}.$$
Expressed as mixed numbers these are
$$1\frac{1}{7} \text{ and } 3\frac{1}{8}, 1\frac{6}{7} \text{ and } 1\frac{12}{13}, 3\frac{3}{7} \text{ and } 1\frac{1}{24}.$$

Exercise 5.5

In this exercise, write your answers as proper fractions in their simplest form or mixed numbers where appropriate.

Level 1   GCSE Grade **3**

1. Calculate these values.
   (a) $\frac{4}{7} \div 2$
   (b) $\frac{4}{7} \div 4$
   (c) $\frac{6}{11} \div 3$
   (d) $\frac{6}{11} \div 9$

   Solution

   (a) $\frac{4}{7} \div 2$
   $$= \frac{^2 4}{7} \times \frac{1}{2_1}$$
   $$= \frac{2}{7}$$

   (b) $\frac{4}{7} \div 4$
   $$= \frac{^1 4}{7} \times \frac{1}{4_1}$$
   $$= \frac{1}{7}$$

   (c) $\frac{6}{11} \div 3$
   $$= \frac{^2 6}{11} \times \frac{1}{3_1}$$
   $$= \frac{2}{11}$$

   (d) $\frac{6}{11} \div 9$
   $$= \frac{^2 6}{11} \times \frac{1}{9_3}$$
   $$= \frac{2 \times 1}{11 \times 3}$$
   $$= \frac{2}{33}$$

2. Work out these values.
   (a) $3 \div \frac{1}{2}$
   (b) $8 \div \frac{4}{7}$
   (c) $\frac{1}{3} \div \frac{1}{2}$
   (d) $\frac{1}{3} \div 1\frac{1}{2}$

   Solution

   (a) $3 \div \frac{1}{2}$
   $$= 3 \times \frac{2}{1}$$
   $$= 6$$

   (b) $8 \div \frac{4}{7}$
   $$= \frac{^2 8}{} \times \frac{7}{4_1}$$
   $$= 2 \times 7$$
   $$= 14$$

   (c) $\frac{1}{3} \div \frac{1}{2}$
   $$= \frac{1}{3} \times \frac{2}{1}$$
   $$= \frac{2}{3}$$

   (d) $\frac{1}{3} \div 1\frac{1}{2}$
   $$= \frac{1}{3} \div \frac{3}{2}$$
   $$= \frac{1}{3} \times \frac{2}{3}$$
   $$= \frac{1 \times 2}{3 \times 3}$$
   $$= \frac{2}{9}$$

3. Find these values.
   (a) $\frac{3}{4} \div \frac{1}{6}$
   (b) $\frac{2}{5} \div \frac{3}{20}$
   (c) $\frac{2}{3} \div \left(-\frac{5}{6}\right)$
   (d) $\left(-\frac{9}{10}\right) \div (-3)$

Solution

(a) $\dfrac{3}{4} \div \dfrac{1}{6}$

$= \dfrac{3}{{}_2\cancel{4}} \times \dfrac{\cancel{6}^{\,3}}{1}$

$= \dfrac{3 \times 3}{2 \times 1}$

$= \dfrac{9}{2}$

$= 4\dfrac{1}{2}$

(b) $\dfrac{2}{5} \div \dfrac{3}{20}$

$= \dfrac{2}{{}_1\cancel{5}} \times \dfrac{\cancel{20}^{\,4}}{3}$

$= \dfrac{2 \times 4}{1 \times 3}$

$= \dfrac{8}{3}$

$= 2\dfrac{2}{3}$

(c) $\dfrac{2}{3} \div \left(-\dfrac{5}{6}\right)$

$= \dfrac{2}{\cancel{3}_1} \times \left(-\dfrac{\cancel{6}^{\,2}}{5}\right)$

$= -\dfrac{2 \times 2}{1 \times 5}$

$= -\dfrac{4}{5}$

(d) $\left(-\dfrac{9}{10}\right) \div (-3)$

$= \dfrac{\cancel{9}^{\,3}}{10} \times \dfrac{1}{\cancel{3}_1}$

$= \dfrac{3 \times 1}{10 \times 1}$

$= \dfrac{3}{10}$

4. Evaluate these expressions.

(a) $\dfrac{8}{21} \div 1\dfrac{5}{7}$

(b) $1\dfrac{3}{22} \div \left(-\dfrac{10}{33}\right)$

(c) $\left(-4\dfrac{1}{2}\right) \div \left(-1\dfrac{1}{8}\right)$

(d) $\left(-5\dfrac{2}{3}\right) \div 3\dfrac{7}{9}$

Solution

(a) $\dfrac{8}{21} \div 1\dfrac{5}{7}$

$= \dfrac{8}{21} \div \dfrac{12}{7}$

$= \dfrac{\cancel{8}^{\,2}}{{}_3\cancel{21}} \times \dfrac{\cancel{7}^{\,1}}{\cancel{12}_3}$

$= \dfrac{2 \times 1}{3 \times 3}$

$= \dfrac{2}{9}$

(b) $1\dfrac{3}{22} \div \left(-\dfrac{10}{33}\right)$

$= \dfrac{25}{22} \times \left(-\dfrac{33}{10}\right)$

$= -\dfrac{5 \times 3}{2 \times 2}$

$= -\dfrac{15}{4}$

$= -3\dfrac{3}{4}$

(c) $\left(-4\dfrac{1}{2}\right) \div \left(-1\dfrac{1}{8}\right)$

$= \left(-\dfrac{9}{2}\right) \div \left(-\dfrac{9}{8}\right)$

$= \dfrac{9}{2} \times \dfrac{8}{9}$

$= \dfrac{1 \times 4}{1 \times 1}$

$= 4$

(d) $\left(-5\dfrac{2}{3}\right) \div 3\dfrac{7}{9}$

$= \left(-\dfrac{17}{3}\right) \div \dfrac{34}{9}$

$= \left(-\dfrac{17}{3}\right) \times \dfrac{9}{34}$

$= -\dfrac{1 \times 3}{1 \times 2}$

$= -\dfrac{3}{2}$

$= -1\dfrac{1}{2}$

Level 2   **GCSE Grade** **3+**

5. Find these values.

(a) $\dfrac{3}{8} \div \dfrac{9}{16} \div 2$

(b) $1\dfrac{7}{18} \div 5 \div 1\dfrac{2}{3}$

(c) $2\dfrac{2}{9} \div 15 \times 3\dfrac{1}{4}$

(d) $8 \times 4\dfrac{2}{7} \div 6\dfrac{1}{4}$

Hint: Work from left to right. Perform the leftmost calculation first.

Solution

(a) $\dfrac{3}{8} \div \dfrac{9}{16} \div 2$

$= \dfrac{3}{8} \times \dfrac{16}{9} \div 2$

$= \dfrac{1 \times 2}{1 \times 3} \div 2$

$= \dfrac{2}{3} \times \dfrac{1}{2}$

$= \dfrac{1}{3}$

(b) $1\dfrac{7}{18} \div 5 \div 1\dfrac{2}{3}$

$= \dfrac{25}{18} \times \dfrac{1}{5} \div \dfrac{5}{3}$

$= \dfrac{5}{18} \times \dfrac{3}{5}$

$= \dfrac{1}{6}$

(c) $2\dfrac{2}{9} \div 15 \times 3\dfrac{1}{4}$

$= \dfrac{20}{9} \times \dfrac{1}{15} \times \dfrac{13}{4}$

$= \dfrac{1 \times 1 \times 13}{9 \times 3 \times 1}$

$= \dfrac{13}{27}$

(d) $8 \times 4\dfrac{2}{7} \div 6\dfrac{1}{4}$

$= 8 \times \dfrac{30}{7} \div \dfrac{25}{4}$

$= 8 \times \dfrac{30}{7} \times \dfrac{4}{25}$

$= \dfrac{8 \times 6 \times 4}{7 \times 5}$

$= \dfrac{192}{35}$

$= 5\dfrac{17}{35}$

6. A rod is $\dfrac{5}{9}$ m long. It is divided into 10 equal pieces. Find the length of each piece.

Solution
Length of each piece

$= \dfrac{5}{9} \div 10$

$= \dfrac{5}{9} \times \dfrac{1}{10}$

$= \dfrac{1}{18}$ m

7. A bag of flour has mass $2\dfrac{3}{4}$ kg. The flour is divided into six equal portions. What is the mass of each portion?

Solution
Mass of each portion

$= 2\dfrac{3}{4} \div 6$

$= \dfrac{11}{4} \times \dfrac{1}{6}$

$= \dfrac{11}{24}$ kg

8. There are $3\dfrac{1}{2}$ kg of roast turkey breast. How many $\dfrac{1}{4}$ kg servings does the roast provide?

Solution
Number of servings

$= 3\dfrac{1}{2} \div \dfrac{1}{4}$

$= \dfrac{7}{2} \times \dfrac{4}{1}$

$= 7 \times 2$

$= 14$

9. Find these values.

    (a) $7 - 1\frac{4}{11} \div 2\frac{1}{22}$ **(b)** $6\frac{2}{3} \div \frac{5}{9} + 2\frac{1}{4}$

    (c) $4\frac{2}{7} \div 1\frac{1}{14} - 2\frac{3}{10}$ **(d)** $\frac{1}{6} - 1\frac{7}{8} \div \frac{3}{4}$

    Hint: Remember the order of operations.

    Solution

    (a) $7 - 1\frac{4}{11} \div 2\frac{1}{22}$

    $= 7 - \frac{15}{11} \div \frac{45}{22}$

    $= 7 - \frac{15}{11} \times \frac{22}{45}$

    $= 7 - \frac{2}{3}$

    $= 6\frac{1}{3}$

    (b) $6\frac{2}{3} \div \frac{5}{9} + 2\frac{1}{4}$

    $= \frac{20}{3} \times \frac{9}{5} + 2\frac{1}{4}$

    $= 4 \times 3 + 2\frac{1}{4}$

    $= 12 + 2\frac{1}{4}$

    $= 14\frac{1}{4}$

    (c) $4\frac{2}{7} \div 1\frac{1}{14} - 2\frac{3}{10}$

    $= \frac{30}{7} \div \frac{15}{14} - 2\frac{3}{10}$

    $= \frac{30}{7} \times \frac{14}{15} - 2\frac{3}{10}$

    $= 2 \times 2 - 2\frac{3}{10}$

    $= 4 - 2\frac{3}{10}$

    $= 1\frac{7}{10}$

    (d) $\frac{1}{6} - 1\frac{7}{8} \div \frac{3}{4}$

    $= \frac{1}{6} - \frac{15}{8} \times \frac{4}{3}$

    $= \frac{1}{6} - \frac{5}{2}$

    $= \frac{1}{6} - \frac{15}{6}$

    $= -\frac{14}{6}$

    $= -\frac{7}{3}$

    $= -2\frac{1}{3}$

10. Calculate these values.

    (a) $\left(3\frac{3}{4} + 2\frac{1}{2}\right) \div 1\frac{5}{8}$ **(b)** $12\frac{3}{4} \div \left(5\frac{2}{3} - 2\frac{1}{8}\right)$

    (c) $9 \div \left(2\frac{2}{9} + 2\frac{1}{12}\right)$ **(d)** $\left(3\frac{3}{8} - 2\frac{5}{6}\right) \div 2\frac{4}{5}$

    Solution

    (a) $\left(3\frac{3}{4} + 2\frac{1}{2}\right) \div 1\frac{5}{8}$

    $= \left(\frac{15}{4} + \frac{5}{2}\right) \div \frac{13}{8}$

    $= \left(\frac{15}{4} + \frac{10}{4}\right) \times \frac{8}{13}$

    $= \frac{25}{4} \times \frac{8}{13}$

    $= \frac{25 \times 2}{1 \times 13}$

    $= \frac{50}{13}$

    $= 3\frac{11}{13}$

    (b) $12\frac{3}{4} \div \left(5\frac{2}{3} - 2\frac{1}{8}\right)$

    $= 12\frac{3}{4} \div \left(\frac{17}{3} - \frac{17}{8}\right)$

    $= 12\frac{3}{4} \div \left(\frac{136}{24} - \frac{51}{24}\right)$

    $= 12\frac{3}{4} \div \frac{85}{24}$

    $= \frac{51}{4} \times \frac{24}{85}$

    $= \frac{3 \times 6}{1 \times 5}$

    $= \frac{18}{5}$

    $= 3\frac{3}{5}$

    (c) $9 \div \left(2\frac{2}{9} + 2\frac{1}{12}\right)$

    $= 9 \div \left(\frac{20}{9} + \frac{25}{12}\right)$

    $= 9 \div \left(\frac{80}{36} + \frac{75}{36}\right)$

    $= 9 \div \frac{155}{36}$

    $= 9 \times \frac{36}{155}$

    $= \frac{324}{155}$

    $= 2\frac{14}{155}$

    (d) $\left(3\frac{3}{8} - 2\frac{5}{6}\right) \div 2\frac{4}{5}$

    $= \left(\frac{27}{8} - \frac{17}{6}\right) \div \frac{14}{5}$

    $= \left(\frac{81}{24} - \frac{68}{24}\right) \times \frac{5}{14}$

    $= \frac{13}{24} \times \frac{5}{14}$

    $= \frac{65}{336}$

11. A piece of ribbon of length $32\frac{4}{5}$ cm is cut into smaller pieces that are each of length $3\frac{1}{4}$ cm.

    (a) How many complete smaller pieces can be obtained?

    (b) What is the remaining length of the ribbon?

    Solution

    (a) $32\frac{4}{5} \div 3\frac{1}{4}$

    $= \frac{164}{5} \div \frac{13}{4}$

    $= \frac{164}{5} \times \frac{4}{13}$

    $= \frac{656}{65}$

    $= 10\frac{6}{65}$

    10 complete smaller pieces can be obtained.

    (b) Remaining length of the ribbon

    $=$ length of $\frac{6}{65}$ of a smaller piece

    $= \frac{6}{65} \times 3\frac{1}{4}$

    $= \frac{6}{65} \times \frac{13}{4}$

    $= \frac{3 \times 1}{5 \times 2}$

    $= \frac{3}{10}$ cm

12. A drink is made by mixing $2\frac{3}{4}$ litres of orange juice and $\frac{7}{8}$ litres of soda. The drink is served in cups, each holding $\frac{1}{4}$ litres.

    (a) How many complete cups of the drink can be filled?

    (b) How much drink would be left after filling the cups?

    Solution

    (a) $\left(2\frac{3}{4} + \frac{7}{8}\right) \div \frac{1}{4}$

    $= \left(\frac{11}{4} + \frac{7}{8}\right) \times \frac{4}{1}$

    $= \left(\frac{22}{8} + \frac{7}{8}\right) \times \frac{4}{1}$

$$= \frac{29}{8} \times \frac{4}{1}$$

$$= \frac{29}{2}$$

$$= 14\frac{1}{2}$$

14 complete cups of the drink can be filled.

(b) Volume of the drink left

$$= \text{volume of } \frac{1}{2} \text{ a cup}$$

$$= \frac{1}{2} \times \frac{1}{4}$$

$$= \frac{1}{8} \text{ litres}$$

13. Fiona has $2\frac{1}{6}$ kg of flour. She uses $\frac{4}{5}$ kg to make a cake and the rest to make buns. Each bun requires $\frac{2}{15}$ kg of flour.

(a) How many buns can Fiona make?

(b) How many kg of flour is left?

Solution

(a) $\left(2\frac{1}{6} - \frac{4}{5}\right) \div \frac{2}{15}$

$$= \left(\frac{13}{6} - \frac{4}{5}\right) \times \frac{15}{2}$$

$$= \left(\frac{65}{30} - \frac{24}{30}\right) \times \frac{15}{2}$$

$$= \frac{41}{30} \times \frac{15}{2}$$

$$= \frac{41 \times 1}{2 \times 2}$$

$$= \frac{41}{4}$$

$$= 10\frac{1}{4}$$

Fiona can make 10 buns.

(b) Amount of flour left is $\frac{1}{4}$ of a bun's worth of flour

$$= \frac{1}{4} \times \frac{2}{15}$$

$$= \frac{1 \times 1}{2 \times 15}$$

$$= \frac{1}{30}$$

The amount of flour left is $\frac{1}{30}$ kg.

14. (a) When $3\frac{4}{7}$ is divided by a proper fraction, the result is an integer. Find two possible values of the fraction.

(b) When $3\frac{4}{7}$ is divided by a positive improper fraction, the result is an integer. Find a possible value of the fraction.

Solution

(a) Note $3\frac{4}{7} = \frac{25}{7}$. Since multiplication is the inverse of division, you can think of the question as asking for a proper fraction which when multiplied by an integer gives $\frac{25}{7}$.

Some possible values of the fraction are $\frac{1}{7}, \frac{5}{7}, \frac{1}{14}, \frac{5}{14}, -\frac{1}{7}$.

(These would give the integers 25, 5, 50, 10, −25 respectively.)

(b) Looking for a positive improper fraction such that $\frac{25}{7}$ divided by a positive improper fraction = an integer

is the same as looking for one such that $\frac{25}{7}$ = an integer multiplied by a positive improper fraction, or

$\frac{25}{7}$ divided by an integer = a positive improper fraction.

Try dividing $\frac{25}{7}$ by 2, 3, ... to get $\frac{25}{14}, \frac{25}{21}$.

Note: Larger integers would give proper fractions and negative integers would give negative fractions.

So when $3\frac{4}{7}$ is divided by $\frac{25}{14}$ or $\frac{25}{21}$, the result is an integer.

15. Find two possible mixed numbers such that the result of dividing the first one by the second one is $2\frac{5}{9}$.

Solution

Some possible mixed numbers such that the result of dividing the first number by the second number is $2\frac{5}{9}$ are

	First number	Second number
(i)	$3\frac{5}{6}$	$1\frac{1}{2}$
(ii)	$3\frac{11}{27}$	$1\frac{1}{3}$
(iii)	$6\frac{7}{18}$	$2\frac{1}{2}$
(iv)	$3\frac{2}{7}$	$1\frac{2}{7}$
(v)	$4\frac{2}{11}$	$1\frac{7}{11}$

You can apply the idea of the inverse relationship between multiplication and division to get the two numbers.

You have

first number ÷ second number = $2\frac{5}{9}$.

Then

first number = $2\frac{5}{9} \times$ second number.

You can choose any mixed number to be the second number, and multiply it by $2\frac{5}{9}$ to obtain the first number.

In **(i)**, $1\frac{1}{2}$ is chosen as the second number.

Hence, $2\frac{5}{9} \times 1\frac{1}{2}$

$= \frac{23}{9} \times \frac{3}{2}$

$= \frac{23}{6}$

$= 3\frac{5}{6}$

i.e. when $3\frac{5}{6}$ is divided by $1\frac{1}{2}$, the result is $2\frac{5}{9}$.

Exercise 5.6

Use a calculator for this exercise. Give your answers as proper fractions in their simplest form or mixed numbers where appropriate.

Level 1 GCSE Grade **2⁺**

1. Calculate these values.

(a) $\frac{3}{5} + \frac{1}{13}$

(b) $\frac{2}{9} - \frac{7}{16}$

(c) $4 - 5\frac{7}{46}$

(d) $3\frac{22}{35} - 1\frac{43}{84}$

Solution

(a) $\frac{3}{5} + \frac{1}{13} = \frac{44}{65}$

(b) $\frac{2}{9} - \frac{7}{16} = -\frac{31}{144}$

(c) $4 - 5\frac{7}{46} = -\frac{53}{46}$

$= -1\frac{7}{46}$

(d) $3\frac{22}{35} - 1\frac{43}{84} = \frac{127}{60}$

$= 2\frac{7}{60}$

2. Work out these values.

(a) $\frac{2}{5} \times 365$

(b) $\frac{3}{28} \div 2\frac{1}{4}$

(c) $\left(-1\frac{2}{3}\right) \times 2\frac{31}{40}$

(d) $\left(-\frac{25}{49}\right) \div \left(-2\frac{2}{14}\right)$

Solution

(a) $\frac{2}{5} \times 365 = 146$

(b) $\frac{3}{28} \div 2\frac{1}{4} = \frac{1}{21}$

(c) $\left(-1\frac{2}{3}\right) \times 2\frac{31}{40} = -\frac{37}{8}$

$= -4\frac{5}{8}$

(d) $\left(-\frac{25}{49}\right) \div \left(-2\frac{2}{14}\right) = \frac{5}{21}$

Level 2 GCSE Grade **3⁻**

3. Calculate these values.

(a) $5\frac{3}{4} + \frac{7}{8} - 1\frac{5}{6}$

(b) $4\frac{2}{3} - 3\frac{1}{6} \times \frac{3}{4}$

(c) $6\frac{2}{9} - \left(2\frac{1}{3} - \frac{3}{5}\right)$

(d) $5\frac{3}{4} \div \left(2\frac{1}{2} + \frac{4}{5}\right)$

Solution

(a) $5\frac{3}{4} + \frac{7}{8} - 1\frac{5}{6} = \frac{115}{24}$

$= 4\frac{19}{24}$

(b) $4\frac{2}{3} - 3\frac{1}{6} \times \frac{3}{4} = \frac{55}{24}$

$= 2\frac{7}{24}$

(c) $6\frac{2}{9} - \left(2\frac{1}{3} - \frac{3}{5}\right) = \frac{202}{45}$

$= 4\frac{22}{45}$

(d) $5\frac{3}{4} \div \left(2\frac{1}{2} + \frac{4}{5}\right) = \frac{115}{66}$

$= 1\frac{49}{66}$

4. Find these values.

(a) $1\frac{5}{6} \times 2\frac{4}{7} \times 2\frac{5}{22}$

(b) $3\frac{1}{3} \times 2\frac{2}{5} \div 1\frac{1}{4}$

(c) $3\frac{3}{8} \div 5\frac{1}{7} \times \left(-1\frac{3}{5}\right)$

(d) $\left(-6\frac{3}{5}\right) \div 7\frac{1}{3} \div \left(-3\frac{1}{9}\right)$

Solution

(a) $1\frac{5}{6} \times 2\frac{4}{7} \times 2\frac{5}{22}$

$= \frac{21}{2}$

$= 10\frac{1}{2}$

(b) $3\frac{1}{3} \times 2\frac{2}{5} \div 1\frac{1}{4}$

$= \frac{32}{5}$

$= 6\frac{2}{5}$

(c) $3\frac{3}{8} \div 5\frac{1}{7} \times \left(-1\frac{3}{5}\right)$

$= -\frac{21}{20}$

$= -1\frac{1}{20}$

(d) $\left(-6\frac{3}{5}\right) \div 7\frac{1}{3} \div \left(-3\frac{1}{9}\right)$

$= \frac{81}{280}$

Level 3 GCSE Grade **3 / 4⁻**

5. There are $2\frac{1}{4}$ litres of milk in a bottle. The milk is poured into cups, each holding $\frac{3}{8}$ litres. How many cups can be filled?

Solution
Number of cups that can be filled

$= 2\frac{1}{4} \div \frac{3}{8}$

$= 6$

6. During a sale, a jacket costing £200 is reduced to $\frac{3}{4}$ of its usual price and a dress costing £135 is reduced to $\frac{4}{5}$ of its usual price. What is the total sale price for the jacket and the dress?

Solution
Total sale price in £ is

$200 \times \frac{3}{4} + 135 \times \frac{4}{5}$

$= 50 \times 3 + 27 \times 4$

$= 150 + 108$

$= 258$

The total sale price for the jacket and dress is £258.

7. The volume of a silver plate is $18\frac{4}{5}\,\text{cm}^3$. The mass of $1\,\text{cm}^3$ of silver is $10\frac{1}{2}$ grams.

   (a) Find the mass of the plate.
   (b) The mass of a gold spoon is $194\frac{1}{3}$ grams. Determine whether the plate or the spoon is heavier. By how many grams?

   Solution
   (a) The mass of the plate is

   $$18\frac{4}{5}\times10\frac{1}{2}$$
   $$=\frac{94}{5}\times\frac{21}{2}$$
   $$=\frac{1974}{10}$$
   $$=197\frac{2}{5}$$

   The mass of the silver plate is $197\frac{2}{5}$ grams.

   (b) The silver plate is heavier since $197\frac{2}{5}>194\frac{1}{3}$.

   $$197\frac{2}{5}-194\frac{1}{3}=3+\frac{2}{5}-\frac{1}{3}$$
   $$=3+\frac{6}{15}-\frac{5}{15}$$
   $$=3\frac{1}{15}$$

   The silver plate is $3\frac{1}{15}$ grams heavier.

8. Yasmin, Ben and Connor worked on an assignment. Yasmin took $\frac{5}{6}$ hours to complete it. Ben took $1\frac{1}{2}$ times as long as Yasmin. Connor took $\frac{4}{5}$ of the time taken by Ben. Did Yasmin complete the assignment faster than Connor? Explain your answer.

   Solution
   Time taken by Ben
   $$=\left(1\frac{1}{2}\times\frac{5}{6}\right)\text{ hours}$$

   Time taken by Connor
   $$=\frac{4}{5}\times\left(1\frac{1}{2}\times\frac{5}{6}\right)$$
   $$=\frac{4}{5}\times\frac{3}{2}\times\frac{5}{6}$$
   $$=1\text{ hour}$$

   Yes, Yasmin completed the assignment faster than Connor.

   Yasmin took $\frac{5}{6}$ hours which is less than 1 hour, the time taken by Connor.

   $\frac{5}{6}<\frac{6}{6}$, i.e. $\frac{5}{6}<1$

9. Two metal bars of length $3\frac{1}{2}\,\text{m}$ and three metal bars of length $2\frac{1}{4}\,\text{m}$ are used to make a frame. If the price of each metre of the bars is $£2\frac{3}{5}$, find the total cost of the bars for the frame.

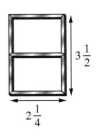

   Solution
   Total cost of frame in £ is

   $$2\frac{3}{5}\times\left(2\times3\frac{1}{2}+3\times2\frac{1}{4}\right)$$
   $$=\frac{13}{5}\times\left(2\times\frac{7}{2}+3\times\frac{9}{4}\right)$$
   $$=\frac{13}{5}\times\left(7+\frac{27}{4}\right)$$
   $$=\frac{13}{5}\times\frac{55}{4}$$
   $$=\frac{13\times11}{1\times4}$$
   $$=\frac{143}{4}$$
   $$=35\frac{3}{4}$$

   The total cost is £35.75.

10. Mary cooks $3\frac{2}{5}\,\text{kg}$ of spaghetti with $1\frac{1}{4}\,\text{kg}$ of mince and $1\frac{1}{2}\,\text{kg}$ of tomato. If each serving is $\frac{3}{10}\,\text{kg}$, how many servings are there?

    Solution
    Number of servings is
    $$\left(3\frac{2}{5}+1\frac{1}{4}+1\frac{1}{2}\right)\div\frac{3}{10}$$
    $$=\left(5+\frac{8}{20}+\frac{5}{20}+\frac{10}{20}\right)\times\frac{10}{3}$$
    $$=\left(\frac{5\times20+23}{20}\right)\times\frac{10}{3}$$
    $$=\frac{123\times1}{2\times3}$$
    $$=\frac{123}{6}$$
    $$=20\frac{1}{2}$$

    There are 20 whole servings.

Revision Exercise 5

In this exercise, give your answers as proper fractions in their simplest form or mixed numbers where appropriate.

1. Determine which fraction in each pair is smaller.

   (a) $\frac{1}{3},\frac{1}{5}$ **(b)** $\frac{9}{11},\frac{6}{11}$

   (c) $\frac{5}{6},\frac{7}{8}$ **(d)** $-\frac{3}{4},-\frac{9}{16}$

Solution

(a) When two fractions have the same numerator, the one with the bigger denominator is smaller.

Hence, $\frac{1}{5}$ is smaller.

(b) When two fractions have the same denominator, the one with the smaller numerator is smaller.

Hence, $\frac{6}{11}$ is smaller.

(c) $\frac{5}{6} = \frac{5 \times 4}{6 \times 4} = \frac{20}{24}$

$\frac{7}{8} = \frac{7 \times 3}{8 \times 3} = \frac{21}{24}$

As $\frac{20}{24} < \frac{21}{24}$,

you have $\frac{5}{6} < \frac{7}{8}$.

Hence, $\frac{5}{6}$ is smaller.

(d) $-\frac{3}{4} = -\frac{3 \times 4}{4 \times 4} = -\frac{12}{16}$

$-\frac{9}{16}$

As $-12 < -9$,

you have $-\frac{12}{16} < -\frac{9}{16}$

i.e. $-\frac{3}{4} < -\frac{9}{16}$.

Hence, $-\frac{3}{4}$ is smaller.

2. There are 18 red jelly beans and 12 green jelly beans in a tube. Find the fraction of green jelly beans in the tube.

 GCSE Grade 2

Solution
Fraction of green jelly beans in the tube

$= \frac{\text{Number of green jelly beans}}{\text{Total number of jelly beans}}$

$= \frac{12}{18 + 12}$

$= \frac{12}{30}$

$= \frac{2}{5}$

3. The price of a vase is £56. The price of a jug is $\frac{3}{8}$ the price of the vase. Find the price of the jug.

GCSE Grade 3⁻

Solution
Price of the jug

$= \frac{3}{8} \times £56$

$= £(3 \times 7)$

$= £21$

---

4. Evaluate these expressions.

 GCSE Grade 3

(a) $\frac{5}{6} + \frac{2}{3}$ **(b)** $\frac{4}{5} - \frac{2}{9}$

(c) $2\frac{1}{2} + 5\frac{3}{7}$ **(d)** $3\frac{5}{8} - 2\frac{9}{10}$

Solution

(a) $\frac{5}{6} + \frac{2}{3}$ **(b)** $\frac{4}{5} - \frac{2}{9}$

$\quad = \frac{5}{6} + \frac{4}{6}$ $\quad = \frac{36}{45} - \frac{10}{45}$

$\quad = \frac{9}{6}$ $\quad = \frac{26}{45}$

$\quad = \frac{3}{2}$

$\quad = 1\frac{1}{2}$

(c) $2\frac{1}{2} + 5\frac{3}{7}$ **(d)** $3\frac{5}{8} - 2\frac{9}{10}$

$= (2 + 5) + \left(\frac{1}{2} + \frac{3}{7}\right)$ $= (3 - 2) + \left(\frac{5}{8} - \frac{9}{10}\right)$

$= 7 + \left(\frac{7}{14} + \frac{6}{14}\right)$ $= 1 + \left(\frac{25}{40} - \frac{36}{40}\right)$

$= 7 + \frac{13}{14}$ $= 1 + \left(-\frac{11}{40}\right)$

$= 7\frac{13}{14}$ $= \frac{40}{40} - \frac{11}{40}$

$\qquad$ $= \frac{29}{40}$

5. Calculate these products.

 GCSE Grade 3

(a) $16 \times \frac{3}{4}$ **(b)** $\frac{5}{14} \times \frac{7}{10}$

(c) $\frac{15}{16} \times 4\frac{4}{9}$ **(d)** $2\frac{1}{12} \times 3\frac{3}{5}$

Solution

(a) $16 \times \frac{3}{4} = 4 \times 3$ **(b)** $\frac{5}{14} \times \frac{7}{10} = \frac{1 \times 1}{2 \times 2}$

$\qquad = 12$ $\qquad = \frac{1}{4}$

(c) $\frac{15}{16} \times 4\frac{4}{9} = \frac{15}{16} \times \frac{40}{9}$ **(d)** $2\frac{1}{12} \times 3\frac{3}{5} = \frac{25}{12} \times \frac{18}{5}$

$\qquad = \frac{5 \times 5}{2 \times 3}$ $\qquad = \frac{5 \times 3}{2 \times 1}$

$\qquad = \frac{25}{6}$ $\qquad = \frac{15}{2}$

$\qquad = 4\frac{1}{6}$ $\qquad = 7\frac{1}{2}$

6. Find these values.

 GCSE Grade 3⁺

(a) $35 \div \frac{5}{6}$ **(b)** $\frac{9}{20} \div 18$

(c) $\frac{28}{33} \div \frac{21}{22}$ **(d)** $5\frac{1}{7} \div 3\frac{3}{14}$

Solution

(a) $35 \div \frac{5}{6} = 35 \times \frac{6}{5}$ **(b)** $\frac{9}{20} \div 18 = \frac{9}{20} \times \frac{1}{18}$

$\qquad = 7 \times 6$ $\qquad = \frac{1 \times 1}{20 \times 2}$

$\qquad = 42$ $\qquad = \frac{1}{40}$

(c) $\dfrac{28}{33} \div \dfrac{21}{22} = \dfrac{28}{33} \times \dfrac{22}{21}$

$= \dfrac{4 \times 2}{3 \times 3}$

$= \dfrac{8}{9}$

(d) $5\dfrac{1}{7} \div 3\dfrac{3}{14} = \dfrac{36}{7} \div \dfrac{45}{14}$

$= \dfrac{36}{7} \times \dfrac{14}{45}$

$= \dfrac{4 \times 2}{1 \times 5}$

$= \dfrac{8}{5}$

$= 1\dfrac{3}{5}$

7. Find these values.

(a) $3\dfrac{1}{2} + 2\dfrac{2}{3} - 1\dfrac{4}{5}$

(b) $5\dfrac{4}{9} - 1\dfrac{1}{3} \times 2\dfrac{3}{4}$

(c) $\dfrac{5}{8} \times \dfrac{2}{15} - \dfrac{1}{6}$

(d) $6\dfrac{3}{5} + 4\dfrac{2}{3} \div 3\dfrac{1}{9}$

Solution

(a) $3\dfrac{1}{2} + 2\dfrac{2}{3} - 1\dfrac{4}{5}$

$= 3\dfrac{3}{6} + 2\dfrac{4}{6} - 1\dfrac{4}{5}$

$= 3 + 2 + \dfrac{3}{6} + \dfrac{4}{6} - 1\dfrac{4}{5}$

$= 5 + \dfrac{7}{6} - 1\dfrac{4}{5}$

$= 5 - 1 + \dfrac{7}{6} - \dfrac{4}{5}$

$= 4 + \dfrac{35}{30} - \dfrac{24}{30}$

$= 4 + \dfrac{11}{30}$

$= 4\dfrac{11}{30}$

(b) $5\dfrac{4}{9} - 1\dfrac{1}{3} \times 2\dfrac{3}{4}$

$= 5\dfrac{4}{9} - \dfrac{4}{3} \times \dfrac{11}{4}$

$= \dfrac{49}{9} - \dfrac{11}{3}$

$= \dfrac{49}{9} - \dfrac{33}{9}$

$= \dfrac{16}{9}$

$= 1\dfrac{7}{9}$

(c) $\dfrac{5}{8} \times \dfrac{2}{15} - \dfrac{1}{6}$

$= \dfrac{1 \times 1}{4 \times 3} - \dfrac{1}{6}$

$= \dfrac{1}{12} - \dfrac{2}{12}$

$= -\dfrac{1}{12}$

(d) $6\dfrac{3}{5} + 4\dfrac{2}{3} \div 3\dfrac{1}{9}$

$= 6\dfrac{3}{5} + \dfrac{14}{3} \div \dfrac{28}{9}$

$= 6\dfrac{3}{5} + \dfrac{14}{3} \times \dfrac{9}{28}$

$= 6\dfrac{3}{5} + \dfrac{3}{2}$

$= 6 + \dfrac{3}{5} + \dfrac{3}{2}$

$= 6 + \dfrac{6}{10} + \dfrac{15}{10}$

$= 6 + \dfrac{21}{10}$

$= 6 + 2\dfrac{1}{10}$

$= 8\dfrac{1}{10}$

8. Calculate these expressions.

(a) $\left(3\dfrac{1}{4} + 2\dfrac{3}{5}\right) \times \dfrac{5}{9}$

(b) $1\dfrac{5}{6} \div \left(3\dfrac{1}{3} - 1\dfrac{1}{2}\right)$

Solution

(a) $\left(3\dfrac{1}{4} + 2\dfrac{3}{5}\right) \times \dfrac{5}{9}$

$= \left(3\dfrac{5}{20} + 2\dfrac{12}{20}\right) \times \dfrac{5}{9}$

$= 5\dfrac{17}{20} \times \dfrac{5}{9}$

$= \dfrac{117}{20} \times \dfrac{5}{9}$

$= \dfrac{13 \times 1}{4 \times 1}$

$= \dfrac{13}{4}$

$= 3\dfrac{1}{4}$

(b) $1\dfrac{5}{6} \div \left(3\dfrac{1}{3} - 1\dfrac{1}{2}\right)$

$= 1\dfrac{5}{6} \div \left(\dfrac{10}{3} - \dfrac{3}{2}\right)$

$= 1\dfrac{5}{6} \div \left(\dfrac{20}{6} - \dfrac{9}{6}\right)$

$= \dfrac{11}{6} \div \dfrac{11}{6}$

$= \dfrac{11}{6} \times \dfrac{6}{11}$

$= 1$

9. The ingredients in a dish are $\dfrac{3}{8}$ kg of beef, $\dfrac{1}{2}$ kg of onion and $\dfrac{5}{16}$ kg of potato. Find the total mass of the ingredients.

Solution

Total mass of the ingredients

$= \dfrac{3}{8} + \dfrac{1}{2} + \dfrac{5}{16}$

$= \dfrac{6}{16} + \dfrac{8}{16} + \dfrac{5}{16}$

$= \dfrac{19}{16}$

$= 1\dfrac{3}{16}$ kg

10. In a garden, $\dfrac{1}{3}$ of the area is planted with trees, $\dfrac{2}{5}$ of the area is for flowers and the rest is the lawn.

(a) What fraction of the garden is the lawn?

(b) If the area of the garden is $5\dfrac{5}{8}$ acres, find the area of the lawn.

Solution

(a) Fraction of the garden that is the lawn

$= 1 - \dfrac{1}{3} - \dfrac{2}{5}$

$= \dfrac{15}{15} - \dfrac{5}{15} - \dfrac{6}{15}$

$= \dfrac{4}{15}$

(b) Area of the lawn

$= \dfrac{4}{15} \times 5\dfrac{5}{8}$

$= \dfrac{4}{15} \times \dfrac{45}{8}$

$= \dfrac{3}{2}$

$= 1\dfrac{1}{2}$ acres

11. 25 m of wire is on a roll. Sections of wire, each $1\frac{1}{3}$ m long, are cut from the roll.

(a) How many sections can be cut from the roll?

(b) How many metres of wire are left over?

Solution

(a) $25 \div 1\frac{1}{3}$

$= 25 \div \frac{4}{3}$

$= 25 \times \frac{3}{4}$

$= \frac{75}{4}$

$= 18\frac{3}{4}$

Hence, 18 sections of wire can be cut from the roll.

(b) Length of wire that is left over

$=$ length of $\frac{3}{4}$ of a section

$= \frac{3}{4} \times 1\frac{1}{3}$

$= \frac{3}{4} \times \frac{4}{3}$

$= 1 \text{ m}$

12. Tom has $2\frac{1}{12}$ kg of coffee. His family consumes $\frac{1}{25}$ kg of coffee each day.

(a) How many days will the coffee last?

(b) How much coffee will be left over?

Solution

(a) $2\frac{1}{12} \div \frac{1}{25}$

$= \frac{25}{12} \times \frac{25}{1}$

$= \frac{625}{12}$

$= 52\frac{1}{12}$

The coffee will last 52 days.

(b) Amount of coffee that will be left over

$= \frac{1}{12} \times \frac{1}{25}$

$= \frac{1}{300} \text{ kg}$

13. A hammer is $27\frac{1}{2}$ cm long. A screwdriver is $19\frac{1}{4}$ cm long. The difference between the lengths of the hammer and the screwdriver is equal to the total length of five screws. What is the length of each screw?

Solution

Screw length in cm is given by

$\left(27\frac{1}{2} - 19\frac{1}{4}\right) \div 5$

$= \left(27 - 19 + \frac{1}{2} - \frac{1}{4}\right) \times \frac{1}{5}$

$= \left(8 + \frac{2-1}{4}\right) \times \frac{1}{5}$

$= \frac{8 \times 4 + 1}{4} \times \frac{1}{5}$

$= \frac{33}{20}$

$= 1\frac{13}{20}$

The length of each screw is $1\frac{13}{20}$ cm.

14. Diana uses $2\frac{1}{4}$ litres of a solution for three experiments. The first experiment uses $\frac{1}{3}$ of the solution. The second experiment uses $\frac{5}{9}$ of the remaining solution. The third experiment uses the rest. Find the volume of the solution used for each experiment.

Solution

The first experiment uses

$\frac{1}{3} \times \left(2\frac{1}{4}\right)$

$= \frac{1}{3} \times \frac{9}{4}$

$= \frac{3}{4}$

The second experiment uses

$\left(2\frac{1}{4} - \frac{3}{4}\right) \times \frac{5}{9}$

$= \left(\frac{9}{4} - \frac{3}{4}\right) \times \frac{5}{9}$

$= \frac{6}{4} \times \frac{5}{9}$

$= \frac{1 \times 5}{2 \times 3}$

$= \frac{5}{6}$

The third experiment uses

$2\frac{1}{4} - \frac{3}{4} - \frac{5}{6}$

$= \frac{9 \times 3}{4 \times 3} - \frac{3 \times 3}{4 \times 3} - \frac{5 \times 2}{6 \times 2}$

$= \frac{27 - 9 - 10}{12}$

$= \frac{8}{12}$

$= \frac{2}{3}$

The first, second and third experiments use $\frac{3}{4}, \frac{5}{6}$ and $\frac{2}{3}$ litres respectively.

15. In a lever system, two loads of mass $13\frac{1}{4}$ kg and

$15\frac{5}{8}$ kg at one end are balanced by a ball at the other end. The mass of the ball is $\frac{2}{11}$ of the total mass of the two loads. Find the mass of the ball.

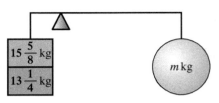

Solution

Mass of the ball is

$$\frac{2}{11}\times\left(15\frac{5}{8}+13\frac{1}{4}\right)$$

$$=\frac{2}{11}\times\left(\frac{125}{8}+\frac{53\times2}{4\times2}\right)$$

$$=\frac{2\times231}{11\times8}$$

$$=\frac{1\times21}{1\times4}$$

$$=5\frac{1}{4}$$

The mass of the ball is $5\frac{1}{4}$ kg.

6 Decimals

Class Activity 1

Objective: To investigate the rule for multiplication of decimals.

Tasks

1. Copy and complete these calculations.

   (a) **(i)** 3×4

   $= \boxed{12}$

   (ii) $0.3 \times 4 = \dfrac{3}{10} \times 4$

   $= \dfrac{\boxed{12}}{10}$

   $= \boxed{1.2}$ Express the answer as a decimal.

   (b) **(i)** 2×9

   $= \boxed{18}$

   (ii) $0.2 \times 0.9 = \dfrac{2}{10} \times \dfrac{9}{10}$

   $= \dfrac{\boxed{18}}{100}$

   $= \boxed{0.18}$ Express the answer as a decimal.

   (c) **(i)** 6×13

   $= \boxed{78}$

   (ii) $0.6 \times 0.13 = \dfrac{6}{10} \times \dfrac{13}{100}$

   $= \dfrac{\boxed{78}}{1000}$

   $= \boxed{0.078}$ Express the answer as a decimal.

   (d) **(i)** 2417×4

   $= \boxed{9668}$

   (ii) $2.417 \times 0.4 = \dfrac{2417}{1000} \times \dfrac{4}{10}$

   $= \dfrac{\boxed{9668}}{10000}$

   $= \boxed{0.9668}$ Express the answer as a decimal.

2. What is the relationship between the results in **(i)** and **(ii)** in each part of Question **1**?

   The results in **(i)** and **(ii)** in each part of Question **1** have the same digits but they are of different place values.

3. Suggest a rule for determining the number of decimal places in the product of a multiplication.

   The number of decimal places in the product of two decimals is the total number of decimal places in the two decimals.

Class Activity 2

Objective: To explore the method of division of a decimal by a whole number.

Tasks

1. Copy and complete these expressions.

   (a) (i) $546 \div 3$

   $= \boxed{182}$

   (ii) $54.6 \div 3 = \left(54 + \dfrac{6}{10}\right) \div 3$

   $= 54 \div 3 + \dfrac{6}{10} \div 3$

   $= \boxed{18} + \dfrac{\boxed{2}}{10}$

   $= \boxed{18.2}$ **Express the answer as a decimal.**

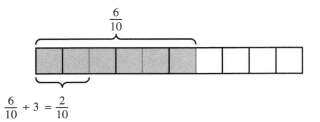

   $$\frac{6}{10} \div 3 = \frac{2}{10}$$

   (b) (i) $824 \div 4$

   $= \boxed{206}$

   (ii) $8.24 \div 4 = \left(8 + \dfrac{24}{100}\right) \div 4$

   $= 8 \div 4 + \dfrac{24}{100} \div 4$

   $= \boxed{2} + \dfrac{\boxed{6}}{100}$

   $= \boxed{2.06}$ **Express the answer as a decimal.**

   (c) (i) $1236 \div 2$

   $= \boxed{618}$

   (ii) $1.236 \div 2 = \left(1 + \dfrac{236}{1000}\right) \div 2$

   $= \dfrac{1236}{1000} \div 2$

   $= \dfrac{\boxed{618}}{1000}$

   $= \boxed{0.618}$ **Express the answer as a decimal.**

2. What is the relationship between the results in **(i)** and **(ii)** in each part of Question **1**?

   The results in **(i)** and **(ii)** in each part of Question **1** have the same digits. The division of a decimal by a whole number in **(ii)** has the same digits as if the decimal was a whole number.

3. Suggest a rule for placing the decimal point in the quotient of a division of a decimal by a whole number.

   Line up the decimal point in the quotient with the decimal point in the dividend.

Class Activity 3

Objective: To identify a method for multiplying a decimal by 10, 100 or 1000.

Tasks

1. Copy and complete the place value table.

Number	Ten thousands	Thousands	Hundreds	Tens	Ones	Tenths
7200 × 10	7	2	0	0	0	
720 × 10		7	2	0	0	
72 × 10			7	2	0	
7.2 × 10				7	2	
0.72 × 10					7	2

2. Copy and complete the place value table.

Number	Ten thousands	Thousands	Hundreds	Tens	Ones	Tenths
184 × 100	1	8	4	0	0	
18.4 × 100		1	8	4	0	
1.84 × 100			1	8	4	
0.184 × 100				1	8	4

3. Copy and complete the place value table.

Number	Ten thousands	Thousands	Hundreds	Tens	Ones	Tenths
93 × 1000	9	3	0	0	0	
9.3 × 1000		9	3	0	0	
0.93 × 1000			9	3	0	
0.093 × 1000				9	3	
0.0093 × 1000					9	3

4. What do you observe about the change in the place value of each digit in a number when it is multiplied by
   (a) 10, **(b)** 100, **(c)** 1000?

The place value of each digit in a number

(a) shifts one place to the left when the number is multiplied by 10,

(b) shifts two places to the left when it is multiplied by 100,

(c) shifts three places to the left when it is multiplied by 1000.

Class Activity 4

Objective: To identify a method for dividing a decimal by 10, 100 or 1000.

Tasks

1. Copy and complete the place value table.

Number	Thousands	Hundreds	Tens	Ones	Tenths	Hundredths
72 000 ÷ 10	7	2	0	0		
7200 ÷ 10		7	2	0		
720 ÷ 10			7	2		
72 ÷ 10				7	2	
7.2 ÷ 10				0	7	2

2. Copy and complete the place value table.

Number	Hundreds	Tens	Ones	Tenths	Hundredths	Thousandths
3500 ÷ 100		3	5			
350 ÷ 100			3	5		
35 ÷ 100			0	3	5	
3.5 ÷ 100			0	0	3	5

3. Copy and complete the place value table.

Number	Tens	Ones	Tenths	Hundredths	Thousandths	Ten thousandths
18 000 ÷ 1000	1	8				
1800 ÷ 1000		1	8			
180 ÷ 1000		0	1	8		
18 ÷ 1000		0	0	1	8	
1.8 ÷ 1000		0	0	0	1	8

4. What do you observe about the change in the place value of each digit in a number when it is divided by
   (a) 10,   **(b)** 100,   **(c)** 1000?

The place value of each digit in a number

(a) shifts one place to the right when the number is divided by 10,

(b) shifts two places to the right when it is divided by 100,

(c) shifts three places to the right when it is divided by 1000.

Try It!

Section 6.1

1. Write these decimal numbers in expanded form. Then write the expanded form in words.
   (a) 0.0347   **(b)** 6.200 108

Solution

(a) $0.0347 = \dfrac{3}{100} + \dfrac{4}{1000} + \dfrac{7}{10\,000}$

The number is three hundredths, four thousandths and seven ten-thousandths.

(b) $6.200\,108 = 6 + \dfrac{2}{10} + \dfrac{1}{10\,000} + \dfrac{8}{1\,000\,000}$

The number is six ones, two tenths, one ten-thousandths and eight millionths.

2. Write down the value of the digit 8 in each of these numbers.
   (a) 326.85   **(b)** 0.034 819

Solution

(a) In the number 326.85, the value of the digit 8 is $\dfrac{8}{10}$.

(b) In the number 0.034 819, the value of the digit 8 is $\dfrac{8}{10\,000}$.

3. What is the reading indicated on the clinical thermometer in degrees Celsius?

Solution

The reading indicated on the thermometer is 37.5 degrees Celsius.

4. Arrange the numbers 2.38, 2.47 and 2.381 in descending order.

Solution

You can display the given numbers in a place value table.

Ones	Tenths	Hundredths	Thousandths
2	3	8	0
2	4	7	0
2	3	8	1

The numbers in descending order are 2.47, 2.381, 2.38.

5. **(a)** The length of a rod is 40.61 cm. Round the length to the nearest cm.

   (b) Round −3.298 to the nearest integer.

   Solution

   (a) 40.61 cm = 41 cm (to the nearest cm)

   (b) −3.298 = −3 (to the nearest integer)

Section 6.2

6. Calculate these expressions.
   (a) 5.256 + 9.784   **(b)** 5.926 − 21.37

   Solution

   (a)
   $$\begin{array}{r} 5.256 \\ +\ 9.784 \\ \hline 15.040 \\ \hline \end{array}$$

   ∴ 5.256 + 9.784 = 15.04

   (b)
   $$\begin{array}{r} \overset{1\ 10\ \ 1\ 6\ 1}{21.370} \\ -\ 5.926 \\ \hline 15.444 \\ \hline \end{array}$$

   ∴ 5.926 − 21.37 = −(21.37 − 5.926) = −15.444

7. A car travels back and forth along a straight road running in an east-west direction. It first travels 10.76 km due east, then it travels 13.28 km due west. Finally, it travels 2.51 km due east. Determine the final position of the car from the starting point.
   Hint: You may draw a diagram to help you understand the problem.

   Solution
   Take distance travelled due east to be positive and distance travelled due west to be negative.
   The final position of the car from the starting point
   = 10.76 + (−13.28) + 2.51
   = 10.76 − 13.28 + 2.51
   = −(13.28 − 10.76) + 2.51
   = −2.52 + 2.51
   = −0.01 km
   The car is 0.01 km due west from the starting point in its final position.

Section 6.3

8. Calculate these products.
   (a) 0.54 × 6
   (b) (−8.05) × 0.034

   Solution

   (a)
   $$\begin{array}{r} 54 \\ \times\ \ 6 \\ \hline 324 \\ \hline \end{array}$$

   ∴ $\underbrace{0.54 \times 6}_{\uparrow} = 3.24$

   total of 2
   decimal places

   (b)
   $$\begin{array}{r} 805 \\ \times\ \ 34 \\ \hline 24150 \\ 3220 \\ \hline 27370 \\ \hline \end{array}$$

   ∴ $\underbrace{-8.05 \times 0.034}_{\uparrow} = -0.273\,70$
   = −0.2737

   total of 5
   decimal places

9. Given that 543 × 139 = 75 477, write down the value of 0.543 × 0.0139.

   Solution
   0.543 has 3 decimal places and 0.0139 has 4 decimal places.
   Their product should have 3 + 4 = 7 decimal places.
   Hence, 0.543 × 0.0139 = 0.007 5477.

10. A bottle contains 1.85 litres of milk. The milk is poured into three cups so that each cup has 0.253 litres. Find the volume of milk remaining in the bottle.

    Solution
    Volume of milk in the 3 cups = 0.253 × 3 litres
    Volume of milk remaining in the bottle
    = 1.85 − 0.253 × 3
    = 1.85 − 0.759
    = 1.091 litres

Section 6.4

11. Calculate 0.5676 ÷ 12.

    Solution
    $$\begin{array}{r} 0.0473 \\ 12\overline{)0.5676} \\ 48\ \ \ \ \ \\ \hline 87\ \ \ \\ 84\ \ \ \\ \hline 36\ \\ 36\ \\ \hline 0 \\ \end{array}$$

    ∴ 0.5676 ÷ 12 = 0.0473

12. The total mass of eight identical packs of sugar is 6.2 kg. Find the mass of each pack.

    Solution
    Mass of each pack
    = 6.2 ÷ 8
    = 0.775 kg

    $$\begin{array}{r} 0.775 \\ 8\overline{)6.200} \\ 0\ \ \ \ \ \\ \hline 6\ 2\ \ \\ 5\ 6\ \ \\ \hline 60\ \\ 56\ \\ \hline 40 \\ 40 \\ \hline 0 \\ \end{array}$$

Section 6.5

13. Work out these values.
    (a) 72.83×10
    (b) 0.506×100
    (c) 1.749×1000
    Hint: Draw a place value table to help you if needed.

Solution
    (a) $72.83 \times 10 = 728.3$

    (b) $0.506 \times 100 = 50.6$

    (c) $1.749 \times 1000 = 1749$

14. Calculate these expressions mentally.
    (a) 0.756×2000 (b) 8.93×25

Solution
    (a) 0.756×2000
        $= 0.756 \times 2 \times 1000$
        $= 1.512 \times 1000$
        $= 1512$

    (b) 8.93×25
        $= 8.93 \times 100 \div 4$
        $= 893 \div 2 \div 2$
        $= 446.5 \div 2$
        $= 223.25$

15. Work out these values.
    (a) $20.9 \div 10$
    (b) $16.38 \div 100$
    (c) $345 \div 1000$

Solution
    (a) $20.9 \div 10 = 2.09$

    (b) $16.38 \div 100 = 0.1638$

    (c) $345 \div 1000 = 0.345$

16. Calculate mentally $9.48 \div 200$.

Solution
    $9.48 \div 200$
    $= 9.48 \div 2 \div 100$
    $= 4.74 \div 100$
    $= 0.0474$

17. (a) Express 875 ml in litres.
    (b) Express 3.62 kg in grams.

Solution
    (a) $875 \text{ ml} = 875 \div 1000 \text{ litres}$
                  $= 0.875 \text{ litres}$

    (b) $3.62 \text{ kg} = 3.62 \times 1000 \text{ g}$
                 $= 3620 \text{ g}$

18. (a) The height of a building is 138 m. Express the height in
        (i) km,   (ii) cm.

    (b) The time taken to get to school is 0.35 hours. Express the time taken in minutes.
    (c) The price for 1 kg of steak is £15. Find the price for 1 gram of steak in pence.

Solution
    (a) (i) Height of the building
             $= 138 \text{ m}$
             $= 138 \div 1000 \text{ km}$
             $= 0.138 \text{ km}$

        (ii) Height of the building
             $= 138 \text{ m}$
             $= 138 \times 100 \text{ cm}$
             $= 13\,800 \text{ cm}$

    (b) Time taken
        $= 0.35 \text{ hours}$
        $= 0.35 \times 60 \text{ minutes}$
        $= 21 \text{ minutes}$

    (c) Price for 1 kg of steak
        $= £15$
        $= 15 \times 100\text{p}$
        $= 1500\text{p}$
        $\therefore$ price for 1 gram of steak
        $= 1500 \div 1000$
        $= 1.5\text{p}$

Section 6.6

19. Calculate $(-37.12) \div (-0.4)$.

Solution
$$(-37.12) \div (-0.4) = \frac{37.12}{0.4}$$
$$= \frac{37.12 \times 10}{0.4 \times 10}$$
$$= \frac{371.2}{4}$$
$$= 371.2 \div 4$$

$$
\begin{array}{r}
92.8 \\
4\overline{)371.2} \\
36 \\ \hline
11 \\
8 \\ \hline
3\,2 \\
3\,2 \\ \hline
0
\end{array}
$$

$\therefore (-37.12) \div (-0.4) = 92.8$

20. Given that $457 \div 8 = 57.125$, work out
    (a) $457 \div 0.8$,   (b) $45.7 \div 0.08$.

Solution
    (a) $457 \div 0.8$
        $= \dfrac{457}{0.8}$
        $= \dfrac{457 \times 10}{0.8 \times 10}$
        $= \dfrac{457}{8} \times 10$
        $= 57.125 \times 10$
        $= 571.25$

    (b) $45.7 \div 0.08$
        $= \dfrac{45.7}{0.08}$
        $= \dfrac{45.7 \times 100}{0.08 \times 100}$
        $= \dfrac{45.7 \times 10 \times 10}{8}$
        $= \dfrac{457}{8} \times 10$
        $= 57.125 \times 10$
        $= 571.25$

21. The price for 0.3 kg of fish is £3.78. Find the price for 1 kg of fish.

Solution

Price for 1 kg of fish
= £3.78 ÷ 0.3
= £12.60

$$\begin{array}{r} 12.6 \\ 3\overline{)37.8} \\ \underline{3} \\ 07 \\ \underline{6} \\ 1\,8 \\ \underline{1\,8} \\ 0 \end{array}$$

Section 6.7

22. Convert each decimal to a fraction in its simplest form.

(a) 0.75

(b) 7.125

Solution

(a) $0.75 = \dfrac{75}{100}$

$= \dfrac{3}{4}$

(b) $7.125 = 7 + \dfrac{125}{1000}$

$= 7 + \dfrac{1}{8}$

$= 7\dfrac{1}{8}$

23. Write the fraction $\dfrac{4}{25}$ as a decimal.

Solution

$$\begin{array}{r} 0.16 \\ 25\overline{)4.00} \\ \underline{2\,5} \\ 1\,50 \\ \underline{1\,50} \\ 0 \end{array}$$

$\therefore \dfrac{4}{25} = 4 \div 25$

$= 0.16$

Alternatively,

$\dfrac{4}{25} = \dfrac{4 \times 4}{25 \times 4}$

$= \dfrac{16}{100}$

$= 0.16$

24. Convert these fractions to decimals without using a calculator.

(a) $\dfrac{7}{9}$

(b) $\dfrac{13}{22}$

Solution

(a)
$$\begin{array}{r} 0.7777 \\ 9\overline{)7.0000} \\ \underline{6\,3} \\ 70 \\ \underline{63} \\ 70 \\ \underline{63} \\ 70 \\ \underline{63} \\ 7 \end{array}$$

$\dfrac{7}{9} = 0.7777...$

$= 0.\dot{7}$

(b)
$$\begin{array}{r} 0.590909 \\ 22\overline{)13.000000} \\ \underline{11\,0} \\ 2\,00 \\ \underline{1\,98} \\ 20 \\ \underline{0} \\ 200 \\ \underline{198} \\ 20 \\ \underline{0} \\ 200 \\ \underline{198} \\ 2 \end{array}$$

$\dfrac{13}{22} = 0.590909...$

$= 0.5\dot{9}\dot{0}$

Exercise 6.1

Level 1   GCSE Grade 1⁺/2

1. Write each decimal number in expanded form. Then write the expanded form in words.

(a) 7.841

(b) 0.010973

Solution

(a) $7.841 = 7 + \dfrac{8}{10} + \dfrac{4}{100} + \dfrac{1}{1000}$

The number is seven ones, eight tenths, four hundredths and one thousandth.

(b) $0.010973 = \dfrac{1}{100} + \dfrac{9}{10\,000} + \dfrac{7}{100\,000} + \dfrac{3}{1\,000\,000}$

The number is one hundredth, nine ten-thousandths, seven hundred-thousandths and three millionths.

2. Write each expression as a decimal.

(a) $\dfrac{3}{10} + \dfrac{8}{100} + \dfrac{1}{1000}$

(b) $8 + \dfrac{3}{100} + \dfrac{5}{1000} + \dfrac{9}{100\,000}$

(c) $\dfrac{5}{10} + \dfrac{7}{1000} + \dfrac{2}{100\,000}$

(d) $15 + \dfrac{6}{1000} + \dfrac{2}{10\,000} + \dfrac{4}{1\,000\,000}$

Solution

(a) 0.381

(b) 8.035 09

(c) 0.507 02

(d) 15.006 204

3. Write down the value of the digit 5 in each number.
   (a) 0.4589   (b) 23.400 578
   (c) 290.51   (d) 0.003 075

Solution

(a) $\dfrac{5}{100}$ (b) $\dfrac{5}{10\,000}$

(c) $\dfrac{5}{10}$ (d) $\dfrac{5}{1\,000\,000}$

4. Write down the reading indicated on the scales below.
   (a) 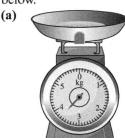   (b)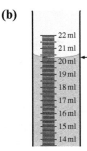

   Hint: You measure liquids accurately from the bottom of the dip in the surface.

Solution

(a) 3.7 kg   (b) 20.3 ml

5. Copy and fill in the blanks with '<' or '>'.
   (a) 2.407 _____ −3.466
   (b) 17.345 _____ 17.369
   (c) 0.043 256 _____ 0.043 219
   (d) −0.3485 _____ −0.348 53

Solution

(a) 2.407 > −3.466

(b) 17.345 < 17.369

(c) 0.043 256 > 0.043 219

(d) −0.3485 > −0.348 53

6. Which is the smaller number in each pair?
   (a) 0.289, 0.293   (b) 3.4458, 3.4178
   (c) −12.908, −12.9083   (d) −0.345, −0.317

Solution

(a) 0.289   (b) 3.4178

(c) −12.9083   (d) −0.345

7. Round each number to the nearest integer.
   (a) 3.5803   (b) 29.134
   (c) 147.9001   (d) 407.2019

Solution

Rounded to the nearest integer,
(a) 3.5803 = 4   (b) 29.134 = 29

(c) 147.9001 = 148   (d) 407.2019 = 407

Level 2   **GCSE Grade** 2^- / 2

8. Write the given numbers in ascending order.
   (a) 2.645, 2.525, 2.54
   (b) −0.9796, −0.9793, −0.979

Solution

(a)

Ones	Tenths	Hundredths	Thousandths
2	6	4	5
2	5	2	5
2	5	4	0

The numbers in ascending order are 2.525, 2.54, 2.645.

(b)

Ones	Tenths	Hundredths	Thousandths	Ten-thousandths
−0	9	7	9	6
−0	9	7	9	3
−0	9	7	9	0

The numbers in ascending order are −0.9796, −0.9793, −0.979.

9. Write the given numbers in descending order.
   (a) 53.81, 53.18, 53.08
   (b) −4.76, −2.89, 3.67

Solution

(a)

Tens	Ones	Tenths	Hundredths
5	3	8	1
5	3	1	8
5	3	0	8

The numbers in descending order are 53.81, 53.18, 53.08.

(b)

Ones	Tenths	Hundredths
−4	7	6
−2	8	9
3	6	7

Comparing the ones, 3 > −2 > −4.
Hence the numbers in descending order are 3.67, −2.89, −4.76.

10. The times recorded by Boris in three 100 m sprint races were 10.98 s, 11.07 s and 10.67 s respectively.
    (a) Which time has a place value of 0 tenths?
    (b) What is Boris's best time in these three races?

Solution

(a) 11.07 s has a place value of 0 tenths.

(b) 10.67 < 10.98 < 11.07 that is, 10.67 is the smallest number. Hence, Boris's best time is 10.67 s.

11. The area of a living room floor is 20.78 m². Round the area to the nearest m².

Solution
20.78 m² = 21 m² (to the nearest m²)

12. The mass of a cat is 3.417 kg. Round the mass to the nearest kg.

Solution
3.417 kg = 3 kg (to the nearest kg)

Level 3   GCSE Grade **2⁺ / 3**

13. The masses of three pieces of diamond are 0.1932 grams, 0.193 grams and 0.195 grams.
(a) Arrange the masses in ascending order.
(b) Round the mass of 0.1932 grams to the nearest gram.

Solution
(a)

Ones	Tenths	Hundredths	Thousandths	Ten-thousandths
0	1	9	3	2
0	1	9	3	0
0	1	9	5	0

The masses in ascending order are 0.193 grams, 0.1932 grams and 0.195 grams.

(b) 0.1932 = 0 (to the nearest gram)

14. From 1 May 2016 to 5 May 2016, one British pound (GBP) could be exchanged to US dollars (USD) as shown in the table.

1 May 2016	1.4592 USD
2 May 2016	1.4667 USD
3 May 2016	1.4544 USD
4 May 2016	1.45 USD
5 May 2016	1.4488 USD

(a) Which amount in the table has a place value of 4 hundredths USD?
(b) On which date was the exchange rate the highest?
Note: The **exchange rate** means the amount of a currency that can be exchanged for one unit of another currency.

Solution
(a) 1.4488 USD has a place value of 4 hundredths.

(b) 1.4667 USD to 1 GBP was the highest exchange rate in the given time period. Hence, the exchange rate was the highest on 2 May 2016.

15. At very low temperatures, the elements nitrogen and oxygen are liquids. When boiled, they become gases. The boiling point of nitrogen is −195.80 °C. The boiling point of oxygen is −182.96 °C.
(a) What is the value of the digit 6 in the number −182.96?
(b) Round the boiling points of nitrogen and oxygen to the nearest °C.
(c) Which of these two elements has a lower boiling point?

Solution
(a) In the number −182.96, the value of the digit 6 is $\frac{6}{100}$.

(b) The boiling point of nitrogen, −195.80 °C = −196 °C (to the nearest °C). The boiling point of oxygen, −182.96 °C = −183 °C (to the nearest °C).

(c) −195.80 < −182.96, so −195.80 °C is the lower boiling point. Nitrogen has a lower boiling point.

16. Write two decimal numbers between 1.285 and 1.286.
Hint: You can use a magnified number line to help you.

Solution
Possible decimal numbers between 1.285 and 1.286 are
1.2851,
1.2852,
1.285 08,
1.285 37,
1.285 49.

17. Write two decimal numbers between −0.9314 and −0.9782.

Solution
Possible decimal numbers between −0.9782 and −0.9314 are
−0.94,
−0.9652,
−0.9315,
−0.977 999,
−0.958.

18. If 0.001 07 > 0.0 ☐ ☐ 09, what are the two missing digits?

Solution

Ones	Tenths	Hundredths	Thousandths	Ten-thousandths	Hundred-thousandths
0	0	0	1	0	7
0	0	?	?	0	9

The two numbers have equal values in the ones and tenths digit place.

For 0.001 07 to be larger than 0.0??09, the missing hundredths digit must be 0.

Since the two values in the ten-thousandths place are equal and the hundred-thousandths digit in the second number is larger than in the first, the thousandths digit of the first number must be larger than in the second number. In other words, the missing thousandths digit is 0 as well.

This gives 0.001 07 > 0.000 09.

Exercise 6.2

Level 1

1. Calculate these sums.

   (a) $\begin{array}{r} 1.456 \\ + \ 5.824 \end{array}$ (b) $\begin{array}{r} 7.6385 \\ + \ 0.3916 \end{array}$

   (c) $4.345 + 6.23$ (d) $13.4529 + 8.1476$

   Solution

   (a) $\begin{array}{r} 1.456 \\ + \ 5.824 \\ \hline 7.280 \\ {\scriptstyle 1 \ \ 1} \end{array}$ (b) $\begin{array}{r} 7.6385 \\ + \ 0.3916 \\ \hline 8.0301 \\ {\scriptstyle 1 \ 1 1 1} \end{array}$

   (c) $\begin{array}{r} 4.345 \\ + \ 6.230 \\ \hline 10.575 \end{array}$ (d) $\begin{array}{r} 13.4529 \\ + \ \ 8.1476 \\ \hline 21.6005 \\ {\scriptstyle 1 \ \ \ 1 1 1} \end{array}$

2. Copy and complete these calculations.

   (a) $\begin{array}{r} 6.538 \\ - \ 3.476 \end{array}$ (b) $\begin{array}{r} 17.8923 \\ - \ \ 8.9275 \end{array}$

   (c) $23.459 - 9.671$ (d) $4.25 - 8.371$

   Solution

   (a) $\begin{array}{r} {\scriptstyle 4\ 1} \\ 6.538 \\ - \ 3.476 \\ \hline 3.062 \end{array}$ (b) $\begin{array}{r} {\scriptstyle 16 \ \ 1\,8\,11 1} \\ 17.8923 \\ - \ \ 8.9275 \\ \hline 8.9648 \end{array}$

   (c) $\begin{array}{r} {\scriptstyle 1 12 \ 13 1} \\ 23.459 \\ - \ \ 9.671 \\ \hline 13.788 \end{array}$

   (d) $\begin{array}{r} 8.371 \\ - 4.250 \\ \hline 4.121 \end{array}$

   $\therefore 4.25 - 8.371 = -(8.371 - 4.25) = -4.121$

Level 2

3. Calculate these expressions.

   (a) $0.35 + 0.9 + 0.28$ (b) $3.761 + 0.98 + 2.435$
   (c) $13.76 + 11 - 20.34$ (d) $5 - 6.781 - 2.13$

   Hint: Work out in pairs first. For example, calculate $0.35 + 0.9$ and then add 0.38 to your answer.

   Solution

   (a) $\begin{array}{r} 0.35 \\ 0.90 \\ + \ 0.28 \\ \hline 1.53 \\ {\scriptstyle 1 \ 1} \end{array}$

   $\therefore 0.35 + 0.9 + 0.28 = 1.53$

   (b) $\begin{array}{r} 3.761 \\ 0.980 \\ + \ 2.435 \\ \hline 7.176 \\ {\scriptstyle 2 \ 1} \end{array}$

   $\therefore 3.761 + 0.98 + 2.435 = 7.176$

   (c) $\begin{array}{r} 13.76 \\ + \ 11.00 \\ \hline 24.76 \\ - \ 20.34 \\ \hline 4.42 \end{array}$

   $\therefore 13.76 + 11 - 20.34 = 24.76 - 20.34$
   $\qquad\qquad\qquad\qquad = 4.42$

   (d) $\begin{array}{r} 1.781 \\ + \ 2.130 \\ \hline 3.911 \end{array}$

   $\therefore 5 - 6.781 - 2.13 = -3.911$

4. The masses of Tom and Zoe are 64.8 kg and 51.7 kg respectively. What is their total mass?

   Solution
   Their total mass
   $= (64.8 + 51.7)\,\text{kg}$
   $= 116.5\,\text{kg}$

5. Joan walks 5.63 km on Monday and 3.92 km on Tuesday. What is the total distance walked on these two days?

   Solution
   The total distance walked in the two days
   $= (5.63 + 3.92)\,\text{km}$
   $= 9.55\,\text{km}$

6. Lisa spends £13.75 on her shopping and pays with a £20 note. How much change should she get?

Hint: You may want to use a mental method instead of the column method.

Solution

Amount of change
= £20 − £13.75
= £6.25

7. The length of a rope is 6.72 metres. If 3.89 metres are cut off, what is the remaining length of the rope?

Solution

Remaining length of the rope
= (6.72 − 3.89) m
= 2.83 m

Level 3   GCSE Grade **3⁻** / **3**

8. Calculate these expressions.
 (a) $6.281 − 9.34 + 4.605$
 (b) $11.92 − 8.3 − 7.416$

Solution
 (a) $6.281 − 9.34 + 4.605$
  $= −(9.34 − 6.281) + 4.605$
  $= −3.059 + 4.605$
  $= 4.605 − 3.059$
  $= 1.546$

 (b) $11.92 − 8.3 − 7.416$
  $= 3.62 − 7.416$
  $= −(7.416 − 3.62)$
  $= −3.796$

9. A family pays £68.43 for their electricity bill, £34.25 for their gas bill and £26.70 for their water bill in a month.
 (a) What is the total amount of these bills in the month?
 (b) If the family has reserved £108 for bills, how much more money is required to settle these bills?

Solution
 (a) Total amount of these bills in the month
   = £68.43 + £34.25 + £26.70
   = £129.38

 (b) Additional amount required
   = £129.38 − £108
   = £21.38

10. The diagram shows the distances between three London Underground stations in km.
 (a) If you travel around the three stations from Piccadilly Circus back to Piccadilly Circus, what is the total distance travelled?
 (b) If you travel from Oxford Circus to Holborn via Piccadilly Circus instead of directly from Oxford Circus to Holborn, how many extra km would you travel?

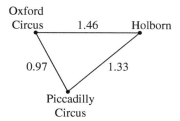

Solution
 (a) Distance travelled is

     0.97
     1.46
   + 1.33
   ⎯⎯⎯⎯
     3.76

   The distance travelled around the three stations is 3.76 km.

 (b) Extra distance travelled is
   $(0.97 + 1.33) − 1.46 = 2.30 − 1.46$
          $= 0.84$

   $$\begin{array}{r} {}^{1\ 12\ 1}2.30 \\ −\ 1.46 \\ \hline 0.84 \end{array}$$

   The extra distance is 0.84 km.

11. A company has a profit of £3.18 million in the first year, a loss of £0.94 million in the second year and a loss of £2.65 million in the third year. Find its overall profit or loss in these three years, giving your answer in millions of pounds.

Solution

Take profit to be positive and loss to be negative.
£3.18 + (−£0.94) + (−£2.65)
= £(3.18 − 0.94 − 2.65)
= £(2.24 − 2.65)
= −£(2.65 − 2.24)
= −£0.41
The company has an overall loss of £0.41 million in the three years.

12. In the Swimming World Cup 2013, Katinka Hosszú broke the world record for the Women's 400 m Individual Medley. Medleys have several types of strokes all in one race. The time for the first 100 m in butterfly was 59.79 s, the next 100 m in backstroke was 65.20 s, the next 100 m in breaststroke was 75.69 s and the final 100 m in freestyle was 60.17 s.

(a) What was her world record time for the medley in seconds?

(b) In which style did she take the least time to complete 100 m?

(c) By how many seconds was her freestyle faster than her breaststroke?

Solution

(a) Her record time for the medley
= (59.79 + 65.20 + 75.69 + 60.17) seconds
= 260.85 seconds

(b) 59.79 is the smallest of the four numbers, i.e. she took the least time to complete the 100 m in butterfly.

(c) Her freestyle was faster than her breaststroke by (75.69 − 60.17) seconds
= 15.52 seconds

13. Aiden, Bella, Carter and Dylan donate a total of £1382.95 to a charity. Aiden donates £432.80, Bella donates £291.75 and Dylan donates £381.20. How much does Carter donate?

Solution
Aiden, Bella and Dylan donate a total of
432.80 + 291.75 + 381.20 = 1105.75
The amount Carter donates is

```
  1382.95
− 1105.75
   277.20
```

Carter donates £277.20.

14. Write two decimal numbers with tenths, hundredths and thousandths such that the answer is 2.38 when the second decimal is subtracted from the first decimal.

Solution
You have
number 1 − number 2 = 2.38.
Then 2.38 + number 2 = number 1.
You can pick any decimal number to be number 2, then add to 2.38 to create number 1.
For instance, if number 2 is 4.015,
you have 2.38 + 4.015 = 6.395
　　　　　　　　　　　　↑
　　　　　　　　　　number 1

Checking: 6.395 − 4.015 = 2.38
i.e. two possible decimal numbers are 6.395 and 4.015.

15. 1.253 kg of tomato, 0.875 kg of onion and 1.86 kg of beef are used to prepare two dishes of food.
If the total mass of these foods in the first dish is 1.95 kg, find the total mass of these foods in the second dish.

Solution
Total mass of food is
1.253 + 0.875 + 1.86 = 3.988
Total mass in the second dish is

```
  3.988
− 1.950
  2.038
```

The mass of foods in the second dish is 2.038 kg.

Exercise 6.3

Level 1　　　**GCSE Grade 2 / 2⁺**

1. Work out these products.
   (a) 0.18×9　　　　　**(b)** 3.142×5
   (c) $0.06 \times (-0.8)$　　**(d)** 4.7×0.25

   Solution

   (a) 0.18×9
   $= 1.62$
   ```
       18
   ×    9
      162
   ```

   (b) 3.142×5
   $= 15.710$
   $= 15.71$
   ```
     3142
   ×    5
    15710
   ```

   (c) $0.06 \times (-0.8)$　　$6 \times 8 = 48$
   $= -0.048$

   (d) 4.7×0.25
   $= 1.175$
   ```
       47
   ×   25
      940
      235
     1175
   ```

2. Find these values.
   (a) 0.003×0.8　　　**(b)** 0.0062×0.7
   (c) 0.005×0.004　　**(d)** $(-0.925) \times (-0.102)$

   Solution
   (a) $3 \times 8 = 24$
   $\therefore 0.003 \times 0.8 = 0.0024$

   (b)
   ```
      62
   ×   7
     434
   ```
   $\therefore 0.0062 \times 0.7 = 0.00434$

   (c) $5 \times 4 = 20$
   $\therefore 0.005 \times 0.004$
   $= 0.000020$
   $= 0.00002$

   (d) 925×102
   $= 925 \times (100 + 2)$
   $= 925 \times 100 + 925 \times 2$
   $= 92\,500 + 1850$
   $= 94\,350$
   $\therefore (-0.925) \times (-0.102) = 0.925 \times 0.102$
   $= 0.094\,350$
   $= 0.09435$

Level 2 GCSE Grade 2⁺/3⁻

3. Given that $85 \times 731 = 62\,135$, write down the values of these expressions.
   (a) 8.5×7.31 **(b)** 0.85×0.731

   Solution
   (a) $8.5 \times 7.31 = 62.135$

   (b) $0.85 \times 0.731 = 0.621\,35$

4. Given that $926 \times 347 = 321\,322$, work out
   (a) 0.926×0.347,   **(b)** $(-0.0926) \times 3.47$.

   Solution
   (a) $0.926 \times 0.347 = 0.321\,322$

   (b) $(-0.0926) \times 3.47 = -0.321\,322$

5. **(a)** Work out the value of 50.7×3.9.
   (b) Use your answer in **(a)** to find the value of 5.07×0.39.

   Solution
   (a)
   $$\begin{array}{r} 507 \\ \times\ 39 \\ \hline 15210 \\ 4563 \\ \hline 19773 \end{array}$$
   $\therefore 50.7 \times 3.9 = 197.73$

   (b) $5.07 \times 0.39 = 1.9773$

6. Calculate these expressions.
   (a) $2.5 \times 4 + 7.89$
   (b) $6.532 - 3.9 \times 2.1$
   (c) $0.05 \times 0.3 + 1.7 \times 0.006$
   (d) $16.37 - 5.8 \times 0.005 + 7.619$

   Solution
   (a) $2.5 \times 4 + 7.89$
   $= 10.0 + 7.89$
   $= 17.89$

   (b) $6.532 - 3.9 \times 2.1$
   $= 6.532 - 8.19$
   $= -(8.19 - 6.532)$
   $= -1.658$

   (c) $0.05 \times 0.3 + 1.7 \times 0.006$
   $= 0.015 + 0.0102$
   $= 0.0252$

   (d) $16.37 - 5.8 \times 0.005 + 7.619$
   $= 16.37 - 0.0290 + 7.619$
   $= 16.341 + 7.619$
   $= 23.96$

7. A gymnasium charges a monthly membership fee of £24.95. What is the total fee for four months?

Solution
Total fee for 4 months
$= £24.95 \times 4$
$= £99.80$

8. Unleaded petrol costs 102.3 pence per litre. David fills his car with 35 litres of unleaded petrol. How much does he pay for the petrol? Give your answer to the nearest penny.

Solution
Amount that David pays for the petrol
$= £1.023 \times 35$
$= £35.81$ (to the nearest penny)

9. The price of steak is £24.95 per kg. Find the price of a piece of steak that is 0.23 kg. Give your answer to the nearest penny.

Solution
Price of the piece of steak
$= £24.95 \times 0.23$
$= £5.7385$
$= £5.74$ (to the nearest penny)

Level 3 GCSE Grade 3⁻/3⁺

10. An electrician charges £30 for a call-out to attend a job and £28.50 an hour for her services. She takes 0.6 hours to install two lights for a family. How much is the bill for the job?

Solution
Amount paid
$= £30 + £28.50 \times 0.6$
$= £(30 + 28.50 \times 0.6)$
$= £(30 + 17.10)$
$= £47.10$

11. The temperature of water in a kettle is 21.5 °C. When the kettle is heated, the temperature rises 10.2 °C every minute. What is the temperature of the water after four minutes?

Solution
Temperature of water after 4 minutes
$= 21.5\,°\text{C} + 10.2 \times 4\,°\text{C}$
$= 21.5\,°\text{C} + 40.8\,°\text{C}$
$= 62.3\,°\text{C}$

12. The mass of a £1 coin is 8.76 grams. The mass of a £2 coin is 12.0 grams. What is the total mass of nine £1 coins and seven £2 coins?

Solution
Total mass is
$9 \times 8.76 + 7 \times 12.0$
$= 78.84 + 84$
$= 162.84$

$$\begin{array}{r} 876 \\ \times\ 9 \\ \hline 7884 \end{array}$$

The total mass of the coins is 162.84 grams.

13. A piece of wire is 8 m long. A net is made by cutting four pieces of length 1.35 m and three pieces of length 0.72 m from the wire. What is the remaining length of the wire?

Solution
Remaining length of the wire
$= (8 - 1.35 \times 4 - 0.72 \times 3)\,m$
$= (8 - 5.40 - 2.16)\,m$
$= 0.44\,m$

14. The potential energy of an object is given by the formula $E = mgh$ joules, where m is the mass of the object, g is the acceleration due to gravity and h is the height of the object. If $m = 0.4$, $g = 9.8$ and $h = 1.02$, find the value of E.

Solution
$E = 0.4 \times 9.8 \times 1.02$
$\quad = 3.92 \times 1.02$
$\quad = 3.9984$ joules

15. The quantity of heat, Q joules, required to raise m kg of water from $t\,°C$ to $F\,°C$ is given by the formula $Q = 4200m(F - t)$. If $m = 0.5$, $t = 23.1$ and $F = 72.9$, find the value of Q.

Solution
$Q = 4200 \times 0.5 \times (72.9 - 23.1)$
$\quad = 2100 \times (49.8)$
$\quad = 2100 \times (50 - 0.2)$
$\quad = 105\,000 - 420$
$\quad = 104\,580$ joules

16. The perimeter of a square is 8 m to the nearest metre. Write down two possible lengths of a side of the square to 2 decimal places.

Solution
Perimeter of a square of side s cm is given by $4s$ cm.
Given that $4s = 8$ (to the nearest m), you have $7.5 \leq 4s < 8.5$,
i.e $1.875 \leq s < 2.125$.
Some possible lengths of a side s cm of the square to 2 decimal places are
1.88 cm,
1.91 cm,
1.99 cm,
2.05 cm,
2.12 cm.
Checking:
If $s = 1.88$,
perimeter of the square
$= 1.88 \times 4$ cm
$= 7.52$ cm
$= 8$ m (to the nearest m)

17. Copy and complete this calculation and correctly place the missing decimal point in the first number.
$$8\,6\,\square\,\square \times 3.\,\square = 277.088$$

Solution
There are 3 decimal places in 277.088 and 1 decimal place in the second number.
Therefore, there must be 2 decimal places in the first number.

Let the missing digits be a, b and c, from left to right.
Working without the decimal points, you have
$$(8600 + ab) \times (30 + c) = 277088$$
$$8600 \times 30 + 8600 \times c + 30 \times ab + ab \times c = 277088$$
$$258\,000 + 8600 \times c + 30 \times ab + ab \times c = 277088$$
$$8600 \times c + 30 \times ab + ab \times c = 19088$$

∴ c must equal 2 (other values would give answers that are too small or too large, e.g. $8600 \times 3 = 25800$).

$$30 \times ab + ab \times 2 = 19088 - 8600 \times 2$$
$$32ab = 1888$$
$$ab = 1888 \div 32$$
$$ab = 59$$

So $8659 \times 32 = 277088$
and $86.59 \times 3.2 = 277.088$
The missing digits are 5, 9 and 2, from left to right.

Exercise 6.4

Level 1   GCSE Grade **2** / **2⁺**

1. Calculate these expressions.
  (a) $25.6 \div 4$ **(b)** $0.006\,12 \div 8$
  (c) $(-0.7799) \div 11$ **(d)** $44.4 \div 12$

Solution
(a)
$$\begin{array}{r} 6.4 \\ 4\overline{)25.6} \\ \underline{24} \\ 16 \\ \underline{16} \\ 0 \end{array}$$

∴ $25.6 \div 4 = 6.4$

(b)
$$\begin{array}{r} 0.000765 \\ 8\overline{)0.006120} \\ \underline{56} \\ 52 \\ \underline{48} \\ 40 \\ \underline{40} \\ 0 \end{array}$$

∴ $0.006\,12 \div 8 = 0.000\,765$

(c) Start by finding $0.7799 \div 11$.

$$
\begin{array}{r}
0.0709 \\
11\overline{)0.7799} \\
\underline{77} \\
09 \\
\underline{0} \\
99 \\
\underline{99} \\
0
\end{array}
$$

$\therefore (-0.7799) \div 11 = -0.0709$

(d)

$$
\begin{array}{r}
3.7 \\
12\overline{)44.4} \\
\underline{36} \\
8\,4 \\
\underline{8\,4} \\
0
\end{array}
$$

$\therefore 44.4 \div 12 = 3.7$

Level 2 — GCSE Grade 2⁺ / 3⁻

2. Calculate these expressions.

(a) $36.75 \div 3 \div 5$ **(b)** $69.48 \div 2 \div 6$

(c) $0.0406 \times 0.2 \div 4$ **(d)** $-7.056 \div 7 \times 0.3$

Solution

(a)

$$
\begin{array}{r}
12.25 \\
3\overline{)36.75} \\
\underline{36} \\
0\,7 \\
\underline{6} \\
15 \\
\underline{15} \\
0
\end{array}
\qquad
\begin{array}{r}
2.45 \\
5\overline{)12.25} \\
\underline{10} \\
2\,2 \\
\underline{2\,0} \\
25 \\
\underline{25} \\
0
\end{array}
$$

$\therefore 36.75 \div 3 \div 5 = 2.45$

(b)

$$
\begin{array}{r}
34.74 \\
2\overline{)69.48} \\
\underline{68} \\
1\,4 \\
\underline{1\,4} \\
08 \\
\underline{8} \\
0
\end{array}
\qquad
\begin{array}{r}
5.79 \\
6\overline{)34.74} \\
\underline{30} \\
4\,7 \\
\underline{4\,2} \\
54 \\
\underline{54} \\
0
\end{array}
$$

$\therefore 69.48 \div 2 \div 6 = 5.79$

(c) $406 \times 2 = 812$

0.0406 has 4 decimal places and 0.1 has 1 decimal place. Their product should have 5 decimal places.

Hence, $0.0406 \times 0.2 = 0.00812$.

$$
\begin{array}{r}
0.00203 \\
4\overline{)0.00812} \\
\underline{8} \\
01 \\
\underline{0} \\
12 \\
\underline{12} \\
0
\end{array}
$$

$\therefore 0.0406 \times 0.2 \div 4 = 0.00203$

(d) $-7.056 \div 7 \times 0.3$

Start by finding $7.056 \div 7$.

$$
\begin{array}{r}
1.008 \\
7\overline{)7.056} \\
\underline{7} \\
0\,0 \\
\underline{0} \\
05 \\
\underline{0} \\
56 \\
\underline{56} \\
0
\end{array}
$$

$7.056 \div 7 = 1.008$

Hence, $-7.056 \div 7 = -1.008$.

$-1008 \times 3 = -3024$

-1.008 has 3 decimal places and 0.3 has 1 decimal place. Their product should have 4 decimal places.

Hence, $-1.008 \times 0.3 = -0.3024$.

3. Work out these values.

(a) $13.7 + 3.81 \div 5$ **(b)** $0.0168 \div 6 - 2$

(c) $(13.7 + 3.81) \div 5$ **(d)** $0.0168 \div (6 - 2)$

Solution

(a)

$$
\begin{array}{r}
0.762 \\
5\overline{)3.810} \\
\underline{3\,5} \\
31 \\
\underline{30} \\
10 \\
\underline{10} \\
0
\end{array}
\qquad
\begin{array}{r}
13.700 \\
+\ 0.762 \\
\hline
14.462 \\
\scriptstyle 1
\end{array}
$$

$\therefore 13.7 + 3.81 \div 5 = 14.462$

(b)

$$
\begin{array}{r}
0.0028 \\
6\overline{)0.0168} \\
\underline{12} \\
48 \\
\underline{48} \\
0
\end{array}
$$

$0.0028 - 2 = -1.9972$

$\therefore 0.0168 \div 6 - 2 = -1.9972$

(c) $(13.7 + 3.81) \div 5$

$$
\begin{array}{r}
13.70 \\
+\ 3.81 \\
\hline
17.51 \\
\scriptstyle 1
\end{array}
\qquad
\begin{array}{r}
3.502 \\
5\overline{)17.510} \\
\underline{15} \\
2\,5 \\
\underline{2\,5} \\
01 \\
\underline{0} \\
10 \\
\underline{10} \\
0
\end{array}
$$

$\therefore (13.7 + 3.81) \div 5 = 3.502$

(d) $6 - 2 = 4$

```
        0.0042
    4⟌0.0168
         16
         08
          8
          0
```

$\therefore\ 0.0168 \div (6 - 2) = 0.0042$

4. Four people share a taxi from Heathrow Airport to an address in London. The taxi fare is £54.40. Find the charge per person if they split the taxi fare equally.

Solution

The charge per person
$= £54.40 \div 4$
$= £13.60$

```
        13.60
    4⟌54.40
      4
      14
      12
       24
       24
       00
       00
        0
```

5. 4.68 kg of mince is divided into nine equal portions. Find the mass of each portion.

Solution

Mass of each portion
$= 4.68 \div 9$
$= 0.52$ kg

```
       0.52
    9⟌4.68
      4 5
       18
       18
        0
```

6. A loan of £3170.40 is repaid in 12 equal monthly instalments. Find the amount of each instalment.

Solution

Amount of each instalment
$= £3170.40 \div 12$
$= £264.20$

```
        264.20
    12⟌3170.40
       24
       77
       72
        50
        48
         2 4
         2 4
         00
          0
          0
```

Level 3

7. A washing machine repair technician charges a basic price of £15 for a home visit and £30 per hour for the repair job. If the total charge for a job is £33, how long has the technician worked on the repair?

Solution

Length of time that the technician has worked on the repair
$= (33 - 15) \div 30$
$= 18 \div 30$
$= \dfrac{18}{30}$
$= \dfrac{6}{10}$
$= 0.6$ hours

8. 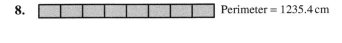 Perimeter = 1235.4 cm

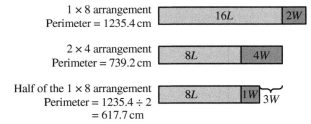 Perimeter = 739.2 cm

The two diagrams above display the arrangements of eight identical desks. When the desks are lined up in a row, the perimeter is 1235.4 cm. When the desks are arranged in a two by four format, the perimeter is 739.2 cm. Find the length and the width of each desk. **Hint**: You may use a bar model to solve the problem.

Solution

Let L cm be the length of each desk and W cm be its width. In the 1×8 arrangement, the perimeter is the sum of $16L$ cm and $2W$ cm.
In the 2×4 arrangement, the perimeter is the sum of $8L$ cm and $4W$ cm.

1×8 arrangement
Perimeter = 1235.4 cm | 16L | 2W |

2×4 arrangement
Perimeter = 739.2 cm | 8L | 4W |

Half of the 1×8 arrangement
Perimeter = 1235.4 ÷ 2 | 8L |1W| 3W
= 617.7 cm

From the bar model diagrams above, you can see that the difference between the perimeter of the 2×4 arrangement and the perimeter of half of the 1×8 arrangement is given by $3W$.
Therefore, $3W = 739.2 - 617.7$
$$3W = 121.5$$
$$W = 40.5$$
Substituting $W = 40.5$ into $8L + W = 617.7$,
$$8L + 40.5 = 617.7$$
$$8L = 577.2$$
$$L = 72.15$$
Hence, the length of each desk is 72.15 cm and the width is 40.5 cm.

9. Create a decimal and a whole number such that the quotient is 0.53 when the decimal is divided by the whole number.

Solution

You have decimal ÷ whole number = 0.53.
So, decimal = 0.53 × whole number.
You can pick any whole number and then multiply it by 0.53 to create the decimal.
For instance, if the whole number is 2, you have
$0.53 \times 2 = 1.06$.
Checking: $1.06 \div 2 = 0.53$.

10. A bottle containing 90 tablets weighs 89.4 grams. After taking 25 tablets, the bottle containing the remaining tablets weighs 67.9 grams. Find the mass of each tablet and the mass of the bottle.

Solution

Let t and b be the masses of a tablet and the bottle respectively.
You have
$90t + b = 89.4$
$65t + b = 67.9$

Subtracting these two equations gives
$(90 - 65)t = 89.4 - 67.9$
$25t = 21.5$
$t = 0.86$

$$
\begin{array}{r}
86 \\
25\overline{)2150} \\
\underline{200} \\
150 \\
\underline{150} \\
0
\end{array}
$$

Substituting $t = 0.86$ into $90t + b = 89.4$,
$90 \times 0.86 + b = 89.4$

$90 \times 86 = 7740$
0.86 has 2 decimal places, so $90 \times 0.86 = 77.4$.

Hence, $b = 89.4 - 77.4$
$= 12$

Each tablet weighs 0.86 grams and the bottle weighs 12 grams.

Exercise 6.5

Level 1   GCSE Grade 2^- / 2^+

1. Work out these values.
(a) 18.3×10
(b) 0.183×10

Solution
(a) $18.3 \times 10 = 183$

(b) $0.183 \times 10 = 1.83$

2. Work out these values.
(a) 0.684×100 (b) $0.068\,04 \times 100$

Solution

(a) $0.684 \times 100 = 68.4$

(b) $0.068\,04 \times 100 = 6.804$

3. Work out these values.
(a) 0.0649×1000
(b) $0.000\,649 \times 1000$

Solution
(a) $0.0649 \times 1000 = 64.9$

(b) $0.000\,649 \times 1000 = 0.649$

4. Find the values of these expressions.
(a) $3.67 \div 10$ (b) $0.030\,67 \div 10$

Solution
(a) $3.67 \div 10 = 0.367$

(b) $0.030\,67 \div 10 = 0.003\,067$

5. Find the values of these expressions.
(a) $9.86 \div 100$
(b) $0.0986 \div 100$

Solution
(a) $9.86 \div 100 = 0.0986$

(b) $0.0986 \div 100 = 0.000\,986$

6. Find the values of these expressions.
(a) $9.17 \div 1000$
(b) $0.917 \div 1000$

Solution
(a) $9.17 \div 1000 = 0.009\,17$

(b) $0.917 \div 1000 = 0.000\,917$

7. Calculate these products mentally.
(a) 0.38×20
(b) 12.39×200
(c) 0.947×4000
(d) $(-0.0317) \times 25$

Solution
(a) 0.38×20
$= 0.38 \times 2 \times 10$
$= 0.76 \times 10$
$= 7.6$

(b) 12.39×200
$= 12.39 \times 2 \times 100$
$= 24.78 \times 100$
$= 2478$

(c) 0.947×4000
$= 0.947 \times 4 \times 1000$
$= 3.788 \times 1000$
$= 3788$

(d) $(-0.0317) \times 25$
$= -(0.0317 \times 100 \div 4)$
$= -3.17 \div 2 \div 2$
$= -1.585 \div 2$
$= -0.7925$

8. Calculate these quotients mentally.
(a) $9.36 \div 20$
(b) $9.36 \div 40$
(c) $52.1 \div 50$
(d) $(-52.1) \div (-25)$

Solution

(a) $9.36 \div 20$
$= 9.36 \div 2 \div 10$
$= 4.68 \div 10$
$= 0.468$

(b) $9.36 \div 40$
$= 9.36 \div 4 \div 10$
$= 9.36 \div 2 \div 2 \div 10$
$= 4.68 \div 2 \div 10$
$= 2.34 \div 10$
$= 0.234$

(c) $52.1 \div 50$
$= 52.1 \div 5 \div 10$
$= 10.42 \div 10$
$= 1.042$
Alternatively,
$52.1 \div 50$
$= 52.1 \div \dfrac{100}{2}$
$= 52.1 \times \dfrac{2}{100}$
$= 104.2 \div 100$
$= 1.042$

(d) $(-52.1) \div (-25)$
$= 52.1 \div 25$
$= 52.1 \div 5 \div 5$
$= 10.42 \div 5$
$= 2.084$

9. Express the given measurements in the specified units.
   (a) 345 cm in metres
   (b) 1.7 litres in ml
   (c) 3890 grams in kg
   (d) £28 in pence
   (e) 0.45 hours in minutes
   (f) 3.7 km in metres

Solution

(a) 345 cm
$= 345 \div 100$ m
$= 3.45$ m

(b) 1.7 litres
$= 1.7 \times 1000$ ml
$= 1700$ ml

(c) 3890 grams
$= 3890 \div 1000$ kg
$= 3.89$ kg

(d) £28
$= 28 \times 100$p
$= 2800$p

(e) 0.45 hours
$= 0.45 \times 60$ minutes
$= 27$ minutes

(f) 3.7 km
$= 3.7 \times 1000$ m
$= 3700$ m

Level 2 | **GCSE Grade 2 / 3⁻**

10. The length of a room is 583 cm. Express the length in
    (a) mm,
    (b) metres.

Solution

(a) Length of the room
$= 583$ cm
$= 583 \times 10$ mm
$= 5830$ mm

(b) Length of the room
$= 583$ cm
$= 583 \div 100$ m
$= 5.83$ m

11. A bottle contains 1.8 litres of milk. It is poured equally into six cups. Find the volume of milk in each cup in millilitres.

Solution
Volume of milk in each cup
$= 1.8$ litres $\div 6$
$= 0.3$ litres
$= 0.3 \times 1000$ ml
$= 300$ ml

12. The price of 320 g of prawns is £8.96. Find the price of one kilogram of prawns.

Solution
320 grams
$= 320 \div 1000$ kg
$= 0.32$ kg
i.e. the price of 0.32 kg of prawns is £8.96.
∴ the price of 1 kg of prawns
$= £(8.96 \div 0.32)$
$= £\left(\dfrac{8.96 \times 100}{0.32 \times 100}\right)$
$= £\left(\dfrac{896}{32}\right)$
$= £(896 \div 32)$
$= £28$

$$\begin{array}{r} 28 \\ 32\overline{)896} \\ 64 \\ \hline 256 \\ 256 \\ \hline 0 \end{array}$$

13. The length of a stick is 38 cm. Find the total length of four identical sticks in metres.

Solution
The length of 4 sticks $= 4 \times 38$ cm
$= 152$ cm
$= 152 \div 100$ m
$= 1.52$ m

Level 3 | **GCSE Grade 3**

14. A boy saves 80p a day. How many days does it take him to save £40?

Solution
£40 $= 40 \times 100$p
$ = 4000$p
Number of days needed
$= 4000 \div 80$
$= 50$

15. The diagram shows a car of length 4.686 m. The distance from the front to the centre of the front wheel is 0.790 m. The distance from the rear to the centre of the rear wheel is 1.056 m.
    (a) Express the length of the car in mm.
    (b) Find the distance between the centres of the front wheel and rear wheel. Express your answer in cm.

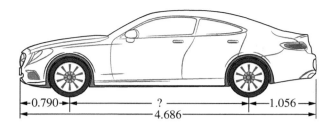

←0.790→ ←———— ? ————→ ←1.056→
←——————— 4.686 ———————→

Solution
(a) Length of car = 4.686 m
= 4.686 × 1000 mm
= 4686 mm

(b) Distance required = (4.686 − 0.790 − 1.056) m
= (3.896 − 1.056) m
= 2.84 m
= 2.84 × 100 cm
= 284 cm

$$\begin{array}{r} \overset{3\ \ ^{15}1^{18}}{4.686} \\ -\ 0.790 \\ \hline 3.896 \end{array} \qquad \begin{array}{r} 3.896 \\ -\ 1.056 \\ \hline 2.840 \end{array}$$

16. The exchange rate between pounds and euros was £1 = €1.14 in June 2017. If you exchange £400 for a trip to Paris at that rate, how many euros do you get?

Solution
Number of euros = 400 × 1.14
= 100 × 4 × 1.14
= 100 × 4.56
= 456
You get 456 euros.

17. A 2 litre bottle of milk costs £2.40. A latte needs 125 ml of milk.
(a) How many lattes can be prepared using the bottle of milk?
(b) Find the cost of milk for one latte in pence.
Hint: You may draw a picture to help you solve the problem.

Solution
(a) 2 litres
= 2 × 1000 ml
= 2000 ml
Number of lattes that can be prepared
= 2000 ÷ 125
= 16

(b) The cost of 2 litres of milk is £2.40, hence the cost of milk in 16 lattes is £2.40.
∴ the cost of milk for one latte
= £2.40 ÷ 16
= (2.40 × 100p) ÷ 16
= 240p ÷ 16
= 15p

18. A sum of prize money is divided equally among 1000 winners. Each winner receives £495, rounded to the nearest pound. Write two possible amounts for the total prize money.

Solution
£494.50 ≤ each prize < £495.50
Hence,
£494.50 × 1000 ≤ total prize < £495.50 × 1000
£494 500 ≤ total prize < £495 500
For example, the total prize money could be £494 640 or £495 210.

Exercise 6.6

Level 1   **GCSE Grade 2⁺**

1. Work out these values.
(a) 9.18 ÷ 0.3
(b) 0.84 ÷ (−0.05)
(c) 2.03 ÷ 0.001
(d) (−9.02) ÷ (−0.004)

Solution
(a) $9.18 \div 0.3 = \dfrac{9.18}{0.3}$

$= \dfrac{9.18 \times 10}{0.3 \times 10}$

$= \dfrac{91.8}{3}$

$$\begin{array}{r} 30.6 \\ 3\overline{)91.8} \\ 90 \\ \hline 1\ 8 \\ 1\ 8 \\ \hline 0 \end{array}$$

∴ 9.18 ÷ 0.3 = 30.6

(b) 0.84 ÷ (−0.05)

$= -\dfrac{0.84}{0.05}$

$= -\dfrac{0.84 \times 100}{0.05 \times 100}$

$= -\dfrac{84}{5}$

$$\begin{array}{r} 16.8 \\ 5\overline{)84.0} \\ 5 \\ \hline 34 \\ 30 \\ \hline 4\ 0 \\ 4\ 0 \\ \hline 0 \end{array}$$

∴ 0.84 ÷ (−0.05) = −16.8

(c) 2.03 ÷ 0.001

$= \dfrac{2.03}{0.001}$

$= \dfrac{2.03 \times 1000}{0.001 \times 1000}$

$= \dfrac{2030}{1}$

$= 2030$

(d) $(−9.02) \div (−0.004) = 9.02 \div 0.004$

$= \dfrac{9.02}{0.004}$

$= \dfrac{9.02 \times 1000}{0.004 \times 1000}$

$= \dfrac{9020}{4}$

$= 2255$

∴ (−9.02) ÷ (−0.004) = 2255

$$\begin{array}{r} 2255 \\ 4\overline{)9020} \\ 8 \\ \hline 10 \\ 8 \\ \hline 22 \\ 20 \\ \hline 20 \\ 20 \\ \hline 0 \end{array}$$

GCSE Grade 2^+ / 3^-

2. Work out these values.

(a) $0.375 \div 25$ (b) $0.0375 \div 2.5$

(c) $13.2 \div (-0.11)$ (d) $0.03484 \div 0.013$

Solution

(a)
$$
\begin{array}{r}
0.015 \\
25\overline{)0.375} \\
25 \\
\hline
125 \\
125 \\
\hline
0
\end{array}
$$

$\therefore 0.375 \div 25 = 0.015$

(b) $0.0375 \div 2.5$

$= \dfrac{0.0375}{2.5}$

$= \dfrac{0.0375 \times 10}{2.5 \times 10}$

$= \dfrac{0.375}{25}$

$= 0.375 \div 25$

$= 0.015$

(c) $13.2 \div (-0.11)$

$= -\dfrac{13.2}{0.11}$

$= -\dfrac{13.2 \times 100}{0.11 \times 100}$

$= -\dfrac{1320}{11}$

$\therefore 13.2 \div (-0.11) = -120$

$$
\begin{array}{r}
120 \\
11\overline{)1320} \\
11 \\
\hline
22 \\
22 \\
\hline
00 \\
0 \\
\hline
0
\end{array}
$$

(d) $0.03484 \div 0.013$

$= \dfrac{0.03484}{0.013}$

$= \dfrac{0.03484 \times 1000}{0.013 \times 1000}$

$= \dfrac{34.84}{13}$

$= 34.84 \div 13$

$\therefore 0.03484 \div 0.013 = 2.68$

$$
\begin{array}{r}
2.68 \\
13\overline{)34.84} \\
26 \\
\hline
88 \\
78 \\
\hline
104 \\
104 \\
\hline
0
\end{array}
$$

3. Calculate these expressions.

(a) $36.75 \div 3 + 0.5$

(b) $0.84 \div 7 \times 1.3$

(c) $0.045 + 2.34 \div 0.9$

(d) $0.063 \div 0.05 - 13.76$

(e) $3.2 \times 0.7 - 0.0086 \div 0.02$

(f) $20.25 \div (3.12 + 1.38)$

Note: Remember the order of operations.

Solution

(a) $36.75 \div 3 + 0.5$

$$
\begin{array}{r}
12.25 \\
3\overline{)36.75} \\
36 \\
\hline
07 \\
6 \\
\hline
15 \\
15 \\
\hline
0
\end{array}
\qquad
\begin{array}{r}
2.45 \\
5\overline{)12.25} \\
10 \\
\hline
22 \\
20 \\
\hline
25 \\
25 \\
\hline
0
\end{array}
$$

$36.75 \div 3 + 5 \times 10$

$= 12.25 + 5 \times 10$

$= 2.45 \times 10$

$= 24.5$

(b)
$$
\begin{array}{r}
0.12 \\
7\overline{)0.84} \\
7 \\
\hline
14 \\
14 \\
\hline
0
\end{array}
\qquad
\begin{array}{r}
12 \\
\times\ 13 \\
\hline
120 \\
36 \\
\hline
156
\end{array}
$$

$12 \times 13 = 156$

$0.12 \times 1.3 = 0.156$

$\therefore 0.84 \div 7 \times 1.3$

$= 0.12 \times 1.3$

$= 0.156$

(c) $0.045 + 2.34 \div 0.9$

$= 0.045 + 23.4 \div 9$

$= 0.045 + 2.6$

$= 2.645$

$$
\begin{array}{r}
2.6 \\
9\overline{)23.4} \\
18 \\
\hline
54 \\
54 \\
\hline
0
\end{array}
\qquad
\begin{array}{r}
0.045 \\
+\ 2.600 \\
\hline
2.645
\end{array}
$$

(d) $0.063 \div 0.05 - 13.76$

$= 6.3 \div 5 - 13.76$

$= 1.26 - 13.76$

$= -12.5$

(e)
$$
\begin{array}{r}
32 \\
\times\ 7 \\
\hline
224
\end{array}
$$

$32 \times 7 = 224$

$3.2 \times 0.7 = 2.24$

$\therefore 3.2 \times 0.7 - 0.0086 \div 0.02$

$= 2.24 - 0.86 \div 2$

$= 2.24 - 0.43$

$= 1.81$

(f) $20.25 \div (3.12 + 1.38)$

$= 20.25 \div 4.50$

$= \dfrac{20.25}{4.5}$

$= \dfrac{20.25 \times 10}{4.5 \times 10}$

$= \dfrac{202.5}{45}$

$= 4.5$

$$
\begin{array}{r}
4.5 \\
45\overline{)202.5} \\
180 \\
\hline
22\,5 \\
22\,5 \\
\hline
0
\end{array}
$$

4. Given that $483 \div 16 = 30.1875$, work out

(a) $483 \div 1.6$,

(b) $48.3 \div 1.6$.

Explain your steps.

Solution

(a) $483 \div 1.6$

$= \dfrac{483}{1.6}$

$= \dfrac{483 \times 10}{1.6 \times 10}$

$= \dfrac{483}{16} \times 10$

$= 483 \div 16 \times 10$

$= 30.1875 \times 10$

$= 301.875$

(b) $48.3 \div 1.6$

$= \dfrac{48.3}{1.6}$

$= \dfrac{48.3 \times 10}{1.6 \times 10}$

$= \dfrac{483}{16}$

$= 483 \div 16$

$= 30.1875$

5. Emma has 4.7 kg of coffee. She stores the coffee in jars of capacity 0.25 kg each. How many jars does she need?

Solution

$4.7 \div 0.25$

$= \dfrac{4.7}{0.25}$

$= \dfrac{4.7 \times 100}{0.25 \times 100}$

$= \dfrac{470}{25}$

$= 18.8$

```
        18.8
  25 ⟌ 470.0
       25
       ───
       220
       200
       ───
        20 0
        20 0
        ────
           0
```

i.e. there are 18.8 portions of 0.25 kg.

Hence, 19 jars will be needed.

6. A roll of cable is 25.5 m long. How many pieces of cable of length 1.5 m can be cut from the roll?

Solution

$25.5 \div 1.5$

$= \dfrac{25.5}{1.5}$

$= \dfrac{25.5 \times 10}{1.5 \times 10}$

$= \dfrac{255}{15}$

$= 17$

```
       17
  15 ⟌ 255
       15
       ───
       105
       105
       ───
         0
```

Hence, 17 pieces of cable can be cut from the roll.

Level 3   **GCSE Grade 3 / 3⁺**

7. The cost of petrol is £1.20 per litre. Alice buys £48 worth of petrol.
 (a) How many litres of petrol does she buy?
 (b) In the city, Alice can drive 8.5 km for every litre of petrol. How many km can she drive using the petrol she bought?

Solution

(a) Amount of petrol bought
   $= 48 \div 1.20$
   $= 480 \div 12$
   $= 40$ litres

(b) Using the 40 litres of petrol Alice bought, she can drive 8.5×40
   $= 340.0$
   $= 340$ km

8. An iron cube has a mass of 26.52 grams and a volume of 3.4 cm^3. Find the mass of an iron cube of volume
 (a) 1 cm^3,
 (b) 5.6 cm^3.

Solution

(a) $26.52 \div 3.4$

$= \dfrac{26.52}{3.4}$

$= \dfrac{26.52 \times 10}{3.4 \times 10}$

$= \dfrac{265.2}{34}$

```
         7.8
  34 ⟌ 265.2
       238
       ───
        27 2
        27 2
        ────
            0
```

Hence, the mass of an iron cube of volume 1 cm^3 is 7.8 grams.

(b) You need to calculate 7.8×5.6.

78×56
$= 4368$

```
       78
   ×   56
   ─────
      468
     3900
   ─────
     4368
```

7.8 has 1 decimal place and 5.6 has 1 decimal place, so the result must have 2 decimal places. Hence, $7.8 \times 5.6 = 43.68$.

The mass of an iron cube of volume 5.6 cm^3 is 43.68 grams.

9. Create two decimals such that the quotient is 0.4 when the first decimal is divided by the second decimal.

Solution

Using the inverse relationship between multiplication and division, you have

1st decimal ÷ 2nd decimal = 0.4,

i.e. 1st decimal = 0.4 × 2nd decimal.

You can pick any decimal number to be the 2nd decimal, then multiply it by 0.4 to create the 1st decimal.

If the 2nd decimal = 3.2,

then the 1st decimal = 0.4 × 3.2 = 1.28.

You have 1.28 ÷ 3.2 = 0.4.
         ↑   ↑
   1st decimal 2nd decimal

Below are some other possible 1st and 2nd decimals such that their quotient is 0.4:

1st decimal	2nd decimal
0.492	1.23
1.08	2.7
2.46	6.15
3.69	9.225

10. The diagram shows a lever system. The beam AB is in equilibrium, i.e. horizontal, when the two masses m and n and two distances p and q have the relationship $mp = nq$. When $m = 43.8$ grams, $p = 0.24$ metres and $q = 0.36$ metres, find the value of n required for the beam to be in equilibrium.

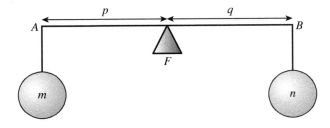

Solution

Substituting $m = 43.8$, $p = 0.24$ and $q = 0.36$ into $mp = nq$ gives

$$43.8 \times 0.24 = n \times 0.36$$
$$n = 43.8 \times 0.24 \div 0.36$$
$$= 43.8 \times \frac{0.24 \times 100}{0.36 \times 100}$$
$$= 43.8 \times \frac{24}{36}$$
$$= 43.8 \times \frac{2}{3}$$
$$= \frac{87.6}{3}$$
$$= 29.2$$

For equilibrium, $n = 29.2$ grams.

Exercise 6.7

For recurring decimals, students could be allowed to use calculators if they find the division difficult.

Level 1   GCSE Grade **3 / 4**

1. Write these decimals as fractions in their simplest form.
    (a) 0.2   **(b)** 0.05
    (c) 0.36   **(d)** 0.375

    Solution

    (a) $0.2 = \frac{2}{10}$ **(b)** $0.05 = \frac{5}{100}$
    $\qquad = \frac{1}{5}$ $\qquad = \frac{1}{20}$

    (c) $0.36 = \frac{36}{100}$ **(d)** $0.375 = \frac{375}{1000}$
    $\qquad = \frac{9}{25}$ $\qquad = \frac{3}{8}$

2. Write these decimals as fractions in their simplest form.
    (a) 3.4   **(b)** −9.45
    (c) 60.008   **(d)** −7.5625

    Solution

    (a) $3.4 = 3 + \frac{4}{10}$ **(b)** $-9.45 = -\left(9 + \frac{45}{100}\right)$
    $\qquad = 3 + \frac{2}{5}$ $\qquad = -\left(9 + \frac{9}{20}\right)$
    $\qquad = 3\frac{2}{5}$ $\qquad = -9\frac{9}{20}$

    (c) $60.008 = 60 + \frac{8}{1000}$ **(d)** $-7.5625 = -\left(7 + \frac{5625}{10\,000}\right)$
    $\qquad = 60 + \frac{1}{125}$ $\qquad = -\left(7 + \frac{9}{16}\right)$
    $\qquad = 60\frac{1}{125}$ $\qquad = -7\frac{9}{16}$

3. Express these fractions as decimals without using a calculator.
    (a) $\frac{1}{4}$ **(b)** $\frac{2}{3}$
    (c) $\frac{17}{20}$ **(d)** $\frac{5}{7}$

    Solution

    (a) $\frac{1}{4} = \frac{1 \times 25}{4 \times 25}$
    $\qquad = \frac{25}{100}$
    $\qquad = 0.25$

    (b)
    $$\begin{array}{r} 0.6666 \\ 3\overline{)2.0000} \\ \underline{1\,8} \\ 20 \\ \underline{18} \\ 20 \\ \underline{18} \\ 20 \\ \underline{18} \\ 2 \end{array}$$

    $\therefore \frac{2}{3} = 0.6666...$
    $\qquad = 0.\dot{6}$

    (c) $\frac{17}{20} = \frac{17 \times 5}{20 \times 5}$
    $\qquad = \frac{85}{100}$
    $\qquad = 0.85$

    (d)
    $$\begin{array}{r} 0.714285714 \\ 7\overline{)5.000000000} \\ \underline{4\,9} \\ 10 \\ \underline{7} \\ 30 \\ \underline{28} \\ 20 \\ \underline{14} \\ 60 \\ \underline{56} \\ 40 \\ \underline{35} \\ 50 \\ \underline{49} \\ 10 \\ \underline{7} \\ 30 \\ \underline{28} \\ 2 \end{array}$$

$$\therefore \frac{5}{7} = 0.714285714...$$
$$= 0.\dot{7}1428\dot{5}$$

4. Convert these fractions to decimals without using a calculator.

(a) $\frac{10}{3}$ **(b)** $-\frac{31}{25}$

(c) $-4\frac{6}{11}$ **(d)** $5\frac{7}{12}$

Solution

(a)
```
      3.3333
  3 ) 10.0000
      9
      ──
      1 0
        9
      ──
      10
       9
      ──
      10
       9
      ──
      10
       9
      ──
       1
```
$$\therefore \frac{10}{3} = 3.3333...$$
$$= 3.\dot{3}$$

(b) $-\frac{31}{25} = -1\frac{6}{25}$
$$= -1\frac{24}{100}$$
$$= -1.24$$

(c)
```
      0.5454
  11 ) 6.0000
       5 5
       ──
        50
        44
        ──
        60
        55
        ──
        50
        44
        ──
         6
```
i.e. $\frac{6}{11} = 0.5454...$
$$= 0.\dot{5}\dot{4}$$
$$\therefore -4\frac{6}{11} = -\left(4 + \frac{6}{11}\right)$$
$$= -\left(4 + 0.\dot{5}\dot{4}\right)$$
$$= -4.\dot{5}\dot{4}$$

(d)
```
      0.5833
  12 ) 7.0000
       6 0
       ──
       1 00
         96
       ──
         40
         36
       ──
         40
         36
       ──
          4
```
i.e. $\frac{7}{12} = 0.5833...$
$$= 0.58\dot{3}$$
$$\therefore 5\frac{7}{12} = 5 + \frac{7}{12}$$
$$= 5 + 0.58\dot{3}$$
$$= 5.58\dot{3}$$

5. Given the numbers -6, $-4\frac{1}{2}$, 2, $\sqrt{2}$, 0.38 and $0.4\dot{7}$, list the
   (a) integers,
   (b) positive numbers,
   (c) recurring decimals,
   (d) irrational numbers.

Solution

(a) -6 and 2 are integers.

(b) 2, $\sqrt{2}$, 0.38 and $0.4\dot{7}$ are positive numbers.

(c) $0.4\dot{7}$ is a recurring decimal.

(d) $\sqrt{2}$ is an irrational number.

Level 2   **GCSE Grade** $\boxed{4^-}$

6. Arrange the numbers $\sqrt{10}$, $3\frac{7}{20}$ and $\frac{41}{13}$ in ascending order.
   Hint: You may use a calculator to help you for this question.

Solution

$\sqrt{10} = 3.16227...$

$3\frac{7}{20} = 3.35$

$\frac{41}{13} = 3.15384...$

The numbers in ascending order are $\frac{41}{13}$, $\sqrt{10}$, $3\frac{7}{20}$.

7. Andrew's best time for running 100m is 10.28 seconds. Express this time as a mixed number.

Solution

10.28 seconds
$$= 10\frac{28}{100}$$
$$= 10\frac{7}{25} \text{ seconds}$$

8. Erica eats $\frac{5}{32}$ of a pizza. Express her share as a decimal.

Solution

```
        0.15625
32 | 5.00000
     3 2
     ‾‾‾‾
     1 80
     1 60
     ‾‾‾‾
       200
       192
       ‾‾‾
        80
        64
        ‾‾
        160
        160
        ‾‾‾
          0
```

$\therefore \frac{5}{32} = 0.15625$

9. The wing-span of a honey bee is $2\frac{7}{8}$ cm. Express the wing-span as a decimal.

Solution

```
      0.875
8 | 7.000
    6 4
    ‾‾‾
     60
     56
     ‾‾
     40
     40
     ‾‾
      0
```

The wing-span is 2.875 cm.

Level 3

GCSE Grade 4

10. One yard is about 0.9144 m.
    (a) Express one yard as a fraction of a metre in its simplest form.
    (b) When a golf ball is hit, it flies a horizontal distance of 150 yards. Express this distance as a mixed number in metres.

Solution

(a) 0.9144

$= \frac{9144}{10000}$

$= \frac{9144 \div 8}{10000 \div 8}$

$= \frac{1143}{1250}$

Hence, one yard is $\frac{1143}{1250}$ of a metre.

(b) From (a),
$\therefore 150 \text{ yards} = \frac{1143}{\overset{}{\underset{25}{1250}}} \times \overset{3}{\cancel{150}} \text{ metres}$

$= \frac{1143 \times 3}{25}$

$= \frac{3429}{25}$

$= 137\frac{4}{25}$ metres

Alternatively,
150 yards $= 0.9144 \times 150$ metres
$= 137.16$
$= 137\frac{16}{100}$
$= 137\frac{4}{25}$ metres

11. Write down one rational number between 1.4 and 1.5.

Solution

Some possible rational numbers between 1.4 and 1.5 are 1.41, 1.409, 1.4789, $1\frac{9}{20}$, $1\frac{11}{25}$.

12. (a) Express $\frac{4}{9}$ and $\frac{5}{9}$ as recurring decimals.

   (b) Is it true that $0.\dot{9} = 1$? Justify your answer.

Solution

(a)
```
      0.444              0.555
9 | 4.000           9 | 5.000
    3 6                 4 5
    ‾‾‾                 ‾‾‾
     40                  50
     36                  45
     ‾‾                  ‾‾
     40                  50
     36                  45
     ‾‾                  ‾‾
      4                   5
```

$\frac{4}{9} = 0.\dot{4}$ and $\frac{5}{9} = 0.\dot{5}$

(b) From (a) you can see

$$\frac{1}{9} = 0.\dot{1}$$

So $\frac{1}{9} \times 9 = 0.\dot{1} \times 9$

$$1 = 0.\dot{9}$$

Revision Exercise 6

1. (a) Write the decimal 3.8192 in expanded form.

   (b) Write the value of the digit 9 in the decimal 3.8192.

Solution

(a) $3.8192 = 3 + \frac{8}{10} + \frac{1}{100} + \frac{9}{1000} + \frac{2}{10000}$

(b) The value of the digit 9 in the decimal 3.8192 is $\frac{9}{1000}$.

2. The heights of three boys, Dicky, Jason and Peter, are 1.73 m, 1.70 m and 1.82 m respectively.
   (a) Arrange the names of the boys in ascending order of their heights.

(b) Subtract the height of the shortest boy from the height of the tallest boy.

Solution

(a) The heights arranged in ascending order are 1.70 m, 1.73 m, 1.82 m. The names of the boys corresponding to this order are Jason, Dicky, Peter.

(b) $(1.82 - 1.70)\,\text{m}$
$= 0.12\,\text{m}$

3. The results of the Rio 2016 Olympics Men's 100 m sprint final race are shown.

Lane	Name	Nationality	Time
2	Trayvon Bromell	United States	10.06 s
3	Akani Simbine	South Africa	9.94 s
4	Justin Gatlin	United States	9.89 s
5	Jimmy Vicaut	France	10.04 s
6	Usain Bolt	Jamaica	9.81 s
7	Andre De Grasse	Canada	9.91 s
8	Ben Youssef Meïté	Côte d'Ivoire	9.96 s
9	Yohan Blake	Jamaica	9.93 s

(a) Whose race time has a place value of 9 hundredths of a second?
(b) Who are the gold, silver and bronze medallists of the race?
(c) What is the difference between the fastest time and the slowest time?

Solution

(a) Justin Gatlin's race time of 9.89 s has a place value of 9 hundredths of a second.

(b) The medallists are Gold: Usain Bolt, Silver: Justin Gatlin, Bronze: Andre De Grasse.

(c) The required difference
$= 10.06 - 9.81$
$= 0.25\,\text{s}$

4. Calculate these expressions.
(a) $3.457 + 0.982 - 0.17$
(b) $2.4 \times 0.7 + 0.786 \div 0.03$
(c) $\dfrac{25.92 - 3.47}{0.05}$
(d) $0.1 \times 1.6 - 2.56$

Solution

(a)
$$\begin{array}{r} 3.457 \\ + 0.982 \\ \hline 4.439 \\ \hline \end{array} \qquad \begin{array}{r} {}^{3\ 1}\!4.439 \\ - 0.170 \\ \hline 4.269 \end{array}$$

$3.457 + 0.982 - 0.17$
$= 4.439 - 0.17$
$= 4.269$

(b) $2.4 \times 0.7 + 0.786 \div 0.03$
$= 1.68 + 26.2$
$= 27.88$

(c) $\dfrac{25.92 - 3.47}{0.05}$
$= \dfrac{22.45}{0.05}$
$= 449$

(d) $0.1 \times 1.6 - 2.56$
$= 0.16 - 2.56$
$= -2.4$

5. Calculate these expressions mentally.
(a) 0.0938×100
(b) $62.7 \div 1000$
(c) $(-5.14) \times (-25)$
(d) $702.8 \div 50$

Solution

(a) $0.0938 \times 100 = 9.38$ **(b)** $62.7 \div 1000 = 0.0627$

(c) $(-5.14) \times (-25)$
$= 5.14 \times 25$
$= 5.14 \times 100 \div 4$
$= 514 \div 2 \div 2$
$= 257 \div 2$
$= 128.5$

(d) $702.8 \div 50$
$= 702.8 \div \dfrac{100}{2}$
$= 702.8 \times \dfrac{2}{100}$
$= 702.8 \times 2 \div 100$
$= 1405.6 \div 100$
$= 14.056$

6. **(a)** Estimate the value of $3.47 + 2.3 \times 15.6$.
(b) Calculate $3.47 + 2.3 \times 15.6$.
(c) Does your estimate suggest your calculation is correct?

Solution

(a) To estimate the value of the expression, you can first round each number to the nearest integer.
$3.47 + 2.3 \times 15.6$
$\approx 3 + 2 \times 16$
$= 3 + 32$
$= 35$

(b) $3.47 + 2.3 \times 15.6$
$= 3.47 + 35.88$
$= 39.35$

(c) Yes, the estimate suggests that the calculation is correct as the values in **(a)** and **(b)** are quite close to each other.

7. Convert these fractions to decimals without using a calculator.
(a) $\dfrac{4}{5}$ **(b)** $\dfrac{5}{9}$
(c) $1\dfrac{13}{20}$ **(d)** $-3\dfrac{8}{11}$

Solution

(a) $\dfrac{4}{5} = \dfrac{4 \times 2}{5 \times 2}$

$\quad = \dfrac{8}{10}$

$\quad = 0.8$

(b)
```
    0.5555
9 ) 5.0000
    4 5
    ___
     50
     45
    ___
     50
     45
    ___
     50
     45
    ___
      5
```

$\therefore \dfrac{5}{9} = 0.5555...$

$\quad = 0.\dot{5}$

(c) $1\dfrac{13}{20} = 1\dfrac{65}{100}$

$\quad = 1.65$

(d) $-3\dfrac{8}{11} = -\left(3 + \dfrac{8}{11}\right)$

```
    0.7272
11 ) 8.0000
     7 7
     ___
      30
      22
     ___
      80
      77
     ___
      30
      22
     ___
       8
```

i.e. $\dfrac{8}{11} = 0.7272...$

$\quad = 0.\dot{7}\dot{2}$

$\therefore -3\dfrac{8}{11} = -\left(3 + \dfrac{8}{11}\right)$

$\quad = -\left(3 + 0.\dot{7}\dot{2}\right)$

$\quad = -3.\dot{7}\dot{2}$

8. Convert these decimals to fractions in their simplest form.

(a) 0.9 (b) −0.68

(c) 4.375 (d) 12.06

Solution

(a) $0.9 = \dfrac{9}{10}$

(b) $-0.68 = -\dfrac{68}{100}$

$\quad = -\dfrac{17}{25}$

(c) $4.375 = 4 + \dfrac{375}{1000}$

$\quad = 4 + \dfrac{3}{8}$

$\quad = 4\dfrac{3}{8}$

(d) $12.06 = 12 + \dfrac{6}{100}$

$\quad = 12 + \dfrac{3}{50}$

$\quad = 12\dfrac{3}{50}$

---

9. A frame consists of eight rods, each of length 65.1 cm. Find the total length of the rods in metres.

Solution

Total length of the rods

$= (65.1 \times 8)\,\text{cm}$

$= 520.8\,\text{cm}$

$= 520.8 \div 100\,\text{metres}$

$= 5.208\,\text{metres}$

10. Mrs Black buys steak for £4.83, sausages for £1.76 and carrots for 75 pence from a supermarket.

(a) Find the total cost of the food in pounds.

(b) How much change would she get if she pays with a £20 note at the till?

Solution

(a) $75p = 75 \div 100$ pounds

$\quad = £0.75$

Total cost of the food

$= £(4.83 + 1.76 + 0.75)$

$= £7.34$

(b) Amount of change

$= £(20 - 7.34)$

$= £12.66$

11. A roll of cable is 20 m long. Short cables of length 1.32 m are cut from the roll.

(a) How many complete short cables can be cut?

(b) What is the remaining length of cable on the roll?

Solution

(a) $20 \div 1.32 = \dfrac{20}{1.32}$

$\quad = \dfrac{20 \times 100}{1.32 \times 100}$

$\quad = \dfrac{2000}{132}$

$\quad = 2000 \div 132$

$\therefore 20 \div 1.32 = 15.1515...$

$\quad = 15.\dot{1}\dot{5}$

Hence, 15 complete short cables can be obtained.

```
       15.1515
132 ) 2000.0000
      132
      ___
      680
      660
      ___
       20 0
       13 2
      ____
        6 80
        6 60
      ____
         200
         132
      ____
         680
         660
      ____
          20
```

(b) Remaining length of cable on the roll

$= 20 - 1.32 \times 15$

$= 20 - 19.8$

$= 0.2\,\text{m}$

12. Given the formula $s = \dfrac{1}{2}(2.1 + v)t$, find the value of s when $v = 5.3$ and $t = 3.6$.

Solution

$s = \dfrac{1}{2}(2.1 + 5.3) \times 3.6$

$\quad = \dfrac{1}{2} \times 7.4 \times 3.6$

$\quad = 3.7 \times 3.6$

$\quad = 13.32$

13. **(a)** A pill capsule consists of a body part and a cap part. For a 00 size capsule, the body length is 20.1 mm and the cap length is 10.8 mm. When the two parts join together, the overall length of the capsule is 23.4 mm. What is the length that the body and the cap overlap when the capsule is formed?

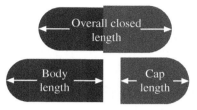

(b) Each empty 00 size capsule weighs 0.123 grams. The mass of medicine powder that can fit inside it is 0.76 grams. Find the total mass of 90 filled capsules.

Solution

(a) Length of overlap = $(20.1 + 10.8 - 23.4)$ mm
$$= (30.9 - 23.4)\,\text{mm}$$
$$= 7.5\,\text{mm}$$

(b) Total mass in grams = $90 \times (0.123 + 0.76)$
$$= 90 \times 0.883$$
$$= 79.47$$
The total mass of 90 filled capsules is 79.47 grams.

14. The thickness of a £1 coin is 2.8 mm. The thickness of a £2 coin is 2.5 mm.

(a) A stack has seven £1 coins and eight £2 coins. Find its height in cm.

(b) A stack has five £1 coins and some £2 coins. The height of the stack is 41.5 mm. Find the number of £2 coins in the stack.

Solution

(a) Height of stack = $(7 \times 2.8 + 8 \times 2.5) \div 10$ cm
$$= (19.6 + 20) \div 10\,\text{cm}$$
$$= 39.6 \div 10\,\text{cm}$$
$$= 3.96\,\text{cm}$$

(b) Let c be the number of £2 coins in the stack. You are given that
$$5 \times 2.8 + c \times 2.5 = 41.5$$
$$c \times 2.5 = 41.5 - 5 \times 2.8$$
$$c = (41.5 - 14) \div 2.5$$
$$c = \frac{27.5}{2.5}$$
$$c = \frac{275}{25}$$
$$c = 11$$
There are 11 £2 coins in the stack.

7 Percentages

Class Activity 1

Objective: To understand the meaning of percentage in some daily life examples and make connections between percentages and fractions/decimals.

1. Between 2013 and 2017 inclusive, Andy Murray won the 2013 and 2016 Wimbledon Championships. What percentage of annual Wimbledon Championships during this period did Andy Murray win?

    Andy Murray won $\frac{2}{5} \times 100\% = 40\%$

2. The Department for Education report *School Workforce in England: November 2016* contains the following paragraph.

    The percentage of female teachers has increased over time. In 2010, 72.9 per cent of full-time equivalent teachers were female and this percentage has increased in each year. By 2016, 73.9 per cent of full-time equivalent teachers were female.

    A school has 37 female teachers and 13 male teachers. Determine whether the percentage of female teachers in this school agrees with the report.

    Percentage of female teachers is $\frac{37}{37+13} \times 100\% = \frac{37}{50} \times 100\% = 74\%$. Therefore, this percentage agrees with the report.

3. Here is some nutrition information from a can of vegetable soup.

	1 serving of 200 g contains	% RI*	RI* of an average adult
Energy	100 kcal	5%	2000 kcal
Fat	2.0 g	3%	70 g
Salt	1.0 g	17%	6 g

    *RI - Reference Intake in a day of an average adult.

    Explain how to work out the percentage column B (% RI) from the columns A (1 serving of 200 g contains) and C (RI of an average adult).

    Divide the number in column A by the number in column C and multiply by 100%

    e.g. $\frac{100}{2000} \times 100\% = 5\%$.

Class Activity 2

Objective: To compare two quantities using percentages.

The price of a book is £12. The price of a DVD is 50% more than the price of the book.

1. Find the price of the DVD and the price difference between the DVD and the book.

    Price of the DVD = price of the book + 50% of the price of the book

    $$= £12 + \frac{50}{100} \times £12$$
    $$= £12 + £6$$
    $$= £18$$

    Price difference between the DVD and the book = £18 − £12
    $$= £6$$

2. Express the price difference as a percentage of the price of the DVD.

    $$\frac{6}{18} \times 100\% = \frac{1}{3} \times 100\% = 33\frac{1}{3}\%$$

3. By how many per cent is the price of the book less than the price of the DVD?

    $33\frac{1}{3}\%$

4. Discuss whether the statement 'If A is 50% more than B, then B is 50% less than A' is correct.

    No, as shown in the above example.

5. Use an example to show whether the statement 'If A is 20% less than B, then B is 20% more than A' is correct.

    e.g. the price of a ticket A to sit in the balcony of a theatre is £80 and the price of a ticket B to sit in the stalls is £100. The price of ticket A is 20% less than the price of ticket B.
    But 20% of the price of ticket A is 20% x £80 = £16 so 20% more than the price of ticket A is £80 + £16 = £96, which is not equal to ticket price B. Therefore, this statement is not correct.

Class Activity 3

Objective: To study VAT on goods and services.

1. Use the Internet to search for VAT on goods and services in the UK.

    Student's independent research.

2. Write down three items which are charged at the standard rate of 20% VAT.

    Biscuits, bottled water and takeaway food are all charged at the standard rate of 20% VAT. Students may come up with different answers.

3. Write down three items which are charged at the reduced rate of 5% VAT.

    The installation of energy-saving materials, mobility aids for the elderly and children's car seats are all charged at the reduced rate of 5% VAT. Students may come up with different answers.

4. Write down three items which have no VAT added.

    Goods sold in charity shops, equipment for disabled people and children's clothes and footwear all have no VAT added. Students may come up with different answers.

Try It!

Section 7.1

1. Express these fractions as percentages.

    (a) $\dfrac{1}{5}$ (b) $2\dfrac{9}{10}$

    Solution

    Method 1

    (a) $\dfrac{1}{5} = \dfrac{1 \times 20}{5 \times 20}$

    $= \dfrac{20}{100}$

    $= 20\%$

    Method 2

    $\dfrac{1}{5} = \dfrac{1}{\cancel{5}} \times \cancel{100}^{\,20}\% \quad (1 = 100\%)$

    $= 1 \times 20\%$

    $= 20\%$

    (b) $2\dfrac{9}{10} = \dfrac{2 \times 100 + 9 \times 10}{10 \times 10}$

    $= \dfrac{290}{100}$

    $= 290\%$

    $2\dfrac{9}{10} = 2 \times 100\% + \dfrac{9}{\cancel{10}} \times \cancel{100}^{\,10}\%$

    $= 200\% + 9 \times 10\%$

    $= 290\%$

2. Express these percentages as fractions or mixed numbers in their simplest form.
    (a) 80% (b) 468%

    Solution

    (a) $80\% = \dfrac{80}{100} \quad \left(1\% = \dfrac{1}{100}\right)$

    $= \dfrac{4}{5}$

    (b) $468\% = \dfrac{468}{100}$

    $= \dfrac{117}{25}$

    $= 4\dfrac{17}{25}$

3. In an aquarium tank, $\dfrac{86}{200}$ of the fish are goldfish. Find the percentage of fish that are
    (a) goldfish, (b) not goldfish.

    Solution

    (a) $\dfrac{86}{200} = \dfrac{86}{_{2}\cancel{200}} \times \cancel{100}^{\,1}\%$

    $= \dfrac{86}{2} \times 1\%$

    $= 43\%$

    $\therefore$ the percentage of goldfish is 43%.

    (b) The percentage of fish that are not goldfish
    $= 100\% - 43\%$
    $= 57\%$

4. Express these decimals as percentages.
    (a) 0.6 (b) 2.06

Solution

Method 1

(a) $0.6 = \dfrac{6}{10}$

$= \dfrac{6 \times 10}{10 \times 10}$

$= \dfrac{60}{100}$

$= 60\%$

Method 2

$0.6 = 0.6 \times 100\%$

$= 60\%$

(b) $2.06 = \dfrac{206}{100}$

$= 206\%$

$2.06 = 2.06 \times 100\%$

$= 206\%$

5. Express these percentages as decimals.
    (a) 19% (b) 402%

    Solution

    (a) $19\% = \dfrac{19}{100}$

    $= 0.19$

    (b) $402\% = \dfrac{402}{100}$

    $= 4.02$

Section 7.2

6. There are 12 students with dark hair in a group of 40 students. Find the percentage of students with dark hair.

    Solution
    Fraction of dark hair students $= \dfrac{12}{40}$

    Percentage of dark hair students $= \dfrac{12}{40} \times 100\%$

    $= 30\%$

7. The length of a spanner is 50 cm. The length of a screwdriver is 20 cm. Express
    (a) the length of the screwdriver as a percentage of the length of the spanner,
    (b) the length of the spanner as a percentage of the length of the screwdriver.

    Solution
    (a) Length of the screwdriver as a percentage of the length of the spanner

    $= \dfrac{20}{50} \times 100\%$

    $= 40\%$

    (b) Length of the spanner as a percentage of the length of the screwdriver

    $= \dfrac{50}{20} \times 100\%$

    $= 250\%$

8. In a 25 km cross-country training route, Paul ran 16 km and walked 9 km. Find
    (a) the percentage of running distance in the route,
    (b) the percentage of walking distance in the route,

(c) the sum of the percentages of running distance and walking distance.

Solution

(a) Total distance in the route $= 25\,\text{km}$

∴ the percentage of running distance in the route

$= \dfrac{16}{25} \times 100\%$

$= 64\%$

(b) The percentage of walking distance in the route

$= \dfrac{9}{25} \times 100\%$

$= 36\%$

(c) Sum of the percentages of running distance and walking distance

$= (64 + 36)\%$

$= 100\%$

9. Find 6% of 1800 seconds.

Solution

Method 1

6% of 1800 seconds

$= \dfrac{6}{100} \times 1800$

$= 108$ seconds

Method 2

$100\% \;\to\; 1800$ seconds

$1\% \;\to\; \dfrac{1800}{100}\,\text{s} = 18\,\text{s}$

$6\% \;\to\; 18\,\text{s} \times 6$

$\qquad = 108$ seconds

i.e. 6% of 1800 seconds = 108 seconds

10. Harry, Ella and Owen invest a sum of £25 000 to run a business. Harry contributes 45% and Ella contributes 36% of the sum. Find the amount invested by
(a) Harry, **(b)** Ella, **(c)** Owen.

Solution

(a) The amount invested by Harry

$= 45\% \times £25\,000$

$= \dfrac{45}{100} \times £25\,000$

$= £11\,250$

(b) The amount invested by Ella

$= 36\% \times £25\,000$

$= \dfrac{36}{100} \times £25\,000$

$= £9000$

(c) Amount invested by Owen

$= £(25\,000 - 11\,250 - 9000)$

$= £4750$

11. The area of room A is $200\,\text{m}^2$. The area of room B is 15% less than the area of room A. The area of room C is 25% more than the area of room A.
(a) Find the area of room B.
(b) Find the area of room C.

Solution

(a) Area of room B

$=$ area of room A $-$ 15% of the area of room A

$= 200 - 15\% \times 200$

$= 200 - \dfrac{15}{100} \times 200$

$= 200 - 30$

$= 170\,\text{m}^2$

(b) Area of room C

$=$ area of room A $+$ 25% of the area of room A

$= 200 + 25\% \times 200$

$= 200 + \dfrac{25}{100} \times 200$

$= 200 + 50$

$= 250\,\text{m}^2$

12. Tank A has 20 goldfish and tank B has 25 goldfish. Both tanks have the same number of goldfish with a short tail fin. If the percentage of goldfish with a short tail fin in tank B is 36%, find the percentage of goldfish with a short tail fin in tank A.

Solution

Number of goldfish with a short tail fin in tank B

$= 36\% \times 25$

$= \dfrac{36}{100} \times 25$

$= 9$

Percentage of goldfish with a short tail fin in tank A

$= \dfrac{9}{20}$

$= \dfrac{9 \times 5}{20 \times 5}$

$= \dfrac{45}{100}$

$= 45\%$

Section 7.3

13. The price of a necklace increases by 6%. If its original price was £1700, find
(a) the increase in price,
(b) the new price of the necklace.

Solution

(a) Increase in price

$= 6\% \times £1700$

$= \dfrac{6}{100} \times £1700$

$= £102$

(b) New price of the necklace
= original price + increase
= £1700 + £102
= £1802

14. An ice cream stall sells 2600 ice cream cones on Sunday. The sales decrease by 33% on Monday. Find
(a) the decrease in sales on Monday,
(b) the number of ice cream cones sold on Monday.

Solution
(a) Decrease in sales
= 33% × 2600
= $\frac{33}{100} \times 2600$
= 858

(b) Sales after the decrease
= original sales − decrease
= 2600 − 858
= 1742

15. The price of a watch is £450. Find the new price if it is reduced by 40% during a clearance sale.

Solution
Reduction in price
= 40% × £450
= $\frac{40}{100} \times £450$
= £180

New price = £450 − £180
= £270

16. There are 125 customers in a café at noon. The number of customers increases by 20% between noon and 1 pm and then decreases by 30% between 1 pm and 2 pm. Find the number of customers at 2 pm.

Solution
Increase in number of customers between noon and 1 pm
= 20% × 125
= $\frac{20}{100} \times 125$
= 25
The number of customers at 1 pm = 125 + 25
= 150
Decrease in number of customers between 1 pm and 2 pm
= 30% of 150
= $\frac{30}{100} \times 150$
= 45
The number of customers at 2 pm
= 150 − 45
= 105

17. The price of a TV set excluding VAT is £1500. Find its price including 20% VAT.

Solution
VAT on the TV set
= 20% × £1500
= £300
Price including VAT
= price excluding VAT + VAT
= £1500 + £300
= £1800

18. The price of a child's car seat excluding VAT is £60. Find its price including 5% VAT.

Solution
VAT on the children's car seat
= 5% × £60
= £3
Price including VAT
= £60 + £3
= £63

19. The price of a computer notepad including 20% VAT is £840. Find the amount of VAT and the price of the computer notepad excluding VAT.

Solution
You can represent the situation using a bar model.

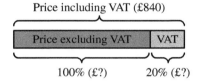

The price including VAT may be considered as 120 parts. 100 parts are the price excluding VAT and 20 parts are the VAT.

120 parts → £840

1 part → $£\left(\frac{840}{120}\right) = £7$

20 parts → £7 × 20
= £140

100 parts → £7 × 100
= £700

Hence, the VAT on the computer notepad is £140 and its price excluding VAT is £700.

Exercise 7.1
Level 1   GCSE Grade 2 / 3⁻

1. Express these fractions and mixed numbers as percentages.
(a) $\frac{8}{100}$ (b) $\frac{9}{50}$
(c) $1\frac{17}{20}$ (d) $2\frac{6}{25}$

Solution

(a) $\frac{8}{100} = 8\%$

(b) $\frac{9}{50} = \frac{9}{50} \times 100\%$
$= 18\%$

(c) $1\frac{17}{20} = 1 \times 100\% + \frac{17}{20} \times 100\%$
$= 185\%$

(d) $2\frac{6}{25} = 2 \times 100\% + \frac{6}{25} \times 100\%$
$= 224\%$

2. Express these percentages as fractions or mixed numbers in their simplest form.
(a) 60%
(b) 25%
(c) 156%
(d) 374%

Solution

(a) $60\% = \frac{60}{100}$
$= \frac{3}{5}$

(b) $25\% = \frac{25}{100}$
$= \frac{1}{4}$

(c) $156\% = \frac{156}{100}$
$= \frac{39}{25}$
$= 1\frac{14}{25}$

(d) $374\% = \frac{374}{100}$
$= \frac{187}{50}$
$= 3\frac{37}{50}$

3. Express these decimals as percentages.
(a) 0.6
(b) 0.28
(c) 1.06
(d) 0.01

Solution

(a) Method 1
$0.6 = \frac{6}{10}$
$= \frac{6 \times 10}{10 \times 10}$
$= \frac{60}{100}$
$= 60\%$

Method 2
$0.6 = 0.6 \times 100\%$
$= 60\%$

(b) $0.28 = 0.28 \times 100\%$
$= 28\%$

(c) $1.06 = 1.06 \times 100\%$
$= 106\%$

(d) Method 1
$0.01 = \frac{1}{100}$
$= 1\%$

Method 2
$0.01 = 0.01 \times 100\%$
$= 1\%$

4. Express these percentages as decimals.
(a) 40%
(b) 35%
(c) 221%
(d) 599%

Solution

(a) $40\% = \frac{40}{100}$
$= 0.4$

(b) $35\% = \frac{35}{100}$
$= 0.35$

(c) $221\% = \frac{221}{100}$
$= 2.21$

(d) $599\% = \frac{599}{100}$
$= 5.99$

Level 2 | **GCSE Grade** 2^+ / 3^-

5. (a) Express $\frac{11}{20}$ and 0.54 as percentages.
(b) Which of these two numbers is smaller?

Solution

(a) $\frac{11}{20} = \frac{11}{20} \times 100\%$
$= 55\%$
$0.54 = 0.54 \times 100\%$
$= 54\%$

(b) 0.54 is the smaller of the two numbers.

6. Arrange these numbers from the smallest to the largest.

77% $\frac{7}{100}$ 0.7

Solution
77%
$\frac{7}{100} = \frac{7}{100} \times 100\% = 7\%$
$0.7 = 0.7 \times 100\% = 70\%$
The numbers arranged from the smallest to largest are
$\frac{7}{100}$, 0.7, 77%.

7. Express the fraction of the area that is shaded as a
(a) percentage,
(b) decimal.

Solution
In the figure, 3 out of 5 parts are shaded
i.e. the fraction of the area that is shaded $= \frac{3}{5}$.
(a) As a percentage,
$\frac{3}{5} = \frac{3}{5} \times 100\%$
$= 60\%$

(b) As a decimal,
$\frac{3}{5} = \frac{3 \times 2}{5 \times 2}$
$= \frac{6}{10}$
$= 0.6$

8. A plot of land has a house and garden built on it. The garden is $\frac{9}{25}$ of the plot. What percentage of the plot is the garden?

Solution

$$\frac{9}{25} = \frac{9}{25} \times 100\%$$
$$= 36\%$$

36% of the plot is the garden.

9. $\frac{7}{50}$ of the total residents in a town are blood type B positive. Find the percentage of residents with blood type B positive.

Solution

$$\frac{7}{50} = \frac{7}{50} \times 100\%$$
$$= 14\%$$

14% of the residents are blood type B positive.

10. Calculate $18\% + 1\frac{4}{25} + 2.06$ and express the answer as a percentage.

Hint: First express the mixed number and decimal as percentages.

Solution

$$18\% + 1\frac{4}{25} + 2.06$$
$$= 18\% + 116\% + 206\%$$
$$= 340\%$$

Level 3　　**GCSE Grade 3⁻ / 3**

11. In a school fundraising campaign, the amount raised is $\frac{5}{4}$ of the target amount. Express the amount raised as a percentage of the target amount.

Solution

$$\frac{5}{4} = \frac{5 \times 25}{4 \times 25} = \frac{125}{100} = 125\%$$

The amount raised is 125% of the target.

12. Admiralty brass is an alloy of copper, zinc and tin. It contains 30% zinc and 1% tin. What is the percentage of copper in the alloy?

Solution

The whole is 100%.
The percentage of copper in the alloy
$$= (100 - 30 - 1)\%$$
$$= 69\%$$

13. Amy, Ben and Carmen are candidates for class prefect. Amy gets $\frac{3}{10}$ of all the votes, Ben gets $\frac{3}{5}$ of all the votes and Carmen gets the rest of the votes. Find the percentage of votes won by
    (a) Amy,　　　　(b) Carmen.

Solution

(a) $\frac{3}{10} = \frac{3 \times 10}{10 \times 10} = \frac{30}{100} = 30\%$

Amy won 30% of the votes.

(b) $\frac{3}{5} = \frac{3 \times 20}{5 \times 20} = \frac{60}{100} = 60\%$

Ben won 60% of the votes.
Carmen won the rest of the votes
$$= 100\% - 30\% - 60\%$$
$$= 10\%$$
Carmen won 10% of the votes.

14. Naseem donates 10% of his income to a charity, he spends $\frac{3}{4}$ of his income and he saves the rest. What percentage of his income does he save?

Solution

Percentage of his income he spends $= \frac{3}{4} \times 100\%$
$$= 75\%$$

∴ the percentage of his income he saves
$$= (100 - 10 - 75)\%$$
$$= 15\%$$

15. In a bag of coins, 0.45 of the total number of coins are £2 coins and $\frac{3}{20}$ of them are £1 coins. Find
    (a) the total percentage of £2 coins and £1 coins in the bag,
    (b) the percentage of other coins in the bag.

Solution

(a) Percentage of £1 coins
$$= \frac{3}{20} \times 100\%$$
$$= 15\%$$
Percentage of £2 coins
$$= 0.45 \times 100\%$$
$$= 45\%$$
∴ the total percentage of £1 coins and £2 coins in the bag
$$= 15\% + 45\%$$
$$= 60\%$$

(b) The percentage of other coins in the bag
$$= 100\% - 60\%$$
$$= 40\%$$

16. Write down a fraction (in its simplest form) and a decimal such that their sum is 36%.

Solution

Sum = 36%
You may have 20% + 16% = 36%.
Convert 20% to a fraction and 16% to a decimal.

$$20\% = \frac{20}{100} = \frac{1}{5}$$

$$16\% = \frac{16}{100} = 0.16$$

Hence, the sum of fraction $\frac{1}{5}$ and decimal 0.16 is 36%.

You can also convert 20% to a decimal and 16% to a fraction to get another possible set of numbers such that their sum is 36%.

17. Write down a fraction (in its simplest form) and a decimal such that their product is 36%.

Solution

$36\% = \frac{36}{100}$

One example can be found by noting

$\frac{36}{100} = \frac{9}{10} \times \frac{4}{10}$

$\frac{4}{10} = 0.4$

So multiplying $\frac{9}{10}$ and 0.4 gives 36%.

Exercise 7.2
Level 1 ┃ GCSE Grade 2⁺ / 3 ┃

1. Express the first quantity as a percentage of the second quantity.
   (a) 32 cm, 64 cm   (b) 3 hours, 10 hours
   (c) 27 kg, 36 kg   (d) 42 litres, 50 litres
   (e) £20, £16   (f) 4 m², 10 m²

Solution
   (a) The required percentage
       $= \frac{32}{64} \times 100\%$
       $= 50\%$

   (b) The required percentage
       $= \frac{3}{10} \times 100\%$
       $= 30\%$

   (c) The required percentage
       $= \frac{27}{36} \times 100\%$
       $= 75\%$

   (d) The required percentage
       $= \frac{42}{50} \times 100\%$
       $= 84\%$

   (e) The required percentage
       $= \frac{20}{16} \times 100\%$
       $= 125\%$

   (f) The required percentage
       $= \frac{4}{10} \times 100\%$
       $= 40\%$

2. In a class of 30 students, 27 students pass an examination. Find the percentage of students who pass.

Solution
The percentage of students who pass
$= \frac{27}{30} \times 100\%$
$= 90\%$

3. There are 12 men and eight women in a queue. Find the percentage of men in the queue.

Solution
Total number of people in the queue
$= 12 + 8$
$= 20$

The percentage of men in the queue
$= \frac{12}{20} \times 100\%$
$= 60\%$

4. The price of a chair is £36 and the price of a table is £90. Express
   (a) the price of the chair as a percentage of the price of the table,
   (b) the price of the table as a percentage of the price of the chair.

Solution
   (a) The price of the chair as a percentage of the price of the table is
       $\frac{36}{90} \times 100\% = \frac{36}{9} \times 10\% = 40\%$

   (b) The price of the table as a percentage of the price of the chair is
       $\frac{90}{36} \times 100\% = \frac{10}{4} \times 100\% = 10 \times 25\% = 250\%$

5. Find the value of each of these amounts.
   (a) 30% of 240 cm
   (b) 45% of 300 grams
   (c) 6% of 200 minutes
   (d) 9% of £120
   (e) 117% of 400 litres
   (f) 204% of 75 km

Solution
   (a) 30% of 240 cm
       $= \frac{30}{100} \times 240$
       $= 72 \text{ cm}$

       Alternatively,
       100% → 240 cm
       1% → $\frac{240}{100}$ cm $= 2.4$ cm
       30% → 2.4 cm × 30 = 72 cm
       i.e. 30% of 240 cm = 72 cm

(b) 45% of 300 grams

$= \frac{45}{100} \times 300$

$= 135$ grams

Alternatively,

$100\% \rightarrow 300$ grams

$1\% \rightarrow \frac{300}{100}$ grams $= 3$ grams

$45\% \rightarrow 3$ grams $\times 45 = 135$ grams

i.e. 45% of 300 grams $= 135$ grams

(c) 6% of 200 minutes

$= \frac{6}{100} \times 200$

$= 12$ minutes

Alternatively,

$100\% \rightarrow 200$ minutes

$1\% \rightarrow \frac{200}{100}$ minutes $= 2$ minutes

$6\% \rightarrow 2$ minutes $\times 6 = 12$ minutes

i.e. 6% of 200 minutes $= 12$ minutes

(d) 9% of £120

$= \frac{9}{100} \times £120$

$= £10.80$

Alternatively,

$100\% \rightarrow £120$

$1\% \rightarrow £\left(\frac{120}{100}\right) = £1.20$

$9\% \rightarrow £1.20 \times 9 = £10.80$

i.e. 9% of £120 $= £10.80$

(e) 117% of 400 litres

$= \frac{117}{100} \times 400$

$= 468$ litres

Alternatively,

$100\% \rightarrow 400$ litres

$1\% \rightarrow \frac{400}{100}$ litres $= 4$ litres

$117\% \rightarrow 4$ litres $\times 117 = 468$ litres

i.e. 117% of 400 litres $= 468$ litres

(f) 204% of 75 km

$= \frac{204}{100} \times 75$

$= \frac{204}{4} \times 3$

$= 51 \times 3$

$= 153$ km

Alternatively,

$100\% \rightarrow 75$ km

$1\% \rightarrow \frac{75}{100}$ km $= 0.75$ km

$204\% \rightarrow 0.75$ km $\times 4 + 75$ km $\times 2 = 153$ km

i.e. 204% of 75 km $= 153$ km

6. There are 150 vases in a delivery van. If 12% of the vases are broken, find the number of broken vases.

Solution

Number of broken vases

$= 12\% \times 150$

$= \frac{12}{100} \times 150$

$= 18$

7. A drink contains 68% orange juice. Find the amount of orange juice in 300 ml of the drink.

Solution

Amount of orange juice

$= 68\% \times 300$

$= \frac{68}{100} \times 300$

$= 204$ ml

Level 2 GCSE Grade $\boxed{3^-}/\boxed{3}$

8. There are eight oranges, seven apples and five pears in a basket. Find the percentage of

(a) apples in the basket,

(b) pears in the basket.

Solution

(a) Total number of fruits

$= 8 + 7 + 5$

$= 20$

$\therefore$ the percentage of apples in the basket

$= \frac{7}{20} \times 100\%$

$= 35\%$

(b) The percentage of pears in the basket

$= \frac{5}{20} \times 100\%$

$= 25\%$

9. Anna's weekly salary is £600 and she spends all of it. She spends £150 on rent and £210 on food. Find the percentage of her salary she spends on

(a) rent,

(b) food,

(c) other items.

Solution

(a) The percentage of the salary Anna spends on rent

$= \frac{150}{600} \times 100\%$

$= 25\%$

(b) The percentage of the salary she spends on food

$= \frac{210}{600} \times 100\%$

$= 35\%$

(c) The percentage of the salary she spends on other items
$$= 100\% - 25\% - 35\%$$
$$= 40\%$$

10. In a shop, cookies are sold in small, medium and large boxes. One day, a total of 200 boxes are sold. 130 of the boxes sold are small and 48 are medium. Find the percentage of boxes sold that are
   (a) small,　　　　**(b)** large.

Solution

(a) The percentage of small boxes sold
$$= \frac{130}{200} \times 100\%$$
$$= 65\%$$

(b) Number of large boxes sold
$$= 200 - 130 - 48$$
$$= 22$$
∴ the percentage of large boxes sold
$$= \frac{22}{200} \times 100\%$$
$$= 11\%$$

11. Pablo got 64 out of 80 marks in an English test and 43 out of 50 marks in a mathematics test.
   (a) Express his English mark as a percentage.
   (b) Express his mathematics mark as a percentage.
   (c) In which test did he perform better? Explain your answer.

Solution

(a) Pablo's English test mark as a percentage
$$= \frac{64}{80} \times 100\%$$
$$= 80\%$$

(b) Pablo's mathematics test mark as a percentage
$$= \frac{43}{50} \times 100\%$$
$$= 86\%$$

(c) Pablo performed better in the mathematics test as he got a higher percentage of marks in the mathematics test; $86\% > 80\%$.

12. There are two recipes to cook chicken. Recipe A uses 135 grams of chicken and 165 grams of other ingredients. Recipe B uses 120 grams of chicken and 130 grams of other ingredients.
   (a) Find the percentage of chicken in recipe A.
   (b) Find the percentage of chicken in recipe B.
   (c) Which recipe has a greater percentage of chicken?

Solution

(a) The percentage of chicken in recipe A
$$= \frac{135}{135+165} \times 100\%$$
$$= \frac{135}{300} \times 100\%$$
$$= 45\%$$

(b) The percentage of chicken in recipe B
$$= \frac{120}{120+130} \times 100\%$$
$$= \frac{120}{250} \times 100\%$$
$$= 48\%$$

(c) Recipe B has a greater percentage of chicken.

13. In a survey, 1200 people were interviewed about customer service in a bank. It was found that 69% of interviewees were satisfied with the service, 22% were not satisfied with the service and the rest had no opinion. Find the number of interviewees who
   (a) were satisfied with the service,
   (b) were not satisfied with the service,
   (c) had no opinion of the service.

Solution

(a) The required number
$$= 69\% \text{ of } 1200$$
$$= \frac{69}{100} \times 1200$$
$$= 828$$

(b) The required number
$$= 22\% \text{ of } 1200$$
$$= \frac{22}{100} \times 1200$$
$$= 264$$

(c) The required number
$$= 1200 - 828 - 264$$
$$= 108$$

Level 3　　GCSE Grade **3⁺ / 4⁻**

14. The area of a flat is $80\,\text{m}^2$.
   (a) The area of the living room is 25% of the area of the flat. Find the area of the living room.
   (b) The area of the kitchen is $12\,\text{m}^2$. Express the area of the kitchen as a percentage of
   (i) the area of the flat,
   (ii) the area of the living room.

Solution

(a) Area of the living room = 25% of $80\,\text{m}^2$
$$= \frac{25}{100} \times 80\,\text{m}^2$$
$$= 20\,\text{m}^2$$

(b) **(i)** The kitchen as a percentage of the flat is
$$= \frac{12}{80}$$
$$= \frac{3}{20}$$
$$= \frac{15}{100}$$
$$= 15\%$$

(ii) The kitchen as a percentage of the living room is

$$= \frac{12}{20}$$
$$= \frac{60}{100}$$
$$= 60\%$$

15. Paula's normal working hours are 35 hours each week at a rate of £12 per hour. For overtime, the rate is 30% more.
    (a) What is the pay for one hour of overtime?
    (b) How much is her total pay if she works 40 hours in a particular week?

Solution
(a) The pay for one hour overtime
= normal rate per hour + 30% of the normal rate
= £12 + 30% of £12
$$= £12 + \frac{30}{100} \times £12$$
= £12 + £3.60
= £15.60

(b) Number of hours that Paula works overtime
= 40 − 35
= 5
∴ her total pay for the week
= 35 × £12 + 5 × £15.60
= £498

16. The price for a set dinner is £28 and there is a 10% service charge on the bill. Mr and Mrs Fahey order two set dinners.
    (a) What is the total service charge?
    (b) What is the total amount of the bill?

Solution
(a) The total service charge for two set dinners
$$= (10\% \times £28) \times 2$$
$$= \left(\frac{10}{100} \times £28 \right) \times 2$$
= £2.80 × 2
= £5.60

(b) Total amount of the bill
= price of two set dinners + total service charge
= £28 × 2 + £5.60
= £56 + £5.60
= £61.60

17. Andy's monthly salary is £5000. Hannah's salary is 10% less than Andy's. Megan's salary is 20% more than Andy's.
    (a) Find Hannah's monthly salary.
    (b) Find Megan's monthly salary.

Solution
(a) Hannah's monthly salary
= Andy's monthly salary − 10% of Andy's monthly salary
= £5000 − 10% of £5000
$$= £5000 - \frac{10}{100} \times £5000$$
= £5000 − £500
= £4500

(b) Megan's monthly salary
= Andy's monthly salary + 20% of Andy's monthly salary
= £5000 + 20% of £5000
$$= £5000 + \frac{20}{100} \times £5000$$
= £5000 + £1000
= £6000

18. Air is a mixture of gases. 78% of air is nitrogen, 21% is oxygen and the rest is a mixture of other gases. The volume of air intake in a breath is $400 \, cm^3$. Find the amount of
    (a) oxygen in the breath,
    (b) gases other than oxygen and nitrogen in the breath.

Solution
(a) The amount of oxygen in the breath
= 21% of $400 \, cm^3$
$$= \frac{21}{100} \times 400$$
$$= 84 \, cm^3$$

(b) Percentage of air that is made up of other gases
= 100% − 78% − 21%
= 1%
∴ the amount of other gases in the breath
= 1% of $400 \, cm^3$
$$= \frac{1}{100} \times 400$$
$$= 4 \, cm^3$$

19. A department store has a Christmas sale. All garments are 20% less than their usual prices. All electrical appliances are 5% less than their usual prices. Mrs McMillan buys a dress and a washing machine. The usual prices of the dress and the washing machine are £120 and £420 respectively. Find
    (a) the sale price of the dress,
    (b) the sale price of the washing machine,
    (c) the total amount that Mrs McMillan pays.

Solution
(a) The sale price of the dress
= £120 − 20% of £120
$$= £120 - \frac{20}{100} \times £120$$
= £96

(b) The sale price of the washing machine
$$= £420 - 5\% \text{ of } £420$$
$$= £420 - \frac{5}{100} \times £420$$
$$= £399$$

(c) The total amount that Mrs McMillan pays
$$= £96 + £399$$
$$= £495$$

20. Tom plays a computer game three times. His score in the first game is 800. His score in the second game is 10% more than his score in the first game. His score in the third game is 10% less than his score in the second game.
(a) Find his score in the third game.
(b) Express his score in the third game as a percentage of the score in the first game.

Solution
(a) Tom's score in the second game
$$= 800 + 10\% \text{ of } 800$$
$$= 800 + \frac{10}{100} \times 800$$
$$= 880$$

His score in the third game
$$= 880 - 10\% \text{ of } 880$$
$$= 880 - \frac{10}{100} \times 880$$
$$= 792$$

(b) The required percentage
$$= \frac{792}{800} \times 100\%$$
$$= 99\%$$

21. A dance club has 30 members of which 60% are female. A drama club has 40 members. The number of female members in both clubs are equal. Find the percentage of female members in the drama club.

Solution
The number of females in the dance club
$$= 60\% \text{ of } 30$$
$$= \frac{60}{100} \times 30$$
$$= 18$$

So number of females in the drama club = 18.
The percentage of female members in the drama club is
$$= \frac{18}{40}$$
$$= \frac{9 \times 5}{20 \times 5}$$
$$= \frac{45}{100}$$
$$= 45\%$$

Exercise 7.3
Level 1
GCSE Grade **3**

1. Find the amount when
(a) 600 increases by 21%,
(b) £320 increases by 15%,
(c) $2500\,\text{m}^2$ increases by 13%.

Solution
(a) New amount
$$= 600 + 21\% \times 600$$
$$= 600 + \frac{21}{100} \times 600$$
$$= 600 + 126$$
$$= 726$$

(b) New amount
$$= £320 + 15\% \times £320$$
$$= £320 + \frac{15}{100} \times £320$$
$$= £320 + £48$$
$$= £368$$

(c) New amount
$$= 2500\,\text{m}^2 + 13\% \times 2500\,\text{m}^2$$
$$= \left(2500 + \frac{13}{100} \times 2500\right)\text{m}^2$$
$$= (2500 + 325)\,\text{m}^2$$
$$= 2825\,\text{m}^2$$

2. Find the amount when
(a) 200 decreases by 18%,
(b) 40 cm decreases by 55%,
(c) £4500 decreases by 9%.

Solution
(a) New amount
$$= 200 - 18\% \times 200$$
$$= 200 - \frac{18}{100} \times 200$$
$$= 200 - 36$$
$$= 164$$

(b) New amount
$$= 40\,\text{cm} - 55\% \times 40\,\text{cm}$$
$$= \left(40 - \frac{55}{100} \times 40\right)\text{cm}$$
$$= (40 - 22)\,\text{cm}$$
$$= 18\,\text{cm}$$

(c) New amount
$$= £4500 - 9\% \times £4500$$
$$= £\left(4500 - \frac{9}{100} \times 4500\right)$$
$$= £(4500 - 405)$$
$$= £4095$$

3. The value of a painting is £2600. If its value rises by 40%, find its new value.

Solution

New value of the painting
$= £2600 + 40\% \times £2600$
$= £\left(2600 + \dfrac{40}{100} \times 2600\right)$
$= £(2600 + 1040)$
$= £3640$

4. The price of a mobile phone is £500. If the price drops by 18%, find its new price.

   Solution

   New price of the mobile phone
   $= £500 - 18\% \times £500$
   $= £\left(500 - \dfrac{18}{100} \times 500\right)$
   $= £(500 - 90)$
   $= £410$

5. Isaac's annual salary is £38 000. If the salary increases by 7%, find his new annual salary.

   Solution

   Isaac's new annual salary
   $= £38\,000 + 7\% \times £38\,000$
   $= £\left(38\,000 + \dfrac{7}{100} \times 38\,000\right)$
   $= £(38\,000 + 2660)$
   $= £40\,660$

6. The price of a skirt excluding 20% VAT is £80. Find
   (a) the amount of VAT,
   (b) the price including VAT.

   Solution
   (a) VAT $= 20\% \times £80$
             $= £16$

   (b) Price including VAT
             $= £80 + £16$
             $= £96$

7. The price of a haircut excluding VAT is £15. The VAT on the haircut is 20%. Find
   (a) the amount of VAT,
   (b) the price including VAT.

   Solution
   (a) VAT $= 20\% \times £15$
             $= £3$

   (b) Price including VAT
             $= £15 + £3$
             $= £18$

Level 2   GCSE Grade **3⁺/4⁻**

8. The initial height of a plant is 100 cm.
   (a) The height increases by 20% in the first month. Find its height at the end of the first month.

   (b) The height then increases by 15% during the second month. Find its height at the end of the second month.

   Solution
   (a) Height of the plant at the end of the first month
       = initial height + increase
       $= 100\,\text{cm} + 20\% \times 100\,\text{cm}$
       $= (100 + 20)\,\text{cm}$
       $= 120\,\text{cm}$

   (b) Increase in height during the second month
       $= 15\% \times 120\,\text{cm}$
       $= 18\,\text{cm}$
       $\therefore$ height of the plant at the end of the second month
       $= (120 + 18)\,\text{cm}$
       $= 138\,\text{cm}$

9. The price of a new car was £48 000. Its value decreased by 15% in the first year and then by 8% in the second year. Find
   (a) the value of the car at the end of the first year,
   (b) the value of the car at the end of the second year.

   Solution
   (a) Decrease in value in the first year
       $= 15\% \times £48\,000$
       $= £7200$
       $\therefore$ the value of the car at the end of the first year
       $= £48\,000 - £7200$
       $= £40\,800$

   (b) Decrease in value in the second year
       $= 8\% \times £40\,800$
       $= £3264$
       $\therefore$ the value of the car at the end of the second year
       $= £40\,800 - £3264$
       $= £37\,536$

10. A rectangular field is 120 m long and 80 m wide. The length of the field is reduced by 15% and the width is extended by 20%.
    (a) Find the new length of the field.
    (b) Find the new width of the field.
    (c) Does the perimeter of the field increase or decrease? Show working to explain your answer.

    Solution
    (a) New length of the field
        $= 120\,\text{m} - 15\% \times 120\,\text{m}$
        $= (120 - 18)\,\text{m}$
        $= 102\,\text{m}$

(b) New width of the field
$= 80\,\text{m} + 20\% \times 80\,\text{m}$
$= (80 + 16)\,\text{m}$
$= 96\,\text{m}$

(c) Initial perimeter $= (2 \times 120 + 2 \times 80)\,\text{m}$
$= (240 + 160)\,\text{m}$
$= 400\,\text{m}$
New perimeter $= (2 \times 102 + 2 \times 96)\,\text{m}$
$= (204 + 192)\,\text{m}$
$= 396\,\text{m}$
Since $396 < 400$, the perimeter of the field has decreased.

11. The price of a jacket including 20% VAT is £312. Find
(a) the amount of VAT,
(b) the price of the jacket excluding VAT.

Solution
(a) Consider the price including VAT as 120 parts and the price excluding VAT as 100 parts. The VAT is 20 parts.
120 parts → £312
1 part → $£\left(\dfrac{312}{120}\right) = £2.60$
20 parts → $£2.60 \times 20 = £52$
100 parts → $£2.60 \times 100 = £260$
∴ the amount of VAT on the jacket is £52.

(b) The price of the jacket excluding VAT is £260.

12. The price of an item excluding VAT is £380.
(a) If there is 20% VAT on the item, find its price including VAT.
(b) If there is 5% reduced rate VAT on the item, find its price including VAT.
(c) How much tax is saved if the VAT is 5% instead of 20%?

Solution
(a) Price of the item including 20% VAT
$= £380 + 20\% \times £380$
$= £(380 + 76)$
$= £456$

(b) Price of the item including 5% VAT
$= £380 + 5\% \times £380$
$= £(380 + 19)$
$= £399$

(c) Amount of tax saved
$= £456 - £399$
$= £57$

Level 3 GCSE Grade $4^- / 5^-$

13. The population of a town is 96 000. If the annual birth rate is 5% and the annual death rate is 2%, find
(a) the number of births in a year,
(b) the number of deaths in a year,

(c) the population of the town at the end of the year, assuming no one moves in or moves out of the town.

Solution
(a) Number of births in a year
$= 5\% \times 96\,000$
$= 4800$

(b) Number of deaths in a year
$= 2\% \times 96\,000$
$= 1920$

(c) Population of the town at the end of the year
$= 96\,000 + 4800 - 1920$
$= 98\,880$

14. Henry earns £5000 a month. His savings are usually 20% of his income and he spends the rest. In a certain month, his expenditure increases by 15% while his income remains the same.
(a) Find his expenditure after the increase.
(b) Express the increase in expenditure as a percentage of his income.
Hint: You may draw bar models to help illustrate the problem.

Solution
(a) Henry's usual expenditure is £5000 less his savings
$= £5000 - 20\% \times £5000$
$= £5000 - £1000$
$= £4000$
After the increase his expenditure is
$= £4000 + 15\% \times £4000$
$= £4000 + £600$
$= £4600$

(b) The increase in expenditure is £600.
As a percentage of his income this is
$= \dfrac{600}{5000}$
$= 12\%$
Alternatively, his expenditure is 80% of his income $(100\% - 20\%)$ and this has increased by 15%, i.e $15\% \times 80\% = 12\%$.

15. A club has 500 members, of which 60% are male. If the number of male members drops by 10% and the number of female members rises by 18%, find
(a) the new number of male members,
(b) the new number of members in the club.

Solution
(a) Initial number of male members
$= 60\% \times 500$
$= 300$
New number of male members
$= 300 - 10\% \times 300$
$= 300 - 30$
$= 270$

(b) Initial number of female members
$$= 500 - 300$$
$$= 200$$
New number of female members
$$= 200 + 18\% \times 200$$
$$= 200 + 36$$
$$= 236$$

Hence, the new number of members in the club
$$= 270 + 236$$
$$= 506$$

16. A baker sells 400 buns a day when the price of a bun is £2. He increases the price of a bun by 50% and the number of buns he sells in a day drops by 30%.
    (a) Find the new price of a bun.
    (b) Find the number of buns sold in a day after the price increase.
    (c) Is the revenue from selling the buns after the price increase less than before? Explain your answer.

Solution
(a) The new price of a bun
$$= £2 + 50\% \times £2$$
$$= £2 + £1$$
$$= £3$$

(b) After the price increase, the number of buns sold in a day
$$= 400 - 30\% \times 400$$
$$= 400 - 120$$
$$= 280$$

(c) Revenue from the sales of buns before the price increase
$$= 400 \times £2$$
$$= £800$$
Revenue from the sales of buns after the price increase
$$= 280 \times £3$$
$$= £840$$
No, the revenue from selling the buns after the price increase is more than before as £840 > £800.

17. The price of an electricity bill including 5% VAT is £315. Find
    (a) the amount of VAT on the bill,
    (b) the bill excluding VAT,
    (c) the new amount of VAT if the bill excluding VAT increases by 25%.

Solution
(a) A bar model can be drawn to represent the situation.

Price including VAT (£315)

Price excluding VAT	VAT
100% (£?)	5% (£?)

Consider the price including 5% VAT as 105 parts. 100 parts are the price excluding VAT and 5 parts are the VAT.

105 parts $\rightarrow$ £315

1 part $\rightarrow$ $£\left(\dfrac{315}{105}\right) = £3$

5 parts $\rightarrow$ £3 × 5 = £15

100 parts $\rightarrow$ £3 × 100 = £300

Hence, the amount of VAT = £15.

(b) The price excluding VAT is £300.

(c) New price of bill after increase
$$= £300 + 25\% \times £300$$
$$= £300 + £75$$
$$= £375$$
The new VAT
$$= 5\% \times £375$$
$$= £18.75$$

18. Sophie reads an advertisement for pet insurance.

> Pay £n each month for 12 months
> or
> pay one annual fee and receive 10% discount.

She chooses to pay the insurance annual fee of £199.80 for her cat. What is the value of n in the advertisement?

Solution
$$12n - 10\% \text{ of } 12n = £199.80$$
$$12n - \frac{10}{100} \times 12n = £199.80$$
$$12n \times \left(1 - \frac{1}{10}\right) = £199.80$$
$$12n \times \frac{9}{10} = £199.80$$
$$n = £199.80 \times \frac{10}{12 \times 9}$$
$$n = \frac{£1998.00}{108}$$
$$n = £18.50$$

19. The price of an item increases by a given percentage and, after the increase, the price is £360. Find one possibility for the original price and the percentage increase that would give this final price.

Solution
You can use a method similar to the method used in Questions **11** and **17**.
Consider a 25% increase in the price of the item such that the price after the increase is £360.
The following bar model represents this situation.

Price after increase (£360)

Original price	Increase
100% (£?)	25%

You have
125 parts → £360

1 part → £$\left(\frac{360}{125}\right)$ = £2.88

100 parts → £2.88 × 100 = £288
i.e. the original price of the item is £288.
Some possible percentages of increase on the
original prices of the item such that the price after
the increase is £360 are shown here.

Original price	Percentage increase	Final price
£240	50%	£360
£288	25%	£360
£300	20%	£360
£320	12.5%	£360

20. A department store has a n% sale. A jacket is
offered at £315 during the sale. Find a possible
original price and the value of n.

Solution
For example consider a 10% sale.
original price − 10% of original price = £315

$(100\% - 10\%) \times$ original price = £315
$90\% \times$ original price = £315
$\frac{9}{10} \times$ original price = £315
original price = £315 × $\frac{10}{9}$
original price = £350

Some other possibilities are shown in the table.

Percentage decrease	Original price	Sale price
20%	£393.75	£315
30%	£450	£315
40%	£525	£315
50%	£630	£315

Revision Exercise 7

1. **(a)** Which of these percentages is equivalent to $\frac{3}{5}$?

GCSE
Grade
2 / 3⁻

   30%   40%   60%   75%

   (b) Which of these percentages is equivalent
   to 0.25?

   2.5%   4%   25% $\frac{1}{4}$%

   (c) Which of these fractions is **not** equivalent to
   160%?

   $1\frac{6}{10}$ $1\frac{3}{5}$ $\frac{16}{20}$ $\frac{320}{200}$

Solution
(a) $\frac{3}{5} = \frac{3}{5} \times 100^{20}$%

   = 3 × 20%

   = 60%

   ∴ 60% is equivalent to $\frac{3}{5}$.

(b) 0.25 = 0.25 × 100%
   = 25%
   ∴ 25% is equivalent to 0.25.

(c) $160\% = \frac{160}{100}$

   $= 1\frac{6}{10}$

   $= 1\frac{3}{5}$

   $\frac{16}{20} = \frac{4}{5} \neq 160\%$

   $\frac{320}{200} = \frac{320 \div 2}{200 \div 2}$

   $= \frac{160}{100}$

   $= 160\%$

Hence, $\frac{16}{20}$ is not equivalent to 160%.

2. Tara played three computer games. Here are her
results.

GCSE
Grade
2⁺

Game A	Game B	Game C
$\frac{17}{20}$	72 out of 75	258 out of 300

(a) Write the results as percentages.
(b) In which game did she perform the best?

Solution
(a) Game A: $\frac{17}{20} \times 100\%$

   = 85%

   Game B: $\frac{72}{75} \times 100\%$

   = 96%

   Game C: $\frac{258}{300} \times 100\%$

   = 86%

(b) He performed the best in Game B as 96% is
the greatest of the three percentages in **(a)**.

3. **(a)** In a jar of jelly beans, 7 out of 25 jelly beans
are red. Find the percentage of red jelly beans
in the jar.

GCSE
Grade
2⁺

   (b) A jar has 60 jelly beans. If Ava has eaten 35%
   of them, how many jelly beans remain in the
   jar?

Solution
(a) The required percentage

   $= \frac{7}{25} \times 100\%$

   = 28%

(b) Percentage of jelly beans that are remaining in
     the jar = 100% − 35%
                = 65%
     Number of jelly beans remaining in the jar
     = 65% × 60
     = 39

4. A test consists of 30 multiple choice questions.

Each question is worth one mark. Xander scores
24 out of 30 marks. Ben scores $\frac{7}{10}$ of the total
marks.
   (a) Express Xander's mark as a percentage.
   (b) Express Ben's mark as a percentage.
   (c) Whose performance is better in the test?

Solution
   (a) Xander's mark as a percentage
          $=\frac{24}{30}\times100\%$
          $= 80\%$

   (b) Ben's mark as a percentage
          $=\frac{7}{10}\times100\%$
          $= 70\%$

   (c) Xander's performance in the test is better.

5. A school has 32 male and 48 female staff.

   (a) Find the percentage of male staff.
   (b) Express the number of female staff as a
          percentage of the number of male staff.

Solution
   (a) Total staff
          = 32 + 48
          = 80
          ∴ the percentage of male staff $=\frac{32}{80}\times100\%$
                                          $= 40\%$

   (b) The number of female staff as a percentage of
          the number of male staff
          $=\frac{48}{32}\times100\%$
          $=\frac{3}{2}\times100\%$
          $=150\%$

6. A bottle of drink is 750 ml, of which 24% is orange

juice. It is poured into a bowl of water to prepare a
punch. The volume of water is 60% of the volume
of the drink. Find
   (a) the volume of water in the bowl,
   (b) the percentage of orange juice in the punch.
   Hint: You may draw a bar model to help you.

Solution
   (a) A bar model may be drawn to represent the
          situation.

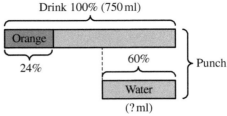

     Volume of water
     = 60% × 750 ml
     = 450 ml

   (b) Volume of the punch
          = volume of the drink + volume of the water
          = 750 + 450
          = 1200 ml
          Volume of orange juice in the bottle of drink
          = 24% × 750 ml
          = 180 ml
          Hence, the percentage of orange juice in the punch
          $=\frac{180}{1200}\times100\%$
          $= 15\%$

7. A tower block has 120 flats. 40% of the flats have

two bedrooms, 35% have three bedrooms and the
rest have four bedrooms.
   (a) Find the number of two-bedroom flats.
   (b) Find the number of four-bedroom flats.
   (c) Express the number of two-bedroom flats as a
          percentage of the number of four-bedroom flats.

Solution
   (a) Number of two-bedroom flats = 40% × 120
                                          = 48

   (b) Percentage of the flats that have four bedrooms
          = 100% − 40% − 35%
          = 25%
          ∴ the number of four-bedroom flats = 25% × 120
                                                = 30

   (c) The number of two-bedroom flats as a percentage
          of the number of four-bedroom flats
          $=\frac{48}{30}\times100\%$
          $=160\%$

8. The price of a table is £200 and the price of a chair

is £50. The price of the table is reduced by 20%
while the price of the chair is unchanged.
   (a) Find the reduction in the price of the table.
   (b) Kent bought a table and four chairs. Express
          his purchase price as a percentage of the
          original total price of the items.

Solution
   (a) The reduction in the price of the table
          = 20% × £200
          = £40

(b) Reduced price of the table = £200 − £40
$$= £160$$
Purchase price of a table and four chairs
$$= £160 + 4 × £50$$
$$= £360$$
Original total price of a table and four chairs
$$= £200 + 4 × £50$$
$$= £400$$
The required percentage
$$= \frac{360}{400} × 100\%$$
$$= 90\%$$

9. (a) The amount of a gas bill for a household is £160 excluding VAT. The VAT on the bill is 5%. Find the amount of the bill including VAT.

(b) The price of a designer handbag including 20% VAT is £300. Find

    (i) the amount of VAT,

    (ii) the price of the handbag excluding VAT.

Solution

(a) The amount of the gas bill including VAT
$$= £160 + 5\% × £160$$
$$= £160 + £8$$
$$= £168$$

(b) 120 parts → £300
$$1 \text{ part} → £\left(\frac{300}{120}\right) = £2.50$$

    (i) VAT = £2.50 × 20
$$= £50$$

    (ii) Price of the handbag excluding VAT
$$= £300 − £50$$
$$= £250$$

10. The monthly income of each waiter in a restaurant is the sum of the basic salary and a share of tips. The basic salary is £1600. The tips are 10% of the total amount of customers' orders and they are divided equally among the 15 staff in the restaurant. If the total amount of customers' orders in one month is £60 000, find one waiter's income for that month.

Solution

Total amount of tips for 15 staff
$$= 10\% × £60\,000$$
$$= £6000$$
∴ the amount of tips received by each waiter
$$= £6000 ÷ 15$$
$$= £400$$
Hence, a waiter's monthly income
$$= £1600 + £400$$
$$= £2000$$

11. A factory has 250 staff, of which 40% are male. The number of male staff increases by 20% while the number of female staff is cut by 10%. Find

(a) the new number of male staff,

(b) the new total number of staff.

Solution

(a) Original number of male staff
$$= 40\% × 250$$
$$= 100$$
New number of male staff
$$= 100 + 20\% × 100$$
$$= 100 + 20$$
$$= 120$$

(b) Original number of female staff
$$= \text{total staff} − \text{number of male staff}$$
$$= 250 − 100$$
$$= 150$$
New number of female staff
$$= 150 − 10\% × 150$$
$$= 150 − 15$$
$$= 135$$
New total number of staff = 120 + 135
$$= 255$$

12. The usual price of a necklace is £150. Its price is marked up by 20% and then it is sold at 20% discount. Find

(a) the marked-up price,

(b) the selling price,

(c) the selling price as a percentage of the usual price.

Solution

(a) Marked-up price
$$= \text{usual price} + \text{increase}$$
$$= £150 + 20\% × £150$$
$$= £150 + £30$$
$$= £180$$

(b) Discount = 20% × £180
$$= £36$$
∴ the selling price
$$= £180 − £36$$
$$= £144$$

(c) The required percentage
$$= \frac{144}{150} × 100\%$$
$$= 96\%$$

13. A raw news video clip is 250 seconds long. An editor decreases its length by 20% and then presents it to her boss. The boss then decreases the length of the video she was given by 10%.

(a) Find the length of the video clip after editing by

    (i) the editor,

    (ii) the boss.

(b) Express the length of the final video clip as a percentage of the length of the raw video clip.

Solution

(a) (i) Length of the video clip after editing by the editor
$$= 250 − 20\% × 250$$
$$= 250 − 50$$
$$= 200 \text{ seconds}$$

(ii) Length of the video clip after editing by
the boss
$$= 200 - 10\% \times 200$$
$$= 200 - 20$$
$$= 180 \text{ seconds}$$

(b) The required percentage
$$= \frac{180}{250} \times 100\%$$
$$= 72\%$$

14. A rectangle is 50 cm long and 40 cm wide. Its length
is extended by 12% and its width is reduced by 15%.

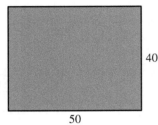

40

50

(a) Find the new length and width of the rectangle.
(b) Paddy said that the perimeter of the rectangle
remains the same after the changes. Do you
agree? Give your reason.
(c) Mara said that the area of the rectangle
remains the same after the changes. Do you
agree? Give your reason.

Solution
(a) New length of the rectangle
$$= 50 + 12\% \times 50$$
$$= 50 + 6$$
$$= 56 \text{ cm}$$
New width of the rectangle
$$= 40 - 15\% \times 40$$
$$= 40 - 6$$
$$= 34 \text{ cm}$$

(b) Original perimeter of the rectangle
$$= 2 \times 50 + 2 \times 40$$
$$= 100 + 80$$
$$= 180 \text{ cm}$$
Perimeter of the rectangle after the changes
$$= 2 \times 56 + 2 \times 34$$
$$= 112 + 68$$
$$= 180 \text{ cm}$$
The original perimeter and the perimeter after
the changes are the same. Paddy is correct.

(c) Original area of the rectangle
$$= 50 \times 40$$
$$= 2000 \text{ cm}^2$$
Area of the rectangle after the changes
$$= 56 \times 34$$
$$= 1904 \text{ cm}^2$$
Mara is incorrect.
$2000 \text{ cm}^2 \neq 1904 \text{ cm}^2$
The original area is different from the area
after the changes.

15. Iris's income is 25% more than Alice's income.
Express Alice's income as a percentage of Iris's
income.
Hint: You may assume that Alice's income is £100.

Solution
Assume that Alice's income is £100.
Iris's income = Alice's income + 25% × Alice's income
$$= £100 + 25\% \times £100$$
$$= £100 + £25$$
$$= £125$$
Hence, Alice's income as a percentage of Iris's income
$$= \frac{100}{125} \times 100\%$$
$$= 80\%$$

General method:
Let £A be Alice's income.
Iris's income = £A + 25% × £A
$$= £\left(A + \frac{25}{100} \times A\right)$$
$$= £\left(A + \frac{1}{4}A\right)$$
$$= £\left[\left(1 + \frac{1}{4}\right)A\right]$$
$$= £\left[\frac{5}{4}A\right]$$

The required percentage $= \dfrac{A}{\frac{5}{4}A} \times 100\%$

$$= \frac{1}{\frac{5}{4}} \times 100\% \qquad \frac{1}{\frac{5}{4}} = 1 \div \frac{5}{4}$$
$$= \frac{4}{5} \times 100\% \qquad \qquad = 1 \times \frac{4}{5}$$
$$= 80\% \qquad \qquad \qquad = \frac{4}{5}$$

16. An aluminium rod is 250 cm long. A copper rod is
20% shorter than the aluminium rod. An iron rod
is 20% longer than the copper rod. Are the lengths
of the aluminium rod and the iron rod the same?
Justify your answer.

Solution
The length of the copper rod is
250 cm − 20% of 250 cm
$$= (100\% - 20\%) \times 250 \text{ cm}$$
$$= 80\% \times 250 \text{ cm}$$
The length of the iron rod is
(100% + 20%) of the length of the copper rod
$$= 120\% \times 200 \text{ cm}$$
$$= \frac{120}{100} \times 200 \text{ cm}$$
$$= 240 \text{ cm}$$
$$= 240 \text{ cm} < 250 \text{ cm}$$
Therefore the lengths of the aluminium rod and the
iron rod are not the same.

1. (a) Write these numbers in ascending order.

    0.8   −0.543   −0.96

    (b) Work out 0.9 − 0.416.

    (c) Work out 0.305 × 0.7.

Solution

(a) The numbers arranged in ascending order are
−0.96, −0.543, 0.8.

(b)
$$\begin{array}{r} \overset{8\;9\;10}{0.9\,0\,0} \\ -0.4\,1\,6 \\ \hline 0.4\,8\,4 \end{array}$$

∴ 0.9 − 0.416 = 0.484

(c)
$$\begin{array}{r} 305 \\ \times\;7 \\ \hline 2135 \end{array}$$

∴ $\underbrace{0.305 \times 0.7}_{\substack{\text{total of 4}\\\text{decimal places}}} = \underset{\substack{\uparrow\\4\text{ decimal}\\\text{places}}}{0.2135}$

2. (a) Arrange $\frac{3}{7}$, 0.3 and 41% in descending order.

    (b) Find the value of $\frac{3}{7} - 41\% + 0.3$. Give your answer as a fraction in its simplest form.

Solution

(a) $\frac{3}{7} = 0.\dot{4}2857\dot{1}$

0.3

$41\% = \frac{41}{100} = 0.41$

The numbers arranged in descending order are

$\frac{3}{7}$, 41%, 0.3.

(b) $\frac{3}{7} - 41\% + 0.3$

$= \frac{3}{7} - \frac{41}{100} + \frac{3}{10}$

$= \frac{300}{700} - \frac{287}{700} + \frac{210}{700}$

$= \frac{223}{700}$

3. $2\frac{1}{4}$ litres of vinegar are poured equally into three bottles.

    (a) Find the volume of vinegar in each bottle. Give your answer in millilitres.

    (b) If 500 ml of water is added to one of the bottles, find the percentage of vinegar in this bottle.

Solution

(a) Volume of vinegar in each bottle

$= \left(2\frac{1}{4} \div 3\right)$ litres

$= \frac{9}{4} \times \frac{1}{3}$ litres

$= \frac{3}{4}$ litres

$= \frac{3}{4} \times 1000$ ml

$= 750$ ml

(b) Volume of vinegar and water in the bottle

$= 750 + 500$

$= 1250$ ml

∴ the percentage of vinegar in this bottle

$= \frac{750}{1250} \times 100\%$

$= 60\%$

4. A company has 50 staff. If 36% of the staff cycle to the office and 20% drive to the office, find the number of staff who go to the office by other means. Compare your method with others in your class.

Solution

Method 1

Percentage of staff who go by other means
$= 100\% - 36\% - 20\%$
$= 44\%$

Number of staff who go by other means
$= 44\%$ of 50
$= \frac{44}{100} \times 50$
$= 22$

Method 2

Number of staff who cycle $= 36\% \times 50$
$= \frac{36}{100} \times 50$
$= 18$

Number of staff who drive $= 20\% \times 50$
$= \frac{20}{100} \times 50$
$= 10$

Number who go to the office by other means
$$= 50 - 18 - 10$$
$$= 22$$

5. Richard attempted two job application tests with the following results.

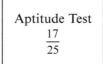

| Aptitude Test $\dfrac{17}{25}$ | Literacy Test 105 out of 150 |

(a) Write the results as percentages.
(b) In which test did he perform better?

Solution
(a) Aptitude test result $= \dfrac{17}{25} \times 100\% = 68\%$

Literacy test result
$= \dfrac{105}{150} \times 100\% = 105 \times \dfrac{2}{3}\% = 70\%$

(b) 70% > 68% so Richard performed better in the literacy test.

6. The carbon dioxide emission in a journey of one km from a diesel car is 125 grams and that from a petrol car is 150 grams.
(a) Express the emission from the petrol car as a percentage of the emission from the diesel car.
(b) Calculate the amount of carbon dioxide emission from the petrol car in a journey of 20.8 km.

Solution
(a) Emission from the petrol car as a percentage of the emission from the diesel car

$= \dfrac{150}{125} = \dfrac{150 \times \frac{4}{5}}{125 \times \frac{4}{5}} = \dfrac{120}{100} = 120\%$

(b)
```
      208
    × 150
    20800
    10400
    31200
```
1 decimal place in product so 1 decimal place in the answer.
$150 \times 20.8 = 3120$
The amount of emission is 3120 grams.

7. The load capacity of a new forklift is 2500 kg.
(a) If the forklift uses 85% of its capacity to lift a load, find the mass of the load.
(b) The load capacity of an older forklift is 1700 kg. Express this as a percentage of the load capacity of the new forklift.

Solution
(a) Mass of the load in kg = 85% of 2500
$= \dfrac{85}{100} \times 2500$
$= 85 \times \dfrac{100}{4}$
$= 2125$
The mass of the load is 2125 kg.

(b) Load capacity of older forklift as a percentage of capacity of new forklift
$= \dfrac{1700}{2500} \times 100\%$
$= \dfrac{17}{25} \times 100\%$
$= 68\%$

8. The volume of a red balloon is 400 cm³.
(a) The volume of a blue balloon is 20% more than the volume of the red balloon. Find the volume of the blue balloon.
(b) The volume of a green balloon is 25% less than the volume of the red balloon. Find the volume of the green balloon.

Solution
(a) Volume of blue balloon = volume of red balloon + 20% of volume of red balloon
$= 400 + 20\% \times 400$
$= 400 + 80$
$= 480$
Volume of blue balloon is 480 cm³.

(b) Volume of green balloon = volume of red balloon − 25% of volume of red balloon
$= 400 - 25\% \times 400$
$= 400 - 100$
$= 300$
Volume of green balloon is 300 cm³.

9. A sample survey about a community issue is conducted and 1200 residents are interviewed. It is found that $\dfrac{7}{10}$ of the residents agree with the issue and the rest disagree with the issue. For those who agree, the fraction that are male is $\dfrac{5}{14}$. For those who disagree, the fraction that are male is $\dfrac{4}{9}$. Find
(a) the total number of residents who disagree with the issue in the survey,
(b) the number of male residents in the survey.

Solution

(a) The fraction who disagree

$$= 1 - \frac{7}{10} = \frac{3}{10}$$

Number of residents who disagree

$$= \frac{3}{10} \times 1200$$

$$= 360$$

(b) The number of residents who agree
$$= 1200 - 360 = 840$$

The number of males is

$$840 \times \frac{5}{14} + 360 \times \frac{4}{9}$$

$$= 60 \times 5 + 40 \times 4$$

$$= 300 + 160$$

$$= 460$$

The number of male residents in the survey is 460.

10. In a choir there are 60 girls, of which 24 have short hair and the others have long hair.

(a) Find the percentage of the girls in the choir who have long hair.

(b) $\frac{1}{4}$ of the girls who have short hair are sopranos.

There are equal numbers of girls with long hair and girls with short hair among the sopranos. Find out what fraction of the girls with long hair are sopranos.

Solution

(a) The percentage of girls in the choir with long hair

$$= \frac{60 - 24}{60}$$

$$= \frac{36}{60} \times 100\%$$

$$= 60\%$$

(b) Number of short-haired girls who are sopranos
$$= \frac{1}{4} \times 24 = 6$$

Number of long-haired sopranos = 6
Fraction of long-haired girls who are sopranos

$$= \frac{6}{36}$$

$$= \frac{1}{6}$$

11. The thickness of a sheet of glass A is $\frac{3}{8}$ cm.

The thickness of a sheet of glass B is 0.35 cm.

(a) Which sheet of glass is thicker? Give your reason.

(b) Find the total thickness of two sheets of glass A and three sheets of glass B. Express your answer in mm.

(c) The price of a sheet of glass A is £28 excluding VAT. The VAT on it is 20%. Find its price including VAT.

Solution

(a) $\frac{3}{8} = 3 \div 8$
$$= 0.375$$
The thickness of glass A is 0.375 cm.
Since 0.375 > 0.35, glass A is thicker.

(b) Total thickness
$$= (0.375 \times 2 + 0.35 \times 3) \text{cm}$$
$$= (0.75 + 1.05) \text{cm}$$
$$= 1.8 \text{cm}$$
$$= 1.8 \times 10 \text{mm}$$
$$= 18 \text{mm}$$

(c) Price including VAT
$$= £28 + £28 \times 20\%$$
$$= £28 + £5.60$$
$$= £33.60$$

12. The price of a dress is £250. A customer can pay using either of the following methods.

A. Pay cash and have a 4% discount on the price.

B. Pay by 12 monthly instalments and each payment is 10% of the price.

(a) How much does it cost if the customer pays in cash?

(b) What is the total payment if the customer pays in monthly instalments?

(c) Express the cost of paying by cash as a percentage of the total payment in **(b)**.

Solution

(a) Amount of discount
$$= 4\% \times £250$$
$$= £10$$
∴ the cost of paying the dress by cash
$$= £250 - £10$$
$$= £240$$

(b) Each monthly instalment
$$= 10\% \text{ of } £250$$
$$= £25$$
Hence, the total of 12 monthly instalments
$$= £25 \times 12$$
$$= £300$$

(c) The required percentage

$$= \frac{240}{300} \times 100\%$$

$$= 80\%$$

13. A rod is 75 cm long. Lengths of 4.5 cm are cut from it.

    (a) How many lengths can be cut?

    (b) What is the remaining length of the rod?

    (c) Express the remaining length as a fraction of the original length. Give your answer in its simplest form.

Solution

(a) $75 \div 4.5 = \dfrac{75}{4.5}$

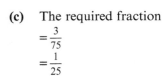

$$= \frac{75 \times 10}{4.5 \times 10}$$

$$= \frac{750}{45}$$

$$= \frac{750 \div 15}{45 \div 15}$$

$$= \frac{50}{3}$$

$$= 16 \frac{2}{3}$$

Hence, 16 complete lengths can be cut.

(b) Remaining length of the rod

$$= \frac{2}{3} \text{ of a short length}$$

$$= \frac{2}{3} \times 4.5$$

$$= \frac{2 \times 4.5}{3}$$

$$= \frac{9}{3}$$

$$= 3 \text{ cm}$$

(c) The required fraction

$$= \frac{3}{75}$$

$$= \frac{1}{25}$$

14. Alan's salary is 20% more than Bowen's. Bowen's salary is 15% less than Carol's. Bowen's monthly salary is £3060.

    (a) Find Alan's monthly salary.

    (b) Find Carol's monthly salary.

Solution

(a) Alan's monthly salary

    = Bowen's monthly salary

       + 20% of Bowen's monthly salary

    = £3060 + 20% × £3060

    = £3060 + £612

    = £3672

(b) Bowen's salary is 15% less than Carol's i.e. Bowen's salary is (100 − 15)% = 85% of Carol's salary

∴ 85% of Carol's salary = £3060

$$1\% \text{ of Carol's salary} = £\left(\frac{3060}{85}\right)$$

$$= £36$$

Hence, Carol's salary (100%) = £36 × 100

$$= £3600$$

15. A shop sells four types of juice: apple, mango, orange and watermelon juice. It sells 560 cups of juice in a day. $\frac{2}{7}$ of the cups are apple juice. 25% of the cups are mango juice.

    (a) Find the total number of cups of orange juice and watermelon juice sold.

    (b) The number of cups of orange juice sold is three times that of watermelon juice. Find the number of cups of watermelon juice sold.

Solution

(a) Total number of cups of orange and watermelon juice

$$= \left(1 - \frac{2}{7} - 25\%\right) \times 560$$

$$= \left(1 - \frac{2 \times 4}{7 \times 4} - \frac{1 \times 7}{4 \times 7}\right) \times 560$$

$$= \left(\frac{28 - 8 - 7}{28}\right) \times 560$$

$$= 13 \times 20$$

$$= 260$$

(b) For every 1 cup of watermelon juice sold, 3 cups of orange juice are sold, i.e. 1 out of a total of 4 sold is watermelon.

So the fraction of the cups sold which are watermelon $= \dfrac{1}{1+3} = \dfrac{1}{4}$.

The number of cups of watermelon juice sold is

$$= \frac{1}{4} \times 260$$

$$= 65$$

8 Angles, Parallel Lines and Triangles

Class Activity 1

Objective: To describe the features of points, lines, rays and line segments.

Task

Point, Line, Ray and Line Segment

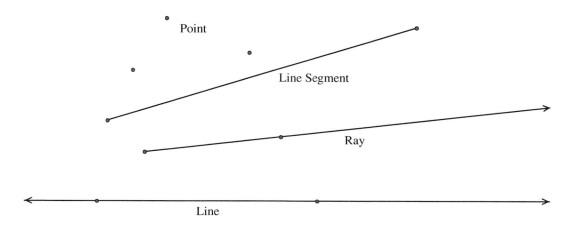

Using the following tools in your geometry software, create each of the geometric objects and hence describe what you see. (Your teacher will guide you on the use of each tool.)

Tool	Object	Observations
Point tool	Point	A point has position but no size.
Segment tool	Line Segment	A line segment has length with two end points.
Ray tool	Ray	A ray has length with one end point.
Line tool	Line	A line has length and no end points.

Questions

1. Based on your observations, describe the differences between a line, a line segment and a ray.

   A line consists of infinitely many points. A ray is a part of a line and has a fixed end point. A line segment is a part of a line with two fixed end

   points.

2. In this task, the points and the lines lie on a flat surface. What is the name of a flat surface in geometry?

   A flat surface in geometry is called a plane.

Class Activity 2

Objective: To investigate the properties of angles formed by two parallel lines and a transversal.

Tasks

Angles Formed by Two Parallel Lines and a Transversal

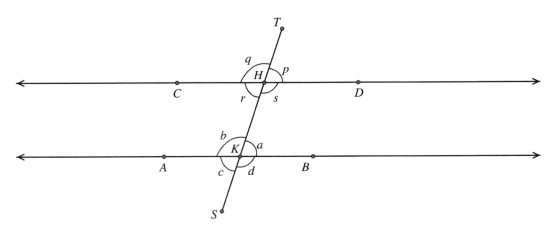

1. Draw a pair of parallel lines (lines *AB* and *CD*) and a transversal (line *ST*) using geometry software.

2. Measure the eight angles, $\angle a$, $\angle b$, $\angle c$, $\angle d$, $\angle p$, $\angle q$, $\angle r$ and $\angle s$ formed by the line *ST*, and the lines *AB* and *CD*.

3. Drag the points *T* and *B* around. Observe how the values of the angles change.

Questions

1. Observe and name a pair of corresponding angles between the parallel lines. What is the relationship between the corresponding angles?

   The pairs of corresponding angles are $\angle q$ and $\angle b$, $\angle r$ and $\angle c$, $\angle p$ and $\angle a$, $\angle s$ and $\angle d$. Corresponding angles are equal.

2. Observe and name a pair of alternate angles between the parallel lines. What is the relationship between the alternate angles?

   The pairs of alternate angles are $\angle s$ and $\angle b$, $\angle r$ and $\angle a$. Alternate angles are equal.

3. Observe and identify a pair of co-interior angles between the parallel lines. What can you say about the sum of the co-interior angles?

   The pairs of co-interior angles are $\angle r$ and $\angle b$, $\angle s$ and $\angle a$.

   The sum of each pair of co-interior angles is 180°.

Class Activity 3

Objective: To investigate the properties relating the sides and angles of a triangle.

Tasks

1. Use a ruler and a pair of compasses to construct these triangles where possible.
   - **(a)** $\triangle ABC$ with $AB = 6$ cm, $BC = 5$ cm and $CA = 3$ cm
   - **(b)** $\triangle DEF$ with $DE = 5$ cm, $EF = 2$ cm and $FD = 3$ cm
   - **(c)** $\triangle GHK$ with $GH = HK = 4$ cm and $KG = 7$ cm
   - **(d)** $\triangle PQR$ with $PQ = 7$ cm, $QR = 2$ cm and $RP = 4$ cm
   - **(e)** $\triangle XYZ$ with $XY = YZ = ZX = 5$ cm

2. Observe the properties of the triangles above in Task **1**. Copy and complete the table below. Part of **(a)** has been done for you.

(a)	$AB = 6$ cm	$AB + BC = 11$ cm	$AB + BC$ > CA
	$BC = 5$ cm	$BC + CA =$ 8 cm	$BC + CA$ > AB
	$CA = 3$ cm	$CA + AB =$ 9 cm	$CA + AB$ > BC
(b)	$DE = 5$ cm	$DE + EF =$ 7 cm	$DE + EF$ > FD
	$EF = 2$ cm	$EF + FD =$ 5 cm	$EF + FD$ = DE
	$FD = 3$ cm	$FD + DE =$ 8 cm	$FD + DE$ > EF
(c)	$GH = 4$ cm	$GH + HK =$ 8 cm	$GH + HK$ > KG
	$HK = 4$ cm	$HK + KG =$ 11 cm	$HK + KG$ > GH
	$KG = 7$ cm	$KG + GH =$ 11 cm	$KG + GH$ > HK
(d)	$PQ = 7$ cm	$PQ + QR =$ 9 cm	$PQ + QR$ > RP
	$QR = 2$ cm	$QR + RP =$ 6 cm	$QR + RP$ < PQ
	$RP = 4$ cm	$RP + PQ =$ 11 cm	$RP + PQ$ > QR
(e)	$XY = 5$ cm	$XY + YZ =$ 10 cm	$XY + YZ$ > ZX
	$YZ = 5$ cm	$YZ + ZX =$ 10 cm	$YZ + ZX$ > XY
	$ZX = 5$ cm	$ZX + XY =$ 10 cm	$ZX + XY$ > YZ

Questions

1. Identify the triangles that cannot be constructed in Task **1**. Use your own words to explain why you are having difficulty constructing them.

   DEF and PQR could not be constructed as triangles, because the length of the longest side is less than or equal to the sum of the lengths of the other

   two sides.

2. Identify the triangles that can be constructed in Task **1**. Describe a relationship between the sides of each triangle.

   Triangles ABC, GHK and XYZ can be constructed. For each of these, the sum of the lengths of two sides of the triangle is more than the length

   of the third side.

3. For each triangle that can be constructed in Task **1**, locate the longest side and the largest angle. What pattern do you notice?

The longest sides are *AB, KG* and any side of *XYZ*. The longest side is opposite the largest angle.

4. What can you say about the angles in an isosceles triangle?

The angles the two equal sides make with the third side (the 'base angles') are equal.

5. What can you say about the angles in an equilateral triangle?

All three angles of an equilateral triangle are equal. Since the angles of any triangle add up to 180°, each angle in an equilateral triangle is 60°.

Class Activity 4

Objective: To make connections between an exterior angle of a triangle and its interior angles.

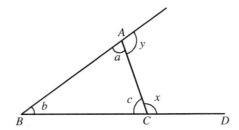

Questions
In the diagram above, $\angle x$ and $\angle y$ are exterior angles of $\triangle ABC$.
1. What is the sum of $\angle a$, $\angle b$ and $\angle c$? Give your reason.

$\angle a + \angle b + \angle c = 180°$ (Angles in a triangle add up to 180°.)

2. What is the sum of $\angle c$ and $\angle x$? Give your reason.

$\angle c + \angle x = 180°$ (Angles on a straight line add up to 180°.)

3. Derive the relationship between $\angle a$, $\angle b$ and $\angle x$ from the two results obtained above. Explain your answer.

$\angle x = 180° - \angle c$ (from 2)
$\angle x = 180° - (180° - \angle a - \angle b)$ (substituting for *c* from 1)
$\angle x = 180° - 180° + \angle a + \angle b$
$\angle x = \angle a + \angle b$

4. Similarly, what is the sum of $\angle a$ and $\angle y$? Derive the relationship between $\angle b$, $\angle c$ and $\angle y$.

$\angle a + \angle y = 180°$ (Angles on a straight line add up to 180°.)
$\angle y = 180° - \angle a$
$\angle a + \angle b + \angle c = 180°$ (Angles in a triangle add up to 180°.)
$\angle b + \angle c = 180° - \angle a$
So from the equation above,
$\angle b + \angle c = \angle y$
In other words, the exterior angle is equal to the sum of the interior opposite angles.

Try It!

Section 8.1

1. The figure shows four points A, B, C and D on a plane.
   (a) Draw the lines formed by these points. How many lines are there?
   (b) Name the line segments that can be formed by the points A, B and C.
   (c) Name three rays that can be formed by the points B, C and D.

Solution
(a) There are six lines.

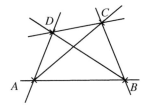

(b) The line segments that can be formed by the points A, B and C are AB, BC and CA.

(c) Rays BC, CB, CD, DC, DB and BD can be formed by points B, C and D.

Section 8.2

2. (a) Draw an angle of $95°$.
   (b) Measure the reflex angle formed by the arms of the $95°$ angle drawn.
   (c) Draw a reflex angle of $210°$.

Solution
(a) *Steps*
   1. Draw a line segment AB.

   2. Align the base line of a protractor with AB so the centre of the protractor is at B. Plot a point C at the $95°$ mark on the outer scale of the protractor.

   3. Draw the line segment BC. Then $\angle ABC = 95°$.

(b) Produce AB to a point D and measure $\angle DBC$ using the inner scale of a protractor. This gives $\angle DBC = 85°$.

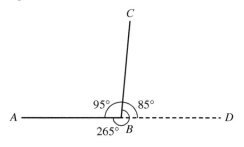

Hence, the reflex $\angle ABC = 180° + 85°$
$\qquad\qquad\qquad\qquad = 265°$

(c) $360° - 210° = 150°$
Draw an obtuse $\angle POQ$ of $150°$. Then reflex $\angle POQ = 210°$.

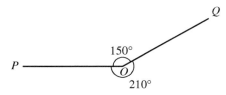

3. In the figure, XYZ is a straight line. Find the angle w.

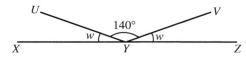

Solution
$w + 140° + w = 180°$ (Angles on a straight line add up to $180°$.)
$\qquad\qquad 2w = 180° - 140°$
$\qquad\qquad 2w = 40°$
$\qquad\qquad\ w = 20°$

4. Find the angle x in the figure.

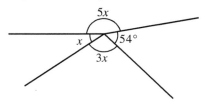

Solution
$5x + x + 3x + 54° = 360°$ (Angles at a point add up to $360°$.)
$\qquad\qquad 9x + 54° = 360°$
$\qquad\qquad\qquad 9x = 306°$
$\qquad\qquad\qquad\ x = 34°$

5. In the figure, *PS*, *QT* and *RU* are straight lines intersecting at *V*. Find the angle *z*.

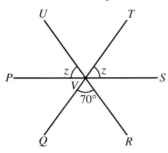

Solution

$$\angle UVT = 70°$$ (Vertically opposite angles are equal.)

$$z + \angle UVT + z = 180°$$ (Angles on a straight line add up to 180°.)

$$z + 70° + z = 180°$$

$$2z = 110°$$

$$z = 55°$$

Section 8.3

6. In the figure, *AB // CD*. Find the angles *p*, *q* and *r*.

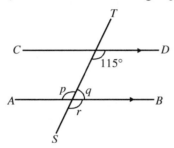

Solution

$$\angle p = 115°$$ (Alternate angles are equal, *AB // CD*.)

$$\angle q + 115° = 180°$$ (Co-interior angles add up to 180°, *AB // CD*.)

$$\angle q = 65°$$

$$\angle r = 115°$$ (Corresponding angles are equal, *AB // CD*.)

7. In the figure, *AB // DE* and *BC // EF*. *BHC* and *DHE* are straight lines. Find the angles *x* and *y*.

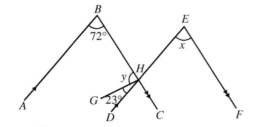

Solution

$$\angle DHC = \angle ABH$$ (Corresponding angles are equal, *AB // DE*.)

$$= 72°$$

$$\angle x = \angle DHC$$ (Corresponding angles are equal, *BC // EF*.)

$$= 72°$$

$$\angle ABH + \angle DHB = 180°$$ (Co-interior angles are equal, *AB // DE*.)

$$72° + \angle y + 23° = 180°$$

$$\angle y = 85°$$

8. In the figure, *BA // DE*. Find the angle *x*.

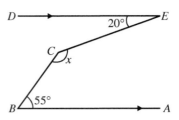

Solution

Construct a line *CF* with *F* between *E* and *A* such that *CF // BA // DE* and let $x_1 = \angle BCF$ and $x_2 = \angle ECF$ so $x = x_1 + x_2$.

$$x_1 = 180° - 55°$$ (Co-interior angles add up to 180°, *CF // BA*.)

$$= 125°$$

$$x_2 = 20°$$ (Alternate angles are equal, *CF // DE*.)

So $x = x_1 + x_2$

$$= 145°$$

Section 8.4

9. Find the unknown angle *x* in △*DEF*.

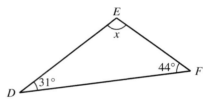

Solution

$$\angle x + 31° + 44° = 180°$$ (Angles in a triangle add up to 180°.)

$$\angle x = 180° - 31° - 44°$$

$$\angle x = 105°$$

10. In the figure, *AB = AC* and *DA // BC*. Find the angles *x*, *y* and *z*.

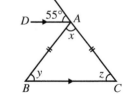

Solution

$$\angle z = \angle EAD$$ (Corresponding angles are equal *DA // BC*.)

$$= 55°$$

$$\angle y = \angle z$$ (Base angles of an isosceles triangle are equal.)

$$= 55°$$

$$\angle x + \angle y + \angle z = 180°$$ (Angles in a triangle add up to 180°.)

$$\angle x = 180° - \angle y - \angle z$$

$$= 180° - 55° - 55°$$

$$= 70°$$

Chapter 8 Angles, Parallel Lines and Triangles

11. In the figure, BCD is a straight line, $\triangle ABC$ is an equilateral triangle, $CE = DE$ and $\angle CED = 90°$. Find the angles x and y.

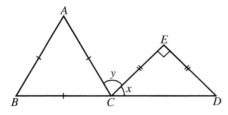

Solution

$$\angle CDE = \angle x \quad \text{(Base angles of an isosceles triangle are equal.)}$$
$$\angle x + \angle CDE + \angle CED = 180° \quad \text{(Angles in a triangle add up to 180°.)}$$
$$\angle x + \angle x + 90° = 180°$$
$$2\angle x = 90°$$
$$\angle x = 45° \quad \text{(Angles in an equilateral triangle are equal.)}$$
$$\angle ACB = 60°$$
$$\angle y + \angle x + \angle ACB = 180° \quad \text{(Angles on a straight line add up to 180°.)}$$
$$\angle y = 180° - \angle x - \angle ACB$$
$$= 180° - 45° - 60°$$
$$= 75°$$

12. In the figure, BCD is a straight line. Find $\angle ACD$.

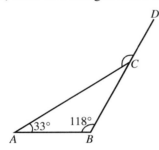

Solution

$$\angle ACD = 33° + 118° \quad \text{(An exterior angle of a triangle is equal to the sum of the interior opposite angles.)}$$
$$= 151°$$

13. In the figure, $ABCD$ is a straight line. $BE \parallel CF$. Find $\angle DCF$.

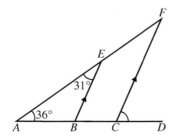

Solution

$$\angle EBD = \angle EAB + \angle AEB \quad \text{(An exterior angle of a triangle is equal to the sum of the interior opposite angles.)}$$
$$= 36° + 31°$$
$$= 67°$$
$$\angle FCD = \angle EBD \quad \text{(Corresponding angles are equal, } BE \parallel CF.\text{)}$$
$$= 67°$$

14. In the figure, ABC, CDE, AFD and BFE are straight lines. Find $\angle CAD$.

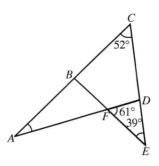

Solution

$$\angle CDA = 39° + 61° \quad \text{(An exterior angle of a triangle is equal to the sum of the interior opposite angles, triangle } DEF.\text{)}$$
$$\angle CDA = 100°$$

$$\angle CAD = 180° - 52° - 100° \quad \text{(Angles in a triangle add up to 180°, triangle } ACD.\text{)}$$
$$\angle CAD = 28°$$

Exercise 8.1

Level 1

1. In the figure, A and B are two points on a plane. How many lines can be drawn passing through
  (a) A,
  (b) both A and B?

Solution
  (a) Infinitely many   (b) 1

2. In the figure, C and D are two points on a plane. Copy the points and draw the ray CD, where C is the end point.

Solution

Level 2

3. In the figure, A, B and C are three points not on a straight line.
  (a) Name the straight lines that can be formed.
  (b) Name the rays with the end point A.

Solution
  (a) AB, BC and CA (b) AB and AC

4. In the figure, A, B and C are three points on a straight line.

    (a) Find the number of different line segments that can be formed by these points.

    (b) Find the number of different rays that can be formed by these points.

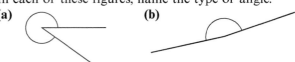

Solution

    (a) Three line segments can be formed. They are AB, BC and AC.

    (b) Four rays can be formed. They are $AB = AC$, BC, $CA = CB$ and BA.

Level 3
GCSE Grade **2**

5. In the figure, M is a point on the line segment PQ such that $PM = \frac{1}{2}PQ$. Show that $PM = MQ$.

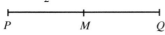

Solution
Line segment PQ is made up of line segments PM and MQ.

$PM + MQ = PQ$

$\frac{1}{2}PQ + MQ = PQ$

$\qquad MQ = PQ - \frac{1}{2}PQ$ Subtract $\frac{1}{2}PQ$.

$\qquad MQ = \frac{1}{2}PQ$ Replace $\frac{1}{2}PQ$ with PM.

$\qquad MQ = PM$ **(shown)**

6. The figure shows a line segment $ABCD$ in which $AB = CD$.

    (a) State the relationship between AC and BD.

    (b) Give the reason for the result in **(a)**.

Solution

    (a) $AC = BD$

    (b) $AB = CD$ (given)

$\qquad AB + BC = BC + CD$

$\qquad \therefore \quad AC = BD$

7. In the figure, AB and CD are two line segments, and AB is shorter than CD.

    (a) How many points are on the line segment
        (i) AB,   **(ii)** CD?

    (b) Is it true that there are more points on CD than on AB?

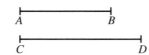

Solution

    (a)   **(i)** Infinitely many

         (ii) Infinitely many

    (b) May not be true

Exercise 8.2
Level 1   GCSE Grade **2⁺/3⁻**

1. In each of these figures, name the type of angle.

    (a)   **(b)**

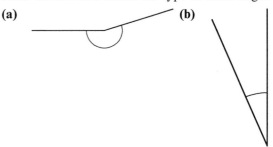

Solution

    (a) Reflex angle   **(b)** Obtuse angle

2. Using a protractor, measure each of these angles. State the size and name the type of each angle.

    (a)   **(b)**

Solution

    (a) First measure the obtuse angle. This measures $161°$. So the reflex angle required is
$360° - 161° = 199°$

    (b) Acute angle of $23°$

3. Use a protractor to draw these angles accurately. Then name the type of each angle.

    (a) $\angle ABC = 23°$ **(b)** $\angle PQR = 161°$

    (c) $\angle XYZ = 307°$ **(d)** $\angle MNO = 190°$

Solution

    (a) Acute angle of $23°$.

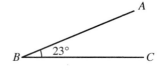

    (b) Obtuse angle of $161°$.

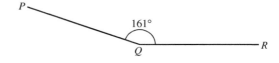

(c) Reflex angle of 307°.

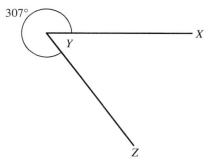

(d) Reflex angle of 190°.

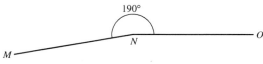

4. In each figure, AOB is a straight line. Find each unknown marked angle.

(a) 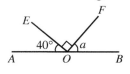 **(b)**

Solution

(a) $40° + 90° + \angle a = 180°$ (Angles on a straight line add up to 180°.)
$\angle a = 180° - 90° - 40°$
$= 50°$

(b) $61° + \angle b + 31° + 18° = 180°$ (Angles on a straight line add up to 180°.)
$\angle b = 180° - 61° - 31° - 18°$
$= 70°$

5. Find the unknown angle x in each figure.

(a) 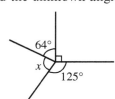 **(b)**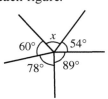

Solution

(a) $\angle x + 64° + 90° + 125° = 360°$ (Angles at a point add up to 360°.)
$\angle x = 81°$

(b) $\angle x + 54° + 89° + 78° + 60° = 360°$ (Angles at a point add up to 360°.)
$\angle x = 79°$

6. In each of these figures, the straight lines AB and CD intersect at a point. Find the unknown marked angles.

(a) 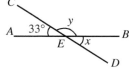 **(b)**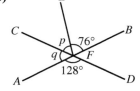

Solution

(a) $\angle x = 33°$ (Vertically opposite angles are equal.)
$33° + \angle y = 180°$ (Angles on a straight line add up to 180°.)
$\angle y = 147°$

(b) $\angle BFC = \angle AFD$ (Vertically opposite angles are equal.)
$\angle p + 76° = 128°$
$\angle p = 52°$
$\angle q + 128° = 180°$ (Angles on a straight line add up to 180°.)
$\angle q = 52°$

Level 2   GCSE Grade **3**

7. In the figure, ABC is a straight line.
   (a) Find the angle x.
   (b) What type of angle is $\angle ABD$?

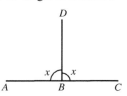

Solution

(a) $x + x = 180°$ (Angles on a straight line add up to 180°.)
$2x = 180°$
$x = 90°$

(b) $\angle ABD$ is a right angle.

8. In the figure, LMN is a straight line.
   (a) Find the angle y.
   (b) What type of angle is
       (i) $\angle PMN$,
       (ii) $\angle LMN$?

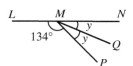

Solution

(a) $134° + y + y = 180°$ (Angles on a straight line add up to 180°.)
$2y = 46°$
$y = 23°$

(b) **(i)** $\angle PMN = 2y$
$= 46°$
$\angle PMN$ is an acute angle.
   (ii) $\angle LMN = 180°$
$\angle LMN$ is a straight angle.

9. In the figure, PQR is a straight line.
   (a) Find the angle x.
   (b) What type of angle is $\angle SQT$?

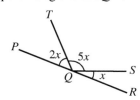

Solution

(a) $2x + 5x + x = 180°$ (Angles on a straight line add
$8x = 180°$ up to 180°.)
$x = 22.5°$

(b) $\angle SQT = 5 \times 22.5°$
$= 112.5°$
$\therefore \angle SQT$ is an obtuse angle.

10. Find the angle x in the figure.

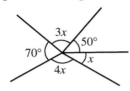

Solution

$x + 50° + 3x + 70° + 4x = 360°$ (Angles at a point add up
$8x = 240°$ to 360°.)
$x = 30°$

11. In each figure, three lines intersect at a point. Find the angle x.

(a)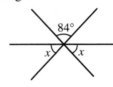

(b)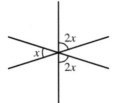

Solution

(a)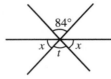

$t = 84°$ (Vertically opposite angles are equal.)
$x + t + x = 180°$ (Angles on a straight line add up to 180°.)
$2x + 84° = 180°$
$2x = 96°$
$x = 48°$

(b)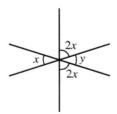

$y = x$ (Vertically opposite angles are equal.)
$2x + y + 2x = 180°$ (Angles on a straight line add
$5x = 180°$ up to 180°.)
$x = 36°$

12. In the figure, the lines AD, BE and CF intersect at the point G. Find the angles a, b and c.

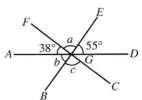

Solution

$38° + a + 55° = 180°$ (Angles on a straight line add up to 180°.)
$a = 87°$
$b = 55°$ (Vertically opposite angles are equal.)
$c = a$ (Vertically opposite angles are equal.)
$c = 87°$

Level 3   **GCSE Grade 3⁺/4⁻**

13. In the figure, what type of angle is
(a) $\angle a$,   **(b)** $\angle b$,
(c) $\angle c$,   **(d)** $\angle d$?

Solution

(a) Right angle

(b) Reflex angle

(c) Acute angle

(d) Obtuse angle

14. A circular pizza is divided into 10 equal pieces by five cuts through its centre as shown. Find $\angle x$.

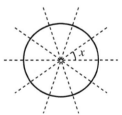

Solution

$\angle x = \frac{360°}{10}$
$\angle x = 36°$

15. To make the corner of a wooden frame, $ABCD$ and $EFGH$ are cut to form an angle x such that $\angle ABC + \angle FGH$ is a right angle. Find the value of x.

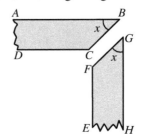

Solution

$\angle ABC + \angle FGH = 90°$

$x + x = 90°$

$2x = 90°$

$x = 45°$

16. The figure shows a logo. Find angle y.

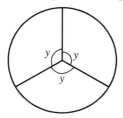

Solution

$3y = 360°$ (Angles at a point add up to 360°.)

$y = 120°$

17. The clock shows 4 o'clock. Find $\angle x$ and $\angle y$.

Solution

$\angle x = \dfrac{4}{12} \times 360°$

$= 120°$

$\angle y = \dfrac{8}{12} \times 360°$

$= 240°$

18. In the figure, AB is a plane mirror. A light ray PQ hits the mirror at Q and is reflected along QR such that $\angle AQP = \angle BQR = x$. If $\angle PQR = 110°$, find the angle x.

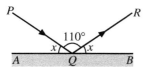

Solution

$x + 110° + x = 180°$ (Angles on a straight line add up to 180°.)

$2x = 70°$

$x = 35°$

19. The figure shows the outline of a pair of tongs. Find the angles x and y.

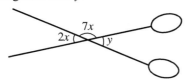

Solution

$2x + 7x = 180°$ (Angles on a straight line add up to 180°.)

$9x = 180°$

$x = 20°$

$y = 2x$ (Vertically opposite angles are equal.)

$y = 40°$

20. In the figure, ABC is a straight line. Write down

   (a) two acute angles,

   (b) two obtuse angles.

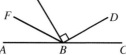

Solution

   (a) $\angle ABF$, $\angle FBE$, $\angle ABE$ and $\angle CBD$ are acute angles.

   (b) $\angle ABD$, $\angle FBD$, $\angle FBC$ and $\angle EBC$ are obtuse angles.

21. In the figure, AD, BE and CE are straight lines which intersect at G.

   (a) Find two pairs of possible angles x and y.

   (b) If y is three times x, find the angles x and y.

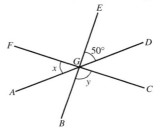

Solution

   (a) $\angle AGB = 50°$ (Vertically opposite angles are equal.)

      $x + y + 50° = 180°$ (Angles on a straight line add up to 180°.)

      $x + y = 130°$

      Possible values of x and y are: 60° and 70°, 50° and 80°, or any two numbers which add up to 130°.

   (b) Given $y = 3x$, from $x + y = 130°$

      $x + 3x = 130°$

      $x = \dfrac{130°}{4}$

      $= 32.5°$

      $y = 3 \times 32.5 = 97.5°$

      So $x = 32.5°$ and $y = 97.5°$.

Exercise 8.3

Level 1   **GCSE Grade 3**

1. Find the unknown marked angles in each figure.

   (a)   **(b)**

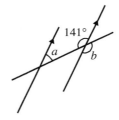
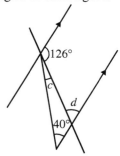

Solution

(a) $\angle a + 141° = 180°$ (Co-interior angles add up to 180°, // lines.)
$\angle a = 39°$
$\angle b = 141°$ (Vertically opposite angles are equal.)

(b) $\angle c + 126° + 40° = 180°$ (Co-interior angles add up to 180°, // lines.)
$\angle c = 14°$
$\angle d + 126° = 180°$ (Co-interior angles add up to 180°, // lines.)
$\angle d = 54°$

2. Find the unknown marked angles in each figure.

(a) 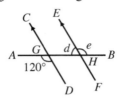 **(b)**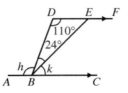

(c) 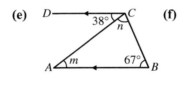 **(d)**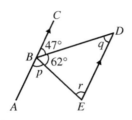

(e) 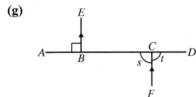 **(f)**

(g)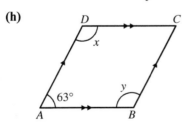

(h)

Solution

(a) $\angle a = 50°$ (Vertically opposite angles are equal.)
$\angle b = \angle a$ (Alternate angles are equal, *AB // CD*.)
$\therefore \ \angle b = 50°$
$\angle c + \angle a = 180°$ (Co-interior angles add up to 180°, *AB // CD*.)
$\angle c + 50° = 180°$
$\angle c = 130°$

(b) $\angle AHF = \angle AGD$ (Corresponding angles are equal, *DC // FE*.)
$= 120°$
$\angle d + \angle AHF = 180°$ (Angles on a straight line add up to 180°.)
$\angle d + 120° = 180°$
$\angle d = 60°$
$\angle e = \angle AHF$ (Vertically opposite angles are equal.)
$= 120°$

(c) $\angle f = 113°$ (Alternate angles are equal, *DE // CF*.)
$\angle g + \angle f = 180°$ (Angles on a straight line add up to 180°.)
$\angle g + 113° = 180°$
$\angle g = 67°$

(d) $\angle h = 110°$ (Alternate angles are equal, *AC // DF*.)
$\angle h + 24° + \angle k = 180°$ (Angles on a straight line add up to 180°.)
$110° + 24° + \angle k = 180°$
$\angle k = 46°$

(e) $\angle m = 38°$ (Alternate angles are equal, *BA // CD*.)
$\angle ABC + \angle BCD = 180°$ (Co-interior angles add up to 180°, *BA // CD*.)
$67° + 38° + \angle n = 180°$
$\angle n = 75°$

(f) $\angle p + 62° + 47° = 180°$ (Angles on a straight line add up to 180°.)
$\angle p = 71°$
$\angle q = 47°$ (Alternate angles are equal, *AC // ED*.)
$\angle r = \angle p$ (Alternate angles are equal, *AC // ED*.)
$\angle r = 71°$

(g) $\angle EBC = 90°$ (Angles on a straight line add up to 180°.)
$s = 90°$ (Alternate angles are equal, *BE // FC*.)
$t = 90°$ (Angles on a straight line add up to 180°.)

(h) $x = 180° - 63°$ (Co-interior angles add up to 180°, *DC // AB*.)
$x = 117°$
$y = 180° - 63°$ (Co-interior angles add up to 180°, *AD // BC*.)
$y = 117°$

Level 2   GCSE Grade **3⁺ / 4⁻**

3. Find the unknown angle x in each figure.

(a) 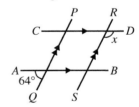 **(b)**

(c)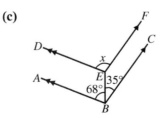

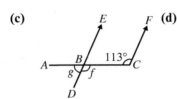

(d)

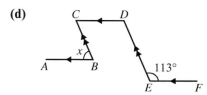

Solution

(a) $\angle GEF = \angle ABE$ (Corresponding angles are equal, *BA* // *EG*.)
    $= 75°$
    $\angle x = \angle GEF$ (Corresponding angles are equal, *EF* // *CD*.)
    $\angle x = 75°$

(b) Label $\angle y$ and $\angle z$ in the diagram.

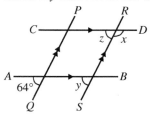

    $\angle y = 64°$ (Corresponding angles are equal, *QP* // *SR*.)
    $\angle z = \angle y$ (Corresponding angles are equal, *AB* // *CD*.)
    $\angle z = 64°$
    $\angle x + \angle z = 180°$ (Angles on a straight line add up to 180°.)
    $\angle x + 64° = 180°$
    $\angle x = 116°$

(c) $\angle BED = 180° - 68°$ (Co-interior angles add up to
    $= 112°$ 180°, *ED* // *BA*.)
    $\angle BEF = 180° - 35°$ (Co-interior angles add up to
    $= 145°$ 180°, *EF* // *BC*.)
    $x + \angle BED + \angle BEF = 360°$ (Angles at a point add
                    up to 360°.)
    $x = 360° - 112° - 145°$
    $x = 103°$

(d) $\angle CDE = 113°$ (Alternate angles are equal,
                    DC // *FE*.)
    $\angle BCD + \angle CDE = 180°$ (Co-interior angles add up
    $\angle BCD + 113° = 180°$ to 180°, *BC* // *ED*.)
    $\angle BCD = 67°$
    $\angle x = \angle BCD$ (Alternate angles are
    $\therefore \quad \angle x = 67°$ equal, *BA* // *DC*.)

4. Find the unknown angle y in each of these figures.

(a)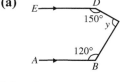

(b)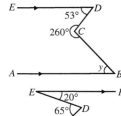

(c)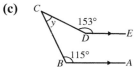

(d)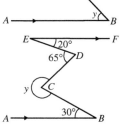

Solution

(a) Construct a line *FC* with *F* between *E* and *A*
    such that *FC* // *AB* // *ED* and let $y_1 = \angle BCF$
    and $y_2 = \angle DCF$ so $y = y_1 + y_2$.
    $y_1 = 180° - 120°$ (Co-interior angles add up to
    $= 60°$ 180°, *FC* // *AB*.)
    $y_2 = 180° - 150°$ (Co-interior angles add up to
    $= 30°$ 180°, *FC* // *DE*.)
    So $y = 60° + 30°$
    $= 90°$

(b) Construct a line *FC* with *F* between *D* and *B*
    such that *FC* // *AB* // *ED*.
    $\angle BCD = 360° - 260°$ (Angles at a point add up to 360°.)
    $= 100°$
    $\angle FCD = 53°$ (Alternate angles are equal, *ED* // *FC*.)
    $\angle BCF = \angle BCD - \angle FCD$
    $= 100° - 53°$
    $= 47°$
    $y = 47°$ (Alternate angles are equal, *AB* // *FC*.)

(c) Construct a line *CF* with *F* above *D* and *E*
    such that *CF* // *DE* // *BA*.
    $\angle BCF = 180° - 115°$ (Co-interior angles add
    $= 65°$ up to 180°, *CF* // *AB*.)
    $\angle DCF = 180° - 153°$ (Co-interior angles add
    $= 27°$ up to 180°, *CF* // *DE*.)
    $y = \angle BCD = \angle BCF - \angle DCF$
    $= 65° - 27°$
    $= 38°$

(d) Construct a line *CG* with *G* between *D* and *B*
    such that *CG* // *AB* // *EF*.
    Construct a line *HD* with *H* between *E* and *C*
    such that *HD* // *EF* // *AB* // *CG*.
    $\angle BCG = 30°$ (Alternate angles are equal, *AB* // *CG*.)
    $\angle EDH = 20°$ (Alternate angles are equal, *EF* // *HD*.)
    $\angle CDH = \angle CDE - \angle EDH$
    $= 65° - 20°$
    $= 45°$
    $\angle GCD = \angle CDH$ (Alternate angles are equal, *CG* // *HD*.)
    $= 45°$
    $y = 360° - \angle BCG - \angle GCD$ (Angles at a point
    $= 360° - 30° - 45°$ add up to 360°.)
    $= 285°$

5.

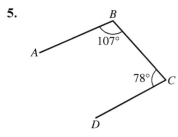

Alex claims that the lines *AB* and *DC* are parallel.
His friend, Anna, thinks that the lines are not
parallel. Who is correct? Explain your answer.

Solution

If AB and DC are parallel lines, the sum of the co-interior angles on the same side of the transversal is $180°$. Since $107° + 78° \neq 180°$, the lines AB and DC cannot be parallel. Anna is correct.

6. In the figure, $AB \parallel CD$ and $SEFT$ is a straight line. Find the angles x and y.

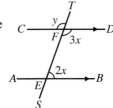

Solution

$$2x + 3x = 180° \quad \text{(Co-interior angles add up to } 180°, AB \parallel CD.)$$
$$5x = 180°$$
$$x = 36°$$
$$y = 3x \quad \text{(Vertically opposite angles are equal.)}$$
$$y = 108°$$

7. In the figure, $AC \parallel DE$ and BCD is a straight line. Find the angles x and y.

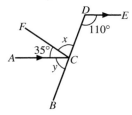

Solution

$$x + 35° = 110° \quad \text{(Alternate angles are equal, } AC \parallel DE.)$$
$$x = 75°$$
$$x + 35° + y = 180° \quad \text{(Angles on a straight line add up to } 180°.)$$
$$y = 180° - 110°$$
$$= 70°$$

Level 3   GCSE Grade **4⁻ / 4⁺**

8. In the figure, $ABCDE$ is the roof of a house. If $GB \parallel FD$ and $\angle ACE = 106°$, find the angles w, x, y and z.

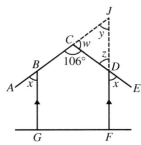

Solution

$$w + 106° = 180° \quad \text{(Angles on a straight line add up to } 180°.)$$
$$w = 180° - 106°$$
$$w = 74°$$
$$y = x \quad \text{(Corresponding angles are equal, } GB \parallel FD.)$$
$$z = x \quad \text{(Vertically opposite angles are equal.)}$$
$$x + x + 74° = 180° \quad \text{(Angles in a triangle add up to } 180°.)$$
$$2x = 106°$$
$$x = 53°$$
$$x = y = z = 53°$$

9. In a mechanical system, rods are joined together as shown in the figure. If $AB \parallel DC$ and $AD \parallel BC$, find $\angle ADY$.

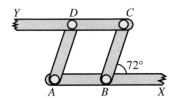

Solution

$$\angle BCD = 72° \quad \text{(Alternate angles are equal, } AX \parallel DC.)$$
$$\angle ADY = \angle BCD \quad \text{(Corresponding angles are equal, } AD \parallel BC.)$$
$$\therefore \quad \angle ADY = 72°$$

10. The figure shows two steps in which $BC \parallel DE$, $BA \parallel CD \parallel EF$ and $\angle ABC = 105°$. Find the angles x and y.

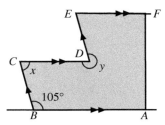

Solution

$$\angle x + 105° = 180° \quad \text{(Co-interior angles add up to } 180°, CD \parallel BA.)$$
$$\angle x = 180° - 105°$$
$$= 75°$$
$$\angle CDE = \angle x \quad \text{(Alternate angles are equal, } BC \parallel DE.)$$
$$= 75°$$
$$\angle y + \angle CDE = 360° \quad \text{(Angles at a point add up to } 360°.)$$
$$\angle y = 360° - \angle CDE$$
$$= 360° - 75°$$
$$= 285°$$

11. In the figure, a line PQ is drawn through the vertex A parallel to the side BC of $\triangle ABC$.
    (a) Which angle is equal to $\angle b$?
    (b) Which angle is equal to $\angle c$?
    (c) Find $\angle a + \angle p + \angle q$.
    (d) Find $\angle a + \angle b + \angle c$.
    (e) What can you conclude from the result in **(d)**?

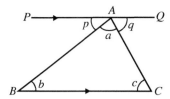

Solution
(a) $\angle p = \angle b$ (Alternate angles are equal, *PQ // BC*.)
(b) $\angle q = \angle c$ (Alternate angles are equal, *PQ // BC*.)
(c) $\angle a + \angle p + \angle q = 180°$ (Angles on a straight line add up to 180°.)
(d) $\angle a + \angle b + \angle c = \angle a + \angle p + \angle q$ (from **(a)** and **(b)**)
                $= 180°$
(e) Angles in a triangle sum to 180°.

12. Perform these tasks using geometry software.
    (a) Draw two parallel lines L_1 and L_2.
    (b) From a point A on the line L_1, draw a ray perpendicular to L_1 to cut the line L_2 at D.
    (c) From a point C on the line L_2, draw a ray perpendicular to L_2 to cut the line L_1 at B.
    (d) What can you say about the line segments AD and BC?

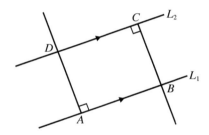

Solution
(a) to (c) Student's own drawing.
(d) AD and BC are parallel, e.g. $\angle L_1BC = 90°$
               (Alternate angles are equal, *AB // DC*.)

Exercise 8.4
Level 1   **GCSE Grade** $2^+/3$

1. Draw each of these triangles if possible and state the type of the triangle according to its sides. If it is not possible to draw the triangle, explain why.
    (a) $\triangle ABC$ with $AB = 7$ cm, $BC = 4$ cm and $CA = 5$ cm
    (b) $\triangle DEF$ with $DE = 6$ cm, $EF = 3$ cm and $FD = 2$ cm
    (c) $\triangle GHK$ with $GH = 4$ cm, $HK = 3$ cm and $KG = 4$ cm
    (d) $\triangle LMN$ with $LM = 4$ cm, $MN = 4$ cm and $NL = 4$ cm
    (e) $\triangle XYZ$ with $XY = 5$ cm, $YZ = 12$ cm and $ZX = 7$ cm

Solution
(a) $\triangle ABC$ is a scalene triangle.

(b) $EF + FD = 3 + 2$
             $= 5$ cm
    $DE = 6$ cm
    Since $EF + FD < DE$, it is not possible to draw $\triangle DEF$.

(c) $\triangle GHK$ is an isosceles triangle.

(d) $\triangle LMN$ is an equilateral triangle.

(e) $XY + ZX = 7 + 5$
              $= 12$ cm
    Since $XY + ZX = YZ$, it is not possible to draw $\triangle XYZ$. The result would be a straight line.

2. State the biggest angle in each of these triangles.
    (a) $\triangle ABC$ with $AB = 7$ cm, $BC = 10$ cm and $CA = 6$ cm
    (b) $\triangle PQR$ with $PQ = 5$ cm, $QR = 5$ cm and $PR = 7$ cm

Solution
(a) $\angle BAC$ (b) $\angle PQR$

3. (a) Draw an isosceles right-angled triangle ABC with $AC = BC = 3$ cm and $\angle ACB = 90°$.
    (b) Find $\angle ABC$.

Solution
(a)

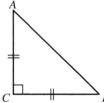

(b) $\angle ABC = \angle BAC$ (Base angles of an isosceles triangle are equal.)
    $\angle ABC + \angle BAC + 90° = 180°$ (Angles in a triangle add up to 180°.)
    $\angle ABC + \angle ABC = 90°$
           $2\angle ABC = 90°$
            $\angle ABC = 45°$

4. Find the unknown angle x in each figure.
    (a)   (b)

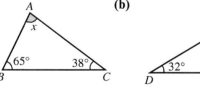

    (c)   (d)

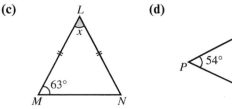

Solution

(a) $\angle x + 65° + 38° = 180°$ (Angles in a triangle add up to 180°.)
$\angle x = 77°$

(b) $\angle x + 35° + 32° = 180°$ (Angles in a triangle add up to 180°.)
$\angle x = 113°$

(c)
$\angle LNM = 63°$ (Base angles of an isosceles triangle are equal.)
$\angle x + 63° + \angle LNM = 180°$ (Angles in a triangle add
$\angle x + 63° + 63° = 180°$ up to 180°.)
$\angle x = 54°$

(d)
$\angle PRQ = \angle x$ (Base angles of an isosceles triangle are equal.)
$54° + \angle x + \angle PRQ = 180°$ (Angles in a triangle
$54° + \angle x + \angle x = 180°$ add up to 180°.)
$2\angle x = 126°$
$\angle x = 63°$

5. Find the unknown angle y in each figure.

(a)
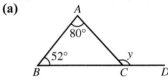

(b)
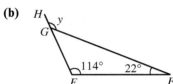

(c)
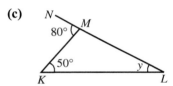

(d)
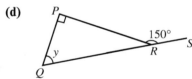

Solution

(a) $\angle y = 52° + 80°$ (An exterior angle of a triangle is equal to
$= 132°$ the sum of the interior opposite angles.)

(b) $\angle y = 114° + 22°$ (An exterior angle of a triangle is equal to
$= 136°$ the sum of the interior opposite angles.)

(c) $\angle y + 50° = 80°$ (An exterior angle of a triangle is equal to
$\angle y = 30°$ the sum of the interior opposite angles.)

(d) $\angle y + 90° = 150°$ (An exterior angle of a triangle is equal to
$\angle y = 60°$ the sum of the interior opposite angles.)

6. Find the unknown angles x and y in each figure.

(a)   **(b)**
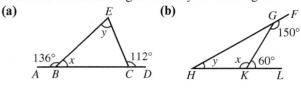

(c)   **(d)**
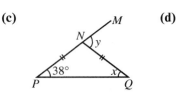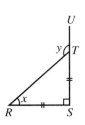

Solution

(a) $\angle x + 136° = 180°$ (Angles on a straight line
$\angle x = 180° - 136°$ add up to 180°.)
$= 44°$
$\angle x + \angle y = 112°$ (An exterior angle of a triangle is equal to
$44° + \angle y = 112°$ the sum of the interior opposite angles.)
$\angle y = 68°$

(b) $\angle x + 60° = 180°$ (Angles on a straight line
$\angle x = 180° - 60°$ add up to 180°.)
$= 120°$
$\angle x + \angle y = 150°$ (An exterior angle of a triangle is
$120° + \angle y = 150°$ equal to the sum of the interior
$\angle y = 30°$ opposite angles.)

(c) $\angle x = 38°$ (Base angles of an isosceles triangle are equal.)
$\angle y = 38° + \angle x$ (An exterior angle of a triangle is equal to
$= 38° + 38°$ the sum of the interior opposite angles.)
$= 76°$

(d)
$\angle RTS = \angle x$ (Base angles of an isosceles triangle are equal.)
$\angle RTS + \angle x + 90° = 180°$ (Angles in a triangle add
$\angle x + \angle x + 90 = 180°$ up to 180°.)
$2\angle x = 90°$
$\angle x = 45°$
$\angle y = \angle x + 90°$ (An exterior angle
$= 45° + 90°$ of a triangle is
$= 135°$ equal to the sum of the interior opposite angles.)

Level 2   **GCSE Grade 3 / 3⁺**

7. Find the unknown angle x in each figure.

(a)
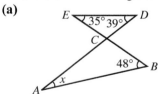

(b)
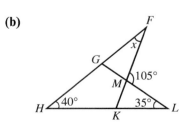

(c)

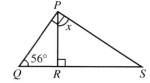

Solution

(a) In $\triangle CDE$,
$\angle BCD = 35° + 39°$ (An exterior angle of a triangle is
$= 74°$ equal to the sum of the interior
In $\triangle ABC$,   opposite angles.)
$\angle x + 48° = \angle BCD$ (An exterior angle of a triangle is
$\angle x + 48° = 74°$ equal to the sum of the interior
$\angle x = 26°$ opposite angles.)

(b) In $\triangle HLG$,
$\angle FGM = 40° + 35°$ (An exterior angle of a triangle is
$= 75°$ equal to the sum of the interior
In $\triangle FGM$,   opposite angles.)
$\angle x + \angle FGM = 105°$ (An exterior angle of a triangle is
$\angle x + 75° = 105°$ equal to the sum of the interior
$\angle x = 30°$ opposite angles.)

(c) In $\triangle PQS$,
$56° + 90° + \angle PSQ = 180°$ (Angles in a triangle
$\angle PSQ = 34°$ add up to 180°.)
In $\triangle PRS$,
$\angle x + 90° + \angle PSR = 180°$ (Angles in a triangle
$\angle PSR = \angle PSQ$ add up to 180°.)
$\angle x + 90° + 34° = 180°$
$\angle x = 56°$

8. Find the unknown angles x and y in each figure.

(a)

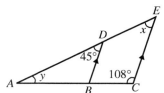

(b)

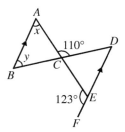

(c)

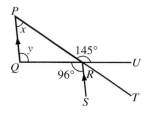

(d)

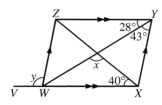

Solution

(a) In $\triangle EAC$,
$\angle x = 45°$ (Corresponding angles are
   equal, *BD // CE*.)
$\angle x + \angle y + 108° = 180°$ (Angles in a triangle add up
$45° + \angle y + 108° = 180°$ to 180°.)
$\angle y = 27°$

(b) In $\triangle ABC$,
$\angle x + 123° = 180°$ (Co-interior angles add up to
$\angle x = 57°$ 180°, *BA // FD*.)
$\angle x + \angle y = 110°$ (An exterior angle of a triangle is
$57° + \angle y = 110°$ equal to the sum of the interior
$\angle y = 53°$ opposite angles.)

(c) $\angle y = 96°$ (Alternate angles are equal, *SR // QP*.)
$\angle x + \angle y = 145°$ (An exterior angle of a triangle is
$\angle x = 145° - 96°$ equal to the sum of the interior
$= 49°$ opposite angles.)

(d) $28° + 43° + 40° + \angle YXZ = 180°$ (Co-interior angles add
$\angle YXZ = 69°$ up to 180°, *WX // ZY*.)
$\angle y = 40° + 69°$ (Corresponding angles are
$= 109°$ equal, *WZ // XY*.)
$\angle x + 40° = \angle y$ (An exterior angle of a triangle
$\angle x = 109° - 40°$ is equal to the sum of the
$= 69°$ interior opposite angles.)

Level 3   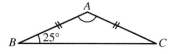 **GCSE Grade 4⁻/4**

9. The figure shows a section of a roof in which
$AB = AC$ and $\angle ABC = 25°$. Find $\angle BAC$.

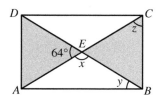

Solution
$\angle ACB = \angle ABC$ (Base angles of an isosceles triangle are equal.)
$= 25°$
$\angle BAC + 25° + 25° = 180°$ (Angles in a triangle add up to 180°.)
$\angle BAC = 180° - 25° - 25°$
$= 130°$

10. The figure shows a rectangular flag. AC and BD
intersect at E such that $AE = BE = CE = DE$. If
$\angle AED = 64°$, find the angles x, y and z.

269

Solution

$\angle x + 64° = 180°$ (Angles on a straight line add up to 180°.)

$\angle x = 180° - 64°$

$= 116°$

In $\triangle EAB$, $AE = BE$ (given)

$\angle EAB = \angle y$ (Base angles of an isosceles triangle are equal.)

$\angle EAB + \angle EBA = 64°$ (An exterior angle of a triangle is equal to the sum of the interior opposite angles.)

$\angle y + \angle y = 64°$

$2\angle y = 64°$

$\angle y = 32°$

In $\triangle EBC$, $BE = CE$ (given)

$\angle EBC = \angle z$ (Base angles of an isosceles triangle are equal.)

$\angle EBC + \angle ECB = \angle x$ (An exterior angle of a triangle is equal to the sum of the interior opposite angles.)

$\angle z + \angle z = 116°$

$2\angle z = 116°$

$\angle z = 58°$

11. In the figure, AC and BC are two equal legs of a pair of compasses. If $\angle ACB = x$ and $\angle CAB = 2x$, find the value of x.

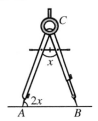

Solution

Given $AC = BC$, $\angle CBA = 2x$ (Base angles of an isosceles triangle are equal.)

$2x + 2x + x = 180°$ (Angles in a triangle add up to 180°.)

$5x = 180°$

$x = 36°$

12. The figure shows a simple device in which AMB is a straight rod and CM is a rod pivoted at M with $AM = BM = CM$.

(a) Find $\angle ACB$ in each of these different cases.

(i) $\angle CAM = 60°$

(ii) $\angle AMC = 36°$

(iii) $\angle BMC = 100°$

(b) What can you generalise from the results in (a)?

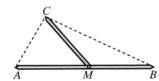

Solution

(a) (i) Label $\angle x$, $\angle y$, $\angle z$ and $\angle t$ in the diagram.

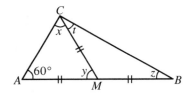

When $\angle CAM = 60°$,   (Base angles of an isosceles triangle are equal.)

$\angle x = 60°$

$\angle y + \angle x + 60° = 180°$ (Angles in a triangle add up to 180°.)

$\angle y + 60° + 60° = 180°$

$\angle y = 60°$ (Base angles of an isosceles triangle are equal.)

$\angle t = \angle z$

$\angle t + \angle z = \angle y$ (An exterior angle of a triangle is equal to the sum of the interior opposite angles.)

$\angle t + \angle t = 60°$

$\angle t = 30°$

$\therefore \angle ACB = \angle x + \angle t$

$= 60° + 30°$

$= 90°$

(ii) Label $\angle p$, $\angle q$, $\angle r$ and $\angle s$ in the diagram.

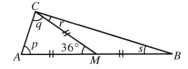

When $\angle AMC = 36°$,   (Base angles of an isosceles triangle are equal.)

$\angle p = \angle q$

$\angle p + \angle q + 36° = 180°$ (Angles in a triangle add up to 180°.)

$\angle q + \angle q + 36° = 180°$

$\angle q = 72°$ (Base angles of an isosceles triangle are equal.)

$\angle r = \angle s$

$\angle r + \angle s = 36°$ (An exterior angle of a triangle is equal to the sum of the interior opposite angles.)

$\angle r + \angle r = 36°$

$\angle r = 18°$

$\angle ACB = \angle q + \angle r$

$= 72° + 18°$

$= 90°$

(iii) Label $\angle a$, $\angle b$, $\angle c$ and $\angle d$ in the diagram.

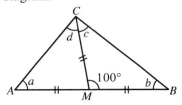

When $\angle BMC = 100°$, along the same line of reasoning in (i) and (ii),

$\angle d = \frac{1}{2} \times 100°$

$= 50°$

$\angle c = \frac{1}{2} \times (180° - 100°)$

$= 40°$

$\therefore \angle ACB = \angle c + \angle d$

$= 40° + 50°$

$= 90°$

(b) $\angle ACB$ is always 90°.

13. In the figure, *BA // CD*, *BE* is the angle bisector of ∠*ABC*, and *CE* is the angle bisector of ∠*BCD*.
   (a) Construct the figure using geometry software.
   (b) Measure ∠*BEC* and write down the result.
   (c) Drag the points *B* and *C* around. What do you observe?
   (d) Derive the size of ∠*BEC* by reasoning.
   Hint: An angle bisector is a line which divides an angle into two equal angles.

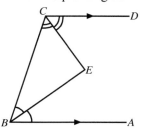

Solution
   (a) Student's own drawing
   (b) ∠*BEC* = 90°
   (c) The angle does not change.
   (d) Because *BE* and *CE* divide the angles equally you are given
   ∠*ABE* = ∠*EBC* and ∠*BCE* = ∠*ECD*
   and ∠*EBC* + ∠*ABE* + ∠*BCE* + ∠*ECD* = 180°
   (Co-interior angles add up to 180°, *BA // CD*.)
   So 2∠*EBC* + 2∠*BCE* = 180°
   ∠*EBC* + ∠*BCE* = 90°
   But ∠*BEC* + (∠*EBC* + ∠*BCE*) = 180°
   (Angles in a triangle add up to 180°, triangle *EBC*.)
   So ∠*BEC* + 90° = 180°
   ∠*BEC* = 90°

14. In △*ABC*, ∠*BAC* = 65° and *BI* and *CI* are the angle bisectors of ∠*ABC* and ∠*ACB* respectively.
   (a) Construct △*ABC* using geometry software.
   (b) Measure ∠*BIC* and write down your answer.
   (c) Drag the point *B* or the point *C* to vary its position while keeping ∠*BAC* = 65°. What do you observe?
   (d) Derive the size of ∠*BIC* by reasoning.

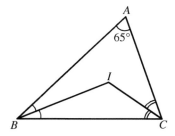

   (a) Student's own drawing
   (b) ∠*BIC* = 122.5°
   (c) ∠*BIC* does not change.

   (d) ∠*ABC* + ∠*ACB* = 180° − 65° (Angles in a triangle
   ∠*ABC* + ∠*ACB* = 115°   add up to 180°, triangle *ACB*.)

   $\frac{1}{2}$∠*ABC* + $\frac{1}{2}$∠*ACB* = $\frac{115°}{2}$

   (Since *IB* and *IC* bisect the angles.)
   ∠*IBC* + ∠*ICB* = 57.5°
   Also ∠*IBC* + ∠*ICB* = 180° − ∠*BIC* (Angles in a
   57.5° = 180° − ∠*BIC*   triangle add
   ∠*BIC* = 180° − 57.5°   up to 180°,
   = 122.5°   triangle *ICB*.)

Revision Exercise 8

1. Find the angle *x* in each of these figures.
   (a) *ABC* is a straight line.

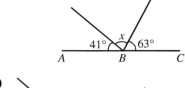

   (b)

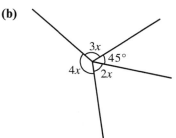

Solution
   (a) 41° + *x* + 63° = 180°   (Angles on a straight line
   x = 76°   add up to 180°.)

   (b) 3*x* + 4*x* + 2*x* + 45° = 360°   (Angles at a point add up
   9*x* + 45° = 360°   to 360°.)
   9*x* = 315°
   x = 35°

2. Find the angles *x* and *y* in each of these figures.
   (a) *AOB* and *COD* are straight lines.

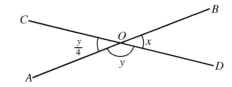

   (b) *AD // BC*, *DC // AB* and *ABE* is a straight line.

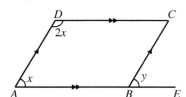

Solution

(a) $\frac{y}{4} = x$ (Vertically opposite angles are equal.)

$y = 4x$

$x + y = 180°$ (Angles on a straight line add up to 180°.)

$x + 4x = 180°$

$5x = 180°$

$x = 36°$

$y = 144°$

(b) $x = y$ (Corresponding angles are equal, *AD // BC*.)

$2x + x = 180°$ (Co-interior angles add up to 180°, *AB // DC*.)

$3x = 180°$

$x = 60°$

$y = 60°$

3. In the figure, a squash ball hits a vertical wall *HK* along the path *AB* and rebounds along the path *BC*. It is given that $\angle ABC = 56°$. Find the angle *y*.

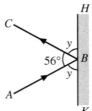

Solution

$56° + 2y = 180°$ (Angles on a straight line add up to 180°.)

$2y = 124°$

$y = 62°$

4. A piece of wire is bent into the shape shown in the figure. If $\angle ABC = 110°$, find $\angle x$ and $\angle y$.

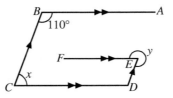

Solution

$\angle x + 110° = 180°$ (Co-interior angles add up to 180°,

$\angle x = 70°$ *BA // CD*.)

$\angle x + \angle EDC = 180°$ (Co-interior angles add up to 180°,

$70° + \angle EDC = 180°$ *CB // DE*.)

$\angle EDC = 110°$

$\angle EDC + \angle DEF = 180°$ (Co-interior angles add up to 180°,

$110° + \angle DEF = 180°$ *CD // FE*.)

$\angle DEF = 70°$

$\angle DEF + \angle y = 360°$ (Angles at a point add up to 360°.)

$70° + \angle y = 360°$

$\angle y = 360° - 70°$

$\angle y = 290°$

5. It is given that $AB = 7\,cm$, $BC = 2\,cm$, $CA = 4\,cm$, $PQ = 5\,cm$, $QR = 6\,cm$ and $RP = 4\,cm$.

(a) Determine which triangle, $\triangle ABC$ or $\triangle PQR$, can be constructed.

(b) Draw the triangle.

(c) State the biggest angle of the triangle.

Solution

(a) $BC + CA = 6\,cm;\ AB = 7\,cm$

$BC + CA < AB$

Hence *ABC* cannot be constructed as a triangle.

$PQ + RP = 9\,cm;\ QR = 6\,cm$

$PQ + RP > QR$

Since the sum of the two shortest sides is greater than the third side, the sum of any two sides will be greater than the third side. Hence, *PQR* can be drawn as a triangle.

(b) Student's own drawing

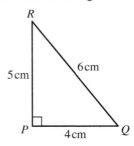

(c) The biggest angle is at *P*, opposite the longest side.

6. Find the angles *x* and *y* in these figures.

(a)

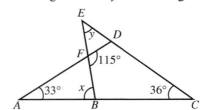

(b)

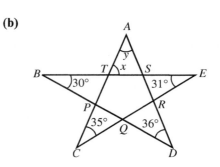

Solution

(a) $33° + \angle x = 115°$ (An exterior angle of a triangle is

$\angle x = 115° - 33°$ equal to the sum of the interior

$= 82°$ opposite angles, triangle *FBA*.)

Considering triangle *ECB*, an exterior angle of a triangle is equal to the sum of the interior opposite angles.

$\angle y + 36° = 82°$

$\angle y = 82° - 36°$

$= 46°$

(b) $\angle x = 31° + 35°$
            $= 66°$
$\angle AST = 30° + 36°$
$\angle AST = 66°$

(An exterior angle of a triangle is equal to the sum of the interior opposite angles, triangle *TEC*.)
(An exterior angle of a triangle is equal to the sum of the interior opposite angles, triangle *SDB*.)

$\angle y = 180 - \angle x - \angle AST$
$\angle y = 180° - 66° - 66°$
$= 48°$

(Angles in a triangle add up to 180°, triangle *AST*.)

7. Find the angle x in the figure.

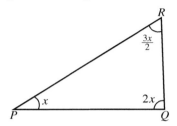

Solution

$\angle x + 2\angle x + \dfrac{3\angle x}{2} = 180°$ (Angles in a triangle add up to 180°.)

$\dfrac{9}{2}\angle x = 180°$

$\angle x = 40°$

8. Find the angle x in the figure.

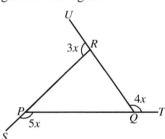

Solution

$\angle PRQ = 180° - 3\angle x$ (Angles on a straight line add up to 180°.)
$\angle RQP = 180° - 4\angle x$ (Angles on a straight line add up to 180°.)
$5\angle x = 180° - 3\angle x + 180° - 4\angle x$ (An exterior angle of
$12\angle x = 360°$ a triangle is equal to
$\angle x = 30°$ the sum of the interior
                                                    opposite angles.)

9. Find the angle x in each of these figures.

(a)

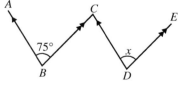

(b)

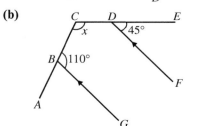

Solution

(a) $\angle BCD = 75°$ (Alternate angles are equal, *BA // DC*.)
          $x = \angle BCD$ (Alternate angles are equal, *BC // DE*.)
          $\therefore$ $x = 75°$

(b)   Extend lines AC and FD to meet at point H.
          $\angle CHD = 180° - 110°$ (Co-interior angles add up
          $= 70°$ to 180°, *GB // FD*.)
          $\angle HDC = 45°$ (Vertically opposite angles are equal.)
          $\angle x = \angle CHD + \angle HDC$ (An exterior angle of a
          $= 70° + 45°$ triangle is equal to the sum
          $= 115°$ of the interior opposite
                                                  angles, triangle *HDC*.)

10. Find the angles p and q in the figure.

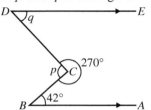

Solution

$\angle p = 360° - 270°$ (Angles at a point add up to 360°.)
$= 90°$

Extend line DC to intersect AB at F.

$\angle CFB = \angle q$ (Alternate angles are equal, *DE // BA*.)
$\angle p = 42° + \angle q$ (An exterior angle of a triangle is equal
$90° = 42° + \angle q$ to the sum of the interior opposite
$\angle q = 48°$ angles, triangle CFB.)

11. In the figure, *ACE*, *BCF* and *DCG* are straight lines and *AB // HC*. Find the angles p, q, r and s.

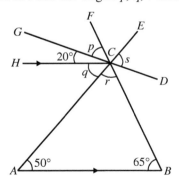

Solution

$\angle q = 50°$ (Alternate angles are equal, *HC // AB*.)
$\angle r = 180° - 50° - 65°$ (Angles in a triangle
$= 65°$ add up to 180°.)
$\angle p + 20° + 50° + 65° = 180°$ (Angles on a straight line
                                       add up to 180°, line *FB*.)
$\angle p = 45°$

$\angle BCD = 45°$ (Vertically opposite angles are equal.)
$\angle s + 45° + 65° = 180°$ (Angles on a straight line
$\angle s = 70°$ add up to 180°, line *EA*.)

12. In the figure, ABC is a straight line, $\angle ABD = 150°$,

GCSE
Grade
4⁻

$\angle CBE = 70°$, $AE \,/\!/\, BD$ and $BE \,/\!/\, CD$.
(a) Find $\angle x$, $\angle y$ and $\angle z$.
(b) Name an exterior angle of $\triangle ABE$.

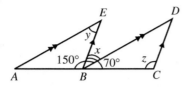

Solution
(a) $\qquad \angle ABE + \angle CBE = 180°$ (Angles on a straight line
$\qquad (150° - \angle x) + 70° = 180°$ add up to $180°$.)
$\qquad\qquad\qquad \angle x = 40°$
$\qquad\qquad\qquad \angle y = \angle x$ (Alternate angles are
$\qquad\qquad\qquad \angle y = 40°$ equal, $AE \,/\!/\, BD$.)
$\qquad\qquad \angle z + 70° = 180°$ (Co-interior angles add
$\qquad\qquad\qquad \angle z = 110°$ up to $180°$, $BE \,/\!/\, CD$.)

(b) $\angle EBC$

Class Activity 1

Objective: To explore the relationship between the shape and size of an object and its image under a translation.

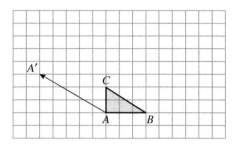

1. Use geometry software to draw a triangle ABC on a grid.

2. Create a directed line segment, AA'.

3. Use the translation command to translate triangle ABC in the distance and direction of AA'.

4. Observe the object triangle ABC and the image triangle $A'B'C'$.

5. Vary the shape of triangle ABC and observe the change in triangle $A'B'C'$.

6. Vary the directed line segment AA' and observe the change in triangle $A'B'C'$.

7. In a translation, what can you say about the relationship between
   (a) the orientation of the object and the image,
   (b) the shape and size of the object and the image?

   In a translation,
   (a) the image has the same orientation as the object,
   (b) the image has the same shape and size as the object.

Class Activity 2

Objective: To explore the relationship between the shape and size of an object and its image after a reflection.

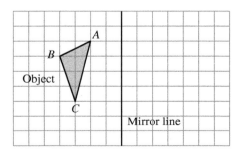

1. Use geometry software to draw a triangle ABC on a grid.

2. Draw a line as the mirror line.

3. Use the reflection command to reflect triangle *ABC* in the mirror line.

4. Observe the object triangle *ABC* and the image triangle *A′B′C′*.

5. Vary the shape of triangle *ABC* and observe the change in triangle *A′B′C′*.

6. Move the mirror line and observe the change in triangle *A′B′C′*.

7. In a reflection, what can you say about the relationship between
   (a) the orientation of the object and the image,
   (b) the shape and size of the object and the image?

   In a reflection,
   (a) the orientation of the image is a flip of the object in the mirror line,
   (b) the image has the same shape and size as the object.

Class Activity 3

Objective: To explore the relationship between the shape and size of an object and its image after a rotation.

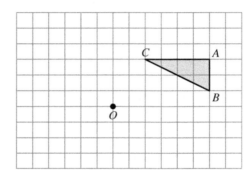

1. Use geometry software to draw a triangle *ABC* on a grid.

2. Mark a point *O* outside the triangle.

3. Taking *O* as the centre of rotation, rotate triangle *ABC* through an angle of
   (a)   90° anticlockwise,   **(b)**   120° anticlockwise,
   (c)   180° anticlockwise,   **(d)**   270° anticlockwise,
   (e)   90° clockwise,   **(f)**   180° clockwise,
   (g)   240° clockwise,   **(h)**   270° clockwise.

4. Move the point *O* so that it is inside the triangle and repeat the rotations in Step 3.

5. Move the point *O* to be a point on the side *AB* and repeat the rotations in Step 3.

6. Move the point *O* to the point *C* and repeat the rotations in Step 3.

7. Which pairs of rotations in Step 3 give the same image? Explain why.

   Angles at a point add up to 360°, so a 180° anticlockwise rotation and a 180° clockwise rotation will give the same image.

   Similarly, a 90° anticlockwise rotation and a 270° clockwise rotation will give the same image.

   A 120° anticlockwise rotation and a 240° clockwise rotation will give the same image.

   A 270° anticlockwise rotation and a 90° clockwise rotation will give the same image.

8. In a rotation, what can you say about the relationship between
   (a) the orientation of the object and the image,
   (b) the shape and size of the object and the image?

   In a rotation,
   (a) the image may have an orientation different from the object,
   (b) the image has the same shape and size as the object.

Class Activity 4

Objective: To examine whether two given figures are congruent by checking if one figure can be obtained from the other by a sequence of translations, rotations and reflections.

Tasks

1. **(a)** Create a triangle ABC, a line MN and a point P using geometry software.

   (b) Reflect $\triangle ABC$ in the line MN and then rotate the image through a certain angle about the point P to get the image $\triangle A'B'C'$.

   (c) What do you observe about $\triangle ABC$ and $\triangle A'B'C'$? What can you say about the shape and size of these two triangles? Explain your answer.

   The shape and size of $\triangle ABC$ and $\triangle A'B'C'$ are the same. $\triangle A'B'C'$ is obtained by reflecting

   and rotating $\triangle ABC$, thus there is no change in its shape and size.

   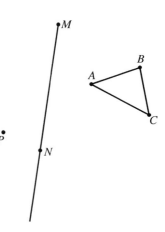

   (d) What can you conclude about $\triangle ABC$ and $\triangle A'B'C'$? Explain your answer.

   $\triangle ABC$ and $\triangle A'B'C'$ are congruent. This is because $\triangle A'B'C'$ is obtained from $\triangle ABC$ by a

   reflection and rotation.

2. **(a)** Draw a quadrilateral $ABCD$ using geometry software. Transform it by first rotating it about a point, then applying a translation and then reflecting it in a line.

   (b) Do you observe any change in the quadrilateral $ABCD$ under the transformation? Explain your observation.

   No, the lengths and angles of quadrilateral $ABCD$ remain the same after the transformation.

   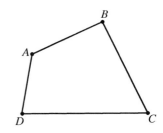

   (c) What can you conclude about the quadrilateral $ABCD$ and its final image? Explain your answer.

   The two figures are congruent. The image is obtained from the quadrilateral $ABCD$ by a

   rotation, translation and reflection.

Try It!

Section 9.1

1. **(a)** Copy the square *ABCD* onto square grid paper. Translate it 7 units right and 4 units up.

    (b) Describe the translation that moves the point *D* to *D″*.

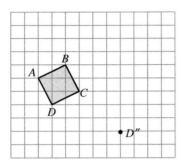

    Solution

    (a) The image square *A′B′C′D′* formed under the given translation is shown below.

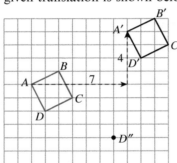

    (b) The translation from *D* to *D″* is 5 units right and 2 units down.

2. Copy the shape *ABCD* and the mirror line *PQ* onto square grid paper. Reflect the shape *ABCD* in the mirror line *PQ*. Draw and label its image *A′B′C′D′*.

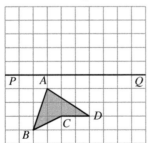

    Solution

    The image *A′B′C′D′* is shown in the diagram below.

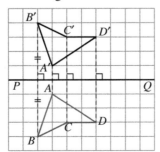

3. △*PQR* is reflected in a mirror line to give the image △*P′Q′R′*. Copy the diagram and draw the mirror line in your diagram.

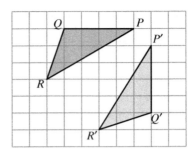

    Solution

    L, *M* and *N* are the midpoints of *PP′*, *QQ′* and *RR′* respectively.

    The mirror line *AB* is the line passing through *L*, *M* and *N*.

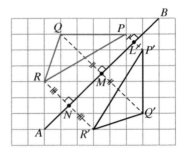

4. The diagram shows triangle *PQR*. Rotate triangle *PQR* 270° anticlockwise about *O* and draw its image.

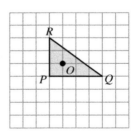

    Solution

    The image *P′Q′R′* is shown below.

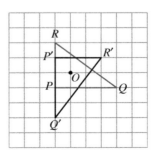

5. Rectangle *ABCD* in the diagram is reflected in the line *MN* and then is rotated 90° anticlockwise about the point *O*. Copy the diagram onto square grid paper and draw the image of *ABCD* after the combined transformations.

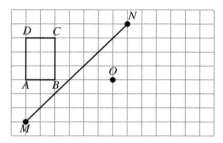

Solution

First do the reflection of the object *ABCD* to get image *A′B′C′D′*. Then do the rotation of the new object *A′B′C′D′* to get the image *A″B″C″D″*.

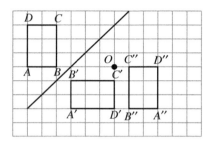

Section 9.2

6. Determine whether these shapes have reflection symmetry. If so, copy and draw the line(s) of symmetry.

(a) Square

(b) Arrow

(c) Right-angled triangle

Solution

(a)

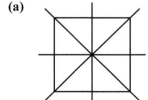

The square has reflection symmetry. It has 4 lines of symmetry.

(b)

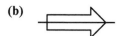

The arrow has reflection symmetry. It has one line of symmetry.

(c) There is no line that can divide this right-angled triangle into two identical halves. Hence, it has no reflection symmetry.

7. Determine whether each of these shapes has rotation symmetry. If so, state the order of rotation symmetry.

(a) Square

(b) Three-arrow shape

(c) Club symbol

Solution

(a) In one full turn about its centre, the square repeats itself four times. It has rotation symmetry of order 4.

(b) The three-arrow shape repeats itself only once in one full turn. It has no rotation symmetry.

(c) The club symbol repeats itself only once in one full turn. It has no rotation symmetry.

8. Describe the symmetry of these objects.

(a) Recycle sign

(b) Saint George's Cross

Solution

(a) There is no line that can divide this recycle sign into two identical halves. Hence, it has no reflection symmetry.
The sign repeats itself three times in one full turn about its centre. It has rotation symmetry of order 3.

(b)

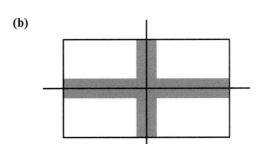

This flag has 2 lines of symmetry. Hence, it has reflection symmetry.
In one full turn about its centre, this flag repeats itself twice. It has rotation symmetry of order 2.

Section 9.3

9. Determine whether these pairs of figures are congruent and give a reason.

(a)

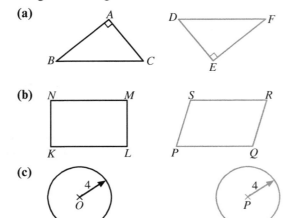

(b)

(c)

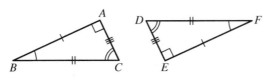

Solution

(a) By measuring the sides and angles of $\triangle ABC$ and $\triangle EFD$, you have

$AB = EF,$ $BC = FD,$ $CA = DE,$
$\angle A = \angle E,$ $\angle B = \angle F,$ $\angle C = \angle D.$

Hence, $\triangle ABC \equiv \triangle EFD.$

(b) Rectangle $KLMN$ has right angles at its vertices. The angles of the parallelogram $PQRS$ are not right angles. Hence, these figures are not congruent as their angles are not the same.

(c) These figures are both circles of the same radius. Hence, they have the same shape and size. They are congruent.

10. The parallelograms $EFGH$ and $TXYZ$ are congruent. The lengths are in centimetres. Find
(a) the length of YZ,   **(b)** the size of $\angle TXY$.

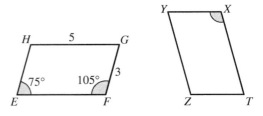

Solution
(a) $EFGH \equiv TXYZ$ (given)
$YZ = GH$ (Corresponding sides of congruent figures are equal.)
$\therefore YZ = 5\,cm$

(b) $\angle TXY = \angle EFG$ (Corresponding angles of congruent figures are equal.)
$\therefore \angle TXY = 105°$

Exercise 9.1
Level 1   **GCSE Grade** $2^+ / 3$

1. In each pair of diagrams, the diagram on the left is transformed to the diagram on the right. State the name of the transformation.

(a)

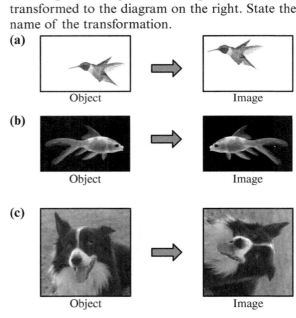
Object   Image

(b)

Object   Image

(c)

Object   Image

(d)

Object   Image

(e)

Object   Image

Solution
(a) Translation
(b) Reflection
(c) Rotation
(d) Rotation
(e) Reflection

For Questions **2** to **6**, copy the given diagram onto square grid paper and draw its image after the transformation.

2. Translate rectangle *PQRS* 4 units left and 2 units up.

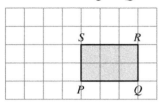

Solution
The image rectangle *P'Q'R'S'* is shown in the diagram below.

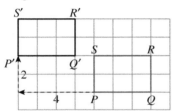

3. Reflect square *TXYZ* in the mirror line *AB*.

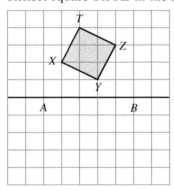

Solution
The image square *T'X'Y'Z'* is shown in the diagram below.

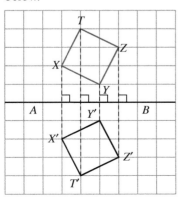

4. Reflect the shape *ABCDEF* in the mirror line *PQ*.

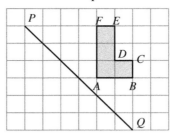

Solution
Shape *A'B'C'D'E'F'* is the image.

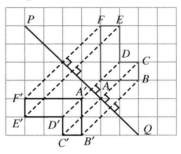

5. Rotate the flag 90° clockwise about the point *O*.

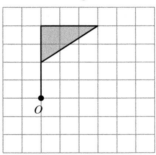

Solution
The image flag is shown in the diagram below.

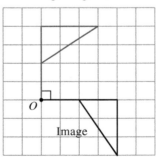

6. Rotate the letter N 180° anticlockwise about the point *O*.

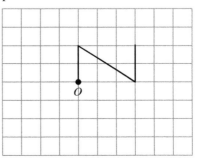

Solution

The image of the letter N is shown in the diagram below.

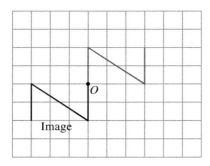

Image

Level 2   GCSE Grade 3 / 4⁻

7. The line $A'B'$ is the image of the line AB after a transformation.
    (a) Describe the transformation.
    (b) Copy the diagram and draw the image of the triangle ABC.

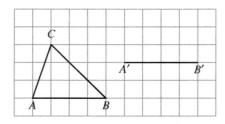

Solution

(a) The transformation is a translation of 5 units right and 2 units up.

(b) The image of $\triangle ABC$ is $\triangle A'B'C'$ as shown in the diagram below.

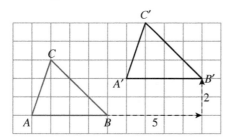

8. Point C' is the image of the point C after a reflection. Copy the diagram and draw
    (a) the mirror line,
    (b) the image $A'B'C'$ of the triangle ABC.

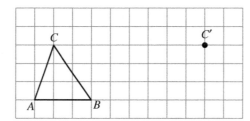

Solution

In the diagram
(a) MN is the mirror line,
(b) $\triangle A'B'C'$ is the image of $\triangle ABC$.

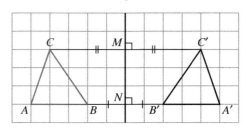

9. In the diagram, the shape $ABCD$ is rotated to $AB'C'D'$. State
    (a) the centre of rotation,
    (b) the angle and direction of the rotation.

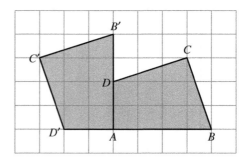

Solution

(a) The centre of rotation is point A. (It remains unchanged under the rotation.)

(b) 90° anticlockwise

Level 3   GCSE Grade 4⁻

10. In an animation, a girl walks 7 units right, jumps up 3 units and then walks 2 units right again to land on some treasure. Describe the single transformation from her initial position to her final position.

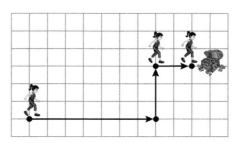

Solution

The single transformation is a translation of 9 units right and 3 units up.

11. Shape $ABCD$ is reflected in the line OX and then reflected in the line OY. Copy the diagram and draw the image after the combined transformation.

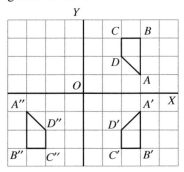

Solution

Shape $ABCD$ is reflected in the line OX to give shape $A'B'C'D'$. $A'B'C'D'$ is then reflected in OY to give $A''B''C''D''$.

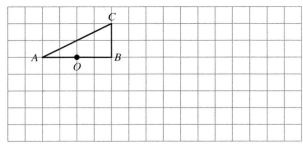

12. $\triangle ABC$ is rotated $180°$ anticlockwise about the point O and then is translated by the vector $\begin{pmatrix} 7 \\ -2 \end{pmatrix}$. Copy the diagram and draw the image after the combined transformation.

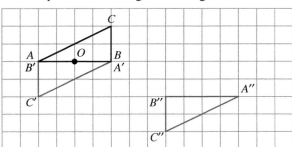

Solution

First rotate the triangle ABC to get image $A'B'C'$. Then translate the triangle $A'B'C'$ 7 squares right and 2 squares down to get the image $A''B''C''$.

13. Copy the diagram.
   (a) Show how you can use one or two transformations to transform the red shape to the green shape.

   (b) What other combined transformations can you use to transform the red shape to the green shape? Compare your answer with another student.

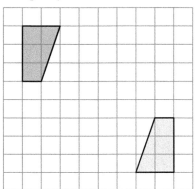

Solution

Student's own diagrams, e.g. you could rotate the shape $180°$ about O. Alternatively, you could reflect the shape twice as shown in the diagram.

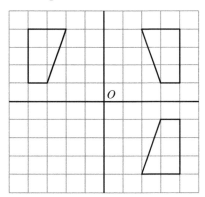

Exercise 9.2
Level 1   GCSE Grade **1 / 2⁺**

1. Which of these shapes have reflection symmetry? For those that have
   (i) copy the shape and draw the lines of symmetry,
   (ii) write down the number of lines of symmetry.

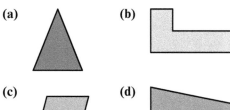

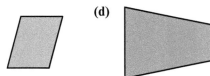

Solution

Shapes in **(a)** and **(d)** have reflection symmetry.

(a) **(i)**

(ii) The shape has one line of symmetry.

(d) **(i)**

(ii) The shape has one line of symmetry.

2. Which of these letters have reflection symmetry? For those that have, copy and draw their lines of symmetry.

(a) **A** (b) **B** (c) **F** (d) **Z**

Solution

Letters in **(a)** and **(b)** have reflection symmetry.

(a) **(b)**

Each of the letters has one line of symmetry.

3. Which of these shapes have rotation symmetry? For those that have, state their order of rotation symmetry.

(a)   (b)

(c)   (d)

Solution

(a) This triangle is an equilateral triangle. It has rotation symmetry of order 3.

(b) The square has rotation symmetry of order 4.

(c) This shape has no rotation symmetry.

(d) This star has rotation symmetry of order 5.

4. Which of these letters have rotation symmetry? For those that have, state their order of rotation symmetry.

(a) **C** (b) **I** (c) **X** (d) **Y**

Solution

Letters in **(b)** and **(c)** have rotation symmetry of order 2.

Letters in **(a)** and **(d)** have no rotation symmetry.

Level 2 GCSE Grade **3⁻**

5. Name two capital letters which have rotation symmetry and
   (a) reflection symmetry with exactly 2 lines of symmetry,
   (b) the order of rotation symmetry is 2.

Solution

(a) Possible letters which have rotation symmetry and reflection symmetry with exactly 2 lines of symmetry are **H**, **I** and **X**.

(b) Possible letters which have rotation symmetry of order 2 are **H**, **I**, **N**, **S**, **X** and **Z**.

6. **(a)** Describe the symmetry of a regular pentagon (5-sided polygon).
   (b) Describe the symmetry of a regular hexagon (6-sided polygon).
   (c) Generalise the above results for the symmetry of a regular *n*-sided polygon.
   Note: A polygon with equal sides and equal angles is called a regular polygon.

Solution

(a) A regular pentagon has rotation symmetry of order 5. It has 5 lines of reflection symmetry (one through each vertex and the midpoint of the opposite side).

(b) A regular hexagon has rotation symmetry of order 6. It has 6 lines of reflection symmetry (one through each opposite pair of vertices and one through each pair of midpoints of opposite sides).

(c) In general, a regular *n*-sided polygon has rotation symmetry of order *n* and *n* lines of reflection symmetry.

7. Here are some road signs.

A B C D

   (a) Which sign has reflection symmetry only?
   (b) Which sign has rotation symmetry only?
   (c) Which sign has both reflection symmetry and rotation symmetry?

Solution

(a) Sign D has reflection symmetry only.

(b) Sign B has rotation symmetry only.

(c) Sign A has both reflection symmetry and rotation symmetry.

8. Describe the symmetry of each flag. State the number of lines of symmetry and order of rotation symmetry, if they have any.

(a) Scotland

(b) Canada

(c) Switzerland

(d) United Kingdom

Solution

(a) The flag of Scotland has 2 lines of symmetry. It has rotation symmetry of order 2.

(b) The flag of Canada has one vertical line of symmetry. It has no rotation symmetry.

(c) The flag of Switzerland has 4 lines of symmetry. It has rotation symmetry of order 4.

(d) The flag of the United Kingdom has no reflection symmetry.
It has rotation symmetry of order 2.

Level 3   **GCSE Grade 3⁻ / 3⁺**

9. Copy each diagram onto square grid paper. Complete the shape so that it has reflection symmetry with the black line as a line of symmetry.

(a)

(b)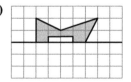

Solution

(a)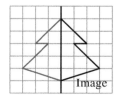

(b)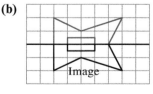

10. Copy each diagram onto square grid paper. Complete the shape so that it has rotation symmetry about the centre *O*.

(a)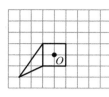

(b)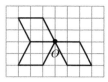

Solution

(a) Possibility 1: One triangle is added to the shape so that it has rotation symmetry, about the centre *O*, of order 2.

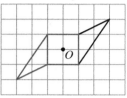

Possibility 2: Three triangles are added to the shape so that it has rotation symmetry, about *O*, of order 4.

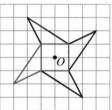

(b) One parallelogram is added to the shape so that it has rotation symmetry of order 2.

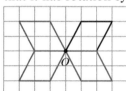

11. Copy and shade four more squares on the grid so that the grid has rotation symmetry but no reflection symmetry.

Solution

Student's diagram. e.g.

12. The word BIKE has reflection symmetry. Create another four-letter word which has reflection symmetry.

Solution

Possible four-letter words which have reflection symmetry are

BECK,

BIDE,

DECK,

DICE,

HIKE.

Hint: First gather all the capital letters that have a horizontal line of symmetry, then form the words.

13. Create a shape which has both reflection symmetry and rotation symmetry using four copies of the tile shown. How many different shapes can you make?

Solution

Four possible different shapes are shown below.

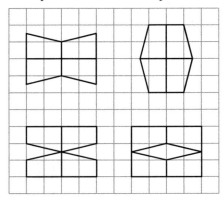

14. Fold a square sheet of paper twice to form four small squares. Use a pair of scissors to cut some shapes from the folded edges. Unfold the paper.

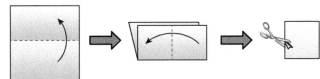

(a) Does the resulting sheet have reflection symmetry? Write down its number of lines of symmetry.

(b) Does the resulting sheet have rotation symmetry? Write down its order of rotation symmetry.

Solution

(a) Yes, the resulting sheet has reflection symmetry. It has 2 lines of symmetry.

(b) Yes, the resulting sheet has rotation symmetry of order 2.

15. Create a shape which has reflection symmetry with 4 lines of symmetry and rotation symmetry of order 4.

Solution

Accept any correct shapes.

16. Create a shape which has rotation symmetry of order 3 and has no reflection symmetry.

Solution

Accept any correct shapes.

Exercise 9.3
Level 1   GCSE Grade **3⁻**

1. Which of these pairs of figures are congruent? Explain your answers.

(a)

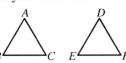

(b)
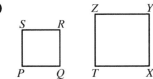

(c)
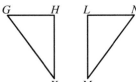

(d)
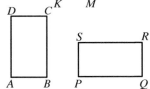

(e)
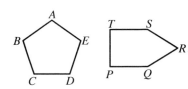

(f)
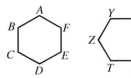

Solution

Tracing paper may be used to check if the figures fit exactly, or measuring the sides and angles of the figures may be done to determine if they are congruent.

(a) $AB = DE$, $BC = EF$, $CA = FD$,
$\angle A = \angle D$, $\angle B = \angle E$, $\angle C = \angle F$.
$\therefore \triangle ABC \equiv \triangle DEF$.

(b) Since the lengths of sides of *PQRS* are not equal to the sides of *TXYZ*, the two figures are NOT congruent.

(c) $GH = NL$, $HK = LM$, $GK = NM$, $\angle G = \angle N$, $\angle H = \angle L$, $\angle K = \angle M$.
∴ $\triangle GHK \equiv \triangle NLM$.

(d) When the quadrilateral *SPQR* is drawn on tracing paper and rotated until *SP* is horizontal, *SPQR* fits the quadrilateral *ABCD* exactly.
∴ $ABCD \equiv SPQR$.

(e) The two figures do not fit exactly. Their angles are not equal. Hence, the two figures are NOT congruent.

(f) Figure *ABCDEF* fits figure *XYZTUV* exactly.
∴ $ABCDEF \equiv XYZTUV$.

2. Name the pairs of figures that are congruent.

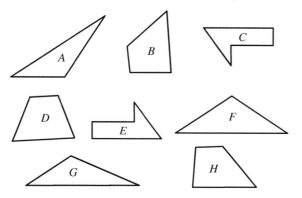

Solution
Figures *A* and *G* are congruent.
Figures *B* and *H* are congruent.
Figures *C* and *E* are congruent.

Level 2   **GCSE Grade 3 / 3⁺**

3. Determine whether $\triangle ABC$ is congruent to $\triangle A'B'C'$ in each case. Explain your answers.

(a)

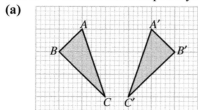

(b)

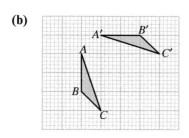

(c)

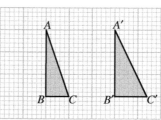

(d)

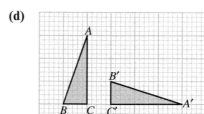

Solution

(a) $AB = A'B'$, $BC = B'C'$, $CA = C'A'$
$\angle A = \angle A'$, $\angle B = \angle B'$, $\angle C = \angle C'$
Hence, $\triangle ABC \equiv \triangle A'B'C'$.

(b) $AB = A'B'$, $BC = B'C'$, $CA = C'A'$
$\angle A = \angle A'$, $\angle B = \angle B'$, $\angle C = \angle C'$
Hence, $\triangle ABC \equiv \triangle A'B'C'$.

(c) $BC \neq B'C'$
The size and shape of $\triangle ABC$ and $\triangle A'B'C'$ are different.
Hence, $\triangle ABC$ is NOT congruent to $\triangle A'B'C'$.

(d) $AB = A'B'$, $BC = B'C'$, $CA = C'A'$
$\angle A = \angle A'$, $\angle B = \angle B'$, $\angle C = \angle C'$
Hence, $\triangle ABC \equiv \triangle A'B'C'$.

4. Determine whether the quadrilateral *ABCD* is congruent to the quadrilateral *A'B'C'D'* in each case. Explain your answers.

(a)

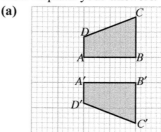

(b)

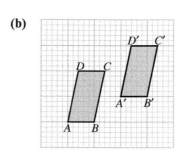

(c)

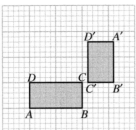

(d)

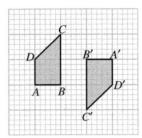

(d)

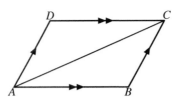

Solution

(a) $\triangle ABC \equiv \triangle CDA$

(b) $\triangle ABD \equiv \triangle ACD$

(c) $\triangle ABC \equiv \triangle ADC$

(d) $\triangle ABC \equiv \triangle CDA$

6. $\triangle ABC \equiv \triangle DEF$, $AB = 4\,$cm, $BC = 3\,$cm, $CA = 5\,$cm, $\angle ABC = 90°$ and $\angle BAC = 36.9°$.

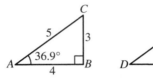

Find
(a) the length of DE, **(b)** the length of FD,
(c) the size of $\angle DFE$.

Solution

Solution

(a) $AB = A'B'$, $BC = B'C'$, $CD = C'D'$, $DA = D'A'$
$\angle A = \angle A'$, $\angle B = \angle B'$, $\angle C = \angle C'$, $\angle D = \angle D'$
Hence, $ABCD \equiv A'B'C'D'$.

(b) $AB = A'B'$, $BC = B'C'$, $CD = C'D'$, $DA = D'A'$
$\angle A = \angle A'$, $\angle B = \angle B'$, $\angle C = \angle C'$, $\angle D = \angle D'$
Hence, $ABCD \equiv A'B'C'D'$.

(c) $CD \neq C'D'$ and $AB \neq A'B'$
Hence, $ABCD$ and $A'B'C'D'$ are NOT congruent.

(d) $AB = A'B'$, $BC = B'C'$, $CD = C'D'$, $DA = D'A'$
$\angle A = \angle A'$, $\angle B = \angle B'$, $\angle C = \angle C'$, $\angle D = \angle D'$
Hence, $ABCD \equiv A'B'C'D'$.

Solution

(a) $\triangle ABC \equiv \triangle DEF$ (given)
$\quad DE = AB$ (Corresponding sides of
$\quad\quad = 4\,$cm congruent triangles are
$\quad\quad\quad$ equal.)

(b) $FD = CA$ (Corresponding sides of
$\quad\quad = 5\,$cm congruent triangles are
$\quad\quad\quad$ equal.)

(c) $\angle DFE = \angle ACB$ (Corresponding angles of
$\quad\quad\quad\quad$ congruent triangles are
$\quad\quad\quad\quad$ equal.)
$\quad\quad = 180° - 36.9° - 90°$ (Angles in a
$\quad\quad = 53.1°$ triangle add up to
$\quad\quad\quad\quad$ $180°$.)

5. State a pair of congruent triangles in each of these diagrams.

(a)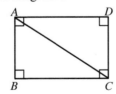

(b)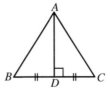

(c)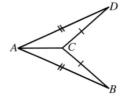

GCSE Grade 3^+ / 4^-

7. Create a tile pattern using each of these shapes.

(a) **(b)**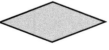

(c) **(d)**

(e)

Solution

(a)

(b)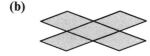

(c)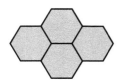

(d)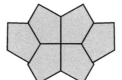

(e)

8. An instrument consisting of two equal pivoting rods is used to measure the internal diameter of a bottle. The pivot *M* is the midpoint of both rods *AC* and *BD*. It is known that △*ABM* and △*CDM* are congruent and *CD* = 7 cm. Find the internal diameter of the bottle.

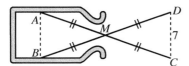

Solution
△*ABM* ≡ △*CDM*   (given)
 AB = *CD*   (Corresponding sides of
   = 7 cm   congruent triangles are equal.)
The internal diameter of the bottle is 7 cm.

9. An engineer wants to find the distance *AB* across a river in the diagram. She walks along a bank from *A* to *C*, and then walks, perpendicular to *AC*, to a point *D* such that *B*, *M* and *D* are on a straight line, where *M* is the midpoint of *AC*. It is known that △*ABM* and △*CDM* are congruent, *AM* = *CM* = 14 m and *CD* = 30 m. Find the distance *AB*.

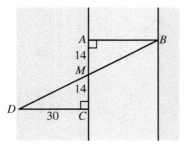

Solution
△*ABM* ≡ △*CDM*   (given)
 AB = *CD*   (Corresponding sides of
   = 30 m   congruent triangles are equal.)
The distance *AB* is 30 m.

10. Many logos are made up of congruent figures, arranged in a symmetrical way.
    (a) Draw the basic figure that forms the given logo.
    (b) Design another logo using four of the basic figures in **(a)**.

Solution
(a) The basic figure is the trapezium.

(b) Accept any correct logo design. One possible logo is shown here.

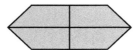

11. Create a tessellation using congruent figures.

    Solution
    Accept any correct design.

12. Find a wallpaper pattern that involves congruent figures.

    Solution
    Accept any correct pattern.

Revision Exercise 9

1. In each pair of diagrams, the diagram on the left is transformed to the diagram on the right. State the transformation.

    (a)

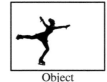

    Object   Image

    (b)

    Object   Image

    (c)

    Object   Image

Solution

(a) Translation

(b) 180° rotation about the centre of the clock face

(c) Reflection

---

2. What transformation will correctly change the postage stamp so that it is the right way up?

Solution

180° rotation about the centre of the portrait.

---

3. Copy these shapes and draw their lines of symmetry.

(a) 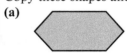   **(b)**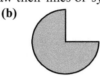

Solution

(a) 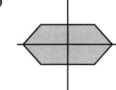   **(b)**

---

4. Describe the rotation symmetry of each shape.

(a)   **(b)**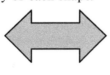

Solution

(a) This shape has no rotation symmetry.

(b) In one full turn about its centre, this shape repeats itself twice, once at 180° and once at 360°. It has rotation symmetry of order 2.

---

5. Describe the symmetry of each sign.

(a)   **(b)**

Solution

(a) This sign has one line of symmetry. Therefore, it has reflection symmetry.
It repeats itself only once in one full turn about its centre. It has no rotation symmetry.

(b) This sign has 2 lines of symmetry. Hence, it has reflection symmetry.
It repeats itself twice in one full turn about its centre. It has rotation symmetry of order 2.

---

6. Describe the symmetry of each flag.

(a) Sweden   **(b)** Israel

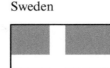   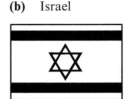

Solution

(a) The flag of Sweden has one horizontal line of symmetry. Hence, it has reflection symmetry.
It has no rotation symmetry.

(b) The flag of Israel has reflection symmetry, with 2 lines of symmetry (one horizontal and one vertical).
It has rotation symmetry of order 2.

---

7. The image of triangle ABC after a reflection in the line PQ is triangle $A'B'C'$. Copy the diagram onto square grid paper. Draw the triangle ABC and the triangle $A'B'C'$.

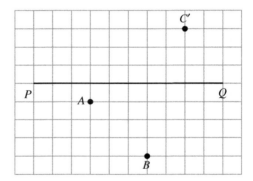

Solution

Triangles ABC and $A'B'C'$ are shown in the diagram below.

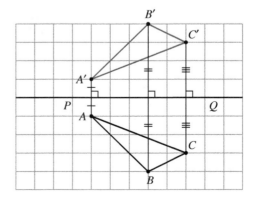

8. Copy the diagram. Reflect $\triangle ABC$ in the line MN
and then translate the image using the vector $\begin{pmatrix} -5 \\ 3 \end{pmatrix}$.

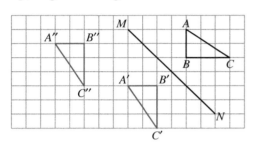

Solution

First do the reflection of the object ABC to get
image $A'B'C'$. Then do the translation of the new
object $A'B'C'$, 5 squares to the left and 3 squares
up, to get the image $A''B''C''$.

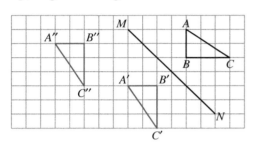

9. Copy and shade two more squares on each grid so
that each grid has rotation symmetry.

(a) **(b)**

Solution

(a) **(b)**

10. Copy and shade three more squares on the grid so
that the grid has
(a) reflection symmetry,
(b) rotation symmetry.

Solution

(a) 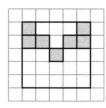 **(b)**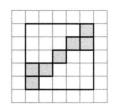

11. $\triangle ABC$ is congruent to $\triangle PQR$. Find $\angle x$ and $\angle y$.

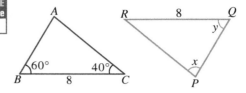

Solution

Advise students to re-draw the second triangle so
that both triangles are in the same orientation. It
will help them greatly when they are comparing the
sides and angles of the two congruent triangles.

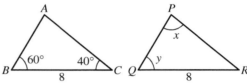

$\triangle ABC \equiv \triangle PQR$ (given)

$\angle x = \angle A$ (Corresponding angles of
congruent triangles are equal.)

In $\triangle ABC$,

$\angle A = 180° - 60° - 40°$ (Angles in a triangle

$= 80°$ add up to 180°.)

$\therefore \angle x = 80°$

$\angle y = \angle B$ (Corresponding angles of

$= 60°$ congruent triangles are equal.)

12. The diagram shows two quadrilaterals. In $ABCD$,
$AB = 4$ cm, $BC = 5$ cm, $CD = 2$ cm and $DA = 3$ cm.
In $PQRS$, $PQ = 4$ cm, $QR = 2$ cm, $RS = 3$ cm and
$SP = 5$ cm. Are these two quadrilaterals congruent?
Explain why.

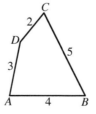 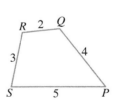

Solution

No, these two quadrilaterals are not congruent. The
lengths of the sides do not follow the same order.

13. $\triangle DEF$ is congruent to $\triangle LMN$,
$DE = 5\,\text{cm}$, $MN = 12\,\text{cm}$ and $LN = 13\,\text{cm}$.

(a) Find the lengths of DF and LM.

(b) Given that $\angle DEF = 90°$ and $\angle EFD = 22.6°$, find $\angle NLM$.

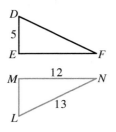

Solution

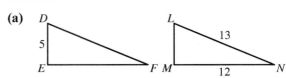

(a)

$$\triangle DEF \equiv \triangle LMN \quad \text{(given)}$$

$$\begin{aligned} DF &= LN \quad &&\text{(Corresponding sides of congruent} \\ &= 13\,\text{cm} &&\text{triangles are equal.)} \\ LM &= DE &&\text{(Corresponding sides of congruent} \\ &= 5\,\text{cm} &&\text{triangles are equal.)} \end{aligned}$$

(b)

$$\begin{aligned} \angle DEF + \angle EFD + \angle FDE &= 180° \quad &&\text{(Angles in a triangle} \\ 90° + 22.6° + \angle FDE &= 180° &&\text{add up to } 180°.) \\ \angle FDE &= 67.4° &&\text{(Corresponding} \\ \angle NLM &= 67.4° &&\text{angles in congruent} \\ & &&\text{triangles are equal.)} \end{aligned}$$

Perimeter and Area of Triangles and Circles

Class Activity 1

Objective: To observe the relationship between the area of a triangle and the area of a rectangle, and derive a formula for the area of a triangle.

Tasks

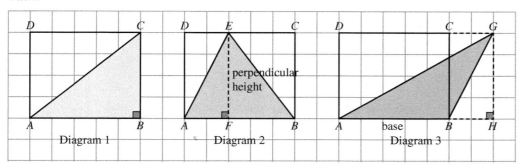

Diagram 1   Diagram 2   Diagram 3

In each of the diagrams, $ABCD$ is a rectangle with length $AB = 5\,\text{cm}$ and width $BC = 4\,\text{cm}$. Copy and complete the following expressions.

1. Look at Diagram 1.
   (a) Area of the rectangle $ABCD = 5 \times \boxed{4}$
   $$= \boxed{20}\ \text{cm}^2$$

   (b) Area of $\triangle ABC = \boxed{\tfrac{1}{2}} \times$ area of $ABCD$
   $$= \boxed{\tfrac{1}{2}} \times \boxed{20}$$
   $$= \boxed{10}\ \text{cm}^2$$

2. Look at Diagram 2.
   (a) Area of $\triangle AFE = \boxed{\tfrac{1}{2}} \times$ area of $AFED$
   $$= \boxed{\tfrac{1}{2}} \times \boxed{8}$$
   $$= \boxed{4}\ \text{cm}^2$$

   (b) Area of $\triangle BFE = \boxed{\tfrac{1}{2}} \times$ area of $BCEF$
   $$= \boxed{\tfrac{1}{2}} \times \boxed{12}$$
   $$= \boxed{6}\ \text{cm}^2$$

   (c) Area of $\triangle ABE =$ area of $\triangle AFE + \boxed{\text{area of } \triangle BFE}$
   $$= \boxed{4} + \boxed{6}$$
   $$= \boxed{10}\ \text{cm}^2$$

3. Look at Diagram 3.

   (a) Area of $\triangle AHG = \boxed{\frac{1}{2}} \times$ area of $AHGD$

   $= \boxed{\frac{1}{2}} \times \boxed{28}$

   $= \boxed{14}$ cm^2

   (b) Area of $\triangle BHG = \boxed{\frac{1}{2}} \times$ area of $BHGC$

   $= \boxed{\frac{1}{2}} \times \boxed{8}$

   $= \boxed{4}$ cm^2

   (c) Area of $\triangle ABG =$ area of $\triangle AHG - \boxed{\text{area of } \triangle BHG}$

   $= \boxed{14} - \boxed{4}$

   $= \boxed{10}$ cm^2

4. What do you notice about the areas of the triangles ABC, ABE and ABG?

   The areas are the same.

   i.e. area of $\triangle ABC =$ area of $\triangle ABE =$ area of $\triangle ABG$.

5. In each triangle:
   Look at the side AB. Take this to be the **base** of the triangle.
   Look at the sides CB, EF and GH. These are the heights of the triangles, perpendicular to the base.
   How would you use the base and the **perpendicular height** to find the area of each triangle?

   In the three diagrams, $CB = EF = GH$.

   From the results in **1(b)** and **4**, you have

   $$\text{area of } \triangle ABC = \frac{1}{2} \times \text{area of } ABCD$$

   $$= \frac{1}{2} \times AB \times CB$$

   Hence, $\text{area of } \triangle ABE = \frac{1}{2} \times AB \times EF$

   $$\text{area of } \triangle ABG = \frac{1}{2} \times AB \times GH$$

   $\therefore$ i.e. area of a triangle $= \frac{1}{2} \times$ base $\times$ perpendicular height.

Class Activity 2

Objective: To find the relationship between the diameter and the circumference of a circle.

1. Draw circles of diameters 3 cm, 4 cm, 5 cm and 6 cm.

2. Wrap a piece of string carefully around each circle to measure its circumference. Use a ruler to measure its length to the nearest mm.

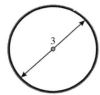

3. Copy the table below and record the readings.

Circle	Diameter (*d*)	Circumference (*C*)	*C ÷ d*
1	3 cm	9.4 cm	3
2	4 cm	12.6 cm	3
3	5 cm	15.7 cm	3
4	6 cm	18.8 cm	3

4. Use a calculator to divide the circumference of each circle by its diameter and fill in the column '*C ÷ d*' of the table. Give your answers to the nearest integer.

5. What do you observe from the values of *C ÷ d*?

$C ÷ d = 3$ (to the nearest integer)

6. Measure the diameters and circumferences of the bases of some circular objects around you such as a waste bin or a water bottle. Check whether the measurements agree with your observation in Question **5**.

Try It!

Section 10.1

1. In $\triangle PQR$, $PQ = 15$ cm, $QR = 8$ cm and $RP = 17$ cm. Find the perimeter of $\triangle PQR$.

   Solution
   Perimeter of $\triangle PQR$
   $= PQ + QR + RP$
   $= 15 + 8 + 17$
   $= 40$ cm

2. Calculate the area of these triangles, where the unit of length is cm.
   (a) $\triangle DEF$
   (b) $\triangle XYZ$

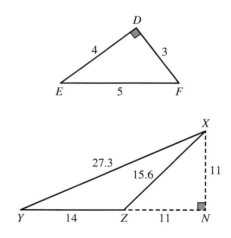

Solution

(a) In $\triangle DEF$, if FD is taken as the base, ED is its perpendicular height.

$$\text{Area of } \triangle DEF = \frac{1}{2} \times FD \times ED$$
$$= \frac{1}{2} \times 3 \times 4$$
$$= 6 \, \text{cm}^2$$

(b) In $\triangle XYZ$, if YZ is taken as the base, XN is its perpendicular height.

$$\text{Area of } \triangle XYZ = \frac{1}{2} \times YZ \times XN$$
$$= \frac{1}{2} \times 14 \times 11$$
$$= 77 \, \text{cm}^2$$

3. The diagram shows a triangular board LMN and the lengths are in metres.
  (a) Find the perimeter of the board.
  (b) Find the area of $\triangle LMN$.
  (c) The mass of the material of the board is 7 kg per square metre. Find the mass of the board.

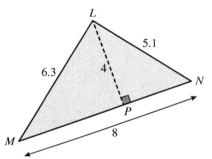

Solution

(a) Perimeter of the board
$$= LM + MN + NL$$
$$= 6.3 + 8 + 5.1$$
$$= 19.4 \, \text{m}$$

(b) Area of the board
$$= \frac{1}{2} \times MN \times LP$$
$$= \frac{1}{2} \times 8 \times 4$$
$$= 16 \, \text{m}^2$$

(c) Mass of the board
$$= 16 \times 7$$
$$= 112 \, \text{kg}$$

Section 10.2

4. Find the circumference of a circle of radius 21 cm. Use $\pi = \frac{22}{7}$.

Solution

$$C = 2\pi r$$
$$= 2 \times \frac{22}{7} \times 21$$
$$= 132 \, \text{cm}$$

5. The diameter of a car wheel including the tyre is 64 cm. How far does it go in one complete revolution? Give your answer to the nearest cm. Use $\pi = 3.142$.

Solution

Distance covered in one complete revolution
= circumference of the tyre
$$= \pi d$$
$$= 3.142 \times 64$$
$$= 201.088$$
$$= 201 \, \text{cm (to the nearest cm)}$$

6. A flower bed is in the shape of a quarter of a circle of radius 3 m. Use your calculator to find the perimeter of the flower bed. Give your answer to the nearest metre.

Solution

Perimeter of the flower bed
= length of the curve + radius × 2
$$= \frac{1}{4} \times 2\pi r + \text{radius} \times 2$$
$$= \frac{1}{4} \times 2 \times \pi \times 3 + 3 \times 2$$
$$= \frac{3}{2}\pi + 6$$
$$= 10.712\ldots$$
$$= 11 \, \text{m (to the nearest m)}$$

Section 10.3

7. Find the area of a circle of radius 7 cm. Use $\pi = \frac{22}{7}$.

Solution

Area of the circle
$$= \pi r^2$$
$$= \frac{22}{7} \times 7^2$$
$$= \frac{22}{7} \times 7 \times 7$$
$$= 22 \times 7$$
$$= 154 \, \text{cm}^2$$

8. A semicircular piece of a pizza has a diameter of 30 cm. Using $\pi = 3.14$, calculate
  (a) the radius of the pizza,
  (b) the area of the top surface of the piece of pizza.

Solution

(a) Radius of the pizza

$= \frac{1}{2} \times$ diameter of the pizza

$= \frac{1}{2} \times 30$

$= 15 \, \text{cm}$

(b) Area of the top of the semicircular piece of the pizza

$= \frac{1}{2} \times \pi r^2$

$= \frac{1}{2} \times 3.14 \times 15^2$

$= 353.25 \, \text{cm}^2$

9. A circular flower bed has a diameter of 4 m. It is surrounded by a ring of pebbles of width 0.5 m. Using your calculator, work out the area of the ring of pebbles
(a) in m²,
(b) in cm².
Give your answers to the nearest integer.

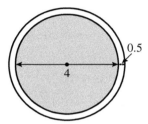

Solution

(a) Radius of the flower bed
$= 4 \div 2$
$= 2 \, \text{m}$
Radius of the outer circle
$= 2 + 0.5$
$= 2.5 \, \text{m}$
Area of the ring of pebbles
= area of the outer circle – area of the flower bed
$= \pi \times 2.5^2 - \pi \times 2^2$
$= 7.06858...$
$= 7 \, \text{m}^2$ (to the nearest integer)

(b) Radius of the flower bed
$= 2 \, \text{m}$
$= 2 \times 100 \, \text{cm}$
$= 200 \, \text{cm}$
Radius of the outer circle
$= 2.5 \, \text{m}$
$= 2.5 \times 100 \, \text{cm}$
$= 250 \, \text{cm}$
Area of the ring of pebbles
$= \pi \times 250^2 - \pi \times 200^2$
$= 70\,685.8...$
$= 70\,686 \, \text{cm}^2$ (to the nearest integer)

Section 10.4

10. **(a)** The area of a square is 169 cm². Calculate the perimeter of the square.
    (b) The area of a rectangle $PQRS$ is 140 cm² and the length of $QR = 10$ cm. Work out the length of PQ.

Solution

(a) Let x cm be the length of a side of the square.

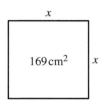

Since the area of the square $= 169 \, \text{cm}^2$,
$$x^2 = 169$$
$$x = \sqrt{169}$$
$$x = 13$$
The length of a side of the square is 13 cm.
Hence, the perimeter of the square $= 4x$
$$= 4 \times 13$$
$$= 52 \, \text{cm}$$

(b) Let y cm be the length of PQ.

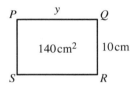

Since the area of $PQRS = 140 \, \text{cm}^2$,
$$y \times 10 = 140$$
$$y = \frac{140}{10}$$
$$y = 14$$
The length of PQ is 14 cm.

11. In the diagram, XYZ is a straight line, $XY = 8$ cm and $YZ = 16$ cm. The area of $\triangle TYZ = 96 \, \text{cm}^2$. Calculate
    (a) the length of TX,
    (b) the area of $\triangle TXY$.

Solution

(a) Area of $\triangle TYZ = 96 \, \text{cm}^2$
$$\frac{1}{2} \times YZ \times TX = 96$$
$$\frac{1}{2} \times 16 \times TX = 96$$
$$8 \times TX = 96$$
$$TX = \frac{96}{8}$$
$$\therefore TX = 12 \, \text{cm}$$

(b) Area of $\triangle TXY$

$$= \frac{1}{2} \times XY \times TX$$

$$= \frac{1}{2} \times 8 \times 12$$

$$= 48 \, \text{cm}^2$$

12. The circumference of a wheel is 108 cm. Using your calculator, find the diameter of the wheel to the nearest cm.

Solution

Let d cm be the diameter of the wheel.
Circumference of wheel = 108 cm

$$\pi d = 108$$

$$d = \frac{108}{\pi}$$

$$d = 34.377\ldots$$

∴ the diameter of the wheel is 34 cm (to the nearest cm).

13. In the diagram, $AB = AE = 5$ cm, $AF = 3$ cm, $BCDE$ is a square of side 8 cm. Find
(a) the perimeter of the shape $ABCDE$,
(b) the area of the shape $ABCDE$.

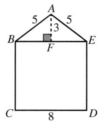

Solution

(a) Perimeter of the shape $ABCDE$
$$= AB + BC + CD + DE + EA$$
$$= 5 + 8 + 8 + 8 + 5$$
$$= 34 \, \text{cm}$$

(b) Area of the shape $ABCDE$
$$= \text{area of } \triangle ABE + \text{area of } BCDE$$
$$= \frac{1}{2} \times BE \times AF + BC \times CD$$
$$= \frac{1}{2} \times 8 \times 3 + 8 \times 8$$
$$= 76 \, \text{cm}^2$$

14. In the diagram, $LMNO$ is a square of side 2 cm. The shaded shape is formed by cutting $LMNO$ from the quarter circle $OABC$ of radius 6 cm. Find
(a) the perimeter of the shaded shape,
(b) the area of the shaded shape.
Give your answers to the nearest integer.

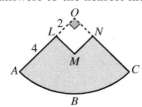

Solution

(a) Length of arc ABC is
$$= \frac{1}{4} \times 2\pi \times 6$$
$$= 3\pi$$
Perimeter of shaded shape
$$= \text{length of arc } ABC + 2 \times LM + 2 \times LA$$
$$= 3\pi + 2 \times 2 + 2 \times 4$$
$$= 3\pi + 12$$
$$= 21.424\ldots$$
$$= 21 \, \text{cm (to the nearest integer)}$$

(b) Area of the shaded shape is
$$= \text{area of quarter circle} - \text{area of square } LMNO$$
$$= \frac{1}{4}\pi \times 6^2 - 2^2$$
$$= 9\pi - 4$$
$$= 24.274\ldots$$
$$= 24 \, \text{cm}^2 \text{ (to the nearest integer)}$$

Exercise 10.1

Level 1   **GCSE Grade** $2^+ / 3^-$

1. In each diagram, $ABCD$ is a square or a rectangle and the unit of length is in cm. Find
(i) the area of $ABCD$,
(ii) the area of the shaded triangle.
(a)

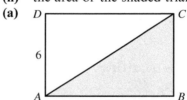

(b)

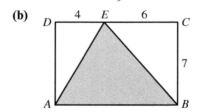

(c)

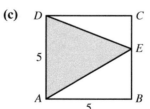

(d)

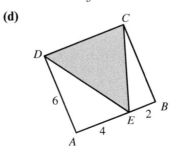

Solution

(a) **(i)** Area of $ABCD$
$= AB \times DA$
$= 9 \times 6$
$= 54\,\text{cm}^2$

(ii) Area of the shaded triangle
$= \frac{1}{2} \times$ area of $ABCD$
$= \frac{1}{2} \times 54$
$= 27\,\text{cm}^2$

(b) **(i)** Area of $ABCD$
$= DC \times CB$
$= (4 + 6) \times 7$
$= 10 \times 7$
$= 70\,\text{cm}^2$

(ii) $AB = DC$ (opposite sides of a rectangle)
$= 10\,\text{cm}$
Area of the shaded triangle
$= \frac{1}{2} \times AB \times CB$
$= \frac{1}{2} \times 10 \times 7$
$= 35\,\text{cm}^2$

(c) **(i)** Area of $ABCD$
$= DA \times AB$
$= 5 \times 5$
$= 25\,\text{cm}^2$

(ii) Area of the shaded triangle
$= \frac{1}{2} \times DA \times AB$
$= \frac{1}{2} \times 5 \times 5$
$= 12.5\,\text{cm}^2$

(d) **(i)** Area of $ABCD$
$= AD \times AB$
$= 6 \times (4 + 2)$
$= 6 \times 6$
$= 36\,\text{cm}^2$

(ii) $DC = AB$ (opposite sides of a rectangle)
$= 6\,\text{cm}$
Area of the shaded triangle
$= \frac{1}{2} \times DC \times AD$
$= \frac{1}{2} \times 6 \times 6$
$= 18\,\text{cm}^2$

2. In each triangle, the perpendicular height is shown. Name the side that is the base.

(a)

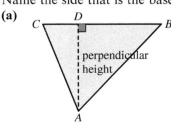

(b)

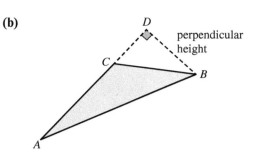

(c)

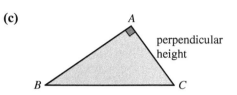

(d)

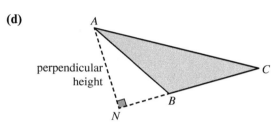

Solution

(a) The base is BC.

(b) The base is AC.

(c) The base is AB.

(d) The base is BC.

3. In each triangle, the base AB is given. Name the perpendicular height corresponding to the base.

(a)

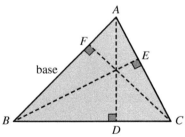

(b)

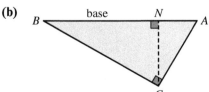

(c)

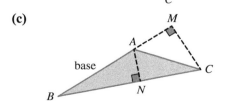

299

(d)

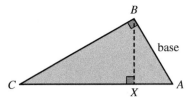

Solution
The perpendicular height corresponding to the base AB is
(a) CF,

(b) CN,

(c) CM,

(d) CB.

4. Calculate the perimeter and area of each shaded triangle. The given lengths are in mm.

(a)

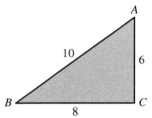

(b)

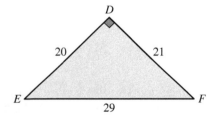

(c)

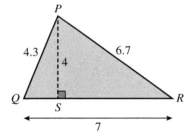

(d)

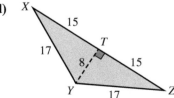

Solution
(a) Perimeter of $\triangle ABC$
$= AB + BC + CA$
$= 10 + 8 + 6$
$= 24\,\text{mm}$

Area of $\triangle ABC$
$= \frac{1}{2} \times BC \times AC$
$= \frac{1}{2} \times 8 \times 6$
$= 24\,\text{mm}^2$

(b) Perimeter of $\triangle DEF$
$= DE + EF + FD$
$= 20 + 29 + 21$
$= 70\,\text{mm}$
Area of $\triangle DEF$
$= \frac{1}{2} \times DE \times FD$
$= \frac{1}{2} \times 20 \times 21$
$= 210\,\text{mm}^2$

(c) Perimeter of $\triangle PQR$
$= PQ + QR + RP$
$= 4.3 + 7 + 6.7$
$= 18\,\text{mm}$
Area of $\triangle PQR$
$= \frac{1}{2} \times QR \times PS$
$= \frac{1}{2} \times 7 \times 4$
$= 14\,\text{mm}^2$

(d) Perimeter of $\triangle XYZ$
$= XY + YZ + ZX$
$= 17 + 17 + (15 + 15)$
$= 17 + 17 + 30$
$= 64\,\text{mm}$
Area of $\triangle XYZ$
$= \frac{1}{2} \times ZX \times YT$
$= \frac{1}{2} \times 30 \times 8$
$= 120\,\text{mm}^2$

5. Work out the area of each shaded triangle. The given lengths are in cm.

(a)

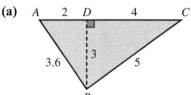

(b)

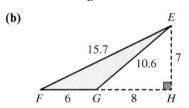

(c)

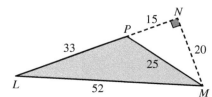

(d)

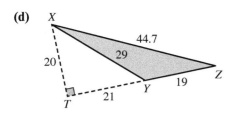

Solution

(a) Area of $\triangle ABC$

$= \frac{1}{2} \times AC \times BD$

$= \frac{1}{2} \times (2 + 4) \times 3$

$= \frac{1}{2} \times 6 \times 3$

$= 9\,\text{cm}^2$

(b) Area of $\triangle EFG$

$= \frac{1}{2} \times FG \times EH$

$= \frac{1}{2} \times 6 \times 7$

$= 21\,\text{cm}^2$

(c) Area of $\triangle LMP$

$= \frac{1}{2} \times LP \times MN$

$= \frac{1}{2} \times 33 \times 20$

$= 330\,\text{cm}^2$

(d) Area of $\triangle XYZ$

$= \frac{1}{2} \times YZ \times XT$

$= \frac{1}{2} \times 19 \times 20$

$= 190\,\text{cm}^2$

Level 2 **GCSE Grade 3⁻**

6. A wire of length $18\,\text{cm}$ is bent into a right-angled triangle ABC with $AB = 8.2\,\text{cm}$ and $BC = 8\,\text{cm}$. Find
(a) the length of AC,
(b) the area of the triangle.

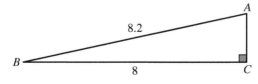

Solution

(a) Length of the wire
= perimeter of the triangle
$= 8.2 + 8 + AC = 18\,\text{cm}$
$AC = 18 - 8.2 - 8$
$\quad\;\; = 1.8\,\text{cm}$

(b) Area of the triangle
$= \frac{1}{2} \times 8 \times 1.8$
$= 7.2\,\text{cm}^2$

7. The diagram shows a piece of glass ABC where $AB = 50\,\text{cm}$, $BD = 30\,\text{cm}$, $DC = 42\,\text{cm}$, $CA = 58\,\text{cm}$ and $AD = 40\,\text{cm}$. Calculate
(a) the perimeter of $\triangle ABC$,
(b) the area of $\triangle ABC$.

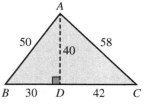

Solution

(a) Perimeter of $\triangle ABC$
$= AB + BC + CA$
$= 50 + (30 + 42) + 58$
$= 50 + 30 + 42 + 58$
$= 180\,\text{cm}$

(b) Area of $\triangle ABC$
$= \frac{1}{2} \times BC \times AD$
$= \frac{1}{2} \times 72 \times 40$
$= 1440\,\text{cm}^2$

8. **(a)** Construct a triangle ABC with $AB = 3\,\text{cm}$, $BC = 5\,\text{cm}$ and $CA = 7\,\text{cm}$.
(b) Draw and measure the perpendicular height CD from C to AB.
(c) Hence, calculate the area of $\triangle ABC$, giving your answer to the nearest cm^2.
Hint: You may draw a sketch first, and construct using a pair of compasses and a ruler.

Solution

(a) First draw the longest side, CA, with your ruler. Use your compasses to draw an arc of radius $5\,\text{cm}$ from C and an arc of radius $3\,\text{cm}$ from A. Mark the point where the arcs intersect as B. Draw in the sides BC and AB, extending line AB beyond B.

(b) You can see the perpendicular height CD is going to be outside the triangle ABC. To find D, fix your compasses and draw two arcs from C, with the same radius, to intersect the extended line AB, at say E and F. Finding the midpoint of where these two arcs cross AB will give you the position of D. To find the midpoint, draw arcs from E and F of the same radius, both sides of line AB. With your ruler, draw a line through where these arcs cross and C. You can now measure CD.

$CD = 4.3\,\text{cm}$

(c) Area of $\triangle ABC = \frac{1}{2} \times AB \times CD$
$= \frac{1}{2} \times 3 \times 4.3$
$= 6.45$
$= 6\,\text{cm}^2$ (to the nearest cm^2)

GCSE Grade **3** / **3⁺**

9. The diagram shows a triangular field, where BCD is a straight edge and AC is a straight fence. $AD = 12\,\text{m}$, $BC = 19\,\text{m}$, $CD = 16\,\text{m}$, $AC = 20\,\text{m}$ and $AB = 37\,\text{m}$. Work out
   (a) the perimeter of $\triangle ABC$,
   (b) the area of $\triangle ACD$,
   (c) the area of $\triangle ABC$.

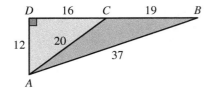

Solution
(a) Perimeter of $\triangle ABC$
   $= AB + BC + CA$
   $= 37 + 19 + 20$
   $= 76\,\text{m}$

(b) Area of $\triangle ACD$
   $= \frac{1}{2} \times CD \times AD$
   $= \frac{1}{2} \times 16 \times 12$
   $= 96\,\text{m}^2$

(c) Area of $\triangle ABC$
   $= \frac{1}{2} \times BC \times AD$
   $= \frac{1}{2} \times 19 \times 12$
   $= 114\,\text{m}^2$

10. ABC is a right-angled triangle with $AB = 6\,\text{cm}$, $BC = 10\,\text{cm}$ and $CA = 8\,\text{cm}$. Find
    (a) the area of $\triangle ABC$,
    (b) the perpendicular height AD from A to BC.

Solution
(a) Area $= \frac{1}{2} \times$ base $\times$ perpendicular height
   $= \frac{1}{2} \times CA \times AB$
   $= \frac{1}{2} \times 8 \times 6$
   $= 24\,\text{cm}^2$

(b) From the area calculated in (a) and using BC as the base of the triangle,
   $24 = \frac{1}{2} \times 10 \times AD$
   $24 = 5 \times AD$
   $AD = \frac{24}{5}$
   $AD = 4.8$

   So, perpendicular height AD is $4.8\,\text{cm}$.

11. Field PQR is in the shape of an isosceles triangle with $PQ = PR = 17\,\text{m}$ and the perpendicular height $PT = 15\,\text{m}$. It is known that $QT = RT$ and the area of the field is $120\,\text{m}^2$.

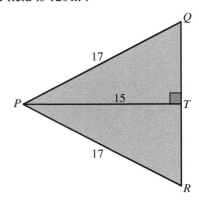

(a) Find the length of QT.
(b) The cost of fencing the field is £13 per metre. Calculate the total cost of fencing all three edges of the field.

Solution
(a) Since the area of the field $PQR = 120\,\text{m}^2$,
   $\frac{1}{2} \times QR \times PT = 120$
   $\frac{1}{2} \times QR \times 15 = 120$
   $QR \times 15 = 120 \times 2$
   $QR = \frac{120 \times 2}{15}$
   $= 16\,\text{m}$
   Since $QT + RT = QR$ and $QT = RT$,
   $QT = \frac{1}{2}QR$
   $\therefore$ $QT = \frac{1}{2} \times 16$
   $= 8\,\text{m}$

(b) Length of the fencing $=$ perimeter of the field PQR
   $= PQ + QR + RP$
   $= 17 + 16 + 17$
   $= 50\,\text{m}$
   $\therefore$ the total cost of fencing all three edges of the field $=$ £13 $\times$ 50
   $=$ £650

12. Draw one acute-angled triangle, one right-angled triangle, one obtuse-angled triangle and one isosceles triangle such that the area of each triangle is $12\,cm^2$. Explain your answer.

Hint: You may use square grid paper to help you.

Solution

To have the area of any triangle as $12\,cm^2$, it is necessary to have the product of the lengths of its base (b) and its perpendicular height (h) as $24\,cm^2$.

Then, the area of the triangle $= \frac{1}{2} \times b \times h$

$$= \frac{1}{2} \times 24\,cm^2$$

$$= 12\,cm^2$$

One possibility is to have base $= 4\,cm$ and perpendicular height $= 6\,cm$ $\left(\frac{1}{2} \times 4 \times 6 = 12\ cm^2\right)$.

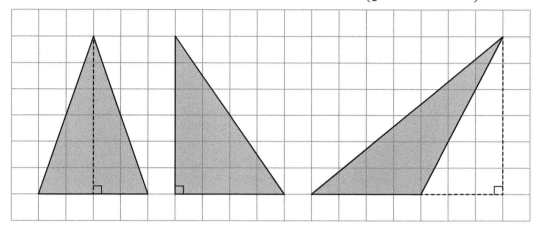

Other possible triangles with the appropriate bases and perpendicular heights are shown below.

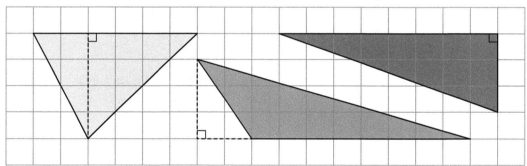

13. In the diagram, OX and OY are two walls perpendicular to each other. A rod of length $75\,cm$ is placed against the two walls to form a triangle, either $\triangle AOC$ or $\triangle BOD$. $AB = 12\,cm$, $BO = 60\,cm$, $OC = 21\,cm$, $CD = 24\,cm$, and $AC = BD = 75\,cm$.

(a) Which triangle has the greater perimeter?

(b) Which triangle has the greater area?

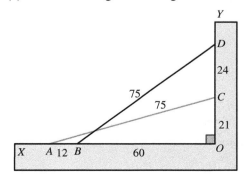

Solution

(a) Perimeter of $\triangle AOC = (12 + 60 + 21 + 75)\,cm$
$= 168\,cm$

Perimeter of $\triangle BOD = (60 + 21 + 24 + 75)\,cm$
$= 180\,cm$

$168 < 180$

Therefore $\triangle BOD$ has the greater perimeter.

(b) Area of $\triangle AOC$

$$= \frac{1}{2} \times 72 \times 21$$

$$= 756$$

Area of $\triangle BOD$

$$= \frac{1}{2} \times 60 \times 45$$

$$= 1350$$

$1350 > 756$

Therefore $\triangle BOD$ has the greater area.

Exercise 10.2

If the value of π is not given, use the π button on your calculator in this exercise.

Level 1 `GCSE Grade 3`

1. Calculate the circumference of each circle with the given diameter. Use $\pi = \frac{22}{7}$.

   (a) 7 cm   (b) 28 cm
   (c) 84 m   (d) 105 mm

   Solution
   (a) Circumference of the circle
   $= \pi d$

   $= \frac{22}{7} \times 7$

   $= 22$ cm

   (b) Circumference of the circle
   $= \pi d$

   $= \frac{22}{7} \times 28$

   $= 88$ cm

   (c) Circumference of the circle
   $= \pi d$

   $= \frac{22}{7} \times 84$

   $= 264$ m

   (d) Circumference of the circle
   $= \pi d$

   $= \frac{22}{7} \times 105$

   $= 330$ mm

2. Find the circumference of each circle with the given radius. Use $\pi = 3.14$.
   (a) 2 cm   (b) 9 m
   (c) 20 mm   (d) 1.5 m

   Solution
   (a) Circumference of the circle
   $= 2\pi r$
   $= 2 \times 3.14 \times 2$
   $= 12.56$ cm

   (b) Circumference of the circle
   $= 2\pi r$
   $= 2 \times 3.14 \times 9$
   $= 56.52$ m

   (c) Circumference of the circle
   $= 2\pi r$
   $= 2 \times 3.14 \times 20$
   $= 125.6$ mm

   (d) Circumference of the circle
   $= 2\pi r$
   $= 2 \times 3.14 \times 1.5$
   $= 9.42$ m

3. Work out the circumference of each circle. Give your answers to the nearest m.
   (a) Radius = 3 m   (b) Diameter = 1.8 m

   Solution
   (a) Circumference of the circle
   $= 2\pi r$
   $= 2\pi \times 3$
   $= 18.8495...$
   $= 19$ m (to the nearest m)

   (b) Circumference of the circle
   $= \pi d$
   $= \pi \times 1.8$
   $= 5.6548...$
   $= 6$ m (to the nearest m)

Level 2 `GCSE Grade 3⁺/4⁻`

4. Find the perimeter of this semicircle with diameter 6 cm. Use $\pi = 3.14$ and give your answer to the nearest cm.

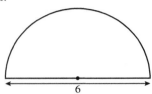

6

   Solution
   Length of the semicircular curve
   $= \frac{1}{2} \times$ circumference of a whole circle

   $= \frac{1}{2} \times \pi d$

   Perimeter of the semicircle
   $= \frac{1}{2} \times \pi d +$ diameter

   $= \frac{1}{2} \times 3.14 \times 6 + 6$

   $= 15.42$
   $= 15$ cm (to the nearest cm)

5. Calculate the perimeter of this semicircle with radius 8 m. Use $\pi = 3.142$ and give your answer to the nearest metre.

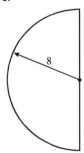

8

   Solution
   Length of the semicircular curve

   $= \frac{1}{2} \times 2\pi r$

   $= \pi r$

Perimeter of the semicircle
$= \pi r + \text{diameter}$
$= 3.142 \times 8 + 8 \times 2$
$= 41.136$
$= 41\,\text{m}$ (to the nearest metre)

6. (a) Work out the perimeter of a quarter of a circle with radius 35 cm.
Use $\pi = \frac{22}{7}$.

35

(b) Does it matter if you use $\pi = 3.14$, $\pi = 3.142$ or $\pi = \frac{22}{7}$ to work out **(a)**?
Do you get the same answer? Explain.

Solution

(a) Length of the quarter curve of a circle
$= \frac{1}{4} \times \text{circumference of a whole circle}$

$= \frac{1}{4} \times 2\pi r$

$= \frac{1}{2}\pi r$

Perimeter of a quarter of the circle
$= \frac{1}{2}\pi r + \text{radius} \times 2$

$= \frac{1}{2} \times \frac{22}{7} \times 35 + 35 \times 2$

$= 55 + 70$

$= 125\,\text{cm}$

(b) Using $\pi = 3.14$ gives

$\text{perimeter} = \frac{1}{2} \times 3.14 \times 35 + 35 \times 2$

$= 124.95$

Using $\pi = 3.142$ gives

$\text{perimeter} = \frac{1}{2} \times 3.142 \times 35 + 35 \times 2$

$= 124.985$

The answer is different depending on which value of π is used. However, if all answers are given to the nearest cm, the answers would all be 125.

Level 3 **GCSE Grade 4⁻ / 5⁻**

7. The diameter of a wheel of a trolley is 30 cm. Find the distance covered by the wheel in 20 revolutions. Give your answer to the nearest metre.

Solution

Distance covered in one complete revolution
= circumference of the wheel
$= \pi d$
$= 30\pi\,\text{cm}$
$\therefore$ the distance covered by the wheel in 20 revolutions
$= 30\pi \times 20$
$= 1884.955...\,\text{cm}$

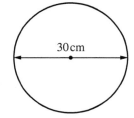

30cm

$= 1884.955... \div 100\,\text{m}$
$= 18.84955...\,\text{m}$
$= 19\,\text{m}$ (to the nearest m)

8. The diameter of a 10p coin is 24.5 mm. The diameter of a £2 coin is 28.4 mm. How much greater is the circumference of a £2 coin than the circumference of a 10p coin? Give your answer to the nearest mm.

Solution

Difference in the circumferences of the two coins
$= \pi \times 28.4 - \pi \times 24.5$
$= 28.4\pi - 24.5\pi$
$= 12.2522...$
$= 12\,\text{mm}$ (to the nearest mm)
The circumference of a £2 coin is 12 mm greater than the circumference of a 10p coin.

9. A ring of diameter 5 cm is made from a piece of wire. The mass of 1 cm of the wire is 4 grams. Work out the mass of the ring to the nearest gram.

Solution

Length of the piece of wire
= circumference of the ring
$= \pi \times 5$
$= 5\pi\,\text{cm}$
Mass of the ring
$= 5\pi \times 4$
$= 20\pi$
$= 62.831...$
$= 63\,\text{grams}$ (to the nearest gram)

10. The London Eye has a diameter of 120 m. It takes 30 minutes to make one complete revolution.
(a) Find the circumference of the wheel.
(b) What is the distance that a person sitting in a capsule travels in one minute?
Give your answers to the nearest metre.

Solution

(a) Circumference of the wheel
$= 120\pi$
$= 376.9911...$
$= 377\,\text{m}$ (to the nearest m)

(b) Distance covered in one revolution $= 120\pi\,\text{m}$
The distance travelled in 30 minutes $= 120\pi\,\text{m}$
$\therefore$ the distance travelled in one minute
$= 120\pi \div 30$
$= 12.566...$
$= 13\,\text{m}$ (to the nearest m)

11. The diagram shows a bend in a road, where ABC and DEF are curved parts of a quarter circle with centre O. $OB = 6\,\text{m}$ and the width of the road is 4 m. How much longer would a walk along the curve DEF be than a walk along the curve ABC? Leave your answer in terms of π.

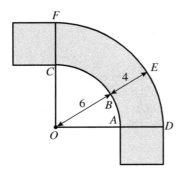

Solution
The outer bend, *DEF*, has length
$$= \frac{1}{4} \times 2\pi \times (6+4)$$
$$= \frac{1}{2}\pi \times 10$$
$$= 5\pi$$

The inner bend, *ABC*, has length
$$= \frac{1}{4} \times 2\pi \times 6$$
$$= 3\pi$$

So the difference in the two distances is
$$= 5\pi - 3\pi$$
$$= 2\pi$$

Walking along *DEF* is 2π m longer than walking along *ABC*.

12. A wire is 38 cm long. It is bent into a circle. Find the radius of the circle, giving your answer to the nearest cm.

Solution
Let *r* be the radius of the circle of wire, in cm.
$$2\pi r = 38$$
$$r = \frac{19}{\pi}$$
$$r = 6.04788\ldots$$
$$r = 6 \text{ cm (to the nearest cm)}$$

13. A piece of wire is shaped into a semicircle and its diameter. The diameter of the semicircle is 7 m. The same piece of wire is then bent into a circle. Find the diameter of the circle. Use $\pi = \frac{22}{7}$.

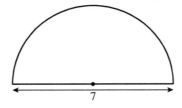

Solution
Length of the wire
$$= \frac{1}{2}\pi \times 7 + 7$$
$$= \frac{1}{2} \times \frac{22}{7} \times 7 + 7$$
$$= 11 + 7$$
$$= 18$$
Let *d* be the diameter of the circle.
$$\pi d = 18$$
$$d = \frac{18}{\pi}$$
$$d = 18 \times \frac{7}{22}$$
$$d = \frac{63}{11}$$
$$d = 5\frac{8}{11}$$
The diameter is $5\frac{8}{11}$ m.

14. The radius of a circle is doubled. Does the circumference of the circle double? Explain your answer.

Solution
Let *r* cm be the radius of a circle and *C* cm be its circumference.
$$C = 2\pi r$$
When the radius is doubled, the radius = 2*r* cm.
Hence, the circumference will be $2\pi \times 2r = 4\pi r$
$$= 2 \times 2\pi r$$
i.e. the new circumference is double the original circumference when the radius doubles.

Exercise 10.3

If the value of π is not given, use the π button on your calculator in this exercise.

Level 1   **GCSE Grade 3**

1. Calculate the area of each circle with the given radius. Use $\pi = \frac{22}{7}$.
   (a)   14 cm
   (b)   28 mm
   (c)   35 m
   (d) $1\frac{3}{4}$ cm

Solution
(a)   Area of the circle
$$= \pi r^2$$
$$= \frac{22}{7} \times 14^2$$
$$= \frac{22}{7} \times 14 \times 14$$
$$= 22 \times 2 \times 14$$
$$= 616 \text{ cm}^2$$

(b) Area of the circle
$= \pi r^2$
$= \dfrac{22}{7} \times 28 \times 28$
$= 22 \times 4 \times 28$
$= 2464 \text{ mm}^2$

(c) Area of the circle
$= \pi r^2$
$= \dfrac{22}{7} \times 35 \times 35$
$= 22 \times 5 \times 35$
$= 3850 \text{ m}^2$

(d) Area of the circle
$= \pi r^2$
$= \dfrac{22}{7} \times 1\dfrac{3}{4} \times 1\dfrac{3}{4}$
$= \dfrac{\cancel{22}^{11}}{\cancel{7}_1} \times \dfrac{\cancel{7}^1}{\cancel{4}_2} \times \dfrac{7}{4}$
$= 11 \times \dfrac{1}{2} \times \dfrac{7}{4}$
$= \dfrac{77}{8}$
$= 9\dfrac{5}{8} \text{ cm}^2$

2. Find the area of each circle with the given diameter. Use $\pi = 3.142$.
(a) 6 cm   **(b)** 10 mm
(c) 40 cm   **(d)** 12 m

Solution
(a) Radius of the circle
$= 6 \div 2$
$= 3 \text{ cm}$
Area of the circle
$= \pi r^2$
$= 3.142 \times 3^2$
$= 3.142 \times 3 \times 3$
$= 28.278 \text{ cm}^2$

(b) Radius of the circle
$= 10 \div 2$
$= 5 \text{ mm}$
Area of the circle
$= 3.142 \times 5^2$
$= 3.142 \times 5 \times 5$
$= 78.55 \text{ mm}^2$

(c) Radius of the circle
$= 40 \div 2$
$= 20 \text{ cm}$
Area of the circle
$= 3.142 \times 20^2$
$= 3.142 \times 20 \times 20$
$= 1256.8 \text{ cm}^2$

(d) Radius of the circle
$= 12 \div 2$
$= 6 \text{ m}$
Area of the circle
$= 3.142 \times 6^2$
$= 3.142 \times 6 \times 6$
$= 113.112 \text{ m}^2$

3. Find the area of each circle. Give your answers to the nearest integer.
(a) Radius = 5 m
(b) Diameter = 5 m
(c) Diameter = 9 mm
(d) Radius = 9 mm
Hint: You might find it useful to sketch the circle.

Solution
(a) Area of the circle
$= \pi r^2$
$= \pi \times 5^2$
$= 25\pi$
$= 78.5398\ldots$
$= 79 \text{ m}^2$ (to the nearest integer)

(b) Area of the circle
$= \pi r^2$
$= \pi \times \left(\dfrac{5}{2}\right)^2$ $r = \dfrac{d}{2}$
$= 19.6349\ldots$
$= 20 \text{ m}^2$ (to the nearest integer)

(c) Area of the circle
$= \pi \times \left(\dfrac{9}{2}\right)^2$ $r = \dfrac{d}{2}$
$= 63.6172\ldots$
$= 64 \text{ mm}^2$ (to the nearest integer)

(d) Area of the circle
$= \pi \times 9^2$
$= 81\pi$
$= 254.469\ldots$
$= 254 \text{ mm}^2$ (to the nearest integer)

Level 2   **GCSE Grade** $3^+/4$

4. Find the area of a semicircle of diameter 8 cm. Give your answer to the nearest cm^2.

Solution
Area of the semicircle
$= \dfrac{1}{2} \times$ area of a whole circle
$= \dfrac{1}{2} \times \pi r^2$
$= \dfrac{1}{2} \times \pi \times \left(\dfrac{8}{2}\right)^2$ $r = \dfrac{d}{2}$
$= 25.1327\ldots$
$= 25 \text{ cm}^2$ (to the nearest cm^2)

5. Calculate the area of a quarter of a circle of radius 2 m. Use $\pi = 3.14$. Give your answer to the nearest m².

Solution
Area of a quarter of a circle
$$= \frac{1}{4} \times \text{area of a whole circle}$$
$$= \frac{1}{4} \times \pi r^2$$
$$= \frac{1}{4} \times 3.14 \times 2^2$$
$$= 3.14 \, \text{m}^2$$
$$= 3 \, \text{m}^2 \text{ (to the nearest m}^2)$$

6. The diagram shows a circular plate of diameter 16 cm. It has an interior border of 3 cm. Work out the area of the border to the nearest cm².

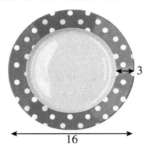

Solution
Radius of the plate = 16 ÷ 2 = 8 cm
Radius of the inner circle = 8 − 3 = 5 cm
Area of the border = area of the plate − area of the inner circle
$$= \pi \times 8^2 - \pi \times 5^2$$
$$= 122.5221\ldots$$
$$= 123 \, \text{cm}^2 \text{ (to the nearest cm}^2)$$

7. The diagram shows a logo in the shape of three-quarters of a circle of radius 4.5 cm. Find
  (a) the perimeter of the logo,
  (b) the area of the logo.
  Give your answers to the nearest integer.
  Hint: Find $\frac{3}{4}$ of the perimeter and area of the circle.
  For perimeter, remember to include the radii.

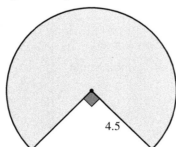

Solution
(a) Length of the curve of the logo
$$= \frac{3}{4} \times \text{circumference of the whole circle}$$
$$= \frac{3}{4} \times 2\pi r$$
$$= \frac{3}{4} \times 2 \times \pi \times 4.5$$
$$= \frac{27}{4} \times \pi \, \text{cm}$$
The perimeter of the logo
= length of the curve of the logo + radius × 2
$$= \frac{27}{4}\pi + 4.5 \times 2$$
$$= 30.20575\ldots$$
$$= 30 \, \text{cm} \text{ (to the nearest integer)}$$

(b) Area of the logo
$$= \frac{3}{4} \times \text{area of the circle}$$
$$= \frac{3}{4} \times \pi \times 4.5^2$$
$$= 47.7129\ldots$$
$$= 48 \, \text{cm}^2 \text{ (to the nearest integer)}$$

8. The diagram shows an arch formed by two semicircles. The inner semicircle has a radius of 1.9 m and the width of the arch is 0.5 m. Find the area of the arch to the nearest m².
Hint: Find the area of the large semicircle first, with radius 1.9 m + 0.5 m.

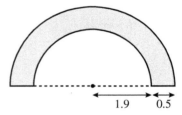

Solution
Radius of the outer semicircle
= 1.9 m + 0.5 m
= 2.4 m
Area of the arch
= area of the outer semicircle − area of the inner semicircle
$$= \frac{1}{2} \times \pi \times 2.4^2 - \frac{1}{2} \times \pi \times 1.9^2$$
$$= 3.377212\ldots$$
$$= 3 \, \text{m}^2 \text{ (to the nearest integer)}$$

9. The diagram shows a poster board formed by two quarters OBC and OAD with centre O. Quarter OAD is the printing area and the region $ABCD$ bounded by the two quarters is the border. $OA = 3$ m and $AB = 80$ cm. Find
    (a) the printing area in m²,
    (b) the area of the border in cm²,
    (c) the perimeter of the poster board in cm.
    Give your answers to the nearest integer.

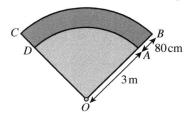

Solution
(a) Printing area $= \frac{1}{4} \times \pi r^2$

$$= \frac{1}{4} \times \pi \times 3^2$$

$$= \frac{1}{4} \times \pi \times 9$$

$$= \frac{9}{4}\pi$$

$$= 7.068\ldots$$

$$= 7\,\text{m}^2 \text{ (to the nearest integer)}$$

(b) Radius of quarter $OBC = 3$ m $+ 80$ cm
$= 300$ cm $+ 80$ cm
$= 380$ cm
Radius of quarter $OAD = 300$ cm
Area of the border = area of quarter $OBC -$
area of quarter OAD

$$= \frac{1}{4} \times \pi \times 380^2 - \frac{1}{4} \times \pi \times 300^2$$

$$= 42\,725.66\ldots$$

$$= 42\,726\,\text{cm}^2 \text{ (to the nearest integer)}$$

(c) Length of arc $BC = \frac{1}{4} \times \pi d$

$$= \frac{1}{4} \times \pi \times (380 \times 2)$$

$$= \frac{760}{4}\pi$$

$$= 190\pi$$

Perimeter of poster board
$=$ length of arc $BC + 2 \times 380$
$= 1356.90\ldots$
$= 1357$ cm (to the nearest integer)

10. In the diagram, O is the centre of the circle of radius 6 cm. OA is a diameter of the small circle. Find the area of the shaded region. Give your answer to the nearest integer.

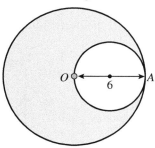

Solution
Radius of the big circle $= 6$ cm
Radius of the small circle $= 6 \div 2$
$= 3$ cm
Area of the shaded region
$=$ area of the big circle $-$ area of the small circle
$= \pi \times 6^2 - \pi \times 3^2$
$= 27\pi$
$= 84.823\ldots$
$= 85\,\text{cm}^2$ (to the nearest integer)

11. In the diagram, a circle with centre O is inscribed in a square $ABCD$ of side 16 cm. Work out
    (a) the difference between the perimeter of the square and the circumference of the circle,
    (b) the total area of the shaded parts.
    Give your answers to the nearest integer.

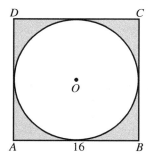

Solution
(a) Diameter of the circle $= 16$ cm
Hence, its radius $= 16 \div 2$
$= 8$ cm
Perimeter of the square
$= 4 \times 16$
$= 64$ cm
Circumference of the circle
$= \pi \times 16$
$= 16\pi$
$= 50.265\ldots$
The difference between the perimeter of the square and the circumference of the circle
$= 64 - 16\pi$
$= 13.7345\ldots$
$= 14$ cm (to the nearest integer)

(b) Total area of shaded parts
= area of the square − area of the circle
$= 16 \times 16 - \pi \times 8^2$
$= 256 - 64\pi$
$= 54.938...$
$= 55 \, \text{cm}^2$ (to the nearest integer)

12. *ABCD* is a square sheet of side 24 cm. Four equal circles are cut from the sheet as shown. Find

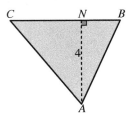

(a) the diameter of each circle,
(b) the total circumference of the four circles,
(c) the area of each circle,
(d) the remaining area of the sheet after cutting out the circles.
Give your answers to the nearest integer.

Solution
(a) Diameter of each circle
$= 24 \div 2$
$= 12 \, \text{cm}$

(b) Total circumference of the four circles
$= 4 \times (\pi \times 12)$
$= 48\pi$
$= 150.796...$
$= 151 \, \text{cm}$ (to the nearest integer)

(c) Area of each circle
$= \pi \times 6^2$ $d = 12$
$= 36\pi$ $\therefore r = 12 \div 2 = 6$
$= 113.097...$
$= 113 \, \text{cm}^2$ (to the nearest integer)

(d) Remaining area
= area of *ABCD* − area of the four circles
$= 24 \times 24 - 4 \times 36\pi$
$= 576 - 144\pi$
$= 123.610...$
$= 124 \, \text{cm}^2$ (to the nearest integer)

Exercise 10.4

If the value of π is not given, use the π button on your calculator in this exercise.

Level 1   GCSE Grade **3 / 3⁺**

1. The area of a square is 225 cm². Find the length of a side of the square.

Solution
Let *x* cm be the length of a side of the square.
Since area of the square = 225 cm²,
$$x^2 = 225$$
$$x = \sqrt{225}$$
$$x = 15$$
The length of a side of the square is 15 cm.

2. A rectangle has an area of 108 cm². If its length is 12 cm, work out its width.

Solution
Let *y* cm be the width of the rectangle.
Since the area of the rectangle is 108 cm²,
$$12 \times y = 108$$
$$y = \frac{108}{12}$$
$$y = 9$$
The width is 9 cm.

3. The area of $\triangle ABC$ is 20 cm². The perpendicular height *AN* is 4 cm. Calculate the length of *BC*.

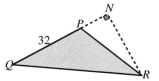

Solution
Area of $\triangle ABC = 20 \, \text{cm}^2$
$$\frac{1}{2} \times BC \times AN = 20$$
$$\frac{1}{2} \times BC \times 4 = 20$$
$$2BC = 20$$
$$BC = \frac{20}{2}$$
$$\therefore BC = 10 \, \text{cm}$$

4. The area of $\triangle PRQ$ is 480 cm². The length of *PQ* is 32 cm.
Find the length of the perpendicular height *RN* from *R* to *PQ*.

Solution
Area of $\triangle PRQ = 480 \, \text{cm}^2$
$$\frac{1}{2} \times PQ \times RN = 480$$
$$\frac{1}{2} \times 32 \times RN = 480$$
$$16RN = 480$$
$$RN = \frac{480}{16}$$
$$\therefore RN = 30 \, \text{cm}$$

5. The circumference of a circular pond is 7 m. Find the radius of the pond to the nearest metre.

Solution
Let r metres be the radius of the pond.
Circumference of the pond = 7 m
$$2\pi r = 7$$
$$r = \frac{7}{2\pi}$$
$$r = 1.11408\ldots$$
The radius of the pond is 1 metre (to the nearest m).

6. In the shape $ABCD$, $ABND$ is a rectangle, $AB = 15$ cm, $AD = 10$ cm, $CN = 8$ cm and $CD = 17$ cm. Calculate
(a) the perimeter of the shape,
(b) the area of the shape.

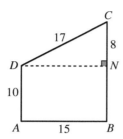

Solution
(a) $BN = AD = 10$ cm (opposite sides of a rectangle)
Perimeter of the shape
$= AB + BN + NC + CD + DA$
$= 15 + 10 + 8 + 17 + 10$
$= 60$ cm

(b) $DN = AB = 15$ cm (opposite sides of a rectangle)
Area of the shape
$=$ area of $ABND +$ area of $\triangle CND$
$= 10 \times 15 + \frac{1}{2} \times 15 \times 8$
$= 150 + 60$
$= 210$ cm^2

Level 2 GCSE Grade **3⁺ / 4**

7. In the shape $ABCDE$, $ABDE$ is a square. $AB = 10$ cm, $BC = 8$ cm and $CD = 6$ cm. Work out
(a) the perimeter of $ABCDE$,
(b) the area of $ABCDE$.

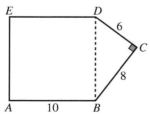

Solution
(a) $DE = EA = AB = 10$ cm (sides of a square)
Perimeter of $ABCDE$
$= AB + BC + CD + DE + EA$
$= 10 + 8 + 6 + 10 + 10$
$= 44$ cm

(b) Area of the $ABCDE$
$=$ area of $ABDE +$ area of $\triangle BCD$
$= 10 \times 10 + \frac{1}{2} \times 8 \times 6$
$= 100 + 24$
$= 124$ cm^2

8. The diagram shows a bookmark which consists of a rectangle $ABDE$ and a semicircle BCD. $AB = 6$ cm and $AE = 4$ cm. Find
(a) the perimeter of the bookmark,
(b) the area of the bookmark.
Give your answers to the nearest integer.

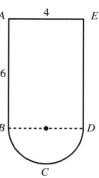

Solution
(a) BD is the diameter of the semicircle BCD.
$BD = AE = 4$ cm (opposite sides of a rectangle)
i.e. the diameter of the semicircle = 4 cm and the radius = 4 ÷ 2 = 2 cm
Perimeter of the bookmark
$= DE + EA + AB +$ length of the curve BCD
$= 6 + 4 + 6 + \frac{1}{2} \times (\pi \times 4)$
$= 16 + 2\pi$
$= 22.283\ldots$
$= 22$ cm (to the nearest integer)

(b) Area of the bookmark
$=$ area of $ABDE +$ area of semicircle BCD
$= 6 \times 4 + \frac{1}{2} \times (\pi \times 2^2)$
$= 24 + 2\pi$
$= 30.2831\ldots$
$= 30$ cm^2 (to the nearest integer)

9. The area of a square board is 9 m^2. Calculate the perimeter of the board.

Solution
Let x metres be the length of a side of the square board.
Area of the square board = 9 m^2
$$x^2 = 9$$
$$x = \sqrt{9}$$
$$x = 3$$
The length of a side of the board is 3 m.
Perimeter of the board $= 4x$
$$= 4 \times 3$$
$$= 12 \text{ m}$$

10. A rectangular field has an area of 3360 m^2. The length of one of its sides is 70 m. What is the perimeter of the field?
Hint: You may want to sketch the field and label it with the information you know.

Solution
Let y metres be the length of the other side of the rectangle.
Area of rectangular field = 3360 m^2
$$70 \times y = 3360$$
$$y = \frac{3360}{70}$$
$$y = 48$$

The length of the other side of the field is 48 m.
Perimeter of the field
$= 2 \times 70 + 2 \times 48$
$= 236$ m

11. The circumference of a disc is 30 cm. Find the area of the disc to the nearest cm^2.

Solution
Let r cm be the radius of the disc.
Circumference of the disc = 30 cm
$$2\pi r = 30$$
$$\pi r = 15$$
$$r = \frac{15}{\pi}$$
The radius of the disc is $\frac{15}{\pi}$ cm.
Area of the disc
$= \pi r^2$
$= \pi \times \left(\frac{15}{\pi}\right)^2$
$= 71.6197...$
$= 72\, cm^2$ (to the nearest cm^2)

12. The shape $VACB$ is formed by a semicircle ACB and a triangle ABV. $AB = 10$ cm, $AV = BV = 13$ cm and $NV = 12$ cm.
Find
(a) the perimeter of the shape,
(b) the area of the shape.
Give your answers to the nearest integer.

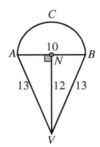

Solution
(a) Diameter of the semicircle is $AB = 10$ cm
i.e. the radius = 10 ÷ 2 = 5 cm
Perimeter of the shape
$= AV + BV + $ length of the curve ACB
$= 13 + 13 + \frac{1}{2} \times (\pi \times 10)$
$= 26 + 5\pi$
$= 41.7079...$
$= 42$ cm (to the nearest integer)

(b) Area of the shape
$= $ area of $\triangle ABV + $ area of the semicircle ACB
$= \frac{1}{2} \times 10 \times 12 + \frac{1}{2} \times (\pi \times 5^2)$
$= 60 + \frac{25}{2}\pi$
$= 99.2699...$
$= 99\, cm^2$ (to the nearest integer)

13. The diagram shows a face of a hut. Rectangle $EFGH$ is a space for a door measuring 2 m by 1 m. The height AM of the hut is 3 m.
$AB = AC = 3.9$ m,
$BE = FC = 2$ m.
Calculate
(a) the perimeter of the shaded region,
(b) the area of the shaded region.

Solution
(a) Perimeter $= AC + CF + FG + GH + HE$
$\qquad\qquad\quad + EB + BA$
$= 3.9 + 2 + 2 + 1 + 2 + 2 + 3.9$
$= 16.8$ m

(b) Area of the shaded region
$= $ area of $\triangle ACB - $ area of rectangle $GFEH$
$= \frac{1}{2} \times (2 + 1 + 2) \times 3 - 2 \times 1$
$= \frac{5}{2} \times 3 - 2$
$= 5.5\, m^2$

Level 3 | GCSE Grade **4 / 5⁻**

14. In the diagram, $BCDN$ is a straight line, $BC = 5$ cm and $CD = 2$ cm. The area of $\triangle ABC$ is $10\, cm^2$.
Work out
(a) the length of AN,
(b) the area of $\triangle ACD$.

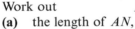

Solution
(a) Area of $\triangle ABC = 10\, cm^2$
$$\frac{1}{2} \times BC \times AN = 10$$
$$\frac{1}{2} \times 5 \times AN = 10$$
$$5AN = 20$$
$$AN = \frac{20}{5}$$
$$\therefore AN = 4\, cm$$

(b) Area of $\triangle ACD$
$= \frac{1}{2} \times CD \times AN$
$= \frac{1}{2} \times 2 \times 4$
$= 4\, cm^2$

15. The diagram shows a board *ABCDE*. *ABCD* is a square of side 6 m and *DAE* is a quarter of a circle with centre *D*. Find

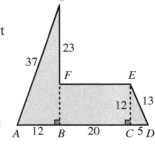

    (a) the perimeter of the board,
    (b) the area of the board.

Give your answers to the nearest integer.

Solution

(a) Radius of quarter of circle, *DA* = 6 m (sides of the square)
    i.e. *DE* is also 6 m.
    Perimeter of the board
    = *AB* + *BC* + *CD* + *DE* + length of curve *EA*

$$= 6 + 6 + 6 + 6 + \frac{1}{4} \times (2 \times \pi \times 6)$$

$$= 24 + 3\pi$$
$$= 33.4247\ldots$$
$$= 33 \text{ m (to the nearest integer)}$$

(b) Area of the board
    = area of *ABCD* + area of the quarter of circle

$$= 6 \times 6 + \frac{1}{4} \times (\pi \times 6^2)$$

$$= 36 + 9\pi$$
$$= 64.2743\ldots$$
$$= 64 \text{ m}^2 \text{ (to the nearest integer)}$$

16. In the shape, *OABC* is a square of side 5 cm and *AOD* is the diameter of the semicircle with centre *O*. Work out

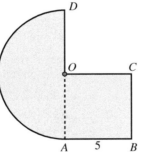

    (a) the perimeter of the shape,
    (b) the area of the shape.

Give your answers to the nearest integer.

Solution

(a) Radius of the semicircle, *OA* = 5 cm (sides of the square)
    i.e. *OD* is also 5 cm.
    Perimeter of the shape
    = *AB* + *BC* + *CO* + *OD* + length of curve *DA*

$$= 5 + 5 + 5 + 5 + \frac{1}{2} \times (2 \times \pi \times 5)$$
$$= 20 + 5\pi$$
$$= 35.7079\ldots$$
$$= 36 \text{ cm (to the nearest integer)}$$

(b) Area of the shape
    = area of *OABC* + area of the semicircle

$$= 5 \times 5 + \frac{1}{2} \times (\pi \times 5^2)$$

$$= 25 + \frac{25}{2}\pi$$
$$= 64.2699\ldots$$
$$= 64 \text{ cm}^2 \text{ (to the nearest integer)}$$

17. In the diagram, △*ABG*, rectangle *BCEF* and △*CDE* are on the straight line *ABCD*. *AB* = 12 cm, *BC* = 20 cm, *CD* = 5 cm, *CE* = 12 cm, *DE* = 13 cm, *FG* = 23 cm and *GA* = 37 cm. Find

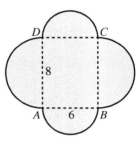

    (a) the perimeter of the shape,
    (b) the area of the shape.

Solution

(a) Perimeter of the shape
    = *AB* + *BC* + *CD* + *DE* + *EF* + *FG* + *GA*
    = 12 + 20 + 5 + 13 + 20 + 23 + 37
    = 130 cm

(b) Area of the shape
    = area of △*ABG* + area of *BCEF* + area of △*CDE*

$$= \frac{1}{2} \times 12 \times (23 + 12) + 20 \times 12 + \frac{1}{2} \times 5 \times 12$$

    = 210 + 240 + 30
    = 480 cm²

18. In the shape, *ABCD* is a rectangle with *AB* = 6 cm and *AD* = 8 cm. Four semicircles are on the sides of the rectangle. Work out

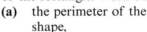

    (a) the perimeter of the shape,
    (b) the area of the shape.

Give your answers to the nearest integer.

Solution

(a) The two semicircles on the length of the rectangle form a whole circle of diameter 8 cm, i.e. radius 4 cm.
    Also, the two semicircles on the width of the rectangle form a whole circle of diameter 6 cm, i.e. radius 3 cm.
    Perimeter of the shape
    = circumference of the two circles
    = π × 8 + π × 6
    = 8π + 6π
    = 14π
    = 43.9822…
    = 44 cm (to the nearest integer)

(b) Area of the shape
    = areas of the two circles + area of rectangle *ABCD*
    = π × 4² + π × 3² + 8 × 6
    = 16π + 9π + 48
    = 25π + 48
    = 126.5398…
    = 127 cm² (to the nearest integer)

19. *ABCD* is a rectangle 9 cm by 5 cm. A quarter of a circle of radius 1.5 cm is cut from each corner to form a plate.

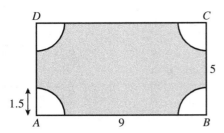

Calculate
(a) the perimeter of the plate,
(b) the area of the plate.
Give your answers to the nearest integer.

Solution
(a) Together the curves at the four corners of the plate make a whole circle. Therefore the total of the lengths of the curved parts is the length of the circumference of a circle, radius 1.5 cm.
Perimeter of the plate
= perimeter of rectangle *ABCD*
$- 8 \times 1.5 + 2 \times \pi \times 1.5$
$= 2 \times 9 + 2 \times 5 - 12 + 3\pi$
$= 16 + 3\pi$
$= 25.4247...$
$= 25$ cm (to the nearest integer)

(b) Area of the plate
= area of rectangle *ABCD* − area or circle, radius 1.5
$= 9 \times 5 - \pi \times 1.5^2$
$= 45 - 2.25\pi$
$= 37.9314...$
$= 38$ cm^2 (to the nearest integer)

20. The diagram shows a view of a house. *ABE* is an isosceles triangle on the rectangle *BCDE*, *BC* = 3 m, *AN* = 1.6 m and *AB* = 3.4 m. The area of *BCDE* is 18 m^2. Find
(a) the length of *BE*,
(b) the area of *ABCDE*.

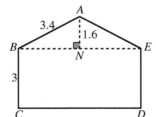

Solution
(a) Area of *BCDE* = 18 m^2
$BC \times BE = 18$
$3 \times BE = 18$
$BE = \dfrac{18}{3}$
$\therefore BE = 6$ m

(b) Area of *ABCDE*
= area of △*ABE* + area of rectangle *BCDE*
$= \dfrac{1}{2} \times 6 \times 1.6 + 18$
$= 4.8 + 18$
$= 22.8$ m^2

21. In the diagram, *ABCD* is a square of area 196 mm^2 and *AED* is a semicircle. Using $\pi = \dfrac{22}{7}$, find
(a) the length of *AD*,
(b) the perimeter of the shape *ABCDE*,
(c) the area of the shape *ABCDE*.

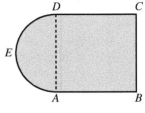

Solution
(a) Let *x* cm be the length of a side of the square *ABCD*.
Area of *ABCD* = 196 mm^2
$x^2 = 196$
$x = \sqrt{196}$
$x = 14$
Hence, the length of *AD* is 14 mm.

(b) $AB = BC = CD = AD$ (sides of square)
Perimeter of the shape *ABCDE*
= $AB + BC + CD$ + length of curve *DEA*
$= 14 + 14 + 14 + \dfrac{1}{2} \times \dfrac{22}{7} \times 14$
$= 42 + 22$
$= 64$ mm

(c) Area of the shape *ABCDE*
= area of *ABCD* + area of the semicircle
$= 196 + \dfrac{1}{2} \times \dfrac{22}{7} \times 7^2$
$= 196 + 77$
$= 273$ mm^2

22. In the diagram, the shaded shape is formed by cutting a semicircle of radius 2 cm from △*ABE*. *AB* = *AE* = 5.66 cm and *BE* = 8 cm. Calculate
(a) the perimeter of the shaded shape,
(b) the area of the shaded shape.
Give your answers to the nearest integer.

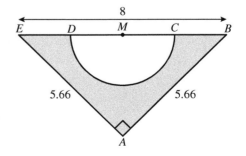

Solution

(a) $BC = \frac{1}{2} \times 8 - 2 = 2\,\text{cm}$

Perimeter of shaded shape
$= AB + BC + \text{semicircle } CD + DE + EA$
$= 5.66 + 2 + \frac{1}{2} \times 2 \times \pi \times 2 + 2 + 5.66$
$= 15.32 + 2\pi$
$= 21.6031...$
$= 22\,\text{cm (to the nearest integer)}$

(b) Area of the shaded shape
$= \text{area of } \triangle ABE - \text{area of semicircle } CD$
$= \frac{1}{2} \times 5.66 \times 5.66 - \frac{1}{2} \times \pi \times 2^2$
$= 16.0178 - 2\pi$
$= 9.7346...$
$= 10\,\text{cm}^2 \text{ (to the nearest integer)}$

Revision Exercise 10

If the value of π is not given, use the π button on your calculator in this exercise.

1. Calculate the perimeter and area of each triangle, where the lengths are in cm.

GCSE Grade 2⁺

(a)

(b)
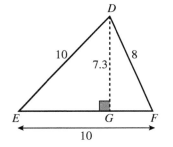

Solution

(a) Perimeter of $\triangle ABC$
$= AB + BC + CA$
$= 25 + 24 + 7$
$= 56\,\text{cm}$

Area of $\triangle ABC$
$= \frac{1}{2} \times BC \times AC$
$= \frac{1}{2} \times 24 \times 7$
$= 84\,\text{cm}^2$

(b) Perimeter of $\triangle DEF$
$= DE + EF + FD$
$= 10 + 10 + 8$
$= 28\,\text{cm}$

Area of $\triangle DEF$
$= \frac{1}{2} \times EF \times DG$
$= \frac{1}{2} \times 10 \times 7.3$
$= 36.5\,\text{cm}^2$

2. The dimensions in the triangle are in mm. Find the perimeter and area of

GCSE Grade 3⁻

(a) $\triangle ABC$,   (b) $\triangle ACD$.

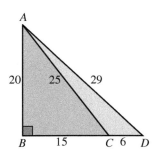

Solution

(a) Perimeter of $\triangle ABC$
$= AB + BC + CA$
$= 20 + 15 + 25$
$= 60\,\text{mm}$

Area of $\triangle ABC$
$= \frac{1}{2} \times BC \times AB$
$= \frac{1}{2} \times 15 \times 20$
$= 150\,\text{mm}^2$

(b) Perimeter of $\triangle ACD$
$= AC + CD + DA$
$= 25 + 6 + 29$
$= 60\,\text{mm}$
Area of $\triangle ACD$
$= \frac{1}{2} \times CD \times AB$
$= \frac{1}{2} \times 6 \times 20$
$= 60\,\text{mm}^2$

3. In $\triangle PQR$, $PQ = 8\,\text{cm}$, $QR = 3.6\,\text{cm}$, $RS = 1.8\,\text{cm}$, $SP = 5.4\,\text{cm}$ and $QS = 4\,\text{cm}$. Find

GCSE Grade 3⁻

(a) the perimeter of $\triangle PQR$,
(b) the area of $\triangle PQS$.

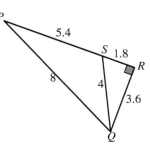

Solution

(a) Perimeter of $\triangle PQR$
$= PQ + QR + RS + SP$
$= 8 + 3.6 + 1.8 + 5.4$
$= 18.8\,\text{cm}$

(b) Area of $\triangle PQS$

$$= \frac{1}{2} \times SP \times QR$$

$$= \frac{1}{2} \times 5.4 \times 3.6$$

$$= 9.72 \, \text{cm}^2$$

4. The diameter of a circular pond is 2.8 m.

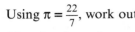

Using $\pi = \frac{22}{7}$, work out

(a) the circumference of the pond,

(b) the area of the top surface of the pond.

Solution

(a) Circumference of the pond

$$= \frac{22}{7} \times 2.8$$

$$= 8.8 \, \text{m}$$

(b) Radius of the pond

$$= 2.8 \div 2$$

$$= 1.4 \, \text{m}$$

Area of the top surface of the pond

$$= \frac{22}{7} \times 1.4^2$$

$$= 6.16 \, \text{m}^2$$

5. The length of the minute hand on a clock is 10 cm. Using $\pi = 3.14$, calculate

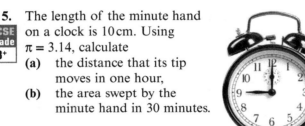

(a) the distance that its tip moves in one hour,

(b) the area swept by the minute hand in 30 minutes.

Solution

(a) Distance that the tip moves in one hour

= circumference of the circle with radius 10 cm

$$= 2 \times 3.14 \times 10$$

$$= 62.8 \, \text{cm}$$

(b) Area swept by the minute hand in 30 minutes

= area of the semicircle of radius 10 cm

$$= \frac{1}{2} \times 3.14 \times 10^2$$

$$= 157 \, \text{cm}^2$$

6. The Equator of the Earth can be modelled as a circle of radius 6371 km. Find the length of the Equator to the nearest km.

Equator

Solution

Length of the Equator

= circumference of the circle

$$= 2 \times \pi \times 6371$$

$$= 40030.173\ldots$$

$$= 40030 \, \text{km (to the nearest km)}$$

7. The radius of a round pizza is 15 cm. After eating a quarter, three quarters are left as shown. O is the centre of the pizza. Work out

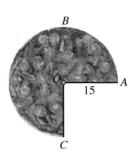

(a) the perimeter of $OABC$,

(b) the area of $OABC$.

Give your answers to the nearest integer.

Solution

(a) Length of curve ABC

$$= \frac{3}{4} \times \text{circumference of the whole circle}$$

$$= \frac{3}{4} \times 2 \times \pi \times 15$$

$$= \frac{45}{2} \pi \, \text{cm}$$

Perimeter of $OABC$

= $OA + OC$ + length of curve ABC

$$= 15 + 15 + \frac{45}{2} \pi$$

$$= 30 + \frac{45}{2} \pi$$

$$= 101 \, \text{cm (to the nearest integer)}$$

(b) Area of $OABC$

$$= \frac{3}{4} \times \text{area of whole circle}$$

$$= \frac{3}{4} \times \pi \times 15^2$$

$$= \frac{675}{4} \pi$$

$$= 530 \, \text{cm}^2 \text{ (to the nearest integer)}$$

8. In the diagram, $ABCD$ is a rectangle, $AB = 18$ cm and $BC = 24$ cm. VAD is an isosceles triangle, $AV = DV = 37$ cm and $VN = 35$ cm.

Find

(a) the perimeter of the shape $VABCD$,

(b) the area of the shape $VABCD$.

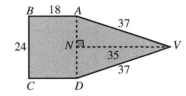

Solution

(a) $CD = AB = 18$ cm (sides of a rectangle)

$AD = BC = 24$ cm (sides of a rectangle)

Perimeter of the shape

$$= AB + BC + CD + DV + VA$$

$$= 18 + 24 + 18 + 37 + 37$$

$$= 134 \, \text{cm}$$

(b) Area of the shape

= area of $ABCD$ + area of $\triangle VAD$

$$= 24 \times 18 + \frac{1}{2} \times 24 \times 35$$

$$= 432 + 420$$

$$= 852 \, \text{cm}^2$$

9. A circular pool of radius 2 m is surrounded by a border of width 1 m.

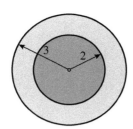

Calculate, in terms of π,
(a) the difference between the external circumference of the border and the circumference of the pool,
(b) the area of the border.

Solution
(a) Difference between the two circumferences
$$= 2 \times \pi \times 3 - 2 \times \pi \times 2$$
$$= 6\pi - 4\pi$$
$$= 2\pi \, \text{m}$$

(b) Area of the border
$$= \pi \times 3^2 - \pi \times 2^2$$
$$= 9\pi - 4\pi$$
$$= 5\pi \, \text{m}^2$$

10. ABD is a right-angled triangle and BDC is a semicircle. $AB = 30$ cm, $BD = 16$ cm and $DA = 34$ cm.

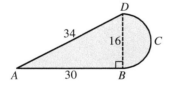

Calculate
(a) the perimeter of the shape,
(b) the area of the shape.
Give your answers to the nearest integer.

Solution
(a) Perimeter of the shape
$$= \text{length of curve } BCD + AB + AD$$
$$= \frac{1}{2} \times (\pi \times 16) + 30 + 34$$
$$= 8\pi + 64$$
$$= 89.1327\ldots$$
$$= 89 \, \text{cm (to the nearest integer)}$$

(b) Area of the shape
$$= \text{area of the semicircle} + \text{area of } \triangle DAB$$
$$= \frac{1}{2} \times (\pi \times 8^2) + \frac{1}{2} \times 30 \times 16$$
$$= 32\pi + 240$$
$$= 340.5309\ldots$$
$$= 341 \, \text{cm}^2 \text{ (to the nearest integer)}$$

11. $ABCD$ is a square of side 6 cm. Equal quarters with centres at the vertices are drawn to form the shaded shape. Work out
(a) the perimeter of the shaded region,
(b) the area of the shaded region.
Give your answers to the nearest integer.

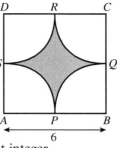

Solution
(a) The four equal quarters form a whole circle of radius $6 \div 2 = 3$ cm.
Perimeter of the shaded region
$$= \text{circumference of the circle}$$
$$= 2\pi \times 3$$
$$= 6\pi$$
$$= 18.8495\ldots$$
$$= 19 \, \text{cm (to the nearest integer)}$$

(b) Area of the shaded region
$$= \text{area of } ABCD - \text{area of the circle}$$
$$= 6 \times 6 - \pi \times 3^2$$
$$= 36 - 9\pi$$
$$= 7.7256\ldots$$
$$= 8 \, \text{cm}^2 \text{ (to the nearest integer)}$$

12. Triangle ABC has an area of 84 mm². $AB = 17$ mm, $AC = 10$ mm and the perpendicular height $AN = 8$ mm. Find the perimeter of $\triangle ABC$.

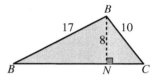

Solution
Area of $\triangle ABC = 84 \, \text{cm}^2$
$$\frac{1}{2} \times BC \times AN = 84$$
$$\frac{1}{2} \times BC \times 8 = 84$$
$$4BC = 84$$
$$BC = \frac{84}{4}$$
$$BC = 21 \, \text{cm}$$
$\therefore$ perimeter of $\triangle ABC$
$$= AB + BC + CA$$
$$= 17 + 21 + 10$$
$$= 48 \, \text{cm}$$

13. $ABCD$ is a rectangle with $AB = 16$ cm and $BC = 10$ cm. Two semicircles of radii 3 cm and diameters on AD and BC are cut from the rectangle.

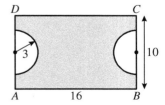

Calculate

(a)   the perimeter of the shaded part,

(b)   the area of the shaded part.

Give your answers to the nearest integer.

Solution

(a)   Together the two semicircles make a whole circle so the sum of the curved lengths is the circumference of a circle, radius 3 cm.
The perimeter of the shaded part is
$= 2 \times \pi \times 3$ + perimeter of rectangle $ABCD$
$\qquad - 2 \times$ diameter of semicircle
$= 6\pi + 2 \times 16 + 2 \times 10 - 2 \times 6$
$= 6\pi + 32 + 20 - 12$
$= 6\pi + 40$
$= 58.8495...$
$= 59$ cm (to the nearest integer)

(b)   The area of the shaded part is
$=$ area of rectangle $ABCD$ $-$ area of circle, radius 3
$= 16 \times 10 - \pi \times 3^2$
$= 160 - 9\pi$
$= 131.7256...$
$= 132$ cm^2 (to the nearest integer)

14.   A wire encloses a square of area 324 cm^2. If the wire is bent to form a circle, work out the area of the circle. Give your answer to the nearest cm^2. Explain your working.

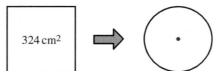

Solution

Let x cm be the length of a side of the square.
Area of the square $= 324$ cm^2
$$x^2 = 324$$
$$x = \sqrt{324}$$
$$x = 18 \text{ cm}$$

Length of the wire
$=$ perimeter of the square
$= 4 \times 18$
$= 72$ cm

When the wire is bent to form a circle,
the circumference of the circle $= 72$ cm.
Let r cm be the radius of the circle.
$$2\pi r = 72$$
$$\pi r = 36$$
$$r = \frac{36}{\pi}$$

i.e. the radius of the circle is $\frac{36}{\pi}$ cm.
Area of the circle
$$= \pi \times \left(\frac{36}{\pi}\right)^2$$
$= 412.5296...$
$= 413$ cm^2 (to the nearest cm^2)

Volume and Surface Area of Cuboids, including Cubes

Class Activity 1

Objective: To observe the nets of cubes and cuboids.

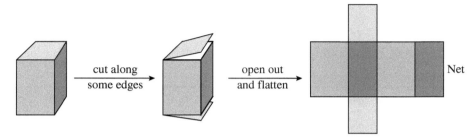

cut along some edges → open out and flatten → Net

1. Collect three cardboard boxes, such as cereal boxes, that are cuboids (some may be cubes).

2. Cut each box along the necessary edges so that each face is still connected with at least one other face and the faces can be laid flat on your desk.

3. Lay the faces flat on your desk. The plane figure formed is called a **net** of the box.

4. Compare the shapes and sizes of your nets with your classmates' nets.

5. Is there only one net for the same box? Explain your answer.

   There is more than one net for the same box. Cuboids (including cubes) have more than one net.

6. How can you tell that a particular net is a net of a cube?

   A net of a 3D shape can be folded up to make the shape. In the net of a cube, every face will be the same shape and size.

Class Activity 2

Objective: To derive the formulae for the surface area of cuboids, including cubes.

1.
 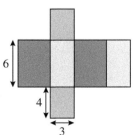

The diagram shows a cuboid of length 6 cm, width 3 cm and height 4 cm and its net.
Copy and complete these expressions.

(a) Area of a yellow face = $\boxed{6} \times \boxed{3\,\text{cm}^2}$

(b) Area of a pink face = $\boxed{6} \times \boxed{4\,\text{cm}^2}$

(c) Area of a green face = $\boxed{4} \times \boxed{3\,\text{cm}^2}$

(d) Surface area of the cuboid
= area of the net
= $\boxed{2}$ × (area of a yellow face + area of a pink face + area of a green face)
= $\boxed{2}$ × $\boxed{6 \times 3 + 6 \times 4 + 4 \times 3}$
= $\boxed{108}$ cm^2

2. If a cuboid has a length of l cm, a width of w cm and a height of h cm, express in terms of l, w and h,

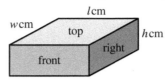

(a) the area of each face of the cuboid,

Area of the top/bottom face = $l \times w = lw$ cm^2

Area of the front/back face = $l \times h = lh$ cm^2

Area of the right/left face = $w \times h = wh$ cm^2

(b) the surface area of the cuboid.
Hint: You can draw a sketch of the cuboid to help you find the answers.

Surface area of the cuboid = $2(lw + lh + wh)$ cm^2

3.

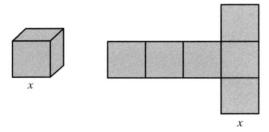

If the cuboid is a cube with length, width and height equal to x cm, express the surface area of the cube in terms of x.

Area of a square on the net = x^2 cm^2

Surface area of the cube = area of the net
= 6 × area of a square on the net
= 6 × x^2
= $6x^2$ cm^2

Chapter 11 Volume and Surface Area of Cuboids, including Cubes

Try It!

Section 11.1

1. Which of these is a net of a cube? Explain your answer.

(a)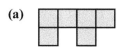

(b)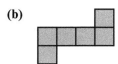

Solution
(a) The figure is not a net of a cube. The two squares at the bottom would overlap each other. There would be no square forming the top.

(b) The figure is a net of a cube. The four central squares form the four side faces, the top square forms the top face and the bottom square forms the base.

2. Which of these is a net of a cuboid? Explain your answer.

Hint: Look carefully at the dimensions of the edges on each face.

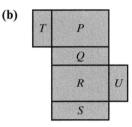

(a)

(b)

Solution
(a) The two squares on the right and left of the figure (E and F) should be rectangles to form the end faces of the cuboid.
Hence, this figure cannot form a cuboid.

(b) The four central rectangles (P, Q, R and S) fold to form the top, bottom, front and back faces. The other two rectangles (T and U) form the end faces on the left and right.
Hence, this figure can form a cuboid.

Section 11.2

3. A cereal box is 23 cm long, 7 cm wide and 30 cm high. Calculate the surface area of the cereal box.

Solution
Surface area of the cereal box
$= 2(lw + lh + wh)$
$= 2 \times (23 \times 7 + 23 \times 30 + 7 \times 30)$
$= 2122 \text{ cm}^2$

4. (a) The length of each edge of a cube is 4 cm. Find the surface area of the cube.

(b) A rectangular box is 8 cm long and 2 cm high. If the box has the same surface area as the cube in (a), find the width of the box.

Solution
(a) Surface area of the cube $= 6x^2$
$= 6 \times 4^2$
$= 96 \text{ cm}^2$

(b) Let w be the width of the box.
Surface area of the box is
$$2(lh + lw + hw) = 96$$
$$2 \times (8 \times 2 + 8 \times w + 2 \times w) = 96$$
$$2 \times (16 + 8w + 2w) = 96$$
$$16 + 10w = 48$$
$$10w = 32$$
$$w = \frac{32}{10}$$
$$w = 3.2 \text{ cm}$$

Section 11.3

5. This solid is formed by 1 cm cubes. Find the volume of the solid.

Solution
Altogether there are 18 cubes in the solid.
Hence, the volume of the solid is 18 cm^3.

6. Find the volume of a cube with edges of length 6 cm.

Solution
Volume of the cube $= 6 \times 6 \times 6$
$= 216 \text{ cm}^3$

7. The internal dimensions of a sink are 43 cm by 32 cm by 10 cm.
(a) Find the volume of water that the sink can hold.
(b) What is the mass of water that the sink can hold?

Solution

(a) Volume of the sink = length × width × height
$$= 43 \times 32 \times 10$$
$$= 13\,760\,\text{cm}^3$$

(b) Mass of $1\,\text{cm}^3$ water = 1 g
Mass of water in the sink $= 13\,760 \times 1\,\text{g}$
$$= 13\,760 \times \frac{1}{1000}\,\text{kg}$$
$$= 13.76\,\text{kg}$$

8. (a) A tank is a cube shape. Its volume is $27\,\text{m}^3$. Find its side length.

(b) Another tank is a cuboid shape. It is 4 m long and 2 m wide. If the volume of the cube and the cuboid tanks are the same, find the height of the cuboid tank.

Solution

(a) Let x be the side length of the tank.
$$x^3 = 27$$
$$x = \sqrt[3]{27}$$
$$x = 3$$
The side length of the tank is 3 m.

(b) Let h be the height of the cuboid tank. Since the two tanks have the same volume,
$$4 \times 2 \times h = 27$$
$$h = \frac{27}{8}$$
$$h = 3\frac{3}{8}$$
The height of the tank is $3\frac{3}{8}\,\text{m}$.

9. In the diagram, the solid is formed by removing a cuboid of dimensions 1 cm by 1.5 cm by 2 cm from a cuboid of dimensions 6 cm by 5 cm by 4 cm.

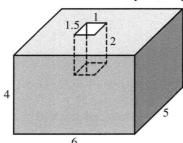

Find
(a) the volume of the solid,
(b) the surface area of the solid.

Solution

(a) Volume of the shape
= volume of the large cuboid − volume of the small cuboid
$$= 6 \times 5 \times 4 - 1 \times 1.5 \times 2$$
$$= 120 - 3$$
$$= 117\,\text{cm}^3$$

(b) Surface area of the shape
= surface area of the large cuboid + area of the 4 vertical faces of the small cuboid
$$= 2 \times (6 \times 5 + 6 \times 4 + 5 \times 4)$$
$$\quad + 2 \times (2 \times 1 + 2 \times 1.5)$$
$$= 148 + 10$$
$$= 158\,\text{cm}^2$$

Exercise 11.1

Level 1   **GCSE Grade 2⁺**

1. Which of these are nets of a cube? Explain.
Hint: You may copy these figures onto square grid paper, cut them out and see if they make cubes.

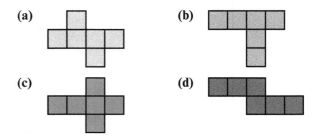

Solution
Generally, figures with a square on each side of four central squares are likely to be nets of a cube. However, advise students to copy the figures on to square grid paper, cut them out and fold them to see if they make cubes.
Figures **(a)**, **(c)** and **(d)** are nets of a cube.
Figure **(b)** is not a net of a cube.

2. Which of these are nets of a cuboid? Explain.
Hint: You may copy these figures onto square grid paper, cut them out and see if they make cuboids.

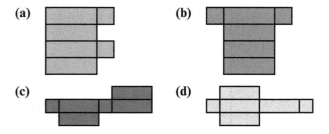

Solution
Generally, figures with a rectangle/square on each side of four central rectangles/squares are likely to form a cuboid.
Figures **(b)** and **(c)** can form cuboids.
Figures **(a)** and **(d)** cannot form a cuboid.
In **(d)**, the two rectangles on the right are in the wrong dimensions.

3. Three of the faces of the cuboid shown are each painted a particular colour, while the other faces are not painted. Which of these are nets of this cuboid?

(1) (2) (3)

Solution

Nets (2) and (3) are nets of the given cuboid.

4. This is the net of a dice that is a cube. The sum of every pair of numbers on opposite faces of the dice is 7. What are the values of *a*, *b* and *c*?

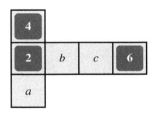

Solution

The values 4 and *a* will be on opposite faces.
$4 + a = 7$
$a = 3$
The values *b* and 6 will be on opposite faces.
$b + 6 = 7$
$b = 1$
The values 2 and *c* will be on opposite faces.
$2 + c = 7$
$c = 5$
So, $a = 3$, $b = 1$ and $c = 5$.

5. Draw a net of a cube different from that in Question **4** which forms a dice with numbers on opposite faces that total 7.

Solution

Some possible nets are shown here.

			3			
		5	1	2	6	
				4		
					4	
		6	2	1	5	
		3				
				6		
			3	2	4	
				1		
				5		

6. Which rectangle has to be removed from the diagram so that the remaining shape is a net of a cuboid?
   Hint: Remember a square is a rectangle too. It is sometimes called a special rectangle.

A	B	C
	D	
	E	F
	G	

Solution

There should be only two square 'ends' of the cuboid. *C* and *F* would overlap when the shape was folded to form a cuboid. Either *C* or *F* should be removed to make the net.

7. Reduce the sizes of two rectangles in the diagram so that the diagram becomes a net of a cuboid. Draw your net.

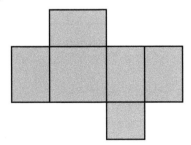

Solution

The face at the top and the face directly below it need to be reduced in width for the diagram to become a net.

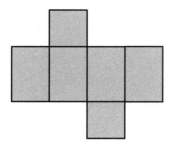

Level 3

GCSE Grade 3⁻/3

8. Draw a net for a cuboid of length 4 cm, width 2 cm and height 1 cm.

Solution

Two possible nets for a cuboid of length 4 cm, width 2 cm and height 1 cm are shown here.

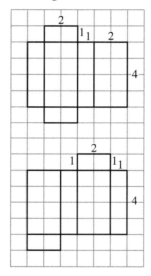

9. When this net is folded into a cube,
    (a) which vertices will join together with the vertex F,
    (b) which line segment in the net will join with AN?

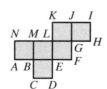

Solution

(a) Vertices D and H will join together with the vertex F.

(b) Line segment IJ will join with AN.

10. **(a)** Copy the diagram and add a square to make it a net of a cube.
    (b) How many different possible ways can you do this?

Solution

(a) Some possible ways to add a square to the given figure to make it a net of a cube are shown here.

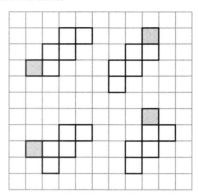

(b) There are 4 different ways to make this a net of a cube.

11. Copy the diagram and add a rectangle to make it a net of a cuboid.

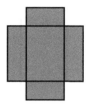

Solution

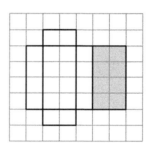

The shaded rectangle is added to make the given figure a net of a cuboid. Alternatively, you can also add the rectangle on the left side of the given figure, or the top or bottom of the figure.

12. Copy the diagram and add a rectangle to make it a net of a cuboid.

Solution

Two possible ways to add a rectangle to the given figure to make it a net of a cuboid are shown here.

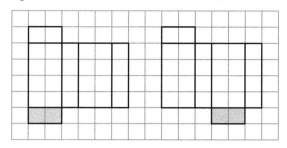

Exercise 11.2

Level 1 **GCSE Grade 3**

1. Find the surface area of a cube if the length of each edge is
   (a) 3 cm, (b) 6 cm,
   (c) 4.5 cm, (d) $2\frac{3}{5}$ cm.

   Hint: You can draw a sketch of the cubes to help you find the answers.

   Solution
   (a) Surface area of the cube
   $$= 6x^2$$
   $$= 6 \times 3^2$$
   $$= 54\,\text{cm}^2$$

   (b) Surface area of the cube
   $$= 6 \times 6^2$$
   $$= 216\,\text{cm}^2$$

   (c) Surface area of the cube
   $$= 6 \times 4.5^2$$
   $$= 121.5\,\text{cm}^2$$

   (d) Surface area of the cube
   $$= 6 \times \left(2\frac{3}{5}\right)^2$$
   $$= 40\frac{14}{25}\,\text{cm}^2 \text{ or}$$
   $$= 40.56\,\text{cm}^2$$

2. Find the surface area of a cuboid with
   (a) length = 8 cm, width = 5 cm and height = 4 cm,
   (b) length = 16 cm, width = 5 cm and height = 4 cm,
   (c) length = 16 cm, width = 10 cm and height = 4 cm,
   (d) length = 16 cm, width = 10 cm and height = 8 cm.
   Hint: You can draw a sketch of the cuboids to help you find the answers.

Solution
(a) Surface area of the cuboid
$$= 2(lw + lh + wh)$$
$$= 2 \times (8 \times 5 + 8 \times 4 + 5 \times 4)$$
$$= 184\,\text{cm}^2$$

(b) Surface area of the cuboid
$$= 2 \times (16 \times 5 + 16 \times 4 + 5 \times 4)$$
$$= 328\,\text{cm}^2$$

(c) Surface area of the cuboid
$$= 2 \times (16 \times 10 + 16 \times 4 + 10 \times 4)$$
$$= 528\,\text{cm}^2$$

(d) Surface area of the cuboid
$$= 2 \times (16 \times 10 + 16 \times 8 + 10 \times 8)$$
$$= 736\,\text{cm}^2$$

Level 2 **GCSE Grade 3 / 4⁻**

3. A wooden cube has edges of length 3.2 cm. Find the surface area of the cube.

   Solution
   Surface area of the cube $= 6 \times 3.2^2$
   $$= 61.44\,\text{cm}^2$$

4. The side length of a dice that is a cube is $2\frac{1}{4}$ cm. Find the surface area of the dice.

   Solution
   Surface area of the dice $= 6 \times \left(2\frac{1}{4}\right)^2$
   $$= 6 \times \left(\frac{9}{4}\right)^2$$
   $$= 30.375\,\text{cm}^2$$

5. A rectangular box is 20 cm long, 13 cm wide and 8 cm high. Find the surface area of the box.

   Solution
   Surface area of the box
   $$= 2 \times (20 \times 13 + 20 \times 8 + 13 \times 8)$$
   $$= 1048\,\text{cm}^2$$

6. A brick is 21.5 cm long, 10.25 cm wide and 6.5 cm high. Calculate the surface area of the brick.

   Solution
   Surface area of the brick
   $$= 2 \times (21.5 \times 10.25 + 21.5 \times 6.5 + 10.25 \times 6.5)$$
   $$= 853.5\,\text{cm}^2$$

7. A rectangular ornamental box is $15\frac{1}{2}$ cm long, $10\frac{4}{5}$ cm wide and $7\frac{3}{5}$ cm wide. Find the surface area of the box.

   Solution
   Surface area of the box
   $$= 2 \times (15.5 \times 10.8 + 15.5 \times 7.6 + 10.8 \times 7.6)$$
   $$= 734.56\,\text{cm}^2$$

8. An open top aquarium tank is 45 cm long, 36 cm wide and 40 cm high. Find the total external surface area of its five sides.

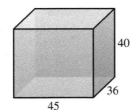

Solution
Surface area of the tank
$= 45 \times 36 + 2 \times 45 \times 40 + 2 \times 40 \times 36$
$= 8100 \, \text{cm}^2$

Level 3   **GCSE Grade** $4^- / 4^+$

9. A cuboid is 10 cm long and 5 cm high. The surface area of the cuboid is 310 cm².

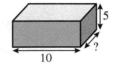

    (a) Find the width of the cuboid.
    (b) Express the width as a percentage of the length.

Solution
(a) Let x cm be the width of the cuboid.
    Given that the surface area of the cuboid = 310 cm²,
    $$2 \times (10 \times 5 + 10 \times x + 5 \times x) = 310$$
    $$2 \times (50 + 10x + 5x) = 310$$
    $$50 + 15x = 155$$
    $$15x = 105$$
    $$x = \frac{105}{15}$$
    $$x = 7$$
    ∴ the width of the cuboid is 7 cm.
(b) $\dfrac{7}{10} = 70\%$
    The width is 70% of the length.

10. The external dimensions of a rectangular tray are 30 cm long, 18 cm wide and 9 cm high. It is made with wooden planks which are 2 cm thick. If the whole tray is painted, what is the painted area?

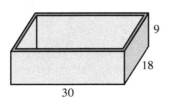

    Note: A tray has no top face. It is called an open 3D shape.

Solution
The surface area of the inside base plus the top edges of 2 cm thickness is the same area as the external base.
Therefore, the surface area of the whole tray is the surface area of a cuboid of dimensions $30 \times 18 \times 9$ plus the area of the 4 inside side faces.

The inside side faces are of height $(9 - 2) = 7 \, \text{cm}$ and width $(18 - 2 - 2) = 14 \, \text{cm}$ or $(30 - 2 - 2) = 26 \, \text{cm}$.
Hence, the surface area of the tray
$= 2 \times (30 \times 18 + 30 \times 9 + 18 \times 9)$
$\quad + 2 \times 7 \times 14 + 2 \times 7 \times 26$
$= 2504 \, \text{cm}^2$

11. A hut is a cuboid of length 3.5 m and width 1.5 m. The total area of the four vertical walls is 25 m². Find
    (a) the area of the roof of the hut,
    (b) the height of the hut.

Solution
(a) Area of roof $= 3.5 \times 1.5$
    $\qquad\qquad\quad = 5.25 \, \text{m}^2$
(b) Let h be the height of the hut.
    Area of the walls $= 2 \times$ length $\times$ height
    $\qquad\qquad\qquad\quad + 2 \times$ width $\times$ height.
    Given the area of the walls is 25 m²,
    $$2 \times 3.5 \times h + 2 \times 1.5 \times h = 25$$
    $$7h + 3h = 25$$
    $$10h = 25$$
    $$h = 2.5 \, \text{m}$$

12. Cuboid A is 15 cm long, 10 cm wide and 8 cm high. Cuboid B is 12 cm wide and 6 cm high. If the surface areas of the two cuboids are equal, find the length of cuboid B.

Solution
Surface area of cuboid A
$= 2 \times (15 \times 10 + 15 \times 8 + 10 \times 8)$
$= 700$
Let l be the length of cuboid B. The surface area of cuboid B is
$$2 \times (l \times 12 + l \times 6 + 12 \times 6) = 700$$
$$2(12l + 6l + 72) = 700$$
$$18l + 72 = 350$$
$$18l = 278$$
$$l = 15\frac{4}{9} \, \text{m}$$

13. The surface area of a cuboid is 136 cm². Work out a possible set of dimensions and sketch the cuboid.

Solution

If the surface area of a cuboid = 136 cm²,
$2(lh + lw + wh) = 136$
where l is the length, w is the width and h is the height of the cuboid.
$lh + lw + wh = \frac{136}{2}$
$lh + lw + wh = 68$

Hint: Similar to the skill used in Question **9**, you can fix the lengths of two sides of the cuboid, say the length and the width, and calculate the height using $lh + lw + wh = 68$.

Some possible dimensions of a cuboid with a surface area of 136 cm² are listed here.

Length l cm	Width w cm	Height h cm
4	4	6.5
5	5	4.3
6	4	4.4
7	5	2.75
8	3	4
10	2	4

Student's sketch

Exercise 11.3

Level 1   GCSE Grade **3**

1. Each solid is formed by 1 cm cubes. Find its volume.

(a) 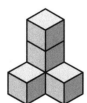 **(b)**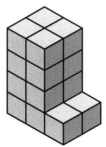

Solution

(a) Altogether there are 5 cubes in the solid. Hence, the volume of the solid is 5 cm³.

(b) Altogether there are 18 cubes in the solid. Hence, the volume of the solid is 18 cm³.

2. Find the volume of a cube with edges that are
(a) 3 cm,   **(b)** 4 m,
(c) 4.8 cm,   **(d)** $1\frac{2}{5}$ m.

Hint: It may be useful to sketch the cubes and write the dimensions on them.

Solution

(a) Volume of the cube
= 3 × 3 × 3
= 27 cm³

(b) Volume of the cube
= 4 × 4 × 4
= 64 m³

(c) Volume of the cube
= 4.8 × 4.8 × 4.8
= 110.592 cm³

(d) Volume of the cube
$= 1\frac{2}{5} \times 1\frac{2}{5} \times 1\frac{2}{5}$
$= \frac{7}{5} \times \frac{7}{5} \times \frac{7}{5}$
$= \frac{343}{125}$
$= 2\frac{93}{125}$ or 2.744 m³

3. Find the volume of a cuboid with the given dimensions.
(a) Length = 6 cm, width = 4 cm, height = 5 cm
(b) Length = 7.1 cm, width = 3.6 cm, height = 4 cm
(c) Length = 2.4 m, width = 1.1 m, height = 0.5 m
(d) Length = $2\frac{2}{5}$ m, width = $1\frac{1}{6}$ m, height = $2\frac{1}{7}$ m

Hint: It may be useful to sketch the cuboids and write the dimensions on them.

Solution

(a) Volume of the cuboid
= length × width × height
= 6 × 4 × 5
= 120 cm³

(b) Volume of the cuboid
= 7.1 × 3.6 × 4
= 102.24 cm³

(c) Volume of the cuboid
= 2.4 × 1.1 × 0.5
= 1.32 m³

(d) Volume of the cuboid
$= 2\frac{2}{5} \times 1\frac{1}{6} \times 2\frac{1}{7}$
$= \frac{12}{5} \times \frac{7}{6} \times \frac{15}{7}$
= 6 m³

4. A paper-weight is a cube of side length 5 cm. Find the volume of the paper-weight.

Solution

Volume of the paper-weight
= 5 × 5 × 5
= 125 cm³

5. The diagram shows a Rubik's cube with sides of length 5.7 cm. Find
  (a) its surface area,
  (b) its volume.

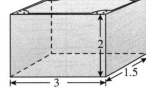

Solution
(a) Surface area of the cube
$$= 6 \times 5.7^2$$
$$= 194.94 \, \text{cm}^2$$

(b) Volume of the cube
$$= 5.7 \times 5.7 \times 5.7$$
$$= 185.193 \, \text{cm}^3$$

6. A carton of juice measures 16 cm by 8 cm by 5 cm. Calculate
  (a) its surface area,
  (b) the volume of juice it can hold.

Solution
(a) Surface area of the carton
$$= 2 \times (16 \times 8 + 16 \times 5 + 8 \times 5)$$
$$= 496 \, \text{cm}^2$$

(b) Volume of juice
$$= 16 \times 8 \times 5$$
$$= 640 \, \text{cm}^3$$

7. A rectangular living room is 6 m long, 4 m wide and 3 m high. Work out
  (a) the area of the ceiling,
  (b) the volume of space in the living room.

Solution
(a) Area of the ceiling $= 6 \times 4$
$$= 24 \, \text{m}^2$$

(b) Volume of space in the room $= 6 \times 4 \times 3$
$$= 72 \, \text{m}^3$$

8. A dice is in the shape of a cube. The volume of the dice is 8 cm³. Find
  (a) the length of an edge of the dice,
  (b) the surface area of the dice.

Solution
(a) Let x cm be the length of an edge of the dice.
Volume of the dice $= 8 \, \text{cm}^3$
$$x^3 = 8$$
$$x = \sqrt[3]{8}$$
$$x = 2$$
Hence, the length of an edge is 2 cm.

(b) Surface area of the dice $= 6x^2$
$$= 6 \times 2^2$$
$$= 24 \, \text{cm}^2$$

9. A rectangular water tank with no top is 3 m long, 1.5 m wide and 2 m high. Calculate
  (a) the internal surface area of the tank,
  (b) the volume of water that the tank can hold,
  (c) the mass of water in the tank when full, given that the mass of 1 m³ of water is 1000 kg.

Solution
(a) Surface area of the 4 sides and the base of the tank
$$= 2lh + 2wh + lw$$
$$= 2 \times 3 \times 2 + 2 \times 2 \times 1.5 + 3 \times 1.5$$
$$= 22.5 \, \text{m}^2$$

(b) Volume of the tank
$$= 3 \times 2 \times 1.5$$
$$= 9 \, \text{m}^3$$

(c) Mass of the water $= 9 \times 1000$
$$= 9000 \, \text{kg}$$

10. A rectangular aquarium tank is 1.2 m long, 80 cm wide and 60 cm deep. Given that 1 litre = 1000 cm³, how many litres of water does the tank hold?

Solution
Length of tank $= 1.2 \, \text{m}$
$$= 120 \, \text{cm}$$
Volume of tank in cm³ $= 120 \times 80 \times 60$
$$= 576 \, 000$$
Volume of tank $= (576\,000 \div 1000)$ litres
$$= 576 \text{ litres}$$

11. A rectangular biscuit tin is 20 cm long, 12 cm wide and 6 cm high. A rectangular sweet tin is 18 cm long and 10 cm wide. Both tins have the same volume.
  (a) Find the height of the sweet tin.
  (b) Do both tins have the same surface area? Explain your answer.

Solution
(a) Volume of the biscuit tin $= (20 \times 12 \times 6) \, \text{cm}^3$
$$= 1440 \, \text{cm}^3$$
Let h be the height of the sweet tin.
$$18 \times 10 \times h = 1440$$
$$180h = 1440$$
$$h = 8 \, \text{cm}$$

(b) Surface area of the biscuit tin
$$= 2 \times (20 \times 12 + 20 \times 6 + 12 \times 6)$$
$$= 2 \times 432$$
$$= 864 \, \text{cm}^2$$

Surface area of the sweet tin
$= 2 \times (18 \times 10 + 18 \times 8 + 10 \times 8)$
$= 2 \times 404$
$= 808\,\text{cm}^2$
The two tins do not have the same surface area.

12. In the diagram, a rectangular hole that is 5 cm long, 1.5 cm wide and 2 cm high is cut through a cube of side length 5 cm.

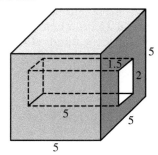

Find
(a) the volume of the solid formed,
(b) the surface area of the solid formed.

Solution
(a) Volume of the solid = volume of the cube −
volume of the hole
$= 5 \times 5 \times 5 - 5 \times 1.5 \times 2$
$= 125 - 15$
$= 110\,\text{cm}^3$
(b) Surface area of the solid
= surface area of the cube
− area of the two ends of the hole
+ area of 4 horizontal faces of the hole
$= 6 \times 5 \times 5 - 2 \times 1.5 \times 2 + 2 \times 5 \times 2$
$\quad + 2 \times 5 \times 1.5$
$= 150 - 6 + 20 + 15$
$= 179\,\text{cm}^2$

13. The diagram shows an open rectangular container. It is made of wooden planks which are 1 cm thick. The external dimensions are 16 cm by 10 cm by 6 cm. Find
(a) the volume of wood in the container,
(b) the total surface area of the container.

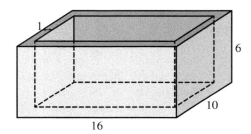

Solution
(a) You can calculate this a few different ways –
just be careful not to double-count the edges!

Volume of wood
= volume of base + volume of 2 short sides
+ volume of 2 long sides
$= 16 \times 10 \times 1 + 2 \times (6 - 1) \times 10 \times 1$
$\quad + 2 \times (6 - 1) \times (16 - 1 - 1)$
$= 160 + 100 + 140$
$= 400\,\text{cm}^3$
(b) Surface area of container
= surface area of cuboid 16 by 10 by 6
(imagine the inside base pulled up to meet
the top edges) + surface area of the 4 vertical
inside walls of the container
$= 2 \times (16 \times 10 + 16 \times 6 + 10 \times 6)$
$\quad + 2 \times 5 \times (10 - 1 - 1) + 2 \times 5 \times (16 - 1 - 1)$
$= 632 + 80 + 140$
$= 852\,\text{cm}^2$

14. A rectangular chocolate box is 20 cm long, 8 cm wide and 5 cm high.
(a) What happens to the volume if the width is doubled? Is the same true if the height is doubled? Show your working.
(b) Show what happens to the surface area if the width is doubled. Is the same true if the height is doubled? Show your working.

Solution
(a) Volume of the original box $= 20 \times 8 \times 5$
$\qquad\qquad\qquad\qquad = 800\,\text{cm}^3$
If the width is doubled, volume of the new box
$= 20 \times (8 \times 2) \times 5$
$= 20 \times 16 \times 5$
$= 1600\,\text{cm}^3$
Comparing the two volumes, you see that the volume of the box is doubled if the width is doubled.

Now, if the height is doubled, the volume of the new box $= 20 \times 8 \times (5 \times 2)$
$\qquad\qquad\qquad = 20 \times 8 \times 10$
$\qquad\qquad\qquad = 1600\,\text{cm}^3$
Comparing this volume and the original volume, you see that the volume of the box is doubled if the height is doubled.

(b) Surface area of the original box
$= 2 \times (20 \times 8 + 20 \times 5 + 8 \times 5)$
$= 600\,\text{cm}^2$
If the width is doubled, the surface area of the new box $= 2 \times (20 \times 16 + 20 \times 5 + 16 \times 5)$
$\qquad\qquad\qquad = 1000\,\text{cm}^2$
If the height is doubled, the surface area of the new box $= 2 \times (20 \times 8 + 20 \times 10 + 8 \times 10)$
$\qquad\qquad\qquad = 880\,\text{cm}^2$
If the width or height is doubled, the surface area of the box will increase but the amount or ratio of increase is not the same in each case.

15. A closed rectangular box has a length of 15 cm and a width of 8 cm. The volume of the box is 840 cm³. Find the surface area of the box.

Solution
Let h cm be the height of the box.
Volume of the box = 840 cm³
$$15 \times 8 \times h = 840$$
$$120h = 840$$
$$h = \frac{840}{120}$$
$$h = 7$$
The height of the box is 7 cm.
∴ the surface area of the box
$$= 2 \times (15 \times 8 + 15 \times 7 + 8 \times 7)$$
$$= 562 \text{ cm}^2$$

16. A small parcel box is 45 cm long, 35 cm wide and 16 cm high.
   (a) Find the volume of the box.
   (b) The box is filled with as many glass cubes as possible. Each glass cube has edges of length 5 cm.
       (i) How many glass cubes fit into the box?
       (ii) What is the volume of the remaining space in the box?
   Hint: You may draw a picture to help you understand the problem.

Solution
   (a) Volume of the box
$$= 45 \times 35 \times 16$$
$$= 25\,200 \text{ cm}^3$$

   (b) (i) The number of cubes that fit:
       along the length of the box is $\frac{45}{5} = 9$

       along the width of the box is $\frac{35}{5} = 7$

       along the height of the box is $\frac{16}{5} = 3$, r 1
       Therefore the number of cubes that fit inside the box
$$= 9 \times 7 \times 3$$
$$= 189$$
   (ii) The total volume taken up by the cubes
$$= 189 \times \text{volume of a single cube}$$
$$= 189 \times 5 \times 5 \times 5$$
$$= 23\,625$$
       Therefore the volume of the remaining space is
$$= 25\,200 - 23\,625$$
$$= 1575 \text{ cm}^3$$

17. A silver bar, in the shape of a cuboid, has rectangular ends of 5 cm by 2 cm. The mass of 1 cm³ of silver is 10.5 grams. If the mass of the bar is 630 grams, find the length of the bar.

Solution
Let l be the length of the bar.
Volume of the bar = $5 \times 2 \times l$
$$= 10l \text{ cm}^3$$
Mass of the bar = $10l \times 10.5$
$$= 105l \text{ grams}$$
$$630 = 105l$$
$$l = 6$$
The length of the bar is 6 cm.

18. A rectangular bucket with length 18 cm, width 12 cm and height 15 cm is completely filled with water. The water is then poured into a rectangular tank with length 45 cm and width 24 cm. Calculate the height of the water in the tank.

Solution
Volume of water in the bucket = $18 \times 12 \times 15$
$$= 3240 \text{ cm}^3$$
Let h be the height of water in the tank.
Volume of water in the tank = $45 \times 24 \times h$
$$3240 = 45 \times 24 \times h$$
$$3240 = 1080h$$
$$h = 3$$
The height of water in the tank = 3 cm.

Revision Exercise 11

1. (a) Which of these is a net of a cube?

   (i)

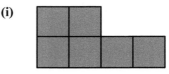

   (ii)

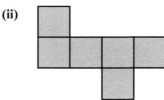

   (b) If each edge of the cube formed in **(a)** is 8 cm, find
       (i) the total surface area of the cube,
       (ii) the volume of the cube.

Solution
   (a) (i) The figure is not a net of a cube. The two squares at the top would overlap each other. There would be no square forming one of the faces.
       (ii) The figure is a net of a cube. The four central squares form the four side faces, the top square forms the top and the bottom square forms the base.

(b) **(i)** The total surface area of the cube
$$= 6 \times 8^2$$
$$= 384 \, \text{cm}^2$$
(ii) Volume of the cube
$$= 8 \times 8 \times 8$$
$$= 512 \, \text{cm}^3$$

2. The diagram shows the net of a dice.

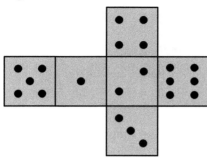

Which of the following dice is made from the net?
Hint: Look carefully at the nets. Which faces will be
opposite each other when the dice is made?

(a)   **(b)**   **(c)**

Solution
Dice **(a)** is formed from the given net.

3. The diagram shows the net of a cuboid where
$AB = 3 \, \text{cm}$, $CD = 1 \, \text{cm}$ and $DE = 2 \, \text{cm}$.

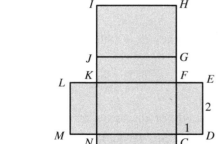

(a) When folded into a cuboid,
  (i) which vertices meet with the vertex B,
  (ii) which edge joins with the edge IJ?
(b) Calculate the surface area of the cuboid.
(c) Calculate the volume of the cuboid.

Solution
(a) **(i)** Vertex B meets with vertices D and H.

  (ii) The edge IJ joins with the edge ML.

(b) Surface area of the cuboid
$$= 2 \times (3 \times 1 + 3 \times 2 + 1 \times 2)$$
$$= 22 \, \text{cm}^2$$

(c) Volume of the cuboid
$$= 3 \times 2 \times 1$$
$$= 6 \, \text{cm}^3$$

4. A wooden plank is $30 \, \text{cm}$ long, $20 \, \text{cm}$ wide and $4 \, \text{cm}$ thick.

(a) Find its surface area.
(b) If the mass of $1 \, \text{cm}^3$ of wood is 0.5 grams, work out the mass of the wooden plank.

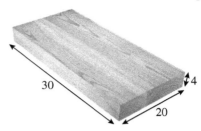

Solution
(a) Surface area of the plank
$$= 2 \times (30 \times 20 + 30 \times 4 + 20 \times 4)$$
$$= 1600 \, \text{cm}^2$$

(b) Volume of the plank
$$= 30 \times 20 \times 4$$
$$= 2400 \, \text{cm}^3$$
∴ the mass of the plank
$$= 2400 \times 0.5$$
$$= 1200 \, \text{grams}$$

5. A garden shed is in the shape of a cuboid. It is $3 \, \text{m}$ long, $2 \, \text{m}$ wide and $2.5 \, \text{m}$ tall. Calculate
(a) the volume of the space inside the shed,
(b) the total area of the four walls and the roof of the shed.
Hint: You may draw a diagram with the dimensions on it to help you.

Solution
(a) Volume of the space inside the shed
$$= 3 \times 2 \times 2.5$$
$$= 15 \, \text{m}^3$$

(b) Total area of the four walls and the roof
$$= 2 \times 3 \times 2.5 + 2 \times 2 \times 2.5 + (3 \times 2)$$
$$= 31 \, \text{m}^2$$

6. A rectangular swimming pool is $25 \, \text{m}$ long, $10 \, \text{m}$ wide and $2 \, \text{m}$ deep.
(a) What is the volume of water required to fill the pool?
(b) Find the total area of the four walls and the base of the pool.

Solution
(a) Volume of water required to fill the pool
$$= 25 \times 10 \times 2$$
$$= 500 \, \text{m}^3$$

(b) Total area of the four walls and the base
$$= 2 \times 25 \times 2 + 2 \times 10 \times 2 + (25 \times 10)$$
$$= 390 \, \text{m}^2$$

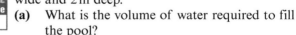

7. A rectangular room is 5 m by 4 m and has a height of 3 m.

(a) Find the volume of space in the room.

(b) Jason plans to paint the two longer walls and the ceiling of the room. One tin of paint covers 6 m². How many tins of paint does he need?

Solution

(a) Volume of space in the room
$$= 5 \times 4 \times 3$$
$$= 60 \text{ m}^3$$

(b)
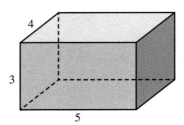

Total area of the two longer walls and the ceiling of the room
$$= 2 \times (5 \times 3) + (5 \times 4)$$
$$= 50 \text{ m}^2$$

One tin of paint covers 6 m².
To find the number of tins of paint required for 50 m², you divide 50 m² by 6 m².
$50 \div 6 = 8$, r 2
Check: $8 \times 6 = 48$
8 tins of paint can cover only 48 m², leaving 2 m² of the surface not painted.
Hence, 9 tins of paint are required.

8. A rectangular water tank has a base of 30 cm by 25 cm. The depth of water in it is 17 cm.

(a) Find the volume of water in the tank.

(b) Tammy adds 1500 cm³ of water to the tank. Calculate the new depth of water.

Solution

(a) Volume of water in the tank
$$= 30 \times 25 \times 17$$
$$= 12\,750 \text{ cm}^3$$

(b) Let d cm be the depth covered by 1500 cm³ of water in the tank.
Volume of water added = 1500 cm³
$$30 \times 25 \times d = 1500$$
$$750d = 1500$$
$$d = \frac{1500}{750}$$
$$d = 2$$
i.e. when Tammy adds 1500 cm³ of water to the tank, the depth of water rises by 2 cm.
Hence, the new depth of water $= 17 + 2$
$$= 19 \text{ cm}$$

9. A solid is formed by placing a cube of edge 5 cm on top of a cube of edge 8 cm. Find

(a) the volume of the solid,

(b) the surface area of the solid.

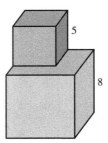

Solution

(a) Volume of the solid
= sum of the volumes of the two cubes
$$= (5 \times 5 \times 5) + (8 \times 8 \times 8)$$
$$= 125 + 512$$
$$= 637 \text{ cm}^3$$

(b) Surface area of the solid.
$$= 5 \times 8^2 + 5 \times 5^2 + (8^2 - 5^2)$$
$$= 320 + 125 + 39$$
$$= 484 \text{ cm}^2$$

10. A closed rectangular box is 12 cm long and 8 cm wide. The volume of the box is 480 cm³. Find

(a) the height of the box,

(b) the surface area of the box.

Hint: A closed rectangular box means the box has six faces.

Solution

(a) Let h cm be the height of the box.
Volume of the box = 480 cm³
$$12 \times 8 \times h = 480$$
$$96h = 480$$
$$h = 480 \div 96$$
$$h = 5$$
∴ the height of the box is 5 cm.

(b) The surface area of the box
$$= 2 \times (12 \times 8 + 12 \times 5 + 8 \times 5)$$
$$= 392 \text{ cm}^2$$

11. (a) A shipping container is a cuboid of length 6.1 m, width 2.44 m and height 2.59 m. Using a calculator, find

(i) the surface area of the container to the nearest m²,

(ii) the volume of the container to the nearest m³.

(b) Another shipping container is a cuboid of length 12.2 m, width 2.44 m and height 2.59 m. Explain whether this container has

(i) double the volume of the container in (a),

(ii) double the surface area of the container in (a).

Solution

(a) **(i)** Surface area = $2 \times (6.1 \times 2.44 + 6.1 \times 2.59$
$\qquad\qquad\qquad + 2.44 \times 2.59)$
$\qquad\qquad = 74.0052$
$\qquad\qquad = 74\,m^2$ (to the nearest m²)

(ii) Volume = $6.1 \times 2.44 \times 2.59$
$\qquad\qquad = 38.549\,56$
$\qquad\qquad = 39\,m^3$ (to the nearest m³)

(b) **(i)** Volume of second container
$\qquad\quad = 12.2 \times 2.44 \times 2.59$
$\qquad\quad = 2 \times (6.1 \times 2.44 \times 2.59)$
$\qquad\quad = 2 \times$ volume of first container

(ii) Surface area of second container
$\qquad\quad = 2 \times (12.2 \times 2.44 + 12.2 \times 2.59 +$
$\qquad\qquad 2.44 \times 2.59)$
$\qquad\quad = 135.3712$
Surface area of first container doubled
$\qquad\quad = 2 \times 74.0052 = 148.0104$
The surface area of the second container is larger than the first, but the surface area is not doubled when one of the dimensions is doubled.

12. In the diagram, the solid is formed by removing a cuboid of dimensions 2 cm by 2 cm by 1 cm from a cube of side 4 cm.

GCSE Grade 4+

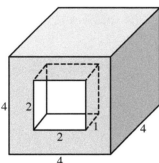

Find
(a) the volume of the solid,
(b) the surface area of the solid.

Solution

(a) Volume of the solid
$\quad$ = volume of cube − volume of small cuboid
$\quad = 4 \times 4 \times 4 - 2 \times 2 \times 1$
$\quad = 64 - 4$
$\quad = 60\,cm^3$

(b) Surface area of the solid
$\quad$ = surface area of the cube (imagine the base of the hole brought up to the top of the hole) + surface area of 4 inside faces of the cuboid
$\quad = 6 \times 4 \times 4 + 4 \times 2 \times 1$
$\quad = 96 + 8$
$\quad = 104\,cm^2$

13. Each carton of juice is a cuboid of height 12 cm, length 6 cm and width 4 cm. Six cartons of juice are packed together using some wrapping material.

GCSE Grade 4−

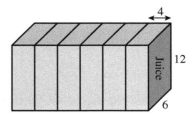

Diagram 1

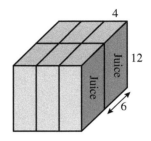

Diagram 2

(a) If six cartons are packed in a row as shown in Diagram 1, what is the area of the wrapping material in contact with the cartons?
(b) If six cartons are packed three by two as shown in Diagram 2, what is the area of the wrapping material in contact with the cartons?
(c) Which of the above packaging methods uses less wrapping material?

Solution

(a) The packaging in Diagram 1 has length
$6 \times 4 = 24$ cm, width 6 cm and height 12 cm.
The surface area of the wrapping material
$= 2 \times (24 \times 6 + 24 \times 12 + 6 \times 12)$
$= 1008\,cm^2$

(b) The packaging in Diagram 2 has length
$3 \times 4 = 12$ cm, width $2 \times 6 = 12$ cm and height 12 cm.
The surface area of the wrapping material
$= 6 \times 12^2$
$= 864\,cm^2$

(c) The packaging method used in Diagram 2 uses less wrapping material.

14. A piece of cheese is a cuboid with square ends. The height of the cheese is 13 cm and its volume is 637 cm³. Find

GCSE Grade 4

(a) the side length of the ends,
(b) the total surface area of the cheese.

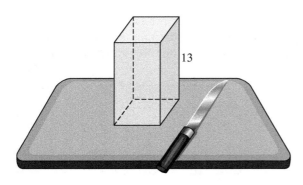

Solution

(a) Let x cm be the length of a side of the square end.

Volume of cheese cuboid $= 637\,\text{cm}^3$

$$x \times x \times 13 = 637$$
$$13x^2 = 637$$
$$x^2 = 637 + 13$$
$$x^2 = 49$$
$$x^2 = \sqrt{49}$$
$$x = 7$$

Hence, the length of a side of each end is 7 cm.

(b) Total surface area of the cheese
$$= 2 \times (7 \times 7 + 7 \times 13 + 7 \times 13)$$
$$= 462\,\text{cm}^2$$

15. An iron block is 15 cm long, 8 cm wide and 6 cm high. It is melted and recast into a rectangular bar measuring 5 cm wide and 2 cm high.

(a) What is the length of the bar?

(b) Find the surface area of the iron block.

(c) Express the surface area of the block as a percentage of the surface area of the bar.

Solution

(a) Let l be the length of the bar. Since the volume of iron is the same as for the block,
$$5 \times 2 \times l = 15 \times 8 \times 6$$
$$10l = 720$$
$$l = 72\,\text{cm}$$

(b) Surface area of the block
$$= 2 \times (15 \times 8 + 15 \times 6 + 8 \times 6)$$
$$= 2 \times 258$$
$$= 516\,\text{cm}^2$$

(c) Surface area of the bar
$$= 2 \times (72 \times 5 + 72 \times 2 + 5 \times 2)$$
$$= 2 \times 514$$
$$= 1028\,\text{cm}^2$$

Surface area of the block as a percentage of the surface area of the bar

$$= \frac{516}{1028} \times 100\%$$

$$= 50.194...\%$$
$$= 50\% \text{ (to the nearest \%)}$$

12 Collecting, Organising and Displaying Data

Class Activity 1

Objective: To select an appropriate data collection method.

Task

Discuss and suggest an appropriate way (e.g. taking measurements, observing outcomes, conducting surveys, reading publications) to collect data about

(a) favourite sports of Year 7 students in your school,

Conducting a survey

(b) body temperatures of a group of patients,

Taking measurements

(c) popularity of a singer,

Conducting surveys

(d) restaurant customer service,

Conducting surveys

(e) effectiveness of a new medicine,

Taking measurements

(f) population of Thailand, Malaysia and Indonesia in 2010.

Reading publications

Class Activity 2

Objective: To discuss the advantages and disadvantages of using pictograms and bar charts.

1. The following table shows the number of different types of trees on a farm.

Tree	Apple	Peach	Pear	Plum
Number of trees	32	16	20	9

You are the owner of the farm and would like to present the data by a graph to visitors. If the data is to be represented by a pictogram or a bar chart, which graph

(a) is easier to draw,

The bar chart is easier to draw.

(b) is more appealing to the public,

The pictogram is more appealing to the public.

(c) is easier to read the number of trees from?

It is easier to read the number of trees from the bar chart.

2. The following table shows the ages of students in a youth centre.

Age (years)	12	13	14	15	16
Number of male students	16	23	16	19	8
Number of female students	12	17	20	15	13

Would a pictogram or a bar chart be more appropriate to represent the data? Explain your answer.

A pictogram uses an icon to represent quantities. An icon cannot effectively represent both male and female students. Also, a pictogram is not able

to show an exact number of students accurately. Therefore, a bar chart would be more appropiate for representing the data.

Try It!

Section 12.1

1. The question below is used in a survey about the number of gym visits in a month made by some clerks.

> **How many times do you go to a gym?**
> ○ 2 to 4
> ○ 10 to 20
> ○ 20 to 25

What is wrong with this question design?

Solution
Student's answer. Examples of possible answers: There are gaps (between 4 and 10 times) and overlap (for 20 times) in the categories. The categories do not cover the possible range of responses (there could be a response of fewer than 2 or more than 25 times). The question is ambiguous because it does not explicitly ask about visits over the period of a month.

Section 12.2

2. A sweet shop has 18 bags of jelly beans. The number of jelly beans in each bag is inspected and recorded as shown.

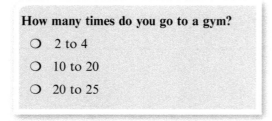

```
49   50   49   50   50   51
48   51   50   49   50   49
51   50   48   51   50   49
```

Construct a frequency table to represent the data.

Solution

Number of jelly beans	Tally	Frequency
48	//	2
49	###	5
50	### //	7
51	////	4
Total		18

3. This list shows the fitness grades ranging from A to E of 36 students.

B	B	A	C	D	C	A	B	E
C	A	D	B	C	E	D	C	B
D	E	E	A	D	B	C	B	A
E	C	B	C	E	C	D	C	D

Construct a frequency table to represent the data.

Solution

Fitness grade	Tally	Frequency
A	###	5
B	### ///	8
C	### ###	10
D	### //	7
E	### /	6
Total		36

4. The following list shows the prices (in pounds) of 24 skirts.

```
23   45   19   18   33   36   25   37
47   30   29   40   34   25   38   12
32   13   41   20   36   34   28   22
```

(a) Represent the data in a frequency table with class intervals $10 < x \le 20$, $20 < x \le 30$ and so on.

(b) Find the percentage of skirts with prices higher than £30.

Solution

(a)

Price (£)	Tally	Frequency
$10 < x \leq 20$	ﬀ	5
$20 < x \leq 30$	ﬀ //	7
$30 < x \leq 40$	ﬀ ////	9
$40 < x \leq 50$	///	3
	Total	24

(b) Percentage of skirts with prices higher than £30

$$= \frac{3+9}{24} \times 100\%$$

$$= \frac{12}{24} \times 100\%$$

$$= 50\%$$

Section 12.3

5. The pictogram below shows the number of plants in a flowerbed.

Number of plants in a flowerbed

Daffodil	✿ ✿ ✿ ✿ ✿
Marigold	✿ ✿ ✿ ✾
Rose	✿ ✿ ✿ ✿ ✿ ✿ ✿ ✾
Tulip	✿ ✿ ✿ ✿ ✿ ✿ ✿ ✾

✿ represents 5 plants

(a) Which type of plant is the most common in the flowerbed?

(b) Find the difference between the numbers of marigolds and tulips in the flowerbed.

Solution

(a) The row of roses has the most symbols. Therefore, roses are the most common in the flowerbed.

(b) Difference = 32 − 18
= 14
There are 14 more tulips than marigolds.

6. The following table shows the number of holidays booked with a travel company from May to August.

Month	May	June	July	August
Number of holidays booked	193	201	258	182

(a) Represent the data in a pictogram.

(b) Read from the pictogram the month in which the number of holidays booked was the lowest.

Solution

(a) Number of holidays booked from May to August

May	•••• •• •• ••• ••
June	••• •• •• •••
July	••• •• •• ••• •• ••• •
August	••• •• •• •• •••

•• represents 50 booked holidays

(b) The number of holidays booked is the lowest in August.

7. Lindsey asks a group of students in her class how they travelled to school that day. She records the results in this frequency table shown. The vertical line chart below is incomplete.

Method of transport	Number of students
Walk	13
Car	10
Bus	4
Train	6
Bicycle	8
Taxi	1

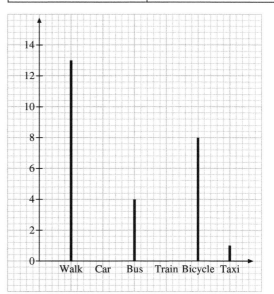

(a) Copy and complete the vertical line chart.

(b) How many students travelled to school by bicycle that day?

(c) Which type of transport was most common that day?

Solution

(a)

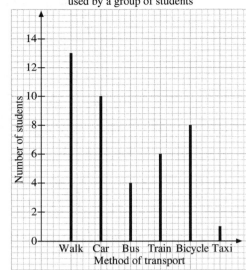

Method of transport to school
used by a group of students

(b)   8 students travelled to school by bicycle that day.

(c)   The tallest line in the vertical line chart indicates the highest frequency.
∴ the most common type of transport that day was walking.

8.   The stock (in kg) of tea, graded A, B, C and D, in a shop is shown in the table.

Grade of tea	Mass (kg)
A	5
B	10
C	13
D	8

(a)   Find the total mass of tea in stock.
(b)   Display the data in a bar chart.
(c)   Which grade of tea has the lowest stock?

Solution

(a)   Total mass of tea = 5 + 10 + 13 + 8
            = 36 kg

(b)

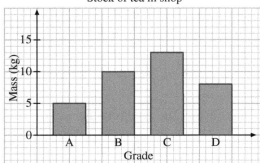

Stock of tea in shop

(c)   Grade A has the lowest stock.

9.   The compound bar chart shows the sales of coffee and tea in a café over four hour sessions on a certain morning.

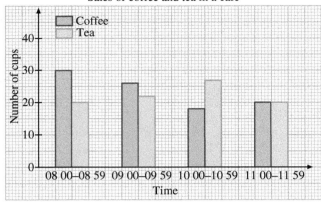

Sales of coffee and tea in a café

(a)   Compare the sales of coffee over the four hour sessions.
(b)   During which period were the sales of tea more than those of coffee?
(c)   How many cups of coffee were sold during the four hour sessions?

Solution

(a)   The sales of coffee (30 cups) were highest between 08 00 and 08 59. The sales of coffee (18 cups) were lowest at between 10 00 and 10 59.

(b)   The sales of tea were more than those of coffee between 10 00 and 10 59.

(c)   Total number of cups of coffee sold
       = 30 + 26 + 18 + 20
       = 94

Exercise 12.1

Level 1   GCSE Grade 2⁺

1.   Roma wanted to determine whether a dice was biased. She threw the dice 120 times and recorded the results.
(a)   What kind of data collection method did she use?
(b)   What are the possible results for each throw?

Solution

(a)   She used the method of observing outcomes in an experiment.

(b)   The possible scores for each throw are 1, 2, 3, 4, 5 or 6.

2. A teacher wants to find out the number of his Year 7 students who have birthdays falling in each month of the year. He collects the data in the following ways.

  (a) Checking the date of birth of each student in the class register.

  (b) Asking the students to raise their hands if their birthdays fall within a certain month.

  (c) Getting the students to fill out a form which asks for their birth dates and return the forms to him.

Name the data collection method used in each case.

Hint: Choose from these methods: taking measurements, observing outcomes, conducting surveys, reading publications.

Solution

  (a) Reading publications

  (b) Observing outcomes

  (c) Conducting surveys

Level 2   **GCSE Grade** 2⁺ / 3⁻

3. A hospital conducts a study on the causes of sports injuries.
  (a) Which data collection method would be appropriate for conducting this study?
  (b) What might be the purpose of this study?

Solution

  (a) The data can be collected by conducting a survey on patients with sports injuries.

  (b) The purpose of the study may be to educate the public on the prevention of sports injuries.

4. A zoologist studies the growth rates of chickens on different feeds.
  (a) Which data collection method should be used?
  (b) What data should be collected?

Solution

  (a) The data can be collected by taking measurements of the masses of chickens on different feeds.

  (b) The data which should be collected is the masses of chickens taken at regular time intervals.

5. A survey is conducted about the Underground services in London during peak hours.
  (a) Which kind of people should be included in the sample? Explain your choice.

  Senior citizens   Commuters   Students

  (b) In what way should a questionnaire be completed? Explain your choice.

  Postal   Telephone   Personal
  questionnaire   inquiry   interview

Solution

  (a) Commuters should be included in the sample. They will be the users of the Underground in London during peak hours.

  (b) The questionnaire should be completed by personal interview as commuters can be easily identified.

Level 3   **GCSE Grade** 3⁻ / 3

6. Consider the following question taken from a questionnaire conducted by a hotel.

How do you rate our services?

1   2   3   4   5   6   7

Point out two areas for improvement in the design of this question.

Solution
Student's answer, e.g. state whether 1 or 7 is the best rating, detail which services are being asked about.

7. Consider the following question taken from a questionnaire about the pocket money that students receive.

How much pocket money do you have?

☐ £10 – £20   ☐ £20 – £30   ☐ £30 – £40

Point out two mistakes in the design of this question.

Solution
Student's answer, e.g. there is an overlap in the categories for values £20 and £30, the questionnaire does not say if, for instance, the amount is per week or per month, not all possible responses are covered.

8. A restaurant manager requests that her customers fill in the following questionnaire.

ABC Restaurant
Customer Satisfaction Survey

1. How would you rate our food?
   ☐ Very good   ☐ Good   ☐ OK
   ☐ Bad   ☐ Very bad

2. Does the level of customer service meet your expectations?

(a) What type of data collection method does the manager use?

(b) Which question in the survey form is better? Why?

(c) Is it a good idea to include the date of visit in the survey form? Explain your answer.

Solution

(a) Conducting surveys

(b) The first question is better since it gives more information about the customer's opinion. For instance, a customer could answer 'no' to the second question when they were unexpectedly delighted by the service.

(c) Including the date would mean that the results could be tracked over time to check for any trends in results or if any particular actions by the manager have had an effect on the results, e.g. introducing a new menu or a staff training programme.

9. Design your own survey form and answer the following questions about your form.
  (a) State the objective of the survey.
  (b) Describe the styles of the questions included.
  (c) Describe some of its good features.

Solution
Student's answer

10. Suggest data that you could collect in your school using the method of
  (a) taking measurements,
  (b) observing outcomes,
  (c) conducting surveys,
  (d) reading publications.

Solution

(a) Student's answer, e.g. heights of classmates, times taken to run 100m, classroom temperature

(b) Student's answer, e.g. record the number of visitors to the library each day, the number of vehicles driving past the school between certain hours of the day

(c) Student's answer, e.g. satisfaction with school lunches, views on school uniform, favourite school subjects

(d) Student's answer, e.g. the number of children taking various exam subjects in Year 11 across the UK, the number of children receiving free school meals in the UK

Exercise 12.2

Level 1   `GCSE Grade 1 / 1⁺`

1. This list shows the ages, measured to the nearest year, of students in a Taekwondo class.

13	14	13	12	15	14	13	13
12	13	13	14	14	15	12	13
13	12	14	14	13	14	13	12
14	15	13	13	12	13	14	13

Construct a frequency table for the data.

Solution

Age (years)	Tally	Frequency
12	⑷ /	6
13	⑷ ⑷ ////	14
14	⑷ ////	9
15	///	3
	Total	32

2. This list shows the number of pets in 30 different families.

3	1	2	1	1	0	1	4	2	1
1	0	0	1	2	3	0	1	1	0
3	2	4	1	0	0	2	1	3	2

Construct a frequency table for the data.

Solution

Number of pets	Tally	Frequency
0	⑷ //	7
1	⑷ ⑷ /	11
2	⑷ /	6
3	////	4
4	//	2
	Total	30

3. Ali, Ben and Cili are candidates for the post of class representative. This list shows the votes received by the three candidates from the other 40 students in the class.

Ben	Ben	Ali	Ben	Cili	Cili	Ali	Ben	Cili	Ali
Ali	Cili	Cili	Ben	Ben	Ali	Cili	Ben	Ali	Cili
Cili	Ben	Ben	Ali	Cili	Ben	Ali	Cili	Ben	Ben
Ali	Ben	Cili	Cili	Ben	Ben	Ali	Cili	Cili	Ben

(a) Construct a frequency table for the data.
(b) Who will be the class representative according to the votes?

Solution

(a)

Candidate	Tally	Frequency
Ali	### ###	10
Ben	### ### ### /	16
Cili	### ### ////	14
	Total	40

(b) Ben will be the class representative.

Level 2   GCSE Grade 2

4. This list is a record of the grades of 40 students in a maths exam.

B	C	A	D	E	A	B	C	C	B
D	C	C	A	B	D	E	C	D	C
B	B	D	E	A	D	B	D	E	E
C	E	C	B	D	C	C	A	D	C

(a) Construct a frequency table for the data.
(b) What was the grade obtained by the highest number of students?
(c) Find the percentage of students who obtained grade A or grade B.

Solution

(a)

Grade	Tally	Frequency
A	###	5
B	### ///	8
C	### ### //	12
D	### ////	9
E	### /	6
	Total	40

(b) Grade C is obtained by the most students.

(c) Percentage of students who obtained grade A or grade B

$$= \frac{5+8}{40} \times 100\%$$

$$= 32.5\%$$

5. This list shows the distances (in km) covered by 30 passengers who took taxis.

7.2	2.8	4.2	6.0	6.5	3.3	5.3	9.0	7.1	0.8
4.1	3.7	8.1	3.6	4.7	6.4	8.4	1.5	5.5	7.9
9.3	5.8	6.9	5.7	1.6	2.3	4.8	4.0	9.2	6.5

(a) Construct a frequency table of uniform intervals for the data, using the intervals $0 < x \le 2$, $2 < x \le 4$ and so on.
(b) Find the percentage of passengers who covered more than 6 km.

Solution

(a)

Distance (km)	Tally	Frequency
$0 < x \le 2$	///	3
$2 < x \le 4$	### /	6
$4 < x \le 6$	### ////	9
$6 < x \le 8$	### //	7
$8 < x \le 10$	###	5
	Total	30

(b) Percentage of passengers who covered more than 6 km $= \frac{7+5}{30} \times 100\%$

$$= 40\%$$

Level 3   GCSE Grade 2⁺/3⁻

6. This list is a record of the scores of 32 students in a science test.

63	56	32	41	66	79	45	91
33	68	75	47	78	61	83	49
85	42	77	86	63	60	95	54
62	88	57	38	64	73	72	55

(a) Construct a frequency table of uniform intervals for the data, using the intervals $29 < x \le 39$, $39 < x \le 49$ and so on.
(b) The pass mark for the test is 50. Find the percentage of students who passed the test.

Solution

(a)

Test scores (x)	Tally	Frequency
$29 < x \le 39$	///	3
$39 < x \le 49$	###	5
$49 < x \le 59$	////	4
$59 < x \le 69$	### ///	8
$69 < x \le 79$	### /	6
$79 < x \le 89$	////	4
$89 < x \le 99$	//	2
	Total	32

(b) Number of students whose scores are greater than or equal to the pass mark

$= 4 + 8 + 6 + 4 + 2$

$= 24$

Percentage of students who passed

$= \dfrac{24}{32} \times 100\%$

$= 75\%$

7. A quality control officer inspected 30 boxes of vases produced by a factory. The list below shows the number of defective vases found in each box of 10 vases.

1	3	1	4	1	2	0	0	4	0
4	2	0	1	3	0	1	3	1	2
0	1	3	0	2	1	0	1	2	1

(a) Construct a frequency table for the data.
(b) Find the percentage of boxes which have 0 or 1 defective vases.

Solution

(a)

Number of defective vases	Tally	Frequency
0	### ///	8
1	### ###	10
2	###	5
3	////	4
4	///	3
	Total	30

(b) Number of boxes with 0 or 1 defective vases $= 8 + 10 = 18$

Percentage of boxes with 0 or 1 defective vases

$= \dfrac{18}{30} \times 100\%$

$= 60\%$

8. The list shows the scores in Round 1 of the first 30 golfers in the 2017 UK Masters Tournament.

70	70	69	69	65	67	68	69	70	69
69	70	69	69	68	65	70	70	69	68
67	69	65	70	67	68	69	69	67	69

(a) Construct a frequency table for the data.
(b) What is the winning score in Round 1 if the game was won by the golfers with the lowest score?

(c) Find the percentage of golfers who scored 69 in this round.

Solution

(a)

Scores	Tally	Frequency
65	///	3
67	////	4
68	////	4
69	### ### //	12
70	### //	7
	Total	30

(b) The winning score is 65.

(c) Percentage of golfers who scored 69

$= \dfrac{12}{30} \times 100\%$

$= 40\%$

9. A survey investigates the number of hours that a person surfs the Internet per day. This list shows the survey results of 25 people.

1.5	3.2	2.1	3.0	0.8
4.2	11.6	2.7	6.6	4.1
1.6	6.3	2.5	2.0	5.8
2.4	8.8	5.4	0.4	9.2
2.9	5.7	7.8	1.0	3.9

(a) Construct a frequency table of uniform intervals, using the intervals $0 < x \leq 3$, $3 < x \leq 6$ and so on.
(b) Find the percentage of people in the survey who spend more than three hours but fewer than or equal to nine hours per day surfing the Internet.

Solution

(a)

Time (x h)	Tally	Frequency
$0 < x \leq 3$	### ### //	12
$3 < x \leq 6$	### //	7
$6 < x \leq 9$	////	4
$9 < x \leq 12$	//	2
	Total	25

(b) Percentage of people who surf the Internet for hours in the range $3 < x \leq 9$

$= \dfrac{7+4}{25} \times 100\%$

$= 44\%$

10. This list shows the monthly shopping bills (in £) of 35 families.

236.49	315.37	256.88	104.56	418.30	176.40	198.95
367.90	187.80	54.73	467.32	238.89	356.60	245.71
287.59	314.90	267.80	378.24	480.43	69.78	135.60
78.40	178.10	245.67	314.90	83.20	472.10	174.30
267.80	69.30	134.70	314.60	180.90	245.60	430.15

(a) Construct a frequency table of uniform intervals for the data, using the intervals $0 < x \leq 100$, $100 \leq x < 200$ and so on.

(b) Find the percentage of families whose bills are more than £200 but less than or equal to £400. Give your answer to the nearest 1%.

Solution

(a)

Shopping bill (£x)	Tally	Frequency
$0 < x \leq 100$	⧕	5
$100 < x \leq 200$	⧕ ////	9
$200 < x \leq 300$	⧕ ////	9
$300 < x \leq 400$	⧕ //	7
$400 < x \leq 500$	⧕	5
	Total	35

(b) Shopping bills which are more than £200 but less than or equal to £400
$= 9 + 7$
$= 16$
Required percentage $= \dfrac{16}{35} \times 100\%$
$= 46\%$ (to nearest 1%)

11. In a factory, the lifetimes of 30 batteries were tested. The results (in hours) are shown below.

9.2	3.2	7.7	8.0	5.2	8.8	6.9	7.6	3.8	4.1
7.6	8.4	9.9	3.6	8.4	9.0	5.1	7.5	4.9	9.5
8.1	4.5	7.2	9.5	6.4	6.9	7.4	5.7	7.9	6.3

(a) Construct a frequency table using four or five uniform intervals for the data.
(b) Compare your table with those of your classmates.

Solution

(a) Student's frequency table e.g.

Lifetime (x h)	Tally	Frequency
$3 < x \leq 5$	⧕ /	6
$5 < x \leq 7$	⧕ //	7
$7 < x \leq 9$	⧕ ⧕ ///	13
$9 < x \leq 11$	////	4
	Total	30

(b) If a classmate uses a different set of class intervals, the frequencies may not be the same.

12. A survey is conducted on the rating of the quality of food in a school canteen. The results are summarised in the table.

Rating	Frequency
Very good	22
Good	57
Fair	61
Poor	35
Very poor	25

Write a brief report about the survey based on the information in the table.

Solution

Student's report. This could include:
Total number of respondents in the survey
$= 22 + 57 + 61 + 35 + 25$
$= 200$
Most respondents selected 'fair' for the rating on the quality of food.
Percentage of respondents with 'very good' rating
$= \dfrac{22}{200} \times 100\%$
$= 11\%$
The percentage of respondents who selected 'poor' or 'very poor' ratings is very high (30%).
$$\dfrac{35 + 25}{200} \times 100\% = 30\%$$

Exercise 12.3

Level 1 GCSE Grade **1 / 2⁻**

1. The pictogram below shows the number of books read by four students in a month.

Number of books read in a month

represents 2 books

(a) Who read the fewest books in the month?
(b) How many more books did Ali read than Cathy?

Solution

(a) Brian read the fewest books.

(b) Number of books read by Ali = 11
Number of books read by Cathy = 8
Difference = 11 − 8
= 3
Ali read 3 more books than Cathy.

2. The pictogram shows the goals scored by four teams in a football season.

Number of goals scored in a football season

Dragon	⚽ ⚽ ⚽ ⚽ ◖
Hawk	⚽ ⚽ ◖
Lion	⚽ ⚽ ⚽ ⚽ ⚽ ◢
Tiger	⚽ ⚽ ⚽ ⚽

⚽ represents 4 goals

(a) Which team scored the most goals?
(b) How many more goals did Dragon score than Hawk?

Solution

(a) Lion scored the most number of goals.

(b) Number of goals scored by Dragon = 18
Number of goals scored by Hawk = 11
Difference = 18 − 11
= 7
Dragon scored 7 more goals than Hawk.

3. The pictogram shows the number of apples produced by four farms.

Number of apples

Evergreen	🍎 🍎 🍎 🍎 🍎 🍎
Good Harvest	🍎 🍎 🍎 🍎 🍎
Reddish	🍎 🍎 🍎 ◗
Sunny	🍎 🍎 🍎 🍎 ◗

🍎 represents 200 apples

(a) Which farm produced the greatest number of apples?
(b) Find the total number of apples produced by the four farms.

Solution

(a) Farm Evergreen produced the greatest number of apples.

(b) Total number of apples produced by the four farms
$$= 200 \times 6 + 200 \times 5 + \left(200 \times 3 + 200 \times \frac{1}{2}\right)$$
$$+ \left(200 \times 4 + 200 \times \frac{1}{2}\right)$$
$$= 3800$$

4. The vertical line chart shows the number of members in each leisure club at a community centre.

Number of members in leisure clubs

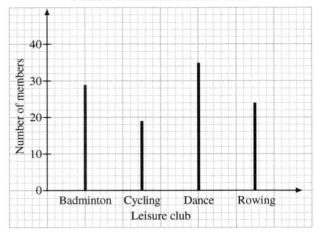

(a) Which leisure club has the greatest number of members?
(b) What is the total number of members in the four clubs?

Solution

(a) The dance club has the greatest number of members.

(b) Total number of members = 29 + 19 + 35 + 24
= 107

5. The following table shows the number of incoming telephone calls received by an office in a working week.

Day	Number of calls
Monday	24
Tuesday	15
Wednesday	19
Thursday	16
Friday	21

(a) Construct a vertical line chart to display the data.
(b) Construct a bar chart to display the data.

Solution

(a)

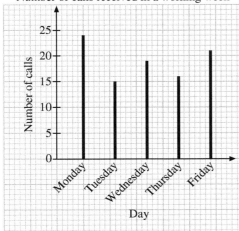

Number of calls received in a working week

(b)

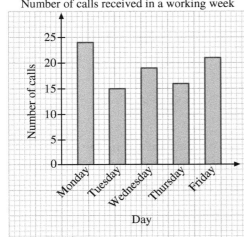

Number of calls received in a working week

6. The bar chart shows the number of rainy days in a city over a period of four months.

Number of rainy days in the city

(a) Which month had the smallest number of rainy days?

(b) How many more rainy days were there in August than in May?

(c) Find the total number of rainy days in these four months.

Solution

(a) May had the smallest number of rainy days.

(b) Number of rainy days in August = 10
Number of rainy days in May = 3
Difference = 10 − 3
$\qquad$ = 7
There are 7 more rainy days in August than in May.

(c) Total number of rainy days = 3 + 5 + 8 + 10
$\qquad\qquad\qquad\qquad\qquad$ = 26

Level 2 $\quad$ **GCSE Grade** **2** / **3**

7. The following table shows the scores obtained by four students in a quiz which has 20 true/false questions.

Student	Scores
Eric	8
Florence	19
Gloria	20
Harry	15

The data is represented by a pictogram and the number of symbols in each row should not exceed 10.

(a) What is the lowest score that can be represented by each symbol?

(b) Draw the pictogram using the result in **(a)**.

Solution

(a) 2 is the lowest score that can be represented by each symbol.

(b)

Quiz scores

Eric	✓✓✓✓
Florence	✓✓✓✓✓✓✓✓✓◗
Gloria	✓✓✓✓✓✓✓✓✓✓
Harry	✓✓✓✓✓✓✓◗

✓ represents 2 points

8. The compound bar chart shows Ahmad's monthly income and expenditure from January to March.

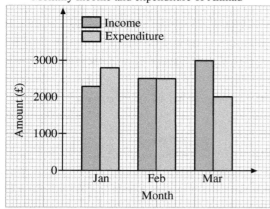

Monthly income and expenditure of Ahmad

(a) Compare Ahmad's monthly income over the three months.

(b) In which month was his income less than his expenditure and by how much?

(c) Determine whether his total income over the three months was greater than his total expenditure over the same period.

Solution

(a) Ahmad's monthly income increased steadily from January to March.

(b) In January, Ahmad's income was £500 less than his expenditure.

(c) Total income in 3 months = £(2300 + 2500 + 3000)
$$= £7800$$
Total expenditure in 3 months
$$= £(2800 + 2500 + 2000)$$
$$= £7300$$
Hence, his total income was greater than his total expenditure.

Level 3   `GCSE Grade 3 / 4⁻`

9. The following table shows the number of medals won by the top three countries in the 2016 Rio Summer Olympics.

Country	Gold	Silver	Bronze
USA	46	37	38
Great Britain	27	23	17
China	26	18	26

(a) Display the data in a bar chart.

(b) Express the total number of medals won by Great Britain as a percentage of the total number of medals won by the USA. Give your answer to the nearest 1%.

Solution

(a)

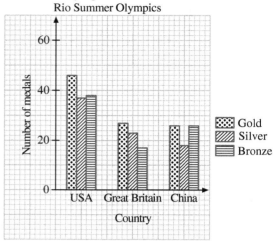

Medals won by top three countries in 2016 Rio Summer Olympics

(b) Total number of medals won by Great Britain
$$= 27 + 23 + 17$$
$$= 67$$
Total number of medals won by the USA
$$= 46 + 37 + 38$$
$$= 121$$
The required percentage $= \dfrac{67}{121} \times 100\%$
$$= 55\% \text{ (to the nearest 1\%)}$$

10. The table shows the monthly maximum temperature and minimum temperature in Edinburgh from June to September 2017.

Month	June	July	August	September
Maximum (°C)	25	25	21	19
Minimum (°C)	5	6	4	3

Display the data in a compound bar chart.

Solution

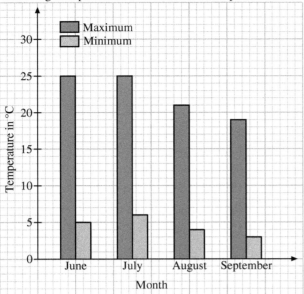

Edinburgh temperatures in °C from June to September 2017

11. The table shows the match results of the first four clubs in the Premier League 2016/17.

Club	Won	Drawn	Lost
Chelsea	30	3	5
Tottenham Hotspur	26	8	4
Manchester City	23	9	6
Liverpool	22	10	6

Draw a compound bar chart to display the data.

Solution

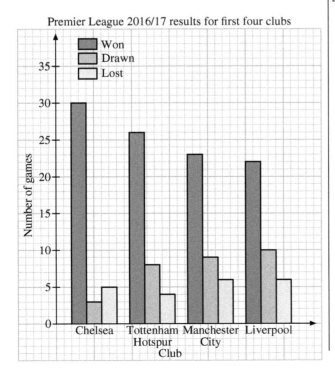

Premier League 2016/17 results for first four clubs

12. Visit a shopping centre or mall near your home. Count the number of different shops and tabulate your results. Draw an appropriate diagram to display your results.

Hint: You could classify the shops based on what they sell e.g. food, clothes, appliances, etc. Tabulate means enter the results in a table.

Solution

The answer depends on the data collected.

Revision Exercise 12

1. Suggest a method of data collection which could be used to find the following information.

  (a) The birth rates and death rates in England.

  (b) The quantity of water a sunflower needs for optimum growth.

  (c) The opinions of local residents on the construction of a nearby motorway.

  (d) The number of passengers in each carriage of a train travelling from London to York.

Hint: Choose from these methods: taking measurements, observing outcomes, conducting surveys, reading publications.

Solution

  (a) Reading statistical publications

  (b) Taking measurements in experiments

  (c) Conducting a survey

  (d) Observation

2. The table shows the number of hybrid cars registered in the UK from 2014 to 2016.

Year	2014	2015	2016
Number of hybrid cars registered	2815	3246	3646

  (a) Round the number of hybrid cars in each year to the nearest hundred.

The pictogram represents the rounded data.

Number of hybrid cars in the UK

2014	🚗🚗🚗🚗🚗🚗🚗
2015	🚗🚗🚗🚗🚗🚗🚗🚗
2016	🚗🚗🚗🚗🚗🚗🚗🚗🚗

🚗 represents n cars

  (b) Find the value of n (the number of cars represented by each symbol in the pictogram).

Solution

(a)   Number of cars in 2014
    = 2815
    = 2800   (to the nearest hundred)
    Number of cars in 2015
    = 3246
    = 3200   (to the nearest hundred)
    Number of cars in 2016
    = 3646
    = 3600   (to the nearest hundred)

(b) $n = \dfrac{2800}{7}$
    = 400

3. Students in a class were asked about their favourite games. The results of the survey are shown in the bar chart.

Favourite games of students

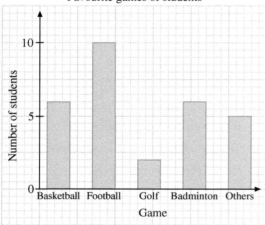

(a)   How many students are there in the class?
(b)   Which game is the most popular among the students?

Solution

(a)   Number of students in the class
    = 6 + 10 + 2 + 6 + 5
    = 29

(b)   Football is the most popular game.

4. This list shows the time taken (in minutes) by 20 students to get ready for school on a certain morning.

GCSE Grade 2+

25	12	17	45	53
30	28	39	51	58
48	15	55	23	46
35	47	32	40	44

(a)   Represent the data in a frequency table with class intervals $10 < x \le 20$, $20 < x \le 30$ and so on.
(b)   Find the percentage of students who took longer than 40 minutes to get ready.

Solution

(a)

Time (x minutes)	Frequency
$10 < x \le 20$	3
$20 < x \le 30$	4
$30 < x \le 40$	4
$40 < x \le 50$	5
$50 < x \le 60$	4
Total	20

(b)   Number of students who took longer than 40 minutes to get ready = 5 + 4 = 9

Percentage of students who took longer than 40 minutes to get ready = $\dfrac{9}{20} \times 100\%$
    = 45%

5. The compound bar chart shows the number of students who participated in some club activities at a school.

GCSE Grade 3

Participation in club activities

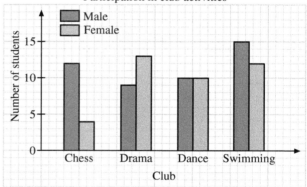

(a)   Which club is the most popular among all the students?
(b)   Which club has an equal number of male and female students?
(c)   Find the total number of students in the four clubs.

Solution

(a)   The swimming club is the most popular.

(b)   The dance club has an equal number of male and female students.

(c)   Total number of male students in the four clubs = 12 + 9 + 10 + 15 = 46
    Total number of female students in the four clubs = 4 + 13 + 10 + 12 = 39
    Hence, the total number of students = 46 + 39
                = 85

6. The incomplete compound bar chart shows the maths and science test scores for four students in Year 7. Calin scored 25 in the maths test and 35 in the science test. Joey scored 18 in the maths test.

Maths and science test scores for four Year 7 students

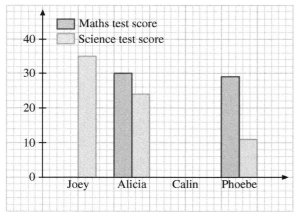

(a) Copy and complete the bar chart.
(b) Which students scored higher in the science test than in the maths test?
(c) Which student had the highest combined score for the maths and science tests?

Solution
(a) Maths and science test scores for four Year 7 students

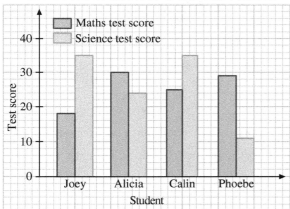

(b) Joey and Calin scored higher in the science test than in the maths test.

(c) Joey's combined score = 18 + 35 = 53
Alicia's combined score = 30 + 24 = 54
Calin's combined score = 25 + 35 = 60
Phoebe's combined score = 29 + 11 = 40
The student with the highest combined score is Calin.

7. The following table shows the results of a survey conducted to investigate the opinions of local people on a particular issue.

Opinion	Number of responses
Strongly agree	38
Agree	42
No idea	20
Disagree	79
Strongly disagree	71

(a) How many people responded to the survey?
(b) How many more people strongly disagreed than strongly agreed?
(c) Find the percentage of people who disagreed with the issue.

Solution
(a) Number of responses
= 38 + 42 + 20 + 79 + 71
= 250

(b) Number of strongly agree = 38
Number of strongly disagree = 71
Difference = 71 − 38
= 33

(c) Number of people who disagreed = 79 + 71
= 150

Percentage of people who disagree = $\frac{150}{250} \times 100\%$
= 60%

8. Ross asks a group of friends how many pieces of fruit they have eaten that day. He records the results in the frequency table below. He also starts to draw a vertical line chart to display the data.

Number of fruits	Frequency
1	4
2	6
3	8
4	5
5	2

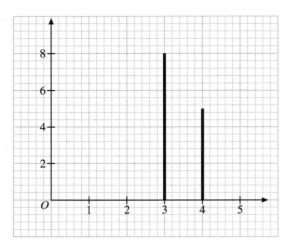

(a) Copy and complete the vertical line chart.
(b) What percentage of the group of friends has eaten five pieces of fruit that day?

Solution

(a)

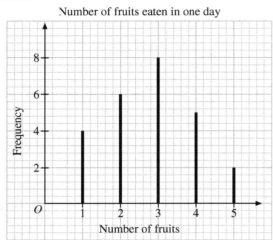

Number of fruits eaten in one day

(b) Total number of friends asked
= 4 + 6 + 8 + 5 + 2
= 25

Percentage of the group of friends who have eaten five pieces of fruit that day

$= \dfrac{2}{25} \times 100\%$

$= 8\%$

9. The bar chart shows the number of friends of four students on a social networking website.

GCSE Grade 3

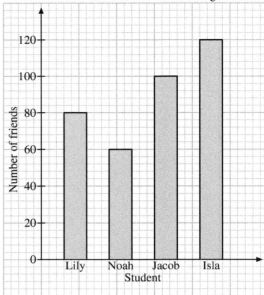

Number of friends on a social networking website

(a) How many more friends does Jacob have than Noah on the social networking site?
(b) Name two students such that one of them has twice as many friends as the other.
(c) By using one symbol to represent 20 friends, construct a pictogram to display this data.

Solution

(a) Number of friends Jacob has = 100
Number of friends Noah has = 60
Difference = 100 − 60
= 40

(b) Isla has twice as many friends as Noah.

(c) Symbol chosen by student.

Number of friends on a social networking website

Lily	☺ ☺ ☺ ☺
Noah	☺ ☺ ☺
Jacob	☺ ☺ ☺ ☺ ☺
Isla	☺ ☺ ☺ ☺ ☺ ☺

☺ represents 20 friends

Review Exercise 3

1. Five line segments are shown on the square grid.

   (a) Which two line segments are parallel?
   (b) Which two line segments are perpendicular to each other?
   (c) Which two line segments are equal in length?

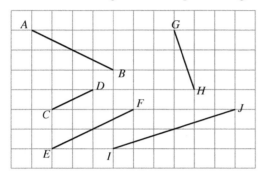

Solution

(a) CD and EF are parallel.

(b) GH and IJ are perpendicular to each other.

(c) AB and EF are equal in length.

2. In the diagram,

   $AB \parallel CF \parallel DE$,
   $\angle ABC = 125°$ and
   $\angle CDE = 110°$.
   Find $\angle x$ and $\angle y$.

Solution
$\angle x + 110° = 180°$ (Co-interior angles add up
$\quad\angle x = 70°$ to 180°, $DE \parallel CF$.)
$\angle y + \angle x = 125°$ (Alternate angles are equal,
$\angle y + 70° = 125°$ $\quad AB \parallel CF$.)
$\quad\quad\angle y = 55°$

3. In the diagram, $BCDE$ is a straight line,

   $\angle ACB = 128°$ and $\angle ADE = 103°$. Find angle x.

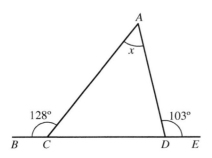

Solution
$\angle ADC = 180° - 103°$ (Angles on a straight
$\quad\quad\quad = 77°$ line add up to 180°.)

$x + \angle ADC = 128°$ (The exterior angle of a
$\quad\quad\quad x = 128° - 77°$ triangle is the sum of the
$\quad\quad\quad = 51°$ opposite interior angles.)

4. The diagram shows an L-shape.

(a) Four L-shapes are placed together to make the shape below. Copy this shape and draw all the lines of symmetry of the shape.

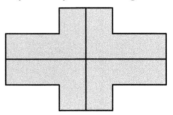

(b) Four L-shapes are placed to form the following shape. State the order of rotation symmetry of this shape.

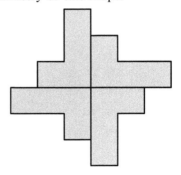

Solution
(a)

The shape has 2 lines of symmetry.

(b) This shape repeats itself four times in one full turn about its centre. It has rotation symmetry of order 4.

5. (a) Copy the diagram and draw the image of △*ABC* after a reflection in the line *PQ*.

(b) Find the area of △*ABC*.

GCSE Grade 4⁻

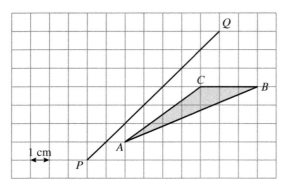

Solution

(a)

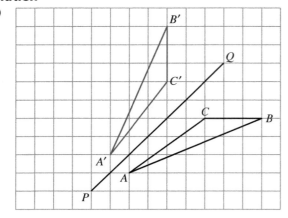

(b) Area of △*ABC*

$$=\frac{1}{2}\times BC\times \text{ perpendicular height}$$

$$=\frac{1}{2}\times 3\times 3$$

$$=4.5\,\text{cm}^2$$

6. (a) Copy the diagram and draw the image *A′B′C′D′* of *ABCD* after a rotation of 90° anticlockwise about the point *A*.

GCSE Grade 3⁺

(b) *A′B′C′D′* is translated by the vector $\begin{pmatrix}6\\-3\end{pmatrix}$ to the image *A″B″C″D″*. Draw *A″B″C″D″* on the diagram.

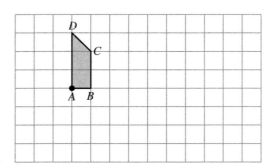

Solution

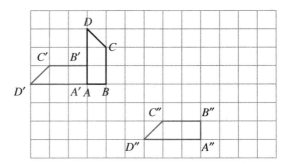

7. In △*ABD*, *C* is a point on *BD*, *AB* = 37 cm, *BC* = 19 cm, *CD* = 16 cm, *AC* = 20 cm and *AD* = 12 cm. Find

GCSE Grade 3⁻

(a) the area of △*ACD*,

(b) the perimeter of △*ABC*,

(c) the area of △*ABC*.

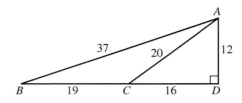

Solution

(a) Area of △*ACD*

$$=\frac{1}{2}\times CD\times AD$$

$$=\frac{1}{2}\times 16\times 12$$

$$=96\,\text{cm}^2$$

(b) Perimeter of △*ABC*

= *AB* + *BC* + *CA*

= 37 + 19 + 20

= 76 cm

(c) Area of △*ABC*

$$=\frac{1}{2}\times BC\times AD$$

$$=\frac{1}{2}\times 19\times 12$$

$$=114\,\text{cm}^2$$

8. The diagram shows a face of a cube. The edges of the cube are (20 − 2*x*) cm, where *x* = 7.

GCSE Grade 3⁺

20 − 2*x*

Find

(a) the perimeter of the face,

(b) the surface area of the cube,

(c) the volume of the cube.

Solution

(a) Substitute $x = 7$ into $20 - 2x$
The length of an edge of the cube
$= 20 - 2 \times 7$
$= 6\,\text{cm}$
$\therefore$ the perimeter of the face $= 4 \times 6$
$= 24\,\text{cm}$

(b) Surface area of the cube
$= 6 \times$ area of a face
$= 6 \times (6 \times 6)$
$= 6 \times 6 \times 6$
$= 216\,\text{cm}^2$

(c) Volume of the cube
$= 6 \times 6 \times 6$
$= 216\,\text{cm}^3$

9. A square and a circle each have a perimeter of 20 cm.

(a) Calculate the area of the square.
(b) Find the radius of the circle in terms of π.
(c) Using a calculator, find the area of the circle, giving your answer to the nearest cm^2.
(d) Which figure has the larger area?

Solution

(a) Let the length of a side of the square be x cm.
Perimeter $= 20\,\text{cm}$
$4x = 20$
$x = 5$
i.e. each side of the square is 5 cm.
Area of the square
$= 5 \times 5$
$= 25\,\text{cm}^2$

(b) Let the radius of the circle be r cm.
Circumference $= 20\,\text{cm}$
$2\pi r = 20$
$\pi r = 10$
$r = \dfrac{10}{\pi}$
The radius of the circle is $\dfrac{10}{\pi}$ cm.

(c) Area of the circle
$= \pi r^2$
$= \pi \times \left(\dfrac{10}{\pi}\right)^2$
$= 31.8309\ldots$
$= 32\,\text{cm}^2$ (to the nearest cm^2)

(d) The circle has the larger area.

10. *ABCD* is a rectangle of length 9 cm and width 5 cm. Quarter circles *BPQ* and *DRS* of radii 2 cm and centres *B* and *D* are cut out of the rectangle at the corners *B* and *D*. Find

(a) the perimeter of the shaded shape,
(b) the area of the shaded shape.
Give your answers to the nearest integer.

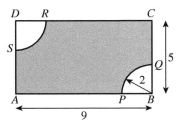

Solution

(a) Note the two quarter circles together would make a semicircle.
The perimeter of the shaded shape
$= 2 \times AS + 2 \times AP +$ perimeter of semicircle, radius 2
$= 2 \times 3 + 2 \times 7 + \pi \times 2$
$= 26.2831\ldots$
$= 26\,\text{cm}$ (to the nearest cm)

(b) The area of the shaded shape
$=$ area of rectangle *ABCD* $-$ area of a semicircle, radius 2
$= 9 \times 5 - \pi \times 2^2 + 2$
$= 45 - 2\pi$
$= 38.716\ldots$
$= 39\,\text{cm}^2$ (to the nearest cm^2)

11. The bar chart shows the average maximum temperature in London from January to May.

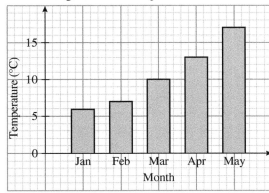

(a) Write down the lowest average maximum temperature in these five months. In which month does it occur?
(b) Which two months have an average maximum temperature between 9 °C and 15 °C?

(c) The table shows the average minimum temperature in London from January to May.

Month	Average minimum temperature (°C)
January	2
February	2
March	3
April	5
May	8

Draw a compound bar chart to show both the average maximum temperature and average minimum temperature in these five months.

Solution

(a) The lowest average maximum temperature is 6 °C.
It occurs in January.

(b) March and April have an average maximum temperature between 9 °C and 15 °C.

(c) The following bar chart shows the average maximum and average minimum temperatures in London from January to May.

Average maximum and minimum temperature in London

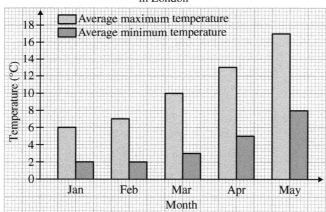

12. Here is a question from a questionnaire about students' weekly pocket money.

> How much pocket money do you receive?
> ☐ £1 – £10   ☐ £10 – £20
> ☐ £20 – £30   ☐ £30 – £40

(a) What is missing from the question?
(b) Suggest three ways to improve the question options.

Solution

(a) The question does not state whether the amounts are weekly or monthly.

(b) Three possible ways to improve the question options would be: (i) ensure the options do not overlap e.g. £1 – £9.99, £10 – 19.99 etc., (ii) include other options so all possibilities are covered e.g. less than £1 and £40 or more, (iii) state a period e.g. per week or per month.

13. The pictogram shows the number of students who are learning a second language.

Number of students learning a second language

French	🌐 🌐 🌐 🌐 🌐 🌐 ◖
German	🌐 🌐 🌐 ◕
Italian	🌐 🌐 🌐 🌐 🌐 🌐
Spanish	🌐 🌐 🌐 ◔

🌐 reprersents *n* students

There are 15 students learning German.
(a) Find the value of *n*.
(b) Find the difference between the number of students learning French and the number learning Spanish.
(c) Display the data in a vertical line chart.

Solution

(a) There are $3\frac{3}{4}$ globe symbols for German.
Therefore
$$3\frac{3}{4}n = 15$$
$$\frac{15}{4}n = 15$$
$$n = 4$$

(b) The number of students learning French
$$= 6\frac{1}{2} \times 4 = 26$$
The number of students learning Spanish
$$= 3\frac{1}{4} \times 4 = 13$$
Therefore the difference between the number of students learning French and the number learning Spanish
$$= 26 - 13$$
$$= 13$$

(c) Student's vertical line chart

14. The diagram shows a net of a cuboid. $AG = 10$ cm, $LM = 2$ cm and $AN = 4$ cm.

(a) When the net is folded into a cuboid, which points would meet with the point N?
(b) Calculate the length of BE.

(c) Find the surface area of the cuboid.
(d) Find the volume of the cuboid.

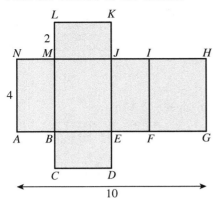

Solution

(a) L and H would meet with N when the net is folded into a cuboid.

(b) Since the net makes a cuboid, you know $NM = LM = 2$ cm and $IJ = KJ = 2$ cm. MJ and IH must be equal and $MJ = BE$. You have

$$NH = AG = 10$$
$$NM + MJ + JI + IH = 10$$
$$2 + BE + 2 + BE = 10$$
$$2BE = 6$$
$$BE = 3 \text{ cm}$$

(c) The dimensions of the cuboid are 4 cm by 3 cm by 2 cm.
Surface area of the cuboid
$$= 2 \times (4 \times 3 + 4 \times 2 + 3 \times 2)$$
$$= 2 \times 26$$
$$= 52 \text{ cm}^2$$

(d) Volume of the cuboid
$$= 4 \times 3 \times 2$$
$$= 24 \text{ cm}^3$$

15. $ABCD$ is a square table with side length 80 cm. Two semicircular boards at its two ends can be flipped up to form a table top $ABPCDQ$ as shown. Find
(a) the increase in the perimeter of the table when the two ends are flipped up,
(b) the area of the table top $ABPCDQ$.

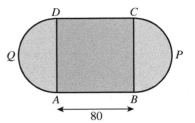

Solution

(a) Note that the semicircle ends of the table top have diameter 80 cm and radius $80 \div 2 = 40$ cm. Together they would make a whole circle.
Perimeter of square table $ABCD$ is
$$= 4 \times 80$$
$$= 320 \text{ cm}$$

Perimeter of table top $ABPCDQ$ is
$$= \pi \times 80 + 2 \times 80$$
$$= 80\pi + 160$$
$$= 411.327\ldots$$
$$= 411 \text{ cm (to the nearest cm)}$$

Increase in the perimeter is
$$= 411 - 320$$
$$= 91 \text{ cm (to the nearest cm)}$$

(b) Area of table top $ABPCDQ$ is
$$= \pi \times 40^2 + 80^2$$
$$= 1600\pi + 6400$$
$$= 11\,426.548\ldots$$
$$= 11\,427 \text{ cm}^2 \text{ (to the nearest cm}^2)$$

Problems in Real-world Contexts

A. Paper Sizes

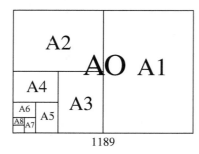

1189

The diagram shows the dimensions of 'A series' paper sizes. The complete sheet is of size A0 with length 1189 mm and area 1 000 000 mm² (or 1 m²). The dimensions of this series of paper have the special property that one piece of A0 paper can be divided into two pieces of A1 paper, one piece of A1 paper can be divided into two pieces of A2 paper and so on.

1. Find the width of a piece of A0 paper. Give your answer to the nearest mm.

GCSE Grade **2**

2. **(a)** Find the area of a piece of A4 paper in m², expressing your answer as a fraction.
(b) Find the length and width of a piece of A4 paper to the nearest mm.

GCSE Grade **3+**

3. The mass of a piece of A0 paper is 80 grams. Find the mass of a piece of A4 paper of the same thickness and quality.

GCSE Grade **3**

4. Sam puts some A4 posters in an envelope. The envelope has mass 25 grams. To minimise the cost of the postage, the total mass should not be greater than 100 grams. How many A4 posters can be placed in the envelope?

GCSE Grade **3+**

Solution

1. Let x mm be the width of a piece of A0 paper.
As the area of a piece of A0 paper is 1 000 000 mm²,
$$1189 \times x = 1\,000\,000$$
$$x = \frac{1\,000\,000}{1189}$$
$$x = 841.04\ldots$$
$$x = 841 \text{ (to the nearest mm)}$$
∴ the width of a piece of A0 paper is 841 mm.

2. **(a)** A0 paper = 2 A1 paper
= 2 × 2 A2 paper
= 2 × 2 × 2 A3 paper
= 2 × 2 × 2 × 2 A4 paper
= 16 A4 paper
You can see how a piece of A0 paper is divided into 16 pieces of A4 paper in the diagram.
∴ area of a piece of A4 paper
$$= \frac{1}{16} \times \text{area of a piece of A0 paper}$$
$$= \frac{1}{16} \times 1\,\text{m}^2$$
$$= \frac{1}{16}\,\text{m}^2$$

(b) Length of a piece of A4 paper
$$= \frac{1}{4} \times \text{length of a piece of A0 paper}$$
$$= \frac{1}{4} \times 1189$$
$$= 297.25$$
$$= 297\,\text{mm (to the nearest mm)}$$

Width of a piece of A4 paper
$$= \frac{1}{4} \times \text{width of a piece of A0 paper}$$
$$= \frac{1}{4} \times 841.04$$
$$= 210.26$$
$$= 210\,\text{mm (to the nearest mm)}$$

3. Mass of a piece of A4 paper
$$= \frac{1}{16} \times \text{mass of a piece of A0 paper}$$
$$= \frac{1}{16} \times 80$$
$$= 5\,\text{g}$$

4. Let n be the number of A4 posters in the envelope. Consider the total mass of the envelope and the posters:
$$25 + 5n = 100$$
$$5n = 75$$
$$n = \frac{75}{5}$$
$$n = 15$$
∴ 15 A4 posters can be placed in the envelope.

B. Brick Wall

The standard size of bricks in the UK is 215 mm long, 102.5 mm wide and 65 mm high. When laying bricks, mortar of 10 mm thick is used to hold the bricks together. One-half running bond is the basic pattern when laying a wall, i.e. approximately half of a brick's length overlaps the brick below.

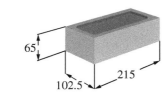

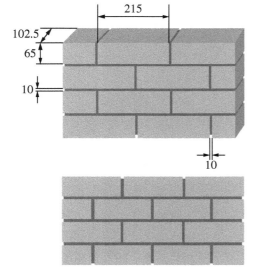

1. In the diagram, the top and the third rows use three whole bricks, while bricks in the second and bottom rows have to be cut at both ends. Find

GCSE Grade 3

    (a)   the length and height of this arrangement in cm,

    (b)   the volume of this arrangement to the nearest 10 cm³ if the thickness of this arrangement is one brick width.

2. Mr Tamworth is going to build a wall 2 m high, 5 m long and 102.5 mm thick. Estimate the number of bricks required. State any assumptions you make in your calculation.

GCSE Grade 3⁺

3. Mr Tamworth wants to buy 5% more bricks than the number required to allow for breakage and waste. How many bricks should he buy?

GCSE Grade 4⁻

Solution

1. **(a)** Length = 3 × length of brick + 2 × thickness of mortar

      = 3 × 21.5 + 2 × 1 cm

      = 66.5 cm

      Height = 4 × height of brick + 3 × thickness of mortar

      = 4 × 6.5 + 3 × 1 cm

      = 29 cm

    (b) Volume = lhw

      = 66.5 × 29 × 10.25

      = 19 767.125

      = 19 770 cm³ (to the nearest 10 cm³)

2.

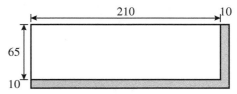

Make the assumption that each brick is a 'nominal brick' with mortar of thickness 10 mm on the bottom and on the right side as shown above i.e. each nominal brick is 225 mm long and 75 mm high.

Area of the front face of a nominal brick

= 0.225 × 0.075 m²

= 0.016 875 m²

Area of the wall = 5 × 2 m²

                   = 10 m²

Number of nominal bricks required

= 10 ÷ 0.016 875

= 593 (to the nearest integer)

∴ an estimate of the number of bricks required for the wall is 593.

3. Number of bricks that should be bought

= 593 + 593 × 5%

= 623 (to the nearest integer)

357

C. Magazine Holder

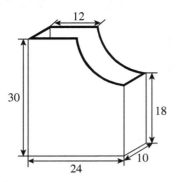

Jenny makes a magazine holder using wooden board 1 cm thick. The two side pieces are cut from a board of 60 cm by 24 cm as shown below. A quarter of a circle of radius 12 cm is cut from each side in the middle.

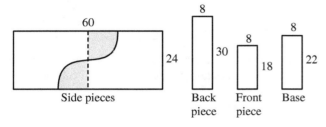

Side pieces   Back   Front   Base
piece   piece

The back end piece is 30 cm high and 8 cm wide. The front end piece is 18 cm high and 8 cm wide. The base piece is 22 cm long and 8 cm wide. A piece of wood of 90 cm by 24 cm by 1 cm is ordered to make the magazine holder.

1. Find the volume of the piece of wood ordered.

2. Find the perimeter of each side piece to the nearest cm.

3. Find the percentage of wastage from the piece of wood that is ordered to the nearest 1%.

Solution

1. Volume of the piece of wood ordered $= 90 \times 24 \times 1$
$$= 2160 \,\text{cm}^3$$

2. Perimeter of each side piece
$$= 30 + 24 + (30 - 12) + \frac{1}{4} \times 2 \times \pi \times 12 + (24 - 12)$$
$$= 84 + 6\pi$$
$$= 103 \,\text{cm (to the nearest cm)}$$

3.

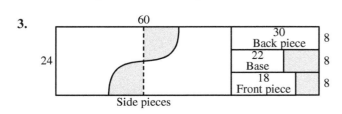

Side pieces

The diagram shows the way to cut the pieces from the piece of wood bought.
The shaded part is the wastage.
Total area of the two quarters cut out $= \frac{1}{2} \times \pi \times 12^2$
$$= 72\pi \,\text{cm}^2$$

Total area of the shaded rectangles
$$= (30 - 22) \times 8 + (30 - 18) \times 8$$
$$= 160 \,\text{cm}^2$$

Percentage of wastage $= \frac{72\pi + 160}{90 \times 24} \times 100\%$
$$= 18\% \text{ (to the nearest 1\%)}$$

D. The Gherkin

30 St Mary Axe is better known by its popular name the Gherkin. It is a skyscraper in London. It was designed using mathematical modelling by a computer and has won many awards for its architecture. The building is 180 m tall, has 41 floors and its distinctive curved shape has a circular body. It is smaller at the bottom. Its largest circumference is at the 16th floor.

1. Although the Gherkin has an overall curved glass shape, there is actually only one piece of curved glass used at the very top of the building. It is covered by 24 000 m² of external flat panes of glass.

(a) The external glass is enough to cover five typical football pitches. What is the area of a typical football pitch?

(b) There are 7429 panes of glass covering the exterior. If each pane has equal area, what is the area of each pane? Give your answer to the nearest m².

2. The largest circumference is 2 m less than the height of the building.

GCSE Grade 3+

(a) Find the largest circumference.

(b) Find the largest diameter of the building. Give your answer to the nearest metre.

(c) The footprint of the building is a circle with diameter 50 m. By what percentage is the largest diameter greater than the diameter of the footprint? Give your answer to the nearest 1%.

3. Due to its shape and design, the Gherkin is energy efficient. It was designed to use up to 50% less energy than a typical skyscraper. Assume that it achieves this energy saving and that a typical skyscraper's energy consumption is 348 kWh per m² per annum. The total floor area of the Gherkin is 47 950 m². How much energy is saved because of the design of the Gherkin in a year? Give your answer to the nearest 1000 kWh.

GCSE Grade 4−

Solution

1. **(a)** Area of a typical football pitch $= \dfrac{24\,000}{5}$
$$= 4800\,\text{m}^2$$

(b) Area of each pane $= 24\,000 \div 7429$
$$= 3\,\text{m}^2 \text{ (to the nearest m}^2\text{)}$$

2. **(a)** The largest circumference $= 180 - 2$
$$= 178\,\text{m}$$

(b) Let D m be the largest diameter.
$$\pi D = 178$$
$$D = \frac{178}{\pi}$$
$$D = 56.659\ldots$$
$$D = 57 \text{ (to the nearest integer)}$$
∴ the largest diameter is 57 m.

(c) The required percentage
$$= \frac{56.659 - 50}{50} \times 100\%$$
$$= 13\% \text{ (to the nearest 1\%)}$$

3. Amount of energy saved
$$= 348 \times 47\,950 \times 50\%$$
$$= 8\,343\,300$$
$$= 8\,343\,000\,\text{kWh (to the nearest 1000 kWh)}$$

E. SD Memory Card

SD memory cards are widely used in computers, cameras and mobile phones for storing and sharing digital content such as photos, videos, music and data. It is typically a rectangular card 32 mm long, 24 mm wide and 2.1 mm thick. A corner, which is half of a square, is cut off; this means it is not symmetrical.

1. The storage capacity of an SD card is 64 GB. The card is used to store photos. The memory size of each photo is 5 MB. How many photos can be stored on the card?
Hint: 1 GB = 1000 MB.

GCSE Grade 3+

2. Find the volume of an SD card.

GCSE Grade 4−

3. A plastic case is designed to protect the card. It leaves a gap of 2 mm on each side and on the top face of the card. The material of the case is 1 mm thick. Estimate the volume of material for the case, giving your answer to the nearest 10 mm³. State any assumptions you make.

GCSE Grade 4

Solution

1. Storage capacity of the SD card $= 64\,\text{GB}$
$$= 64 \times 1000\,\text{MB}$$

Memory size of each photo $= 5\,\text{MB}$

Number of photos it can store $= 64 \times 1000 \div 5$
$$= 12\,800$$

2. Area of the top face of a SD card
$$= 32 \times 24 - \frac{1}{2} \times 4 \times 4$$
$$= 760\,\text{mm}^2$$

Volume of a SD card $= 760 \times 2.1$
$$= 1596\,\text{mm}^3$$

3. Assume that the internal space and the external part of the case are cuboids.

Length of the internal space $= 2 + 32 + 2$
$$= 36\,\text{mm}$$

Width of the internal space = 2 + 24 + 2

                             = 28 mm

Thickness of the internal space = 2.1 + 2

                             = 4.1 mm

As the material is 1 mm thick,
length of the external part = 1 + 36 + 1

                             = 38 mm

width of the external part = 1 + 28 + 1

                             = 30 mm

thickness of the external part = 1 + 4.1 + 1

                             = 6.1 mm

Volume of material for the case
= 38 × 30 × 6.1 − 36 × 28 × 4.1
= 2821.2 mm³
= 2820 mm³ (to the nearest 10 mm³)

F. Turn Left Sign

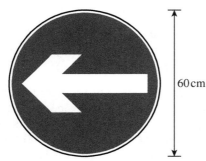

60 cm

Diagram 1

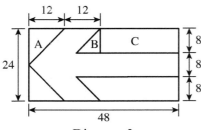

12   12

A   B   C

24

8

8

8

48

Diagram 2

The road sign shown in Diagram 1 is a circle with diameter 60 cm. The sign is used to indicate that vehicular traffic must turn left. The arrow is cut from a rectangle 48 cm by 24 cm. Diagram 2 shows the dimensions of the arrow in centimetres.

1. **(a)** Copy the sign and draw the line of symmetry on it.

GCSE Grade 2+

   (b) Does the sign possess rotation symmetry? Explain your answer.

2. Find the area of the arrow.

GCSE Grade 4

3. Find the percentage of the area of the sign occupied by the arrow. Give your answer to the nearest 1%.

GCSE Grade 4−

Solution

1. **(a)**

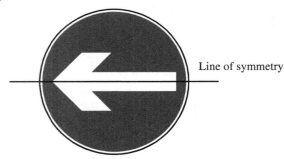

Line of symmetry

   (b) The sign does not possess rotation symmetry. This is because it only repeats itself once when rotating 360° about its centre.

2.

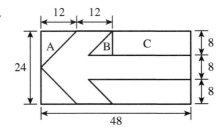

12   12

A   B   C

24

8

8

8

48

In the diagram, the triangle A is an isosceles right-angled triangle with two equal sides of length 12 cm.

Area of triangle A = $\frac{1}{2}$ × 12 × 12

                            = 72 cm²

In the trapezium at the top right, draw a perpendicular line to divide the trapezium into an isosceles right-angled triangle B and a rectangle C.

Triangle B is an isosceles right-angled triangle with two equal sides of length 8 cm.

Area of triangle B = $\frac{1}{2}$ × 8 × 8

                           = 32 cm²

Length of rectangle C = 48 − 12 − 12

                             = 24

Area of rectangle C = 24 × 8

                           = 192 cm²

Area of the rectangle enclosing the arrow = 48 × 24

                                               = 1152 cm²

Area of the arrow
= area of the rectangle enclosing the arrow
   − 2 × (area of triangle A + area of triangle B
   + area of rectangle C)
= 1152 − 2 × (72 + 32 + 192)
= 560 cm²

Note: There are other ways to calculate the area of the arrow.

3. Area of the sign = $\pi \times 30^2$
$= 900\pi\,\text{cm}^2$

Percentage of the area of the arrow
$= \dfrac{560}{900\pi} \times 100\%$
$= 20\%$ (to the nearest 1%)

G. Window Frame

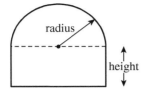

A worker makes a metal window frame of perimeter 150 cm. The frame is in the shape of a semicircle on top of a rectangle as shown in the diagram. For ease of calculation, the worker uses $\pi = 3$ for his rough workings and sets the radius of the semicircle to be an integer.

1. If the radius of the semicircle is 20 cm, find

    (a) the length of the semicircular curve,
    (b) the height of the rectangular part,
    (c) the area of the frame.

2. If the worker makes a square window frame of perimeter 150 cm, what is the area of the square window frame?

3. Another window frame is a circular one with

circumference 150 cm. Compare it with the window frames in Question **1** and Question **2**. Which window frame has the largest area?

Solution

1. **(a)** When radius = 20 cm,
length of the semicircular curve = πr
$= 3 \times 20$
$= 60\,\text{cm}$

    (b) Let h cm be the height of the rectangular part.
Length of the base of the frame = $2r$
$= 2 \times 20$
$= 40\,\text{cm}$

$2h$ + length of the semicircular arc + length of the base = perimeter of the frame
$2h + 60 + 40 = 150$
$2h = 50$
$h = 25$
∴ height of the rectangular part = 25 cm

    (c) Area of the frame
= area of the semicircle + area of the rectangle
$= \dfrac{1}{2} \times \pi r^2 + 2r + h$
$= \dfrac{1}{2} \times 3 \times 20^2 + 2 \times 20 \times 25$
$= 1600\,\text{cm}^2$

2. Length of a side of the square window frame
$= \dfrac{150}{4}$
$= 37.5\,\text{cm}$

Area of the square window frame = 37.5×37.5
$= 1406.25\,\text{cm}^2$

3. Let R cm be the radius when the frame is a circle.
$2\pi R = 150$
$2 \times 3 \times R = 150$
$6R = 150$
$R = 25$

Area of the circular frame = πR^2
$= 3 \times 25^2$
$= 1875\,\text{cm}^2$

∴ the circular frame has the largest area.

H. Population Pyramid for the UK

A population pyramid shows the age and sex of a population. The diagram shows the population pyramid for the UK in 2015.

Population pyramid for the UK in 2015

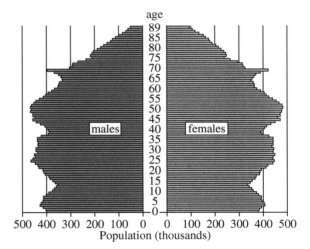
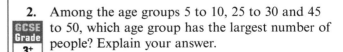
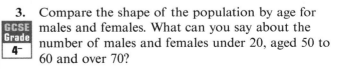

Source: Office for National Statistics

1. Assume all Year 7 students are 11 years old. Estimate the total number of Year 7 students from the population pyramid.

2. Among the age groups 5 to 10, 25 to 30 and 45 to 50, which age group has the largest number of people? Explain your answer.

3. Compare the shape of the population by age for males and females. What can you say about the number of males and females under 20, aged 50 to 60 and over 70?

Solution

1. Reading from the graph,
    number of boys at age 11 ≈ 370 000
    number of girls at age 11 ≈ 370 000
    Therefore, the total number of Year 7 students
    = the total number of boys and girls at age 11
    ≈ 370 000 + 370 000
    = 740 000

    Note: In fact, most students in Year 7 are age 11 or 12, and most students in Year 8 are age 12 or 13, and so on. You can estimate the total number of students in Year 7 by considering all the children who are 11 or all the children who are 12.

2. The bars for the age group 45 to 50 for both male and female are longer than the bars for the other two age groups.
    Therefore, the age group 45 to 50 has the largest number of people.

3. For people under 20 and aged 50 to 60, the lengths of the bars for males for females are nearly the same for each age. Therefore, the numbers of males and females at these ages are more or less the same. However, the numbers of women over 70 begin to outnumber men. In particular, this is quite obvious for ages over 80. This means, in general, the lifetime of women is longer than the lifetime of men.